C0-CBZ-404

THE WAYNESBURG COLLEGE STORY
1849-1974

LD
5891
W37
.D8

The Waynesburg College Story

1849-1974

William Howard Dusenberry

The Kent State University Press

Copyright © 1975 by Waynesburg College
All rights reserved
ISBN 0-87338-173-4
Library of Congress Catalog Card Number 74-27386
Manufactured in the United States of America

Library of Congress Cataloging in Publication Data

Dusenberry, William Howard.
The Waynesburg College story, 1849-1974.

Includes bibliographical references and index.
1. Waynesburg College, Waynesburg, Pa.—History.
I. Title.
LD5891.W42D87 378.748'83 74-27386
ISBN 0-87338-173-4

118235

BELMONT COLLEGE LIBRARY

LD
5891
W42
D87

To the alumni of Waynesburg College

CONTENTS

LIST OF ILLUSTRATIONS

FOREWORD

THE APPROACH OF THE ACADEMIC YEAR 1974-75 SIGNALED THE ARRIVAL of the 125th anniversary of Waynesburg College. Classes were begun in September 1849; a state charter was granted in March 1850. To provide continuously a program of higher education for a century and a quarter is an accomplishment of no small magnitude. The preparation of a history of the College was suggested as an appropriate recognition of this important milestone. Following trustee endorsement of the project, Dr. William Howard Dusenberry was asked to write the history.

Dr. Dusenberry's qualifications for the task were unusual. A native of Greene County, an alumnus of the College, with a doctorate in history from the University of Michigan, for many years a member of the history faculty and departmental chairman at Waynesburg, he had achieved national recognition in 1962 while a member of the faculty at the University of Pittsburgh. In that year he received the annual award of the Agricultural History Society for his study, *The Mexican Mesta, The Administration of Ranching in Colonial Mexico*. The study was published in 1963 by the University of Illinois Press.

Early in 1971, Dr. Dusenberry began systematically to collect and to organize source materials. Trustee minutes, faculty minutes, local newspapers, various student and alumni publications, — these and many other sources had to be painstakingly searched. In addition, knowledge of the educational scene generally was important in terms of maintaining perspective. Thus, a large amount of reading was necessary over and above the extensive examination required of materials which were of particular relevance to Waynesburg College.

During the academic year 1971-72, Dr. Dusenberry was relieved of his teaching responsibilities, although he continued to discharge the not inconsiderable duties of department chairman. Following his retirement in June 1973, he worked on a full-time basis, without any remuneration whatsoever, until the history was completed.

On behalf of the College family—trustees, faculty and administration, students, alumni, and friends—I wish to thank him and to express appreciation for an extraordinary demonstration of dedication to a cause in which he deeply believed—the care and nurture of Waynesburg College.

Bennett M. Rich
President

PREFACE

As the title of this book indicates, my purpose in writing it is to tell simply and objectively the story of Waynesburg College from its founding in 1849 to its 125th Anniversary in 1974. After brief treatment of the background institutions in Chapter I, the narrative begins with the first president, the Reverend Joshua Loughran, and continues chronologically with each succeeding administration. To balance the book properly, four main facets of the story are covered. First is academics, including matters relating to admissions, the curriculum, the faculty, the Library, registration, and student records. Second is business and finance, including supervision and maintenance of buildings and grounds; business management; campus security; and food service. Third is planning and development, including alumni relations, development of the physical plant, fund-raising, public relations, and sports information. Fourth is student life, including athletic programs, counseling, health services, the literary societies and other student groups, social fraternities and sororities, student government, and so on.

This book is based primarily on voluminous source materials available on the campus, including trustees' minutes, faculty minutes, minutes of the Board of Trust, minutes of literary societies, letters, memoranda, college catalogues and bulletins, and college newspapers and yearbooks. Newspapers have been very valuable as sources: the *Cumberland Presbyterian*, published by that church, threw much light on the founding of the college and on its development late in the nineteenth century; and local newspapers have been helpful. Several histories dealing with the local area helped to show the relationship of the college to the community. Two histories of the Cumberland Presbyterian Church were enlightening on the origin and early decades of the college: one was produced by Benjamin

W. McDonnold in 1888; the other by Ben M. Barrus, Milton L. Baughn, and Thomas H. Campbell in 1972. The work by George P. Schmidt, entitled *The Liberal Arts College: A Chapter in American Cultural History* was most useful in placing the college in its proper setting in American higher education. Throughout this study I have attempted to show how affairs at the college were related to contemporary events on the national scale.

The story of Waynesburg College is essentially one of human interest. It is a story of struggle and success, of defeat and victory, of despair and happiness. The college was fortunate to have a few dedicated individuals who asked only for the privilege of spending their energies and their lives in unselfish service for their fellowmen. As a result, of some twelve institutions of higher learning founded by the Cumberland Presbyterian Church prior to the Civil War, Waynesburg College is the only one that survived that conflict and operated continuously to the present day.

No study of this kind would be possible without help from others. Dr. Bennett M. Rich, President of the College, and Dr. G. Wayne Smith, Academic Dean, whose specialties respectively are political science and American history, took time in their extremely crowded schedules to read all chapters and give me the benefit of careful criticism. Robert W. Cahn, Dean of Student Life, read Chapter XXI; and Charles B. Stoy, Jr., Vice President, Business and Finance, read Chapter XXII. I am deeply indebted to these men for their helpful comments and suggestions. Michael K. Talpas, Registrar, constantly made available the file of catalogues and original documents in his office. May P. Clovis, Librarian, and her successor, Teresa Viarengo, aided me in locating materials in the Library. The Athletic Department provided complete brochures on all sports in which the college has engaged. Edward A. Marotta, Director of College Relations, reproduced certain old pictures and took a number of new ones for the book. Evalyn B. Fowler, Secretary to the Academic Dean, typed the entire manuscript; she was able to decipher my hand-written scrawl and to transform it into cleanly typed pages. Lois Westfall helped by typing research notes and by making available old pictures and documents. Others who helped were Martha M. Bissett, Shirley Haines, Donna Porterfield and Mardy J. Rush.

Many other persons came to my assistance. Local newspaper men and women were most cooperative. The office which houses *The Waynesburg Republican* and the *Observer-Reporter* was always open to me; likewise I had free access to the *Democrat Messenger* file. Personnel in the local courthouse were willing to help me look for materials there. Clergymen in several area churches, which formerly were of the Cumberland Presbyterian denomination, gave valuable assistance. Several of my students guided me to reliable sources and offered to help in other ways. Alumni and friends of the college, on learning that the project was under way, sent old newspapers, yearbooks, pictures, and original documents which were highly valuable.

My heartfelt thanks go to all who helped me in any way. Finally I enjoyed complete freedom in my research and writing. I alone am responsible for any errors.

William Howard Dusenberry
27 June 1974

I
THE BACKGROUND INSTITUTIONS

THE CUMBERLAND PRESBYTERIAN (HEREINAFTER ABBREVIATED TO CP) Church founded Waynesburg College in 1849, but this college is rooted in developments which occurred over the three preceding decades. The CP Church, a child of the Presbyterian Church, like others, established colleges, chiefly for the training of its ministers. Its first two attempts in the tri-state area were fruitless: one was Madison College, in Uniontown, Pennsylvania; the other was Beverly College, in Beverly, in southeastern Ohio. It next became interested in Greene Academy at Carmichaels, in eastern Greene County, Pennsylvania, but lack of a legal title to that institution was the main drawback to its transformation into a college. Finally, CP leaders resolved to establish an institution of higher learning in Waynesburg. Waynesburg College matured in the latter half of the nineteenth century, declined during the first twenty years in the twentieth, was resurrected, beginning in 1921, and, despite periods of stress and storm, thrived thenceforth. In 1974, its 125th Anniversary, it has a selected student body, a strong faculty, modern facilities for teaching and research, an excellent physical plant, a sound financial structure, and worthy objectives as a liberal arts institution.

In order to understand the origin of Waynesburg College, we must first be aware of the CP Church's "parent," the Presbyterian Church, established in Scotland in 1560 by John Knox, earlier a protégé of John Calvin in Geneva, Switzerland; Knox became thoroughly instilled with Calvin's teachings. Scotch Presbyterians, all ardent Calvinists, kept fleeing from religious persecution which they suffered, first in their homeland at the hands of Englishmen; next in Ulster (Northern Ireland) where they were given the name "Scotch-

Irish"; and next in New England to which they began migrating late in the seventeenth century. Even the strongly Calvinist Puritans did not welcome them. In quest of freedom, they finally moved to the American frontier, chiefly western Pennsylvania, where they greatly outnumbered Baptists, Methodists, and other denominations. By 1790 the Scotch-Irish and Scotch made up seven per cent of the population of the United States, then totaling nearly 4,000,000. The Presbyterian Church felt responsible for these settlers.[1]

After leaving New England, the Presbyterians first concentrated in the New York and Philadelphia areas. By 1706 they organized the Presbytery of Philadelphia, which became the base of operations to the West and South.[2] The "Father of American Presbyterianism" was the Reverend Francis Makemie, educated in Glasgow University, who arrived in America in 1683, did missionary work throughout the coastal colonies, and became moderator of the Presbytery of Philadelphia. Another notable Presbyterian was the Reverend John Witherspoon, a lineal descendant of John Knox, and the only clergyman to sign the Declaration of Independence. A devout Calvinist, Witherspoon came to Princeton, New Jersey, in 1768, and he was the sixth president of the College of New Jersey (later Princeton University), founded chiefly to train Presbyterian ministers.[3]

Beginning in 1763, the Presbyterian Church sent missionaries to preach in the West and to prepare the way for permanent pastorates. The first four "settled ministers," all Princeton-trained, to come to the transmontane area were: John Power who came in 1776 and preached to congregations in Mount Pleasant and Sewickley; John McMillan who toured western settlements in 1775, became pastor of the Pigeon Creek and Chartiers churches, and was dubbed "the Apostle of the West"; Thaddeus Dodd who, in 1778, organized and ministered to the Upper Ten Mile and the Lower Ten Mile churches, located respectively at Prosperity and Amity in Washington County; and Joseph Smith whose churches were at Buffalo and Cross Creek, beginning in 1779. In September 1781 McMillan, Power, and Dodd established the Presbytery of Redstone at a meeting in the Pigeon Creek Church. Princeton could not train enough ministers for frontier service. Two moves were made, therefore, to meet the demand: in 1808 a Calvinist seminary was established at Andover, Massachusetts; and McMillan founded Jefferson Academy[4] (later Jefferson College) at Canonsburg, Pennsylvania, which was approved by the Presbytery of Redstone in 1792 as its official training school for its ministers. Here Princeton-trained men turned out others who served ably as missionaries.[5]

Presbyterian clergymen consistently preached the basic tenets of Calvinism. First was the depravity of man. Since Adam fell, all human beings, including even babes in the womb, fell and were doomed to hell for eternity. Second was the doctrine of predestination. God was merciful, however, and He foreordained that a few, "the elect," would be saved, because of their faith in Christ's sacrifice. These beliefs were embodied in the Westminster Confession, the fundamental document of the Presbyterian Church.[6] Third was Presbyterian insistence that their ministers should be well-educated men. John Calvin's work entitled *The Institutes of the Christian Religion*, published in 1536, was the product of thorough research in the ancient languages. It was he who set an example of sound scholarship at the outset, which all Presbyterian clergymen felt impelled to follow.[7]

The religious ferment of the frontier first fragmented Presbyterians in New England in the "Great Awakening" beginning in the 1730's. The chief cause of dissension was the attitude toward revivals. In 1741 the Presbyterians, and some Congregationalists, split into two groups over the revival question: (1) the New Lights who wanted revivals and whose emotionalism appealed to the poor; and (2) the Old Lights who opposed them, and were chiefly of the rich class.[8]

By 1800 the "Second Awakening" was under way. It began in New England and reached its peak after crossing the Appalachians. The leader of this movement was the Reverend James McGready of Scotch parentage, and trained by McMillan at Canonsburg. After preaching in Pennsylvania and North Carolina, McGready went to Kentucky in 1796 and conducted camp meetings in clearings here and there in the forest. He attracted crowds as large as 20,000 who came from all around in wagons and camped out for as long as three weeks in one location. Aping Methodist and Baptist preachers, he became highly emotional in his preaching; his listeners "got religion" by falling, jerking, dancing, shouting, testifying, running, and rolling. Presbyterians, who adhered to Calvinist doctrine, opposed McGready's revivals and persecuted him wherever he preached.[9]

Reasons for establishing the CP Church are found in McGready's movement. First was the controversy over revivals. In Kentucky and Tennessee, Presbyterians split into revival and anti-revival parties.

The revivalists, led by McGready, insisted on emotionalism in religion. The anti-revivalists opposed emotionalism and all its manifestations.[10]

Second was the issue of predestination, a doctrine always unpopular on the frontier. The dissenters condemned Calvin's fatalistic view that only "the elect" would be saved. They believed that Christ died for all and that all who believed in Him, and lived by His teachings, would reap salvation.[11]

Third was the disagreement over the education of ministers. Presbyterians maintained they should be classically educated in colleges and seminaries. But such men could not cope with frontier conditions. Every congregation and its minister had to be armed and alert to any eventuality, for in their meetings they were constantly endangered by Indians and even by white desperadoes. Pistol-packing preachers, who had some religious training and who were dedicated, were most desirable. They could be found in nearly every congregation. As one commentator put it: "The hardy backwoodsman required a new type of preacher—one who could shoulder an axe or musket with his congregation, preach in his shirt sleeves, and take the stump for a pulpit. Men of this stamp could not be made to order in colleges. They must of necessity be trained up in the field."[12]

Fourth was a dispute over constitutional rights. By 1802 there were enough Presbyterians in Kentucky to establish the Synod of Kentucky with three presbyteries—West Lexington, Washington, and Transylvania. Later that year this Synod formed the Cumberland Presbytery from the southern portion of Transylvania. In the Cumberland Presbytery there was so much "hell-fire-and-brimstone" preaching that, in 1805, the Synod appointed a commission to investigate affairs of that Presbytery. After listening to a pulpit-pounding preacher who held his audience spellbound for three hours, the commission decided that such men were not qualified. And the Synod of Kentucky, in October 1806, dissolved the Cumberland Presbytery, and reannexed that area to the Transylvania Presbytery. This move aggravated a situation that was already tense. Consequently, early in February 1810, four young revivalists, namely, Finis Ewing, Samuel King, Ephraim McClean, and Samuel McAdow met in McAdow's home, an old log house in Dixon County, Tennessee, and proposed the founding of a new presbytery. They and their followers withdrew from the other Presbyterians in Kentucky and organized the independent Presbytery of Cumberland. Not intending to form a new sect, they still hoped for reconciliation with the Kentucky Synod. But their hopes were in vain, and the breach widened. The "Cumberland Schism" became a new denomination. And the General Assembly of the Presbyterian Church regarded the secessionists as a separate church to be treated like any other branch of Christianity.[13]

The CP Church was definitely a trans-Appalachian institution. Its home base was in the Nashville area in Tennessee. On the east it extended, by the 1830's into the foothills of the Appalachians; on the west to the Pacific Ocean. It borrowed its scheme of organization and government from the parent church: several congregations in a given area were called a presbytery; at least three presbyteries made up a synod; and annually delegates from these bodies met in the General Assembly, which drew up their constitution and Confession of Faith, made policies, and governed the denomination as a whole. Through unwearied toil, the CP Church grew rapidly. By 1845 it had 19 synods, 62 presbyteries, 700 ministers, 1,000 congregations, and a total membership of some 500,000, despite its weak financial structure. In the early years the church depended chiefly on the meager collections taken up at camp meetings. And CP members looked upon contributions to their church as matters of charity—not as binding Christian duties. For example, in 1846, a prosperous Mississippi farmer, when called upon for a donation for the circuit-riding preacher, refused to give. "He blessed GOD (capitals in original) that his religion was free. He had been a Christian fifteen years and his religion had cost him only one bit, that is twelve and a half cents." Customarily circuit-riders were housed and fed by the church members. Beyond this they received little or nothing; they were reluctant to mention pay, lest the members become suspicious that they were materialistic, selfish, and "out for money." Some compensations are notable. In 1824 the Reverend Robert Sloan, a circuit-rider in Missouri, received "*one three-cornered, white, cotton cravat*" for six months' preaching (italics in original). Another circuit-rider said that from 20 April to 12 November 1826, he rode 1,038 miles, preached 161 times, and received as pay $27.25; his expenses totaled $3.62.[14] Such financial practices were detrimental to the CP Church, and they tended to stigmatize permanently its institutions of learning.

Like all denominations, the CP Church did missionary work among whites, Indians and blacks in America, and in the foreign field. During the 1860's and 1870's it established missions in China,

Japan, Liberia, Mexico, and Turkey. By far the most important area was Japan, where five CP missionaries, all trained at Waynesburg College, rendered excellent service in the spread of Christianity—despite strong opposition from Buddhists and the government. Most noteworthy was Dr. M. L. Gordon, '68, a medical missionary who went to Japan in 1872.[15]

The CP missionary movement into western Pennsylvania led to the founding of Waynesburg College. Early in 1829, the Reverends Jacob Lindley and Cornelius Loughran, who served Presbyterian churches in the Ten Mile Creek area of Washington County, read about CP doctrines and liked them. In June 1829, the Reverends Matthew H. Bone and John W. Ogden, CP ministers from Cumberland College in Princeton, Kentucky, came to southwestern Pennsylvania in search of funds for their institution, and they met a number of Presbyterians who concurred in CP doctrine. In January 1831 a "Committee of Five" elders representing Presbyterians on the borderland between Greene and Washington counties wrote to the Reverend F. R. Cossitt, President of Cumberland College, saying they had learned something of the CP Church "of the West"; their adherents sincerely approved CP doctrine; and they viewed CP members as "brothers in Christ." This committee invited Cossitt to send them a missionary, so they could learn more about the CP Church.[16]

The letter from the Committee of Five was laid before the CP General Assembly at Princeton, Kentucky, in May 1831. That body promptly appointed the Reverends Alfred Bryan, Reuben Burrow, Alexander Chapman, Robert Donnell, and John Morgan as missionaries to visit Pennsylvania congregations. Shortly Bryan, Chapman, and Morgan started on their mission. Traveling on horseback, they preached here and there enroute to congregations in Tennessee, Kentucky, and southern Ohio. They reached Washington, Pennsylvania by 15 July 1831; Burrow and Donnell followed that fall. Regardless of denominations, they evangelized not only in churches in the area, but also "from house to house and grove to grove . . . and convictions multiplied daily in every direction."[17]

At the outset of their work in western Pennsylvania, they did not intend to establish churches of their faith; they planned to conduct a series of revivals, then return to their home base. But their methods of preaching and their doctrine appealed to the people, and the movement quickly gathered momentum—to the disgust and disapproval of Presbyterians who condemned emotionalism in religion. CP churches in the area originated mainly from opposition by the old hierarchy toward these popular missionaries.[18]

They worked north and south from Washington. After a bout with illness Bryan recovered, went to Pittsburgh, preached to several congregations, and won over many people to the faith. Simultaneously Morgan and Chapman, by invitation, met with two Presbyterian congregations, one in the Lower Ten Mile Presbyterian Church, where the Reverend Thaddeus Dodd had preached; and the other at the Upper Ten Mile Presbyterian Church, where now the Reverend Jacob Lindley preached. At Lindley's church Chapman and Morgan held forth with great emotionalism. Despite two elders who said there was "too much excitement," 192 came forward and sought salvation. After these meetings Morgan and Chapman preached in the area where the Committee of Five resided. On 18 August 1831 they met with their converts in a grove on the farm of William Stockdale and organized the first CP Church in Pennsylvania. Called the "First Church," it consisted of two congregations—one at Old Concord, the other at West Union. Each congregation had four ruling elders, two of whom served both; three ruling elders were members of the Committee of Five who first invited CP missionaries to visit their area. These congregations were "500 miles away from other CP churches." But the new field was considered so important that Bryan and Morgan remained, and they "married girls who weren't afraid to work—different from southern belles."[19]

Encouraged by the success of their crusade, the CP missionaries proposed a camp meeting in order to accommodate the great throngs of people. But Presbyterians objected, said it would be a tactic "too much like Methodism," and predicted chaos and evil consequences. Nevertheless, after much discussion, plans were made to hold a camp meeting to begin on 1 September 1831, "at Upper Ten Mile . . . about one-half mile from where the Concord Church now stands." Some 250 families from all around the countryside came in wagons, carriages, and on horseback, and tented on the campground. They were of all ages from "ten years to the hoary-headed sinner; children, skeptics, blasphemers *all* became penitent (italics in original)." The meeting lasted seven days during which Morgan preached zealously about the torments of an eternal hell, and some 250 persons were converted, most of whom became members of the CP Church.[20]

Of all converts to the CP denomination in western Pennsylvania, the most notable was the Reverend Jacob Lindley. Born and reared as a devout Presbyterian, with all the earmarks of Calvinism, he was educated under McMillan at Canonsburg. Subsequently, after serving fifteen years as the first president of Ohio University, he became pastor of the Upper Ten Mile Presbyterian Church. At first he was alarmed at the approach of the CP missionaries, but after listening to them preach he was "fully convinced that they sought only God's glory, and would never harm a single lamb of his flock." He became friendly with them, entertained them in his home and had them preach to his congregation. He even participated with Morgan in conducting services in churches of other denominations. Strait-laced Presbyterian authorities were cold toward Lindley, because of his cordial relations with Morgan and other CP missionaries. Calling CP members "excommunicated heretics," they directed the session of the Upper Ten Mile congregation to close its doors to CP preachers. They ordered Lindley to join the session in ousting these men, but he would not do so. Instead, by 20 May 1833, he joined the CP denomination and took most of his flock with him from the Presbyterian Church at Prosperity and organized them into the Bethel CP Church, on present Route 18, some three miles north of Prosperity. Lindley's departure with most of his followers shocked and saddened many "old Presbyterians."[21] Similar moves soon were made at other churches in Washington, Greene, and Fayette counties.

The CP churches in Greene County were most closely associated with Waynesburg College. A few people from Waynesburg, including Mrs. Mary Campbell, attended the camp meeting near Old Concord, and they were most favorably impressed with the services. At the request of Mrs. Campbell, Morgan came to Waynesburg in November 1831, "and preached in the old court house." He was warmly welcomed and, as a result, the CP congregation in Waynesburg was organized later that month. It started with only 22 members, but they built a small church, known as the "Brick Church on the Hill." The first church in town to be built of bricks, it was located in what is now the town park, with its back approximately a hundred feet east of the Civil War Memorial Monument, and fronting toward the present Wayne Street. The building was not pretentious, but it became an important element in the life of the college, particularly during the first two years when some classes met there and some students used it as a dormitory. As the years went on, many students attended the church, and the presidents of the college often served also as its pastors. By 1880, a new CP Church was completed. An excellent building, it was located on what is now West High Street at the present site of the Atlantic and Pacific Supermarket. It was razed in 1941, long after the merger of the CP and Presbyterian churches in town.[22]

The CP Church in Waynesburg remained strong, despite two drawbacks. First, there were periods of apathy among the congregation, but these were remedied by revivals. Second was the westward movement. After the passage of the Homestead Act in 1862, many people went west in quest of free land and better economic opportunities. The Waynesburg congregation, like others regardless of denomination, declined in numbers by such emigrations. Erstwhile members of the local CP Church were "scattered all the way from Waynesburg to the Pacific shore."[23]

CP missionaries and their converts toiled to establish and maintain their churches. By 1888 they had founded ten churches in Greene County; in southwestern Pennsylvania they outnumbered Presbyterian congregations by two to one. All CP churches in the area were interested in the welfare of Waynesburg College and they contributed regularly, if sparingly, to its support.[24]

The administrative organization of the CP Church in this area followed the usual pattern. First was the Pennsylvania Presbytery which embraced churches in Washington and Greene counties and extended southward and westward a short distance into what is now West Virginia, northward into Allegheny County, and westward to include Athens, Ohio. Second was Union Presbytery, lying east of the Monongahela River and including Fayette County. Third was Allegheny Presbytery which extended northward from Pittsburgh and encompassed Armstrong, Jefferson, Mercer, and Venango counties. These presbyteries made up the Pennsylvania Synod of the CP Church which had jurisdiction over Waynesburg College. The Synod customarily met annually by turns in each presbytery.[25]

Aware of the need for education of their ministers, early leaders in the CP Church made plans to establish and maintain institutions of learning. But in this respect they occupied a "medium ground, believing that many men have been eminently successful who have not received a classical education. . . . "[26] The first CP college opened at Princeton, Kentucky, in March 1826 with six students enrolled. The CP Church there was weak, and many believed Princeton was a poor location for a college. Shortly it was moved to Lebanon, Tennessee, where classes began in 1842, and the name was changed to "Cumberland University." The institution was completely wrecked during the Civil War, but, after that conflict, Cumberland rebounded strongly and established the preparatory department, the collegiate program, and schools of engineering, law, and theology.[27] Another strong CP institution was Lincoln University, founded in February 1865 at Lincoln, Illinois.[28] The CP institution destined to be the most affluent was Trinity University in Texas. As the name indicates, it originated from three institutions founded before the Civil War, namely, Ewing College, in 1848; Chapel Hill College, in 1849; and Larissa College, in 1855. All three were war casualties. After the war three CP Synods established Trinity, with the motto *E Tribus Unum*. Chartered by the legislature of Texas in August 1870, and located in the town of Tehuacana, it prospered and grew until a more advantageous site seemed desirable. In 1902 it was moved to Waxahachie and, in 1942, it was moved again to San Antonio.[29] The leading CP collegiate institutions might well be called "The Big Four," namely, Cumberland, Lincoln, and Trinity Universities, and, "in the eastern quarter," Waynesburg College. The CP Church founded several other institutions of higher learning, but most of them closed because of lack of funds; a few were taken over by other denominations.[30] The Big Four, however, remained stable while under the aegis of the CP Church. Of all these establishments Waynesburg is the only one which survived the Civil War and operated continuously to the present day.

Within less than a decade after the CP Church spread into the tri-state area, it attempted to establish a college in that quarter. Though CP control over Madison College was short-lived, that institution was the chief precursor of Waynesburg College. The origin of Madison College can be traced back to 1791, when John Hopwood laid out a plan for a village, later to bear his name, at the foot of the mountain east of Uniontown, and "set aside part of the area for an academy under the patronage of Baptists. . . . " After Hopwood's death on 2 June 1802, the academy was moved nearer to Uniontown and named "Union Academy"; it was chartered by the state legislature in 1808. Finally renamed "Madison College" on 7 March 1827, when it received a new charter, it was located on the present site of St. John the Baptist Greek Catholic Church on East Main Street, nearly two blocks east of the Fayette County courthouse.[31]

Madison College was named not in honor of James Madison, President of the United States, but rather in memory of his relative, the Reverend James Madison, who had been president of William and Mary College, bishop of the Protestant Episcopal Church of Virginia, and one of the four commissioners from Virginia who collaborated with four from Pennsylvania in settling the boundary controversy (the completion of the Mason and Dixon line), from 1767 to 1784.[32] Madison College was sponsored, at various periods of time, by four denominations—the Methodist Episcopal Church, the Cumberland Presbyterians, for a brief interlude by the Presbyterians, and finally by the Methodist Protestant Church.

The Methodist Episcopal Church was first to take the college under its care in April 1827.[33] Methodist Episcopal ascendancy over Madison ended in 1832, when that denomination acquired Allegheny College, Meadville, Pennsylvania, from the Presbyterians. Allegheny was much better equipped and more affluent than Madison College; these Methodists did not need both colleges in western Pennsylvania. Their abandonment of Madison coincided with the rise of the CP movement in western Pennsylvania.[34]

By the mid-1830's, the Pennsylvania Synod of the CP Church comprised three presbyteries: Pennsylvania and Union presbyteries in western Pennsylvania; and Athens presbytery in Athens, Ohio. Each of these was making an effort to provide educational facilities for "the youth under its influence." Madison College was in the bounds of Union presbytery. In 1835 the Reverend John Morgan became pastor of the CP Church in Uniontown, which then had a strong congregation. The trustees of Madison College sought the patronage and support of this new church.[35]

In 1838 the CP Church took control of Madison College, then under the nominal jurisdiction of forty-five trustees from four denominations—Presbyterian, Episcopalian, Methodist Episcopal, and Cumberland Presbyterian. They were widely "scattered through a dozen states." J. P. Weethee, age twenty-two, a graduate of Ohio University, at Athens, and a candidate for the CP ministry, was made president. He and three others, including the Reverend John Morgan, made up the faculty. Under CP auspices, the college started with only three students, but it prospered until the enrollment was 150. One main drawback was a rival school established in another part of Uniontown by a talented young Presbyterian minister. According to Weethee, this sectarian opposition continued during the period while "Madison College was under the patronage of our people." Doubtless this competition in the same town hurt Madison's growth and development.[36]

The CP Church introduced coeducation at Madison College, which caused a great deal of controversy. While Oberlin College had already become coeducational, the idea of equal educational opportunities for males and females was generally opposed. The trustees of Madison College were confronted with the question: "Are females, matriculated and pursuing a college course, students in the eyes of the law?" They decided in the affirmative, and Madison was certainly one of the first institutions of higher learning in America to admit female students. They were enrolled in the "female department" and taught by the same faculty that instructed the young men. Classes were separate, however, and "members of the two divisions have no intercourse whatever."[37]

Madison College under CP sponsorship was a liberal arts institution with a Preparatory Department for those who were not ready for college-level work. Then there were the regular four classes for male students: freshman, sophomore, junior, and senior. Classical studies, chiefly Latin and Greek, were stressed. The Female Department had a three-year program: primary, junior, and senior. Its courses were less difficult than those for the male students. By 1840 eighty-six males and thirty-one females were enrolled. The college year was divided into two terms: the first, or summer term, began early in May and ended in late September; the second, or winter term, began early in November and ended in late March. Tuition was sixty dollars per term. Board, which usually included room and laundry, was $1.25 per week; fuel, however, was extra. At commencement, as was the custom everywhere in America, all members of the graduating class participated in the exercises.[38]

Anxious to promote the development of Madison College, its trustees met late in June 1841 and planned to add a new building to the institution. In order to increase enrollment, they provided that school directors in each township in Fayette County could send a student to Madison "free of charge for tuition fees." The faculty members were devout, dedicated, hard-working men. President Weethee, reminiscing some years later, said he often taught twenty classes daily from dawn to dusk. Others on the faculty doubtless had heavy schedules, but they cooperated and the college prospered and was considered "worth having."[39]

For a brief time all seemed well and Madison was on the march. Beginning in the spring of 1842, however, problems arose, which rocked the institution and eventually led to the ouster of Weethee and to the resignation of most of the faculty members. A struggle ensued among the trustees when the Episcopal, Presbyterian, and Methodist members of that body united against the CP members. Such a coalition consistently outvoted the minority group, and thus weakened CP control over the college.[40]

A much more serious blow to CP sponsorship of the college struck when Weethee became a religious fanatic over "Millerism," a new sect started in 1832 by the Reverend William Miller, an eloquent Baptist minister from Massachusetts. The complexities of Millerism are difficult to comprehend. Miller, after carefully studying the Bible, was convinced that Christ's "second coming" was at hand, sometime in 1843 or 1844. Christ "would then raise the righteous dead and judge them together with the righteous living, who would be caught up to meet him [*sic*] in the air." He would purify the earth with fire by burning all the wicked and their property and by sending their souls "to the place prepared for the devil and his angels." The saints would live and reign with Christ in the new earth for a thousand years (the millennium) at the end of which war would rage between saints and sinners. In this struggle the sinners would lose, be judged, "and cast down to hell forever." Weethee and his followers expected Christ to return to Uniontown on 14 April 1843. In imitation of Christ, they donned robes and went to housetops—the nearer to be to God—and watched, prayed, praised the Lord, and awaited all night for His return.[41]

Christ of course did not come. When the appointed time passed and nothing unusual happened, Weethee and his followers must have been sadly disappointed for they had hoped to ascend with Christ to Paradise. Still faithful and undaunted, however, they set other dates, only to be frustrated again and again. The "Adventists" became a subject of ridicule, and their actions were increasingly detrimental to Madison College. Finally, the Honorable John Dawson, a trustee having the interests of the college at heart, called Weethee "to a halt." In addition to his quirks over religion, Weethee was very sensitive about his prerogatives; he constantly feared that someone would interfere with his supremacy. Dawson, backed by a majority of the trustees, forced Weethee and his faculty to resign. In effect they ended CP control over Madison College, which passed briefly into the hands of the Presbyterians.[42]

Within a few months the trustees "repented of their folly of dispossessing the Cumberland Presbyterians and wanted their help again." In 1844 they corresponded with the Pennsylvania Synod of the CP Church, which, at its meeting that fall, took steps again to secure control of Madison College. Their action was reported to the trustees, who, early in 1845, returned the college to the CP Synod's control. The Reverend Milton Bird, editor of *The Cumberland Presbyterian*, then published in Uniontown, Pennsylvania, appealed through this paper to all CP members for help for the college. There was little or no chance of securing state aid, but, as Bird put it: "We have thirty or more churches in Pennsylvania. If each would contribute a small amount, we could sustain one professorship, and all candidates for the ministry could attend tuition free."There was great need for books for the library and apparatus for the laboratory. The few students then enrolled were "studious and moral in habits." With Weethee gone, it was expected that a new president would be appointed, and hopes were high for "a considerable accession of students."[43]

In October 1845 the Pennsylvania Synod of the CP Church met at Old Concord. Previously the trustees of Madison College had empowered this body to nominate the president and faculty, to fix their salaries, and to fill all vacancies on the Board of Trustees. On the nomination of the Synod's Board of Education, the trustees elected the Reverend Azel Freeman, professor of ancient languages, and John N. Lewis, professor of mathematics "and the other branches usually connected with that chair." Prospects of the college seemed good, provided there would be concerted effort on the part of its friends and members of the CP Church.[44]

Appeals to the churches in western Pennsylvania for adequate support, characteristically enough, were fruitless. Freeman and Lewis, the only teachers, could not handle the work load. They resigned in the fall of 1846, and CP control over the college ended and was never revived.[45]

Before the CP Church abandoned Madison College, it gave attention to a college at Beverly, Ohio, in the Athens Presbytery, then within the bounds of the Pennsylvania Synod. There a three-story brick building had been partially erected in 1843 on land donated by John Dodge, who also pledged funds for the institution. In that year it was chartered by the Ohio legislature, and named "Beverly College." After Weethee left Madison College, he went to Beverly to head that institution. When the Pennsylvania Synod met at Old Concord in October 1845, it gave consideration to both colleges—Madison and Beverly. Aware that the CP hold on Madison was weak, as a possible alternative, the Synod expressed its desire to sustain Beverly College. It elected a board of seven trustees, and passed a resolution that the churches in Ohio chiefly should support that institution.[46]

Beverly College was doomed to failure at the outset. The population of Beverly and its environs was divided in its patronage between two strong institutions within a radius of thirty miles, namely, Marietta College at Marietta, and Ohio University at Athens. The

CP denomination was weak in that area, lacking young people who desired a college education. The college building was not finished and, during the winters, classes met in a hotel in Beverly. Most people who had made pledges to the college did not honor them. By the late 1840's there was "no agent in the field to solicit funds for the institution, no endowment fund on hand, no apparatus, no library, no professors or teachers. The institution never had a graduate. And it can scarcely be said that it ever existed as a college."[47]

The CP Church next turned to Greene County, Pennsylvania, which, according to one commentator, was "in many respects the most hopeless of all fields they had hitherto surveyed." The CP authorities became interested in a small, unpretentious institution, namely, Greene Academy.[48] The Pennsylvania legislature chartered a number of academies in the late eighteenth and early nineteenth centuries. Greene Academy was one of several such institutions in the western part of the state. As a contemporary put it, it "was a harbinger of great good, and diffused a halo of light over a then benighted land."[49]

The founders of Greene Academy were pioneers who migrated to eastern Greene County, beginning in 1767. Coming chiefly from Virginia and Maryland, where the Anglican, or Church of England, was strong, many of them adhered to that faith. After the American Revolution the Anglicans were nationally organized into the Protestant Episcopal Church. The "Episcopalians," as they were commonly called, planted missions here and there on the frontier. After the American Revolution, Charles Swan built a slab-sided structure —the first Episcopal meeting house on that part of the frontier. On 12 April 1790 James Carmichael, another Episcopalian, for whom the town was named, conveyed to the Episcopal vestrymen a lot on which a more substantial stone structure was shortly erected.[50]

Charles Swan and fellow Episcopalians were so anxious for an institution of learning in their community that they offered their church for its use. But money was needed, and funds were sought from the state legislature. Accordingly, on 20 March 1810, that body passed "an Act establishing an Academy at Carmichael's town in the County of Greene with an appropriation from the treasury of $2,000 on condition that the Episcopal society there fulfill their offer of their church as a donation for the use of the institution." Largely through the efforts of Hugh Barclay, a local member in the legislature, this appropriation was made, and the institution was chartered. In the charter, the following trustees were appointed: Hugh Barclay, George Evans, James Flenniken, Robert Lewis, Charles Swan and Robert Whitehill, Jr. They were "declared to be one body politic and corporate in Deed and in Law" with powers and duties similar to those of the "trustees of Union Academy in the Borough of Uniontown in the County of Fayette. . . . "[51]

The charter contained other details concerning the institution. Named "Greene Academy," it was intended "for the education of youth in the English and other languages and in the useful arts, science, and literature." Provision was made for the education *gratis* of not more than six poor children at any one time; and if others applied, those already enrolled could remain in school no "longer than two years." The grant of $2,000 was to be divided evenly, with $1,000 for the building and equipment, "and the purchasing of books, mathematical instruments and the necessary philosophical apparatus"; and $1,000 for endowment. Both were contingent on the cession of the lot and church building to the new institution. On 4 September 1810 the Episcopal Church deeded this property to the trustees of the new Academy. Immediately behind the building was a small cemetery in which James Carmichael was buried; his grave "is just eight feet from a window in the wall of the old building." Later more adjacent land was donated to the institution, and the citizens made subscriptions to it and took keen interest in its welfare. These funds, plus the state appropriation, made it possible to add two rooms, built of locally-made brick, to the stone structure.[52]

After the Carmichaels CP congregation was organized in 1832, services were held in Greene Academy until a church could be erected. The first church, a frame structure, was built on land donated by Myers Seaton, approximately a block from the Academy. The CP missionaries—John Morgan, Milton Bird, and Leroy Woods—were as popular there as everywhere. The Episcopalians were too formal, and "their whole system of worship" did not appeal to frontiersmen. During the American Revolution most of them were identified with Tories (Loyalists, colonials loyal to the king), hence they lost prestige after that conflict. Their local congregation declined; and Greene Academy ceased to be Episcopalian by 1836, after the Reverend Joshua Loughran, a CP minister, became its principal. Though the CP Church had no legal claim to Greene Academy, with the exception of Madison College, it was the chief educational center for CP members in Pennsylvania until 1849. The influence of the Reverend

Leroy Woods and his successors "did much to make Greene Academy an ally of Cumberland Presbyterians." The Reverend Loughran doubtless strengthened this relationship.[53]

Greene Academy made its greatest strides forward while Loughran was its principal. Largely through his efforts the curriculum was improved, enrollment of students increased, competent faculty members were employed and more books and apparatus were acquired. Although many of its students came from CP families, particularly after 1836, it was not affected by party or sectarian prejudice. Like other institutions of its kind, it stressed religion and morality.

The trustees of Greene Academy were all leading citizens, keenly interested in the welfare of the institution. In accord with established practice at many older institutions of higher learning east of the Appalachians, the Academy also had a Board of Visitors, consisting of seven members, who at certain times called at the institution to observe its operations and to make suggestions for its improvement. Members of this Board were themselves well educated and qualified to evaluate the institution. Their regular visitations undoubtedly did much to maintain the high academic standards for which the Academy was noted.[54]

The academic year was divided into two terms of five months each with a week's vacation coming near the middle of each term. The Summer Session opened on the first Monday in May; and the Winter Session on the first Monday in November. Expenses appear to have been modest—even for that time. Tuition was ten dollars per term for one taking the Languages and the higher branches of Mathematics; eight dollars for a student in the sciences; and five dollars at the primary level. Boarding, which included room, fuel, and laundry, could be had in town at $1.50 per week; and at a convenient distance from the Academy for $1.25 per week. Clubbing, however, was encouraged. Students could rent rooms and board themselves at a cost of no more than 50 or 62 1/2 cents per week. It was estimated that the "expense of students including boarding and tuition will never exceed $45 per session."[55]

The curriculum laid great stress on classical studies, as was customary everywhere in America, but Greene Academy was fortunate to have a strong science department. Upon completion of its program of studies, one was fully qualified to "honorable entrance into any of the higher classes of the most respectable colleges," or to enter the teaching profession. At the base of the curriculum was the Preparatory Department which students could enter upon the completion of their public school work. The "branches" in that Department were English Grammar, Geography ("with the globes"), Arithmetic, Aids to Compositions, Exposition of the Constitution of the United States, and Primary Physiology. The Academic Department offered a three-year program for male students. The first year covered Latin Grammar, Caesar's *Commentaries*, Virgil, Greek Grammar, Graeca Majora, Arithmetic (completed), Rhetoric, Algebra, and History (Ancient and Modern). The second year included Virgil (completed), Xenophon, Algebra, Geometry, Physiology (with anatomical plates), Natural Philosophy, Horace, Chemistry, Geology, Mensuration and Trigonometry. In the third year the courses were Cicero, Homer, Surveying (theoretical and practical), Astronomy, Logic, Political Economy, Moral Philosophy, Conic Sections, Natural Theology, Orations of Demosthenes, Mental Philosophy, Commentary on the Constitution of the United States, Tacitus, and Evidences of Christianity. Many of these courses were clearly on the college level. For each one the textbook was prescribed in the catalogue. Not many reference books were available, but one educator felt that "fewer books meant deeper impressions on the brain, better scholars, and more definite lines." At the close of each session a final examination was given in each course. In order to enrich the curriculum, additional lectures covered a variety of topics, and experiments were performed in chemistry and philosophy.[56]

Greene Academy was a pioneer in coeducation. Shortly after Loughran became its principal, he started the Female Department with Almira B. Kerr as its head. Reminiscing many years later, she recalled: "Those were primitive times—the beginning of what afterward became a celebrated school."[57] The Female Department, with its own Primary Department for the smaller girls, was "entirely distinct from the MALE (capitals in original), only being subject to the general rules of government for that department." One alumnus lamented many years later that, "While both ladies and gentlemen were admitted to the classic halls of the old Academy, yet we were separated by a wide hall and could only look at the girls sidewise, unless we stole a march and went star-gazing—which no little was done."[58]

While the library, with only a few valuable works, left something to be desired, the Academy was well equipped with "excellent philosophical and chemical apparatus," including a telescope, surveyor's compass and instruments, and globes—both terrestial and celestial. The most notable apparatus was Page's Rotary Generating machine with a large glass wheel, which could generate electricity and store it in a Leyden jar. The students would form a circle and clasp hands. The instructor then would adjust the jar "so as to make contact which would strike students on the wrists." He would then explain how electricity is generated and released. One eminent scholar referred to this equipment as "the best in the West." Estimated to be worth $5,000, it was adequate "to illustrate all that is known about electricity."[59]

The literary societies at Greene Academy added to the intellectual atmosphere, and gave students of both sexes the all-important opportunity to mingle together socially. There were three such organizations, namely, Thalia, Erodelphia, and Clio, and each fitted up its own room in the Academy. Each had regular programs consisting of two select orations, two original orations, two essays, and one debate. There was a tendency to be verbose, florid, and turgid in these performances. Examples of topics for select orations are "Pleasure," and "Progress of Mind"; of essays, "Time's Revolutions" and "The World of Midnight"; of original orations, "Patient Thought" and "The Men and Education for the Times." Programs always opened with prayer and ended with the benediction. It was customary to have musical selections between performances. The students gained much from their preparations for these programs, and the practice in public speaking was most beneficial. They were enthusiastic about their respective societies, particularly at the end of the academic year when the annual contest took place. Each student felt a deep sense of loyalty to his society, and the competition was keen.[60]

The great majority of students at the Academy came from Greene, Fayette, and Washington counties. Some hailed from more distant places in Pennsylvania and in other states. Figures on yearly enrollments are not available, but in 1851 the Male Academic Department had twenty-four classical students, twenty-seven mathematical and scientific students, and sixteen in the Preparatory Department. The Female Department, including those in the primary class, had thirty-four students. George W. Miller was Principal. The Academy had a "quality program" of studies. The catalogue boasted that, "In comparison with other institutions it is believed that few possess its advantages for obtaining a classical or scientific education. . . . To the community, we say, witness its Examinations, Literary performances, and then judge of its merits."[61]

On 23-24 August 1900 alumni and former students of Greene Academy held a reunion and reminisced about the "old days." The most revered speaker was Alfred B. Miller, then President Emeritus of Waynesburg College, who lauded Loughran's long, devoted service at the Academy. With its sound academic standards, its competent faculty, and its selected students, Greene Academy would have been an excellent forerunner of any college. As Miller said, "the spirit which founded and fostered Greene Academy, and the impulse it gave toward higher education led to the founding of Waynesburg College."[62]

II
PRESIDENT LOUGHRAN

AT ITS MEETING AT GREENFIELD (LATER COAL CENTER) IN WASHINGTON County in April 1849, the Pennsylvania Presbytery called attention to the need of an institution of higher learning within its bounds, and appointed a committee of five to receive proposals for the location and establishment of such an institution. Shortly this committee received overtures from Carmichaels and Waynesburg.[1]

As the frontier moved westward there was keen competition among centers of population, both large and small, to have colleges located in or near them. A college would add prestige, maintain high social morality, and be good for business. Small towns were preferred over large cities, for they lacked big crowds and were quieter and more conducive to learning. After the Pennsylvania Presbytery received proposals from Carmichaels and Waynesburg, these towns contended with each other for the college. Carmichaels, with a population of 600, offered to build a three-story brick building sixty feet long and thirty-five feet wide at the present location of the Hathaway home, and to donate considerable acreage in the environs.[2] Waynesburg, with 1,200 souls, was the county seat of Greene County, which in itself was generally considered an advantage. Further, in Waynesburg three prominent men, namely, Jesse Lazear, R. W. Downey, and Jesse Hook, had been raising money for more than a year for the institution. They originally contemplated an academy, for the first subscription list reads: "We the subscribers hereby agree to pay Jesse Lazear . . . the sums of money set opposite to our names respectively for the purpose of erecting a building in the town of Waynesburg . . . for an Academy." Hook and Lazear subscribed $200 each; Downey and nine others, $100 each; and 51 others gave smaller amounts—for a total of $2,794. Available evidence indicates that they upgraded the plan for an academy, raised additional money totaling $5,000, resolved to establish a college, and decided to erect a three-story brick building seventy feet long and fifty feet wide on a lot on College Street for that purpose. The relative merits of the Carmichaels and Waynesburg proposals were weighed and the "offers of citizens of Waynesburg were more considerable than those of Carmichaels, and Waynesburg was accordingly adopted as the seat of the proposed college." After Carmichaels lost its bid the citizens there, still insistent, proposed to erect a three-story brick building sixty feet long and thirty-five feet wide which they would offer to the Pennsylvania Synod of the CP Church for use as a female seminary. But the Synod rejected this offer, and, in collaboration with the Pennsylvania Presbytery, concentrated its efforts on one institution, which "finally became the educational enterprise of the whole church in Pennsylvania."[3]

Waynesburg was an ideal town in which to locate a college. According to legend, Thomas Slater, pioneer settler, purchased some 400 acres now comprising the campus, park, and town from the local Indian chief for a two-year old calf, a flintlock rifle, and a few trinkets. The land was fertile and well situated with a hill to the north and Ten Mile Creek to the south. Standing on the hill, one could look southward and see a beautiful panorama. Appropriately enough, Slater called his claim "Eden." On 28 October 1796 he sold it to the trustees of the newly established Greene County for $2,396. Within the original patent the "Commons," consisting of twelve acres on the northern limits of town, was laid out for the use of the first lot-holders. Covered with primeval forest at first, that area was cleared and used for pasturage on a communal basis. Until the 1870's livestock of all kinds could run and graze freely in the commons and all over town as well. The resulting unsanitary conditions eventually caused many citizens to complain. Accordingly the town council passed two ordinances to improve conditions. One banned hogs from the borough, and the other, cows. The Commons area was not controlled in any way until 1883 when the Court of Common Pleas of Greene County chartered a corporation known as the Waynesburg Park Company, which created and has maintained the parks since that time.[4] These parks have blended into the beauty of the adjacent campus. The college and the town, therefore, have been mutually fortunate.[5]

When the decision was made to establish the college in Waynesburg, no building or facilities existed there for the proposed institution. Moreover, a leader was needed, and Loughran was available for the position. There had been some dissatisfaction with him as an administrator at Greene Academy, but he was an able, popular teacher. Hence two friends, Jesse Lazear, whose son, James B. Lazear, had gone to the Academy, and John A. Gordon, who also had been a student there, invited Loughran "to open a school in Waynesburg with a view to the establishing of the college."[6]

The Reverend Joshua Loughran was born in Armagh, Ireland, 17 March 1808, of Scotch-Irish parents. He came to the United States with his father, Cornelius Loughran, in 1821. The elder Loughran, a Presbyterian minister, preached for several years in Washington County, where he met and came to admire the CP missionaries who arrived there in 1831. As a youth, Joshua attended Plattsburg Academy in New York and, after moving to Washington County, he enrolled in Jefferson College at Canonsburg in 1827. Although he did not graduate from the latter institution, it later awarded him a master's degree. Concentrating in the field of theology and concurring with CP doctrine, doubtless due to the influence of those missionaries, he became a CP minister. After his student days at Jefferson College he taught in subscription schools in Washington County until 1835, when he was called to Greene Academy.[7]

In the fall of 1849 Loughran left Greene Academy and opened "a school of high grade" in Waynesburg. This was the preliminary step in the founding of the college, for this school was merged into the new institution.[8] Classes for males were first held on the second floor of the Hayes building, on the site of the later *Messenger* Building, on the northeast corner of High and Washington Streets.[9] By the beginning of the second year the school was transferred to the CP Church "on the hill north of town," and Loughran had as assistants the Reverend Philip Axtell and James Ryall. Classes met there during the second year, and some students roomed in the building "in order to keep down expenses by doing their own housekeeping and by boarding themselves." According to one commentator, "Some of our best known men not only slept in the church pew on Sunday, but they actually slept behind the pulpit at night."[10]

In line with tradition deeply rooted in English common law, women were not equal to men. But the founders of Waynesburg

College believed that women should have the advantages of higher education. Accordingly in late summer 1850, they employed Miss Margaret Kerr Bell to take charge of a school for female students. In anticipation of her coming, Loughran said to one of his classes, on a summer day in 1850: "Wait 'till Miss Bell comes, and then we will do great things." She became principal of the "Female Seminary" which, at the outset, was separate from Loughran's school, indicating some reluctance to mix males and females in classrooms. In the fall of 1850 Miss Bell started classes for the girls on the second floor of a brick building later called the "Green House," in which a hardware store and a loan company are now located on East High Street. By the summer of 1851, the female school had been transferred to the Baptist Church, located at its present site on West High Street. A separate building, proposed for the female school, was never erected.[11]

During the first two years of operation, the relationship of Loughran's school and that of Miss Bell was not clearly defined. They were separate, yet related, institutions, and both were sponsored by the CP denomination. Meanwhile two developments took place which brought the two schools closer together. First, the new brick building was erected on College Street. Construction began in the spring of 1850 and was completed in the fall of 1851. Classes began in the new building on the first Monday in November 1851. In attendance were Loughran's male students and Miss Bell's female students. The first faculty in the new building consisted of Loughran, President and Professor of Moral and Intellectual Science, Belles Lettres, etc.; the Reverend R. M. Fish, Professor of Mathematics and Adjunct Professor of Greek and Latin Languages; Miss Bell, Principal of the Female Seminary; and Alfred B. Miller and Frank Patterson, while toiling as students, served also as teachers in the Preparatory Department. A year later William E. Gapen became Principal of the Preparatory Department; and Miss M. Fisher was Assistant Tutor, aiding Miss Bell, and teaching Piano.[12]

The second important development was the chartering of the college by an act of legislature, signed by Governor William F. Johnson on 25 March 1850. Entitled "an Act to incorporate the Waynesburg College in Greene County, state of Pennsylvania," it was broad and liberal in nature. It established "a college or public school for the education of youth in the English and other languages, literature, and the useful arts and sciences. . . . " Under a Board of Trustees, the president and professors were empowered to confer all degrees conferred by colleges and universities in the United States and to grant to graduates diplomas as was customary elsewhere. The preamble to the charter notes that its petitioners were erecting a large building for educational purposes, which they desired to place under the control of the Pennsylvania Presbytery of the CP Church upon the condition that a college be started in which at least three professorships should be sustained by the Presbytery. The charter provided that a majority of the trustees should be elected by the Pennsylvania Presbytery of the CP Church, but after commencement in 1853 the college was transferred to control by the Pennsylvania Synod, the larger body which was more capable of sustaining it. This transfer had been delayed, because only one CP Synod had existed for Pennsylvania and Ohio, which had attempted Beverly College. In 1852 this Synod was divided into one for Ohio and one for Pennsylvania. The idea prevailed that a single Synod should support only one college. Therefore, the Beverly attempt at an institution was left to the Ohio Synod; and Waynesburg College "was fully received under the fostering care of the Pennsylvania Synod." The CP Church held that the Pennsylvania Synod should have one well established and influential college. After the transfer all educational efforts of the church in its eastern area were concentrated on Waynesburg College. The charter secured to the Synod the perpetual use of the property, provided Synod sustained at least three professors. But the charter did not specify how the professors were to be supported.[13]

The Act that incorporated the college named the following men as trustees: A. G. Allison, William Braden, R. W. Downey, Mark Gordon, Jesse Hook, John T. Hook, Jesse Lazier [*sic*], Bradley Mahanna, John Phelan, John Rodgers, William W. Sayer [*sic*], A. Shaw, and W. T. E. Webb. They were local men, identified with the community. They were a nonsalaried, self-perpetuating body, which constituted a corporation charged with the execution of the charter that legally created the college. While the college was chartered, by an apparent oversight, the Female Seminary was not.[14]

The budding college was fortunate to have Loughran at the helm and Miss Bell as head of the Female Seminary. James B. Lazear, son of Jesse, was a student in Loughran's classes. Many years later James remarked: "Of course we in Waynesburg recognized how fortunate we were to have such a profound scholar and accomplished professor to assume the great work of building up to prosperity our beloved college."[15] Loughran had an excellent knowledge of Greek and Latin and a keen interest in science. He predicted that electricity would eventually be more important than steam power. He was a fine disciplinarian, who "always commanded the respect, if not the love, of his pupils." He was relatively small of stature with a dark complexion, round head, and thin hair. But he would "attract attention wherever he might be."[16]

Miss Bell, by birth, background, temperament, and training was doubtless one of the most able educators of her day. She was a pioneer in female education and a champion of women's rights. Born on 2 October 1826 at Washington, Pennsylvania, she resided there until she came to Waynesburg. Her father, Andrew Bell, was an elder in the CP congregation in Washington, which was founded shortly after those at Old Concord and West Union. He was deeply pious, and an ardent friend of education. From her father, Miss Bell inherited "that goodness and meekness which shone so conspicuously through her entire history." She attended the Washington Female Seminary, and graduated with honors. One of her classmates described her as a thoughtful, dark-haired girl who was so unselfish that she was glad her sister was prettier than she. Her diligence, motivation, and accuracy as a student "won the admiring notice of sage committees of examination." She naturally loved people, regardless of age. One of her students, Mrs. Estelle Biddle Clark, best described her as "the very impersonation of charity."[17]

The idea of complete equality of educational opportunity for the sexes was slow in coming. Many people believed that college work would place too much strain on females, and lead to nervous breakdowns. Most young women seemed resigned to their lot. Many of their elders feared that mixing the sexes during "the inflammable" teen-age years would be like igniting a powder keg and, therefore, most unwise. Accordingly, during the early years at Waynesburg, there was a great degree of segregation of the sexes. As Principal of the Female Seminary, Miss Bell taught only young women. Her school had a separate seal, separate diplomas, and separate commencement exercises. The course for females was shorter than that for males. The first class, three girls, graduated from the Waynesburg Female Seminary in September 1852 and received diplomas instead of degrees. A year later the second class of females and the first class of males, four each in number, graduated. At their commencement the females were awarded diplomas which were captioned "Waynesburg Female Seminary," but they were signed by the trustees of the college and by Loughran and Miss Bell. Thus the Female

Seminary and the college were becoming more closely integrated. At commencement for males, the young men won baccalaureate degrees, and Alfred B. Miller delivered the main oration. On 14 October 1853 he was employed as professor of mathematics to replace Professor Fish who resigned because of the low salary. In March 1855, Miller and Miss Bell were united in marriage, which was fortunate for Waynesburg College, for they labored together tirelessly, diligently, and unselfishly for the institution until her untimely death in 1874.[18]

Soon after classes started in the new building, the trustees gave careful attention to proper maintenance of the building and grounds. The college was surrounded by a cow pasture, and the need for improvement of the environs was obvious. Accordingly, on 8 April 1852 they made plans to build a fence to enclose the college lot. It was to be a plain board fence on three sides—north, east, and west—built at an estimated cost of forty-two dollars; with a view to aesthetics, the trustees provided that on the south, fronting toward town, the fence was to consist of palings "including painting with oil and sand," to be built for sixty-eight dollars. The trustees also authorized one of their own body "to employ some person to cleanse and take care of the college the coming session." Shortly they appointed a Committee on Buildings and Grounds, with Jesse Lazear, William T. E. Webb, and R. W. Downey as the first members. This committee was charged with seeing that the physical plant was adequately maintained.[19]

The original college building has been referred to variously down through the years. From 1851 to 1879 it was known as the "New College"; from 1879, when Miller Hall was under construction, to 1896 it was called the "Old College"; and from 1896, when the Reverend William Hanna provided funds for its new roof, to the present day, it has been known as "Hanna Hall." Built in the Georgian style of architecture, its beauty stems from its simplicity and symmetry. Such architecture was commonplace in England after the "Georges" came to power. It became standard in America in the late eighteenth and nineteenth centuries in churches, public buildings, and stately mansions. Construction of the top of the building is unique; the ceiling of the third floor is supported by iron rods suspended from rafters under the roof; and the third floor itself, by similar rods which extend from the ceiling vertically through walls running lengthwise. The structure was solidly built. The building was fully utilized from the beginning. (For the floor plan of the original building see page 29) On the first floor in front were two relatively small classrooms; the larger rooms of Loughran, Miss Bell, Professor Fish, Frank Patterson, and Alfred B. Miller occupied most of the space. On the second floor in front were two small rooms, one for the college library, the other for the janitor; toward the back was the chapel with a high wooden partition right down the middle north and south, which separated the girls on the west from the boys on the east; at the north end was a platform with the pulpit, plus chairs for speakers and student performers. Miss Bell's chair was on the platform in front of the girls, the better to observe them; and Loughran's chair likewise was in front of the boys. The third floor housed the literary society halls; in front each had a small room used as its library; occupying approximately the rear two-thirds were the two halls—Philo in the west and Union in the east.[20]

Within the sacred walls of the college the faculty stressed religion, morality, and knowledge, but the greatest of these was morality. A college education was presumed to be terminal, and if one were sound in character, he could get along in life. Upon winning a college degree, one could go directly into teaching, the ministry, or business. He could "read law" in an office of a reputable lawyer, and go to the practice himself. He could be apprenticed for a time under an established physician or dentist, and then practice these professions. With respect to the curriculum, there was a strong classical influence at Waynesburg College—as in all other liberal arts institutions in America. This feature, brought from Europe, can be traced back to Aristotle.[21]

Let us examine Waynesburg's program of studies during the first years of operation. The academic year was in two sessions: the first began on the first Monday in November and lasted through March; the second began the first Monday in May and ran into late September. The vacation months were April and October, timed so the young men could be home to help respectively with much of the labor at seed time and at harvest. Since there were no high schools, pupils could come to college upon the completion of their common school work. They were of course not prepared for college-level work. Hence, after admission they were enrolled in the Preparatory Department in order to make certain that they mastered the fundamentals—and learned much more—before beginning college work. The earliest catalogues gave no duration of the preparatory course. It appeared to have been at least two years, and it was

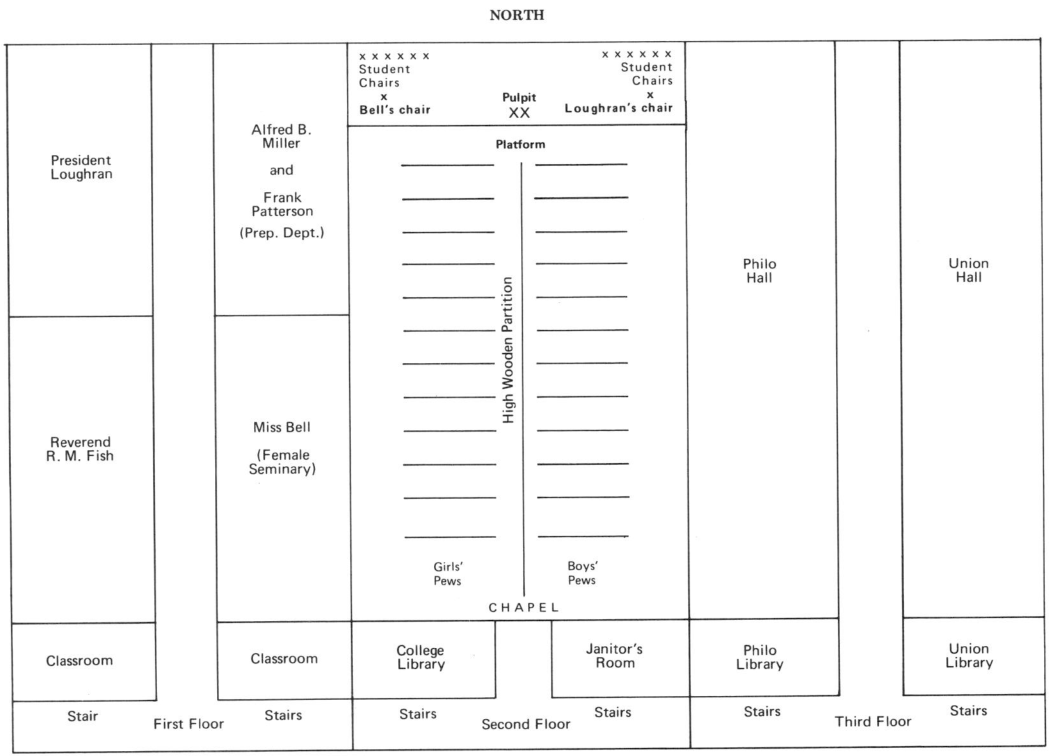

NORTH

President Loughran

Reverend R. M. Fish

Classroom

Stair

First Floor

Alfred B. Miller and Frank Patterson (Prep. Dept.)

Miss Bell (Female Seminary)

Classroom

Stairs

x x x x x x
Student Chairs
x
Bell's chair

Pulpit
XX

x x x x x x
Student Chairs
x
Loughran's chair

Platform

High Wooden Partition

Girls' Pews

Boys' Pews

CHAPEL

College Library

Janitor's Room

Stairs

Second Floor

Stairs

Philo Hall

Philo Library

Stairs

Third Floor

Union Hall

Union Library

Stairs

FLOOR PLAN OF ORIGINAL BUILDING

later lengthened to three and finally to four years after the turn of the century. Courses in the Preparatory Department for male students were English grammar, geography (with globes), arithmetic, bookkeeping, natural philosophy, algebra, geometry, history of the United States, chart of universal history, Latin Ollendorff, Latin grammar, Caesar's *Commentaries*, Sallust, Greek Ollendorff, Greek grammar, Greek testament, and aids to composition. As in all parts of the catalogue, after each course, the name of the author of the textbook is listed. The faculty selected all texts; every effort was made to secure the latest and best ones "prepared by the most accomplished German and American scholars." Supplementary to the textbooks was the small collection in the Library, gathered by three male students from the townspeople. Prior to the Civil War, American colleges were strongly influenced by higher education in Germany, and Americans were compelled to go to Germany for systematic advanced study. The German influence began in 1815 when two Harvard graduates, George Ticknor and Edward Everett, went to Germany to study; later George Bancroft joined them. They all liked the German system of higher education. The first Ph. D. degree in America was granted by Yale in 1861, and by the early 1870's both Yale and Harvard had graduate divisions.[22]

At the college level Waynesburg's curriculum for young men consisted of the regular four-year program—freshman, sophomore, junior, and senior. For freshmen the courses were Modern History, Latin Prose Composition, Plane Geometry, Virgil, Xenophon's *Anabasis*, Arithmetic, Algebra, Cicero's Select Orations, Experimental Philosophy, Homer's *Iliad*, and Livy. For sophomores the courses were Rhetoric, Grammar, Trigonometry (Plane and Spherical), Mensuration, Navigation, Surveying, Demosthenes "On the Crown," Analytical Geometry, Aristotle's Art of Poetry, Chemistry, Odes of Horace, Zoology, Physiology, and Manual of Ancient Geography and History. For juniors the courses were Natural Philosophy, Logic, Select Satires of Horace, Roman and Grecian Antiquities, Select Greek Tragedies, Mineralogy, Botany, Political Economy, Descriptive Geometry, Astronomy, Plato's *Georgius*, Tacitus' *Germania*, and Geology. For seniors, the courses were Intellectual Science, Evidences of Christianity, Natural Theology, Differential and Integral Calculus, Civil Engineering, Hebrew and German Languages, Moral Science, Kame's Elements of Criticism, Butler's *Analogy*, Longinus on the Sublime, and International and Constitutional Law. Throughout the four years, Elocution, Declamation, and English Composition were part of the regular studies.[23]

The program of studies of the Female Seminary consisted of the Preparatory Course and a three-year plan including the primary, junior, and senior classes. The Preparatory Course was essentially a review of the branches covered in public school. Courses in the primary class were Arithmetic, English Grammar, Universal History, Natural Philosophy, Ancient and Modern Geography and History, Physiology, and Botany. Courses in the junior class were Algebra, Geometry, Rhetoric, Latin, Greek, or German Ollendorff (optional), Chemistry, Plane Trigonometry, Mensuration, and Geography of Heavenly Bodies. Courses in the senior class were Political Science, Elements of Criticism, Moral Science, Latin, Greek, Mental Philosophy, Logic, Evidences of Christianity, and Natural Theology.[24]

Expenses at the college were low. In the early years, tuition ranged from $8.00 per session in the Preparatory Department to $15.00 per session for seniors. Anxious that boarding costs could be kept down, the trustees chose a committee from among themselves to assist students in finding boarding houses where the food was good and the prices were reasonable. Good boarding, which generally included room, fuel, lights, and laundry, could be had in Waynesburg and vicinity for $1.50 to $2.00 per week. Clubs could be "formed under proper regulations" and students could obtain board and the usual appurtenances "at an expense not exceeding $1.00 per week for each member." By 1853 the college had a boarding house "prepared in the most beautiful manner for the reception of students—and as other houses will also be ready, gentlemen desiring board are assured that they will find ample accommodations."[25]

The college drew most of its students from Greene County and its neighboring counties in Pennsylvania. By 1854 there were 154 common schools in Greene County with a total enrollment of 4,840 pupils. Most students who came to the college were from these schools. They entered the Preparatory Department around age fourteen. They were not admitted, however, until they passed a thorough entrance examination. Further, each one had to "give a solemn pledge in the presence of the faculty that he will observe all the Laws of the Institution." Students could transfer from other institutions and enter any class, but they had to give evidence of "a thorough acquaintance with the preceding Branches of the course or with such other studies" as the faculty deemed equivalent. Students who wanted to take part-time work could do so by attending classes along with those who aimed to graduate.[26]

With a view to high academic standards certain rules of study were prescribed. Each student was encouraged to apply himself diligently to his studies; he could not absent himself from class without permission of his teacher or without a satisfactory excuse. At the close of each session, students were compelled to take final examinations on all courses taken during the session. If they failed as the "result of idle or careless habits," they were in danger of being "degraded to an inferior class." At commencement, for both males and females, all candidates for graduation had to participate by reading essays or delivering orations under penalty of forfeiting their diplomas, if they refused. Each essay or oration had to be submitted to the president of the college prior to commencement. He customarily gave the candidates the benefit of his criticisms "and no student shall fail to observe such corrections. . . . " The trustees took action to assure that the foregoing rules were enforced. They required each professor to keep a "log book" of the progress of the several students under his charge. At the end of each session these results were reported to parents or guardians of the students.[27]

The students were subjected to rules of conduct which became increasingly numerous and rigorous. Since they entered the Preparatory Department around age fourteen, they were not so mature as today's freshmen. Faculty members and administrators, therefore, had to take the place of parents in caring for the young people entrusted to them. For each and every infraction of the rules students were brought before the faculty where they might be reprimanded, suspended, or expelled, depending on the nature of the case. No expulsion was final, however, without the approval of the Board of Trustees.[28]

The literary societies gave students some respite from the constant vigilance of the faculty and officials. The faculty encouraged these organizations, but students established and maintained them, and hence they flourished. In the early decades before football and other sports and social sororities and fraternities, these were the main extracurricular activities. In them students had opportunities to do research, to write orations and essays, to prepare material for debates, and to practice the art of public speaking. They also filled a social vacuum and, to some extent, developed self-discipline among students. They were considered an indispensable part of one's education, and membership in them was compulsory.

Literary societies were organized at the college shortly after it was chartered. Loughran promoted the first one, and named it the "Lamartine Society" in honor of Alphonse de Lamartine, a liberal republican leader in France in 1848, whom he greatly admired. An organization exclusively for males, it met in the local CP Church prior to the completion of the college building. Shortly plans were made to divide it into two societies, but some members were reluctant to make such a move. One student, writing many years later said there were those who "had regrets that two organizations seemed necessary, as all connected with the Lamertine [*sic*] were warm friends and co-workers in the building up of Waynesburg College. . . . " It appears that most members of the Lamartine Society, however, believed that two organizations were desirable, so they could compete against each other, develop a keen spirit of rivalry, and thus achieve a higher degree of excellence. Hence a "division of the old Lamartine Literary Society" met early in February 1851, for the purpose of organizing a new society. A committee was appointed to draft a constitution and bylaws and to select a suitable name for it. On 21 February this group met in the Baptist Church and presented a regular program consisting of a composition class, a declamation class, an original oration, and a debate. The "committee on the constitution" had drafted a document which was considered and approved by the group. It was then submitted to Loughran for his inspection. Shortly he approved the constitution, and the new organization was named the "Philomathean Literary Society"; by usage the name was abbreviated to "Philo Society." In the early years it was exclusively for males. By September 1851 it had adopted a distinctive badge, which was distributed to members at a cost of thirty-five cents each. Thenceforth no one was allowed to perform on the stage without his badge under penalty of a fine of fifty cents.[29]

In the fall of 1851 those members of the Lamartine Literary Society, who had not become Philomatheans, founded the Union Literary Society. Its object was "the promotion of literature, virtue and friendship, mutual improvement in composition and elocution, and enlarging the fund of information." Shortly both Union and Philo Societies obtained charters from the state legislature. They were corporate bodies within the larger corporation of the college.[30]

Not to be outdone by the young men, the female students organized their own literary societies which remained separate from Union and Philo for more than two decades. On 16 May 1850 students from the Female Seminary met in the Baptist Church, founded the first female organization, and named it the "Emma Willard Literary Society." They asked Loughran to write a constitution for them, which he promptly did. It was adopted on 21 May 1850.[31]

Shortly the other female students founded the Philean Literary Society, which was similar to the Emma Willard organization. In the early years, while there were two societies for males and two for females, the Philos showed a certain affinity for the Emma Willards and the Unions felt likewise about the Phileans. After the college building was completed the Emma Willards held their weekly meetings on Friday afternoons in Philo Hall; the Philo members met there on Friday evenings. Likewise the Phileans met each Friday afternoon in Union Hall; and the Union members met there on Friday evenings.[32]

Membership in literary societies was open to all students; it shortly became compulsory and regular attendance at meetings was required. Each society also could elect honorary members, which was frequently done. A female society could choose honorary members, regardless of sex; for example, on 5 August 1853 the Emma Willard group elected Loughran and Professor Fish to honorary membership. Any important man might be so elected, whether he was well known locally or on the national scene. On 18 September 1851 the Philo Society elected Daniel Webster, Henry Clay, and Lewis Cass as honorary members and, as usual, chose a committee to inform them of their good fortune. Choices of this high caliber were usually made in the hope that those so honored would donate funds to the society.[33]

Each society had a president, vice president, secretary, treasurer, and "reviewers." The task of the reviewers was essential to the production of high quality papers. After weekly programs ended, they received the essays, original orations and other written productions, carefully perused and corrected them, and returned them to the authors at the next meeting. Thus the performers were continually getting the benefit of searching criticism. The president's duties were most onerous for he not only conducted the weekly programs, but was charged with enforcing the rules contained in the constitution and bylaws. No member was allowed to show disrespect to officers of the society, to use bad language, to quote Scripture irreverently, to deface furniture, or to use tobacco during meetings. Other "misdemeanors" were whispering, inattention, walking around the room, lying down, doing unnecessary work, or otherwise "disturbing the society." Constitutions contained rules relative to penalties, fines, and trials of members. Elections of officers were strictly regulated, and anyone found guilty of stuffing a ballot box was fined fifty cents. In all meetings strict rules of order were observed.[34]

Each society was empowered to try its own members for breaking the rules and to impose fines in proportion to the seriousness of each offense. Most fines ranged between 6 1/4 and 50 cents. The most common offense was lying down during meetings, for which the offenders were fined from 6 1/4 to 12 1/2 cents each. At a Philo meeting late in February 1853, a student was fined 12 1/2 cents for lying down, and a second fine was imposed on him "for tumbling a sumerset" [*sic*]. A fine of 12 1/2 cents was standard for talking during performances, leaving the hall or walking around without permission, or being unprepared to perform on a program.[35]

Prior to the completion of the college building the men's societies met in the CP Church and the ladies' groups met in the Baptist Church. Once they moved into the spacious quarters in the new building they set about to furnish them and to "fit them up" for use. Carpet must be obtained; stoves were needed for heating; and candles must be had for light. The members of each gave of their time and money, and they worked hard to put their respective halls in good condition. Funds were obtained by subscriptions of members and friends, by initiation fees at one dollar per member, by fines imposed on offenders, and also from library taxes. Members who did not meet their financial obligations were suspended from societies. Some debt was incurred when the societies purchased furniture. For example, in February 1852 Philo's vice president was authorized to effect a loan to pay for furnishing their hall, but this debt was paid off subsequently by levying a tax of one dollar on each member.[36]

A typical program of a society opened with prayer, followed by the roll call. The program consisted generally of two select orations, two essays, two original orations, and one debate. Any performer who was not prepared was liable to a fine ranging from 12 1/2 to 25 cents. Usually at the end of a program, there was some discussion about the strengths and weaknesses of each participant; and those who were to take part at the next week's meeting were chosen. Some debate questions smacked of medieval times, and were religious or philosophical in nature; others dealt with social problems or current events. As examples, in July 1851, the Philos debated on: "Has the Negro or Indian the greater right to complain of their usage by the whites?" Another was: "Can the Existence of the Creator be Proved without the aid of the Bible?" The young ladies were thinking along different lines. In August 1854 members of the Emma Willard Society debated the question: "Is coqueting excusable in women?" They also tried to resolve the profound question: "Do whiskers add to the appearance of the masculine gender?" Another was: "Should old bachelors be taxed higher than married men?" Each society could, and did, invite visitors. It became customary for Philo members to invite to their programs members of the Emma Willard Society—and vice versa. Likewise members of the Union Society and the Phileans, by invitation, visited each other. Occasionally a society would hold a meeting to which the public was invited.[37]

The climax of the whole year's activities came when the societies held their annual contest. Plans for contests were initiated in the fall of 1851 when members of the Union Society challenged the Philos to a "literary contest at the close of this session." In keeping with a code of honor relative to such things, the Philos considered the challenge and accepted it. Both societies promptly began grooming members to participate in the contest. The Philos set up a series of programs over four weeks to determine who its best contestants would be; likewise the Union Society selected its best contestants. Spirit was high and competition was keen. The contest was held in November 1851. Available evidence indicates that the judges copped out in rendering a definite decision; they seemed fearful that their views might be published in the press. But each society appointed a committee to evaluate its contestants and to make comments upon their performances for publication in local newspapers.[38]

While plans for the contest were under way the college building neared completion and the problem arose over the choice of halls. Philo and Union each appointed a committee to confer on this matter. Philo claimed first choice "under an arrangement entered into at the close of the last session. . . . " If Union would not agree, the Philos suggested that they then cast lots for the choice. The Union Society obviously would not agree to give Philo its choice. Therefore, each chose a committee to cast lots—and Philo won. On motion of Alfred B. Miller, an ardent Philo, that society "elected to take the western hall."[39]

As in other collegiate institutions, each society had its library. Books were acquired by donations from faculty members and interested local citizens. Each society also levied a library tax on its members in order to purchase books; another source of income was in fines collected for overdue books. The vice president of each society usually served also as its librarian. His duties were to keep a record of all books taken out, to collect fines for overdue books, and to keep order in the library.[40]

In the early years the literary societies jointly published a journal of high quality. The first one, entitled *The Literary Visitor* and edited by a joint committee from all such societies in the college, was published in May 1854. Eight pages in length, it contained poetry and articles dealing with social problems, religion, great men of the past, and female education in Japan—where the sexes had equality in this respect. Some four years later the name of the journal was changed to *The Literary Pearl.* Although these publications were temporary, they contained items of interest to all readers.[41]

As everywhere, the college's greatest need was money, and the search for funds was continuous. The Pennsylvania Synod of the CP Church considered fund-raising so important that, in 1850, it chartered a special body of five members, called the "Board of Trust," to take charge of the endowment fund and to raise money for the college. Interest on invested endowment was used to support the faculty. Most members of the Board of Trust were chosen annually from the Waynesburg area. They were reliable, hard-working men with a sincere interest in the welfare of the college. Their main task was to secure and collect pledges most of which ranged from $25 to $100, and were payable over ten years. They had great difficulty in collecting funds, as is shown by notes throughout their records. They categorized pledges as "Collected in full," "Doubtful," "Probably Worthless," "Worthless," "Utterly Worthless," and "Hopelessly Insolvent." Indicating a certain tactfulness on the part of the board, some notes are: "Inquire again"; "Write him in a soothing manner"; "Don't crowd him, he is a good man and a friend of the College"; and "They seem very anxious to pay, but are *poor.* Be careful of them." The Board of Trust was conscientious in discharging its duties. The Synod, however, had an auditing committee which regularly visited the college and examined the accounts.[42]

Some subscriptions for the college building were only partially collected and some were not collected at all. Elijah Adams, Sr., the contractor, was paid partly from money borrowed from the Farmers and Drovers Bank in Waynesburg. As we have seen, the sum of $5,000 was raised for the building, but its actual cost was $6,000. Jesse Lazear was not only one of the most liberal donors to the college, but also cashier of the bank and owner of more than half of its stock. A devout member of the local CP Church and a leading citizen, he helped the college and the church in every possible way. One commentator later said: "It is probable that our life has been shaped and determined more by his influence than by any other man." It was to him that the public was most indebted for the beneficial support that made the college possible.[43]

In addition to donations to the college, the chief means of raising funds in the early years was by the so-called "perpetual scholarships." A practice which was common among all struggling colleges in the nation, it was an expedient to begin the collection of endowment. After the Pennsylvania Synod resolved to establish a college in its area, it decided to raise $30,000 for endowment. Agents were sent out to canvass congregations and to sell scholarships. A perpetual scholarship sold for $100; and a "full course scholarship for $30." The purchaser of a perpetual scholarship was supposed to advance $100 to Waynesburg College. But he was not required to give the cash; he could give his note and retain the principal so long as he paid the annual interest. These scholarships were transferable, and could be used immediately. They granted full tuition to any bearers who wanted to enter Waynesburg College. The interest often was hard to collect, and many notes reported as endowment were worthless. Obviously the greater the number of these scholarships, the more poverty-stricken the condition of the college. Clearly, even $20,000 raised in such a manner "would crowd the College with students, without yielding enough actual income to pay one professor." This system was financially devastating even in the early decades when tuition was low. Holders of perpetual scholarships, according to law, could continue to gain full tuition, regardless of its amount, if they pressed the matter. As the years went on the college's financial condition constantly neared disaster. Miller said it was a great error to permit students to use these scholarships before an adequate fund was raised to pay the required number of teachers.[44]

The college's low income was reflected in faculty salaries, which were comparable to wages of day laborers. Salaries were often in arrears, or not paid at all. When Alfred B. Miller was employed to teach mathematics his starting salary was $150 per session, or

$300 for an academic year. As Principal of the Female Seminary, Miss Bell was to receive the same salary, for late in April 1852 the trustees resolved "that she be allowed $150 for her services the past session." There is evidence that "the full sum of this pittance was not paid in any year." Loughran earned some income by preaching in the local CP Church. But from the outset of his work for the college, he was unhappy about his salary. Aware of this, in April 1853, the trustees promised him $250 for the next session. In the event they could not pay this sum, they hopefully resolved "to pay him as much as can be collected from the funds of the institution which shall amount to at least $150 and that the deficiency, if any, shall be paid to him out of the first surplus funds in the treasury."[45]

Loughran undoubtedly had excellent qualities as a classroom teacher. His chief weakness was his inability or unwillingness to grapple with the financial exigencies that beset the college. He was so discouraged in April 1853 that he resigned. The trustees, however, would not accept his resignation. They assured him of their "entire confidence in his integrity and ability as President," and added "that no dissatisfaction exists here or elsewhere to justify a resignation at this time." In February 1854 the trustees offered him a salary of $250 for the next session, apparently confident they could meet this figure. But Loughran took a defeatist attitude over his salary and the lack of finances. This was the chief reason for his resignation early in August 1855, which the trustees accepted.[46]

Loughran would not stay "and take chances for the future." Ethelbert H. Grabill, valedictorian of the Class of 1855, after exhorting his classmates to live lives of service to humanity and bidding them fond farewell, with the bombast and floridity characteristic of orations at that time, lauded Loughran at great length and assured him:

> "Where'er thou goest, or whate'er thy care,
> Our hearts shall follow, and our spirits share."[47]

Loughran had the respect and admiration of his students. His theological training helped him to maintain good relations with CP leaders in the community. He could preside satisfactorily at all formal functions, give out diplomas, confer degrees, and perform the many other duties of the presidency. But Waynesburg, like all other new colleges, faced a financial crisis. A topflight president was a man who could find ways to raise funds to avert disaster. Loughran could not fulfill this all-important responsibility.

III
WEETHEE AND FLENNIKEN

THE PENNSYLVANIA SYNOD OF THE CP CHURCH NOMINATED THE REVERend Jonathan P. Weethee as Loughran's successor, and the Board of Trustees elected him president of the college in the fall of 1855. They hoped he would be more successful at Waynesburg than he had been at Madison and Beverly Colleges. But he still held peculiar religious views which impaired his work at Waynesburg. Nevertheless, while Loughran had made no attempt to solve the problem of finances, Weethee at least made a feeble effort in that direction. Weethee was a strong supporter of coeducation which was finally achieved. During his administration the relationship between the Female Seminary and the college was clarified. Largely through his efforts the college made its first move to improve the quality of education in the public schools of Greene County.

Born on 6 August 1812, Weethee descended from New England parentage. In 1798 his father, Daniel Weethee, and his mother, Lucy Wilkins Weethee, walked from New Hampshire to their 750-acre grant acquired from the Ohio Company in the environs of Athens in southeastern Ohio. Weethee's parents taught him to read, and he attended the local frontier school with a term lasting only two to three months per year. With this weak background, he entered the Preparatory Department at Ohio University in the fall of 1827. By diligence he earned the A. B. degree there in the fall of 1832. For the next two years he studied medicine, as an apprentice under a practicing physician in Athens, Ohio. In the interim he attended a camp meeting and heard the Reverend John Morgan and other CP ministers preach the Gospel. Weethee was so favorably impressed that he professed his faith in Christ, joined the CP Church in Athens, and resolved to become a CP minister. To this end, in 1834 he came to Uniontown, Pennsylvania, and studied theology under the Reverend Morgan, then pastor of the CP Church there. Ohio University conferred an A. M. on Weethee in 1835. After leaving Beverly College, he preached in several places in Ohio, New York, New England, and Canada prior to coming to Waynesburg.[1]

Weethee was tall and slender with dark hair and piercing eyes. A man of good habits, he did not use tobacco or drink alcoholic beverages, tea, or coffee. Throughout his life he was a crusader in the temperance forces; his wife, the former Ann C. Kreps, aided him in all his work and shared his views. Having studied the Scriptures carefully, he was familiar with the numerous references to the second coming of Christ. Weethee, like many others, believed "that His coming will be personal, bodily, and visible." Hence his watchful waiting in Uniontown and in other places where he preached and taught. Weethee had other eccentricities, however, over religion. A relative of his, writing many years later, said that in Ohio many legends grew up about him. He had constructed a house with doors in the upstairs windows, with a view to making balconies. One legend was that "he flew out of the upstairs windows in the form of a bat." Another story "held that he expected the world to come to an end, and that he had the doors made in order to provide for an immediate exit. (Where, I don't know). Another story maintained that at night the Professor had communications with the Devil, and that he practiced black magic." His relative adds: "Since I grew up in the house, I suffered a good deal of heckling through these stories."[2]

That Weethee was erratic and unstable over religious matters is shown by the fact that, when he became President of Waynesburg College, he "had ceased to be a Cumberland Presbyterian," and did not belong to any denomination. Yet "he professed unabated attachment to our church; and his doctrinal views were thought by the Synod to be no barrier to his nomination." But that body soon became disappointed in him, because of his bizarre religious ideas.[3]

Until Weethee's administration the institution had functioned practically as two entities. One was a chartered college for male students; the other was an unchartered seminary for female students. They were separate, and efforts were made to keep them so—even after the two had moved into the college building. After the advent of Weethee to the campus, there was much discussion as to the nature of the institution. Should it continue in its dual capacity and be a college and a female seminary, or a college admitting both sexes? Sentiment grew in favor of making the female seminary a department in the college, but bitter opponents argued that "this was not in accord with college systems." A strong advocate of complete coeducation, Weethee invited people to the college chapel, gave an address, and held a discussion of the problem. He pointed out that the Female Seminary had no charter and, without one, it could not be publicly recognized. But opposition mounted almost to the point of violence. A public meeting over the matter was later held in the courthouse, where the two sides became boisterous and nearly came to blows. Weethee wanted the young women to have equality of educational opportunity with the young men; he contended that females should have the right to take the same courses as males and to win the bachelor's degree. Opponents countered that it would seem odd to call girls "bachelor," but the word came to be used in the generic sense to embrace the ladies. Shortly a committee consisting of those who favored coeducation and those who opposed it met and compromised. As a result, the trustees decided that the institution was a college with a female department, "the said department to have its own principal." It admitted students, regardless of sex, under one administration. Consequently, Weethee inspired his two nieces, Lydia and Laura Weethee from Chauncey, Ohio, and Margaret Needham from Providence, Rhode Island, to enroll in courses leading to the bachelor of science degree. All three graduated *cum laude* at the end of their college career in September 1857. While several other young ladies graduated from the Female Seminary and, as usual, received diplomas, Weethee's nieces and Miss Needham were the first to receive degrees. A classmate reminisced many years later that "those three girls deserted us and went over to the men." Waynesburg was one of the first colleges in the nation to grant degrees to women. And Weethee was dubbed "Father of Female Education in Pennsylvania."[4]

Weethee tried to solve the problem of finances. Shortly after he became president, the Reverend T. J. Simpson was appointed financial agent of the college. Simpson solicited money from CP congregations in the area and worked hard to increase the endowment fund. He made good contacts among members of the church, brought in a large number of students, and began an era of good feeling which bore fruit in subsequent years. Unfortunately he could not raise enough money even to meet current expenses, and very little was accomplished in raising the endowment fund. Doubtless perpetual scholarships were already detrimental to the financial stability of the college.[5]

As was the custom for most college presidents, Weethee taught Moral and Intellectual Science. His other course was Belles Lettres, which stressed the aesthetic value of literature, rather than its informative content. The Reverend Alfred B. Miller was professor of mathematics and natural science. Rounding out the "male department" was Thomas G. Lazear, professor of Greek and Latin languages. Mrs. Margaret Bell Miller was principal of the female department. She was assisted by Miss Juliet E. Barclay; and Mrs. L. L. D. Jacobs was instructor in music. As usual the great majority of students came from the local area. "Out of state" students included five from that part of Virginia which became West Virginia in 1863, four from Ohio, three from Kansas, two from Illinois, two from Iowa, one from Rhode Island, and one from Missouri. In 1857, total enrollment was 181, 100 being males and 81 females. The scientific course included the same studies as the classical, without the Greek and Latin languages. The 1857 catalogue states that: "Students completing this course, whether ladies or gentlemen, receive the degree of Bachelor of Science." The full collegiate course was open to female students. They could advance beyond the course of study in the female department and take other courses leading toward a degree. At graduation, however, there were separate baccalaureate services and commencement exercises, which indicates that complete equality of the sexes had not been achieved.[6]

From its beginnings Waynesburg College was interested in the welfare of public schools, particularly in Greene County. Loughran had suggested the desirability of a county institute for teachers, but the matter was delayed until after Weethee became president. The Reverend A. J. McGlumphy, a Waynesburg College student, who had taught public school, became Superintendent of Schools of Greene County in 1857. One of his first moves was to call through the local newspapers "for a meeting of the teachers, directors, and other friends of education, to convene in the college hall at Waynesburg to organize a teachers' institute for the county." Poor transportation and impassable roads prevented many teachers from attending this meeting. Nonetheless, the county institute was established, with help from Weethee, Miller, and several students of the college. Early institutes were held in the "College Hall." Subsequently they met in the courthouse or in the town hall; still later they met in the Opera House in Waynesburg. Provision was made for semi-annual meetings, but later only annual meetings were held. The county institute set a pattern for similar such organizations on a smaller scale, which met here and there over the county during the fall and winter. It is to the credit of Weethee, Miller, McGlumphy, and other Waynesburg College men that the county institute was so successfully organized. The benefits which have accrued to public schools in this area over the years are inestimable.[7]

In 1857 the "laws and regulations" of the college were codified. With slight revisions in 1869, they remained in effect through the remainder of the century. They outlined the duties of Weethee and his successors which were similar to those of presidents of other colleges. Weethee had general superintendence of the institution. He could convene the Board of Trustees and lay before them any relevant matters; he could summon faculty members, preside over their meetings, and vote in case of a tie. He was keeper of the college key; the security and maintenance of buildings and grounds were important responsibilities. He presided over all public functions such as commencement or other special exercises. Teaching was also a responsibility in addition to his other duties; and he could drop in and visit any class at will.[8] But a college president had many duties which were not listed in the laws and regulations. He was a fund-raiser, public relations man, chaplain, counselor of students, and so on.

The principal of the female department had the same voice as any other professor in all matters concerning the general welfare of the college. She taught in that department and had special oversight of the conduct of female pupils. And it was "her privilege to deliver an address to each graduating class of ladies on the presentation of diplomas." Professors were responsible for faithful instruction of students and were required to do other work to meet the daily needs of the college. They were to preserve order, secure "obedience to the laws," and promote the welfare of the institution.[9]

Each year was climaxed during commencement week with its several activities. It became customary to hold public examinations; on such occasions each student was assigned a seat in the chapel, and no one could leave without permission. Great care was taken that nothing untoward happened at commencement. If any graduating senior failed to profit by the president's suggestions and criticisms of his essay or oration, or attempted "to deliver in public anything profane or otherwise censurable, the President is authorized to stop him on the stage, and he shall be otherwise punished as the faculty may determine." Persons who received the master's degree also were required to perform. Anyone who held the bachelor's degree for three years and was of good moral character, could win a master's degree simply by paying the usual five dollar fee and by making "such public performances as the Faculty may direct." The hard grind toward a graduate degree was then unknown in America.[10]

Rules relating to religion and morality were greatly detailed by 1857. The faculty was charged to watch over the conduct of students and to encourage them, by precept and example, to lead virtuous lives and to give diligent attention to the duties of religion. Students were required to attend public worship at least once every Sunday, but "not at night." All students had to attend the daily chapel "and to behave with respect and gravity during the same." In teaching religion the faculty was enjoined to avoid controversial points "which have long divided the Protestant world, leaving those of different religious denominations to the peaceful enjoyment of their peculiar views. . . . " But students were warned that "principles of irreligion" were destructive, and anyone who avowed or propagated ideas subversive of morals or religion was liable to "be admonished, suspended, or expelled, as the Faculty may decide." Students who behaved irreverently either in church or in chapel were "liable to the severest penalties."[11]

Rules of conduct were more numerous than, and just as stringent as, those concerning religion. Students were required to demean themselves properly at all times, which meant courtesy to all, respect toward the faculty and officers of the institution, and quiet behavior in or near the college building; and they had to refrain from speaking profane language. The use of tobacco in any form was banned in the building. Students were forbidden to drink intoxicants anywhere or to enter a house where such drinks were sold as a beverage. They were "forbidden to keep company with persons of bad character." They could not board in a hotel without permission of the faculty. Deadly weapons were barred—either on their persons or in their rooms. They were not allowed to "attend a horse race, ball, circus, or other immoral amusement, or take part in any theatrical exhibition." Playing cards "or other sedentary games," rolling dice, and gambling were prohibited. Vandalism was discouraged. Any student who wrote on the walls of the building or otherwise damaged the property was required to pay a sum equal to twice the estimated damage. Students were compelled to attend classes; if one absented himself three times without the instructor's permission or a lawful excuse, he was reported to the faculty to be "dealt with as they may think the case requires." Students could not hold general meetings without the president's permission. Nor could they leave the campus to visit their homes or go elsewhere without his knowledge and approval. The students themselves were required to give all possible assistance in the enforcement of these rules of conduct.[12]

The college adopted special rules for boarders in the female department. The young ladies were allowed to board only in homes designated by the faculty. They could not board where male students boarded "except by special permission." They were forbidden to "go on excursions or visits to the country, attend any party, or be absent from their rooms at night, for any other purpose than to attend religious services, without permission from the Principal." Dating was quite limited. The young women were "not permitted to receive calls from gentlemen except on Saturdays; and in no case shall such company be entertained at a later hour than 10 o'clock, P.M." The young man had to apply to the president's office in writing, stating the name of the girl he wished to visit—and when. His desire for "an appointment" was passed on to the young lady. Her answer—either acceptance or rejection—was returned by the same route. It appears that they were chaperoned even during their brief visit.[13]

The laws of the college indicate the parental role which the faculty and officials felt impelled to assume. If it became clear that a student's connection with the college was answering no valuable purpose to him or that it was injurious to the institution, he was privately notified to withdraw, and his parents or guardian were apprised of the situation. During vacations students were required to be on their good behavior, and were held responsible for their moral conduct, the same as during the terms. The institution was vigilant over them from the time they entered it until they graduated or otherwise severed their connection with it. Though the code of 1857 contains seventy-six rules designed to govern all facets of the institution, one provision reads: "The laws of the College being of necessity few, cases not provided for will occur, in which the Faculty may proceed according to their judgment."[14]

By 1857 the literary societies were flourishing. They were free to conduct their own affairs, but were subject to the laws of the college. The faculty and trustees had power to regulate them, and even to dissolve them if there was good reason to do so. Faculty members could visit the literary societies at their pleasure. Each society was required to report regularly to the faculty concerning its activities, and to aid in the enforcement of rules governing these organizations. Shortly after his administration began, Weethee took an interest in their work. On 7 December 1855 the Philo Society elected him as an honorary member at the end of their weekly program. There was some cooperation between the male and female societies. For example, in December 1856 a committee of five Philo members was appointed to act in conjunction with a like committee from the Emma Willard Society "in taking up and turning the carpet, and cleaning the hall." And Philo's treasurer "was authorized to purchase oil cloth to go under the stove for the protection of the carpet from fire." The practice of presenting diplomas from each society to its outstanding members who graduated also was begun.[15]

Rules relating to student life were predicated on the proposition that no student—even a mellowed senior—was capable of self-discipline. The rigid authoritarianism doubtless caused resentment among many students; rules frequently were violated, and student opposition to the system was revealed in many ways. The wooden partition right down the middle of the chapel, and extending half way to the ceiling, became intolerable to a few. During a spring in the early years, "two males were so lovesick (and so were their girls) that they could no longer endure the partition." One of the males cut a hand-sized hole in it. "Thenceforward students looked forward eagerly to chapel. . . . One affair (through the hole in the partition) culminated in a four-year engagement, then marriage."[16] In this case, at least, the end justified the means.

While Weethee had certain admirable qualities, there were three main drawbacks which were detrimental to him as president of the college. First, his peculiar religious views made him rather unpopular. For this reason he did practically no preaching in local churches. He disavowed membership in the CP denomination and still, like William Miller, awaited the second coming of Christ. Second, he was unable or unwilling to grapple successfully with the financial distress of the institution. During his administration a debt of $3,000 was incurred, and the college was on the brink of disaster. At the end of 1857, his salary for the whole year was unpaid and the treasury was empty. He had a family consisting of "a wife and two lovely daughters," but lacked income to support them. Third, there was still strife and controversy over the relationship of the male and female segments of the college. Those who would stress the male element strongly opposed Weethee's insistence on coeducation in all facets of the institution.[17]

These problems led to Weethee's resignation in the fall of 1858. The prospects were then so gloomy that many friends of the college feared it would terminate—like Madison College and many others in the nation. In this crisis the Pennsylvania Synod of the CP Church shortly met in Carmichaels and revealed its discouragement about the condition of the college. As that body put it: "The educational enterprise within our bounds is considerably embarrassed; there is but a partial faculty; [there is] demand for immediate attention and action that the institution be conducted on the most economical plan possible." The Synod sent a call to Loughran, then head of a school in Wisconsin, and proposed that he return to the presidency of the college, "but having been starved out once, he made conditions which Synod could not accept." Meanwhile, Weethee hoped to collect his salary, but "the trustees had nothing with which to pay." They met in an office in the courthouse and directed the president and secretary, respectively C. A. Black and J. A. J. Buchanan, of that body "to confess judgment to Mr. Weethee to the full amount of his salary, which they did." Actual payment was not forthcoming, however. Weethee even contemplated selling the college property in order to collect his salary. He told Alfred B. Miller: "I could sell it out, but I will not do so now."[18] After this meeting, Black and Buchanan, in desperation, approached Miller and the latter said: "Mr. Black and I have talked the matter over, and we see nothing that can be done with the college but for you and Mrs. Miller to take it, run it if you can." The Synod disbanded without nominating a president, and it was not to meet again for nearly a year. In the interim the trustees chose the president of their own body, the Honorable John C. Flenniken, erstwhile member of the senate of Pennsylvania, to serve as acting president of the college. In addition to Miller, his faculty consisted of the Reverend S. H. Jeffrey, A. M., pastor of the Waynesburg CP Church, Professor of Natural Science; the Reverend A. J. McGlumphy, just graduated from the college, Professor of Mathematics; and Margaret B. Miller, Principal of the Female Department. Flenniken was deeply interested in the college; he frequently visited chapel exercises, but did no teaching. The real work of running the institution fell on Miller, who taught a heavy schedule and did the administrative work.[19]

The college faltered and flagged during the academic year 1858-1859, and some members of Synod and the Board of Trustees feared it would fail. Weethee's peculiar religious views and his inability to raise sufficient funds hurt the institution. The situation was more critical, because the controversy over slavery was threatening to engulf the nation in civil war. Conditions clearly called for a man capable of leading the college out of its morass of difficulties. Such a man would maintain friendly relations with students, their parents, faculty, trustees, alumni, and the public. Above all he would make good contacts with donors and have that all-important quality of coming up with money when it was needed most. He would be undaunted in the face of any adversity. In short he would be totally committed to Waynesburg College.

IV
THE MANY-SIDED MILLER

AFTER WEETHEE'S RESIGNATION THE COLLEGE REACHED THE NADIR, AND A steady hand was needed to see it through its period of stress and storm. The Reverend Alfred Brashear Miller, professor of mathematics, was the "man of the hour" who had the ability, desire, and dedication to meet the great challenge and to set things aright. Many times he has been called the "Moses of Waynesburg College." As Moses, facing incredible adversities over a period of forty years, led the Israelites from slavery in Egypt to independent nationhood in the Promised Land, Canaan, so Miller, in forty years, led the college out of its depths of despair and debt and transformed it into a mature, solidly established institution.

He did so in the face of almost unbelievable handicaps and discouragements. Among the prophets of doom was a proselytizer who tried to induce Miller not to attend Waynesburg College as a student, but rather to come to Washington (later Washington and Jefferson) College instead, which "will be better. They [the CP leaders] failed in Uniontown; they will fail in Waynesburg." Miller resolutely replied: "I will go to Waynesburg College and help to make it succeed." Loughran later advised Miller not to remain at the college when the outlook was so discouraging. The institution was in such desperate straits for money that a piano belonging to it was sold for debt. The treasury was empty, and faculty salaries and other expenses could not be paid. Dissensions had partly turned the community against the college; the public lacked confidence in its future. Even Jesse Lazear, the main financial patron, felt the church had undertaken too much in founding a college; he believed the institution should have been kept at the academy level. During spring vacation in 1855 Lazear wrote to the Millers, and "deplored the fact that money was not foreseeable to pay them for their work if they remained with the college. . . . " If the Millers had acted on this suggestion, the college would have closed then. Plans made by Synod to raise funds proved unsatisfactory. The trustees were willing to consider measures proposed by Synod and the faculty, but "found an easy relief from pecuniary responsibility by simply reiterating that the church is to support the professors." The tendency to pass the buck continued to hurt the college. Such were conditions in 1859 when a committee of Synod nominated Miller to the presidency of the college. Shortly the trustees elected him to the position. During the preceding year he had performed virtually all the duties devolving upon the office of president. With a certain prospect of hard work and little pecuniary reward, he accepted. Thenceforward, particularly for the first fifteen years, he literally "took the College and ran it." He had complete freedom to manage it as he wished and, "without seeming egotistical," he believed this was the only way the college could be saved from hopeless failure. The college became a highly personalized institution with Miller serving as top administrator, financial agent, faculty member, and public relations man. He was chief recruiter of faculty and students. He also assumed most of the duties normally performed by the trustees. Undertaking his responsibilities under such unfavorable circumstances "seemed more like an effort to make a college than the honor of presiding over one. . . . " But Miller was a man who could endure adversities and rise above all obstacles. As a contemporary put it: "His own account of conducting the college and holding together a faculty and paying them would be amusing if it were not so sad."[1] A man of lesser commitment, desire, firmness of purpose, and faith would have given up in vain.

Miller was a many-sided man. In his era the college presidency was an art that one learned to do by doing. In addition to mastering that art, Miller admirably did many other things which redounded, either directly or indirectly, to the glory of Waynesburg College.

Miller was born near Brownsville, Pennsylvania, on 16 October 1829. His parents Moses and Mary (Knight) Miller were respectively of German and English descent. He was the fourth of ten children. His early schooling was very meager; because of dissension the local schools were closed for several years during which he worked on his father's farm. But he spent a good summer in a school in Brownsville, where he started to study Latin. He was a student at Greene Academy in the summers of 1847, 1848, and 1849. During the winters he taught public school—first at Coal Center (Greenfield) in Washington County, where he proved to be an excellent teacher. Before age twenty-one he had become a member of the CP Church and had united with the Union Presbytery of that denomination. He was licensed as a CP minister, and preached first in a schoolhouse in Masontown, Pennsylvania, where he promoted the building of a CP Church. In November 1851, when the college building was ready for use, he came from his home, brought two students along, and reached the campus on the opening day. He began his studies there, and he also taught in the Preparatory Department. According to him, "The first term in the new building was a truly pleasant and auspicious beginning. As I look back upon that winter's work, it seems to me that no set of students and teachers were ever happier or more intent on the faithful discharge of duty. Unbroken harmony prevailed. . . . " At the first commencement for males, 28 September 1853, there were four graduates: A. B. Miller, W. E. Gapen, Clark Hackney, and James Rinehart who won the baccalaureate degree. This was a great occasion, with nearly all members of the Pennsylvania Synod, along with other dignitaries, on the platform. Appropriately the class motto "*Ducimus*" ("We lead") was displayed above the four young men. Aware of the importance of the event, each showed mastery of the art of public speaking. Miller had the privilege of speaking first, and it was here that he, "without being egotistical," considered himself the "first born son of *Alma Mater*." He was later to receive three honorary degrees: a D. D. from Adrian College; a D. D. from Allegheny College; and an LL. D. from Cumberland University. As student, teacher, and administrator right after Weethee left, "he felt the deepest possible interest in the welfare" of the college. Fully cognizant of the unfavorable circumstances confronting the institution in 1859, Miller, without being erratic like Weethee, had a strong conviction of providential direction of his life—that God led him in the course he "pursued in regard to our college."[2]

With respect to religious doctrine, Miller went back to the origin of the CP Church and concurred in its Confession of Faith which abandoned the fatalism of Calvin. He held that the Westminster Confession of Faith could never be reconciled with CP doctrine. He protested "against that cardinal dogma of Calvin, that a God of justice elected out of Adam's fallen race some men, and reprobated others to eternal pain, *thousands of years before they were born*!!! (Miller's italics)." Miller pled for a modification of the Westminster Confession of Faith "to express the plain teaching of God's word and to meet the common sense view of mankind. . . . " If this could be done, he saw no reason why the different branches of the Presbyterian family should not be one in organic union. By August 1869, some Presbyterian ministers suggested that the CP Church "come back into the family"; they contended that there was not too much difference in CP and Presbyterian doctrines. Miller opposed reunion most emphatically: "As to joining any union upon the Westminster standards, so long as . . . our understanding of those standards remains as now, we can never go into such a union, never—never—never." In 1874 he chided Calvinists again: "*Their* system of theology . . . is not our system, and no committees or councils on earth can make them harmonize, while they remain as now. We are not Calvinists. The Calvinist theology and our theology are positive, well defined, irreconcilable antagonisms." To Miller, the Calvinist belief that "infants go to hell because of original sin" was absurd.[3]

Since the great emphasis in higher education was on morality, Miller was deeply concerned about human conduct—why some are more impelled toward sin and wrong-doing than others. In an article entitled "Phrenology *versus* Fatality," he sided with the phrenologists who believed that one's character and mental capacity were determined chiefly by the shape of one's skull. He held that this was "a reliable science which opposes the dangerous theory of fatality." He contended that men could not blame their sins on fate, the devil, heredity, or some other factor. As he put it: "Man's own conscience and his experience furnish strong proof that he is a free moral agent. . . . We are responsible for the right use of the talents we possess." In judging anyone's conduct, the main question was: "Did he live in the fear and love of God?"[4]

One of the most serious problems in the early nineteenth century was the heavy drinking of alcoholic beverages. Liquor had long been considered a social necessity at barn-raisings, corn-huskings, christenings, marriages, and even funerals. When a visitor called, as coffee is usually served today, it was customary in many homes to set out the jug and a glass of water. Whiskey was commonly found on subscription papers for ministers' salaries. Alcohol literally was "King." To eradicate such a deeply rooted social evil called for concerted action of all the temperance forces. Miller joined wholeheartedly in this reform movement. In 1871 he rejoiced when a four-year crusade had been won against the sale and use of intoxicating drinks in Waynesburg; the court had closed the last saloon in town. But this court order did not terminate drinking in town for, in February 1877, Miller held a revival meeting in the CP Church at which the Murphy temperance pledge, so-called for a converted Irish drunkard, was daily "offered and pressed upon the congregations." Some "200 men and boys signed it, many of whom had been given much to strong drink." The Murphy movement was generally hailed as a success, for it reclaimed many men from the evils of alcohol as a beverage.[5] In 1886 Miller was happy that the CP General Assembly declared for prohibition. He then courageously called for political action on a national scale to end the evils of liquor. He urged all temperance people in the nation to use their ballots to divorce government "from its alliance with the gigantic system of legalized wrong known as the liquor traffic."[6]

Miller's opposition to alcoholic beverages was equaled by his repugnance to the widespread use of tobacco. Smoking, chewing, and indelicate spitting became scandalous in the decades before the Civil War; the salivary propensity persisted everywhere in the nation. In 1869 Miller predicted that "the coming Christian" would not use tobacco, and stressed the need for a great crusade against its use in any form. He defined a cigar as "a roll of nasty weed with a fire on one end and a fool on the other." Reform, he contended, must begin with preachers. He was thankful that the use of alcoholic drinks was driven first from the ranks of the ministry. Pleading for preachers to "act like Christian gentlemen," he referred to a cultured lady from Europe who was being entertained in the same home as a local "divine" who "spits tobacco over everything about the house." He urged ministers to practice what they preached. Pointing to the offensive smell of tobacco on their breath and clothing, he told preachers: "You have a whole appearance forcibly reminding one of the back yard of a slaughterhouse after a heavy rain in a wet time in July."[7] Warning that the Gospel commands "Do thyself no harm," Miller maintained that nicotine was a deadly poison and "cannibals will not eat the body of a man who uses it." Furthermore, he wondered "how a lovely woman, the soul of purity," could kiss a man who had just thrown out a quid of tobacco. By 1900 the cigarette was coming into wider use, and Miller declared that its slender form, its nicotine, and its heat would "produce cancer of the lip and do other harm." Research at Amherst and

Yale, he said, proved that the ill effects of cigarette smoking were loss of weight, decrease in chest capacity, and poor scholarship.[8]

Miller coupled his fight against tobacco with support of CP missions in Japan. In January 1873 he appealed to the whole CP Church, through a notice in *The Cumberland Presbyterian*, for sixty dollars in order to purchase a copy of the *American Cyclopedia* for "Brother Gordon" who had gone to that distant land. He waited at length—and received only five dollars. Undaunted, a year later he called through the church newspaper for $106.58 to pay for an organ to be shipped to Gordon. Funds for the organ and the *American Cyclopedia* were slow in coming. Miller then made an impassioned plea to all CP members: "If all addicted to their use would throw away the hurtful quid and pipe, they could thoroughly equip Brother Gordon, and send a dozen more to join him during the year. O for consecration of money now spent on hurtful lusts of the flesh!"[9]

Miller was equally interested in seeking solutions to other great social problems of the day. Most serious was the lot of black people in the nation, many of whom were members of the CP denomination. Since the CP Church geographically straddled the line dividing the North and South over the question of slavery, Miller and other CP leaders were in a better position than those in the Presbyterian Church, North, or the Presbyterian Church, South, to see this problem from an unbiased viewpoint. Miller contended that the CP Church should lead the way in the evangelization of the colored race, and "should extend to them our fostering care. . . . They adhere to our Confession of Faith; they conform to our government; they assume our distinctive name. . . . " Black people were forcibly brought to America and "put under the yoke of servitude," and God "looks to his people in this land to work out the deliverance of his long oppressed race." Political deliverance had come to the blacks—at least on paper—but equality of civil rights had not. Miller insisted that "neither race can manifest a feeling of hostility toward the other without bringing evil on both." He urged equality of the races on three grounds. First was "justice as repayment for what the African race has done for this country." Second was Christian obligation. "God's image 'cut out of ebony' ought to be just as dear to the Christian heart as God's image cut out of any other material." Third was economy. While foreign missions were desirable and should be fostered, more attention should be given to the field at home. Miller maintained that, after blacks in America had been evangelized, black ministers should be trained and sent as missionaries to Africa to Christianize the millions in that vast continent.[10]

Concerned about the education of black ministers, Miller took a practical approach to this problem. In 1869 a convention of black CP ministers met in Murfreesboro, Tennessee, and asked to be organized into separate presbyteries and synods. The CP General Assembly shortly approved this proposition and advised the blacks to establish a theological seminary to educate their ministers. Miller, seeing the obvious impossibility of such a move, asked: "Could they run it, if they had it?" They "are unlearned, homeless, landless, moneyless, and almost friendless." He cautioned that the CP Church must quickly find ways to educate its black ministers, or other denominations would "occupy the field." According to him, the Roman Catholic Church then had "400 colored men in Rome training for the priesthood. How many are Cumberland Presbyterians educating? Not one!" Miller proposed sending black students to the seminary at Cumberland University where professors could "put them in separate classes, if necessary, and teach them the elements of theology. This may seem humiliating, but it is necessary."[11]

In 1869 Miller carried his reform movement into the field of women's rights. Doubtless he had support from his wife, who believed in equality of the sexes. Well into the nineteenth century the status of American married women depended on old English common law. The wife had no rights to make deeds, wills, contracts, or sue in courts without her husband's consent.[12] Women of course had been denied equality of opportunity for education; and they had no political rights.

Miller first pleaded for woman suffrage in September 1869. Pointing out that God created man and woman equal, he quoted Scripture: "There is neither Jew nor Greek; there is neither bond no free; there is neither male nor female." The popular argument against woman suffrage was that females would be demoralized when they go to the polls, where they would see drunkards, hear profane language, smell tobacco smoke, and be targets of careless squirting of tobacco juice. Some believed that as a woman's privileges were enlarged, her purity of life was diminished. Miller said facts disprove this. He alluded to women school teachers and held that the profession did not hurt their morals. He argued "there's nothing about casting a ballot that will demoralize women. Women vote in church elections. Why not for a governor or a president?" Deploring the evils of the day and the "godless spirit of lust and gain," he believed that woman's influence for good could "save the nation . . . through the ballot box." Miller assumed that woman suffrage would in no way hurt the home. He maintained that woman's endowments were the same as man's and, "She is his companion—not his slave."[13]

Knowing that conditions in county almshouses all over the country were deplorable, Miller gave attention to the one in Greene County. In general, insane people were frequently kept in the same space as poor people; attendants were ignorant and inclined to be cruel toward inmates. Conditions in such institutions constituted one of the worst cultural lags in the nation. The Greene County Almshouse, originally a large farmhouse, was no exception to the rule. With a view to improvement, in January 1882, Miller became chairman of a committee of three who visited the "County Home for the poor" several times, inspected it, and made a report to the Board of Public Charities of the state. This report showed that 96 people were crowded into 17 rooms. Some were ill; some were shut up in the attic with no ventilation; the water supply from the nearby run was inadequate; there was no sewage system. Worse still, all inmates regardless of age, sex, and condition of health, mingled together. Obviously the steward could not constantly watch them all. Hence every year there were illegitimate births—"a fact reproachable in the extreme." Miller reported: "We must have a new county home."[14] Two years later, Dr. A. J. Ourt, Secretary of the State Lunacy Commission, verified Miller's findings, and declared the local almshouse was "the worst place in Pennsylvania." Unfortunately the county commissioners would not provide money for a new building. In October 1889 the local grand jury visited the place and "found conditions bad." Miller was still concerned about the almshouse. His efforts were not fruitless, for eventually additions were constructed to the rear of the original home; sewage and water systems were installed; and bathroom facilities and furniture were obtained.[15] Thus the place was made fit for human habitation.

While Miller promoted social reforms, he was successful in solving the all-important problem of raising funds for the college. In so doing he had to resort to many expedients, some of which were most unusual—but all were ethical and commendable. During his first eleven years as president he taught six hours daily, charging and receiving nothing for such dedicated services. He paid the faculty chiefly out of his own pocket; he earned some of this money by preaching in the Waynesburg CP Church; and some by lecturing at teachers' institutes, which often netted him $100 per week. At the same time, Miller took charge of the perpetual scholarship program. He assumed full responsibility for the financial affairs of the college—and fulfilled it most satisfactorily. He commented thus on Waynesburg's unique situation: "If any other college on the continent has been engineered through such a financial strait, more economically, honestly, or successfully, than this one was, I would be glad . . . to take my hat off to the man who did it."[16]

By July 1869 the numerical strength of the CP Church was 130,000 members, who were served by 1,200 ministers. Miller called them a great "army of workers," and urged each one to give one dollar for missionary work. He also proposed a plan whereby select members could donate, on the basis of their abilities over a five year period, to the endowment funds of CP collegiate institutions. In five years, together with other bequests, he estimated, "we could give our struggling institutions $1,000,000—a sum sufficient to relieve them all from want . . . and to endow a theological seminary." Waynesburg College was in the worst circumstances of any CP collegiate institution. It was "hedged in by older, wealthier institutions. . . . To compete with surrounding colleges it must have money. . . . "[17]

In December 1869 Miller appealed to the CP Synod of Pennsylvania for funds for the college. He explained that "Colleges are essentially religious institutions, founded by Christian enterprise, sustained and endowed by Christian liberality, conducted by Christian men and women." Their aim is "to do good" in the world, but all colleges in America—even Harvard—had small beginnings. Some were slower and weaker in starting than others. Miller apprised Synod of Waynesburg's financial needs. First was to increase its library. It had 1,000 volumes, but needed $1,000 to get more reference books so sorely lacking. Second was for apparatus for which $1,000 "could be used to great advantage." Third was to meet faculty salaries. The teachers had "too much work and too little compensation." The endowment fund was $40,000, much of which was not bearing interest; at least $25,000 more was needed for this fund. The annual income then "would support only the teachers absolutely needed at very moderate salaries." Money was raised by tuition and charges for "boarding"; by a matriculation fee set in 1870 at $3.00 per session; by perpetual scholarships, which were not reliable; by donations, which could be for whatever purpose the donor may wish; and by bequests. In the early years the college received but one bequest. It was for $500 from William Hague, a noble young man who was killed in action during the Civil War. It was "sacredly kept to speak of the generous spirit that bestowed it for a purpose so laudable—to aid in the education of indigent youth who have a thirst for knowledge." In his appeal Miller said the CP Church had no rich members like George Peabody to give millions, but many could give smaller sums. He feared that Synod might be lax in its efforts, because the college was getting along satisfactorily. But, he asserted, "it has succeeded by self-denial, sacrifices, and struggles known only to those who have patiently borne the burden of its work. Shall we longer ask them to sacrifice so much? Is it right?"[18]

In response to Miller's plea, the Synod shortly employed the Reverend G. W. McWherter as an authorized agent of the Board of Trust, who was to give full time to fund-raising. Ministers were asked to help him make contact with church members. By Synod's order, once annually each congregation was to take up a special collection for Waynesburg College. By December 1871 the endowment fund was around $50,000, but it was largely on paper—perpetual scholarships. Synod's aim was to double this figure. An enrollment of some 300 students was anticipated, and additional money was greatly needed. Although McWherter worked diligently, funds were slow in coming. Hence, upon the recommendation of Synod, Miller temporarily left his work at the college and went out to raise funds. He urged ministers to set an example by giving not only to Waynesburg College, but to all CP institutions of learning. He maintained that "If ministers will do their duty, so will the people." According to Miller, Yale had recently asked for $500,000, and welcomed subscriptions "from anybody, in any form, of any amount, payable in any manner." Waynesburg was asking for only $50,000, and Miller said it "would ditto Yale's plan."[19]

The fund-raising campaign was abruptly stalled by the Panic of 1873. Business sharply declined, and very little money was in circulation. But Miller took "the panic" in good stride. Revealing his excellent sense of humor, he referred to a rumor rife around town—the "talk in some circles over the discovery of superior iron ore found in large quantities near Waynesburg, which yields, on chemical analysis, fifty per cent, and some as much as seventy-five per cent. Of course this new source of wealth will make us all rich, build us a railroad, and endow our college."[20] Available evidence indicates that no such highly valued ore was ever found in this locality.

In November 1880 Miller appealed, through the press, to all Christians to remember the colleges when making their wills. He urged them to do so while they were still in good health.[21] He was discouraged many times in his efforts to raise money. In an article entitled "Endowment Driblets," he said that "some people use this expression to stigmatize small donations to a college. . . . Waynesburg College will accept gladly and thankfully any 'endowment driblet' that anyone may send it. Until we can receive large gifts we must be content with small ones, trying to secure a greater number of them."[22] He explained that the CP Church, while rich in resources, failed to develop them for two reasons: First was lack of concentration. The church should concentrate on fund-raising for one college at a time. Second was lack of cooperation. A few CP members "do their part, while the greater part by far stand aloof, idle, and indifferent."[23]

Late in his administration, Miller sought funds for a roof for "the old college building." The need was immediate, and he urged donors to make their contributions as soon as possible. In the summer of 1896 the Reverend William Hanna of Canonsburg, Pennsylvania, supplied funds for a good slate roof, and for other improvements on the building. Thenceforth it was called "Hanna Hall." Its walls were sound and, Miller added, "there is no reason why it may not stand for hundreds of years, and it should be sacredly preserved as significant of the humble beginning of the institution. . . ."[24] After the new building was projected, as we shall see, Miller began a special campaign to raise funds to pay for it.

While Miller bore the main burden of fund-raising, he worked diligently as a recruiter of students. A drawback in the early years was the lack of suitable housing for students. In March 1870, however, the Board of Trust purchased several acres of land adjacent to the college building, intending to erect thereon suitable housing for students who desired to board themselves. By so doing, young men could reduce expenses of board and room to about $1.50 per week which "ought to put a college education in the reach of every young man of energy." The aim was to help all students who were able and worthy—though poor financially.[25]

Early in 1871 an unfortunate controversy over student recruiting arose through the press between Miller and the Reverend B. W.

McDonnold, then president of Cumberland University. Some weeks earlier McDonnold had written "that the Civil War erected an impassable wall between North and South. . . . " He implied "that all intercourse between the two sections is forbidden or impracticable." The inference was that students from one section of the nation would not feel free to attend college in the other. Miller took the opposite view, and contended "that the war utterly demolished the wall between the areas." He had just recently urged a Waynesburg College student to attend the Law Department of Cumberland University. Miller believed that students were, and should be, free to attend the college of their choice, regardless of location. McDonnold, claiming that Miller had misconstrued his article in the newspaper, said he "didn't mean that Northern students couldn't come to Cumberland University. We welcome Northern students."[26]

Miller welcomed students from any area. In March 1870 he invited "young friends from the West" to come to the college and to enjoy this part "of our great Keystone State, while pursuing their studies. . . . " Students from the South would benefit by the change of climate, new associations, the advantages of travel, and the distinctive features of Waynesburg College. Miller summarized the advantages offered by Waynesburg College. First was the good environment. The mountain air, pure water, and perfect drainage were conducive to the development of "a sound mind in a sound body." Second was economy. The entire expense of a college year of 39 weeks, including tuition, room, board, fuel, and washing, "need not exceed $180; it can easily be brought under that sum." Waynesburg, he added, "has the best for the least expense." It is "so cheap the poorest could attend, and so good the richest would want to attend." Third was church influence. While students of all denominations were admitted, many were from the CP Church. They had opportunities to hear good preaching, to join student religious associations, and to attend Sunday School and weekly prayer meetings. Fourth was the spirit of the institution. The faculty encouraged intellectual growth, and inspired students of both sexes to a lofty purpose in life. Miller contended that, in recruiting students, "the Synods of Ohio and Pennsylvania should do much more for Waynesburg College than they are doing. How shall we awaken people to the demands upon them?" He urged CP members to help the "college of your own Church. . . . " He warned them not to send their youth to New England colleges "that may not be unjustly styled at least semi-infidel."[27]

Late in his career, in an address to youth on "Shall I Go to College?", Miller called attention to the good, lucrative positions of graduates and those who had just attended Waynesburg College.

> The humbler colleges are the best. . . . Sixty percent of the brainiest Americans . . . are graduates of small colleges whose names are scarcely known outside their own states. . . . Big institutions do a good job, but *it is not the college*; *it is the student*. Earnest *students* will become scholars regardless of the size of the college (Miller's italics).[28]

Miller was a profound philosopher and a clear thinker. He looked upon colleges as institutions where "the principles are inculcated, and the minds are awakened and trained by which society is to be governed." He held that "knowledge steadily increases," and "every generation must write new books and express its own ideas." One of his prize proverbs was: "If an oak be planted in an urn, the urn must break or the oak must die." He believed that "man's progress—printing, railroads, telegraphs, telephones, electric lights, and other great inventions . . . all stand in an important relation to the progress of the Kingdom of God upon the earth. . . . "[29]

As a classroom man, Miller had many talents. An alumnus said of him: "I never met a man . . . in whom I could place greater confidence as a man of God, as a profound thinker, and as a classroom artist. He possessed the two prime factors which make great men, a great brain and a true heart. . . . " Another of his students called Miller "the Mark Hopkins of . . . Waynesburg College," which "was transformed, when he became its President, . . . like an electric shock." He taught students to think, and his clear concepts, logical methods of presentation, and flawless English, "spoke him a master."[30]

Miller urged the church to provide adequate facilities for the education of CP ministers, for "educated audiences demand educated preachers." In 1876 he lamented "that our Church has not been ready, and is not now ready, to sustain a highly educated ministry. Such a ministry is possible only in a church that pays its ministry well, or educates its ministry at its own expense." Some ministerial students supported themselves by preaching to congregations in areas where colleges were located. Several congregations in Waynesburg and its vicinity helped young men in this way, for which Miller was grateful. But he believed ministerial students should have more help. At Waynesburg, for example, some such students did janitorial work. Through the press, Miller recommended that rich families near all CP colleges "board students and help them with clothing and books." He felt that ministerial students should not borrow money, because "the burden of pecuniary debt is by no means favorable to a young man's rapid growth in the ministry. There will be discouragements . . . enough after entering the field without having debts to pay."[31]

The geographic location of Waynesburg College was a disadvantage. As Miller put it in 1876: "Pennsylvania is so far away from the heart of the church that the throbbings of that heart pulsate little life to us. Educationally, however, we are not dead; and our experience may instruct and encourage our bretheren in other sections." He spoke of the many able ministers who graduated from Waynesburg. They had been adequately trained, but Miller wanted the CP Church to have facilities second to none. He urged congregations to "press on the attention of the Church the immediate need" of such facilities. Revealing his great patience, however, he cautioned the people not to be discouraged if the Church was slow in reaching the "point where it will encourage, support and *demand* an educated ministry (Miller's italics)."[32]

Miller led a movement to establish one theological seminary adequate to train all candidates for the CP ministry. This question was raised in the CP General Assembly of 1865, when he chaired a committee to consider the problem. A majority of members of the assembly agreed that one such institution, well endowed and manned, would meet the ministerial needs of the denomination. It should not be a "mere department of any college," but "should have patronage of the whole church." There was some dissension, however, and nothing came of this attempt. The matter was again brought before the General Assembly in 1872, but it was strongly opposed by presidents of two institutions, and dropped; many leaders in the church seemed indifferent to the problem. In 1873 Miller pointed out that one theological seminary was highly desirable, and suggested that "the nucleus at Lebanon affords the only reasonable hope of meeting this need." If the CP Church did not do something for its young men, they would attend seminaries of other churches. Some Waynesburg graduates, who were CP members, for example, went to Allegheny and to Andover theological seminaries. Devout CP leaders shuddered at the thought of students attending them, for they were strongly Calvinist in doctrine.[33]

According to Miller, the effects of geography were detrimental to the establishment of a strong CP theological seminary. Every great denomination had its "centers of power—literary, moral and religious. Large cities became strongholds to denominations that had the greatest number of flourishing congregations." In 1877 he asserted that, "If there were today even four strong [CP] congregations in Pittsburgh, the efficiency of the Pennsylvania Synod would thereby be doubled." The crowning error of the CP Church, he added, was its failure "to entrench ourselves strongly in St. Louis." Large centers of power and wealth were conducive to the most prosperous institutions of learning. Lebanon, Lincoln, Tehuacana, and Waynesburg "are centers of power to our whole body. . . . " But each locality was too small to support a large seminary.[34] Miller wondered: "Why won't some rich man give $100,000 to establish a Cumberland Presbyterian theological seminary in St. Louis?" Such an institution could soon be staffed, and "we could do a great work . . . for God and our cause in that city. . . . "[35]

Apparently assuming that the CP Church would not have such good fortune, early in 1877 Miller proposed a course of study for ministerial students to be used in all CP collegiate institutions; it was not designed to supersede seminary training, "but to prepare a student for a seminary course—and to compensate partially for the lack of a seminary course." He believed such training would give ministerial candidates the culture and knowledge essential to their lifework. This would be a bare minimum, however; Miller held that "the CP church should not ordain anyone unless he had at least three years in a literary course of study." His efforts to have one seminary to serve the entire denomination were in vain. But each of the four CP institutions had its own program of studies for the ministry. The strongest theological department was at Cumberland University. It had "the right relation to the church," but its facilities and faculty were inadequate to meet the needs of the whole denomination.[36]

Miller was interested particularly in the maintenance of high academic standards. Early in 1875 he condemned a plan adopted by Cumberland University whereby students could be granted credits without attending classes. He contended that there was no good substitute for the classroom experience where students could listen to lectures, take notes, join in discussions, and have personal contact with professors and with one another. But authorities at Cumberland explained that the plan was for nonresidents who lacked the means to attend college. They granted that it was not the best way to get an education, but it was better than no way; it was essentially a program of correspondence courses, conducted on the honor system. Cumberland University defended the plan, because it "taps at the door of the lowly, and offers the hungry and thirsty the food and drink they want."[37]

Always with a view to sound scholasticism, Miller chided certain writers who "unjustly disparage our schools." They would set certain standards of endowment, size of faculty, and number of books in the library before an institution "is worthy to be called a college." He reminded such men of Waynesburg's dedicated faculty. "Our course of study is respectable and the instruction is *not* inferior. . . . Freshmen need clear, faithful instruction and *recitation*—not just lecturing. . . . (Miller's italics)." He always stressed character-building. In 1885 total enrollment in American colleges was 31,000. According to Miller, only half of these students were Christians; and Harvard was lowest, with only one-fourth of her students making such a profession. Miller contrasted expenses at Harvard and Waynesburg: "At Harvard the most economical student annually spends $450, while a rich student spends $3,000; at Waynesburg the estimate is $200, but the *Church* is the best thing we offer our students . . . (Miller's italics)". Miller firmly believed that "a young person cannot find between the two oceans better facilities for him than in Waynesburg College."[38]

Miller maintained that all four CP collegiate institutions were best adapted to the needs of the church. Lincoln University, for example, "is better than Harvard would be for us." Yale, Harvard, and Princeton

> would be entirely out of harmony with the state of things in our denomination. Suppose the president of Lincoln University received a salary of six thousand dollars a year, drove a span of blooded horses, and served and drank wine at his dinners, could he command the sympathy and support of our laity, or of a ministry living on an average salary of six hundred dollars and teaching the virtue of total abstinence?

Miller pleaded, however, for better support for the CP collegiate institutions. At Waynesburg, he and the faculty toiled tirelessly, but "double work on half pay is not good. Without meaning it, the church has required of these laborers a double tale of brick, while withholding the straw. But . . . God is not unmindful of the labor of love; and glorious realization must come to the faith

> 'Which, rowing hard against the stream,
> Sees distant gates of Eden gleam,
> And knows full well t'is not a dream.'"[39]

As a minister of the gospel, Miller was just as outstanding as he was in the field of education. He greatly admired the Reverend Henry Ward Beecher, who liked the new rationalism in religion and opposed the unpopular tenets of Calvinism. In December 1873 Miller attended services in Beecher's church, heard him preach, and called him "the most popular preacher in America."[40] Miller did most of his preaching in the CP Church in Waynesburg at a salary of $800 per year, which was a little higher than the income of others in this area. Occasionally he preached at other CP churches in Greene, Fayette, and Washington counties. He also discharged the other duties of a clergyman such as performing marriage ceremonies, visiting the sick, caring for the dying, performing last rites, and comforting the bereaved. His manifold duties as a minister took so much of his time that Synod wanted him to give up preaching so he could give full time to the college.[41]

An important aspect of Miller's ministry was his work as an evangelist. Whenever he felt it necessary he held a protracted meeting in the CP Church in Waynesburg, lasting usually three to four weeks. He customarily invited a minister from a neighboring church to assist him in such meetings. When possible, he visited other churches and helped their ministers in conducting revivals. In February 1877 Miller, aided by the Reverend A. Templeton of the Pittsburgh CP Church, held a successful revival in Waynesburg. According to Templeton, "Truly it was a precious meeting. The Lord was with his people in great power. . . . " Available evidence suggests that some in attendance, like Methodists and Baptists, were inclined to become emotional. But Miller controlled his emotions. Templeton described Miller as "a man of deep feeling. I think he suppresses his feelings too much for his own enjoyment and the good of others."[42]

Miller hoped the CP ministry would remain strong in all churches in the denomination. By 1884 some ministerial students were leaving the CP Church, were going over "to the so-called mother church," and were attending its seminaries. One young man told Miller he changed denominations because of the better salary, which Miller viewed as "not the most worthy motive."[43]

Miller was widely known and highly respected as a lecturer. Most of his lectures were delivered at teachers' institutes in counties in western Pennsylvania. For many years he regularly "went instituting," remained at each place for a week, and lectured on topics which were helpful and interesting to teachers. Through the inspiration of men like Miller, Pennsylvania had one of the best school systems in the nation. By the early 1870's it had outstripped Massachusetts, where Horace Mann had led the way, in the field of public education. It was spending more money annually on public schools than any other state in the union. But there was still a lack of schools—especially to bridge the gap between common school and college. Miller also promoted the program of adult education, which was instituted at Lake Chautauqua, New York, beginning in 1874. Designed chiefly to train Sunday School teachers, and conducted every summer, it "attracted thousands of earnest adults to the lectures of leading scholars. . . . "[44]

If Miller could effectively communicate by the spoken word, he could do equally well with his pen. As writer and publisher he had few peers. His excellent style lacked the great verbosity and floridity so common in the nineteenth century. His book entitled *Doctrines and Genius of the Cumberland Presbyterian Church* is essentially a masterful defense of CP doctrine. A product of thorough, careful research and great depth of thought, it reveals Miller's inspiration by some of the most renowned religious leaders of the past. For example, he quotes Zoroaster, the great Persian prophet of the sixth century B. C., which succintly summarizes Miller's view of man's duty and destiny: "Taking the first footstep with a good thought, the second with a good word, and the third with a good deed, I entered Paradise." Miller pointed to the "inseparable connection between creed and conduct, principle and practice, doctrine and destiny. . . . " He maintained that the works of God are progressive: "Newton knew more about the heavens than did Galileo, and the astronomers of today know vastly more than Newton knew; and we are constrained to believe that the sum of astronomical knowledge will yet be vastly increased."[45]

Miller made a great contribution by supporting the newspapers of the CP Church, chief among which was *The Cumberland Presbyterian*, a publication designed to meet the needs of rural, agrarian America. It contained articles on religion, morality, news items on the national and world scenes, and columns useful to farmers and farm women. In 1869 Miller called attention to total church membership of 130,000. Only some 10,000 were subscribing to this newspaper. Miller made a plea for more subscribers. At two dollars per year, this paper was indeed a bargain; eight pages in length, it was printed on high quality paper. Considering the total church membership, he urged that subscriptions be increased to at least

15,000. He lauded *The Cumberland Presbyterian* and felt that all families should have it so they would not "remain intellectual and moral dwarfs. . . . " He appealed to farmers to take advantage of the many useful articles relating to agriculture and stock raising. This paper was published successively at different places in the trans-Appalachian region. In 1869 it was being published at Alton, a small town in Southwestern Illinois. But Miller believed it should be moved to a large city, like St. Louis, in order to secure "a stronger financial base."[46] Accordingly, ere long it was removed to that city and renamed the *St. Louis Observer*.

From 1855 to the mid-1860's *The Cumberland Presbyterian* was published in *The Messenger* Building in Waynesburg. Miller did most of the editorial work with great efficiency. After doing a day's work as teacher he went directly to the publication office and prepared his editorials. According to a contemporary who knew him, Miller worked fast and "with a precision I have never seen equaled. His copy was the most satisfactory, from the standpoint of a printer, that I have ever seen. That round, clear, beautiful hand, legible to the dullest boy, with seldom an erasure or a correction, was a model, and an emphatic refutation . . . that a man of genius must necessarily write in a scrawl." Miller also aided in working the hand press and in folding and mailing the papers. When the paper was published in centers other than Waynesburg, he was a regular contributor.[47]

Miller always sought ways to improve the quality of the leading CP newspaper. For example, in January 1877, he pointed out its good features, but added that it lacked

> well written, well digested, well thought out, solid articles—such articles as would represent the great currents of thought of the times, the attitude of science toward religion, and the secular influences that are retarding, helping, or modifying the effects of Christianity. . . . Could not each number contain at least one such article? Where are the pens of our college faculties, of our ministers who have leisure, and of our theological professors? We should have something worthy of being copied by other journals.[48]

While Miller was editing *The Cumberland Presbyterian*, performing his duties as president of the college, and shepherding his flock in the Waynesburg CP Church, he found time to serve briefly as Superintendent of Schools of Greene County. In November 1861 John A. Gordon, then in that office, resigned his post, joined the Union Army, and was elected captain by "his companions in arms."

Miller was appointed to complete Gordon's term to end in 1863. This extra duty added greatly to his burdens, for he had no means of transportation. Lacking a horse and buggy, he walked from Waynesburg to all the 160-odd schools in Greene County. It was commonly known "that in visiting the county schools he always traveled afoot." Despite this handicap, he faithfully discharged this duty. In his report in 1863, he summarized the public school situation:

> The war has taken from the county . . . its best teachers, several of whom have discharged the debt of patriotism with their lives; still the schools are supplied, and there is gradual improvement in the general or aggregate qualifications. . . . [Waynesburg College] is exerting a decided and beneficial influence upon the school interests of this county. It has educated many teachers and its professors have ever manifested a most cordial cooperation with those who have had supervision of the public schools.[49]

Miller's income as president was either nil or at most a mere pittance. He received very little money as superintendent of schools, and his salary as a minister was low. He felt impelled to seek other ways to earn money to keep himself and his family, and to maintain the dignity of his office. Hence, by 1871 he had gone into business as a salesman of pianos, organs, and melodeons. Organs costing from $50 to $1,500 were suited to parlors, schools, and churches. In 1874 Miller advertised his instruments in *The Cumberland Presbyterian*, thus making them available to the whole CP denomination as well as to others. He frequently and sorrowfully saw organs in churches costing from $50 to $100 more than he would have charged for them. Showing that he was not interested in excess profits, he "could send organs and pianos of every description and almost any make at prices *much below what is usually paid* (Miller's italics)." Such instruments, shipped to Ohio, Illinois, and other states reached the purchasers in perfect order; and each had Miller's guarantee. In addition to selling musical instruments, Miller also ran a bookstore in Waynesburg; he sold books and other materials chiefly of a religious nature. His "several branches of goods" included equipment for lawn tennis, hammocks, and other essentials of the time. A contemporary note avers that "his neat and well filled bookstore presents a good appearance."[50]

As a result of his manifold interest and abilities, Miller was recognized as a leader in the CP Church, and he constantly sought ways to strengthen the whole denomination. He believed one way to improve the church was to change its name, which touched off considerable controversy. He contended that the word "Cumberland" had geographic significance only—and it was sometimes confusing. Miller was often asked if it had anything to do with Cumberland, Maryland. He then would explain that the name stemmed from the great revival of 1800 along the Cumberland and Tennessee rivers, and was clearly geographic only. But the church had spread over a large part of the nation—and beyond—and the local name should give way to a broader one. Hence Miller would erase the word "Cumberland" and use the word "American."[51] Another name suggested was the "Evangelical Presbyterian." The word "Cumberland" was opposed because it was local in nature, and had no significance as to doctrine or government. The same was said of the word "American," only its geographic boundaries were much larger. But the word "Evangelical" signified *doctrine* (italics in original); it could apply to the church anywhere.[52] The Reverend B. W. McDonnold held that the "proposed substitutes are more objectionable than 'Cumberland.'" The church had spread beyond the Pacific, and "I never heard of anyone refusing to join our church because of its name, no matter how far off from the place of our birth." When the CP General Assembly met in Austin, Texas, on 19 May 1881, many arguments were advanced as to why there should be no change in the name. And a motion was passed that the whole matter be dropped.[53]

Miller desired to improve regular church services. He believed, for example, that the hymn book should be revised; he considered it inferior to most others and made suggestions for its improvement. First, it was badly arranged. Numbering pages at the bottom was "awkward and inconvenient. The index should refer to the *hymn*, not the page (Miller's italics)." Second, some of the hymns and psalms were rarely used. Third, many of the best hymns in the English language were not in the book. Miller suggested several that should have been included, such as "Just As I Am, Without One Plea," "In the Cross of Christ I Glory," "Sweet Hour of Prayer," "Stand Up for Jesus," and above all others, "Nearer My God to Thee." He suggested a revision of the book to include 500 hymns, plus 100 from the Psalms.[54]

Fully aware of man's egotism, irrationalism, and tendency to quarrel, Miller pleaded for peace and cooperation throughout the CP denomination: "Differences in religion are unavoidable. Quarreling costs too much. Christ is crucified thereby." In His name, "let us have peace everywhere and all the time." As a peacemaker, he suggested: "First, hold one another equally honest in his views, equally entitled to respect, equally liable to be mistaken. Second, accord freedom of thought, speech, and press to all equally. Third, when the Church . . . adopts a plan, let us work at it until a better one is found." He concluded that "there can be no reason for strife, and no one knows all the truth."[55]

Miller was most highly respected as a leader in the Pennsylvania Synod of the CP Church. His dedication to that body was revealed in his careful plans for its meeting in Waynesburg in September 1871. A week prior to this assembly he published instructions to delegates concerning the best means of transportation to Waynesburg. Those coming through Pittsburgh were notified that, if they came thence by boat to Rices Landing, they would be "brought from that point and returned to it without charge. The boats leave Pittsburgh daily at 5:00 or 6:00 P.M., and reach the landing by morning, whence the hacks run to Waynesburg by 11:00 A.M." Those who prefer "can take cars at Pittsburgh for Washington, Pennsylvania, and come thence by hack, reaching this place at 7:00 P.M." In order to have enough hacks available for the former route, Miller requested all "who avail themselves of free passage from Rices Landing" to let him know as promptly as possible. "Here we desire a *full* meeting of Synod and will strive to make it pleasant (Miller's italics)."[56]

If Miller was popular in the transmontane West, he was equally so as an international emissary of good will. In him we have a veritable trans-Atlantic handclasp between two denominations with implicit faith in similar doctrines. Many new sects in America had their counterparts in Europe where, to a lesser extent, old faiths were also fragmented. The European counterpart of the CP Church was the Evangelical Union of Scotland, a group which had rebelled against the "established" Presbyterian Church founded by John Knox. For several years there was blissful liaison between them, chiefly through their newspapers and by exchanges of visits of their respective delegates across the Atlantic. Such visits, however, were few because of the distance involved. The zenith of this brotherly relationship was reached late in 1875 when Miller was chosen as the national delegate of the CP Church to the annual Conference of the Evangelical Union.

News of Miller's sojourn was happily received on both sides of the Atlantic. On 12 August 1875 the press reported: "We learn that Dr. Miller of Waynesburg starts to Europe early in September as a delegate to the Evangelical Union of Scotland. We are pleased with this because we wish to cultivate the friendship of our Scotch brethren, whose history and doctrine are so like our own, and because we could not have a better representative."[57]

After a rough voyage in which he suffered a serious case of seasickness, Miller arrived in Glasgow on Monday evening, 27 September 1875, in time for the opening of the annual Conference of the Evangelical Union. The meetings started that evening by a sermon by the Reverend George Gladstone, retiring President of that Conference. At this first meeting, those present were all agog over Miller's arrival. Many, particularly from rural Scotland, were asking, "Has Dr. Miller arrived from America?" The announcement that he had arrived was received with hearty applause. There was a large turnout, attributed chiefly "to the expected presence of the delegate from the CP Church of America. . . . " Miller was introduced to the Conference at its morning meeting on Wednesday by the Reverend Gladstone. Miller was still sick, but he bravely resolved to endure his suffering and to proceed with his role in the Conference. "When he stepped forward to receive the right hand of welcome . . . the whole crowd rose to their feet and were deeply moved. . . . Every heart was touched and not a few were melted in tears. . . . " His reception in the evening "at the large soiree in the City Hall baffled description." The hall, largest in the city, "was crowded to the roof, and hundreds could not gain admittance, who desired to do so." When Miller was introduced and rose to speak, "the vast company rose *en masse*—and their applause was overpowering. The ladies waved their handkerchiefs and gentlemen clapped their hands and cheered for some minutes." At the breakfast meeting on Thursday morning, which was also crowded, Miller was again introduced and "was received in the most enthusiastic way." The climax came when he was introduced to the Conference on Thursday afternoon. Miller then asked that some of his remarks be "off the record." He proceeded to tell the crowd of the new building being erected at Waynesburg College and said he "would be happy if the Evangelical Union would hand over to him, say 20 pounds ($100) so he could put a memorial window in Waynesburg College with a suitable inscription on it." A vote of thanks was extended to Miller and to those who sent him. The next day he was presented a check for the money needed for the stained glass window to be placed in Alumni Hall.[58] These generous Scotsmen knew that, once the building was completed, this window would be a pleasant reminder of Miller's visit. The window is still there—in two sections. On one are the words "Evangelical Union, Scotland"; on the other, "Pennsylvania Synod, C. P. Church."

The Reverend Fergus Ferguson, a Scottish clergyman and leader in the Evangelical Union, gives us the best account of Miller's role in the Conference.

> I take this opportunity, after the close of the Conference, to tell you how delighted we have all been to see Dr. Miller of Waynesburg College and how admirably he has discharged his duties as a delegate from your Church to the Evangelical Union in Scotland. . . . One required only to look at Dr. Miller to perceive that he was a refined, modest Christian gentleman; and . . . by his successive public appearances he left the impression upon all our ministers and people that he was scholarly, fluent, and logical in mind while he endeared himself by his goodness and amiability to all who came in contact with him.[59]

Miller must have suffered miserably throughout the conference. The severe case of seasickness persisted, and was a heavy drain on his energies, but stoically he stood the strain of his several performances and of attendance at meetings. When it was all over he was nearly exhausted. Clearly, he did not reveal his true condition to those present. "We all thought the Doctor looked a little thin," said Ferguson later, "at our Conference meetings, although he seemed wiry and in good health." Miller's condition deteriorated to the point where he had to spend two weeks at the Waverly Hydropathic Establishment located at a small town called Melrose—"a beautiful place on the banks of the Tweed." Here he took the so-called "water cure," in which water was used in therapy. He rapidly recovered and, before embarking for America, he was able to preach to two Evangelical Union congregations at Melrose.[60]

Miller arrived home on Friday, 31 December 1875, after apparently smooth sailing—and no illness. On the following Sunday he preached at morning and evening services in the Waynesburg CP Church. The audience room was "festooned with evergreen" and behind the pulpit was a large sign "Welcome Home." Crowds were large and attentive at both meetings. In the morning service his theme was: "My Grace Shall be Sufficient for You." In the evening he gave an account of his journey "in a religious view only."[61]

Miller's mission to Scotland, his almost regal reception there, and numerous communications through the press attest to the strong spiritual bond and the fraternal relationship between the CP Church and the Evangelical Union. Trans-Atlantic contacts between these two sects resulted in significant developments for Waynesburg College and for its sponsoring church as well. Despite his illness, Miller did more than any individual hitherto to establish brotherhood between these two denominations. Best of all, he advertised Waynesburg College in a most favorable light.

Miller excelled in many fields of endeavor. As administrator, teacher, clergyman, fund-raiser, recruiter of students, social reformer, writer, lecturer, Superintendent of Greene County schools, businessman, leader in the CP denomination, he had no peer. Largely because of his renown, in 1877, he was chosen moderator of the CP General Assembly at Lincoln, Illinois.[62]

When Miller became President of Waynesburg College, there was every sign that it would go the way of the majority of new colleges on the frontier—fail and close its doors. The one trait in him "which was the secret of much of his great achievement was his persistent devotion to duty—even under the most trying circumstances. He told of one crisis after another in the College and how faithful friends advised him to give up the attempt. But his faith and persistence won the victory."[63] He was most appropriately called the "Father of Waynesburg College."

V
STUDENT LIFE, 1859-1899

MILLER AND HIS FACULTY GRAPPLED WITH THE MANY PROBLEMS RELATING to student life in this period. Practices were adopted relative to "boarding" and other services essential to students. While morality was the paramount object, there was stress on religion, knowledge, patriotism, and good manners. The college was designed to achieve these ends; its faculty was deeply pious, and its location in bucolic surroundings removed youth from the distractions and temptations of the large city. Contacts between males and females continued to be greatly limited. While there were many infractions of the rules, and a few students protested against what they believed to be injustices, in general they respected the authority itself. The literary societies reached their peak in power and prestige; certain religious organizations were established; and, largely through the initiative and efforts of students, the athletic program got under way. As time passed, the entire college family became increasingly convinced that co-education was more desirable than separate institutions for men and women.

The catalogue of 1871-1872 boasts:

> Waynesburg College was one of the first to admit both sexes. Many more colleges are adopting this practice. Association of sexes is good. *Association* of sexes is *encouraged* (italics in original). In this institution the two sexes associate under proper restriction . . . . Ladies are permitted to receive the company of gentlemen only one day in a week, and never at a late hour of night. They are allowed outdoor recreation during each day, but must repair to their rooms on the ringing of the evening bell.[1]

The faculty interpreted the laws, which were amended from time to time, and made every effort to enforce them. It met regularly every Friday afternoon from 2:30 to 4:30, while school was in session, and considered students' excuses for infractions of rules during the week. Students were required to submit excuses in writing, to appear in person before the faculty, and to acknowledge their wrongs. They were given the opportunity to make any comments they wished in their defense. The faculty members then judged them on the basis of the evidence, and meted out whatever punishment they deemed necessary. By precept and example, the faculty tried to develop in students the "strongest possible motives to right conduct." The catalogue continues: "The young man is made to feel that if he is a gentleman he will govern himself." And young ladies "are surrounded by circumstances calculated to render them ladies in the truest sense." But students who could not be "stimulated to right doing" were warned that, "after reasonable effort for their reformation," they would be dismissed. A beginning student's ability to manage his own finances was questioned. Parents and guardians were told that "the managers of this Institution urge economy as a duty on the part of pupils. Unrestricted use of money is a temptation that few young persons can withstand. It is better, in the majority of cases, that money for younger pupils be intrusted to some teacher in the Institution."[2]

Problems pertaining to student conduct gradually became more serious. The janitor, who worked under the direction of Miller, among other things, was required to make a prompt report of any "injury to the college buildings or anything therein." And, as an additional safeguard, each student, before entering his first class in any given session, was required to sign a pledge that he would obey the rules and regulations of the college as long as he had any "connection therewith."[3]

Drinking, although not at all widespread among the students, was shocking when it did occur. For example, on a Saturday in June 1888, eleven male students went to Masontown, some twenty miles from Waynesburg, beyond the Monongahela River, and indulged in "drinking beer and other liquors." They were brought before the faculty, acknowledged their offense, and were "allowed to remain students on condition that they sign a pledge of total abstinence."[4] In another case one of the professors smelled liquor several times on a certain student's breath. This offender confessed to drinking alcoholic beverages. He was rude to his fellow students, discourteous to faculty members, and derelict of his scholarly responsibilities. The faculty members concluded "that while his connection with the College is of no obvious advantage to him, it is pernicious in its influence on others." They tried, and expelled, him. The offender then appealed to the trustees, who requested the faculty to revoke the expulsion and to restore the student on three conditions: (1) that the accused acknowledge all charges against him to the faculty; (2) that he sign a pledge of total abstinence from intoxicating drinks, "unless the same be used by requirement of a physician" until the end of the college year; and (3) that he "make at least one recitation daily until the close of the present term. . . . " When one considers the total enrollment of nearly 400 students in the late 1890's, the percentage of those who drank alcoholic beverages was very small.[5]

By the middle 1890's, a few students began frequenting poolrooms, which the faculty considered pitfalls to be avoided by youth. Accordingly, late in May 1895 the faculty passed a motion "that it shall be a misdemeanor for any student of Waynesburg College, whether a resident or nonresident, to visit billiard or pool rooms." Nevertheless, a few students ignored this rule, particularly if they resided in the Downey House, a good hotel in town. In December 1897, at least twenty-three students were cited for visiting poolrooms, four of whom were discovered in the act of breaking into Alumni Hall. All the students admitted their guilt; some were admonished, while others were suspended in accordance with the degrees of their guilt. The faculty pursued this problem without letup, and appeared to have it under control.[6]

The rule that young ladies were not allowed to board where gentlemen boarded was tested early in 1885. A female student had engaged board at a certain home for the remainder of the school year, but several gentlemen came after she had made such arrangements. The young lady was called before the faculty, and ordered to "change her boarding place, obtaining one where gentlemen do not board." Every effort was made to provide boarding for girls in homes of faculty members. Parents and guardians were assured that "your children and wards" could always find good boarding places. Most fortunate were those young women who lived in Miller's house, where they found the "privileges and restraints of a Christian home." One girl who boarded in his home recalled: "You may be sure we followed the rules laid down. We had the room next to Dr. Miller's, so when it was 10:00 o'clock there would come a knock at the door—'Ten o'clock girls.' The lights had to go out then, but we didn't go to sleep just then. In subdued tones, we told our different stories. . . . " From time to time the students implored the faculty to make exceptions to the rules governing boarding—to no avail.[7]

For several years most faculty meetings were concerned with absences from class and chapel. At first students claimed they did not know the rules, and hence most were either excused for the first infraction or "continued on trial." When a student had three unexcused absences, however, he was suspended. Tardiness at class or chapel was not tolerated. Students who did not attend literary society meetings and participate in programs, in addition to fines by those organizations, were liable to disciplinary action by the faculty. Each student was required to report weekly on his attendance at church services on Sunday. In October 1891, the faculty, in order to improve the system, adopted blank forms which were printed and distributed to students. Every Friday evening each student was required to give this form to the secretary of the faculty. The completed form was presumed to be an honest record of the student's attendance at class, chapel, church, and literary society during the preceding week.[8] The faculty resorted to various methods to compel students "to behave with respect and gravity" during chapel services. Occasionally they ordered an offender to change his seat in chapel on account of disorderly conduct. Some violators were required to "sign a pledge to abstain hereafter from all improper conduct in chapel during morning exercises."[9]

It was impossible to make rules to govern all eventualities. Some offenses seemed minor; and others were purely in the nature of pranks. For example, some culprits rang the college bell at night, and they were warned "you must stop it and allow us to sleep peaceably during the little time we have for rest, or we will give you dead away."[10] Girls occasionally violated the "8:00 o'clock" rule which forbade them to be absent from their boarding places without permission after that hour. Each was admonished for this offense.[11] It was considered socially improper for a girl to sit alone in the park at any time; female students who did so received the usual admonition. In February 1898 two female students left town without permission from the principal. As punishment they were "not allowed calls from gentlemen during the remainder of the term."[12]

The faculty not only tried to enforce rules governing behavior, but also exhorted students to maintain high academic standing. If students could be kept busy, they would be less inclined to frivolity or infraction of the rules. Accordingly, the rule "for idle students" was regularly invoked and applied. For example, in May 1895 a student was cited for weak scholarship. The faculty investigated his reason for poor recitations, and warned him "that he must show more preparation in the future, or the President would deem it his duty to report him to his father." Subsequently another student, charged with nonpreparation of lessons, was warned that he "must get to work at once."[13] Available evidence suggests that the great majority of students, however, were well motivated, and threats of this sort were few.

With all the rules and the efforts to enforce them, compassion toward students was revealed, at different times, in individual professors, in the faculty as a whole, and in the Board of Trustees. For example, late in November 1880, the students petitioned the faculty for the Friday "off" following Thanksgiving Day. "After lengthy discussion the petition was granted." In April 1884 the senior class petitioned the faculty for a three-week vacation immediately preceding commencement; such would give them time to prepare for the forthcoming program. Professor Walter G. Scott, the eminent mathematician, who always sided with the students, moved that the petition as read be granted. After careful consideration, the matter of a senior vacation was left to the discretion of each individual professor. During a class early in 1892, a prankster threw a concoction of red pepper, asafetida, and garlic into the stove "and filled the room so full of the obnoxious odor that the class had to be dismissed." The young man was summoned before the faculty where he stood utterly abashed and deeply humbled, and confessed, and threw himself on their mercy. The venerable, compassionate Professor Scott, who "never wanted to see a student punished" then spoke up, saying: "Mr. President, I move the student be excused; if the wind had just been blowing in the other direction, no one would have known anything about it." The motion passed. Imagine the heartfelt gratitude of that student toward Professor Scott.[14]

Instances in which students appealed to the trustees over the faculty and administration were nearly nil. One such case occurred in February 1869 when a student read an essay in chapel which apparently reflected unfavorably on certain faculty members. Miller wrote to the student and told him his essay "was so very disrepectful and so shamefully false" that there was no alternative but to expel him. Miller apprised the student of his right to appeal to the trustees. The student promptly made such an appeal, and explained to them that he "did not refer . . . to any particular individuals in said essay. . . . " He claimed he "was surprised to learn that certain members of the faculty thought . . . that they were attacked. . . . " He petitioned the Board of Trustees to reinstate him as a student. They did so on the condition that he make "a public disclaimer in the college chapel that he did not intend any reference to any member of the faculty. . . . "[15]

Exceptions were made to rules when it was impracticable to apply them, chiefly because of distance and time factors. In the early years, before blank forms were used to indicate absences, on Monday mornings when the roll was called in chapel, students answered "church" if they had attended regular church services on the preceding day. Many students in residence went to their homes in the country on weekends. If no church was located sufficiently near their homes, they were excused from church attendance. The distance had to be quite far, however, so one could not traverse it by horse and buggy in a reasonable time. If a church was located nearby and a Sunday School service only was held, the student was required to attend such a service in lieu of church. By the late 1870's, after the Waynesburg and Washington (W. & W.) Railroad was in operation, many students were traveling by train, leaving town on Friday evenings and returning Monday mornings. In such cases they were excused from chapel on Monday, when the train did not arrive in time. If chapel conflicted with a student's work outside of college, in which he was earning money to pay for his education, he was excused only while engaged in such work. For example, in April 1882, a student was excused from chapel on Thursday and Friday mornings while he was working on *The Democrat*, one of the local newspapers. In May 1882 a student who had no classes on Friday morning was excused from attending literary society, which took place on those evenings, "on account of living so far in the country. . . . "[16]

Female students could be out later than 8:00 P.M., if they went to religious services or to special programs which would enlighten them. For example, in February 1882, the faculty gave permission to the girls "to attend the exhibition in town hall on Thursday night, it being the drama *Uncle Tom's Cabin.*" In another instance, in October 1894, the faculty passed a motion "that the ladies are granted the privilege to attend the evening lectures of the County Institute of next week."[17]

The literary societies gave students some measure of freedom. The number of students in each class varied from two to as high as ten. It became customary for each society to grant trophies to winners "as an incentive to further study and improvement." Many times Miller visited the literary societies; when present, he was usually called upon to read the Scriptures and to pray.[18] While the societies sometimes opened meetings to the public, they occasionally limited visitors. For example, late in July 1863 the Philo Society planned a meeting to "be public only to the Phileans and Emma Willards, [and] all ladies connected with the institution, together with the faculty."[19]

The work of literary societies was considered so important that, in November 1881, the faculty acted favorably on a petition from the students that all Friday afternoons be set aside for their activities. By 1890, however, the students were stressing these activities to the detriment of their regular course work. In addition to regular programs they were presenting theatrical productions which were too time-consuming. Accordingly, at Miller's suggestion, the faculty resolved "that in consequence of the neglect of college requirements and the loss of time occasioned by theatrical exhibitions, all such be henceforth forbidden until further action."[20]

Many debate questions indicate that students were keeping up with current events, such as one in January 1865: "Resolved that the Signs of the Times Indicate a Restoration of the Union within Six Months." Another in late April 1865, after Lee's surrender and Grant's magnanimous offer to allow the ex-Confederate soldiers to take their horses home for the spring plowing, was: "Was it Wise Policy in our Military Authorities in Receiving Lee's Surrender on the Terms Stipulated?" Another during our Cuban crisis of 1873 was: "Resolved that the United States Should Declare War on Spain."[21]

After 1857, when the college first conferred the baccalaureate degree on women, there was increasing sentiment in favor of merging the four literary societies into two. The young ladies themselves seemed reluctant to make such a move.[22]

Gradually, however, there was a closer relationship between the male and the female societies. Finally late in May 1874, the Philo's debated the question: "Resolved that the Philomathean and Emma Willard Societies Should Be United." A week later the Philos passed a resolution "that we extend an invitation to the Emma Willard Society to unite with us and form one society." But the girls did not come en masse to the Philo organization. On 19 June 1874 the Philos opened their door on a voluntary basis by moving that "ladies who left the Emma Willard Society be taken in as members of this Society on their own request." One of the Philos, doubtlessly considering himself lucky, "was appointed to welcome the ladies."[23]

On 10 July 1874 the Philos presented the first program in which the ladies, who had left the Emma Willard group, joined them. In each of four classes—select oration, essay, extemporaneous, and original oration—at least three girls "performed." They did not debate, however, for they were loath to do so. A week later the girls had more courage, and males and females participated in all classes, including debate in which there was one boy and one girl on each side. Shortly other girls left the Emma Willard group and joined the Philos, but the merger was not complete until two more years had passed.[24] Right after the merger some interesting questions were debated, with male and female students on the same teams. For example, in January 1876 they debated the question: "Resolved that the Narrow Gauge Railroad Would be More Beneficial to the People of this County than the New College." Both were projected, and building was in the early stages. The railroad would connect Waynesburg and Washington and touch points in between. The "New College" was the administration building, much later named "Miller Hall." In July 1877, a debate question was: "Resolved that Darwin's Theory of the Origin of Species is a True One." By the 1870's the Darwinian hypothesis was a controversial topic in colleges all over the nation.[25]

The union of the Union and Philean Societies was consummated simultaneously with that of the Philos and Emma Willards. Each new organization had approximately the same number of male and female members.[26]

Heating and lighting the halls with the available means must have been rather cumbersome. On 6 November 1863, when the weather was getting cold, the Philos appointed a committee of six men "to bring in the stove and put the room in order by the next meeting of society." By that time the kerosene lamp was soaring in popularity and rapidly replacing candles.[27]

Customarily each society selected two members to serve as janitors and to see that the halls were properly maintained. On 10 March 1865 Philo's janitors reported humorously on their "highly honorable and lucrative positions. . . . " They took the stove from the garret, set it on its legs, and blacked it; they also procured a large pine box for coal. They encountered difficulties at the hands of certain members of Union Society who committed acts of vandalism; they referred to "incursions of Gauls and Vandals who had broken the lock on the door." Worse still, these flirtatious fellows molested the young ladies who swept the hall: "Our dearly beloved and amiable sisters—the Emma Willards, being overtaxed with domestic duties, were prevented from . . . sweeping, which their smiles and words of commendation assure us they would have rendered under different circumstances." The janitors wittily tell how they "tasted of the mingled honor and labor—the joy and grief—the tribulation and the pay (the latter item not yet tasted, but hope [*sic*] soon will be) of our exalted position."[28]

There were many instances of frivolity which at times led to friction between the societies. Pranksters in one often played practical jokes on the other. For example, in July 1863, the Union Society notified the Philos that a Philo put a snake in Union's water pitcher. Condemning this as "a very ungentlemanly act," the Union Society inquired whether the Philos "upheld or sanctioned" such shenanigans. The Philos promptly replied that they did not authorize "said act, and are therefore not responsible for the same."[29]

The charter of each society provided that the members had full control over the use of their hall, and that only they could "grant the hall for purposes other than Literary." The members jealously guarded this right, and they permitted outsiders to use their halls only on special occasions, which sometimes led to controversies. Most serious was a clash between Miller and the officers of Philo. During the "County Institute" in 1869 Miller "announced there would be a reunion on Thursday evening, provided the societies would grant their halls." On that Thursday morning the Philos held a "call meeting" and rejected Miller's request "by almost unanimous vote." They defiantly ordered "the janitor to close the hall and keep it closed during the evening." But "the janitor opened the hall contrary to the desire of the Society, by order of the President of the College." Incensed at Miller's action, the officers of Philo appealed to the trustees to interpret the existing law, and if no law was applicable, "we pray that you will enact one that will prevent further controversies." The trustees examined the problem, and resolved that "the hall shall be used for no other purpose than such as pertaining to the regular exercises of the societies, except by permission of the faculty."[30]

As in colleges all over the nation, the literary societies were housed in the best halls the college could offer. By 1890 both societies had moved to their more spacious quarters in the new building.

As in the old, the Philos occupied the hall on the third floor, west wing of the new building; and the Union Society, the third floor, east wing. The Union Society was first to complete and dedicate its new hall, some months prior to Philo's dedication on 30 June 1890. These halls were "top-notch in all respects."[31]

Many hours were spent in training for the annual contests. Some students "rehearsed in the solitude of the forest, the cornfield, or the cemetery. Some people thought they were crazy." Contests were held first in the chapel of the old building; and later in Alumni Hall, in the new. If heat were lacking, these meetings were in the old Opera House, "where there was a scramble for seats." There was such enthusiasm in 1886 that the societies disputed as to which performers should speak first, which caused delay in starting for nearly two hours.[32] To be chosen to represent a literary society in contests was a great honor. After hearing the best participants in all categories, the members voted by secret ballot for the contestants they believed would win.[33]

A challenge to a contest was considered an affair of honor to be met, regardless of circumstances.[34] The results of contests were decided by two judges and an umpire. Efforts were made to get well-qualified judges who would render decisions on the basis of merit alone; usually they were professional men of some note, including lawyers, clergymen, and professors. The audience always awaited decisions with breathtaking anticipation. Honors were awarded to winners; and seniors in each society, who were about to graduate, were presented diplomas as awards for their work in their respective organizations.[35]

Despite keen rivalry, in general things went in good stride in the contests. According to Miller, in the contest of March 1876, several young ladies and gentlemen performed in a highly creditable manner. "Good order, good music, and the kindest feelings characterized the evening." The point system was used in calculating the results of contests. The results were cumulative, and late in the nineteenth century the Philos gradually forged ahead of the Unions. By 1903 the honors stood at 217 1/2 for Union and 250 1/2 for Philo.[36]

By the middle 1890's intercollegiate oratorical contests were being sponsored annually, with participants from several collegiate institutions in the tri-state area. Winning orators in contests of the literary societies were excellent timber from whom candidates could be chosen to compete against rivals from neighboring institutions.

To be selected as the college's orator was a distinct honor; winners were looked upon with greatest admiration. For example, in April 1896, William S. Allen was Waynesburg's orator in the contest held at Westminster College. There were eight orators in all, coming from Allegheny, Bethany, Geneva, Thiel, Waynesburg, Westminster, West Virginia University, and Western University of Pennsylvania (later the University of Pittsburgh). Speaking on the topic, "The Scepter of the Titans," Allen won first place. When he returned to Waynesburg he was welcomed as a great hero. A large crowd gathered at the depot to meet him when he stepped from the train; he was taken in a carriage to the campus, with some 200 jubilant, shouting students parading behind. A crowd of at least 500 gathered at the college entrance to listen to speeches by Miller and several others, praising Allen for his victory.[37]

The literary societies continued to increase acquisitions for their libraries. Each had works in biography, religion, history, oratory, science, philosophy, and so on. Primary sources such as census records, state archives, and other government documents were at hand. Dictionaries were available, and were regularly used.[38]

It was difficult to enforce rules relative to membership in literary societies. Some students did not wish to join them; others were not qualified by physical impairment, temperament, or disposition to benefit by membership in them. Some individuals who were not even in college attempted to become members. In February 1874, the faculty resolved that no person could be a member of a literary society "who is not a student in actual attendance in said College," and no diplomas could be tendered to such persons. In October 1878, on Miller's motion, the faculty resolved to excuse students from attending literary societies who were unfit physically or emotionally. But those who were fit in all respects and who could profit from membership and participation were not excused.[39]

Since Waynesburg College was a child of the CP Church, religious influence was strong. The daily chapel, normally led by Miller or a faculty member, consisted of reading the Scriptures, singing, and praying. Students not only attended church "at least once each Lord's day," but also voluntarily joined in work in Sunday Schools and churches.[40] There were weekly Bible classes for all students. On each Sunday afternoon, at 3:30, there was a student prayer meeting attended by nearly all students and "some additions from the young people of the village." These meetings were conducted by students, who read the Scriptures, offered voluntary prayers, and made remarks on the topic at hand. The college welcomed students of all denominations. Each student could attend the church of his choice, but in religious activities at the college, such as Y.M.C.A. and temperance work, students harmoniously united in their efforts.[41]

Apparently seeking something on the lighter side, on 5 March 1873, the students presented a public program purely humorous in nature—the "Annual Exhibition of Alf. Miller's Grand Combination Variety Troupe! Consisting of trained animals, clog dancers, famous singers, jugglers," and so on. The program reads:

> The audience may select from the following performances: Select Oration—"Seventeen Ounces of Brain" by Lobsternozed Campbell; Song—"Mule Chorus" by Lopeared Saunders, Gourdhead Crow, and Spiketail Lantz; Moral Lecture—"What I Know About Women" by the Smiling Parson, Snicker Dicker Woods; Last Performance—"The Spanish Bullfight"—First Bull, Grimes—Second Bull, Patton—As soon as the bulls become ferocious the ladies are earnestly requested to retire.

A year later another humorous program, entitled "The Annual Exposition of the Waynesburg Squirt-Gun Factory," was presented. Students of course were forbidden to use tobacco in any form in the college building; and this show appears to have been a satire on the ubiquitous spittoon. Some thirteen "different styles of Squirt Guns will be tested . . . at this Factory." Most interesting of all was "Rusty Squirt Richards: This specimen of Darwinism left his mother before he was properly weaned; hence his crabbed nature and sour temper. It is only by cheating and hanging on to the President's coattails that he was allowed to graduate." It may well be that such programs were too risque, for there is no indication they were continued.[42]

Though the literary societies remained the main student activity during the latter half of the nineteenth century, a few students became interested in athletics. In the nation as a whole, interest in sports came slowly. Most people believed that play of any sort "was only for children." Hence colleges lacked gymnasiums and other facilities for athletics. For exercise, people generally went for walks in the country, and showed little desire for physical recreation.[43] By 1859, however, Waynesburg College students had developed great skill at cricket, an outdoor game played with a ball, bats, and wickets. This was the first varsity sport—and the first chapter in the long story of athletics at the college. Waynesburg's first intercollegiate athletic event was a cricket game with Washington (later

Washington and Jefferson) College in 1859, played at Washington. Waynesburg won, and her players and few fans there were most joyous. One Waynesburg player was so elated that he went on a veritable marathon, and ran some twenty-five miles from Washington to Waynesburg, shouting "Victory," "Victory" as he neared the courthouse steps. Down to 1880 cricket was the most important intercollegiate sport.[44]

Interest in baseball began during the Civil War, but so few students were available that the college had no well-trained team until after that conflict—and even it left something to be desired. By 1860 the "Grecian Benders," a "town and gown" combination, was organized; this was a motley band with some players who were not enrolled as students. Despite this, one player was Albert B. Cummins, destined to become governor of Iowa and United States Senator from that state. They played barehanded; no gloves, chest-protectors, shinguards, protective helmets, or other equipment were available. The first games were played on the old fairground at the foot of South Morgan and First Streets; later, when the fairgrounds were abandoned, games were played at the present site of College Field. This team played not only intercollegiate ball, but also games with noncollege clubs in the area. For example, in September 1871 they played against the Eagles Club of Morris Cross Roads in Fayette County, for a premium of twenty-five dollars, offered by the Greene County Fair Company.[45]

By the 1890's there was increasing interest in football. The game had been developed and refined at a few eastern institutions. The ball was then oval; there were eleven players on each side; and a few basic rules of the game had been adopted. Football then was a far cry from the first intercollegiate game between Rutgers and Princeton in 1869, which was a mob scene with some twenty players on each side. During the 1890's a total of 104 men went forth from Yale, Harvard and Princeton to teach football in colleges in the nation.[46]

Football at Waynesburg began under the initiative of one student. In the fall of 1894, Thomas D. Whittles transferred from Ursinus College to Waynesburg. He had learned to play football in his preparatory school days. He loved the game, and continued to play it at Ursinus, where he introduced the sport. On arriving in Waynesburg, he was disappointed that there was no football team—and there never had been. Worse still, there was no interest in the game. Waynesburg College attracted him from the first, but he lamented that "no one around appreciated the gentle pastime of the pigskin." He, therefore, "became a Moses and elected myself leader of an unborn cause." Despite the Panic of 1893 and the scarcity of money, he took up a collection totaling $5.25 to pay for a football—"the first resplendent pigskin that ever arrived in your classic confines." It was too late to organize a team in the fall of 1894, but a few students "punted the oval around the campus, much to the annoyance of beloved old Dr. Miller and the unbeloved town cop, who parked himself by the fountain to see that none of us unregenerates interfered with the hay that the Park Board was trying to coax into captivity under the aspiring trees." The fall was spent in passing, punting, getting some vague ideas about formations, and developing a love for the game—which led to the team of '95, "uncouth parent of all other Waynesburg College teams." Whittles also had to overcome much popular prejudice against football, stemming from articles in leading magazines such as the *Ladies Home Journal*, edited by Edward Bok, who opposed the "ungodly game of football," and warned of "the groans of the wounded and shrieks of the dying." Such accounts were widely read in Waynesburg by Miller, the townsmen, the faculty, and the students, who looked upon football as a plague and feared "its introduction would mean an enlargement of the cemetery and a decimation of the student body." Whittles and Miller had many private talks, with Miller stressing moral philosophy, and Whittles instructing him about the game. At length a compromise was reached: the faculty promised not to ban football until a casualty list had been created after the sport was well under way. Whittles felt that Miller wanted to give football a chance, because five members of the squad were ministerial students. The first team was fielded in the fall of 1895, after forty-five dollars had been raised to buy makeshift football suits; this money was "contributed by business men in town by driblets." Even these suits did not arrive on time. Lacking uniforms early in the season, the boys "wore scanty cast off clothing from our none too plethoric wardrobes. . . . " Such clothing was easily torn. After a rough practice session, a player, who had all his clothes torn off, "retired from the field of glory clad in the charitable folds of a Quaker Oats carton. There were no football heroes in Waynesburg at that time. We resembled the rejected recruits of Coxey's army." Despite all drawbacks, the small, inexperienced squad, coached by Whittles, had a successful season. The team was aided greatly by graduate manager Thomas S. Crago, later United States Congressman, and commander of the "Fighting Tenth" Pennsylvania Infantry. It played only three games against second-string teams of nearby institutions, which had had football for some years, namely, one game against Washington and Jefferson College and two against West Virginia University. Score records show that Waynesburg won all three games, but Whittles denies this. According to him, Waynesburg lost at Morgantown by a high score: "The Mountaineer team wiped the earth up with us and taught us a lot of football that we remember."[47]

Compensation came, however, when Waynesburg played at home against West Virginia University that first season. Jesse H. Hazlett, Waynesburg's left end, recalled that the referee weighed 240-odd pounds, and "blundered both ways." One of the Mountaineers, in an attempted end run, fumbled the ball and Hazlett grabbed it "before it hit the ground and ran to pay dirt for Waynesburg College, thus making the first touchdown ever recorded for the Jackets." With this and another touchdown, Waynesburg won by a score of 10-0, since a touchdown then counted five points. The "flying wedge" was a common formation, but it was "later outlawed because of injuries." Hazlett recollected that: "Although part of the game was to knock the other fellow out, it was an infraction of the rules to tackle around the neck for fear of injuries. In those days . . . only two rules had to be observed: keep your eye on the ball, and stay conscious."[48]

The football team made progress during the next five years. In 1897 games were scheduled with Allegheny, Geneva, Grove City, Westminster, and Western University of Pennsylvania. The team that year was considered the strongest "the school has had." But the players lacked knowledge of kicking and punting; and to remedy this weakness, the college employed an expert from LaFayette College, who did excellent work in helping to build the team. By 1899 there were several candidates for each position, and competition was keen. The players were screened, and the team that year was the best to date. It was called the "Fairest Team," because the members were all exceedingly handsome. Their aesthetic qualities were equaled by their abilities on the gridiron. Those early teams competed respectably even against what are today two of the "big time" powerhouses, namely, West Virginia University and the University of Pittsburgh. When Waynesburg won, the good news was made known all over town and vicinity by ringing the college bell—a time-honored custom until the advent of the radio.[49]

By April 1897 the Athletic Association of Waynesburg College had been organized. It was in good running order, and promised "to be a great factor in the future of the college." Its purpose was "to develop the manhood and the womanhood of the college. . . . " The local newspapers praised the efforts of students in the establishment of this association, and held that they "should receive the hearty approbation and cooperation of the trustees and faculty." A move had already been made to organize an intercollegiate athletic association for western Pennsylvania composed of Allegheny, Geneva, Grove City, Thiel, Washington and Jefferson, Waynesburg, Westminster colleges and Western University of Pennsylvania.[50]

While students were promoting athletic sports, the faculty and administration were concerned about housing and boarding for students. By 1870 American colleges in general had the dormitory system under surveillance of the faculty, and governed by rules laid down by that body. But Waynesburg had no dormitory facilities until 1885. Many of her students organized clubs in order to keep expenses down. Some 20 to 30 students would form a club, rent sufficient space, live two in a room, buy their own provisions (or bring some from home), hire a cook, and eat at one table. In so doing, their expenses ranged from $1.80 to $2.50 per week per person. Beginning in 1885, the "Young Men's Boarding Hall" was established in the old college building. With a view to economy, a group of young men organized a club there. Under this arrangement, the cost of living was around two dollars per week each. Shortly several other such clubs were formed in the building. To keep expenses even lower, a student could rent a furnished room there and board himself. Boarding in private homes in Waynesburg and vicinity was considerably higher in cost; it was estimated at $3.25 per week. At this rate, expenses in 1885-1886 for a term of thirteen weeks were: tuition, $7.00; boarding, $42.25; and washing, "probably $4.00." Miller said that some people felt that Waynesburg's expenses were too low and "in the minds of some this tends to lower the estimate of the character of the college." He replied "that young people who have plenty of money can go elsewhere. . . . The salvation of society, morally, socially, and religiously, is in the education of poor young men and young ladies whose noble aspirations to do good lead them to struggle to obtain an education. For all such we have a place . . . at Waynesburg."[51]

Special arrangements were made for candidates for the ministry. Part of the third story of the old college building was fitted out "by the generosity of some ladies in Waynesburg for the free use of candidates. . . . " Young men residing there were under faculty supervision. According to a faculty member of the 1890's, "President Miller had an eye on their conduct and comfort, even down to the intimate item of sufficient covers on cold nights."[52]

The college aided needy, deserving students in finding morning and evening work to help meet expenses, "though applications of this kind generally exceed opportunities." Many students devoted summer vacations to work for book agencies and publishing companies, and thereby realized enough to pay a full year's expenses in college. Some Waynesburg students were highly successful in summer work. For example, in 1892 they "won a cash prize of $500 as the best agents of the Dickerson Publishing Company, at Detroit, Michigan." Some of Waynesburg's best alumni were men and women who "supported themselves by taking care of public buildings and by other honorable work."[53]

Throughout Miller's forty years at the helm, there was a gradual increase in student enrollment. The worst blow was the Civil War. Each call for soldiers drew the more advanced students, resulting in small classes during that struggle. It is reasonable to assume that most students, who were called to arms, served in the Union army, but available evidence shows that some joined the Confederate army. As Miller put it: "Most of our boys fought somewhere during the war, some in the blue, others in the gray." Those who fought for the Union showed the highest sense of patriotism and justice, and were entitled to their share of glory after that "terrible and triumphant conflict." The class of 1862 was smallest with only one graduate, a young lady named Rhoda Yeagley. In the same class was a young man, Edmund Dunn, who was called into the service shortly before his commencement. He rose to the rank of captain in the United States cavalry. He fortunately returned after the war and, we may safely assume, he happily married Miss Yeagley. In 1923 he was residing in Connellsville, Pennsylvania, and "his belated degree was conferred by Waynesburg College as of the Class of 1862.[54]

By the early 1870's co-education had fully come into its own on the Waynesburg campus: "Young ladies here stand up at the same blackboard with gentlemen, and show equal ability to write Greek, Latin, and French, to solve the same problems in Algebra, and to demonstrate the same theorems in Calculus, Descriptive Geometry, and Mechanics." Ladies and gentlemen harmonized in singing the same hymns, and participated in programs before the same audiences. Ladies "sometimes join with gentlemen in a grand promiscuous walk, and sometimes in a grand social gathering. In the discharge of the daily round of college duties, they come and go as gentlemen come and go. In all respects they are equal. . . . "The CP newspaper frequently stressed the advantages of coeducation. One writer literally lauded women to the skies:

> A pious female seems to breathe an atmosphere more allied to heaven than earth. Her presence overawes man in every form. The hardened sinner, who fears no God, will reverence and respect his [*sic*] image as reflected in the life and character of an intelligent, pious lady. . . . Man is coarser and sterner; woman is more refined and milder. Thus the sexes are designed by an all-wise Creator to exert a mutually elevating and refining influence upon each other.[55]

Students were admitted to the college, regardless of race, creed, or color. In March 1885, Miller called attention to an Indian from the West who had entered Waynesburg College, "intending to take a full course of study." This student said "that others from his region will join him directly." A local editor frequently stressed the importance of college students regardless of race, to the town: "Waynesburg could not possibly get along as she does were it not for the College. It should, therefore, receive the hearty support of all citizens."[56]

Fully aware of the low salaries and heavy burdens of the faculty, the students occasionally showed sincere gratitude for the efforts of the most beloved faculty members. For example, in July 1871, a large number of students, both ladies and gentlemen, assembled in the chapel and "marched in procession to the home of the Principal of the Female Department (Mrs. M. K. B. Miller) and placed her in the hands of a committee of ladies, who attired her in a magnificent new dress." The visit was a complete surprise, and "the presentation speech a perfect gem in its way. . . . " After an hour of pleasant conversation, "the crowd dispersed early and orderly, and the whole affair was one of the nicest little episodes known in our college life—especially to the 'Principal.'" A similar gesture of appreciation of Professor Scott was shown in January 1872, while the Greene County Teachers' Institute was under way. Students and several alumni of the college presented a handsome gold watch to Scott "whose services as Professor of Mathematics not only entitle him to such a mark of esteem, but have contributed much to the present enviable reputation of the College."[57]

On another occasion the students sponsored a surprise banquet to be held in the Downey House in Miller's honor "to show their appreciation for his faith and good works." In February 1895 he went to Nashville, Tennessee, to a meeting of CP college presidents. The students then "grasped their chance." In a kind of ruse, they telegraphed to Nashville that his presence was needed on the coming Saturday "to officiate at a wedding. . . . " He promised to return in time to perform the ceremony. But his train was snowbound, and he reached Waynesburg just in time for the banquet, which completely surprised him. Several speeches of welcome were delivered. The President of Union Literary Society spoke first:

> Our president has returned to us a safe, a happy, a whole man. Students may sometimes indulge in pranks, may sometimes disturb midnight stillness by the wild, weird, doleful, unreasonable tones of the college bell, but amid all of this there beats a student heart, undismayed and loyal . . . a heart full of gratitude and love. That is what brings us here tonight. We want to express our gratitude . . . by a practical manifestation of heart-sprung endearments.

He referred to Union Literary Society as "that matchless organization." In the usual emulous spirit, the President of Philo, claiming it "one of the noblest organizations on the face of the earth," uttered peerless rhetorical pearls:

> And now, my dear Doctor Miller, allow me, in behalf of the Philomathean Literary Society, to convey to you our love, our trust, our confidence, and our esteem for you as a gentleman, a scholar, a teacher, a Christian. . . . You, sir, if ever man did, have perceived the true end of living. . . . And . . . your whole life has been spent in the laudable work of pointing the way to others. . . . All hail to the Prince of Wisdom.[58]

Favors of the foregoing sort were not one-way affairs. The Millers frequently sponsored social functions in their home, and other events to which students and faculty were invited. For example, in July 1879, Miller invited the faculty to accompany members of the senior class on an excursion to Carmichaels "to be given in their honor."[59] Since there were only six in the graduating class, and the faculty was small, three or four hacks would readily provide adequate transportation to that town, some fourteen miles from Waynesburg.

Despite all the rules and regulations, in general the relationship among students, faculty, and trustees was cordial. To be sure, at times there was horseplay that alumni often liked to recall. But cases of severe hazing, misbehavior in the classroom, disrespect for faculty members, and insubordination were few. The religious influence probably curbed students in their frivolity, and caused them to have respect for authority. Doubtless there were many who disliked the formal discipline, and yearned for sympathy and understanding, such as they found in Professor Scott. But faculty paternalism and the rigid rules over students persisted through Miller's administration.

VI
THE FACULTY, 1859-1899

LIKE LOUGHRAN AND WEETHEE, MILLER WAS A MINISTER IN KEEPING with a pre-Civil War trend, when ninety percent of the nation's college and university presidents were theologians. On the national scale, many faculty members also were theologians. Contrary to this practice, however, most of Miller's fellow teachers were not clergymen. Most held honorary degrees; a few attended German universities where, in the early years, they could pursue work leading toward earned graduate degrees. Though the trustees had a Committee on Teachers and Salaries, they relied largely on Miller to select members of the faculty. He was an excellent judge of prospective teachers. Many faculty members came from among the best graduates of the college, a practice called "inbreeding" which is frowned upon today. Sometimes they were watched for years before being employed. While scholarship and ability in the classroom were prime considerations, a faculty member had to be tactful, devoted to his work, unselfish, and sound in character. Anyone who used tobacco in any form or drank alcoholic beverages was disqualified for a position on the faculty. Late in the nineteenth century the duties of faculty members were prescribed: "faithful instruction in class; keep order in classes; attendance at daily religious exercises and at faculty meetings; earnest cooperation with the President in enforcing order about buildings, and obedience to regulations and rules of conduct; and prompt, faithful notice to the faculty of known violations of college rules." The faculty also prepared courses of study in all departments. Miller's success, in large measure, was due to his good fortune in finding faculty members who fully cooperated with him.[1]

In October 1870, Azel Freeman, a former student and friend of the college, after an absence of twenty-seven years from Waynesburg, returned for commencement week, and he highly praised the institution:

> Waynesburg College is doing a noble work. President Miller and his excellent and accomplished lady have gathered around them a corps of efficient teachers. The College has just closed its twentieth year, and is sending out a stream of influence for good that is incalculable. As I attended its thorough examinations, and witnessed the performances of its Senior class, and learned the history of the institution, I felt like the Queen of Sheba, when she had seen the magnificence of the temple, and heard the wisdom of Solomon. I had heard of the fame of Waynesburg College, and it was a true report that I had heard, *but the half had not been told me* (Freeman's italics).

Freeman shortly attended the meeting of the Pennsylvania Presbytery, and was greatly pleased to hear six young preachers "of high ability." He expressed his hope that all presbyteries in the CP denomination had set "standards of education as high as that of Pennsylvania. . . . "[2]

In order to maintain these high standards, the Millers and their colleagues labored long, diligently, and devotedly. The majority of them taught five to six hours daily from Monday through Friday, besides attending the daily chapel, enforcing rules relating to student conduct, working on preparations for class, counseling officials of the literary societies, participating in church and Sunday School activities, and serving the community in various ways. Some literally worked themselves to death. Despite such travail, Miller usually gave a favorable account of the college in the press: "Everything here speaks of life, health and growth. Professors are cheerful and earnest. Recitation rooms and halls are clean, neatly papered, and thronged with students, even to the overflowing. . . . The reputation of the college is growing at home and abroad, and its influence expands in ever widening circles."[3]

The trustees continued for many years to rely on Miller almost solely to run the college. At their meetings, little could be done without his presence. The trustees even looked to Miller for suggestions as to how to conduct their own meetings. They resolved, on his recommendation, "that meetings be opened with the reading of the scriptures and with prayer, when any members present will conduct such exercises."[4]

Miller's paramount objects were to get the college out of debt and to establish confidence in its value and permanence. To do so, "and to keep the necessary teaching force in the college without incurring debt, has been the constant, ever perplexing problem through all these years." He adopted "pecuniary expedients that would put ordinary credence out of the question, some of which, aside from my personal knowledge, are known only to Him from whom there is nothing hidden." Verifying the prevailing concept that CP members were financially weak supporters of their church, and, therefore, their colleges suffered, Miller told of his toil and tribulations:

> For the sake of my fellow educators, I wish to say to my church, from my heartfelt sorrows in that respect, that *an incompetent support is a great hindrance to the usefulness of a college president or professor* (Miller's italics). I have been compelled to preach in order to live, sometimes supplying points twenty miles distant; I have been compelled to deny myself books greatly needed; to stay at home when I should have traveled; to walk many miles because I could not pay hack-fare; to be harassed with debts that have eaten up the mind as cancers eat the flesh; in short to do a great many things, and to leave undone a great many things . . . which greatly hindered my usefulness as a public servant of the church. . . . How imperfectly all these things were done, no one is more painfully sensible than the writer, and he sincerely prays that a like apparent necessity of trying to do so many things at the same time may never come again. . . . If there is a position, however, which demands all the service of head and heart that any man can give, that position is the presidency of a college. . . . [5]

Miller added that he was not casting reflections "directly or by implication" on the Pennsylvania Synod, the trustees, or anyone else to whom he looked for funds. He then commented on certain disadvantages—the location of the college far from the heartland of the church, the weak pecuniary resources of the community, the inaccessibility and obscurity of the place at the time, and the fact that the sole ecclesiastical support was from a single, isolated synod. But Miller reaffirmed his "sustaining and abiding conviction that the Lord has signally opened the way for my support and success in this work." Friends had helped him and his family. When he performed marriage ceremonies, he often received "generous sums." His income from lectures generally was liberal, although this was hard work. Much of his money, regardless of the source, was used to pay faculty salaries until the late 1870's.[6]

In the early and middle 1870's Miller's burdens became so heavy that he could no longer bear them. Certain devoted colleagues died prematurely, chiefly from illness brought on by overwork. In April 1870 Miller attended the meeting of the Pennsylvania Presbytery in Pittsburgh. His friends saw that "He is very much worn by the heavy labors and duties of the past Winter; also much pained and afflicted in view of the recent death of a dear personal friend, as well as a beloved fellow laborer in the college, *viz.* Professor M. E. Garrison." Garrison, who held a master's degree from Allegheny College, became professor of ancient languages in 1859 when Miller became president. Miller delivered the funeral discourse at the time of Garrison's burial. He recalled that "we entered upon the work before us at the most trying period in the history of the Institution. . . . The funds available were by no means sufficient to support the number of teachers required. Divisions had been made at home and abroad, and some predicted only failure." Miller then quoted Garrison: "I labored in the College, not for money, but because I loved the business and believed I was doing good."[7]

Miller reached the limit of his endurance and patience late in September 1876, when he presented his resignation as president of the college to the Pennsylvania Synod at its meeting in Mercer County, Pennsylvania. Synod would not accept it. The trustees told of their own shameful neglect. They confessed "that we as a Board of Trustees of Waynesburg College have not been as fully alive and active in our duties as we ought to have been, and as the interests of our institution in the past have demanded. . . . " They then resolved to do all in their power to help Miller, and assured him "our warmest sympathies and strongest support."[8]

But Miller persisted in his determination to quit. On 31 July 1878 he tendered to the trustees his resignation as president of the college. That body promptly referred it to its Committee on Teachers and Salaries. That committee reported:

> Believing that the welfare of the institution demands his retention in this position, we recommend that said resignation be not accepted, but that Dr. Miller be retained as president of the college, and that for the school year beginning October 1, 1878, the board agrees to pay him nine hundred dollars. We further recommend that Dr. Miller be relieved of all burdens pertaining to the future financial management of the institution, so that he may devote his whole time to the departments of teaching and government.[9]

In accord with the committee's recommendation, the trustees would not accept Miller's resignation. Instead, they expressed full confidence in him as president. They were grateful for his faithful service in the past and for declining more lucrative and inviting positions offered him by other institutions.[10]

On 6 August 1878 Miller replied:

> Gentlemen: In response to your request that I continue my labors as president of the institution under your care, I beg leave to say, that

> if in your judgment injury would come to the institution by my withdrawal from it at this time, I will withdraw my resignation on the following conditions:
>
> 1. That the requirement of $1,000 to be paid to me for past services be promptly met by the first day of October.
> 2. That my salary hereafter shall be paid promptly, any balance due at the close of a term to be then fully met.
> 3. That all expense for postage and stationery required in the legitimate correspondence of the College be paid out of the contingent fund of the College.
> 4. That I be allowed the privilege of employing at my own expense a substitute to do my teaching for a part or all of the first term, as may seem to me practicable.
> 5. That any sums paid me for lecturing or other public service that may not conflict with my legitimate work as president of the College shall belong to me aside from my salary.
> 6. That I be allowed a credit of $300 on my subscription for services rendered and expenses incurred in raising $25,000 of subscription for the new building.
> 7. That there be a respectful recognition of my resignation and of the action of the Board in requesting me to continue my labors as president of the College. The same to be published along with such resolutions as may be calculated to cherish confidence in the institution and its president in the papers of this county and of the CP church.[11]

The trustees immediately agreed to retain Miller as president of the institution on his conditions. But the treasury contained only $265, and, therefore, they could not meet his first condition—that $1,000 be paid to him by 1 October 1878. Belatedly, on 11 October the trustees borrowed $735 from the Board of Trust out of the endowment fund to pay the balance of Miller's claim. This loan was for one year at six percent interest "on the corporate security of the college. . . ."[12]

Though this loan was effected, Miller received nothing from it. What happened to this money is not clear. Months passed and he was not paid. On 6 May 1879 he informed the trustees "of his pressing financial need, requesting immediate receipt." He had been using what little money he had to meet essential expenses of the college. For example, in March 1879 he paid $30.50 out of his own pocket "for advertising this term of college in twenty-eight newspapers outside of this county."[13] Since the trustees stalled in paying Miller, he took the matter to the Pennsylvania Synod, in the hope of getting better results. Consequently that body, at its meeting in September 1879, directed "the Board of Trustees to pay him . . . one thousand dollars ($1,000.00), which is to be

BELMONT COLLEGE LIBRARY

a full and final settlement of all matters and for all services rendered by him to September 1878."[14]

Under pressure from the Synod, the trustees met on 24 December 1879 for the purpose of settling with Miller "for the past twenty-five or thirty years." Miller then changed his proposals for a settlement from those of the preceding year. First he asked the trustees to "lift the notes now held by the Board of Trust . . . against me. . . . " These notes totaled $1,200.00. Miller wanted to make certain that he would not be held for their payment. Second, Miller demanded that the trustees pay him $200.00 within thirty days; $200.00 within sixty days; and give him credit for $700.00, the balance of his subscription of $1,000.00 to the building fund of the college. If the trustees would meet these conditions, Miller promised them a receipt in full of all claims against them. But the treasury was empty. The trustees, therefore, proceeded to borrow $1,300.00 from the Board of Trust, with which they made payments according to Miller's plan. They finally "fully complied with their part of said contract" to Miller's entire satisfaction.[15]

The trustees were not alone in their awareness that Miller's services were indispensable to the very life of the college. The CP Church as a whole, the general public, the Pennsylvania Synod, newspaper men, and residents of Waynesburg recognized his merits and his deep devotion to the institution. Different attempts were made to lure him away from Waynesburg. For example, in October 1893 the Pittsburgh Presbytery unanimously recommended him "for election to the chair of Theology at Cumberland University. No man in the denomination is better qualified for this important position." Miller consistently declined overtures of this sort. As a local editor put it: "Waynesburg College can't spare Dr. Miller."[16]

If Miller was indispensable to the life of the college, nearly so was Mrs. Miller. They had a single purpose in life—the development and preservation of Waynesburg College. Mrs. Miller's excellence as a classroom teacher was matched by her great strength of character. According to one of her students, "All Mrs. Miller's graces of speech and manner overlay a very solid substructure of real Puritanism in morals. The girls remembered her intolerance of things paltry and ignoble, and her 'Of course you would not do that'. . . . " Another contemporary described her as "a lady of extraordinary earnestness and devotion, and as one of fine literary taste and culture." Referring to her teaching schedule of six to seven hours daily, he made a heartfelt plea for her: "It is a shame that one so willing to labor should be suffered to waste life's power simply because the 'college treasury' is deficient of funds. Provision, immediate provision ought to be made to remedy this . . . $1,000 should be her salary."[17]

We learn of Mrs. Miller's wise counsel to the graduates of the Female Department in 1859, when evidently a girl's "place was in the home." She reminded the girls that their education was not completed, and expressed her hope that they would be

> life-long students, for I assure you your education has just commenced. I have borrowed you from your mothers for the few years that have passed so pleasantly by. I now propose to return you to the source from which you came, that you may there in your mother's kitchen, dining room, and parlor still pursue your education, for be assured of this one thing, that every young lady, be she high or low, rich or poor, ought to know how to make and mend, wash and iron, bake and scrub, and if she is ignorant of these important duties, an essential part of her education has been omitted.[18]

Thenceforward until her death, Mrs. Miller was a great champion of women's rights. When speaking to the graduating class of girls in 1871, she asserted: "That a life of activity and substantial usefulness is the happiest life, as it is the only true life. . . . Let me remind you that the great practical lesson of this Institution is work—work—work." She then spoke of the traditional discrimination against women:

> It is for you, young ladies, to contribute your part to the great work of woman's emancipation from her hitherto, and yet almost universal thraldom of ignorance and servitude. A kind Providence has opened life's scenes to you in this land which, above all others, recognizes your right to become all that the rational development and use of your powers will permit. When an English university recently offered a handsome prize for the best treatise on a scientific theme, it was unanimously agreed by the judges that a lady had produced the ablest paper offered; but the authorities decided that she was not eligible to the honor, simply *because she was a woman* (Mrs. Miller's italics). In this land your efforts in the literary world will be discouraged by no such stinging injustice. Whatever they may be—and we cannot discuss them now—all the rights consistent with the appointed sphere of your sex will ere long be secured to you by enlightened public sentiment. Let it be your endeavor, with others of your sex, to show that these rights can be enjoyed and exercised with honor to yourselves and benefit to the world.

Mrs. Miller closed by imploring the girls always to love Waynesburg College: "A dying soldier in a Virginia battlefield wrote in his last letter to friends. 'If I am permitted in spirit to return to earth, you will be nearest to me when you walk amid the elms of New Haven.' So may your living and dying thought hover around this, *your* college home, as grand old *Yale* was *his* (Mrs. Miller's italics)."[19]

Within less than three years after delivering this commencement address, Mrs. Miller came to a premature grave from illness, doubtless from exhaustion and overwork. In addition to her heavy teaching schedule and administrative duties as Principal of the Female Department, she was the gracious overseer of social life of the institution; frequently she entertained friends from the faculty, student body, and townspeople. As mother and homemaker she had heavy duties, having borne eight children, none of whom had reached adulthood at the time of her death. She suffered a stroke on 10 February 1874 which disabled her. It nearly resulted in immediate death, and left one side entirely helpless. She received the best possible care, considering medical science and available facilities at that time, and showed some signs of improvement. Hopefully on 4 March a local newspaper announced: "We are glad to inform all readers that Mrs. M. K. B. Miller is slowly recovering from her recent attack of paralysis." This report was overly optimistic, for at no time could Mrs. Miller leave her bed without help. She lingered until 27 April 1874 when she suffered a stroke on the other side and passed peacefully away. She was buried in Greene Mount Cemetery near the campus which was so dear to her heart. She sacrificed her life for the college. As one historian put it: "Without her self-denying work and influence, Waynesburg College might have failed."[20]

Mrs. Miller's death was an irreparable loss. On learning the sad news, the trustees met immediately, resolved to attend her funeral in a body, and appointed a committee "to prepare resolutions expressive of their sense of the worth and services of Mrs. Miller to the college." They also expressed their sympathy and condolences to the "devoted husband and dear children in their sad bereavement." And as a token of respect to Mrs. Miller, they declared that "her vacant chair in chapel be draped in mourning for the space of thirty days."[21]

Mrs. Miller's death was widely mourned. Her funeral was the largest ever known in Waynesburg. The alumni expressed their collective sentiment: "None knew her but to love her; none named her but to praise."[22] When the Alumni Association of the college met in September 1874, it adopted a resolution to erect a monument to the memory of Mrs. Miller. By November 1880 the alumni had "contributed a fund sufficient to erect to the memory of the late Mrs. M. K. B. Miller a beautiful monument."[23]

In 1928, more than a half century after her death, Mrs. Miller was still remembered with the greatest esteem, when a magnificent new high school was built in Waynesburg. Members of the local school board and other friends of education resolved to name the building "'The Margaret Bell Miller High School' in honor of the wife of Dr. A. B. Miller, long time President of Waynesburg College. . . . " The building, located at the corner of Lincoln and Morgan Streets, was dedicated on 1 June 1928.[24]

Of the male members of the faculty the most noted, in addition to Miller, were Professors Walter G. Scott and James R. Rinehart. All three, known as the "Great Triumvirate," usually taught without any salary; each earned his livelihood chiefly from other sources. Professor Scott was born near Washington, Pennsylvania, on 11 December 1832. He moved with the family to the Pursley Creek Valley, near Oak Forest, Greene County, in 1840. His father purchased a farm there, which was partly woodland with choice oaks. From these trees, in 1850 Professor Scott sawed the rough oak timber used in building the first building of the college. He enrolled as a student, pursued his studies diligently, and graduated in the class of 1857. He later received an A.M. degree from Waynesburg College and a Ph.D. from Adrian College. In 1858 he taught Latin at Greene Academy. From 1859 until 1908 he taught mathematics in Waynesburg College. In the latter year he became Professor Emeritus of Mathematics in the college, and held that distinction until his death in 1922 at age ninety. As we have seen, Professor Scott had a kindly, gracious spirit that endeared him to all. "Hate never entered his heart and love never left it." He had a keen intellect "that he used to seek out and illuminate the eternal truths that underlie all things . . . and he had the power to impart his marvellous reasoning powers to his pupils." He was "perfectly at home in all the higher mathematics"; in this specialty he was well known all over the country. He also taught in several areas of the sciences and was dubbed "Father of Science" at the college. Many institutions, including West Point, made offers to lure him away, "but he steadfastly remained true in the service of his Alma Mater." Scott's salary was small, and generally in arrears or not paid. Fortunately he had a small grocery store, founded by his father, which provided his main source of income.[25]

The third man in the "Great Triumvirate," Professor Rinehart, was born on 24 October 1832 at Woodsfield, Ohio. His father was a blacksmith and hardware merchant. While Rinehart was a small boy the family moved to Waynesburg. After the completion of his studies in the local public school, Rinehart entered Waynesburg College, and graduated in the class of 1853, with Miller. Following graduation, Rinehart studied law in the office of the Honorable A. A. Purman in Waynesburg, and subsequently was admitted to the Greene County bar. In 1855 he moved to Illinois, and located his practice at Clinton, county seat of DeWitt County, not far from Springfield, in the same judicial district where Abraham Lincoln practiced law. Rinehart and Lincoln had offices in the same building, and they became good friends. In those days it was customary for circuit judges to call on local lawyers to hold court in their places, if circumstances prevented them from holding it themselves. Poor transportation, inclement weather, or illness often prevented circuit judges from making their rounds at county courts on time. Hence Rinehart, and other lawyers as well, could not always be sure who would be the judge in cases of their clients. He liked to recall one of his first cases in Illinois, prior to which he confidentially gave the facts to Lincoln and sought his advice. Lincoln replied that he feared the law was not on Rinehart's side, but if the judge hearing the case was incompetent, "there might be a chance." Rinehart worked hard on preparations for his case. But on entering the courtroom he found, to his surprise, that Lincoln was on the bench. The case proceeded. When it was concluded, as kindly as possible, and with a certain trace of humor, Lincoln decided against Rinehart. Rinehart was not taken aback too greatly, for he knew that Lincoln was an outstanding lawyer and a capable judge. He spoke of "Mr. Lincoln as being kind-hearted, and in a lawsuit, even his opponents liked him." At that time, however, Rinehart looked on Lincoln only as a great lawyer. He did not believe the "railsplitter" was presidential timber.[26]

Before joining the faculty of Waynesburg College, Rinehart served as lawyer and educator in several other places. He left Clinton, Illinois, and briefly practiced law in St. Louis and St. Joseph, in Missouri. In 1880 he returned to Waynesburg and served for two years as President of Monongahela College, at Jefferson, Pennsylvania. Subsequently he taught briefly in the public schools in Mt. Morris and Waynesburg. He also began law practice with W. A. Hook in Waynesburg. In 1885 he became professor of Latin and Greek in the college, and so served with great dedication and efficiency until 1901. He knew seven languages, including Hebrew and Sanskrit. His *Alma Mater* honored him by conferring the LL. D. degree upon him. In July 1895 the trustees created the office of Vice President of the College and named Rinehart to that post. As they put it: "Professor Rinehart has for years taught in the college, and is a gentleman of high scholarly attainments. He will fill the position with honor." Like his colleagues at the college, his salary was a pittance; he made his living chiefly by practicing law. At the time of his death on 25 November 1910, he was the oldest lawyer at the Greene County bar.[27]

Another noted faculty member was Professor Albert McGinnis, a graduate of the college in the class of 1878. In March 1879 he was employed as registrar, "and also to take charge of the laboratory and apparatus of the college." His salary was $500 per year, but the trustees resolved "that in view of the straitened finances of the College, he along with each of the other professors, be requested to abate his salary for one year in the sum of $50." As the months passed, instead of voluntarily decreasing his salary, McGinnis "proposed to continue his labors in the college only on the condition of an increase of salary" which the trustees "deemed it impracticable to promise to pay. . . . "[28]

Knowing that he could not stand at the top of his profession without taking graduate work in a German university, in 1882 McGinnis took a year's leave and attended the University of Leipzig, where he studied in the sciences and the German and French languages. After returning to Waynesburg, he taught these languages and resumed his teaching in the sciences. He was an excellent teacher. His work at Leipzig greatly strengthened him as a scholar, and resulted in an increase in salary at his *Alma Mater*. But it was still less than $1,000 per year; and he taught the usual schedule of some six hours daily. By contrast, according to a friend of the college:

> In Vanderbilt the professors teach *two* hours per day and receive $2,500 per year (italics in original). Their professors are no better prepared than several men in our church schools who are laboring three times as hard on starving salaries. Our best professors receive less pay than an ordinary coachman in New York. The professors at Waynesburg College have sacrificed ease and comfort and high positions, because they love the Church.

In 1887 McGinnis left to take a similar position at Lincoln University. His departure was deeply regrettable. A local editor expressed the popular sentiment: "An able man, and our town and college will suffer a severe loss in his leaving."[29]

Another competent man who served with Miller for several years, and with his successors after the turn of the century was Professor Andrew J. Waychoff, born in Muddy Creek valley, in Jefferson Township, on 12 April 1849. His early education was obtained at nearby Scott's school, after which he attended Greene Academy. Next he entered Waynesburg College and graduated in the class of 1873. Prior to joining the faculty of his *Alma Mater* in 1882, he had had good experience as an educator, having served as assistant principal of the State Normal School at West Liberty, West Virginia, and as principal of Greene Academy. From 1887 to 1890 he was Superintendent of Schools of Greene County. In this position he aimed at raising educational standards. He regretted that in the schools

> wages during the last three years have been on the decrease. About twenty-five of our best teachers leave the profession every year. The discrimination between good and poor teachers has been so slight that the selection of teachers has come to be regarded as a kind of lottery. . . . Not enough attention is given to moral training in our schools. It seems the great delight of many persons is to weaken the influence of teachers.

Waychoff had a variety of interests, including anthropology, archaeology, geology, local history, and mathematics. His *Local History*, published in 1926, was essentially a collection of interesting items from newspapers. He was an avid collector of geological specimens and Indian artifacts. He

> held several positions in Waynesburg College such as Principal of the Normal Department, Principal of the Preparatory Department, Chair of Mathematics, and, of late years, teacher of Sciences. He has been a general utility man in the college for about twenty-five years and has repeatedly declined the vice-presidency of the college.[30]

A notable female faculty member was Anna Acklin, a native of Carmichaels, where she received her early education and also taught school. Subsequently she entered Waynesburg College and graduated in 1886. She then went westward, and taught at Drury College, Springfield, Missouri, and at the College of the Ozarks, Clarksville, Arkansas. She returned to Waynesburg in 1894; and from then until 1903 she taught English and History in the college and served as Dean of Women. Meanwhile, during summers, she earned an A. M. degree at the University of Chicago. She later attended graduate school at Harvard and Boston Universities, and won the Ph. D. from the latter in 1905. She had all the qualities of a great teacher and scholar. Interestingly enough, she was the first woman in the college to be called "Dean of Women." Until her advent, "those who published the college catalogue were too backward" to use this title. They had persisted in using the title "Principal of the Female Department."[31]

The foregoing faculty members were the most notable ones, who served with Miller, from the standpoints of ability, devotion to the college, and length of service. Of others, briefly affiliated with the college, most noteworthy was the Reverend J. L. Goodnight, pastor of the CP Church in Waynesburg, who attended Cumberland University, and the University of Jena in Germany. After teaching for a short time at Waynesburg, he became president of West Virginia University at a salary of $3,500 per year—a substantial income for that time.[32]

In June 1870 Miller called on "the Synod to help us get two more professors. Relief should be given to those so heavily taxed. One beloved workman has fallen" from "too severe labor in the College." The two additional faculty members were not forthcoming. A year later, when enrollment was 280, Miller begged again for more funds and faculty members. A minister from Kansas sent him five dollars, for which he was grateful, but he needed more. Said Miller: "Endowment is not adequate to support professors now at work. We need two more. . . . There are colleges in the land that, with ten times our endowment, are doing less work, have fewer students, and are accomplishing less good, than ours. . . . In the Pennsylvania Synod there is at least $50,000 that can be secured in the next two years. It will not come to us. We must go after it." Knowing that many alumni and friends of the college had gone westward, in 1871 Miller looked to them also for help:

> Are there not 100 men and women scattered over the West who will send Waynesburg College $5.00 each during the summer to help meet current expenses of the year? We have no Boston, New York, or Philadelphia to which to appeal for help. . . . We are, like California, frontier in our church operations. And yet every year we spare some of our men for the Great West. Will not the West help us?[33]

Concerned over heavy teaching schedules, the trustees, in December 1879, directed their Committee on Teachers and Salaries "to forthwith visit the College and ascertain from each teacher the number of classes taught and number of hours engaged each day; and the number of pupils in each class. . . . "[34] Little or nothing came from this effort, however. During the late decades of the nineteenth century the faculty consisted of from five to seven members, but student enrollment ran between 250 and 400.[35] Clearly the faculty was overloaded by sheer numbers. In order to aid the faculty in bearing their burdens, able, advanced students were sometimes called on to teach underclassmen. For example in 1891, several such students were serving "as teachers in the preparatory department and the best satisfaction is reported. Mr. Stahlman is acting as assistant instructor of the Commercial Department, and goes about his work with a great amount of enthusiasm." Another capable student who helped the faculty was Edward Martin who "frequently taught mathematics as high as trigonometry without thought of compensation." Martin was destined to become one of the most outstanding of all alumni of the college, and one of the greatest Americans. A leader in civilian, military, and political life, he became Governor of Pennsylvania, United States Senator from Pennsylvania, and a Major General in the United States Army. He was a student under Miller, Rinehart, Scott, Waychoff, and Miss Acklin—all of whom he held in highest esteem.[36]

Despite adversity, the overall quality of instruction appears to have been high. Many times Miller called attention to this fact in faculty meetings, in churches, and in the press. At a mass meeting held at the courthouse in June 1879, the speaker, who was familiar with large and small institutions of learning, including Waynesburg, maintained that Waynesburg "is not a one-horse college. Instruction is just as thorough as anywhere, and the graduates get high positions and are just as useful as those of the big universities." At big schools, "Much of the teaching is done by tutors substituted for the distinguished catalogued faculty. . . . "[37]

The trustees, continually confronted with the problem of meeting faculty salaries, operated on a shoestring basis indeed. In July 1878 they attempted "to ascertain the amount of indebtedness of the college to professors for past services." Shortly their Committee on Teachers and Salaries reported that Weethee, who had left the college twenty years earlier, was still pressing a claim. His claim and those of Miller, Scott, R. V. Atkinson and George Frazer were found to total $4,128.50. Frazer, in the worst financial straits, appealed to the trustees for help. He desperately needed money to meet his contract with a life insurance company. The treasury was empty. But the trustees appointed a committee from their own body, which raised funds for Dr. Frazer in the amount of $175.00.

They also urged the Board of Trust to grant the college another loan as speedily as possible.[38]

Faculty salaries ranged between $100 and $600 per year.[39] Sources of income were always inadequate. Tuition was as low as two dollars per student per session. In March 1882, P. H. Crider, Financial Agent of the college, appealed to peoples' pride in the hope of securing funds. More endowment, he held, was absolutely indispensable to the future existence of the college. Crider pleaded for gifts in all amounts, and the Board of Trust wanted the whole field canvassed. In what appears to have been a "buck-passing" system, there was confusion concerning what organization should support faculty members. In March 1879, in the hope of clarification of this matter, the trustees directed their Committee on Teachers and Salaries "to consider and report to the Board at its next meeting what professorships in Waynesburg College the Presbytery or the Board of Trust should support."[40] No clear-cut answer was forthcoming. It seems that responsibility here overlapped, for the Board of Trust raised most of its funds within the Pennsylvania Presbytery.

The various practices relative to faculty salaries seem strange—and pitiful. At times faculty members were employed at certain salaries, and then requested voluntarily to abate them by ten per cent.[41] Some teachers were not promised any salary. For example, in September 1878 the trustees resolved to employ a teacher in the Music Department, "provided that if anyone be engaged, it shall be without cost to the college." A year later an elocutionist, doubtless aware of the salary situation, proposed "to teach elocution while pursuing a course of study, accepting the responsibility of his own salary." Teachers in the fields of music or elocution were permitted to charge their students fees and to keep the money as their incomes. In some instances faculty members were employed at certain salaries and any money earned beyond those figures "on extra duties shall be paid to the treasurer of the Board of Trustees."[42] In the apparent absence of contracts in writing, sometimes there were misunderstandings between trustees and faculty members regarding amounts of salaries.[43] A curious situation arose in December 1880, when the treasury was empty. A certain faculty member's salary was in arrears $225.00. The trustees met and moved to borrow this sum from the Farmers' and Drovers' Bank to pay him. The vote was tied, but the chairman voted "Nay"—and the motion was lost.[44] In some cases when the college was insolvent, faculty members agreed to split equally whatever income there might be from tuition and fees. There is no evidence that they were ever paid in kind such as potatoes, beans, or other produce from farms—as was the practice in some colleges in rural America.[45]

Since the salary situation was so tenuous, it was difficult to recruit and hold faculty members, particularly from outside the local area. The trustees could never be sure how soon certain faculty members might leave. In recruiting faculty members, it was customary to hold personal interviews with candidates prior to employment. By 1880 the college had set an excellent precedent of paying a candidate's travel expenses for the interview, whether or not he was employed.[46]

The faculty members felt sorry for janitors, who received the lowest wages of all. In 1878 the janitor received $50.00 for a full term of sixteen weeks and there is no indication this wage was raised. It was even lower in 1897, when the faculty moved "That we call the attention of the trustees to the meager salary of the janitor, and that we recommend that the work be divided between two janitors and that each be paid a minimum of twenty dollars per term and free tuition, or that the regular janitor employ an assistant to do one-half of the work in terms named above."[47]

Regardless of the bleakness of the financial picture, the optimistic side was always pointed out in the press. In an appeal in 1872 for $50,000 for additional endowment, due to increased patronage, a local editor held that the "college is basically prosperous, with attendance near 300." The institution "has public confidence and sympathy. . . . " Rigid economy in management meant that "Not one dollar of the $50,000 will be used for any purpose but endowment. . . . This institution is among us. It is ours. It has all facilities necessary to a college education."[48]

From catalogues and laws of the college we get a fairly good idea concerning classroom procedure. The library was small; and laboratories in the modern sense were nonexistent. The main sources of subject material were textbooks, supplemented by lectures. The students' notebooks were indispensable tools in the learning process. The Socratic method was in general use; professors asked the students questions on material to which they had been exposed; student participation in class discussions was encouraged. Classes were regularly referred to as "recitations." For example, in the languages "the student's ear is constantly exercised, as well as his eye; and by recitations in concert the mastery of the inflections of words becomes easy. . . . " Language teachers continually stressed the Greek and

Latin roots of innumerable words in the English language, and pointed out similarities and differences "between our own language and those noble languages of antiquity." It was

> assumed that effort is the essential condition of development, and every student is from the first put under the necessity of thinking for himself. . . . Free intercourse among pupils, and between pupils and professors, by question, debate, criticism, and argument, secures interest in the recitation room and develops the students' mental power.

Grades were based on marks for recitations in the classrooms and on tests and examinations. Final examinations generally covered material in entire courses, commonly referred to as "branches."[49]

It is abundantly clear that Miller and his most noted colleagues were not mere timeservers. He would do nothing, and leave nothing undone, that would hurt the college. Referring to his attempts to resign during the depths of discouragement and despondency, he put duty to the college above all other considerations. As he put it about 1888:

> If I had any conviction of Providential direction of my life, it is that God led me in the course I have pursued in regard to our college. . . . At various times I have earnestly desired to see the way open for me to leave; but as there are obstructions to a river on all sides but one, so convictions of duty have ever shut me up to the direction in which my life of labor has been running through all these years. How much better another man could have discharged the duties of the place, I cannot know. It is a source of comfort to have the internal assurance that I have done as well, as was in my power to do, in performing a work to which my Heavenly Father called me, and which I have been able to do only through a sense of his sustaining grace.[50]

Faculty members who worked with Miller, like most others in the nation, of necessity, were familiar with a variety of fields, for an individual might be called on to teach several "branches," some of which were unrelated. All faced the handicaps of low salaries, heavy schedules, and lack of fringe benefits. They had no guild or organization such as the American Association of University Professors of today; a union for faculty members was unknown. While they lacked expertise in narrow specialties and did not "produce" articles and books like modern scholars, by and large, they were dedicated, masterful teachers. There is abundant evidence that they had excellent rapport with students; they were not dull pedants, who bored their students. Their knowledge, practical experience, ability to express themselves clearly, sense of humor, and genuine human sympathy and understanding made for a pleasant, profitable experience in the educational process. Miller was a born leader. As a contemporary put it: "Clear scholarship, tactful teaching, and fellowship with his faculty meant success for President Miller."[51]

VII
THE CURRICULUM AND ACADEME, 1859-1899

As in colleges all over the nation, Waynesburg's curriculum was strongly classical. It stressed the liberal arts and sciences which aimed to aid man in the discovery of the nature of the universe and in an understanding of his role in it. The great emphasis on Latin and Greek, including religious works, stemmed chiefly from the Italian Renaissance of the fourteenth and fifteenth centuries. Classical Latin and Greek poetry and philosophical writings, considered essential to educated, cultured gentlemen, were introduced in the University of Paris, and extended thence to Oxford and Cambridge in England, whence they came to America. The curriculum adopted at Harvard in 1636 spread successively as other colleges were founded in America.[1]

During Miller's administration, apparently by trial and error, the length of the academic year was changed at various times. In the early years the calendar called for two terms of school, totaling thirty-six weeks. In 1879 the academic year was lengthened to forty weeks and divided into three terms. In July 1881 it was shortened to thirty-eight weeks. Some five years later the total time was thirty-nine weeks; the fall, winter, and spring terms were fixed at fourteen, twelve, and thirteen weeks respectively with a short vacation at the end of the first and second terms.[2]

At the preparatory level for male students, by 1870 there was little change in the curriculum. The "three R's" and Latin and Greek were stressed. By the end of the second year, students at this level, having been exposed regularly to Latin and Greek, were able to read most works in these languages. In 1898 the preparatory course was lengthened from two to three years—a junior, middle, and senior year—with three terms annually as in all other programs. Work in the additional year comprised more Greek and Latin, more mathematics and mediaeval and modern history. The emphasis on Latin and Greek was generally believed the best way to train students' minds.[3]

At the college level the classical course for males remained essentially unchanged during the latter half of the nineteenth century. New courses added after 1870 included acoustics, anatomy, art, elocution, English literature, exposition of the United States constitution, mechanics, optics, physical geography, and physiology. Seniors were required to present weekly written dissertations throughout the term.[4]

The scientific course was offered with the "apparatus" at hand; no laboratory in the modern sense existed. There was some variation in the requirements for this course. In the early years it was essentially the same as the classical course, but there was less emphasis on Latin and Greek. As the years went on there was increasing stress on French and German; by 1898 these languages had completely replaced Latin and Greek as the language requirement for the bachelor of science degree. The scientific program at that time called for more mathematics and English, and science courses every year. Courses in history and philosophy also were required.[5]

In any age there are those innovators who advocate change in existing curricula. Such was the case in September 1875 at a joint program of the literary societies when, after the regular performances, James E. Sayers, spoke of the need for reform in the curriculum: "Because of change, it is not judicious to follow the old, beaten track of college studies." He held that courses of study should be adapted to needs after graduation. He "would drop all Greek beyond Homer and all Latin beyond Virgil." He would delete higher mathematics courses, "unless a student would need them later," and would lay greater stress on science. Miller, who was inclined to preserve the classical tradition, agreed with Sayers on the mathematics requirements, "but did not go so far in cutting down the languages." He added that: "No doubt a reform will soon be made in our college," for, "in general, change was needed."[6]

An innovation in 1870 was highly desirable, for its aim was physical culture. Doubtless many on campus welcomed Miller's announcement: "The Dio Lewis System of Gymnastics will hereafter be taught by a gentleman who comes very highly recommended. . . . " He was Professor Welch of Yale's Department of Physical

Culture. Welch launched the program, but evidently did not stay long. A year later the course was being taught by a Professor Wood. In October 1871 Miller happily reported in the press:

> Professor Wood's class in gymnastics gave an entertainment of the Dio Lewis system of physical training, the exercises being timed by the piano and interspersed with essays and brief orations. There is much interest in physical training, and the students under Professor Wood's instruction give striking proof of the benefits derived therefrom. A *sound mind in a sound body* is the true ideal of an educated man (Miller's italics.)[7]

The interest in physical training continued. By 1892 the Gymnasium Association, composed of students, had furnished a spacious room at considerable expense with apparatus, appliances, and other essentials for physical training. This gymnasium was open daily, and an instructor directed the exercises. Physical training was wholly a voluntary matter at the college, but all students were advised to take it. Shortly a Department of Physical Culture was established. The relationship between physical training and oratory is obvious. For some years the college had had a Department of Elocution and Oratory with the most approved methods, such as "drills, deep breathing, tone production, phonic analysis, articulation, gesture, facial expression, and so on." Classes met twice weekly for regular lessons and on Saturday for special work in delivery. The tuition for a thirteen-week term was five dollars. The Department of Physical Culture and the Department of Elocution and Oratory had so much in common that, in 1897, the two were merged into a new one—the Department of Oratory and Physical Culture. In it a student could learn the basics of public speaking, and gain the added training in the gymnasium.[8]

From 1857 until about 1880 young women had the choice of enrolling either in the Female Department or in the "college proper." On completing the course of study in the former, one received a diploma, but no degree; on completing all requirements in the latter, one received the baccalaureate degree. In this Department, at the preparatory level, there was little change from the curriculum of 1850. In advanced classes, by the early 1870's, new courses included anatomy, astronomy, elocution, English literature, French, geology, meteorology, music, and physical geography. An advertisement of the college in February 1875 reminded readers that: "The Female Department offers all the advantages of a first-class Female Seminary. . . . " Another advertisement, relating to the institution as a whole, in March 1881, read: "Waynesburg College: A live institution, affording the *very best facilities* for acquiring a partial or thorough education at the LEAST POSSIBLE EXPENSE (italics and capitals in original)." This advertisement listed the courses as classical, scientific, commercial, ministerial, and one for teacher-training.[9] Available evidence indicates that the curriculum for the Female Department was terminated about 1880. Thenceforward male and female students pursued the same work leading toward the baccalaureate degree.

When Albert McGinnis returned from the University of Leipzig in October 1883, the faculty looked to him for suggestions on curriculum changes. In March 1884 he was appointed chairman of a committee "to make a program of studies for the next term." Available evidence indicates that no radical changes were then made. Unfortunately McGinnis left to take a position at Lincoln University in 1887.[10] But in the long run his suggestions on curriculum changes at the college are evident. Until the end of the century, there was increasing emphasis on science, the modern languages, and on innovations of a practical nature in the curriculum.

One of the most important features of the curriculum was the "Normal Course," designed to train teachers. This program was "one road to continued success" of the college. According to Professor Andrew J. Waychoff: "Before the advent of the university at Morgantown and the nearby normal schools, attendance during summer school frequently rose to 325."[11] In the early years the emphasis was on spelling, geography, grammar, and methods of instruction. Beginning in June 1879, arithmetic was added; and a class in school economy was started with Miller as the instructor. In 1883 a "summer normal" of five weeks duration was established, which proved very successful. The program embraced all common school studies, organization and management of schools, the best methods of teaching, and "careful study of hygiene with special reference to the effects of alcoholic drinks and narcotics." Taught by regular faculty members, "the summer normal" was prosperous and "of great advantage to those who will teach." Despite competition from other collegiate institutions, it remained popular, with an enrollment of at least 100 every summer during the 1880's.[12]

In 1890 the teacher-training program was lengthened to two full academic years, and it was re-named the "Normal Preparatory Department." With Waychoff as principal, its purpose was "to give further efficiency to the work of instruction." Facilities included a spacious room for the sole use of the Department, and an excellent library of reference books. In the first or "junior year" the "branches" were those usually included in good public schools; in the second or "senior year" they were algebra, geometry, rhetoric, composition, natural philosophy, physiology, physical geography, descriptive astronomy, English literature, United States government, science of government, moral science, psychology, English classics, and pedagogics. Some training was offered also in elocution, including reading, reciting, gesture, voice culture, impersonation, and physical culture. Upon completion of this course of study, the degree Master of Didactics was conferred, with a diploma "which will be the equivalent of a diploma from a State Normal School."[13]

If the training of teachers was essential to improvement of education in public schools, equally so was that of preachers who served churches in the CP and other denominations. Since Waynesburg was the only CP college to continue operations without interruption through the Civil War, she played an indispensable role in the life of the whole church; CP churches everywhere, which lacked ministers, were compelled to look to her as the sole source to fulfill their ministerial needs during that holocaust. The Theological School of Cumberland University had been the best institution for the training of CP ministers. Devastated by hostilities, it was forced to close; its students and faculty were scattered; and its funds were gone. Some CP members did not want their sons, who planned on ministerial careers, to attend Andover or other seminaries where they might be tainted with Calvinist doctrine. Hence in 1863 Waynesburg established a Chair of Theology, which was held by the Reverend S. T. Anderson, D. D. He was also Vice President of the college and pastor of the Waynesburg CP congregation. His chair was not endowed, and it was not permanent. No successor to him was elected, and for several years after the Civil War the program was abandoned. In 1876 Miller revived it, and he drew up a course of study for candidates. He knew that some young men were unable to pursue both college and seminary training. One candidate asked Miller which he could "omit with the least disadvantage." Miller advised a mixed course as the next best procedure—a course embracing some of the studies of both college and seminary. He proposed such a program for Waynesburg. It was to be three years in duration, but "may be extended to four years. It should embrace enough Greek so one can handle the Greek testament with ease. Hebrew must be included with a view to study of the Old Testament." In response to the desires of several young men, in September 1877, Miller published the theological course offered by Waynesburg and asked for criticisms and suggestions for its improvement. It was a comprehensive four-year program including courses in aesthetics, Bible, botany, chemistry, Christian doctrine, church history, composition of sermons, critical study of English, elocution, English composition, English grammar, English literature, evidences of Christianity, exegesis of Greek testament, geology, geometry, Greek, Hebrew, hermeneutics, higher algebra, homiletics, Latin, logic, metaphysics, moral science, mythology, physics, plane trigonometry, political economy, rhetoric, surveying, and zoology. Miller believed that the stress on the Greek, Latin, Hebrew, and English languages "imbued one with Christianity."[14] Some old lecture notes, doubtless those of Miller, reveal that the course in homiletics was the most practical one for the beginning minister. It contained many points on how to visit the sick, how to conduct prayer meetings, and how to preach. Among a number of "don'ts" on pulpit manners were: "Don't put your hands in your pockets. Don't finger your watch chain. Don't preach at the ceiling or at the floor. Don't yell. Don't pound the Bible, or slam it shut, or throw it down; treat it as though the very paper and ink were precious. Don't lean on the pulpit or pace to and fro. Don't blow your nose violently. Don't grin; undue familiarity is much more repulsive than undue solemnity." Clearly the ministerial course, which embraced much subject material ordinarily included in seminary training, if successfully completed, would prepare a young minister for a useful career.

The ministerial course also gave young men a finished foundation for further studies if they chose to attend seminaries. Waynesburg was a feeder of other institutions. For example, in 1878 Western Theological Seminary at Pittsburgh had students from twenty-two different colleges. Washington and Jefferson College sent the most; Wooster was second; and Waynesburg, third. The CP newspaper then reported: "Our Eastern College is doing good work for the Presbyterian church, helping to educate her ministry." At that time, unfortunately for the CP denomination, more young men from Waynesburg were attending Presbyterian seminaries in preparation for service for that denomination rather than for the CP Church. In areas other than the ministry, Waynesburg was also a feeder to Yale, Harvard, Leipzig, Princeton, Michigan, and various medical and law schools.[15]

In addition to the standard programs—classical, scientific, normal, and ministerial—other offerings were introduced which strengthened the curriculum. In August 1871 a course in practical engineering was begun. The college had the necessary equipment, including an engineers' transit valued at over $200, plus other essential instruments. Students could practice with them and learn to "survey, grade, level, lay out roads and railroads . . . without having to take additional training after leaving Waynesburg College—as is usually the case." The mathematics courses at the college prepared students thoroughly to succeed in engineering—better than other colleges "and almost coming up to . . . West Point."[16]

Although some business courses had been offered prior to 1885, it was then that the Commercial Department was established. The commercial course lasted a full academic year of three terms. Its offerings were bookkeeping, penmanship, commercial calculations, banking, business forms, commercial law, rapid computation, and commercial correspondence. This Department was housed in Commercial Hall, a spacious room in the new building, which was well lighted and adapted to commercial students.[17]

In 1891 the college instituted a Department of Telegraphy. By that time a vast network of railroads had spread over the nation, and the telegraph system was almost as extensive. A telegraph office was needed at nearly every railway station, and operators were in great demand. This new Department guaranteed positions to all students who became "competent to take charge of offices." The course was relatively easy; the apparatus was "quite simple and easily understood." The income was good; wages ranged "from $40 to $100 per month the year around." The duration of the course was from four to six months. Tuition was $50 in advance and "good until the course is completed." As an inducement to female students to learn telegraphy, the catalogue reads: "A reduction is made in favor of ladies, and special rates will be made for students pursuing other branches in the College."[18]

In the early years the college developed a Music Department which became increasingly popular and widely known, despite lack of funds and equipment. For example, in 1880 the faculty adopted the following resolution: "That in view of the present wants of the Music Department . . . we hereby request the Trustees to procure another piano for the use of the College."[19] The program in music was boosted in 1885 when the Conservatory of Music was established. It offered training in piano, organ, violin, cornet, and various other musical instruments, and in singing as well. At that time the course was of one year's duration.[20] As the years went on, this Conservatory expanded its program. And it was a thriving organization until well into the present century.

Aware that art is universal and an important part of a liberal education, the faculty had developed a good Department of Art by the mid-1880's. A large room, well adapted to the study of art was set aside as a "studio in elegant style in the new building." The emphasis was on drawing, painting, and sketching. The term lasted thirteen weeks; and tuition was five dollars. In 1897 there was greater emphasis on art than ever before. The relationship between art and history was pointed out: "We live in a world of pictures in which we receive impressions that educate us. Through them we preserve and recall the past." The college aimed to make the study of art "truly educational in the highest and best sense of the term" and to develop faculties which open "the mind to the world and the world to the mind." By that time the program consisted of twenty lessons of three hours each. Tuition for the sixty hours was ten dollars.[21]

While the undergraduate program of study was adapted to current needs, work at the graduate level was offered. Prior to 1870 only sixteen earned doctorates, with the exception of the M. D. degree, were granted in the United States. For the most part, graduate schools were superimposed on undergraduate colleges at institutions in the country during the last quarter of the nineteenth century.[22]

In keeping with the provision in its charter which empowered the president and faculty "to grant and confirm such degrees in the arts and sciences . . . as are granted in other colleges or universities in the United States," Waynesburg launched its program of graduate studies in 1891 by offering work leading toward both the A. M. and Ph. D. degrees. The A. M. degree was conferred on any person who had completed the requirements for any of the baccalaureate degrees, plus "one year of recitation in the College or two years of reading and study outside." The Ph. D. was conferred on those who held a baccalaureate degree and "who recite two years in the College or read a three-year course outside the College." The work prescribed for these degrees depended "somewhat on the courses already pursued, and on the designed literary work of the applicant."[23]

The faculty was careful to set high scholarly standards for advanced degrees, and to make certain that requirements for them were similar to those of other institutions. In June 1894 the faculty resolved "that hereafter an examination at the discretion of the faculty be required on subjects studied for the degree of A. M., and that a thesis be submitted on a subject to be assigned by the faculty."[24] The faculty considered the intellectual ability, talent, motivation, and inclination of individual students, and encouraged each one along the line for which he seemed best fitted—sometimes with great success. For example, in 1895 a graduate student named William C. Farabee, of the class of 1894, "asked that the degree A. M. be given him at the close of the school year, provided he comes to College and does what work he can next term, and reads a prescribed course next year." The faculty passed a motion to grant the master's degree to Farabee on these conditions.[25] Farabee's chief interest was in the field of anthropology. After receiving his A. M. at Waynesburg he attended Harvard, won his Ph. D. in anthropology there, taught there for some ten years, and later led two expeditions throughout the length of the Amazon River valley studying aboriginal tribes there and elsewhere in South America. He became one of the most widely acclaimed scientists of all time.[26]

In June 1896 the post graduate courses were spelled out in greater detail. The one-year requirement of additional recitation for the A. M. and two years of additional work for the Ph. D. was clarified to be "residence study" beyond the baccalaureate degree. At Waynesburg, as well as at other institutions, the undergraduate school was a feeder for the graduate level. Qualified persons, who were not Waynesburg graduates, were admitted to work leading toward the A. M. or Ph. D. Such persons were required to submit evidence of qualification for pursuing the required studies and pay an entrance fee of three dollars. The required courses were "largely philosophical" in nature. Substitutions were permitted, and each applicant could choose from three areas of study—scientific, classical, or literary. The catalogue reads: "The works cited below are *to be carefully studied*—not simply read (italics in original). After this study, the student must notify the President of Waynesburg College, submit to examinations, and present a thesis on an assigned subject, then pay the usual graduation fee of $5.00." For the A. M. degree the works were: G. T. Ladd, *Outlines of Physiological Psychology*; Mark Hopkins, *Outline Study of Man*; E. Jaynes, *Human Psychology*; Duke of Argyll, *The Unity of Nature*; and James Seth, *A Study of Ethical Principles*. The program leading to the Ph. D. included all the work for the A. M., plus the following: Mulford, *The Nation*; Whewell, *History of Inductive Sciences*; Weber, *History of Philosophy*;

Diman, *Theistic Argument*; and Cousin, *The True*, *The Beautiful*, *The Good.*[27]

It appears that the foregoing requirements were minimal, and additional work could be mandatory on individual students at the discretion of the faculty. For example, in November 1896 the faculty outlined an M. A. program for Miss Louise Smith, a graduate of the class of that year, which is considerably more exacting than the one above. In epic poetry Miss Smith was required to be familiar with the *Iliad*, the *Song of Roland* (in French), *Beowulf*, *Robin Hood*, *The Idyls of the King*, *Paradise Lost*, and Lytell Geste's *English Ballads*. In the *History of English Lyric Poetry*, she was to study carefully Percy's *Reliques*, Mabere's *Elements of Poetry*, and *English Miscellany*. In language studies, she was to know Whitney, *On Language*, Sweet's *Primer of English*, and Von Ten Brink's *Literature*. In addition, she was required to produce a satisfactory thesis on a subject assigned by the faculty.[28]

The college conferred only a small number of earned graduate degrees in the 1890's. In 1891, one Ph. D. was conferred on an individual listed among the eleven seniors. Granted thenceforward in that decade, and listed separately, were: three Ph. D's, in 1892; one A. M. in 1894; two Ph. D's, and two A. M.'s, in 1895; two A. M.'s, in 1896; and three Ph. D's, and two A. M.'s, in 1899.[29]

The practice of making regular reports to parents and guardians relative to students' scholastic standing and behavior was adopted immediately after the founding of the college. For example, every three months the Waynesburg Female Seminary sent a "certificate of deportment and improvement" to parents of each female enrolled therein. Such a certificate, for a young lady, dated 5 July 1859, records: "Deportment—amiable; perfect lessons—all; deficient lessons—none; drawing and painting—very good improvement; writing, arithmetic, spelling—excellent. Parents are requested to examine this certificate."[30]

The faculty permitted certain students to substitute courses for those required in the several programs of study. In some cases substitutions seem justifiable, and permitted for the convenience of individual students. If some courses required for a given degree were not offered, substitutions could be made. On the other hand, some students were permitted to make substitutions, apparently for no good reasons. For example, in February 1879, the faculty approved a student's request "that he be allowed to substitute three terms of German for three terms of mathematics, *viz.* descriptive geometry, analytical geometry, and calculus."[31] In another case a student requested the faculty to permit him to forgo all mathematics and to substitute language instead. But the faculty required him to take three courses in mathematics and the two in language.[32] In June 1891 the faculty permitted fourteen students "to make various course substitutions, and considered certain individual loads too heavy and advised an extra year of study." In January 1894 a student requested "to be graduated without further attendance by substituting Greek and Latin . . . for work in English yet undone." In view of "his high standing as a student," the faculty acceded to his request.[33]

Occasionally the faculty faced problems relative to student enrollment. At the beginning of each term a deadline date was set by which students must be enrolled, but some evaded this rule. In September 1879 the faculty passed a motion that, after the enrollment deadline, those students not enrolled "will not be permitted to recite."[34] In January 1882 a student desired to take music lessons under a teacher, who was not a member of the college faculty, and get college credit for it. The faculty promptly denied this student's request, resolved that students must be enrolled, and "decided to make no exceptions to the rule that all students . . . are expected to recite in *all* their studies to members of the faculty (italics in original)."[35]

The faculty received many requests from students who wished to be excused from class, and used its discretion in individual cases. Reasons for such excuses are not always clear. Doubtless some students were excused for illness, death in the immediate family, or other urgent reasons; others might have been reluctant to speak in class. For example, in February 1880, a female student was "excused from reciting in evidences of Christianity"; and another, from reciting in algebra. In June of that year, four students were "excused from recitation" in French, physical geography, United States history, and "dictionary class." On 27 June 1881 nine students requested the faculty to permit them "to go home during this week and be absent the remainder of the term," claiming that they were needed to help with the harvest. This request was not granted. On the other hand, in February 1882 the faculty excused a student from his German class during the remainder of the term, "because of the fact that German recites in the afternoon and he is employed by his father at that time."[36]

Available evidence shows that there were no clear-cut steps in progression from one class to another. It was sometimes difficult to ascertain to what class a student belonged. For example, in September 1879, a student requested the faculty "to be allowed to enter the Senior year. . . . " The faculty promptly met and considered the merits and demerits of this student. After considerable discussion, the faculty decided to permit him "to enter the Senior year, conditional on Greek and mathematics."[37] In July 1880 the faculty considered a request from a student "to be allowed to graduate by attending College four more sessions." He was not ready, however, to pursue college work without interruption. After due deliberation the faculty decided that if he "reads a book of *Anabasis* and 1,000 lines of Ovid during the next two terms when he is absent, and pays as much attention as possible to the languages while in College, he may be graduated in that time."[38] In August 1894, a female student, uncertain about the time of her graduation, appealed to the trustees for an answer. That body "directed the faculty to determine within ten days" her right to a College diploma. The faculty, in a called meeting in Professor Scott's store, "found her qualified to graduate in the class of 1894, and upon payment of the customary fee to Dr. Miller. . . . "[39]

Transfer students complicated the problem of classification. The practice of sending transcripts of student's records from one institution to another seems to have been slipshod and irregular. In some cases transcripts were not sent at all, and students' statements of work done elsewhere were accepted by the faculty. For example, in June 1884, the faculty considered a student's request to be graduated that year, and "decided that he be permitted to make a statement to the faculty of all branches of study he has pursued here and elsewhere—and that, if in the opinion of the faculty he can complete the course in one year by studying at home, he may upon examination be graduated in 1885."[40] In October 1891 a transfer student was "asked for an official statement of his standing in previously attended colleges." By 1896 the practice of sending transcripts of academic records of transfer students seems to have been established. In March of that year, two seniors at Grove City desired to transfer to Waynesburg. The faculty moved that "they be admitted to the present Senior class of this College whenever satisfactory papers are filed with the College showing that they are now regular Seniors at Grove City College. . . . " Even before the sending of transcripts of transfer students, Waynesburg's faculty members carefully tried to put such students in classes where they belonged.

Whenever they were in doubt they reserved the right to examine students in any branches pursued at other schools.[41]

Procedures adopted relative to grading were designed to promote high academic standards. In May 1888 the faculty resolved "that all classes shall be held to examinations, and no student shall be accounted to have studied a branch who has not reached at least 60%."[42] Attendance at classes and examinations was a factor in the grading system. Each student who absented himself from a final examination was required to "sign a pledge of obedience to the laws of the college before being admitted next term"; and to restudy the "branch in which the examination was not attended." The faculty also resolved "that no student shall be allowed to appear in any public exercise connected with the College, if he has unexcused absences from class."[43]

Students who faithfully attended class were rewarded, but lazy, irresponsible ones suffered the consequences. In March 1895 the faculty unanimously resolved that:

> Any student who has been present at nine tenths of the recitations of his class, and also at the last three exercises of the same, if his attainment therein be satisfactory to his teacher, may pass without further examination to the work of the next term. Failing, however, in this standard of attendance and attainment, he shall be required to pass a special examination in the work of the term, the minuteness of which shall be in proportion to the degree of his failure.[44]

Grades on final examinations in juncture with daily grades were the bases of grades "to be placed upon the permanent college register."[45]

While the faculty generally was careful to maintain high academic standards, in a few instances it took action which seems inconsistent with sound scholasticism. For example, in April 1884, Miller called a special meeting of the faculty apparently to consider the conditional graduation of two students, with some work to be completed after graduation. One student was "permitted to take mathematical astronomy this session in place of Greek, provided he will agree to do the session's work in Greek after graduation, and render to the faculty such account thereof as they may require." Another student was "permitted to leave such studies as are still necessary in her course, but which she cannot take this session, provided she will agree to complete the same after graduation. . . . "[46] Without giving definite reasons, these students were graduated—even though they did not fulfill all the requirements until after commencement. Specific procedure here is not clear. It is reasonable to assume that diplomas were withheld until all work was completed.

The most important week of the year came at the end of the last term. In the early years it was referred to as the week of "Anniversary Exercises" and later as "Commencement Week." A typical week's events included the baccalaureate sermon on Sunday evening, the annual address before students on Monday evening, literary and musical performances on Tuesday, public examinations on Wednesday, commencement for the Female Department on Wednesday evening, the alumni meeting on Thursday, and gentlemen's commencement on Thursday evening. Until 1873 there were separate commencements for female and male graduating seniors.[47] Thenceforward the two were merged.

All members of each graduating class customarily participated in commencement exercises. A typical commencement program opened with music and prayer. Then came the salutatorians; in the early years frequently three of them spoke—one in English, one in Latin, and one in Greek. Following were orations and essays by members of the class. The valedictorian then spoke, after which degrees were conferred and diplomas were awarded. Musical selections were presented between performances. The program ended with the benediction. We get an insight into some of the essays from those read at the female commencement on 10 September 1867 on such topics as "We Are Going," "After Many Days," and "Clearing Off." The valedictorian then spoke on the subject, "We are Living, We are Dwelling in a Grand and Awful Time." On the following day at the gentlemen's commencement, orations were delivered on "Self Architecture," "A Comparison," "The Pulpit Master's Oration," and "Intellectual Unfoldings of the Age." The valedictorian spoke on "The Elements." At commencement in September 1871 the best oration, dealing with the development of personality in the educational process, was delivered by M. L. Gordon, later the noted missionary to Japan.[48]

As graduating classes grew larger it became impracticable for each member to give a long presentation at commencement. In June 1880 the faculty "moved that graduates be informed that each performance be limited to ten minutes"; two years later the limit was set at eight minutes. In January 1884 the senior class, numbering eighteen, petitioned the faculty for "the privilege of substituting for the regular commencement performances a lecture by some one of our eminent men. . . . " The faculty did not act on this matter, for Miller decided it "comes within the jurisdiction of the Trustees" and could not legally be decided by the faculty; a week later five seniors submitted a counter-petition to the faculty; this minority wanted no change from the traditional commencement.[49] The matter was temporarily dropped. In June 1890 the faculty and seniors again considered the desirability of having an outsider speak at commencement. Again, nothing came of this proposal. In May 1896, however, the faculty agreed to excuse seniors from performance at commencement, if they could give good reasons for not wishing to participate. A year later a committee of seniors broached the subject of selecting a class orator to represent them at commencement, but the faculty felt it "is more satisfactory to the class, to friends, and to others that each member take part in Commencement exercises."[50]

If commencement exercises were lengthy and wearisome, there were many compensations which were most rewarding and pleasant. Contemporary accounts throw light on commencement, and indicate the pleasure derived in travel to Waynesburg, and in being on campus and in town at that time of the year. The Reverend Azel Freeman returned in October 1870, when there was no rail line into Waynesburg. After a visit in Uniontown, he traveled thence to Brownsville, and thence up the Monongahela River "by means of slack water navigation, and at the second lock we stepped from the steamer, and found we were at Rices Landing, in Greene County. Thence we passed by stage over the hills through the village of Jefferson, where the Baptists are laying the foundation of a college in the midst of a beautiful pine grove." Freeman and his friends "wended their way eight miles further through a region of rocks and hills, and we came suddenly in sight of Waynesburg, the Mecca of our pilgrim-land; for all the passengers—and our stage-coach was full and crowded—were going to the College Commencement."[51]

Freeman returned in 1876, expressed his love for the town of Waynesburg and for the college, and told of his exuberance during commencement week: "Waynesburg is the Jerusalem of the CP church in this region, 'whither the tribes go up.' We met many ministers and old friends at the Commencement; and the universal expression coming from every heart was: 'Long live Waynesburg College!' "[52]

It was customary to ring bells at the college and the courthouse on different occasions during commencement week. Sometimes processions formed at the college and, for some activities, marched to the courthouse or to the town hall; at other times, especially for commencement, the reverse was true. The town's brass band was indispensable to these activities.[53] We have a description of the scene on 3 August 1876 at 9:00 o'clock in the morning, when

> the college bell swept hill and valley with its silvery tones and, almost as quickly as if the call had been a fire alarm, the walks leading to the college were thronged with people eager to gain the hall and find a seat while yet there was room—the young and the old, the rich and the poor, all with smiling faces, and many bearing sweet bouquets, all indicating the wave of pleasure such an occasion sweeps over a community.

At sunset on that commencement day the senior class planted a centennial tree on campus to commemorate the founding of the town of Waynesburg in 1776. After that there was a program in College (Hanna) Hall, which contained humorous predictions on the future of each graduating senior. In addition, the members of the class delivered orations in English, French, German, Latin, and Greek—"all interspersed with delightful music."[54]

Commencement exercises were held in the old structure (Hanna Hall) until 1890, when they were moved to spacious Alumni Hall in the new building. By December 1890, after some sixteen years of labor, the new edifice was completed, although it was not fully furnished.[55]

From the standpoint of scholarly endeavor the most important feature of commencement week was the public examination which all students in the institution were required to take. Prior to the merger of commencements separate public examinations were administered—one in the Female Department and one for males in the college. Conducted in chapel, such tests lasted from two to four days. Individual students, taking turns on the rostrum, were quizzed orally by their professors in the several branches. An examination committee, usually of three members, was chosen to evaluate the overall performance of the students. There is every indication that public examinations were not "fixed," and that students "had no idea what the questions would be like" when they went to the rostrum.[56] Accounts in the press show that the students consistently performed well on public examinations. Students and faculty members alike were appreciated by evaluation committees and by the audiences.[57]

In looking at the whole academic picture in the early decades, one gets an impression that it was slipshod and inefficient. As in all colleges in the nation, there were no specific requirements for admission, no "quality points" in grading, no academic quotients, no prerequisites for courses, no rules relative to transfer students, no specified amounts of work to be completed in advancing from one class to another, and no uniform requirements for graduation. The faculty handled cases individually, using their best collective judgment at the moment on a kind of hit-and-miss basis. The overall system may have had some merits. It was flexible enough to permit the faculty to know, and to work with, each student as an individual. This close relationship is something we yearn for in American education today.[58]

VIII
"ARISE AND BUILD"

"I VERILY BELIEVE THAT GOD BIDS US ARISE AND BUILD . . . A MONUMENT that will not only record the liberality of a grateful church, but send a blessed influence through the centuries," said Miller early in November 1881 when construction of the "new college" was well under way.[1] The overall project called for teamwork and perseverance along three major, interrelated lines. First was the seemingly endless task of raising money to pay for the building. Second was construction, which was slow and sporadic on a pay-as-you-go basis. Third was the campaign for endowment, for the new building greatly enlarged the college, and hence a steady, adequate source of income was essential to its permanence.

By the early 1870's a new building was needed for two obvious reasons. First was the inadequacy of the existing edifice. During Miller's first three years as president the college made rapid progress. But during the Civil War student enrollment was very low. After the war the veterans returned, enrollment sharply increased, and the college enjoyed a period of unprecedented prosperity and progress. In the late 1860's "some classes had to meet in inconvenient places —out of the building." And rooms were needed for apparatus, cabinets, and expansion of the library. Second was competition of neighboring institutions. Within a radius of thirty miles from Waynesburg three institutions, namely, West Virginia University, Washington and Jefferson College, and California Normal School were erecting spacious, new buildings. Some twenty miles farther away, in the West Virginia "Panhandle" was Bethany College, which already had a magnificent building. And in 1872 Monongahela College was nearly completed at nearby Jefferson. Founded by Baptists of southwestern Pennsylvania and West Virginia, it had a large, beautiful building on a fourteen-acre plot covered by evergreen trees just outside that borough. In addition to the classical and scientific "courses," the training of public school teachers was offered at all these institutions; and in the early 1870's, added competition was in the offing when special arrangements were made to train teachers at Greene Academy and at Jacksonville Academy, located at Wind Ridge. "To arise and build," Miller said, "was the only way to escape being swallowed up by this encroaching competition." He added: "Put in the one small building, our institution would have been in deplorable contrast with those about us."[2]

Miller told the trustees of his fears of competition from neighbors and of his faith that something could be effectively done to meet it. But "they seemed fearful and of but little faith. . . . " They replied, "if you can present us with reliable subscriptions amounting to $25,000, we suppose the building can be undertaken." Shortly a canvass was made. Immediate responses were favorable, but collections of cash were slow. Nevertheless, it was agreed that "the building might be undertaken."[3]

The original plan called for a building "to be in all respects, beautiful, substantial, convenient, as far as the judicious outlay of the dollar will make it so." To be constructed on the "most approved style of architecture," it was "to contain all rooms necessary for a first class college" and "to cost, furnished, not less than $65,000." Miller believed this project should be supported not only by local citizens, but by all CP members. He gave reasons for affimative action by the trustees. First, he pointed out the usefulness of the college. For twenty-five years its preachers had gone to serve churches all over the nation, and to do missionary work in the foreign field. Waynesburg College had given a president, in the Reverend A. J. McGlumphy,. to Lincoln University, and professors to all the leading CP collegiate institutions. Its graduates were serving ably in pulpits, schools, business enterprises, and other fields all over the nation. Second, the prospects of the college were eminently good. It had an enviable, wide reputation. Alumni and friends spoke kindly of it, and were willing to support it. Third, success of Waynesburg College would mean success of the CP Church in Pennsylvania. Miller contended: "We cannot depend on our colleges in the South and West," or "on men from other *sects*, lest we be *absorbed into other sects* (Miller's italics). . . . Our Synod depends on educational influence. To ignore this fact is fatal. A prosperous college silences the taunt that we are opposed to education." Miller held that "the

Pennsylvania Synod and Waynesburg College had done much for the church—especially in the West." If the college should fail—"and consequently the Synod, such calamities would paralyze the whole church." To build up the college would be to make the CP Church in Pennsylvania "as permanent as the grand hills among which many of our churches are nestled."[4]

A local editor held that in the old building the "chapel and recitation rooms were too small. Some say that the present building can be enlarged to meet demand. I do not think so. An adequate addition would cost as much as a new building." He suggested that the old building "be used as a gymnasium, boarding, and cabinet rooms. We need a building to accommodate 400 students. If we don't get it, students will go elsewhere. If they do, our institution will lose the respect, confidence, and support of the people." He urged the Synod to "shake off its sluggishness now, and put agents in the field immediately to secure an endowment fund of $150,000. With effort this can be done in two years. One man has promised $500 for a new building. Others can do so."[5]

Alumni, faculty members, and former faculty members of the college, strongly supported Miller's building project. For example, in 1877, Professor R. V. Foster, who left the Waynesburg faculty to take a position on the staff of Cumberland University, pointed out that "Waynesburg College is our central point in the East, and is to a great extent the exponent of our denominational influence in western Pennsylvania. The Pennsylvania Synod needs Waynesburg College, the congregations need it, the whole church needs it, hence I am deeply interested in it, and pray with all my heart that the efforts now being made in its behalf may be abundantly successful." Early in 1881, Professor H. D. Patton, a member of Waynesburg's faculty, pointed out that each region should support its college. Residents, particularly CP members, in western Pennsylvania and Ohio "should help Waynesburg College, because it is in their area. . . . The college must live and live well. . . . It has proved its worth—has shown its right to live."[6]

After the decision was reached to build a new edifice, the next step was to decide what kind of building to erect. To that end Miller visited several institutions and examined their buildings. At Bethany College, in West Virginia, he found a building "whose proportions amazed me." Subsequently he visited Swarthmore, Princeton, Rutgers, and a few other campuses. He saw no building, however, which was exactly copied in design. Many college buildings then had mansard roofs, and Miller and the trustees decided on that style. They apprised several architects of the number of rooms desired, and their sizes; and requested them to submit plans for the building, keeping in mind "the two points of convenient internal arrangements and architectural elegance of exterior." After carefully considering several plans, the one submitted by J. W. Drumm, a Pittsburgh architect, was adjudged best, and, by 1874, it "was unanimously adopted by the trustees. . . . " Drumm's architectural plan was faithfully followed with only one minor modification. In the summer of 1880, when stone ornamentation was being constructed on the exterior, in the interests of economy, the trustees requested Drumm "to prepare a plan for less expensive ornamentation on the south entrance."[7]

It was relatively easy to decide on an architectural plan for the building. The main problem was money. Miller and the trustees resolved to proceed on a "pay as you go" basis. Construction would not begin until subscriptions totaling $25,000 were collected. All bills would be paid weekly on Saturday. If funds were short, work would stop. Thus, in avoiding debts, progress on construction of the building was slow, and a quarter century passed before it was completed and furnished.[8] It was agreed that Miller would be the general financial agent of the college. Other such agents were to be employed to work under his supervision.

Miller tapped all conceivable sources of funds for the new building. Beginning in 1872 subscriptions were taken in the local area. Miller thanked local residents for their donations and pointed out that "subscriptions began at home, in the very shadow of the college, but the many friends scattered abroad will in due time, be offered the privilege of completing the work thus well begun at home. Every gift will be gladly received. . . . We shall expect an occasional cheer from the many former students and other friends scattered over the West." Miller asked friends to "second the effort to erect the new building by doubling their efforts to send students."[9]

In August 1878 the trustees employed the Reverend R. J. P. Lemmon as a financial agent to assist Miller in raising funds. Reputed to be "an earnest and efficient agent," Lemmon agreed to raise within three years, beginning on 1 August 1878, $25,000 "or money enough to complete the new building entire, ready to receive the furniture . . . at a salary of $800 per annum." He was to furnish his own horse and buggy; and the trustees were to pay all other necessary expenses. Lemmon was to work locally and to report monthly on his progress. He was not very successful; in some fourteen months he received in pledges, notes, and some cash only $2,308.37. His salary and expenses in that time totaled $1,010. He resigned on 1 October 1879, and shortly was replaced by another agent. Miller, the Building Committee of the Board of Trustees, and other members of that body joined in the task of soliciting subscriptions for the new building "in and about Waynesburg immediately. . . . "[10]

Even children in the CP congregation in Waynesburg helped. Louie Hoskinson, age thirteen, wrote a letter for the "Children's Corner" in the CP newspaper, telling all readers how the children in her church held a "Wood's Sociable" every month, named in memory of their beloved pastor, the Reverend Leroy Woods, to which the public was invited. For an admission fee of fifteen cents, one could get his supper and enjoy an entertainment of music and literary performances. The proceeds were divided between the church and the college. This young lady appealed to all children: "Couldn't some of our little readers of 'the Corner' send us a mite to help the College?"[11]

Adults in Waynesburg helped by making donations, subscriptions, and bequests. For example, Miss M. A. Harvey bequeathed to the trustees the sum of $1,000, to be paid to them immediately, to aid in the erection of the building, on condition that the trustees pay her the interest at six percent annually on that sum "during the term of her natural life." The trustees promptly accepted her offer.[12] Members of the college faculty were among the first Waynesburgers to donate to the building fund. Their salaries were in arrears, and they donated to this fund what the college owed them; in the case of Professor Scott the sum was $400; the other amounts ranged from $100 to $280.[13]

Shortly after the drive for funds for the new building began, residents of Waynesburg and friends of the college faced two major discouragements. A local financial crash, possibly related to the Panic of 1873, resulted in the loss of several large subscriptions. And the death of Mrs. Miller was a blow to students, faculty members, and the whole community. On looking at the architect's plan for the new building, she said prophetically: "I shall never see the erection of such a building as that." Some people thought the building would be too large, and predicted that it "would never be completed in the world."[14] But such skepticism did not deter Miller and the trustees in their efforts.

In 1879 the college sought more aid from the CP Synod of Pennsylvania. In the early years the Pennsylvania Presbytery, consisting of CP churches in Greene and Washington counties, was the chief promoter of the college. The institution had relied largely on those congregations for support; and they had contributed substantially to the new building. In September 1876 this Presbytery met at Jacksonville (Jacktown) in Greene County, and its Education Committee recommended for Waynesburg College: (1) that ministers instruct congregations of the importance of sustaining the college; (2) that ministers urge members to patronize it; (3) that each minister try to get students for it; and (4) that members of the church visit the college "at convenient seasons, learn of its workings, and thus understand its usefulness and its relation to the church." In August 1879, however, the Pennsylvania Presbytery met at the Fairview Church in Washington County and appealed to the CP Synod of Pennsylvania for greater support for the college. Synod had already met in Mercer County, Pennsylvania, where it recommended that Miller be relieved from ministering to the CP congregation in Waynesburg, so he could give full time to his duties as president and chief financial agent of the college. Synod's Board of Trust was eager to promote the building fund and to increase the endowment fund. The trustees invited all "Sabbath schools in the Pennsylvania Synod, and any others . . . to contribute to the new building, and we promise them that, if as much as $1,000 is contributed . . . we will place a beautiful inscription in some prominent place in the new building, as a memorial to their gifts. . . . " And each Sabbath school that gave from $10 to $25 was promised a "nicely framed lithograph of the new building, small size"; each such school that gave over $25 was promised a "lithograph, large size." The trustees requested ladies' organizations "to contribute . . . and promised that, if as much as $5,000 is contributed by them, . . . a beautiful memorial inscription shall be placed in some very prominent part of the building. . . . " The ladies were also encouraged to give individually, for which they were promised lithographs; a small one to a donor giving from $10 to $20; and a large one, to each who gave over $20. The trustees also proposed to name the new library "permanently the name of any person who would donate $3,000" to the college. Likewise they would name the parlor or drawing room in the new building by the name of any person who would give $1,000 "to be applied in furnishing said room."[15]

Despite these inducements, funds accumulated at a snail's pace. By late July 1878, subscriptions to the new building totaled $24,487.88, or nearly the amount required by the trustees before construction could start. An auditing committee of the trustees estimated that

$5,000 of the subscriptions was "worthless"; and the amount paid in cash was only $7,549.26. The trustees waited about nine months in the hope that collections would sharply increase. Finally, in April 1879, some seven years after the project was planned, they resolved "that the Treasurer proceed at once to collect the whole of the subscription to the new college building fund. . . . " They also authorized the building committee "to proceed at once to the erection of the new building." They apprised subscribers of the great need of funds, and warned that "if said subscriptions are not voluntarily paid, they will be collected by law." This threat of legal action evidently brought desired results. Shortly the trustees procured a deed for a lot adjacent to other land, valued at $1,000, already donated by E. M. Sayers, on which the building was to be erected.[16]

After construction started, Miller bent to the task of fund-raising more than ever before. He did not receive any additional salary for soliciting funds. If his total workload became too burdensome, the trustees permitted him to employ "temporary assistance in his department of instruction" and his own salary was increased from the building fund "at least equal in amount to the sum necessary to pay his assistant." Miller's travelling expenses as financial agent were "paid out of funds raised by him." Curiously enough, the trustees still expected him to give to the college any money he received from lectures. While funds were being raised for the new building, money was needed to maintain the old one which, according to plans, would be "used as a boarding hall" when the new structure was completed. In July 1875 a new bell was purchased for $400, including freight. Cast in Cincinnati, Ohio, it weighed 1,000 pounds, and the words "W. C. *Veritate et Virtute*" were emblazoned upon it. To help pay for the bell, an entertainment, consisting of music, readings, essays, and orations, was held at the college. In July 1879 the trustees "resolved that the President of the College be directed to use for the purpose of repairs on the [old] College building any portion of funds he may have realized from lectures . . . not immediately needed for other purposes. . . .[17]

In August 1880, fortunately for Miller, the trustees employed two able men to serve as agents to raise funds for the new building. One was the Reverend J. H. Coulter, of St. Louis, Missouri; the other, the Reverend B. W. McDonaw, of Lebanon, Tennessee. Miller consulted with both men, and delineated the territory in which each was to work. Each agent was paid out of funds he raised. Available evidence indicates that McDonaw did not remain long at his post.

Coulter, however, worked hard in the local area, and reported monthly to the trustees on his progress. In January 1881 an appeal was made to Greene Countians to give "liberally to the completion of the new building." To this end a committee of five persons in each township was created to assist the trustees in finding means to complete the building; and public meetings were planned throughout the county during the summer of 1881. The first such meeting was held at the courthouse on 4 April, where specific plans were made for later meetings. The main speaker at this meeting was Dr. W. K. Pendleton, of Bethany College, who gave constructive suggestions on procedures in fund raising. Coulter unfortunately became ill in July 1881; he lay "prostrate from sickness" in Brownsville, and was unable to continue his service for the college.[18]

The local press fully supported the college in its drive for funds. As a local editor put it in 1881:

> All interested persons, including all Greene Countians, must know that a crisis exists at Waynesburg College. The College will *die* if money is not obtained soon. The work is slowed for lack of money. Massive, imposing buildings have gone up all around us with all modern improvements. All must help Waynesburg College. The *farmers* find a ready market for their produce, largely because of the influx of students. *Complete* the building to the roof at least this year. Some have the idea that the building will go up without our individual aid. Let us get rid of such a false notion (italics in original).[19]

In October 1883 the editor again gave an assist to the college, when he called on subscribers to give $100 each. According to him, there were "men in Waynesburg and environs who have sons and daughters who have given little or nothing at all. The new building must be put in use soon. Give $100 or $200 to help. . . . It will be money well invested and pay heavy interest in the future."[20]

The CP congregation in Waynesburg strongly supported the college. Miller said "if every congregation in the Pennsylvania Synod had given as much per capita as our local people" the sum would greatly boost endowment and "amply support the faculty. Let the good work go on."[21]

Whenever time permitted, Miller traveled to churches relatively far from Waynesburg in search of funds. His visits to CP congregations and to individuals in western Pennsylvania were sometimes quite rewarding. Two ladies in Uniontown, for example, were most generous: Mrs. Isaac Beeson gave him $1,000; and Mrs. Judge Huston, $500. Many others gave smaller sums. In October 1874 Miller visited a number of CP congregations in Ohio. The Ohio Synod, then in session in Covington, praised Waynesburg College for "her fidelity and thoroughness in preparing young men and women for usefulness in the world," and welcomed "heartily the presence of Dr. Miller in our churches to present the financial and other interests of said institution to our people." That group, at its meeting in Covington, again in 1882, recommended

> that this Synod cooperate with the Pennsylvania Synod in sustaining Waynesburg College, both in patronage of students and in financial contributions. . . . The history of Pennsylvania Synod and of Waynesburg College is our history. They have done and are still doing much for the CP church in Ohio. . . . Being contiguous to Pennsylvania Synod . . . and having no other college in our bounds in operation now, we . . . can't stand idly by when our brothers are in need. . . . [22]

Miller hoped to get substantial aid from the CP General Assembly. In June 1877 that body complimented him on his work, and implored the whole church to help him. In April 1878 the trustees called attention to the General Assembly's appointment of the Reverend A. D. Hail to work in foreign missions. With Hail's wife, five missionaries—all trained at Waynesburg College—would then be serving in the foreign field. The influence of the college was not confined to Pennsylvania alone, but "great benefits have already been reaped by the church at large. . . . " The trustees believed that a request to the General Assembly for funds "might probably be looked upon as a privilege. . . . " Accordingly they resolved to ask that group, at its next meeting, to contribute $1,000, "or more, as a memorial of the semi-centennial" of the CP Church in Pennsylvania, which was to take place in 1881. If the General Assembly would give this amount, the trustees promised: "We will have a proper inscription placed in an appropriate part of the new building to commemorate this offering and event."[23] Miller sincerely believed the General Assembly would give him $1,000, but no such donation was made. At its next meeting, which took place in Austin, Texas, in May 1881, no action was taken on the trustees' request. Instead the Assembly adopted a resolution to request all CP congregations to collect "thank-offerings" to be sent to the college during its semicentennial celebration.[24] The amount thus collected is not recorded.

Miller had an approach that would make one almost feel ashamed, if one did not help the college. He logically and repeatedly pointed out that: (1) the new building was indispensable to the college; (2) the college was essential to the CP Synod in Pennsylvania; (3)

the Synod was isolated and, in building the new structure, it needed the help of the whole church; and (4) the Synod was an indispensable arm of the entire denomination. If it fell, the whole church would suffer. At various stages of construction of the building, Miller apprised readers of the newspaper what had been accomplished, and how much money would be needed for the next step. He received numerous letters from people who enclosed small sums, and invariably expressed regrets they could not send more. For example, one man, who had lost all his earthly belongings in a fire, sent Miller one dollar. Miller was thankful for it, but he was even more so for

> words too encouraging not to be winged through the whole church: "I feel that I must have at least one dollar of what is left me . . . in the new college building you propose to erect. The time was when I did not see and feel the influence of this institution on our beloved Church as I now do. . . . Though your enterprise is local, it is of general interest to us all."[25]

Another man, who sent Miller ten dollars, said he regretted he could not send a thousand, as "I am anxious that the new building project shall have entire success."[26]

Miller looked upon every commencement as an opportunity to raise money. For example, in August 1877, he invited all to "come and bring a gift with you for our new building. If you cannot come, don't fail to sit down and write us 'greeting,' enclosing five dollars to give emphasis." While Waynesburgers generously aided Miller, the new building was "conditioned also on gifts of many, many friends far from Waynesburg, some of whom have never looked upon what this money helped to rear." Miller called attention to a report made on 1 April 1881, as an example. It showed a collection of $1,465.80 "which was gathered from eighty-five (85) parties, including collections in congregations and in Sunday Schools, and from individual contributors in Illinois, Missouri, Philadelphia, etc., and in sums ranging from 25 cents to $100." Miller believed "it is better that thousands give a few dollars each, than that a few give thousands each."[27]

For the information of benefactors, Miller explained how funds were handled. On the pay-as-you-go basis money was needed for weekly settlements with contractors, who paid their respective workers every Saturday. There was no single contractor for the overall project, but several contractors, each responsible for a given type of work, were engaged. The trustees, under the charter, were legal guardians of the buildings and grounds. The CP Church controlled the property, had a voice in the election of trustees, entrusted the endowment fund to the Board of Trust, and secured all other funds of the college.[28]

Miller and the trustees considered the ill effects of the Panic of 1873. In March 1876 Miller wrote: "With the present building for use, there is no need for haste, and the financial troubles of the country suggest that subscribers be given more time to pay pledges." A year later the trustees recommended that, because of the depression, "no home subscriber be compelled to pay assessments until the first of May 1878."[29]

Miller and others looked ahead to the semicentennial of the founding of the CP Church in Pennsylvania, to be celebrated in 1881, as an opportunity to raise funds. With undue optimism, the Synod proposed to mark the event by completion of the new building and by the endowment of the Alfred Bryan and John Morgan memorial professorships. Locations considered for this celebration were Pittsburgh, "the old campground" at Hewitt's Church, and the fairground at Waynesburg. The Synod could not agree on any of these places. Instead it recommended that "each church hold special services at home during June and July 1881, as the time of the Semicentennial." The presbyteries also were to meet in August and September 1881 "at such places as each may designate" and to conduct programs with three speeches each—one on CP history and doctrine, one on the introduction of the Church into Ohio and Pennsylvania, and one "on present and immediate wants of Synod, especially on the subject of education. . . . " The Synod recommended "that special efforts be made to raise money for the endowment fund of Waynesburg College."[30]

In March 1881 Miller appealed to the whole church: "As soon as weather permits, work on the new building will resume." He hoped "to complete this beautiful building" as soon as possible. "A kind lady recently sent us a check for $100—*unsolicited*," he said. He then begged: "If you cannot send us $100, send us $50, $25, $10, something, if only $1. Every little helps. Rills make rivers . . . Help us now (Miller's italics)."[31]

Late in August 1881 the Pennsylvania Presbytery, nearest to the college, held two meetings, located geographically for the convenience of congregations within it. The first meeting was in the western part of that Presbytery at Minton's Grove, near the Old Concord Church, on 16-18 August; the second, to accommodate those in the eastern part, was in Hathaway's Grove at Carmichaels, on 30-31 August. At both meetings Miller stressed the need of money not only for the new building, but also to increase the endowment fund by $30,000. He knew that all CP colleges needed money, but he "doubted whether any institution needed immediate help like Waynesburg College."[32]

By the spring of 1881 construction on the building had reached the point where it was imperative to roof it in order to prevent damage to the walls and interior structures. To do so required immediately a large sum of money—much more than could be raised in a relatively short time by collections from donors and subscribers. It was estimated that $8,000 would be sufficient to put the building under roof. Hence the trustees borrowed that sum, and they mortgaged "the whole college proper to secure the repayment of same with interest." They further agreed "to keep an agent in the field to solicit subscriptions which are to be applied to the liquidation of the mortgage as fast as said subscriptions are received." In order to increase collections of funds, some 2,000 printed copies of "an appeal" were obtained for distribution among possible donors. According to Miller, these steps "seemed to the trustees the only practical way of tiding the work over the crisis that was upon them."[33]

News that sufficient funds had been obtained to roof the building was welcomed. The Pennsylvania Synod applauded the plan, and it offered to help pay off the mortgage. The CP editor wrote: "We all rejoice that after a long, hard struggle the Board of Trustees has secured enough money to roof the new building, lay the floors, build the stairways, plaster the walls—and so again the sound of the hammer is heard on the fine edifice."[34] The $8,000 assured a roof on the building, but an additional $2,000 was needed "to put the building beyond danger of exposure in any part—until the finishing touches can be made and all the debt paid." Hence "each friend was asked to sign a note promising to pay Waynesburg College ten dollars—five dollars by 1 March 1887, and the other five by 1 June 1887, for the new building."[35]

Still more money was needed. In May 1890 Miller said that, "with little help the new building can be ready for dedication at the close of the current term." The literary societies, the Y. M. C. A., and the Alumni Association were all pushing their respective parts of the work. "To complete all parts of the building," Miller said, "will require only $1500." He appealed to local citizens "to help finish an undertaking that has been a long time on our hands." The estimated total cost was then $75,000, most of which had come in small sums. Miller urged everyone to help "finish this good work by *harvest* time (Miller's italics)."[36] But he was too optimistic about the time of dedication. That happy day came nearly a decade later.

The pace of construction depended on the availability of funds, on the pay-as-you-go basis, and on the weather. The work was seasonal; it slowed, or stopped, during the coldest weather, and speeded up in the spring, summer, and fall.

The brick-making process began in the spring of 1875, some four years before the foundation was laid. Brick-making then was an art; expert technical know-how and experience were required in order to produce high quality bricks. The materials were handled some seventeen times in the overall process.[37] The clay was obtained from the excavation of the basement, from the back of the campus, and from "Lake Winetta," the pond near the intersection of Wayne and Morris Streets. Three kilns, constructed on the quadrangle behind the present building, could produce 4,000 bricks daily. Miller and some of the students labored on the project, and asked for, and received, no pay. He said: "I did myself a great deal of work, and my boys hauled hundreds of barrels of water. . . . To mould so many bricks almost exhausted Ten Mile creek for water to moisten the clay, and to burn them required a good sized forest, a good deal of which was donated."[38]

After nearly two years of the "burning of brick," Miller prematurely announced:

> We have made all the brick needed, 803,000, which are on the ground, and pronounced of the very best quality. They wait the hands of art to lay them into a spacious and beautiful building. The amount of ornamentation this building will receive must depend somewhat on the contributions that shall yet be made. It will add greatly to its external appearance to trim the front with the fine sandstone in which this locality abounds.

Once completed, the building would be delightful, but Miller "did not want to sacrifice the ornamentation." Therefore he called for many friends to send by 1 April 1877 "as great contributions as they can spare." He was thankful that "a good Providence . . . has always placed the funds in reach as they have been needed" for weekly payments to contractors.[39]

Progress on construction of the building was regularly reported in newspapers. And almost as regularly, appeals were made for more money. By June 1879 work on the foundation was well under way. While sitting in his office in the "old building" in late August 1879, Miller described the operation, and told of his faith:

> Within my sight at this moment, a company of masons are finishing the work of the great foundation of the new building for this institution. The ring of hammers and the creaking of the passing wagon beneath its burden of imperishable blue stones float out on the air. With a beautiful front of one hundred and fifty-eight feet, running due east and west, with a southern exposure commanding an extensive common capable of the highest ornamentation, and in all respects beautiful in architecture, this building, if ever completed, will give to the institution all that can be desired in the way of an attractive exterior. Appearances are now quite hopeful for the early completion of this building, and for this every Cumberland Presbyterian who loves his Church should pray and give something. . . . The conception, even, of the erection of such a building, and much more the determination to undertake it, called for an extraordinary faith—a faith that, resting in God, 'laughs at impossibilities.' If God designed the CP Church to live and go on with its work, then it was His will that this institution—a necessity of the Church—be sustained, and hence that this indispensable building be erected. This was the faith, and the realization of it will be sweet, hopeful, and grand.[40]

By July 1879 work on the foundation reached the point where the trustees could plan for the laying of the cornerstone—an occasion to which all looked forward with pleasure. A significant step in the building process, it afforded an opportunity to raise more money. The trustees hoped to lay the cornerstone on Commencement Day, 30 July 1879, but various delays caused postponement until 10 September. Happily Miller announced the forthcoming event: "Everything here is now working well, and every rill of sympathy from abroad will swell the great current of interest at home." He cordially invited all to the ceremonies: "We say to all the friends of the cause, 'Come and bring a gift with you.' If you cannot come, send the gift. We need yet to raise a great deal of money, and much of it must be made up of the 'littles' that help."[41]

Dignitaries invited to the event included Governor Hoyt of Pennsylvania and Governor Matthews of West Virginia. Hoyt unfortunately could not attend, but Lieutenant Governor Stone represented the Commonwealth of Pennsylvania instead. A "grand procession" started the occasion. Among several speakers on the program were Governor Matthews and Lieutenant Governor Stone. The cornerstone was laid on the southeast corner of the foundation. A box similar in size and shape to a cigar box, containing a small Bible, some old coins, and other appropriate items, was placed in it. Speeches, and the actual laying of the stone, were interspersed with fitting music. The cornerstone hymn, sung to the tune of "Auld Lang Syne," ran in part:

O Thou who didst foundations lay
For Nature's vast domain,
Bless now this cornerstone, we pray,
For learning's sacred fame.
Grant that the walls hereon to rise
Unbroken long may stand,
A temple beauteous in our eyes,
A bulwark of our land.
As year succeeds to prosperous year,
May wisdom's light divine,
Fair sons and daughters gather here,
For culture at this shrine.
O Christ, the living Cornerstone,
In Thee our hopes we rest,
To bring us, when life's toils are done,
To mansions of the blest.[42]

Construction progressed slowly during 1880 and 1881 when funds and the weather permitted. In June 1881 the trustees aimed "to put the building under roof before winter comes."[43] But it was July 1882 before the roof neared completion. Early in 1885 the work force was decreased, while more funds were collected. A local editor lamented that "the building is not finished, and stands as a mockery to the young folks who come here."[44]

Fortunately Miller received a bequest of $500 from a former student, Miss Sallie A. Porter, of Dunbar, Pennsylvania, which advanced the work sufficiently to permit the transfer of some classes to the new building by the opening of the term in September 1886. By February 1887, two fine stairways had been built to the third floor by the Ullom Brothers, "master workmen along this line," and all floors had been laid.[45] A spacious room on the second floor was set aside for a cabinet and museum; and friends were asked "to send fossils, minerals, shells, stuffed birds and quadrupeds, old coins, rare books, Indian relics of all kinds, and everything else of interest in such a place." The library had some 2,000 volumes in the "old building," where it was crowded. In the fall of 1887 the room for the Library was ready on the second floor in the new building. It was called the "Clark Library" in honor of Dr. Byron Clark of Washington, Pennsylvania, who gave liberally toward its furnishings. Students carried the books to the new Library, where the reading room was "capacious." All books of a scholarly nature were gladly received from donors. The new chapel was in process of completion on the second floor. Several donors had each given $1,000 for it; it "will be finished in excellent style, with frescoing and seating." Alumni Hall, the great room on the third floor designed for commencement and other public events, with a projected seating capacity of 1,000, was being completed by the Alumni Association.[46] By 1888 furniture and equipment were being rapidly obtained for classrooms; and by 1890 all classes had been transferred to the new building. Hanna Hall then became a house for "boarding clubs." McDonnold said the new edifice was "the finest single college building in western Pennsylvania, and by far the most beautiful and imposing structure of its kind ever erected by Cumberland Presbyterians."[47]

Alumni Hall was the largest, most magnificent room in the building. The Alumni Association was organized in 1871. At annual meetings in "college hall" in the old building, it had presented programs consisting of essays, orations, poetry-reading, musical selections, and so on. Comprising graduates of all departments of the college, its chief aim always was "mutual improvement and the promotion of the interests of the common *Alma Mater*." Its goal now was raising funds to finish and furnish the hall; to that end the members determined to secure as much money as possible at the annual banquet in June 1889. In the belief that "the best way to a man's heart is through his stomach," and that it "is easier to get money from a man face to face than to write it out of him," they solicited funds right after the banquet, taken up with toasts, speeches, music, and the consumption of much delicious food. The scheme worked. The sum of $1,000 was raised in $50, $25, and $10 subscriptions to be paid within ninety days from date. It was expected that Alumni Hall would be ready for commencement in 1890, "and that the alumni will be invited to gather to participate in its dedication." There is evidence that these hopes were realized, but no permanent seats had been installed—and it appears that removable chairs were used by those present. In June 1895 the alumni expressed their unhappiness about a debt due the architect: "Though we boast about our fine new Hall, it is not ours, but that of the architect, as there is yet due $1,000 to him for which he is badly in need and should be paid at once." They immediately appointed a committee "to raise part of this money on commencement day." They also raised some money during each year. For example, on 25 June 1896 they reported that, during the preceding year, $102.66 had been raised to help furnish the Hall. This sum was given by eighteen persons, including Miller who gave $2.[48]

In the late 1890's the alumni still faced an uphill struggle. In 1897 they claimed to have "finished Alumni Hall . . . in excellent style. . . . " But the hall still had no seats. They worked hard at soliciting contributions from members "for the liquidation of the indebtedness contracted in the completion of the hall. . . . " They fervently hoped that seats could be obtained, and that the debt could be paid in full "by the proposed Semicentennial Celebration in June 1900"—when the founding of the college would be commemorated.[49]

As money was raised to pay for the building and as construction proceeded, it was obvious that the endowment fund must be greatly increased in the hope of assuring permanence of the institution. The new structure, with a much greater capacity and better facilities than the old, would attract a larger student body. More faculty members would be needed; and a reliable source of funds was essential to pay their salaries. There was a clause in the written agreement relative to construction of the building, which called for a certain minimum number of teachers. Failure to meet that condition would mean either that the college would close its doors or the CP Church would lose it "to other hands." Total income from tuition and fees fell far short of the amount needed for salaries and other current expenses. The endowment fund, therefore, was as sorely needed as the building fund.[50]

Drives for both funds proceeded simultaneously, and all conceivable sources were tapped. In December 1874 an appeal for endowment for all CP colleges was made through the press "to all rich members of the church." The contention was "that the best business men put their money where it will do the most good. . . . The value of a well endowed college to the Church and to the world cannot be fully estimated. . . . Poor people cannot give enough. . . . " The advantages to the rich who give generously were "a clear conscience, God's approval, and a great blessing to the church of your choice. . . . " The leading CP institutions of learning were alluded to, and "all are in great need of large additions to their respective endowments." Waynesburg's need was greatest of all. At the CP General Assembly in Lincoln, Illinois, in May 1877, productive endowment figures were given respectively for these four institutions: Cumberland University had $30,000 "and $30,000 prospective"; Lincoln University, $50,000 "with prospective $139,000"; Trinity University, $20,000; and for Waynesburg no productive endowment figure was reported. In October 1880 the Reverend Azel Freeman asserted that Waynesburg "has been running almost without endowment, and President Miller says that from the start no person has ever given as much as $1,000 for endowment." Freeman prayed that rich CP members would give more.[51]

Beginning in the fall of 1879, the Pennsylvania Synod, gratified that the cornerstone had been laid, that construction was progressing, and that work already done was paid for, declared: "God forbid that we or our successors should ever . . . permit this institution of learning to fail for want of funds. . . . " It called attention to "a standing rule of this Synod that ministers in its bounds present the cause of education in *annual* sermons and take up collections *annually* for Waynesburg College on the first and second Sabbaths each May (italics in original)." It also sent a circular letter to all of its churches asking for bequests, and it urged the Board of Trust to employ an agent to work on endowment with a view to endowing five professorships of not less than $20,000 each. The first two were to be named in memory of the revered missionaries, the Morgan and Bryan Professorships. With respect to each of the other chairs, Synod promised that anyone contributing $10,000 or more "will have the privilege of naming said professorship until all are endowed."[52]

In order to promote a spiritual revival and to help with endowment, in October 1880 the Reverend B. W. McDonnold of Cumberland University came to Pennsylvania on an evangelistic tour. Assisted by the Reverend Azel Freeman, McDonnold dynamically preached and fervently prayed at meetings at the Old Concord Church. These men continued evangelistic meetings throughout the bounds of the Synod and planned to assist in the semicentennial services in 1881. They yearned for more endowment and for "an outpouring of the spirit like that of 1831," when Morgan, Bryan, Chapman, and other CP missionaries preached in western Pennsylvania. Results were discouraging, however. Even as Freeman and McDonnold preached at Old Concord, Synod's Education Committee reported that it had "not learned of any increase in the endowment fund."[53]

Early in 1881 the college's endowment fund was estimated to be $10,000. The following August, the editor of the CP newspaper called on all CP churches and leaders in Pennsylvania for aid in adding $30,000 to the endowment fund: "There are, no doubt, thirty persons who could give $1,000 each without any embarrassment. . . . If they will not give, then the money must come in smaller amounts. It can be done by 300 persons giving $100 each." Church memberships in Pennsylvania then were: Allegheny Presbytery, 1,496; Pennsylvania Presbytery, 2,205; and Union Presbytery, 1,382 —a total of 5,083. The editor calculated:

> At $10 each we have $50,830 or almost double the sum asked. . . . Someone will say so many of my members are children or ladies. Any child old enough to belong to the church can subscribe $10 to be paid in five payments of $2 per year. And any lady ought to consider it a shame that she would be thought so stingy as not to raise and save 50 cents every three months to pay to this grand enterprise of the Church.[54]

The college was fortunate to obtain the services of the Reverend P. H. Crider, a resident of North Dakota and an experienced, hard-working financial agent. In cooperation with Miller, his chief task was to raise funds for endowment. At the outset of his work for the college in February 1881, the weather was unfavorable. A deep snow had been on the ground since 20 December 1880. Conditions were good for sleighing; the demand for sleighs was so high that their prices rose. "The young folks loved the snow," Crider wrote. Like McDonnold and Freeman, he combined evangelism with fund-raising. Miller was too busy at the college to join Crider in his first week's meeting, which took place at the West Union Church, where Crider preached powerful sermons and pleaded for money for the college. He won seven converts, but made no mention of the sum collected. Thence he went to the Bethel Church, "where members and friends came in sleds and sleighs from all directions and favored us with a social and *donation* (Crider's italics)." The table was loaded with delicious food, and the repast was most sumptuous. The good people of the Bethel congregation did not have money to give the college. Knowing that it would welcome personal property, however, they gave to Crider many things in kind, including large quantities of "hay, corn, oats, coal, flour, meal, apples, groceries, and many other items—totaling a large sum." As Crider put it: "This was a great token of kindness and love."[55]

In October 1881 the Reverend J. R. Morris was appointed as another financial agent to solicit money and subscriptions to complete the $30,000 fund proposed to endow the Morgan and Bryan chairs. Miller hoped he would be well received everywhere, and asked ministers to cooperate with him. Miller also implored friends of the college to "hold firm through the struggle until the new building and the addition of $30,000 to the endowment fund are completed. . . ."[56] Morris did not long remain at this post, but Crider carried on the work with great enthusiasm.

As the endowment fund was raised, from time to time "matching grants" were made on the condition that certain totals be reached by given dates. In January 1882 Professor R. V. Foster warned the Ohio and Pennsylvania Synods that "it is vital that the full $30,000 to endow two chairs be raised between now and April next." The sum of $15,000 had been promised, conditional on the raising of $15,000. Failure to raise it would mean "the $15,000 will be forfeited. This would be a shame to the whole church. . . . Everybody knows that Waynesburg College has done much good for these two synods, for the whole church, for foreign lands. . . . If people don't go to work, Waynesburg College will fail."[57]

On 1 April 1882 Crider undertook to raise $18,000 in one year. During May, June, and early July 1882 he worked among CP congregations at Rock Lick, in West Virginia, and at Old Concord, Bethel, Harmony, Muddy Creek, Jefferson, Millsboro, Clarksville, Nineveh, Carmichaels, Greenfield, and Hewitt's. In late July and early August he visited Masontown, Salem, Hopewell, and Pleasant View congregations. At each place he preached on Sunday on the subject of "the college and Christian benevolence," and then carefully canvassed the congregation through the week. He asked each congregation to consider facts in relation to endowment. The college "is in fine condition, with a large student enrollment and several ministerial students. . . . The faculty is strong. The new building is going up fast; it will supply present needs and be a blessing to coming generations."[58]

Crider kept records of pledges and the amount of cash received each month, regardless of the sum given. For example, in July 1882 cash was received from individuals, ranging from $100 down to 5 cents. The "banner congregation" was Carmichaels which gave $910 to endowment from 1 April to 1 August 1882; the Hopewell congregation was second, with $744. During the first four months of the campaign, Crider and Miller together averaged $1,500 per month.[59]

Crider was so industrious and efficient that he exceeded his goal early. By February 1883 he had raised more than $25,000 in cash and pledges. In the interim, Blackly Lindley of Prosperity promised to give $5,000 toward endowment, "provided the sum would be increased $25,000, making a total of $30,000" by 1 April 1883. Crider, therefore, secured Lindley's gift of $5,000. And William Thaw of Pittsburgh agreed to give $1,000 "whenever Lindley gives his $5,000." Crider felt fortunate to have secured the Lindley grant. In the belief that his mission was accomplished and because of circumstances at home, he returned to North Dakota in February 1883. He had "done a glorious work here in Pennsylvania for our college."[60]

Unfortunately some persons who made pledges to Crider did not honor them. After he left, the Board of Trust urged Miller "to take up the work and complete it." As a result of Crider's efforts, by November 1883, the amount secured in cash was $21,000, or $4,000 short of the needed sum. Shortly, however, other funds were collected and, by mid-December 1883, only $1,000 was yet to be raised. Miller then sent a plea to the Synod: "We ask all church members in this Synod to help raise the last $1,000—which must be done by the end of *this* December (Miller's italics)." He also appealed to CP members who had moved West to Illinois, Iowa, Kansas, Missouri, and elsewhere "to send a Christmas offering to college endowment. Who will send $100, $50, $20, $10, $5? Send it at once and help us mark 1 January 1884 as a GRAND JUBILEE, the influence of which will strike on through generations (Miller's capitalization)."[61]

Miller's joy that the endowment goal of $30,000 was in sight soon turned into sadness and disappointment. In March 1884 Lindley reneged on his promise. He "took exceptions to the time in which the money had been secured, and in this way crawled out." With Lindley backing out, all that had been raised might be lost; Crider's and Miller's labors might be in vain. Lindley "took his $5,000 and had a great sepulchre built in a cemetery in Washington County, Pennsylvania, in which to put his bones when he is done with money here below." An irate local editor, who loved the college, lambasted Lindley, telling him "to move into his tomb and pull the hole in after him." Fortunately, John R. Rush of East Pittsburgh, a friend of the college, shortly gave $5,000, "thus filling the place left empty by Lindley."[62] The $30,000 figure was thus reached.

In July 1884 Miller happily reported in the press that enough funds had been raised "for the MORGAN and BRYAN endowed professorships (Miller's capitalization)." He also appealed to friends of the college to send funds for memorial windows at appropriate places in the building. He wanted a window in memory of John R. Rush, who completed the $30,000 endowment fund. Eight friends had given $25 each for stained glass windows in the new reading room of the library. One of these had the inscription: "In Memoriam, Rev. P. H. Crider, a faithful agent of the College, Died, April 1884." Miller wanted to fill ten stained glass windows in the new chapel; the central window there was placed by the alumni in memory of Mrs. M. K. B. Miller. "One name that stands among the first," Miller wrote, "is that of the Reverend Milton Bird, D. D.—who has thousands of admirers. Will not someone send $25 to place a window inscribed to his memory? Likewise for the Reverend Leroy Woods, one of our pioneer ministers in Pennsylvania." In the renovation of the building in recent years, most of the stained glass windows on the second floor have been replaced. Those on the third floor, in Alumni Hall, are still intact. One portion of the large, central window bears the inscription: "Rev. John Morgan, Milton Bird, D. D., Alfred Bryan, D. D., Founders of the C. P. Church in Pennsylvania." Concerning this window, Miller said it "will cost $300 or $400 and will be very fine and durable. Such a memorial will commend itself to many who revere these men. . . . "[63]

In 1892 the trustees employed a new financial agent, the Reverend J. S. Keener, who worked hard and enjoyed some success. But the Board of Trustees, the Board of Trust, and the faculty knew that Miller was the most efficient money-raiser. The faculty offered to help him with his duties as teacher, and to cooperate in other ways in order "to relieve the College of financial embarrassment."[64]

Fund-raising was boosted in August 1897, when the first issue of *The Banner of Peace* appeared. An eight-page paper published monthly in the interests of the college and the CP Church, it was edited jointly by the Reverend C. C. Russell, pastor at the Carmichaels CP Church and by the Reverend R. L. Biddle, then assisting Miller as financial agent of the college. This paper included, among other things, news of the Synod's efforts on behalf of the college. Noteworthy was Synod's meeting in September 1899, in the Shady Avenue Church in East End, Pittsburgh, where plans were made for a centennial celebration of the founding of the CP denomination in 1810. The chief aim of this event, to take place in 1910, was "to raise a centennial fund of $1,000,000 for educational purposes, most to go to Waynesburg College." Despite the interest of Synod and the perseverance of Miller, assisted from time to time by other financial agents, funds for the college accumulated very slowly.[65]

While the new building and the concomitant fund-raising campaigns were underway, another local development had a direct bearing on the college, on the Waynesburg community, and on Greene County as a whole. The building of the Waynesburg and Washington (the "W. & W.") Railroad was a boon to all three. So important was this project, and so interested were the students, that the literary societies seized upon it as a question for debate: "Resolved that the new college building will be more beneficial than the railroad to the citizens of Greene County." Aware that outside capital would not be available for the railroad, local citizens put their money into it, and "soon saw their wishes gratified." The narrow gauge (three feet wide) road, and twenty-nine miles long, cost $6,500 per mile. Pulled by the locomotive "General Greene," the first "W. & W." train reached the depot in Waynesburg on 31 October 1877. Miller exulted: "Of course this railroad will be a great help to our college, and we may now at least *invite* the General Assembly of 1879, as there is a way to get here (Miller's italics)."[66]

During the long years of the drive for the building fund, a local editor never hesitated to remind people: "When the railroad was built, nearly every man, woman, and *boy* in the community subscribed and paid something toward securing it. Likewise the college needs help from *all* (italics in original)."[67]

Other projects which greatly improved the environment of the college were the development of the town commons into a park and the end of the "cow question."[68] After a local editor complained, "We have eaten and slept with cows all these years," in August 1884, the town council passed an ordinance which prohibited cows from running at large within the borough limits.[69]

Gradually the commons area was developed into a beautiful park under the supervision of the borough's Park Directors; it was named "College Park." Most imposing was the new monument in the eastern portion of the Park, which was dedicated on 4 July 1899 to the memory of soldiers and sailors who served in the Civil War.[70]

Throughout the period when the new building was under construction, the importance of Waynesburg College to the town and to the CP Church was stressed.[71] In June 1884, the CP newspaper threw light on the local community and the college:

> Waynesburg is a town of 2,500 population. Houses are generally good and substantial without front yards. (The people built houses as was customary in the Old World—without yards). In outward appearance the homes of the wealthy seem about the same as the others. Society is

> uniformly good. The people look well-bred, intelligent, and refined. . . . Doubtless the college has contributed its influence in producing this state of things. . . . A college naturally draws about it the friends of education and refinement. . . . Money invested in a college is more helpful to a community than money invested in a woolen mill, a coal mine, or a cheese factory. . . . Waynesburg College is a smaller institution than the Bessimer [*sic*] Steel Works, which the General Assembly visited in a body, but it has produced better results than they have. . . . The institution is not rich and there is a spirit there that is mighty. . . .[72]

Many friends lauded Miller for bringing the college through its periods of stress and storm. In July 1886 the editor of the CP newspaper, then published in St. Louis, applauded Miller's efforts to recruit and train ministers, urged churches in Pennsylvania and Ohio to help him more, and implored parents to send their sons and daughters to Waynesburg College.[73] In similar vein, McDonnold pointed out how fruitful had been "the money put into this institution, the prayers of the Church in its behalf, and the labors and sacrifices of . . . its faithful instructors. . . . "[74] In 1882 the Reverend William Hanna, an old friend of Miller, praised the college, saying

> I have known its President for the last twenty-five years during which time he has tenaciously hung on to that institution, through evil as well as good report. I believe the initials "W. C." are written on Miller's heart, for I know of no man who has persisted all these long years in rendering so much unrequited service. For it cannot be denied that with the education, talents, energy, and self-denial of Dr. Miller, he could obtain a far more lucrative position any time.[75]

But there were complaints against Miller. When the Pennsylvania Presbytery met at Jefferson on 16 April 1886, Miller offered a resolution "demanding investigation of reports affecting his Christian character and ministerial usefulness." The charges against him were not recorded, but there were a few members in the Synod who questioned Miller's management of the funds, and they wanted to oust him from the presidency of the college. In November 1889, when that body met in the CP Church in Waynesburg, the matter was brought up again. The students and townspeople overwhelmingly supported Miller. After some controversy in the meeting it was resolved that Miller was to remain President "till the close of the college year, and that a committee be appointed to investigate complaints against him." Miller welcomed such an investigation. When Synod met in July 1890, a "well documented" report was made. It was not a condemnation of Miller nor injurious to the college. It read in part: "Public servants are entitled to moral support of the community and of those who put them in power. To secure this their acts, plans, and influence should be open to inspection and correction of the constituting authorities." There was no sound basis to condemn Miller or his handling of the funds. The Synod then advised an end of all complaints, and urged full cooperation "for the crowning success of the college." Nevertheless, complaints continued. Some members of the CP Church "annually sought the scalp of Dr. Miller . . . and found it not." According to a local editor, "they always appear at every synod with their little tomahawks. The public has often wondered what the objections to Dr. Miller really are. Judging by the prosperity of the institution, one would think that Dr. Miller's influence and work had been beneficial and undeserving of scornful treatment."[76]

Despite criticisms against Miller, he remained at his post. Work toward completion of the new building continued without interruption through the 1890's, and it was dedicated on 28 June 1899. The Reverend J. W. McKay, an alumnus of the college, then a faculty member and fund-raiser, attended to details of the dedication service. He invited President McKinley, Governor Stone of Pennsylvania, and Governor Atkinson of West Virginia. Unfortunately McKinley and Stone could not attend, but Governor Atkinson spoke briefly to the large crowd. The dedication address was delivered by the Reverend W. H. Black of Missouri Valley College, Marshall, Missouri. A week later, on 4 July, the monument in the Park was dedicated to Union soldiers who served in the Civil War. Various local organizations, military units, and many townsmen paraded to the Park. Salutes fired by a Civil War battery "made the hills resound with echoes." Big fireworks were set off in the evening. The monument, sixty-five feet in height, was an honor to Greene Countians and a fitting memorial to those who fought, bled, and died in order to save the Union.[77]

After assuming the office of president of the college in 1859, Miller's chief aim was "to get the college out of debt and establish confidence in its value and permanence." The new building was "a must." While looking ahead to its completion, Miller hoped, more than ever, to promote sound learning. To this end his objectives were: (1) to maintain an able faculty and "liberal appliances of apparatus," thus affording the very best educational facilities; (2) to make these facilities available, as far as possible, to young people of limited means "who may have a laudable thirst for knowledge"; and (3) to pervade the whole institution by a "Christian spirit—the most indispensable condition."[78]

During Miller's administration Waynesburg College was greatly enlarged. In 1850 student enrollment was about 100; in 1899 it was nearly 400. In 1850 the "humble building" was worth $6,000; the college suffered from debt, and no one was willing to work hard at fund-raising. In 1899 it had a magnificent new building, and the value of the property was "reasonably estimated at $100,000"; and the college was out of debt. In 1850 there was no endowment fund; in 1899 this fund totaled $50,000 and Miller had faith that this figure would shortly be increased. Sound academic standards had been maintained. The faculty members had been competent and devoted. The students had been "of an unusually good class with respect to both diligence and behavior." Over the years harmony had prevailed; there had been "very little discord" among students, faculty, and trustees.[79]

In June 1899, upon retiring from forty years of struggle as President to assume the duties of Professor of Philosophical Sciences, Miller expressed his sincere thanks for "a favoring and guiding Providence" and for the "sympathy and efficient cooperation of the numerous friends of the College. . . . " He added "that the college is today notably prosperous and has a more hopeful outlook than at any previous stage in its history." It had been useful in educating youth to serve humanity. Miller predicted that under "management reasonably competent," the college would continue to succeed.[80]

Miller put the college on a par with other institutions of its kind; the public had confidence in it. But he did not labor alone. As a contemporary editor put it: "Waynesburg College did not have many wealthy constituents." The building "is a monument to the sacrifices of people of very moderate means, a proof of their profound devotion to the institution and its heroic president." Bates appropriately says that Miller's work "deserves to live on the brightest page in the history of American colleges. Such devotion as this meant success for Waynesburg College."[81]

IX
McKAY AND TURNER

Advancing age, declining health, and tiring burdens induced Miller to retire as President of the college, effective 30 June 1899. In addition to his administrative duties and fund-raising labors, he had been teaching a heavy schedule in the fields of psychology, logic, ethics, and evidences of Christianity. Upon his retirement as President, the Synod and trustees conferred upon him the title "President Emeritus"—an honor well deserved. Still mentally alert, deeply devoted to the college, and rich in wisdom that comes only with long experience, he was eminently qualified to serve as adviser and teacher. Hence he was chosen to teach the courses he had long taught. It is obvious that the trustees and Synod sincerely appreciated his hard work, self-sacrifice, and devotion to the college for some forty-six years.[1]

The Reverend J. W. McKay was elected President *pro tempore*, effective 1 July 1899, at a salary of $1,200 per year. The Synod, at its meeting early in October of that year, resolved that he was to be retained in that capacity "until next June."[2] In the interim efforts were made to employ a president. It was 10 September 1900, however, when the trustees elected Professor A. E. Turner, who had been serving as President of Lincoln University, one of the "Big Four," as President of Waynesburg College, at a salary of $1,800 per year. Interestingly enough, $1,200 was to be paid by the trustees and $600 by the Pennsylvania Synod, "provided the college funds are not sufficient to pay the whole $1800."[3] McKay served while the quest for a president was under way. Turner was at the helm nearly four years, during which considerable progress was made in the several facets of the institution—the faculty, fund-raising, student life, the curriculum and academic problems, buildings and grounds, and work of the Alumni Association. Unfortunately Miller died during Turner's administration. His passing from the scene left his children, the entire college family, and friends of the college with a deep sense of bereavement and loss.

McKay '83, was a most loyal alumnus of Waynesburg College. In addition to his duties as President *pro tempore*, he taught courses in Bible and in sociology. Through his efforts, several improvements were made. A pipe organ was procured for the chapel. A good laboratory was installed on the first floor, west, in the old building. Called "Science Hall," Professor Waychoff was "the presiding spirit" over it. A study room was furnished in the new building, where students could read and meditate in quiet surroundings; a room for a museum also was "fitted up." Through the college newspaper, the plea went out: "Let each student bring a contribution for the College Museum." McKay was very popular among the students. They liked him, and they hoped the Pennsylvania Synod would "continue the present administration and trustees."[4] Nevertheless, according to plans, Turner was called to the presidency.

Archelaus E. Turner was born near Greenville, Illinois, 27 April 1861. He received the A. B. degree from Lincoln University at age 20; and later the A. M. was there conferred upon him. He had proved to be an able teacher and administrator, and an influential member of the CP Church. He was friendly, likable, and young—at age thirty-nine—when he came to Waynesburg. As president of Lincoln University he had gained excellent experience, which helped him at Waynesburg—and later. Shortly after his arrival by rail in Waynesburg, Turner addressed the students, faculty, and friends of the college in chapel. He also spoke to the trustees "outlining his general policy, and calling attention to some of the special needs in connection with the work of the institution." To the local people, he was a stranger at first. However, "when he showed them he was *for* Waynesburg College, the people rallied to him (italics in original)."[5]

When Turner assumed the presidency, the duties of that office were outlined as follows: (1) to preserve order at all times; (2) to see that buildings were kept in good condition; (3) to teach as many classes as the needs of the college "may seem to him to require"; (4) to preside at all public exercises of the college; (5) to direct all religious exercises of the college; (6) to attend to needful correspondence, advertising, and public notices; (7) to report to the trustees any observed delinquency or inefficiency by instructors; and (8) to see that all regulations are enforced.[6] Curiously enough, this list omits some of the most important functions, such as fund-raising and the recruiting of students.

Turner's faculty, including himself, numbered some ten members. He taught courses in philosophy and political science. His best faculty members were Miller; W. G. Scott, the mathematician; Anna E. Acklin, in history and English; Ezra D. Stewart, Principal of the Normal Department; A. J. Waychoff, Principal of the Preparatory Department; J. F. Bucher, in biology; and A. L. Darby and J. E. Garvin, both in Latin and Greek. Others taught modern foreign languages and English. On 20 June 1901 the trustees determined faculty salaries for the coming year. Turner's salary remained at $1,800; the other salaries ranged from $700 down to $150. Scott, although reputed to be a topnotch mathematician, received the $150 salary. This seems an amazing paradox. But the trustees knew that Scott had a good business in his grocery store, and that he loved the college so much he would teach, if necessary, without salary; there were instances in which they would reduce his salary in order to increase those of others. For the year beginning in July 1904, Scott received no salary. Miller's salary was $600 per year for teaching "such classes as the President of the College may assign him . . . it being understood that the Synod shall be responsible for this amount." In June 1902 Turner received a raise of $300 per year, but other faculty salaries remained fairly constant—and they were often in arrears. If faculty members were assigned extra duties, there was no increase in salary. Ezra D. Stewart, Waychoff, and Bucher were directed in July 1904 to "conduct a vigorous campaign to secure students for the coming year" without remuneration. These three men came to be known as the "Second Triumvirate," succeeding Miller, Scott, and Rinehart—the First Triumvirate—because of their hard work and devotion to the college.[7]

Turner did his best to raise funds for the college. In September 1900 a committee of three trustees conferred with a like committee of the Board of Trust on ways to increase the endowment fund. A month later Turner and five others chosen from these boards were appointed as a committee "to visit Pittsburgh and interview capitalists with a view to securing additions to the endowment fund of Waynesburg College."[8] The needs of the college were listed as: four endowed professorships, each $25,000; a new science building, $15,000; a gymnasium, $10,000; an athletic field, no cost listed;

a women's dormitory, $10,000; a library endowment, $5,000; a heating plant, $5,000; and an observatory, $2,000. Any one of these gifts entitled the donor "to give a name to the benefaction. Will you help us?" By 1901 several donors had given money for electric chandeliers for Alumni Hall, the president's office, the library and the Y. W. C. A. room.[9]

The semicentennial celebration of the start of classes in the "old college building" was an occasion not only of reunion of alumni and old friends, but also a good opportunity to raise funds.[10] Called the "Waynesburg College Jubilee," in preparation for it, a mass meeting was held in the courthouse on the evening of 7 October 1901. Turner, Miller, Waychoff and several others spoke on this occasion. At the celebration on 6-7 November, scores of alumni returned, and many friends of the college attended. Among the speakers was Miller, in one of his last public appearances. He choked with emotion, and was scarcely audible when he closed his speech with "*Alma Mater, Esto Perpetua.*" Turner announced an increase of $31,000 in endowment, "with promise of getting $20,000 more." The goal was $100,000; on nearing it, the figure would be raised. Late in 1901 it was "confidently expected that within a year the productive endowment will be increased to $150,000."[11]

In December 1901 the trustees notified all persons who had not paid their subscriptions to the college "to pay the same in ten days, else legal proceedings will be instituted to collect same." They also called on Turner "to devote his entire time during the ensuing college term to raising permanent endowment for the college." They moved to secure a substitute to teach Turner's classes. Early in March 1902 Turner announced that pledges for endowment totaled $40,000, and "that the $100,000 mark will be reached by June." In addition was the sum of $25,000, which was to be raised to endow the "A. B. Miller Chair of Philosophy." It was estimated that by the end of 1902, a total of $150,000 would be reached. But this figure was far too optimistic. Some fifteen years later, endowment was only half this sum.[12]

During the drive for increased endowment the college faced difficulties in meeting current expenses. In April 1903, in order to pay such expenses "and to meet debts already contracted" the trustees arranged to borrow "any sum not exceeding $2,500" in the name of the college "and upon its credit."[13]

If money was essential to the existence of the college, even moreso were the students. As ever, the great emphasis was on morality.

There were occasional instances of misconduct in class; and a few frivolous students committed pranks of one kind or another. For example, in April 1902 two students locked the chapel door, which frustrated the faculty and students and created considerable chaos. Students were not permitted to dance. In January 1902 a faculty member reported "that it had come to ear" that a certain female student "was attending dancing school." An investigation was made, but what happened to her was not recorded.[14]

Students were still required to attend class, chapel, church on the Sabbath, and meetings of literary societies. But common sense was used in the application of these rules. On 11 May 1900, for example, a male student "was excused from attending chapel because of difficulty in ascending the stairs." On 1 March 1901 the faculty granted a request, signed by Lieutenant Edward Martin and seventeen students, "that members of Company K be excused from college exercises until 5 March or longer, if necessary, in order to attend the inaugural parade in pursuance of orders from headquarters." This parade was in honor of Theodore Roosevelt at his inauguration on 4 March 1901. At the faculty meeting on 12 December 1902, Turner mentioned the members of the baseball team and wondered "if they would be discredited while absent" from the campus and playing another team. The faculty members pointed out that they had approved the schedule, and *ipso facto* all such absences were excused. A precedent was thus set, which has always been followed in all intercollegiate athletic events.[15]

As time passed, it became increasingly difficult to enforce rules governing absences. At Turner's call, on 10 October 1902, the faculty met "to consider the number of absentees from society, chapel, and church." After long discussion, they decided to appoint a committee "to devise new laws governing absences from college exercises." Shortly the committee's report was adopted. In the final grading of a student, his scholastic work, and attendance at chapel, class, church, and literary society, "as required by the college, shall be the basis." Thenceforward, for each absence from any of these exercises a student received a demerit. Excessive absences meant lower grades.[16] It appears that this was an improvement over the preceding system in which students received "admonitions" for excessive absences.

In 1902 more space in Hanna Hall was set aside for use as a domitory for male students. It meant "an increase in college spirit, better facilities for study, better rooms than usual," and everyone connected with it was to be commended. Regulations relative to student conduct in the dormitory were prescribed. And a housemother was appointed to see that the rules were enforced and to take care of students residing there.[17]

The students took an interest in the buildings and grounds, and occasionally made suggestions for improvement. For example, in December 1902 they requested that a room "in the new building be set apart for a waiting and study room. . . . " In April 1903 members of the senior class requested the trustees for permission "to plant ivy in front of the college building on Class Day. . . . " Their request was granted, and this was the start of the ivy which has increasingly covered, and beautified, the south wall through the years.[18]

Members of the literary societies were especially noted for their efforts to improve their respective halls. There was an excellent spirit of competition to see which would be the better finished and furnished. In March 1900 Philo hall on the third floor, west, in the new building was described as "clean, neat, and it has a newly polished stove which gives evidence of the loyalty of its members." On 20 June 1901, immediately after commencement, the Philo's met to discuss the purchase of a new piano. They believed they could get $25 for the old one as a trade-in. Edward Martin, a member of the graduating class, "said he would subscribe $5 for the new one and that, if it wasn't paid for by next commencement, he would give $5 more." Several other Philos subscribed $5 each. The piano was slow in coming, however. On 4 December 1903, the Philos met in "secret session, the reason being that we make some improvements in the hall—a new carpet, varnishing, frescoing, and a new piano." By meeting secretly the Union members would not know their plans. The Philos might surpass their rivals in elegance of their hall.[19]

Another significant development was a new publication sponsored by students. In January 1891 the first issue of a newspaper entitled *Waynesburg College Crayon* had been published. With Miller as "the general editorial supervisor," it had been a monthly paper at a subscription price of 25 cents per year. Its aim had been to bring "to the attention of the public the wants, the work, and the facilities of the College." But it was short-lived, and for several years the college had no newspaper. Early in 1900 the students took the initiative to start a new one; Edward Martin presented the matter to Philo Society. Shortly each society appointed a publications committee; the two met jointly and made provision for financial support of the paper. The students held a mass meeting, at which the Reverend McKay presided. An executive board and an editorial staff were appointed. John C. Knox, destined to become an eminent federal jurist, was chosen editor-in-chief. Entitled *The Collegian*, this useful student newspaper thrived for more than two decades. Well organized and written in the best English, it included materials on student organizations, athletic events, brief articles of a scholarly nature, and excellent editorials.[20]

As in previous years, all students were required to join the societies. There was some difference of opinion as to whether or not students in the Normal Department should come under this rule. But the faculty decreed that the rule applied to them, and "ordered the Secretary to cite all deliquents."[21]

As always, a few students were frivolous, and inclined to violate the rules of the college and of the literary societies. In February 1901 some students were "engaged in questionable amusement" in Union Hall; they were dancing and indulging in hilarity which "created disturbance in the Building." The faculty took it so seriously that they called on Turner to prepare a pledge to be signed by the offenders, in which they promised to "refrain from such conduct hereafter during our connection with the college." This pledge was signed by eight girls and five boys.[22]

Early in February 1902 it was the Philo's turn to submit debate questions to the Union society for its consideration for the forthcoming contest. The Philos, however, delayed in the matter. The Union society called on the faculty to intercede—to no avail. It appears that the spirit of rivalry between the literary societies became emotional and bitter. The faculty, caught in between, called on Turner, in June 1903, "to call the officers of the two societies together" in order to improve relations between them. A greater degree of faculty supervision over the societies seemed desirable.[23]

One gets the impression that the literary societies considered themselves as important as the college itself. In March 1903, the Philos boasted in the student newspaper: "Every year Philo sends out many earnest boys and girls into the world, and they never fail to make their mark. Most give the Society credit for their success; lawyers, teachers, doctors, ministers, and so on, are doing well."[24]

Two other student organizations which became strong by the turn of the century were the Young Men's Christian Association and the Young Women's Christian Association. The Y.M.C.A. had been organized in 1888, and it occupied a room on the second floor of the new building. Its aim was "to promote Christian fellowship among its members, and aggressive Christian work—especially by and for students to train them for Christian service, and to . . . devote themselves to Jesus Christ, not only in distinctively religious callings, but also in secular pursuits." Each member received a certificate which entitled him to admission to a Y.M.C.A. anywhere. The Y.M.C.A. met daily at 8:30 A.M. for a fifteen-minute service; and held a weekly session of one hour every Friday at 6:30 P.M. Attendance was large; roll was regularly called, and absences were recorded. The programs were religious in nature, with "good music at all meetings."[25]

The Y.W.C.A. had been organized in 1895, after a young lady from Waynesburg had spent a summer at Moody's Summer School at Northfield, Massachusetts. Interest in the organization rapidly increased. In 1896 the trustees set aside a room for it, where brief daily devotional exercises were held, "plus weekly Bible classes and various special meetings." The object of the association was "to develop Christian character and do Christian work, especially at Waynesburg College." It was of great value for it "trained for active Christian work"; the girls critically studied the Bible, and came in contact with other schools. They held frequent receptions; and established a "home committee" which met new students and showed them "kindly attentions so much needed and appreciated when one is among strangers." Occasionally joint meetings were held with the Y.M.C.A. at which students of both sexes could get acquainted. These groups sometimes joined in attending services at the local CP Church. One of the most enjoyable features was the social life. But the girls also benefited by the spiritual uplift. Despite eight o'clock classes, the brief prayer meetings every morning were "felt to be a great source of help by those who are permitted to attend."[26]

If students were interested in the literary societies and Christian associations, equally so were they in athletics at the college. The main problem, however, was a lack of athletic grounds. For many years the college had rented the "old" fairground located on the south side of town, which had a good half-mile track and was sufficiently large for football and baseball. Early in 1900, however, the Uniontown, Waynesburg, and West Virginia Railroad Company planned to take over the grounds for depots. In that event, the college would be compelled to look elsewhere for grounds. In 1902 Turner and a faculty committee began looking for permanent athletic grounds to be college property. They wanted a good location, adequate in size for a football field and a gymnasium.[27]

Early in 1903 plans for the railroad caused a crisis in the athletic situation. It was announced that the grounds, which had been rented for years, would no longer be available. The baseball team looked ahead to the coming season. With no athletic grounds, the whole schedule would, of necessity, be canceled. In February 1903, the editor of the college newspaper wrote: "This problem is very important, and should be solved *now*. It is as important as the endowment (italics in original)."[28] As events were soon to prove, fortunately for the college, the railroad project was abandoned.

Meanwhile Turner and his committee bent to the task of finding an athletic field and funds to pay for it. Friends of the college responded favorably. In March 1903 Turner gladdened the students and faculty when he announced in chapel that athletic grounds had been purchased south of town on the banks of Ten Mile Creek, being part of the "old fairground." It is the present site, located on East Street at the terminus of Elm; in area it is three acres, 159 perches. The price was $5,500—all donated by friends of the college. Businessmen in town gave generously; nearly every townsman supported the enterprise. In 1903 that part of town was growing rapidly, which tended to increase the value of property. The college was the more fortunate, for the purchase included enough lumber to fence the ground. On learning of Turner's deal, "the enthusiasm of the students knew no bounds." That evening they "formed a procession, marched to the residence of President Turner, built a bonfire, sang college songs, gave the college yell, and finally called on the President for a speech." Turner told them about the location, and purchase, and casually mentioned the lumber which was included in the bargain. The students loudly cheered him, and marched past faculty homes singing and blowing horns. "And the old college bell rang as it never rang before." Under the direction of a committee of alumni, the students went to work with enthusiasm to build the fence and do the necessary grading as evidence of their appreciation of Turner's efforts and of the liberality of friends of the college. The boys worked in mud and water, "cheerfully stepping in holes over their shoe tops, getting wet, muddy, and colds." For several days classes were practically suspended "as one and 'most all dug post holes, built fences, or shoveled dirt. 'Twas a most inspiring sight." Plans were made to build a grandstand, and visitors were invited "to see the park for themselves."[29]

The college aimed to promote the several intercollegiate athletic sports and to keep professionalism out of athletics. But this was difficult to do, because neighboring institutions would not adhere to the same policy. As the editor of the college newspaper put it:

> No school in western Pennsylvania can truthfully say that they [*sic*] carry out the provisions of a contract calling for the playing of bona fide students only in athletic contests. . . . We make a great cry for amateur athletics, but don't live up to it. There is strong sentiment in favor of pure athletics. The colleges should work together to keep athletics clean. It takes courage to field amateur teams, for they will lose. But all should demand pure athletics.[30]

To the end that athletic sports would be kept clean and yet competitive, in September 1903, the trustees appointed an executive committee of three to be in charge of athletics "in conjunction with the faculty and subject to the faculty's direction." The three were: two alumni—Edward Martin '01 and A. L. Moredock '97; and a student, John W. Day.[31]

Baseball, for many years the leading sport, was still going strong. The student body supported the teams, which were thoroughly competitive. For example, in May 1900, at a meeting in Alumni Hall the students supplied funds for the team; some "subscribed $5 to $10 to the fund." The spirit of rivalry was keenest with the team of Washington and Jefferson College. The game on 7 May 1901 draws our interest. A special train carried some 200 students and townspeople to the game at a round-trip fare of one dollar—which was half the usual rate. Students who wished to go were excused from classes. Enthusiasm was high. The game was close; unfortunately Waynesburg lost in the ninth inning by one run. But the editor of Waynesburg's newspaper came to the team's defense. He explained that the long ride (twenty-five miles) and "strange grounds" worked to Waynesburg's disadvantage. He really believed Waynesburg "won the game so far as playing alone is concerned." A return game was to be played in Waynesburg; and the editor boasted "we anticipate a good game—a Waterloo for W. & J."[32]

The baseball teams generally scheduled were those of Allegheny, Bethany, California Normal, Grove City, Indiana Normal, Washington and Jefferson, Westminster, Western University of Pennsylvania (the University of Pittsburgh), and West Virginia University. Occasionally independent teams were played, such as those at Carlisle and Homestead. Whenever "W. & J." was defeated in Waynesburg, there was great rejoicing. For example, late in May 1904, Waynesburg won by a score of 3 to 2. Elated over the victory, Waynesburg students celebrated by a "nightgown parade." Clad in such attire, they "traversed several of the streets and assembled in front of the Blair Hotel, where they serenaded the W. & J. baseball players who took it very pleasantly."[33]

Football, the second major sport, had its ups and downs from 1899 to 1904. The main problems were lack of funds, players, and a good coaching staff. For one reason or another, some games were canceled each season; in 1901 no games were played. The 1899 season was the most successful. Of seven games scheduled, five were played; and Waynesburg won three of them. The highlight came on Thanksgiving day of that year, when Waynesburg, in a home game, defeated West Virginia University 20 to 0. A local editor boasted: "The West Virginians were entirely outclassed, standing no show at any stage of the game. The Waynesburg boys pushed them down the field and went through their line at will." Some 600 persons saw the game, "and they were very enthusiastic."[34]

Students, the faculty, and townsmen had confidence in the team. In March 1900 they were optimistic about the forthcoming season. The captain of the team was J. Boyd Crumrine, "the famous fullback," who graduated in Waynesburg's class of 1902. A schedule was arranged. The team practiced, played three games, and won two of them. A local editor then explained what happened on 27 September 1900: "The football team disbanded yesterday, due to lack of funds to see them through the season. . . . The faculty and students want football, but there hasn't been enough time to raise money."[35] John Knox summarized the sentiments in "a eulogy on the deceased football team. . . . " He "ascribed all honor to the unfortunate eleven—and showed that its death was a natural consequence of certain pecuniary complications that baffled all skill." He hoped that "in the future the team might be resurrected to a longer, brighter existence."[36] According to J. Boyd Crumrine, there was a "lack of men coming out for the team, because the school in general doesn't take the interest it should in athletics. We lack college spirit. . . . " He urged people to take an interest in the game, and felt that each class should organize teams.[37]

Crumrine's enthusiasm must have been contagious, for a team was organized for the 1902 season. But it faced insurmountable obstacles. A coach would not come, chiefly because the team was amateur. Two of the best men were lost by the calling out of the National Guard. The fence around the field was not finished, and people could see the game from almost any vantage point; hence gate receipts were low. Consequently the Athletic Association, organized earlier, "decided to cancel the rest of the games after the California game." Only three games were played. Two were against Bethany, with Waynesburg losing one 6-0, and tying the other 0-0; in the third, Waynesburg defeated California 6-5.[38]

In January 1903 the editor of the college newspaper derided those persons who, through ignorance of football, still feared the alleged dangers of the game: "When it's all said and done, when the lists of killed and wounded have been published, when the little sermonettes have been preached, there is fascination which holds us to the noble game of football. It's American in its intensity. It's life in its quickness. Long live football at Waynesburg College."[39]

His words did not fall on deaf ears. By the fall of 1903 the athletic grounds had been greatly improved; the grading was completed; the fence finished; and bleachers to seat several hundred people were erected. Most important, the team had a coach. Fred M. Hatch, who had been football coach at Oberlin College, was employed as football coach and athletic director at a salary of $600 per year. Hatch made a favorable first impression. Such a coach and a "good turnout of men" were harbingers of a successful season. The results, however, were rather mediocre. A schedule of seven games was played—with Waynesburg winning three, losing three, and tying one.[40]

Interest in basketball began around 1900 when baskets were attached to walls in the "gymnasium," a room described as "large, well lighted and accessible. . . . " It contained a piano, parallel bars, horizontal bars, rowing machine, ladders, punching bags, dumb bells, gloves, and other athletic equipment. Of all these sports, the students became most interested in basketball. Six such teams were practicing, and some "expert players" were developed. The coeds had the gymnasium "exclusively two days each week" for basketball practice. Coached by Miss Neonetta Iams, a recent graduate of Radcliffe College, they were "making remarkable progress as well as enjoying a pleasant pastime." The girls, clad in baggy bloomers, blouses, and black stockings, yearned for an adequate basketball floor; the boys also deplored the lack of such a facility. In December 1902 the editor of the college newspaper complained that "basketball season is here, and we have no place to play. This is a sport for both ladies and gentlemen." Turner was then trying to get a suitable hall; and many men and women "have expressed their intention to play." Finally, by 1904, space in the "Old Mill," which was located on the site of the Paul R. Stewart Science Building, had been procured as a basketball floor. Waynesburg's first intercollegiate game was played there in 1904 against "a strong intramural team from West Virginia University."[41]

Spring sports "were slow in starting." In the fall of 1902 an excellent tennis court was constructed to the rear of the new building. Students of both sexes were very enthusiastic about it. In the spring of 1903 the first track team was organized. A number of students joined the team, and practiced running, jumping, putting the shot, and throwing the javelin.[42] Ere long these young men were able to compete respectably with those of other institutions in the tri-state area.

Participation in athletics developed the students' bodies, but the curriculum was essential to the development of their minds. During the McKay and Turner regimes only a few changes were made in the curriculum. Administratively the following departments were created: Greek and Latin; French and German; Mathematics; the Sciences; English and History; Religion and Philosophy; and Political Science. The program in the Preparatory Department was lengthened from two to three years—a junior year, middle year, and senior year. At that level, beginning in 1903, students were not required to take Greek; it became optional, and students could take general history instead. At the college level, the classical course still stressed Latin and Greek, but electives were available in French, German, and English after the sophomore year. This course led to an A. B. degree. In the scientific course, modern languages were substituted for Latin and Greek; science courses were required every year, with some stress on mathematics. This program led to a B. S. degree. The literary-scientific course stressed modern languages and literature, and led to the B. L. degree. Special courses were offered for those who did not wish to pursue a degree. Such courses were purely elective, subject to approval by the faculty.[43]

A significant curriculum change came in October 1902 when the faculty unanimously voted to abolish the course leading toward the Ph. D. degree. While the faculty sincerely tried to maintain respectable standards for a Ph. D., Waynesburg could not compete with the big universities with large libraries, excellent laboratories, and highly specialized faculty members. Students eschewed Waynesburg's graduate program; when Waynesburg "went out of the Ph. D. business" only two students were enrolled in the graduate department. The A. M. program was continued for some time after the Ph. D. was discontinued.[44]

Other aspects of the curriculum are noteworthy. The Normal Department continued to draw many students; in 1901, 89 young people were preparing for careers in teaching. The Conservatory of Music, with 108 students then enrolled, was most popular—under the direction of Professor J. M. Blose. When Blose came to Waynesburg, "the Conservatory was almost expiring. . . . " He "soon made it a prosperous, successful department." There was always harmony and unity between it and the college. The Conservatory offered work in piano, organ, pipe organ, violin, voice culture, and harmony. Recitals were regularly held, "and the students performed very well."[45]

Admission requirements became more rigid. Completion of the "preparatory course," examination in it "or any equivalent course, or certificates from other colleges," would admit a student to the freshman class. Transfer students from other colleges were admitted at the beginning of any term, or "in any year except the senior year." The senior year had to be taken in residence at the college as a requisite for graduation. Students deficient "in not more than two subjects" could be admitted "on conditions—the time for fulfilling them to be determined by the faculty."[46] The faculty adhered strictly to rules governing transfer students.[47]

Despite attempts at more careful selection of students, from 1900 to 1903 a rash of weak students came from the public schools to the college's Preparatory Department. In December 1900 several teachers reported students, who "were failures in almost all work undertaken." Certain faculty members, therefore, agreed "to form classes for said students," in what would be called "special education" today; small classes of "slow learners" were given extra attention by the faculty. In September 1901 the faculty discussed "the propriety of rejecting certain students who had applied for admission in . . . the preparatory school." Several teachers suspected that academic standards in public schools were low. In March 1902 a committee of the faculty was appointed "to look into the system of grading in the public schools." This seemed to be necessary in order to get data for admitting students to the college.[48]

The faculty was troubled by a few lazy, immature students, who had been admitted to college-level work. Such students desired to drop difficult courses and substitute easier ones; they sought ways to evade the rules, and asked for favors of one kind or another. The faculty castigated them. For example, in November 1901 a student who was weak in English was ordered "to take up work in grammar at once" for a term of school. Another student who was "doing no good" in physics, wanted to drop the course. The faculty ordered him to "get into classes regularly and do good work" or they "would inform his father that he could not matriculate his son next term."[49]

One of the most perplexing problems facing the faculty was that of classification of students. In the progression from class to class it was difficult to ascertain just when individual students should be advanced to the next class; this became most serious as students approached the senior class.[50] The most unusual case relative to classification and eligibility for graduation confronted the faculty several weeks prior to commencement in 1901. On 5 April of that year a "Professor Gilmer" and his wife requested to be graduated with that year's class. Professor J. E. Garvin, a member of the Waynesburg College faculty, presented their names for the faculty's consideration. A motion that Gilmer and his wife be graduated, was not seconded; the faculty was reluctant to approve the conferring of degrees upon them. On 17 May Turner, who had secured more information on the Gilmers, informed the faculty that Mrs. Gilmer had done no work above the high school level, and that "Professor Gilmer" was only a normal school graduate. Mrs. Gilmer's name was then dropped, but a motion was made, and seconded, to graduate "Professor Gilmer." At Turner's suggestion, the faculty voted, by secret ballot, four votes for graduation and three votes against. Turner then, with the consent of those voting for Gilmer's graduation, directed that the rule relative to the senior year's study in residence at the college, as a requirement for graduation, be waived; and that Gilmer be graduated with the degree A. B.[51]

The students, on learning the faculty's action to graduate Gilmer, arose almost en masse against such an inequity to them and such a travesty on the educational process. It was so obvious that Gilmer, holding his diploma from a normal school, had about the equivalent education of one who had completed his sophomore year at Waynesburg College. Petitions to the faculty from three classes were quickly forthcoming. The senior class, with Edward Martin's name first, petitioned the faculty to rescind its action, saying that "Gilmer is not according to the laws of the College, entitled to graduation." If the faculty did not concur, and still graduated Gilmer, the seniors "asked that he have no part in commencement exercises." A committee of the junior class, including J. Boyd Crumrine, John C. Knox, and Daniel L. Rich petitioned the faculty not to graduate Gilmer "inasmuch as the named gentleman has not completed the course, nor complied with the stipulations of the catalogue governing the conferring of degrees, and that such action would be lowering the high standard of the institution." The sophomore petition apparently was the most forceful one of all. It was not received "on account of the manner in which the request was made." After all the hullabaloo, Gilmer "expressed the desire that the degree voted him by the faculty be withdrawn on account of the unfavorable comments concerning the matter and the compromise manner in which it was granted. The faculty unanimously concurred with his request. . . . "[52]

By October 1902 the faculty had devised a system to honor students with high scholastic standing. Honor students were rated on a scale above ninety percent. Seniors whose grades in all departments averaged ninety-five percent, or higher, were graduated *magna cum laude*; those with averages between ninety-three and ninety-five percent were graduated *cum laude*; and those with averages between ninety and ninety-three percent received honorable mention.[53]

As was the custom, honorary degrees were conferred at commencement. During Turner's administration, the two most notable men to receive such degrees were A. B. Cummins, '67, Governor of Iowa, who was awarded an LL. D. in June 1903; and Lieutenant General Nelson A. Miles, great and gallant hero of the Spanish American War, who received an LL. D. in June 1904. The visit of General Miles was extraordinary. On 15 June 1904 he came to town on a "W. & W. special" train, and was met at the station by Major T. S. Crago, '92, a loyal alumnus, and by other friends of the college. He was guest of honor at the alumni banquet, a "big meal of fried chicken and roast beef" with all the trimmings. Both Miles and Turner spoke on this occasion. The next day the General delivered the commencement address, and "his genuine good sense and manliness would not permit him to say an uninteresting thing. . . . He spoke from the heart. . . . " During his brief stay General Miles also addressed a large audience, including Grand Army of the Republic (GAR) veterans and Spanish American War Veterans, at the courthouse.[54]

The academic side of the institution was important, but buildings and grounds were equally so. Turner and the trustees put forth sincere efforts to maintain and to improve the physical plant. The new building was a great boon to the college, but the old one needed repairs now and then. In January 1901 the trustees secured a watchman for these buildings. They also moved to pay the janitor's salary, $15 per month, which was three months in arrears. With a view to changing classes more promptly, Turner procured a "program clock with a system of bells for all classrooms." In June 1903 the trustees borrowed $514 from a local bank to pay for the grandstand on the athletic field. A great innovation came in March 1904, when they arranged "for telephone service in the college at $12.00 per annum."[55]

Turner was greatly interested in the museum in the college. Friends were asked to contribute specimens of the various branches of science, or cash. Funds received were entrusted to Professors Waychoff and Bucher, who would "spend the money according to the wishes of the donors." Contributions kept coming in, and the yield in 1903 was excellent. It included selenite and petrified wood; gypsum; carborundum; gold and silver ores; anthracite coal and fossils; asbestos; shells from Japan; fossil ferns; birds' eggs; and a tooth of a megalonyx, a large animal of the Quaternary period, found on Hoover's Run, in Greene County, and loaned by Ezra D. Stewart. Through Turner's efforts more money was raised for the Library. And his wife organized the "Gossip Club," later the Waynesburg Women's Club, for the purpose of helping the Library. Through the years this organization has regularly contributed to it.[56]

The alumni continued to support the college in every way possible. They met annually in Alumni Hall which, by 1900, they had furnished at a cost of $3,000. In June 1900 they appointed a committee to secure portraits of Loughran and Miller to be placed in the chapel; a year later they added Weethee to their list. In the interim "the committee on this had done nothing—and were instructed to go to work at once."[57] The portrait of Miller only was placed in Alumni Hall, and in 1974 those of Rich and Stewart were added.

The ever-increasing body of alumni was boosted on 14 May 1901, when the Pittsburgh Alumni Association was organized in Pittsburgh through the efforts of the Reverend William Q. Rosselle of the Homestead Baptist Church. At that time there were 200 alumni of the college in the Pittsburgh area. Some 50 attended the banquet in the Monongahela House, where this Association was created. Turner and his wife were honored guests. This was the first of several "branch" organizations of the alumni. They multiplied as time passed and the alumni body grew. In March 1903

Turner met with the Pittsburgh group again, and spoke at their banquet attended by some 100 members. On that occasion, Dr. William Beach, Miller's son-in-law, was elected president of the Pittsburgh Association.[58]

As the alumni body increased in numbers and prestige, many members felt that alumni should have some voice in the government of the college. In June 1901 the Alumni Association appointed a committee to request the Pennsylvania Synod of the CP Church "to allow the Alumni Association to elect a portion of the college trustees. . . . " By June 1902 this committee "had done nothing, because Synod seemed unwilling to grant the request." The committee was continued, with two additional members, "and was asked to report next year."[59] In October 1902 Turner attended the Synod's meeting at California, Pennsylvania. On his return he reported that the Board of Trustees of Waynesburg College would be increased from eleven to twenty-one members. Of these, seven were to be chosen annually, two of whom would be elected by the Alumni Association and known as alumni trustees. In April 1903 the charter of the college was amended to include this increase in the number of trustees, and details were worked out concerning the election of alumni trustees. The trustees were organized into five committees: judiciary; finance; accounts; teachers and salaries; and buildings and grounds.[60]

Many alumni were going to the best graduate schools in the nation. Farabee was doing excellent work in Harvard's Department of Anthropology. In 1901 he invented the "Farabee instrument," which made him famous. With it he established a law of racial difference by measuring the angle of twist and torsion of bones of Indians and Mound Builders. Farabee was so brilliant at Harvard that he attracted other alumni of Waynesburg College. By 1904 there were enough Waynesburg graduates attending Harvard to call them the "Waynesburg College colony." Others were going to Boston University, where a similar "colony" was formed. Frequently these alumni recalled Waynesburg College: "We still love to think of her as our *Alma Mater*, and rejoice in her better equipment and increased prosperity." As a local editor put it: "Waynesburg College has an honorable history—rich in men of purpose, who have become men of achievement, rich in loyalty of her sons and daughters to whom her best has been imparted."[61]

The joy of the alumni over the college's "increased prosperity" was turned to sorrow when they received the sad news of Miller's death late in January 1902. During the preceding year he had enjoyed his usual good health. In May 1901 the Pennsylvania Presbytery appointed him as its delegate to the CP General Assembly, which met at West Point, Mississippi. After attending that meeting, he accepted a summer position as chaplain of a large sanitarium near Philadelphia, Pennsylvania. When the fall term opened at the college, he resumed his regular teaching schedule. But illness early in January 1902 forced him to quit teaching. This was naturally a shock to all on campus and to townsmen who knew him. The student editor expressed the sentiment: "It hardly seems like Waynesburg College without the Doctor in his accustomed place. The students and friends of the college sincerely sympathize with him in his illness and all join in the hope of a speedy recovery. . . . " During his sickness, William Jennings Bryan came and addressed the students, and it was the only big event "in the history of the college in which he has not been a central figure."[62] At mid-January 1902, Miller's son-in-law and daughter, Dr. and Mrs. William M. Beach of Allegheny, Pennsylvania, came to Miller's bedside. He had suffered a stroke of paralysis, and was critically ill. There were no signs of improvement, and death came on 30 January 1902—at age seventy-two "in the old college building, which to him was the best loved spot on earth." All school exercises were suspended until after the funeral.[63]

Miller's funeral, on 1 February 1902, was conducted with solemnity and dignity befitting the occasion. In the morning his body lay in state in the college rotunda for three hours. The tolling of the college bell in the afternoon announced the conclusion of the funeral services. Miller was buried in nearby Greene Mount Cemetery, beside "his precious wife long-gone before."[64]

Miller's death was deeply mourned. The faculty and students began a thirty-day period of mourning. Turner told how indispensable Miller was to the college: "If Dr. Miller had died fifty years ago, I suppose no man believes there would today have been a Waynesburg College." Expressions of sympathy came from the Women's Christian Temperance Union, the local press,[65] the faculty of Lincoln University,[66] and the Alumni Association.[67] Waynesburg College was Miller's "foster child," said a faculty resolution: "When others cast it off, he took it to his great heart, nourished it, sacrificed for it, believed in it. . . . As a teacher, as a literary light, as a defender of the faith, he was unsurpassed in the Cumberland Presbyterian Church. His church this day bows her head and weeps."[68]

The college catalogue pointed out how Miller guided the college through the Civil War crisis and the years of financial stress that followed:

> His rare executive and scholarly ability, his uncommon aptness and power as a teacher, his growing fame as a thinker, writer, and educational leader gave prestige and standing to the institution. . . . In spite of meager endowment and a constant need of money he was able to associate with himself a body of teachers imbued with his own spirit of self sacrifice, and thus Waynesburg College has grown to a footing of equality with many older and better endowed institutions.[69]

Shortly after Miller's death, Turner boosted the worthy project to raise $25,000 to endow the "A. B. Miller Chair of Philosophy." An anniversary memorial service was held a year after Miller's passing, at which efforts were made to raise this fund.[70] But, paradoxically enough, attempts to endow this chair ended in failure.

Early in February 1904, Turner attended a meeting of the Pittsburgh Alumni Association in quest of more funds. In May 1904, in order to advertise the college more widely, he promoted a Waynesburg College exhibit at the World's Fair in St. Louis. It was an excellent display consisting of some fifty photographs of the new building, classrooms, grounds, faculty, and athletic groups. It also listed prominent alumni and, on a large map of the world, showed where they were located.[71]

The trustees sincerely appreciated Turner's services. On 6 June 1904 they agreed to furnish him "a suitable house for next year—at a cost not exceeding four hundred dollars." A week later, to the disappointment of many, Turner tendered his resignation to the trustees. His wife had been suffering from "bronchial trouble . . . for several years." She "feared the loss of her beautiful soprano voice" from the condition. Turner told the trustees he had "been advised by a specialist in Chicago . . . that Mrs. Turner would probably be benefited by removal to North Texas. . . . I wish to assure you that no other consideration, save one of health, could have induced me to take this step. . . . " He expressed his deep attachment to Waynesburg College, thanked the trustees for their "constant and loyal support," and said he had signified his willingness to take "the position tendered me in Texas. . . . " He hoped the trustees would accept his "resignation at once." Turner assumed the presidency of Trinity University, then located in Waxahachie.[72] This was the third of the "Big Four" CP institutions of higher learning over which he became president.

The trustees accepted Turner's resignation "with sincere regret and very great reluctance. . . . " They wished him and his wife, "who has so endeared herself to this community," the best in "their new field of labor wherein we trust his efforts may be crowned with . . . success and her health restored to its full vigor."[73]

The trustees immediately began the search for a successor to Turner. Proceeding on a hit-and-miss basis, they appointed an *ad hoc* committee from their own body "to confer with Rev. Ira Landreth, of Chicago, Illinois, with a view to securing him to accept the presidency of the college; and on failure to secure him, then to confer with Rev. J. M. Hubbard, of Marshall, Missouri . . . and on failure to secure him, then to confer with Reverend J. V. Stephens for the same purpose." All three efforts were fruitless. Meanwhile, the trustees fixed the salary of the president of the college at $2,000 "per annum." They also called on Professor J. F. Bucher of the faculty "to take charge of the college correspondence until a president is elected and enters upon his duties." On 5 July 1904 the special committee of trustees was "directed to open negotiations with such persons as they deem suitable and available for the position." Shortly Alvin F. Lewis was chosen as Turner's successor. He accepted the position, and began working with energy and determination.[74]

X
FROM LEWIS TO HUDSON

FROM 1904 TO 1911 TWO PRESIDENTS AND AN ACTING PRESIDENT OF Waynesburg College came and went. Alvin F. Lewis served as president for only one year, 1904-1905; Jacob F. Bucher was acting president from 1905 to 1908; and William M. Hudson was president from 1908 to 1911. In this period, the CP Church merged with the Presbyterian Church in the United States of America, resulting in a new—and more affluent—sponsor of Waynesburg College. A new dormitory for women made the institution much more attractive to young ladies. There was an upsurge in athletics when Edward Martin became Director of Athletics. And social fraternities and sororities were organized on the campus.

On 1 August 1904 the trustees unanimously elected Dr. Alvin F. Lewis President of the college at a salary of $1,800 per year. Born at Bowling Green, Kentucky, he became a member of the CP Church at an early age. He attended Ogden College, in Kentucky, and transferred to Princeton University, where he graduated in 1884 with the A. B. degree. Three years later Princeton conferred the A. M. upon him. He then went south, and, for five years, served as President of West Florida State Seminary, a coeducational school in Tallahassee. He suffered several attacks of malaria there, and hence came north where he regained his health. He took four years of graduate work at Johns Hopkins University and won the Ph. D. there in 1899; his chief interests were in history, political science, and philosophy. Subsequently he did post-doctoral work at the University of Berlin. He returned to America, and began teaching in the fields of history and political science at the University of Arkansas, at a salary of $1,800 per year. On becoming President of Waynesburg College he was forty-two years old; he was unmarried, pleasing in personality, and had excellent social qualities. He came to Waynesburg "with the very highest recommendations and . . . he impresses one at first as an educator in the truest sense of the word. . . . Dr. Lewis is encouraged by large enrollment. A bright era for Waynesburg College is beginning."[1]

Lewis labored diligently for the college. And all seemed to be going well. But he resigned the presidency early in May 1905, ostensibly because of the failure of a bank in Bowling Green where "he had funds deposited." The trustees promptly requested him to withdraw his resignation. But he informed them that "under existing circumstances, it is impossible . . . to do so. . . . " The trustees then accepted his resignation "with sincere regret" at the end of his first year of service. They appreciated his Christian character, his scholarship, his skill as an administrator, and his careful attention to the affairs of the college. After looking after his savings account in Kentucky, Lewis returned to Germany for more post-doctoral work. The trustees quickly appointed a committee of three of their own body to secure another suitable man to fill the vacancy.[2]

The committee of trustees corresponded with several persons in relation to the presidency—apparently to no avail. The committee then suggested that someone be appointed on a temporary basis. Accordingly, the trustees elected Professor Jacob F. Bucher as Vice President of the college and Acting President "for the present at a salary of $1500 per annum." The trustees also chose three from among themselves to serve as an advisory committee to act in conjunction with Bucher "until the presidency is filled. . . . "[3]

Bucher was born in St. Louis, Missouri, 20 January 1869. In 1871 his parents moved to Cleveland, Ohio, where he lived for several years. Subsequently the family moved to Cortland, Ohio. In 1889 Bucher graduated from the classical course of Cortland High School. He then entered the College of Physicians and Surgeons of Baltimore, Maryland, and received the degree M. D. in 1893. He briefly practiced medicine, but failing health terminated his work as a physician in 1894. He then began teaching biology and chemistry at the New Lyme Institute at South New Lyme, Ohio. He remained there until 1898, when he resigned to take a year's graduate work in biology at New York State Normal College, at Albany. He then came to Waynesburg College to take charge of the newly established Department of Biology.[4]

For some six years Bucher had been a popular, successful teacher at the college. He assumed his duties as Vice President and Acting President on 13 September 1905. He also taught biology and chemistry. His salary remained at $1,500 per year until 9 September 1907, when it was raised to $1,600. In January 1908 Bucher became ill, first with grippe and then with typhoid fever. Fortunately he was "getting along favorable, and all hoped for his full recovery."[5]

Meanwhile the search for a president of the institution continued. On 14 January 1908, the trustees chose the Reverend William M. Hudson, President. He assumed his duties on 31 March 1908. The trustees also elected Bucher Vice President and Professor of Biology. Unfortunately he again became ill from overwork, fever, and worries which led to insomnia. For months he had little sleep and, in the fall of 1909, he suffered a serious nervous breakdown. He was sent to St. Francis Hospital in Pittsburgh for treatment by an eminent nerve specialist, but his condition deteriorated. Thence he was sent to The Dixmont Hospital for the Insane, where he continued to suffer until his death on 25 July 1912.[6]

William Mestrezat Hudson was born at Kirby, in Greene County, Pennsylvania, on 26 February 1872. He graduated *magna cum laude* from Waynesburg College in 1892. He then attended McCormick Theological Seminary, in Chicago, for one year; thence he transferred to Princeton Seminary, and graduated *cum laude*, with a degree in theology. Subsequently he received two honorary degrees: a D. D. from Tulsa University; and an LL. D. from Illinois College. He was ordained as a Presbyterian minister in 1896. He earned a Ph. D. at Waynesburg College in 1898. While working toward that degree, he served as pastor of the New Providence (Glades) Presbyterian Church at Carmichaels. After leaving that congregation, Hudson served ably as pastor of the First Presbyterian Church, at Clarksburg, West Virginia.[7]

Faculty members and friends of the college looked favorably on the advent of Hudson as President of the College. As an alumnus, he was dedicated to the institution. With his earned degrees from Waynesburg and Princeton, he was highly qualified from the standpoint of education; he had proved to be a successful clergyman. In addition to his duties as President, he taught courses in religion and philosophy. His starting salary was $1,500 per year, plus house rent, beginning with the spring term in 1908. Elaborate plans were made for his inauguration, which took place in Alumni Hall on

17 June 1908. The trustees, faculty, alumni, students, and friends of the college attended.[8] There was general consensus that the trustees had chosen "the right" man.

Hudson diligently went about his duties, and all seemed to be going well. Strangely enough, however, his salary was cut on 17 June 1910 from $1,500 per year, plus rent, to "$1000 and house for the ensuing year." Despite this setback, Hudson continued to work hard at his manifold tasks. Early in April 1911 he and his family moved into the president's home—a new addition to the women's dormitory. Meanwhile he became ill, and submitted his resignation early in June 1911. The trustees reluctantly accepted it, effective on 1 July 1911. Hudson had a farm near Kirby, his birthplace, to which he wanted to go and rest. He had been an able president. And Mrs. Hudson "had a good influence on the youth. The female students liked her." The trustees offered several resolutions in appreciation of Hudson and his services for the college. Hudson next did some preaching in Greene County for approximately one year. In 1912 he regained his health, and he assumed the presidency of Blackburn College, at Carlinville, Illinois.[9]

One of the most important events during these administrations was the reunion of the CP Church and the Presbyterian Church, U. S. A. After some twenty-five years of controversy, certain events made reunion possible. President Miller, the most vocal opponent of reunion, passed away in January 1902. The Confession of Faith of the Presbyterian Church, U. S. A. was revised in 1903, and its doctrine was changed sufficiently "to warrant a union honorable alike" to both churches. The General Assemblies of both approved the union by May 1905. While negotiations for the merger were under way, the trustees were concerned about the status of the college after reunion. A committee of five from their own body made a study of the effects of reunion on the college.[10] Early in October 1904 the Pennsylvania Synod met in McKeesport, where Lewis spoke of the interests of the college; and the Synod planned to meet next in Waynesburg early in January 1905 to make "some arrangements concerning the control of Waynesburg College in view of the proposed church union. . . ."[11]

The CP Synod met in Waynesburg on 10 January 1905. Lewis made an interesting talk on the work of the college. The matter of amending the college charter in view of the proposed reunion was then considered. The aim was to safeguard the interests of the college "for all time, whatever future changes in church relationship may be brought about." The proposed amendment gave "the college a charter similar to that of Washington and Jefferson and other well known colleges which are known as denominational institutions, though their boards of trustees are self perpetuating."[12]

Power to amend the charter of the college was vested in the Court of Common Pleas of Greene County, Pennsylvania. In a petition to that Court on 22 March 1905, the Board of Trustees of the college and the Board of Trust of the Pennsylvania Synod of the CP Church set forth the desired amendments to the charter. One amendment merged the Board of Trust and the Board of Trustees into "the corporation of Waynesburg College." All endowment funds and property which had been owned and controlled by both boards came under the control of the united corporation. The new corporation consisted of one Board of Trustees of twenty-seven persons, all of whom were to be citizens of the United States; at least fourteen were to be citizens of Greene County; and a majority were to be members of the CP Church "or any denomination with which it may unite. . . . " They were to have perpetual succession. Originally they consisted of the twenty-one members of the Board of Trustees, the five members of the Board of Trust, and the president of the college who was an ex-officio member of the Board of Trustees. Nine members were a quorum competent for the transaction of any business other than the election to fill a vacancy in the board or to elect a president of the college.[13] When the churches merged, Waynesburg College was welcomed as one of the institutions in western Pennsylvania under control of the Presbyterian Church, U. S. A. Thenceforth it reported annually to its Pennsylvania Synod and to its Board of Christian Education. No close affiliation was established, however, until 1949 when the College entered into an agreement with the Synod by which it "came directly under the control of the Presbyterian Church." The college's trustees and president thenceforth were to be approved by the Presbyterian Synod of Pennsylvania.[14] In its operation and administration, the college remained practically unsectarian, however.

During the period from Lewis to Hudson the faculty continued to work for modest salaries and no fringe benefits. The most outstanding faculty members in this period were Lewis, Hudson, Waychoff, Ezra D. Stewart, and Edward Martin.[15]

Bucher's case forcefully brought to the attention of the trustees the need for certain fringe benefits for faculty members and their families. Pensions for teachers and insurance to cover hospital costs would be highly desirable. By 1910 Andrew Carnegie had established the Carnegie Foundation for the Advancement of Teaching, but no church-related college could "be admitted to its benefits." When Bucher suffered so seriously from mental illness, it was ascertained that some colleges "not regularly enrolled in the Foundation had been granted aid in such a case as this. . . . " Hence an application was made for Bucher. But it was refused, "because the charter of the Foundation prohibited such aid to church colleges." The problem stemmed from the fact that Waynesburg College required a majority of its trustees to be Presbyterian. Some trustees then wanted to sever the church relation and to affiliate the college with the Carnegie Foundation. The Synod of Pennsylvania was alerted to this problem, and it worked on a plan "by which the necessary funds may be secured."[16] No documents are at hand to throw light on the results of this effort.

The administration and faculty gave close attention to admissions, the curriculum, and academic matters. By 1908 two significant developments had taken place with respect to entrance requirements: the "Academy" had been established in the college to replace the Preparatory Department; and a number of high schools were in operation in the area from which the college could draw students. One could enter Waynesburg College in one of three ways: (1) by completion of the courses in the Academy; (2) by a certificate from an approved high school or academy; and (3) by examination in subjects covered in the Academy. In order to enter an advanced class in the college, one could do so by presenting a certificate from another college; he could transfer into the college, entering at any term except the senior year. One could also gain admission to advanced standing by examination in work done elsewhere to determine his fitness to enter any given class in the college.[17]

Costs to students remained low. Tuition was fifteen dollars per term "in all departments." "The best" board cost three dollars per week in the college commons. With two students to a room, "the best" room could be had for two dollars weekly. At this rental rate, male students could reside in Hanna Hall; and beginning in September 1908, female students could reside in Women's Hall.[18]

With respect to the curriculum, beginning in 1908, the aim of the Academy was "to prepare a student to enter satisfactorily on college work." Students would be thoroughly drilled in rudiments, "thus laying a sure foundation." Stress was on English, Latin, Greek, science and mathematics. The Academy offered a three-year program, consisting of a junior, middle, and senior year for full time students. It also had some "special" students not enrolled in any class. During the academic year 1908-1909, the Academy had sixty-four students, including sixteen juniors, fifteen middle students, eighteen seniors, and fifteen "specials."[19]

By 1909 the "credit system" of computing a student's academic progress, and of determining his classification, had been established. A "credit" was defined as one hour of class work per week during the college year. In order to win a degree a student was required to complete sixty credits in the Academy, or the equivalent in high school, and seventy-two credits in the college.[20]

The Normal Department, with Waychoff as Principal, continued to offer an excellent program. Many competent young people were sent forth to teach in public schools in Greene County and its environs.[21]

At the graduate level, work leading only to the master's degree was offered. Requirements for the A. M. were the same as in preceding years—and comparable to those of other institutions. But enrollment in the graduate program was small. Not more than two students received master's degrees in any given year; and in most years there were no candidates for this degree.[22]

The administration and faculty made every effort to provide the best facilities for the educational process. Some donations to the Library were most valuable. For example, in May 1911 the late Professor Robert Ferguson left to the Library several hundred valuable volumes including the higher classics in Latin, Greek, German, and French. These books were highly prized, and a special alcove was set apart in the Library for them. Early in 1911 a new museum, with Professor Paul R. Stewart as Curator, was established on the second floor of the new building. A call went forth for mineral specimens, fossils, Indian relics, old firearms, swords, and oriental and other foreign articles; donations in money also were welcomed. The Museum contained many useful training aids, particularly in the several sciences.[23]

Early in 1911 the students, directed by Professor C. W. Freitag, organized a Wireless Telegraph Club. They obtained the necessary equipment and set up a wireless telegraph system by which they could receive messages from a distance up to 600 miles; they could transmit them up to 200 miles. This Club originated the "kite idea": they used kites to make contact higher in elevation, and thus increased the distances of reception and transmission. Members of this Club had carefully studied Marconi's ideas in a scientific magazine. They learned that he had gained greater height for his apparatus on the mast of an ocean vessel, and could receive messages 3,600 miles away. This suggested the "kite idea" to them. It was a real contribution to the development of the radio.[24]

The faculty constantly tried to maintain high academic standards. In 1904 a student's work load was defined: "A diligent student is supposed to be able to recite 18 periods per week and to devote two hours of study to preparation for every recitation." In grading a student, recitations were considered first in importance; other considerations were examinations, deportment, and "attendance at all college exercises and at church service once each Sabbath." In 1909 Waynesburg adopted the grading system which was in use at Bowdoin College; it was considered "the best," and was being used by an increasing number of colleges and universities. Bowdoin used letter grades instead of percentages to indicate a student's scholarship. An A represented "complete grasp of material, plus your own insight." B meant "grasp of material, but lacking your own insight." C stood for "partial and fragmentary information—not complete." D meant "you have a few faint traces which the charity of the examiner is able to identify; poor and pitiful as such an exhibition is, we allow a limited number of D's to count toward a degree." E meant "total failure." Two E's "bring a letter to parents and dismissal." Such a letter read, in part, "if the College were to allow you to remain longer under the impression that you were getting an education, it would be receiving money under false pretenses." In the Bowdoin system the letter grades were reduced to numerals for purposes of computing averages: A counted 1; B, 2; C, 3; D, 4; and E, 5.[25]

By 1909 a system was devised by which students could be classified more specifically than ever before. Students, having completed four-fifths of the work in any given year, were classified with that year. If a student lacked one-fifth of the freshman year's work, he was classified as an Academy student. A student could be conditioned in two subjects each year; in order to be advanced to the next year's class, he had to pass examinations which were given at the opening of each year.[26]

In the belief that physical training was essential to a student's welfare, the faculty encouraged football, baseball, basketball, tennis, and track. The athletic program was under the immediate supervision of the faculty through a committee of that body. The faculty aimed to keep athletics clean. The catalogue read: "Professionalism will not be permitted, and the schedule of games must be approved by the faculty."[27]

The purchase of the athletic grounds was a boost for the athletic program. But a gymnasium and adequate bathing facilities were sorely needed. In 1904 athletics "in all departments reached an all time low without being given up entirely." For the next three years the students recruited teams from among themselves, trained them, and "worked hard without compensation while most others stood around and complained about the weak teams. There was no school spirit." Lack of money was a problem. Some boys waited in vain for many months for donations for a gymnasium. Discouraged by the lethargy, in June 1905 they began to create one themselves on the basement floor of the new building. They "fitted up" two rooms—one with a pine floor and wainscoating; and the other with a concrete floor and shower baths and lockers. The boys gave liberally of their own money. When friends in town knew they "meant business," they too gave the boys "handsome donations." To obtain additional funds the girls made candy "and held a candy sale realizing a neat sum." By the fall of 1905, thanks largely to the work of students, the athletic program was again on the upgrade. Aware of the lack of money for athletics, in the fall of 1907 the trustees raised tuition three dollars per term to support such sports. This made possible the "hiring of an athletic director whose sole duty will be to take charge of athletics." The students and trustees resolved to put athletics on a solid basis "without professionalism."[28]

The football team of 1904 deserves much praise. It was made up of the "best material since McKay was President." There were no "hired professionals" on it. The players were "good *students* (italics in original)." All they needed was a coach, some money, and support of the townsmen and student body. Their "pluck and grit" partially compensated for these indispensables. The editor of the student newspaper appealed to townspeople to attend the games, and he urged the girls to help: "Girls, you don't know how much harder a fellow will play when there are a lot of you standing around rooting for him." Coachless, cashless, and cheerless this team played five games. It tied Bethany and lost all the others.[29] Almost solely on their own resources the Waynesburg squad had made gallant efforts and had played clean games against overwhelming odds. The editor of the student paper then defined college spirit simply as "that quality of a student's character which makes him a good all around college man. It makes a fellow manly, loyal, gallant, popular, scholarly, honest, and upright. It may play an innocent prank, but it never prompts a base deed."[30]

For the next two years the football fortunes of the college dipped nearly to the nadir. In January 1906 some said that "football has already gone from Waynesburg College." To be sure, football-wise the institution faced adversities. Semi-professionalism swept this part of Pennsylvania; teams "everywhere were unaccountably stronger." The college made a hard fight for clean football, but it "seemed a losing one." The press carried accounts of the number of deaths annually from football; during the 1905 season some twenty players were killed in the nation. In 1906 some people felt the college should drop football. But the editor of the college paper said: "Granted some are killed, but there are deaths from hunting, swimming, and from automobiles. . . . Shall football go? *No*, a thousand *No's* (italics in original)."[31]

The long-suffering students undoubtedly were relieved and elated when the trustees employed Edward Martin as Athletic Director and Football Coach. Martin was a natural leader of men. His military training and experience stood him in good stead as a coach; he knew the game of football, and was well qualified to serve as Athletic Director. Being an alumnus, he had the interests of the College at heart; his salary was $500 per year. He was immediately successful. Eschewing professionalism, he recruited a squad of twenty-five students, coached them, and led them through the season, winning five games out of six, including four area colleges and two independent teams; the only loss was to Carnegie Institute of Technology by a score of 12 to 0. Eager to help their excellent coach and Athletic Director, in May 1907, a committee of students presented a plan to the trustees for raising $5,000 to help build a gymnasium. But this goal was not reached.[32] In March 1908 the college basketball team played a game, the proceeds of which were used to purchase sweaters for "last year's college football players." At collegiate institutions, it was "customary to award sweaters with the college letter or monogram" to players who had participated in a certain number of intercollegiate contests. Thus the practice was begun at Waynesburg College.[33] The season record for 1908 was four victories and two defeats; the losses were against Carnegie Institute of Technology and Washington and Jefferson College. Martin yearned for the time to come when the Waynesburg College team would be on a par with the best in western Pennsylvania.[34]

While Martin served as Athletic Director of the college, he was also practicing law and engaged in other work. It appears that the pressure of other duties impelled him to give up his services for the college by mid-1909. He later referred to his good athletes many of whom had

> taken a very prominent part as citizens. Hook became a judge; Ray and Montgomery, outstanding lawyers. Ross, Lippincott, Parkinson, Biddle, Mosca and Clutter became good businessmen. Andrews became a prominent physician. Stewart, Parkinson, and Rinehart became outstanding educators. Stewart is the marvelous President of Waynesburg College. Debolt became a very famous minister.[35]

The college's football fortunes fell immediately after Martin left. The 1909 season was a losing one—with one victory, four defeats, and one tie. The team, coached by a man named Louder, was light in comparison with opposing teams. In June 1910 the trustees employed another coach, Clarence W. Freitag, a "product of Washington and Jefferson College, at an annual salary of $1,200." In addition to his coaching duties, Freitag taught mathematics. He worked hard and was successful; during the 1910 season the team won four games, lost three, and tied one.[36]

A number of men on the football squad also played basketball, which came into its own during the days of Lewis, Bucher, and Hudson. The main handicap to basketball was lack of an adequate floor. By 1904 a basketball court had been improvised on the fourth floor of the new building; located on the west side, it was directly over Philo Hall. It was called the "Chicken Coop," because the rafters were covered with chicken wire to keep the ball from getting away. It was far too small; an average player could stand under one basket and pitch the ball through the hoop on the other end. The floor, made of poor quality pine, was splintery and perforated with knotholes; it was not only too small, but most hazardous. Players frequently came from practice or from games with splinters in their knees and elbows. The games, most of which were intramural, attracted students and townsmen, who ascended the three flights of stairs, climbed a ladder from the third to the fourth floors, and sat on uncomfortable benches on the sidelines. The next basketball court was on the third floor of the Reagan building on South Morris Street. This floor also was inadequate; hoops were located in alcoves at opposite ends of the court, which impeded scoring. Basketball was played next on the ground floor of what was called the "Union Transit Building" also located on South Morris Street;

subsequently, for many years, this floor served as a garage for buses of the Union Transit Company. Later the Armory, located on Washington Street, was used for basketball games. Players on the first varsity basketball team were John I. Hook (later Judge Hook), Bird Clutter, Lloyd Pollock, John Ross, and Harvey Andrew.[37]

Basketball reached one of its highest points in the history of athletics at Waynesburg College while Martin was Athletic Director. During the 1908-1909 season the team lost only one game "to a Hans Wagner team from Carnegie, Pennsylvania." Most games were played against area colleges; a few were against independent teams. The climax came when Waynesburg won against Carnegie Institute of Technology in a game in the Armory. Members of that team had been "acknowledged champions of western Pennsylvania." In defeating them, Waynesburg won "one of the finest victories ever achieved in local athletics."[38] By 1910 the Waynesburg College Basketball League had been formed in order to give more students an opportunity to participate. There was a series of games among these teams; the better teams were ascertained by play-offs. And a championship game was played annually.[39]

In baseball the college continued to play teams in the tri-state area. The chief opponents were Bethany, California Normal, Muskingum, the University of Pittsburgh, and Washington and Jefferson. It was customary to play each opponent twice in a season. Waynesburg's team competed respectably against these formidable opponents.[40]

Among other "spring sports," tennis and track are noteworthy. When Martin became Athletic Director greater emphasis was laid on track. In the belief that as many students as possible should participate, he organized a series of interclass field and track contests of all kinds. Teams from all classes, including the Academy and the Normals, worked-out in these sports and selected the best in each. Then, late in May 1908, an "Inter-class Field Meet" was held, which attracted 1,000 spectators. No records were set. But competition was keen, and many students had the opportunity to participate. The class "Field Day" in the spring of 1909 "far surpassed any preceding event of this sort." Despite a heavy rain, a good crowd attended. Trophies, consisting of letters and flags, were awarded to winners.[41]

In the hope of increasing interest in track, in the spring of 1910 the college initiated "Field Day" for high schools in Greene

County. The interclass contests for college students took place in the morning; and contests with high school students as participants were held in the afternoon. The first "Waynesburg College Field Day" on a county-wide basis was held on 12 May 1910. It attracted wide attention, and was considered "the most important college event of the season. . . . " Five of the six high schools in the County sent contestants. They were Center, Cumberland, Jefferson, Morris, and Richhill; Monongahela did not enter a team.[42] In sponsoring a field day for high schools, the college aided them in the promotion of track, effected better liaison with them, and found an avenue to good public relations.

The athletic program instilled in students the spirit of good sportsmanship and fair play. But students at times engaged in contests of a frivolous nature. For example, in June 1905 there was a "strenuous contest" between the freshmen and sophomores. Early one morning the freshmen flew their flag from the college tower. The sophomores spied it, and soon a battle ensued. The seniors joined the sophomores and juniors joined the freshmen. The contest was waged along the stairways in the building and the colors were captured by the sophomores. The battle was continued upon the campus and in the park, "where a freshman and two sophomores received a ducking in the lake." At the climax of the fray, Lewis appeared upon the scene, and as a result many of the students retreated. A long session of the faculty in the afternoon caused much anxiety on the part of the participants.[43] There is no evidence, however, that the students were punished. Doubtless the faculty felt they were just "letting off steam"—and forgave them.

Interest in the literary societies continued. One of the most popular topics discussed at meetings was football. Most members of both societies regularly attended the games. Debate questions then showed that students were interested in relations between the United States and Latin America, particularly those nations in the Caribbean area.[44] In the annual contests the two literary societies were quite evenly matched. By 1906 the honors stood at 261 1/2 for Philo and 245 1/2 for Union.[45]

In 1906 an ambiguity concerning the relationship of students in the Normal Department to the literary societies was clarified. Students in that Department were defined as those who had "more than half their work in the Normal Department." They were given a choice between doing regular work in a literary society or in a class to meet once weekly for a double period to be called "School Economy and Methods of Instruction," which was designed to aid students who entered the teaching profession.[46]

A new development between 1904 and 1911, which was to affect social life on the campus, was the founding of social fraternities and sororities. These organizations, together with increasing emphasis on athletic sports, eventually led to the decline and fall of literary societies. By 1908 the Phi Sigma Fraternity was thriving on the campus. During commencement week in June of that year it held an elaborate banquet in the Blair Hotel, with seventy-five persons present. Among the speakers were Edward Martin '01, J. Boyd Crumrine '02, and T. S. Crago '92. It was "a most enjoyable affair."[47]

Early in January 1911, Nu Chapter of Delta Sigma Phi, a national fraternity, was organized by students at the college. Officers of the chapter were installed by Richard Toeplitz from the national office in New York City. The eighteen charter members secured rooms in the J. W. Iams Building at the corner of Franklin and Washington Streets. Several members resided there.[48] By May 1911 two sororities, Alpha Gamma Theta and Theta Pi Sigma, had been organized on campus. Although these were essentially social organizations, they promoted scholarship of their members, participated in athletics, and welcomed back alumni who had respectively been members during undergraduate days.[49]

If the several aspects of student life were important, so was the field of finance. Income from tuition remained low, and costs of board and room were kept down. It was estimated that a student's expenses for one year totaled $200.00. Those who cooked for themselves in small groups could live on much less.[50] Children of ministers "not engaged in some other calling," or of foreign missionaries, were charged one-half the regular tuition and fees. Likewise ministerial students were charged one-half the regular fee. They were required to sign a pledge to repay the treasurer of the college all fees remitted to them in the event they entered any profession other than the ministry.[51]

For several years, beginning in 1904, the most urgent financial needs of the college were reiterated in annual catalogues. These included "endowment of $25,000 each for two additional professorships, a women's dormitory costing $10,000, and a heating plant costing about $5,000. These would greatly increase the efficiency of the institution. Any one of these gifts would "entitle the donor to give a name to the benefaction."[52] A year later the estimated amount needed for the dormitory was increased to $30,000. And still a year later, in addition to these requests, a call went forth for $25,000 for a science hall and $10,000 for a gymnasium.[53]

In February 1906, after the reunion of the churches, management of the endowment fund was transferred from the Board of Trust of the Pennsylvania Synod of the CP Church to the treasurer of the trustees' Finance Committee.[54] The college's new sponsor was stronger than the CP Church had ever been. The United Presbyterian Church, U. S. A., though it was strongest in the North, was nationwide in scope; it was not confined to the trans-Appalachian West as the CP Church had been; and its Synod of Pennsylvania was statewide in scope, and not confined to western Pennsylvania as the CP Synod had been. The trustees did not hesitate to ask its new sponsor for funds. On 26 April 1907 they requested $2,000 from the College Board of that church, but there is no evidence that anything was granted. On 3 June 1909 they "most earnestly" requested an appropriation of $2,000 "for maintenance of Waynesburg College for the coming collegiate year." But only $500 was forthcoming, which the trustees happily accepted. On 13 October 1910 they requested an appropriation of $2,000 "for contingent expenses" for the year 1910-1911. Only $1,500 was granted, however.[55]

In June 1906, a campaign was started to raise funds for a new science hall. This drive was greatly boosted when Andrew Carnegie agreed to give the college $25,000 on condition that it would be matched by donations from others. The trustees called on Bucher to head this campaign; and three of their own body agreed to help him. The editor of a local paper referred to Carnegie's generosity, and said: "Friends of Waynesburg College cannot afford to see this offer go by. Join in and push this to success."[56] It appears, however, that his exhortation was fruitless for no science hall was built. A golden opportunity was missed. Bucher must have worried over his lack of success in raising funds, which doubtless contributed to his nervous breakdown three years later.

Simultaneously the drive continued for funds to endow the A. B. Miller Chair of Philosophy. This effort started shortly after his death. Pledges ranging from $10 up to $500 had been made; they were supposed to be "bona fide subscriptions." The amount of endowment originally contemplated for this Chair was $25,000. In June 1909, the trustees considered its establishment, but not all subscriptions had been paid. Late in November 1910, they called on their attorney to notify all subscribers to the A. B. Miller fund "to pay same and, on failure to do so within a reasonable time, to proceed to collect the same."[57] It appears that this effort too fell short of the goal.

Another aim during the administrations of Lewis, Bucher, and Hudson was to secure funds for a women's dormitory. In 1907 the college was fortunate that local members in the state legislature were interested in its welfare; D. S. Walton was a senator; and James Rush, a representative. The trustees applied for an appropriation of $30,000.00 to pay for "a dormitory for the use of young ladies" attending the college. But Governor Stuart had to reduce all appropriation bills that year to keep them within income. He approved an appropriation of $15,000.00 for which the trustees were grateful. On 20 June 1907 they passed a resolution, "That the thanks of this board are due . . . Senator D. S. Walton and Representative James Rush . . . for their earnest and faithful service in securing a state appropriation of $15,000.00 to Waynesburg College to be used in the erection of a Ladies Dormitory." The Alumni Association also extended a vote of thanks to these men for having secured this appropriation. The "lowest and best" bid for construction of the building was $16,990.00 In June 1908, therefore, the trustees borrowed $1,990.00 in order to pay for the building "completed according to contract."[58]

The college welcomed even small fees and donations. In April 1907, the trustees agreed to charge an admission fee of ten cents to the grandstand on the athletic grounds; this income would help finance the athletic program. Beginning in 1904 the Music Department was required to pay two dollars to the college per term for each student enrolled in it. In 1909 the college received ten dollars from the Old Concord Church to purchase maps; and three dollars from the Mapletown Church for the same purpose. Simultaneously the Waynesburg Women's Club made several donations, including a twenty-five volume set of orations from Homer to McKinley; it gave valuable works also to the Science Department. At the same time Hudson gave the college a twenty-nine volume set of the *Encyclopedia Brittanica.*[59]

The trustees frequently were forced to borrow money, giving part of the college's property as security. For example in July 1908, they borrowed $5,000 for two years, at six per cent interest payable semiannually. For security they mortgaged the land on which the girls' dormitory was built. If notes became due and funds were not available to pay them, they would be renewed. The trustees relied on two local banks for help in times of financial crises.[60]

The trustees chose a committee of three from their own body and gave them responsibility for the construction of the ladies' dormitory. This committee presented a plan of a building eighty-five feet long and thirty-nine feet wide; it was to be three stories high with a large veranda. The first floor would have a large dining hall, reception rooms, kitchen, and rooms for the matron. The second and third floors would have twenty-two rooms for students in addition to bathrooms. The basement would have a laundry and storage room. A centralized heating system—either steam or hot water—was to be installed "in the most modern manner." The dining hall was to be large enough to accommodate one hundred boarders. The rooms were to be sufficient for some forty young women. And the president of the college, his family, and two faculty members also could live there. The building would have "a commons" for young men, and forty-odd could meet "around this common table." A special college bulletin described this building and asked: "*Where could you find a school home more suited to the needs of your daughter than here* (italics in original)?" While Hudson was President a wing was added to the women's dormitory. Called "the President's House," it was built at a cost of $6,000 which was raised by Hudson and his immediate successors.[61]

Better housing was also provided for the young men. By 1905 Hanna Hall had "been completely overhauled and repaired so as to make it a dormitory." New, attractive furniture was procured; all rooms and corridors were papered and painted; and bathroom facilities were installed on the third floor. During 1905 and 1906 some thirty young men lived there "at a very low figure." And meals were served to a much larger number at greatly reduced cost.[62]

The trustees made certain that buildings were repaired and properly maintained. For example, in September 1904, they directed their Committee on Buildings and Grounds "to repair stone window caps in [the] new college building that are out of place." At the same time they directed that committee "to make the best contract possible for electric lights for the college, and the two literary societies are required to pay for the electric lighting of their respective halls."[63]

The security of the college buildings was a constant concern of the trustees. In July 1907, they authorized their treasurer to carry $40,000.00 insurance on the buildings. In March 1910, they directed the Committee on Buildings and Grounds "to have two fire escapes erected to the new college building as directed by the factory inspector." In June 1910, they accepted a proposition from a Pittsburgh firm "to erect two fire escapes to the new college building for $455.00 . . . in accordance with requirements of the Factory Inspector of Pennsylvania. . . . "[64]

With respect to college grounds, the trustees made a deal in March 1910, which aided the institution financially. At that time the Waynesburg and Blacksville Railway Company planned to build a railroad through Waynesburg. This firm needed "a certain strip or lot of ground off the southern part of the college athletic grounds" over which to construct a portion of the railroad track. The transfer of this property to the Railroad Company called for the removal of the grandstand on the athletic grounds. The trustees unanimously agreed to sell this strip for $1,600.00. Fortunately for the college, this sum was sufficient to pay off the mortgage on the athletic grounds.[65] The college at last had a clear deed to that property.

During the administrations of Lewis, Bucher, and Hudson the college moved forward on most fronts. But little was accomplished in raising the endowment fund. The terms of these presidents were brief and seemingly transient. After Hudson retired to his farm, the trustees looked for a good man to succeed him.

XI
PATTON AND BAKER

AFTER HUDSON RESIGNED, THE TRUSTEES, IN JUNE 1911, APPOINTED Professor Henry Dudley Patton, a member of the faculty, as Vice President and Acting President of the college. He efficiently handled administrative matters and taught for a year while the quest for a president was under way.[1]

Patton was born near Fayette City, in Fayette County, Pennsylvania, 28 July 1845. As a youth he joined the local CP Church; at the time of reunion of the churches in 1905, he became a Presbyterian. He briefly attended California Normal School, not far from his birthplace. After securing a teacher's certificate, he taught public school in that area for several terms. Later he briefly pursued further studies at Massachusetts State Normal School at Westfield, Massachusetts. Thence he transferred to Waynesburg College, and graduated in the class of 1872, in the classical course. Right after graduation, he was elected to the Waynesburg College faculty, and he taught mathematics and languages until 1875. He then resigned to take a position in the Academy at Jersey Shore, Pennsylvania. A year later he returned to his *Alma Mater* as Professor of Greek and Latin which he taught until 1881. He then became principal of the Youngsville (Pennsylvania) school system, but he soon left teaching to attend Franklin and Marshall Theological Seminary and prepare himself for the clergy; he later received a D. D. from that institution. He also studied law and was admitted to the bar "not with the intention to practice, however." With such a versatile educational background, he decided to go on the lecture platform. For some thirty years he was a reformer, especially in the anti-liquor movement, which, he believed, involved the welfare of the race and perpetuity of free government. For many years he was a national figure in the prohibition movement, and a great lecturer on temperance. From 1895 to 1915 he was Pennsylvania State Chairman of the Prohibition Party. In the election campaign of 1908, he was candidate for Vice President of the United States on the Prohibition ticket. After the trustees employed a president of the college, Patton remained on the faculty until 1919, when he resigned due to age and illness. He had wanted to be in Waynesburg "for the sake of home life, after a long period of travel." Patton lived to see the passage of the Eighteenth Amendment, a great landmark in the cause for which he fought. He died on 8 December 1922, and was buried in Greene Mount Cemetery. Friends of Waynesburg College revered him. He was always willing to sacrifice time, money, and energy for his *Alma Mater.*[2]

During the year Patton served as acting president there were several constructive developments. The Library Committee solicited funds for magazines and periodicals which were greatly needed in the reference department. Subscriptions were small, "but the good spirit with which our citizens respond is very helpful and encouraging." The total amount raised was sufficient to acquire many top magazines including the *Atlantic Monthly*, *American Magazine*, *Century Magazine*, *Current Literature*, *Harpers*, *Ladies Home Journal*, *Literary Digest*, *McClures*, *North American Review*, and *Outlook*. Publishers of local newspapers regularly donated their papers to the college. Encouraged by Patton, the students published an excellent yearbook entitled *The Athenian*, which portrayed many aspects of life on the campus.[3]

In April 1912 Patton and the trustees adopted a method of recruiting students which proved to be helpful. By that time several high schools were in operation in Greene County. The college faculty was requested "to designate one of its members to attend each of the High School Commencements in Greene County in the interest of the College and to solicit students. . . . " The trustees agreed to pay necessary expenses of individuals who went on such missions.[4]

Aware of the agrarian nature of Greene County and surrounding areas, Patton promoted the establishment of an Agriculture Department in the college. The aim was to train students in the basics of agriculture and horticulture and to give information and advice to area farmers and gardeners. This Department, headed by Professor Paul R. Stewart, rendered excellent service not only to students, but also to residents in the Waynesburg area and all over the county. Among other things Stewart and his students produced each spring excellent varieties of plants "for distribution among growers in this neighborhood." Their plants included cabbage, cauliflower, and tomatoes, which were put on sale at Hills Flower Store on Main (now High) Street in Waynesburg at a uniform price of ten cents per dozen plants. There was great demand for these plants. Hence they were limited to two dozen of any variety to one person to get as wide a distribution as possible among Greene County growers. These varieties were carefully selected as a result of experimentation and were "most perfectly adapted to local soil and climatic conditions."[5]

Early in May 1912 the search committee of the trustees recommended the selection of the Reverend Ezra F. Baker, a member of the faculty of Huron College, Huron, South Dakota, "to the presidency at a salary of $1500 per annum and use of the President's house. . . . " On 14 June the trustees unanimously elected him. Born in Butler County, in Kentucky, in 1869, Baker as a youth moved with his parents to Garden City, Kansas, where he completed high school work. He entered Missouri Valley College and graduated in 1898 with the A. B. degree. He next attended the Theological Department of Cumberland University, completed the course there in 1901, and served as pastor of the CP Church in Harrisonville, Missouri, from 1901 to 1903. For the next five years he took graduate work at Columbia University, winning the Ph. D.; simultaneously he spent a part of the time as a student at Union Theological Seminary. On completion of his studies at the latter institution, he was ordained as a Presbyterian preacher. In 1908 he became Professor of Philosophy and Bible at Trinity University, then located at Waxahachie, Texas. He spent the academic year 1910-1911 at the University of Berlin studying philosophy, theology, and the German language. While in Europe he traveled to Egypt, Palestine, and Syria. On returning to America, he held the chair of philosophy at Huron College for the year 1911-1912. Baker obviously was well educated; he had wide experience as a preacher and lecturer, and he apparently had been successful as a teacher at Trinity and Huron. Right after his arrival in Waynesburg, he met with students, faculty, and trustees, and told them his chief aims were to recruit more students and a topflight faculty; he was especially eager to recruit additional faculty members. At Waynesburg, in addition to his duties as president of the college, he taught philosophy and Bible.[6]

A devout clergyman, Baker stressed "the awfulness of sin in the sight of God and the terrible retribution that comes upon the sinner." He regretted that some preachers were drifting away from the fundamentals of the Gospel. He frequently preached in area churches, condemning man's depravity and urging all to seek salvation. He usually asked congregations for donations to Waynesburg College, often with considerable success.[7]

In accord with plans, Baker quickly doubled the faculty. In August 1912 the trustees employed three faculty members, "for the ensuing college year," and authorized Baker "to fill all other vacancies in the faculty of the college on the best terms possible." Baker promptly proceeded to do so, and to employ several additional faculty members. To meet the added expense, he personally began raising funds; he shortly raised $3,000; and he hoped to get $10,000 more from friends in New York City, "provided Waynesburg and Greene County and friends in adjoining counties make a good showing." Hopefully all this money, plus the income from tuition, would go for faculty salaries. All departments would be stronger; the faculty, would be "second to none." If we exclude the Departments of Music and Expression, by August 1913, the faculty consisted of seventeen full-time members, most of whom were hired by Baker. Of these, six held the earned doctorate. A local editor boasted that all faculty members "are most capable." The college bulletin referred to these "strong Christian men and women, educated in the best universities in the nation. . . . " Happy over his success in building the faculty, Baker was the college's first president to refer to his faculty members as "specialists." Unfortunately, within a year, all those with the terminal degree left, except two—one being Baker.[8]

At Baker's behest, five part-time preachers were employed to teach courses in religion and philosophy, requisites for the baccalaureate degree. This seemed an excessive number of teachers, for only sixty-one students were studying toward that goal. Baker explained that these ministers came from local churches and were working gratis. He contended "they have been a great re-enforcement [*sic*] not only from the standpoint of education, but their spiritual and moral influence has been very helpful."[9]

Members of the Music Department had never been considered a part of the regular faculty of the college; they were a separate, yet related, organization. Because they frequently aided in chapel services, in July 1914, Baker recommended that all teachers in that Department "be employed by the Board of Trustees"; that all music students be required to matriculate in the college with the Dean or Registrar; that all music fees and tuitions be paid "to our treasurer"; and that all boarding music students be required to take at least one course in the literary department. The trustees considered Baker's proposals—and dropped them.[10]

Salaries of faculty members were low. In June 1913 the trustees increased Baker's salary by $500, making it $2,000 per year; and he resided in the president's house free from rent. Most other faculty salaries, however, ranged from $1,000 down to $200 per year, depending on the amount of service rendered. The college paid railroad fares of new faculty members who came from distant points such as New York and Chicago. In addition to their salaries, several faculty members were given a home in the dormitory.[11]

Baker made several suggestions which were aimed at academic improvement of the institution. In August 1912 the length of the college year was "fixed at nine months or 36 weeks, instead of ten months or 40 weeks as heretofore." The recitation periods were lengthened from forty-five minutes to one hour. In the grading system, letter grades were continued and were determined on a percentage basis: an A equaled 96 to 100 percent; a B, 90 to 95 percent; a C, 82 to 89 percent; a D, 75 to 81 percent; and E was below 75 percent, or failure. The curriculum in the Academy, the former Preparatory Course, was extended from a three- to a four-year program. It was then considered "equivalent to a *first class high* school (italics in original)." Graduates of the Academy received a diploma which would admit them to the freshman class of the best colleges and universities in the country. Students who completed common school could be admitted to the first year's work in the Academy. Those who graduated from a "second class high school may be admitted to the senior year of the Academy, provided they agree to make up any studies in which they may be deficient." A Course Committee was created to help "irregular students" come up to standards so they "may as quickly as possible become 'regular' either in the Academy or in the College." Other changes included the addition of a Business Department, and the requirement of a thesis for the baccalaureate degree.[12]

In his report to the trustees in June 1913, Baker said he was compelled to double the faculty and to make the foregoing changes "in order to properly standardize Waynesburg College. . . . " He claimed that after coming to Waynesburg, he made an investigation of the college, found that it was a fourth grade institution, and that a graduate from the college had to take about two years of work in a standard college for admission into the graduate department of standard universities. He said that in 1911 Waynesburg

College was dropped from the accredited list of colleges because of its classification. His paramount object was to reestablish its accreditation. In order to do so several new departments had to be opened and several new teachers had to be employed. He then told of his troubles in recruiting faculty members. Between May and September 1912, he made two trips to New York City, and spent several days each time interviewing candidates. But by that time, the best ones had already been employed. By the fall of 1913, however, he was fortunate to employ several capable faculty members.[13]

Despite early difficulties in recruiting faculty members, in November 1912 a visiting committee of the Pennsylvania Synod of the Presbyterian Church came to the college and praised Baker's work. A committee member remarked that "Waynesburg College came to us by inheritance from the Cumberland Church and its revised charter requires that a majority of its Board of Trustees shall be members of the Presbyterian church." The committee referred to Waynesburg's good location in oil, gas, and coal fields. Without raising the cost of education, "it is proposed to raise the college from the fourth grade to that of a second grade institution. This in fact has already been done." Changes in the calendar and curriculum, and attempts to strengthen the faculty, put the college on a par with "any of our higher grade colleges, with the exception of our great universities with which it has no ambition to compete." Members of Synod's committee were pleased with the physical plant—"the large, substantial building, the new dormitory and President's House, and fair equipment, but like all colleges it needs friends and funds." Most important, plans were made by this commiteee and local college and church officials for a meeting of Synod in Waynesburg.[14]

An advertisement of the college in 1914 throws light on the academic program. The college entrance requirements were completion of 14 1/2 "Carnegie Units" or graduation from a first class high school. Normally a student who took all his work at Waynesburg College spent four years in its Academy and four years at the college level. A six-week summer term was offered. Meeting six days weekly, it included courses which were offered during the regular sessions; and credits earned were counted toward graduation.[15]

The problem of student absences still troubled the faculty. It appears that church attendance on the Sabbath was no longer required. After four absences from class or chapel, however, students were compelled to take extra examinations. Students who were tardy at class or chapel were marked absent. Baker wanted to apply these same rules to attendance at literary society, but the faculty took no action in the matter.[16]

In December 1914 the faculty took certain steps to maintain sound academic standards. The practice of excusing students from examinations on account of high grades was discontinued. Athletes were exhorted to be studious and diligent; students holding athletic scholarships were required to take at least the minimum load of ten hours' work, "and otherwise live up to the rules of the school. . . . " They were warned that if they failed to do so, they would be "dropped from the school at once."[17]

The graduate program had been discontinued, but, interestingly enough, in January 1915 the Reverend J. T. Neel of Donora, Pennsylvania, requested the college to confer upon him a Ph. D. He claimed that President Miller had promised him this degree "many years ago . . . for work done, partially at least, under the guidance of the faculty of Cumberland University. . . . " The trustees referred this request to its Committee on Honorary Degrees. But the Ph. D. was conferred, as an earned degree, on Neel on 11 June 1915.[18]

For some years after Miller's administration, certain large universities hesitated to accept graduates of Waynesburg College into their graduate schools. As we have seen, Farabee, a graduate of Waynesburg in 1894, was so brilliant at Harvard that he attracted many other Waynesburg graduates, whom Harvard welcomed. By 1915, however, there was some doubt about the quality of Waynesburg's academic program and the ability of its graduates to pursue successfully the work required in leading graduate schools. An insight into such skepticism came from Columbia University:

> We have gone over the matter of the rating of the Bachelor's degree of Waynesburg College with great care in the light of additional information and have decided to put your college upon our accepted list as entitling the holders of your A. B. and B. S. degrees to matriculate at Columbia University on the normal basis, beginning with 1915 degrees. We . . . shall reserve the right, which, of course, is ours, to scrutinize carefully the records made with us by your students until we are quite satisfied that the rating indicated is the correct one. Students with your degrees before 1915 we think should in every case submit their individual record for such adjustment as may appear to us to be necessary. This does not, of course, mean that your students will be discriminated against in any way. . . . [19]

The most important event during Baker's administration was the meeting of the Pennsylvania Synod of the Presbyterian Church, U. S. A. in Waynesburg. Baker earlier attended Synod's annual meeting held in Butler, Pennsylvania, where he "presented Waynesburg College's claims very well." Arrangements were there made to hold the next annual meeting in Waynesburg; Philadelphia and Uniontown wanted this meeting, but they agreed to withdraw their invitations in the interests of Waynesburg College. In the hope of making a most favorable impression on Synod, Baker was anxious that the buildings be in top condition and that the grounds be beautified. He even wanted the trustees to confer with the town council "to induce them, if possible, to pave Washington Street from the laundry up to First Avenue . . . before the coming of Synod." He was firmly convinced that unless these needed improvements were made, Synod would have a bad impression of the college. He said that many friends had given him money in order to prepare for the advent of this, "the greatest and richest Presbyterian synod in the world." He wanted the trustees and faculty to cooperate with local churches in doing everything possible for the entertainment and comfort of Synod's delegates. The event was considered "a great thing for Waynesburg."[20]

The Synod met in Waynesburg from 21 to 23 October 1913. Statewide in scope, it embraced 21 presbyteries, 1,168 churches, and 283,142 members. The opening meeting was held in the auditorium of the Presbyterian Church, with 175 ministers and delegates present. Sessions during each day took place in Alumni Hall. The general theme was the necessity of increasing church memberships. Near the close of the meeting, Baker stated the needs of the college which included a steam heating plant, a science hall, and a gymnasium. He said he had started a campaign to raise $500,000 of endowment money, and he believed the people in Waynesburg would give $150,000. The visiting delegates considered Baker an able man. They honored him by electing him as Vice Moderator and as a member of the Synod's College Board.[21]

In July 1914 Baker attempted to effect a closer relationship between the Synod and the college. He recommended to the trustees that the college's charter be revised to bring the institution directly under the control of Synod, that members of the Board of Trustees henceforth be elected by Synod, and that two-thirds of them be Presbyterians. He and officers of the Board of Trustees drafted a proposed revision of the charter providing for twenty-five trustees, the manner of their election, and their tenure in office. Simultaneously the alumni presented a new proposal for the election of alumni trustees. But the trustees took no action on these proposals.[22]

Baker believed that closer affiliation with Synod would facilitate fund raising. At its meeting in June 1912, the Alumni Association discussed "things for the betterment of Waynesburg College." That body maintained that all Greene Countians, regardless of denomination, should help the College. For several years, local people seemed to lack interest in the institution. Baker and the trustees looked not only for donations from individuals, but to the state legislature for financial aid. In April 1913 a Committee on Appropriations from the House of Representatives came to inspect the college. The trustees had asked for an appropriation of $25,000 for a gymnasium and $2,000 to install a steam heating plant in the main building. These efforts were fruitless, however.[23]

Late in 1913 Baker launched a campaign to raise endowment to $500,000 within three years. He sought the support of Synod and all Presbyterians interested in giving their children a Christian education. Despite a lack of local interest in the college, Baker believed he could raise at least $100,000 in Waynesburg. If he could do so, he felt sure he could raise $400,000 from outside donors. He contended that some people in Greene County had "plenty of money and no children. They could *help* Waynesburg College (Baker's italics)." But subscriptions over ten months totaled only $8,336.35; and the amount actually paid in that time was $6,366.35. He hoped for heavy contributions in Waynesburg, but in the first ten months the amount subscribed there was only $3,921.35; and the sum actually paid was considerably less.[24]

Baker claimed that his duties at the college greatly limited his work in the field. In July 1914 he told the trustees: "Most all colleges have what is known as a field man whose business it is to travel continually throughout the territory of the college and solicit students and also subscriptions for current expenses. . . . " He said he had already negotiated with the Reverend Clement McKee of Washington, Pennsylvania. McKee's services could be secured for $1,200 per year, plus his traveling expenses. He had an automobile which he would use, if employed. McKee was well acquainted with this area, where he had served for several years as Superintendent of Home Missions. The trustees approved Baker's plan, and McKee got the job.[25]

Meanwhile the college was running in debt. In March 1914 the trustees directed their Finance Committee to examine the college's debts "and ascertain the amount of money needed to liquidate the same. . . . " Tuition and fees were low; and gifts were not generous. The trustees were forced to borrow money to meet current expenses. In January 1915 the college was fortunate to receive $500 from the Presbyterian Church, but this sum was applied on the deficit of the preceding year.[26]

On Baker's recommendation, the trustees adopted certain measures to attract the best graduates of high schools. In July 1914 they approved the awarding of scholarships consisting of free matriculation and tuition fees for one year to first honor graduates of first class high schools.[27] Simultaneously the Alumni Association decided to give a student of Greene County high schools a scholarship to Waynesburg College. To start with the school year beginning in September 1914, it was to be offered on competitive examinations to any student having completed three years' work. The examinations were to be in mathematics, English, and political history of the United States.[28]

In January 1915 the trustees broadened their scholarship program to attract more students. A two-year scholarship was granted to the honor graduate of any first class high school with over 500 students; and a one-year scholarship was available to a student with second highest honors from such high schools. Also a one-year scholarship was tendered to the top honor student from any first-class high school with less than 500 students. All students winning scholarships were required to use them during the year immediately following graduation.[29]

In the belief that brawn as well as brains should be rewarded, Baker would offer scholarships to athletes—to the point of straining the budget and running in the red. All students in the Academy and in the college were urged to participate in athletics. It was generally conceded that students "can study better after exercise." But funds were needed to finance athletics. Other colleges required an athletic fee along with tuition and fees for laboratory and matriculation. Therefore, the trustees, beginning in September 1912, required each student to pay an athletic fee of $1.50 at the beginning of each term for athletic purposes, which entitled a student to a season ticket to all athletic games of the term. The Faculty Athletic Committee assisted the athletic program in every way possible. As a means of raising funds, the student body presented theatrical performances, and all proceeds went for the benefit of athletics. In June 1913 Baker recommended to the trustees that at least two athletic scholarships be provided as an inducement for young men to come from other cities to Waynesburg College. The trustees approved his recommendation, and at first the number was limited to two; in September 1914 three additional scholarships were granted in full to football players. In order further to promote athletics, the college applied for membership in the Western Pennsylvania Athletic Association composed of Allegheny, Geneva, Grove City, and Westminster colleges, and Carnegie Institute of Technology. Membership in this association facilitated better scheduling in all lines of sports.[30]

In the fall of 1914 football at the college became tainted with professionalism. The faculty found that "many football men had not matriculated . . . and some . . . expect to receive salaries for playing on the team. . . . " The faculty was strongly opposed to unclean athletics. Baker verified the findings of the faculty, and said he would demand clean football; and the trustees fully concurred. The Faculty Athletic Committee, considering itself as an advisory group only, consulted with students "to get their views and to help them adjust the matter." Members of this Committee called in several players and were most pleasantly surprised by their attitude. One player said the Athletic Association had recently adopted a constitution containing a provision "that they would get rid of professionalism in the school, and they had adopted a resolution that no one could be on the team unless he were a regular student." The Faculty Athletic Committee believed it best to assist the Athletic Association in solving the problem themselves. The latter declared they "would get all their boys to line up in school, and those receiving salaries would be dropped." The students thus handled the matter; players guilty of these irregularities were dropped. The faculty approved the Athletic Association's action. Professionalism or not, Waynesburg's football team suffered three losing seasons while Baker was President.[31]

The students were enthusiastic about basketball, but their gravest handicap was lack of a suitable floor. In December 1912 the editor of the college newspaper exhorted them: "Let us all get together and give our help toward renting a basketball hall." Unable to secure a suitable court, their only alternative was to practice and play in the "Chicken Coop." They seemed happy to have it. By January 1913 they had greatly improved it; bleachers were constructed which would "easily seat 200 persons"; and electric lights were installed. The college newspaper stretched the truth a bit in saying: "Though the room is small, it is well adapted to basketball." With

George Wisecarver as manager, a league was formed, consisting of teams from the college, from the academy, and from the local high school. The freshmen and juniors combined, and the sophomore and senior teams combined, in order to have four evenly matched teams. From the best players a good varsity team was organized. In the winter of 1913 the varsity played Broaddus, Davis and Elkins, Fairmont Normal, Salem, and West Virginia Wesleyan.[32] Despite having to practice in the "Chicken Coop," this team made a good showing against its neighbors in the "Mountaineer State."

Baseball, track, and tennis dipped to the nadir. The athletic grounds were well suited to baseball and track; on campus there was a suitable tennis court. In June 1913 the trustees secured the use of a half acre of ground for another tennis court.[33] There is no evidence that these sports were stressed, however.

Baker lamented that his most difficult task was to awaken the students spiritually. To that end, in February 1913, he induced a clergyman to spend six days on the campus and to preach "to the faculty and students with the view of deepening their spiritual life and of reaching the unsaved." On the second day after this preacher's arrival, he told Baker "the spiritual atmosphere of the faculty was such that he could not hope to reach the unsaved and the only thing that he might . . . accomplish . . . was to do ground work for the future." Baker reminded the trustees that "every member of the faculty must be a man or woman with a positive Christian influence." He had to vouch for them before the Presbyterian College Board in order to secure appropriations from the church. A sinful faculty, he feared, would mean fewer funds—or none at all—from that important source.[34]

The new Woman's Hall was a boon to student life. Female students were not required to live there; on arriving at the campus, a faculty committee assisted them in finding living quarters either in the dormitory or in approved private homes.[35] Baker wanted all persons residing in the dormitory to adhere to paths of purity and rectitude. He gave the Dean of Women responsibility for overseeing the girls. And he would not allow dancing anywhere on the campus.[36]

By late 1912 social sororities and fraternities and the several athletic sports were waxing while the literary societies were waning. A minority of members, both in the Philo and Union Societies, attempted to keep the organizations going. Those who worked hard for the societies could not inspire others to join sincerely in performances or even to attend meetings. Members of Philo, at times, had good reason not to attend meetings; the "Chicken Coop" was right over their hall, and the basketball bouncing over the floor, and the running and shouting of players were most distracting. Early in December 1913, after the roll call, Philo "adjourned on account of commotion in the basketball room."[37] In a very literal sense, basketball was cutting down the work of the societies.

Rules relating to attendance at society meetings were increasingly difficult to enforce. At Philo's meeting on 3 April 1914 the "crowd was so small, they adjourned to have a joint meeting with Union Society," at which plans were discussed for securing larger attendance. Baker's aid was solicited. In July 1914 he recommended to the trustees "that every student be required to join one of the literary societies within three weeks after entering college, and that any student who is absent from his literary society without a reasonable excuse shall be dealt with by the faculty in the same way as if he were absent from his classes." The trustees adopted this recommendation. In September 1914 Baker reminded the faculty that each society had its own charter and should handle its own affairs. But he asked the faculty to help them "build up attendance and interest in the societies." Apparently feeling that these were the societies' problems, the faculty took no action on Baker's request.[38]

In September 1914 Baker called attention to the work of the Y. M. C. A. and Y. W. C. A., and said these associations wanted faculty help in their work. A Boys' Glee Club and a Girls' Glee Club had been organized. In order to maintain interest in chapel, Baker believed these organizations could assist in chapel services. He exhorted the faculty to aid them all.[39] Anxious to strengthen religious life on the campus, late in February 1915 Baker made plans for a week of prayer; he wanted students to think of this week and get as much benefit from it as possible. He would deemphasize scholasticism and emphasize spiritualism; he asked the faculty to be lenient on class work and to postpone examinations until the close of the meetings. The faculty agreed to do so.[40]

In the spring of 1914 the students took an unscheduled vacation of one week. In March 1915 Baker anticipated such insubordination again; he then announced in chapel that "the students would be held responsible for all absences from the first day of the term." Without hesitation, the faculty unanimously concurred that school would open on time (30 March) and that absences would be counted from that day—both from class and from chapel.[41]

If Baker wanted to improve student behavior, he also wanted better buildings and grounds. In November 1912, he sought "a suitable man to do the landscape gardening for the purpose of grading our grounds preparatory to the planting of grass, shrubbery, and flowers." A specialist from Pennsylvania State College came on 5 March 1913 and looked over the grounds. But his plans for landscaping the campus were not forthcoming until two months later—"entirely too late to think of putting out shrubbery this spring." Therefore, a landscape gardener was summoned from Pittsburgh who quickly designed the grading of the grounds, and put them in condition for planting grass, trees, and shrubbery. A floral company in Pittsburgh did everything possible to help beautify the campus. It donated 600 shrubs and the services of a landscape expert to supervise the planting of these shrubs and other plants.[42]

Baker doubtless was happy that the campus was thus beautified. But he was unhappy about stench from the chemistry laboratory, located on the first floor of the main building, which polluted the air in the halls and penetrated even into adjacent classrooms. In June 1913, he recommended to the trustees that the "Chemical Laboratory be moved to the attic where the fumes from chemical experiments will not fill the corridors. This will involve the finishing of a room in the attic for that purpose."[43] If moved to the attic, however, the chemistry laboratory would be located right under the roof where heat in the summer would be unbearable. The trustees, evidently believing that his idea was impracticable, decided to build the laboratory in the basement of the main building; by December 1913 this work was well under way.[44] It appears that the chemistry laboratory remained there for several years. It later was removed successively to Hanna Hall, to the "Old Mill," and to the Paul R. Stewart Science Building.

While electricity had been brought earlier to the campus, the buildings were not completely wired. Early in 1913, at Baker's suggestion, the trustees entered into a contract with the local Electric Light and Power Company to wire the dormitory and to complete the wiring of the main building. This company generously donated to the college all the necessary materials and the services to install them.[45]

In June 1912 the trustees leased the two lower floors of Hanna Hall to the Board of Directors of the Waynesburg Public Schools for use as an elementary school. Enrollment in the college had dropped to the point where only the third floor was needed as a dormitory.[46] In October 1914 the trustees desired to lease Hanna Hall again to the school board for two years. But the faculty opposed this move because of the need of more classrooms, more blackboard space, more library space, a gymnasium room, and space to relocate the Departments of Music and Expression. Despite the will of the faculty, the trustees proceeded, in January 1915, to rent Hanna Hall, except two rooms on the west side of the third floor, to the local school district for two years, beginning 1 July 1915. The rent was $675.00 per year, and all repairs were to be made by the school board, subject to the approval of the trustees' Committee on Buildings and Grounds.[47]

Additional light is thrown on Baker by an interesting pamphlet published by a committee of loyal alumni of the college in December 1913, some eighteen months after he became president. Entitled "Suggestions by Friends of Waynesburg College," the pamphlet was unsigned, and addressed to alumni and "some other friends" of the college. It contained several allegations against Baker, which doubtless weakened his position and led to his resignation. First was the decrease in enrollment. There was a sharp drop in nonresident students. In the early years of the century, and until Baker came, paid matriculations averaged around 150; the highest was 168, reached in the fall of 1906. After Baker's advent, enrollment dropped to 98 students—the first time in many years that it fell below 100. The alumni committee declared this was an honest count "free from the errors of the late padded lists in the late catalogue." Second was the decline in morality on the campus. The committee deplored "the almost entire collapse of attendance at chapel and at literary society during the past year, and the withdrawal of all attempts to enforce the former regulations concerning gambling, poolrooms, and other dissipations . . . and rules concerning the general morality of the student body outside school hours." Baker was largely to blame for these conditions, because he placed power in the hands of a small committee, then dictated to this committee. Third was the resignation of many faculty members. They were so unhappy they would "not stay long enough to understand the needs of students nor school." Resignations "were wholly due to the mismanagement and ungentlemanly spirit of Pres. [*sic*] Baker. . . . " Fourth was the deemphasis on science courses. Baker forced the cancellation of instruction in agriculture, fruit-growing, dairying, and certain other sciences, which had been popular among students; and the Department of Agriculture had greatly aided local farmers, stock raisers, and gardeners. Fifth was the lack of any standards of scholarship for admission to the college. The alumni committee lamented that "during the last three years there have been admitted without question failures from the sixth, seventh, eighth, and ninth grades of the public schools, as well as pupils from the local high school who were dismissed therefrom because of bad behavior and lack of application." Such action caused "teachers and good pupils of these schools" to lose respect for the college. Sixth was poor financial management. In 1900 the college was out of debt. But thenceforward finances had been a problem, and the situation became serious during Baker's incumbency. The college looked each year to the Presbyterian Church for $1,500, but this sum was decreased in 1912. The church required an annual audit of the general accounts of the college. Baker's "annual report to the Presbyterian Board states that such an audit had been made," when in fact it had not. Seventh was misleading information in the college catalogue. It contained "an extensive printed course of study never taught. . . . " The alumni committee doubted Baker's credibility and maintained

> that deceitful statements are continually being made by the President concerning [the] amount of actual money raised, actual number of students, and reasons for the dismissal and resignations of so many of the Faculty, even going so far as to wrongfully blame the Trustees. Also that deceptions are being practiced by him concerning the so-called raising of the "standards"; the actions . . . of certain members of the Board of Trustees; and acceptance of the College in the graduate departments of certain large universities. Added to these are numerous empty promises to students and faculty, and attempts to blind the Presbyterian Synod in respect to the true state of affairs in this institution. It has been a saying lately that his statements must be put through a sort of decreasing geometrical progression, if even then they can be believed.

The pamphlet alleged further that Baker lost the support of the local newspapers, the Superintendent of Schools of Greene County, the Superintendent of the Waynesburg Public Schools, the Principal of Waynesburg High School, many friends of the college, faculty members who resigned, a majority of the students, and the Woman's Club of Waynesburg. Members of the alumni committee envisioned a much better Waynesburg College, and made several excellent suggestions for its welfare:

> Organize the school under modern ideas of usefulness for the masses of young men and young women. Do not force all students toward the ministry, law, or medicine. Direct all students toward high moral deportment; respect for religion; to a love for the good in literature, history,

> and art; in love for uprightness in public and in private life; in skill in maintaining public utilities in the application of science and knowledge already gained by man; in the best means of acquiring and maintaining an honest income. Instruct them in the vast field of business relations, give them a view of the future outlook, direct each toward his field of greatest usefulness, advise each in his preparation and efficiency for employment in life.[48]

In May 1914, some six months after the alumni committee's suggestions were published, a local editor called for an investigation of Baker's performance. He pointed out the merits of the college and of its Board of Trustees. "We have a splendid college," he declared, "but there is something wrong with either faculty or president. They are not working in harmony." The editor frankly expressed his "belief that the President is at fault—and that is why we feel there should be an investigation. The trustees are capable and should make the investigation."[49]

Available records indicate nothing about an investigation. On 11 June 1915, at the regular annual meeting of the trustees, Baker resigned, and the resignation was accepted. But Baker was not entirely discredited. In that same meeting, possibly to palliate partly the polemics against him, the trustees passed a motion to confer upon him the honorary degree D. D.[50]

XII
PRESIDENT HOUGHTON

IN ANTICIPATION OF BAKER'S RESIGNATION THE TRUSTEES' COMMITTEE ON Teachers and Salaries conferred with a committee from the Alumni Association for the purpose of finding, and recommending, candidates for a new president of the college. Several men were thus screened and, on 11 June 1915, the trustees unanimously elected Dr. Herbert Pierrepont Houghton of Amherst College to the post at a salary of $2,000 per year, plus use of the president's house. He promptly accepted the offer, and his duties began on 1 July 1915.[1] He aimed to make Waynesburg College the "Amherst of the West."

Houghton was born in Brooklyn, New York, on 22 January 1880. He did his undergraduate work at Amherst where he received the baccalaureate degree in 1901. He was a graduate student at Princeton and Johns Hopkins universities; he won his Ph. D. at the latter in 1907. Having studied Greek, Latin, and Sanskrit, he was well grounded in the classics and fully familiar with works of the greatest classical writers. After earning the doctorate, he taught at Amherst and proved to be an excellent classroom man. At Waynesburg, in addition to his duties as president, he taught Greek.[2]

Houghton was a kindly, considerate man. One of his colleagues tells us how he proceeded right after Baker left:

> It is needless to recall the very trying situation that confronted him. Courageously, hopefully, tactfully he gathered up one by one the torn and tangled threads. He did not take any revolutionary, sudden action. Before taking the next step, he acquainted himself patiently and carefully at first hand with all the conditions, and then gradually he introduced the necessary modifications. Thus he has conquered all difficulties, so that there has been now for many months the best feeling within and without Waynesburg College.[3]

Houghton was inaugurated on Wednesday, 14 June 1916, during "Old Home Week" in Waynesburg. Other important events of that week were the Centennial Celebration of the incorporation of the town of Waynesburg as a borough; the dedication of the new Armory; the literary societies' contest; a parade of the Patriotic Order, Sons of America, and other fraternal organizations, followed by a picnic; church reunions; the baccalaureate service; Class Day at the college; and Commencement. The inauguration service, held in Alumni Hall, was open to the public. The program consisted of four addresses, including one by Major Edward Martin, interspersed by musical selections.[4] Then Houghton delivered his inaugural address, entitled "The Business of the College." His words refreshed and renewed all who heard him. His central theme was clear, concise, and cogent:

> What we intend to stand for here at Waynesburg College is the four-sided education. We shall continue to send forth from these halls young men and young women of promise, who shall represent the ideals in which we believe and by which we endeavor to live. . . . We shall aim to make the college the place of the *mind* first, the place of the *spirit* always, the place of *physical* development, and the place of the *heart* forever (Houghton's italics).[5]

Houghton sincerely wished to create a common bond between the college and the community. Hence he cordially invited local people to visit the college. He wanted to minister to the desires of the people at large. To do so he encouraged people of Waynesburg who had completed their studies to elect a course or two in the college as auditors, or as regularly enrolled students. He felt that the college should be the educational and cultural center of Greene County "as it is rapidly coming to be." He suggested several courses including language, history, political science and others which would be of interest. During the winter of 1916-1917 he gave a series of readings at the college on the dramas of Aeschylus, the great Greek author of seven tragedies, which are still extant. Houghton read and interpreted them all to the class. No knowledge of Greek was necessary.[6] Members of the class greatly appreciated, and profited from, his efforts.

Nearly a year after the entrance of the nation into World War I Houghton recalled with pride all Waynesburg College men who had served in our wars since 1861—that fateful date when the nation was divided against itself. His sense of patriotism tugs at the heart-strings and reminds us all that we should venerate these veterans—both living and dead:

> Did they return? Yes, some—maimed and crippled for life, ill, weakened, but still loved, still brave, still the object not of your pity, but of your warm heart, love, and active sympathy. Others more fortunate had been through the worst and yet as by a miraculous dispensation had passed through unharmed. No less heroes than the others; all, all heroes, that they fell and that they returned to tell us the tale of hardship and the toil of battle, and to be an inspiration to their sons and daughters for patriotic devotion and loyal deeds.

Houghton reminded his listeners that out of the old building marched the men of 1861; out of the new building, the men of 1898; and in 1917 many more left the latter building. "Will they come back? They are gone. What are we doing at home?"[7]

Houghton was such an inspiration that public confidence in the college was soon restored. The opening on 26 September 1916 "was the most auspicious in the college for the past fifteen years." Enrollment increased; fortunately two-thirds of the graduating class of Waynesburg High School entered Waynesburg College—"a clear indication that the school is beginning to believe in the college." People in Greene County realized that they could educate their sons and daughters here just as well as elsewhere—and at less expense. Standards of admission and graduation were higher than ever before; they were on an equal footing with all colleges in this area.[8] Individual alumni expressed their full confidence in Houghton. In June 1917 an elderly alumnus remarked: "We have a most excellent President of the College at this time, better than we have had for many years, and under his management the 'Old College' appears to have taken on new life. We hope to be able, within the next few years, to increase our endowment fund and to make it self-sustaining."[9]

The local press praised Houghton. An editor lamented that, "Many people do not show enough loyalty to Waynesburg College." The college "under President Houghton's administration is doing as good work as any college in the neighborhood. . . . Let us . . . send our sons and daughters to Waynesburg College to be educated for higher ideals of life and culture under his direction."[10]

One of Houghton's aims was to recruit a faculty which would be second to none in western Pennsylvania. To that end he retained some of the best of the former faculty members, including Patton and Paul R. Stewart; others were dismissed. To replace them, Houghton recruited topnotch teachers from such universities as Chicago, Clark, Columbia, George Washington, and Harvard. The full-time staff, including Houghton, numbered ten members. The majority received salaries of $1,000 per year.[11] In order to staff the Normal Department, Houghton secured the services of "the most prominent and popular educators in Greene County." Professor J. E. Williamson, Principal of Rogersville High School, was placed in charge of that Department; he also taught mathematics and English. Professor O. C. Mundell, Principal of Rices Landing School, taught history, civil government, and political and physical geography. Professor Charles W. Earnest, Principal of Hanna Hall School, taught the Palmer method of penmanship.[12]

Houghton did not overburden his faculty. He felt that no teacher should be asked to conduct more than five three-hour courses per week and no teacher should be required to offer a course for less than three students.[13] The fifteen-hour schedule per week allowed teachers enough time to work on preparations, to administer examinations and grade the papers, and to perform other tasks in the regular line of duty.

The faculty members revealed their sense of patriotism in April 1917, shortly after the nation entered hostilities in World War I. They voted to send a message to the President of the United States "assuring him of our loyalty and support." A resolution was passed "to grant diplomas to Seniors who may be called away to Service before 14 June 1917."[14]

Houghton examined and reorganized the curriculum so it would best meet the needs of students—and hence society as a whole. Being a deeply religious man, he held that the curriculum should provide in the Bible Department the study of the Bible itself—not just books about the Bible. He deplored the neglect of Bible study in the home, in the public school, and in society in general. He felt that a Christian college should require Bible courses throughout the four-year program. Students would then know the Bible and "come in touch thus closely with divine truth."[15] Accordingly in April 1917 the faculty passed a motion that requirements for graduation from the college "shall be: a course of four years, the work of each year to consist of five three-hour courses, plus one hour of Bible. . . . " Over the four-year period, one had to complete sixty-four hours of work in order to graduate. In November 1917, possibly because of the war situation, a student was permitted to shorten the time to three years. To do so, he had to indicate his intent at the beginning, and take twenty-two hours of work per year—a total of sixty-six hours. One embarking on such a shortened program was put on a trial basis for the first year. He was "judged by his first year's work whether he can continue a three-year program or be transferred to a four-year basis."[16]

In April 1916, to the embarrassment of Houghton and others, a state examiner and a professor from the University of Pittsburgh visited the college and evaluated the Science Department—and found it wanting. They reported that the science equipment and teaching force at Waynesburg College were insufficient to prepare students for graduate school and for medical school. The professor from the University said "it was impossible for a Waynesburg College graduate to enter Pitt Medical School because of above-mentioned inadequacies." Houghton and the faculty thanked these men, and promised to try to get better equipment and staff. They were soon successful. In September 1916 Houghton announced that the pre-medical course was standardized to meet requirements for affiliation with the University of Pittsburgh. For the term beginning on 25 September 1916 the college offered several distinctive pre-vocational courses of study. While all led toward the A. B. or B. S. degree, they offered instruction of from two to four years necessary to further study of agriculture, engineering, journalism, law, library work, medicine, teaching, and theology. Pre-vocational courses in agriculture and in medicine would aid those going into dentistry, pharmacy, and veterinary science.[17]

Fortunately the course in Agriculture, with Professor Paul R. Stewart as teacher, was restored to the curriculum. The plot of ground in the rear of the girls' dormitory was used as an experimental farm for the raising of vegetables and fruits. This course covered the fundamentals of agriculture; fruit-growing, budding, and grafting; and farming and vegetable gardening. Both the scientific and the practical aspects of agriculture and horticulture were stressed. At Houghton's behest, students from Waynesburg High School participated in the program in agriculture. And female students from the college took work in domestic science under the tutelage of Sue Frick, a teacher in the local high school. The combination of training in agriculture and domestic science was excellent.[18]

In 1915 the curriculum was changed in the college's Academy. It was limited to the "last three years of a college preparatory school." Students desiring to enter the Academy were advised to take their first year in Waynesburg High School. In the interests of high academic standards, students with deficiencies in their previous schooling were admitted to the Academy only after removing them.

Further, any graduate of a Pennsylvania State Normal School who came to the college was admitted to standing no higher than the sophomore year. In 1916 the Academy was eliminated. By that time high schools were commonplace—and adequate to prepare people for college. The college gained prestige by getting out of the "preparatory business."[19]

Houghton wanted to do everything possible to strengthen the Normal Department. To that end he joined that teaching staff, and lectured once weekly on "educational problems"; others from the college faculty taught such courses as Educational Psychology, History of Education, and Educational Administration. All these supplemented the work of Professors Earnest, Mundell, and Williamson. College courses taken in addition to the Normal work counted toward a degree. The regular "spring Normal" customarily began about 10 April and lasted twelve weeks. The fee for a term was $20.00, "payable strictly in advance."[20] At Houghton's suggestion, the calendar for the Normal course was changed, beginning on 1 May 1917. Starting then it ran for six weeks, and it was followed by a summer term lasting six weeks. If a high school teacher attended both sessions, he could do college work and get credit for both. The aim was to permit a teacher to hold his position and to make faster progress toward a degree[21]

Through Houghton's initiative and interest, the graduate program leading toward the master's degree was resumed in the fall of 1915. Graduate courses met from four to six o'clock from Monday through Friday, beginning early in October. Eight graduates of Waynesburg College entered the graduate school and worked toward the M. A. degree.[22] Graduate work was also offered on Saturday morning, chiefly to accommodate teachers in Greene County. Graduate courses included Latin, Greek, chemistry, geology, philosophy, psychology, mathematics, history, economics, modern languages, and literature. A graduate of any approved college or university could be admitted. The requirement was completion with high credit of a year's work in residence, following a course of study in chosen, related fields such as science and mathematics, history and economics, and language and literature. It is noteworthy that this standard was more rigorous than the earlier one in which a candidate could do much of the work as a nonresident student. While Houghton was president, the graduate school thrived. In June 1916 three M. A.'s and one M. S. were conferred; and two years later two M. A.'s were awarded.[23]

With a view to rewarding students with high scholastic standing,

Houghton was instrumental in the establishment of an Honor Society on campus. Its membership was limited to juniors with an average of 90 percent, and to seniors with an average of 87 percent. The emblem of the Society was either an appropriate pin or a watch charm. Beginning with graduation in 1918, honors were indicated on diplomas in three grades: highest honors went to graduating seniors with an average of 93 percent, or higher, in all college work; high honors, to the one with an average of 90 percent; and honors, to the one averaging 87 percent.[24]

If some students were honored for high scholastic standing, others were lazy and irresponsible. While the faculty did not "admonish them" as in days of yore, efforts were made to keep them in line. Attendance was required at class and at "prayers conducted daily except Sunday and Monday in the Assembly Hall at 11:50 A.M., lasting from ten to fifteen minutes." Three unexcused absences from class or prayers were permitted each term. Students exceeding this were in danger of being conditioned.[25]

Infinitely more deplorable than absences from class or chapel was a case of tampering with student records, which was discovered early in June 1915. As if trying to confirm Calvin's views on the depravity of man, someone clandestinely gained access to the student records and falsified several transcripts. False grades were added; one student was listed for "four courses *he never took*. . . . (italics in original)." Several low grades were changed to A's; and a number of F's were converted to B's. It is difficult to imagine the consternation of the faculty in this case; the matter of the forgery of grades was in long controversy. The faculty—and Houghton—were at a loss to know what to do. To locate the guilty person seemed impossible. On 20 September 1915 the faculty finally and embarrassingly moved that, "in the matter of the forgeries . . . inasmuch as it is impossible to establish guilt without expert evidence, and inasmuch as the funds of the college do not admit an expert being employed, the matter be dropped *for the present* (italicized part in original, and added in handwriting)."[26] The motion carried. There is no evidence that the reprobate was ever identified.

While Houghton wrestled with academic problems, he gave attention to matters pertaining to student life. The athletic program merits first attention. Houghton opposed professionalism in college athletics. He pointed out how "football taxes the strength of students." He frowned on the great competition among colleges to get top players. He contended that

> a football schedule of six games, free from unnecessary expense and pervaded with good, wholesome college spirit is helpful to any institution, and should suffice for any season. One game of basketball or of baseball a week for a period of ten or twelve weeks should be the limit of our schedules. Thus we should conserve the best powers of our students; thus we should eliminate the preposterous expenses and glaring debts, which often face us at the close of a season. . . . A college without spirit is dead. Athletics certainly do foster college spirit, but when the college appears to be administered for the sake of athletics . . . then athletics become a menace to a real educational institution.

Houghton pleaded for emphasis on scholasticism—not on athletics. He wanted "equal development in mind, body, spirit, and heart." He did not want "a mere mass of students, a majority of whom think more of the pigskin, than they look forward to the sheepskin."[27]

Houghton was opposed to "buying athletes, so prevalent at other colleges." He did not "believe in paid coaching." Basketball and baseball would be continued as main sports. "No one *but students* will play (Houghton's italics)." Houghton asked the alumni for financial aid, and added: "If it is not given, he will not feel encouraged to continue work so successfully begun."[28]

Several moves were made in order to implement Houghton's athletic policy. Intercollegiate football was quickly phased out. In the fall of 1915, the team, coached by Arthur Garrett, played—and lost—two games. Subsequently the faculty passed a motion that the college not participate in intercollegiate football. And no such games were played from 1916 to 1920 inclusive.[29]

Houghton tried to induce other college presidents to use their influence to end all signs of professionalism in intercollegiate athletics. Early in 1917 he attended a meeting of the Association of College Presidents of Pennsylvania. The consensus of those gentlemen was "that colleges in the Association should discourage payment of money to students for athletic ability." On 1 March 1917 Houghton reported to the faculty that other college presidents in our state frowned on professionalism in intercollegiate athletics. The faculty passed a motion "that Waynesburg College sanction this attitude."[30] What the several college heads actually did to end such professionalism is unknown. In June 1917 the trustees resolved "that hereafter no athletic scholarships be granted by Waynesburg College." A few days later they passed a motion that the faculty member, who served also as athletic director, should not receive additional salary as such.[31]

A good move in the implementation of Houghton's athletic program came with his appointment of Professor Paul R. Stewart as Director of Athletics "with full power to reorganize and improve the athletic situation at the college." Thenceforth all students were required to participate in some athletic exercise. Football, baseball, basketball, and tennis were available to the men; and basketball and tennis to the women. The grounds for football and baseball were adequate; several good tennis courts were at hand. But the college gravely needed a gymnasium, one suitable for basketball.[32] The "Chicken Coop" was used as the gymnasium; some new equipment was purchased and it was "fixed up" for gymnastics. Coach Garrett conducted "gymnasium classes" which were open to male students only. Such classes afforded systematic exercise to develop students physically, who did "not care to participate in more strenuous sports." Indoor games such as volleyball were introduced. The whole program was basically intramural, with each class developing teams in the several sports. As an inducement to excellence, winning teams received pennants and other awards.[33]

By December 1915, through tireless efforts of Houghton, Stewart, and Garrett, the Athletic Association secured the local Armory for use in basketball. Occupied by Company K, this building had "the best basketball hall in this part of Pennsylvania." Its use was obtained at considerable expense to the college. But there was room for optimism that Waynesburg College's teams would regain and hold their former position in the basketball world.[34] During 1916 and 1917 the men's varsity basketball team played a variety of opponents including the Epsilon Pi team of Washington, Pennsylvania; an independent team from Spraggtown, in Greene County; Fairmont High School; Y. M. C. A. teams from New Brighton, Pennsylvania, and Wheeling, West Virginia; Grove City College; and Capital University at Columbus, Ohio. The departure of players who entered the armed forces in World War I hurt the team. It appears that no intercollegiate games were played by male students of the college in 1918.[35]

While varsity basketball for male students declined during the war, the girls organized a good team and competed respectably against several area colleges. Called the "Girls Basketeers" and coached by Professor Paul R. Stewart, they made a "gruelling jaunt" in February 1917. They defeated Geneva College 13 to 12, lost to the University of Pittsburgh 18 to 11 and to California Normal 14 to 3. In the Geneva game, Mary Munnell was Waynesburg's star. The other girls were Mary Blair, Edna Faddis, Pauline Lewis,

Ethel McNeely, and Lura Tennant. The editor of the college newspaper praised these girls: "The defeat of Geneva and the close game with Pitt . . . shows the skill of our girls. . . . " They "show good sportsmanship in losing. They are an inspiration." On 21 February 1918 the girls soundly defeated the team from Pennsylvania College for Women by 25 to 7. In the last game of that season, however, they lost to Pitt which had one of the fastest teams in this section of the country.[36]

Despite the war, the students, under Stewart's tutelage, continued spring sports. In April 1918, the editor of the college newspaper exhorted them not to abandon spring sports. He conceded that "we can't have varsity baseball, but we can keep up an intramural program." He suggested three baseball games between two men's teams, three baseball games between two women's teams, a tennis tournament, and a field meet. This plan was followed. The teams were evenly matched, and competition was keen. The program was beneficial to students of both sexes.[37]

Since Houghton frowned on the use of college funds to promote athletics, it was necessary to raise supplementary money by other means. The college's Athletic Association, with Stewart as counselor, worked hard to pay its debts and to keep the organization on a good basis. The students adopted an excellent practice of presenting annual plays, and the proceeds were used to help pay expenses. In December 1915 a local editor lent his support. "Your aid is solicited," he wrote. "Every little added to what they already have will help cancel the debt." He urged everyone to attend the play "What Happened to Jones," a comedy with college students as actors and actresses. Plays took place in the Opera House, the largest theatrical building in Waynesburg. A most interesting—and timely—one was presented in February 1917. Entitled "A Regiment of Two," it was a story related to the mobilization of American troops for duty on the Mexican border in the spring of 1916 in the search for Pancho Villa, the elusive, bandit-type revolutionary, whom President Woodrow Wilson considered a menace to the United States and to political freedom in Mexico. This play was a great success. It was a most amusing comedy; the students played their parts well. A large crowd was delighted—and $80.00 was raised for the Athletic Association. In June 1917 Houghton reported that all debts of this Association had been paid.[38]

When Houghton became president, the literary societies were still conducting regular programs and annual contests—but with less zeal than in former years. In June 1917 Professor Paul R. Stewart spoke before the Philo Society, and said "there was some talk of dropping" both societies. Some people believed they were "too much of a mollycoddle." But Stewart held that "they are the best thing we have in the college."[39] Two moves were made in the hope of saving and strengthening the societies. One, relating to initiation fees and fines imposed by the societies, was a form of coercion. The faculty resolved that students must pay these fees and fines on pain of having their grades withheld. The other was rewarding in nature. In February 1918 the faculty passed a motion "that literary society be made a required course for which credit of one year-hour will be given."[40] As a result the societies continued to operate a little longer.

Deeply religious himself, Houghton gave close attention to religion on the campus. Students were required to attend chapel. The faculty was urged to set an example by attending chapel and by cooperating in every way possible. Interestingly enough, there were still some signs of segregation of the sexes—reminiscent of the old days. Faculty members checked on student attendance at chapel. The faculty minutes for 15 September 1917 record: "Miss Martin will act as monitor for the women's side, and Prof. Day for the men's."[41] Morality, both in private and public life, was still prized above all other values. Houghton wanted to quicken spiritual life on the campus, for he believed "that education is not merely of the mind, but even more of the soul and of the heart." Hence, in February 1916, he began the practice of holding prayer week at least once annually for meditation on things of the spirit. The regular morning chapel, which began at 8:30, was lengthened by fifteen minutes, or time for a brief talk by a devout clergyman. These services were open to the public, especially to parents of local students. The Y. M. C. A. and Y. W. C. A. participated in this work under Houghton's direction.[42] Beyond a doubt, many students gained inspiration and renewal from such meetings.

One of the most important student activities during Houghton's administration was intercollegiate debating. There was keen interest in debating—not only among team members, but among the students, faculty, and townsmen. Topics for debate were timely. For example, about a year before the United States declared war on Germany in World War I, Waynesburg College debated against Washington and Jefferson College on the question: "Resolved that there should be a prompt and substantial increase in the army and navy of the United States." The war was then raging; and our nation was unprepared. Waynesburg upheld the affimative and won.[43] After the United States entered hostilities, Waynesburg debated the University of Pittsburgh on the question: "Resolved that the United States should adopt a system of universal military training." Again Waynesburg upheld the affirmative side, and won unanimously—to the delight of the large crowd in Alumni Hall.[44] A year later, as labor problems loomed on the American scene, Waynesburg lost a decision to a strong team from Westminster College on the question: "Resolved that the United States should adopt the Canadian plan for dealing with industrial disputes." There were able arguments on both sides. The Westminster debaters complimented the Waynesburg team as the "best they had met in two years. . . ."[45]

During World War I a sense of patriotism pervaded the whole student body, the faculty, and the alumni. By January 1918 some forty-nine Waynesburg College men were in the armed forces. Some were alumni; others were students who left the campus. As a symbol of patriotism, the senior class presented to the college a handsome service flag. Made by female students, it contained forty-nine stars and was presented as a tribute to those in the service. Heading the list of these men was the name of Major Edward Martin.[46]

Many alumni yearned to return to the campus, to take an interest in student activities, and to promote other worthy causes. Noteworthy was Farabee's return on 25 April 1917 when he lectured in Alumni Hall to a large crowd on "My Three Years among the Wild Tribes of Brazil." His trip from 1913 to 1916, sponsored by the University of Pennsylvania, took him among natives never before observed by white men. Admission was charged; and the incomparable Farabee generously gave all the proceeds to the benefit of *The Collegian*, the excellent student newspaper.[47]

While students were becoming less interested in literary societies, they were giving more attention to social fraternities and sororities. The year 1916 marked the tenth anniversary of the founding of Phi Sigma fraternity on the campus. In that decade some "eighty-four loyal sons" of the college joined this fraternity. They had gone out into all walks of life and had done credit to themselves, to their fraternity, and to the college. They were in nearly all professions. The other strong fraternity on campus was Delta Sigma Phi. It was steadily expanding "in the face of competition from older and larger fraternities." The culmination of its social activities was the annual banquet held in Hotel Downey.[48]

Houghton gave careful attention to fund raising. In January 1916 he went to New York City, met with the Presbyterian "College Board," and was promised an increase in the appropriation. Shortly it was raised from $1,500 to $1,900 per year. He also discussed plans for an endowment campaign to start in Pittsburgh. He said he would "start with the alumni there and work out." He felt the "time was not yet ripe to attempt raising endowment in Greene County. . . . "[49] He was realistic about the amount of endowment which could be raised locally. Unlike Baker, who tried to raise $500,000, Houghton's goal was $100,000 in addition to the existing endowment fund. In May 1917 the college's endowment was only $75,000, which was less than that of "any other college with a reputation as good as Waynesburg College's." The minimum cost at which the college could be operated each year was about $15,000. Average annual receipts from students totaled $5,200. The income from endowment was $4,300. Therefore, the college needed additional income annually in the amount of $5,500 to keep the budget in balance.[50]

In order to raise this money, the trustees employed Alfred F. Hoffsommer, of Harrisburg, Pennsylvania, an experienced man in fund raising. He was formerly state secretary of the Y. M. C. A. Early in May 1917 a conference of leading citizens was held in Hotel Downey with Judge James Inghram presiding. They planned a campaign in Waynesburg and vicinity, to be directed by Hoffsommer. Houghton told the group that "more than 1,000 people had been educated at Waynesburg College, and 566 were still living." They compared more than favorably with graduates of other institutions. He held that the college must be adequately endowed or it would finally deteriorate and die. Financially the college was falling behind, and "more than $13,000 of accumulated deficits stare us in the face." Hoffsommer said "much work and sacrifice would be necessary." He would concentrate on the best citizens in his quest for funds. For his drive he used four words: "organization, concentration, publicity, sacrifice." He said the problem was one of simple arithmetic. The college needed between $5,000 and $6,000 more income per year. "It cannot go on without it." The only right way to solve the problem was "to put up the money for a permanent endowment and be done with it." Hoffsommer praised Houghton for increasing enrollment in the college department from 71 in 1915 to 115 by 1917. He also called attention to the college as a business enterprise in the community. In 1917, in all departments, enrollment was 269 students. "At a low estimate they spend $1.00

per day for living expenses of all kinds. They bring in at least $75,000 annually, and this does not take into account the faculty."[51]

In May 1917 a plan was presented for raising funds in Waynesburg, in Greene County, in neighboring counties, and elsewhere. The total goal was $100,000. Campaign committeemen consulted several leading citizens in Greene County, and concluded it was best to defer the drive for a year or so "until coal begins to move," and those able to make larger subscriptions could do so more easily. Hoffsommer concurred. But the college was in debt; it needed money immediately. An intensive effort was then made to raise funds for current expenses for a period of three years. Hoffsommer resolved to conduct a four-day "whirlwind campaign" similar to others he had conducted, and found successful, in drives by Y. M. C. A.'s, hospitals, and colleges. Shortly six teams were organized under "captains" A. I. Cooke, W. D. Cottrell, B. N. Freeland, H. P. Houghton, Paul R. Stewart, and T. J. Wisecarver; each team consisted of from five to seven leading citizens. The aim was to make a four-day canvass of all citizens in the community who were able to make even small contributions. It was hoped that at least $18,000 could be raised during 1917, 1918, and 1919. Subscriptions could be paid in three equal installments on 1 September of each year. Each worker chose names of persons he was willing to see; team members worked in pairs, and asked only once, unless the residents refused "in which event they may be seen until they become converted." On each evening of the four-day drive, team members met for supper and made reports. They were judged daily on the number of subscriptions and the totals subscribed. A pennant was offered to the winner each day.[52]

The campaign was a success beyond all expectations. After it ended shouts could be heard: "Hurrah for Waynesburg! What's the matter with Waynesburg? She's all right." The original goal was $18,000. As the campaign showed increasing success, it was raised to $25,000; and the final figure for the four days was $25,132. Houghton praised the public spirit and excellent teamwork, and said it showed that $100,000 could be raised "when the coal begins to move. . . . Our appetites are whetted for the larger task within the next year or two." Hoffsommer said he had repeatedly seen communities do the impossible. He was entirely captivated with Waynesburg and its hospitable people, and he left town with keenest regrets.[53]

While residents of Waynesburg and its environs loyally supported the college, the state legislature was not so inclined. The appropriation made earlier for the girls' dormitory led the trustees to hope for more funds from the state. A science hall had long been needed. The trustees, therefore, appointed a committee consisting of J. W. Ray, D. S. Walton and Houghton, to petition the legislature for $75,000 for the erection of a science and agriculture building. This committee went to Harrisburg to present the project. Walton had been instrumental in getting state funds for the dormitory; since he was a member of the committee, the college might enjoy another blessing by the state. The assemblyman and senator, who represented this area, were available in Harrisburg to help the committee.[54] Available evidence indicates, however, that this attempt was in vain.

Wherever Houghton searched for funds, he also searched for students. He frequently visited high schools in western Pennsylvania, and spoke of the merits of Waynesburg College. He briefly outlined its history, told of recent developments, and of plans for new courses; he stressed religious activities, athletic interests, and social life. In order to induce students to come to the college, full tuition for one year was offered to graduates of area high schools, including Aleppo, Carmichaels, Jefferson, Mt. Morris, Nineveh, Richhill, Rogersville, Smithfield, Waynesburg, and West Alexander. The Presbyterian Synod of Pennsylvania urged publicity of Waynesburg College among young people all over the state. That body held that the college "deserves to be better known and supported." It aided not only in recruiting students, but also in raising funds.[55]

The success of Waynesburg College graduates in many walks of life was one of Houghton's main selling points as he recruited students. By 1915 alumni of the college were teaching in many of the newly established high schools in the tri-state area. Others were filling "eminent positions in colleges and schools in distant states. Invariably they were successful in the classrooms and as leaders in communities where they resided. For example, in August 1915, Houghton received a letter from a town in West Virginia where a Waynesburg graduate was teaching, asking him to recommend another teacher for their high school. An editor in Waynesburg boosted the college: "If you plan to teach, a diploma from Waynesburg College will be a valuable aid in securing a position for you."[56]

If raising funds and recruiting students were important, so were the buildings and grounds. Aware of the constant need for maintenance and for improvements, the trustees kept their Committee on Buildings and Grounds busy. In December 1915 they moved to install lights in recitation rooms. Ever with a view to economy, they authorized the Committee on Buildings and Grounds "to purchase as many electric lamps at the reduced price as they may be able to obtain during the special sale being carried on this week by the West Penn Electric Co."[57] A better heating system was also needed. In June 1917, the Committee on Buildings and Grounds was directed to "equip the main college building with new heating stoves of the best kind for burning gas." Further, a hood costing $65.00 was placed over the chemical laboratory to carry the fumes away.[58]

The only innovation with respect to grounds came in August 1916, when the trustees proposed to open First Avenue through the college grounds from Morris to Washington Streets. This move facilitated access to the women's dormitory. The buildings and grounds were kept in excellent condition, thanks to the efforts of the Buildings and Grounds Committee and to "the efficient work of janitor, Albert Bruce."[59]

While all appeared to be well, on 27 January 1918 Houghton resigned, and told the trustees he wanted to be released by 30 June next. He had accepted an offer of the presidency of Carroll College at Waukesha, Wisconsin. He said he had repeatedly received opportunities "to enter upon fields of larger usefulness and wider responsibilities." He had turned them down, because at Waynesburg "he didn't want to desert the ship before I had it well out into a deeper current." But it was necessary, he felt, to provide his family with the best possible living; at Carroll College he was getting an appreciable increase in salary. He said he was glad to have the good will of the trustees, faculty, and students; and promised he "would *still* do what he could for Waynesburg College (Houghton's italics)." The trustees accepted his resignation, and began the search for his successor.[60]

On the surface there was a spirit of cordiality between Houghton and the trustees. There is evidence, however, of an undercurrent of friction and unhappiness. It appears that the trustees did not grant full power—and responsibility—to Houghton as administrative head of the college. As early as April 1916 there were signs of Houghton's dissatisfaction and discontent. The treasurer of the college had belittled Houghton's authority in the presence of a student. Irate over the matter, Houghton verbally lashed the treasurer later in a telephone conversation. Houghton said: "Students must not be led to feel that the President is the hired man of the Trustees.

In most colleges the president is in command absolutely . . . and it might be better if it were so here. . . . " But then "there are so many things in connection with running this college which need adjustment that one hardly knows where to begin."[61] In March 1917 the trustees chose a committee of five from their own body to act with Houghton as an executive committee "to pass on accounts, issue orders, and have general supervision of college affairs." About a year later, they passed a motion "that no bills be contracted by any teacher, President, or student without same be authorized by this board and that Secretary be authorized to inform Pres. [*sic*] Houghton & teachers." From these actions, it is obvious that Houghton's powers were greatly limited by the trustees.[62]

Houghton was an able president of the college. A thorough scholar, he hoped to make Waynesburg one of the "best in the West." Beyond a doubt, he aroused opposition because of his athletic policy; his termination of intercollegiate football assuredly disappointed many. But he strengthened the academic program by ending the work of the college's Academy, by the restoration of the graduate school, and by strengthening the faculty. As a fund-raiser he gave local people the opportunity to show their faith in, and loyalty to, the college. While the endowment fund, when he left, was still only $75,000, he inspired hopes that appreciable sums would be added in the near future. As a public relations man and a recruiter of students, he was one of the best. He restored public confidence in the college. All things considered, he had been good for the institution.[63]

XIII
McKAY RETURNS

After Houghton resigned, the trustees cast about for his successor—a task they had faced almost triennially for nearly two decades. On 20 May 1918, after carefully considering four candidates, they elected the Reverend J. W. McKay, '83, of Washington, Pennsylvania, to the presidency of the college. McKay was not new to the campus. A loyal alumnus, after serving for a year, beginning on 1 July 1899, as acting president, he had kept in close touch with his *Alma Mater*, and had regularly assisted in raising funds. Early in July 1918 he and his wife moved into the President's home on the campus. Old friends welcomed his return. He told the trustees he believed the future of the college was bright.[1]

McKay was born at Jackson Center, in Mercer County, Pennsylvania, 11 August 1857, the son of John and Jane Hill McKay. His parents were pioneers in the transallegheny West. After his graduation from Waynesburg College he entered Cumberland Theological Seminary where he won a degree in theology and became a CP minister. Waynesburg College awarded him an honorary LL. D. in 1915. He first preached at the CP Church at Franklin, Kentucky. Subsequently he was pastor of the CP Church at Carmichaels. Later he organized the Shady Avenue CP Church in Pittsburgh, Pennsylvania; and the Central CP Church in Washington, Pennsylvania. During all these pastorates, he showed intense loyalty to Waynesburg College; he was ready to extend personal and financial aid "whenever the call was heard." From 1898 to 1900 he led a fund drive which cleared the college of a debt of over $25,000. As acting president of the college, McKay had filled the position with great enthusiasm, raising attendance and student activities. An able journalist and editor while serving as acting president of the college, he also established and edited the *Waynesburg Daily Times*, and edited *The Waynesburg Independent*. In 1906 he became editor of the *Washington Record*. His other interests included the promotion of railroads in this area, and the Washington Fair Association which he organized.[2]

McKay had a strong faculty. In addition to his duties as president, he was Professor of Bible and Philosophy. Andrew J. Waychoff taught economics and mining engineering; Paul R. Stewart taught chemistry and geology; Stewart's father, Ezra D. Stewart, taught Greek and mathematics. These were the most devoted and loyal faculty members. In addition to their duties during the regular academic year, they taught in the Normal Department. As a result of inflation brought on by the war, faculty salaries were raised. For the year 1918-19, most salaries were around $1,100 per year; two years later they ranged between $1,200 and $1,575 per year; and for the year 1921-1922, Paul R. Stewart's salary was set at $2,025—doubtless a merit increase because of his efficiency, hard work, and great devotion to the institution.[3]

Though teaching was the primary responsibility of the faculty, certain members were noted for research, particularly in the field of archaeology. In the summer of 1919, Professor Waychoff, Professor Paul R. Stewart, and Dr. William C. Farabee examined several mounds and village sites in Greene County. Knowing that mounds in the Ohio valley were among the most noted of prehistoric man in the world, they next gave attention to a project in Ohio. On Farabee's recommendation, Waychoff was appointed to work with Dr. William C. Mills and H. O. Shetstone, respectively curator and assistant curator of the Museum of Columbus, Ohio. Beginning in July 1920, they examined Mound City, a group of mounds near Chillicothe, Ohio. Since Waychoff was considered one of the best authorities on primitive man in western Pennsylvania, he was well qualified to aid fellow archaeologists in learning more about the earliest peoples in Ohio. His appointment was an honor to himself and to Waynesburg College.[4]

The faculty of the Music Department continued to function somewhat differently from that of the regular staff. The head of that Department, Helen McGiffin, was employed by the trustees, and in July 1920 her salary was $1,500 per year. She was authorized to employ all assistants in that department. She was also required to pay the college 15 percent of its gross receipts. There was some difficulty in finding space for that department—where there would be the least distraction to students in other classes. The first and second floors of Hanna Hall were contemplated for its use, but in June 1921 space was found in rooms adjacent to Philo and Union Halls on the third floor of the main building.[5]

There was little change in admission requirements. To enter the freshman class, fifteen units or its equivalent of secondary work was "absolutely essential." Conditional admission was permitted, however, to one who had completed thirteen units. Students could transfer from other colleges, but efforts were made to assure that the courses transferred were similar to those offered by Waynesburg.[6]

A significant change was made in the college calendar. The three-term college year gave way to the semester system. The last three-term year (fall, winter, and spring terms) was 1921-1922.[7]

With respect to the curriculum, prospective teachers were reminded of the college's Normal Department. The catalogue boasts: "Waynesburg College . . . was the precursor of state Normal Schools in our state and it still leads along this important line. . . . Teachers, remember where you can get the very best things for the least money." By 1920 students who completed the Normal course received permanent certificates, and periodic examinations by the Superintendent of Greene County Schools were terminated.[8]

The most important innovation in the curriculum was the establishment of the Student Army Training Corps (SATC) by the fall of 1918. With the war raging in Europe, Uncle Sam needed commissioned officers in increasing numbers—hence this new program. Many young men were recruited in Greene County; others came from Pittsburgh and other places in western Pennsylvania. In all they numbered 150. They were housed and fed partly in the college dormitory and partly in the Armory. Military training both in the classroom and on the campus was conducted by United States Army officers. These students were "excellent fellows—poised, refined, polite, and cultured." They had "good table manners: So far no one has been slapped in the face with a butter dish, and no one has cut his mouth with a knife. . . . We are at war, hence we work hard, and patiently wait for our commissions. . . . The dormitory gang thinks the girls of Waynesburg are all belles—not dumb belles either." The young men were hospitable; they invited Waynesburgers to visit them on Sundays. They were also religious: "We have Bible reading and grace at luncheon." They suggested a football team for the college: "Good material seems plentiful. Let's get together and start something."[9]

Early in November 1918 Colonel Edward Martin talked in chapel, and addressed himself chiefly to the SATC men. He stressed the need for discipline, which would always stand them in good stead. He asserted that the men "who went to war have learned how to appreciate America."[10] Fortunately for the SATC men—and for everyone—hostilities soon ended. In December 1918 the unit at the college was demobilized. Shortly the Government suggested the formation of a Reserve Officers Training Corps (ROTC) to take its place. McKay and the trustees favored the organization of such a unit on the campus. The Government would provide training officers, uniforms, supplies, and other equipment. But the college did not meet certain "essential conditions" for the organization of such a unit, and the project was dropped.[11]

In the fall of 1919 a sociology course, which would have been a blueprint for Communism, was included in the college catalogue. To the delight of devotees of Lenin, the Russian Revolution of 1917 was still having repercussions—even on the campus. Professor Nathaniel A. Danowsky, who held a master's degree from Susquehanna University, had been employed to teach sociology. Whether or not he was a Marxist is not clear, but he described the sociology course he was scheduled to teach under five main headings. First, "labor is the only source of value, and the laborer is entitled to all that he produces." Second, "capital . . . is . . . the result of spoliation, legalized by the present forms of political administration." Third, "the true function of government is the solution of the economic problem." Fourth, "land . . . and tools . . . should at once become public property and be held as such." Fifth, "agriculture and manufacturing are to be carried on under governmental inspectors, who shall prevent overproduction and waste; or, as Karl Marx prefers, by voluntary and independent communes, holding governmental leases of land and of fixed capital in the forms of buildings and machinery." In line with Leninists who believed that Communism would quickly spread over the world, Danowsky declared: "These professed changes constitute a definite political issue, fundamental and international."[12]

The trustees reacted immediately. On 17 September 1919 they instructed their Committee on Teachers and Salaries "to investigate the statements made in the College Bulletin . . . under the head of Sociology by Professor Donskey [*sic*] and report to this board." Details relative to this investigation are not available. But Danowsky was not a member of the faculty the following year. And the description of the sociology course was changed to read that it "aimed to study society and develop good citizens."[13]

With the introduction of military training, the curriculum had been adapted to wartime needs. When peace came, the shortened program in which one could win a degree in three years was terminated. Beginning early in 1919 four full years of study in the arts and sciences were required for the baccalaureate degree.[14]

If McKay effected needed changes in the curriculum and in academic matters, he also revamped the athletic program. Prominent men in the community backed the college in all forms of athletic sports. The armory was available to the college for the use of athletes, their coaches, and trainers. The college catalogue declared: "Waynesburg College athletics have been put on a safe and sane foundation for the next five years. . . . A new day has dawned for the outdoor life of our college. All hail the day!"[15]

Under this new athletic policy, Paul R. Stewart continued to toil devotedly as Director of Athletics. In the hope of improving the program, the college gradually raised the athletic fee to $4.00 per student; townspeople made donations to the cause. Efforts were made to secure able coaches for the several sports. For example, in the spring of 1921 Stewart and John G. Dinsmore, the student manager, secured the services of Joe ("Hooker") Phillips as baseball coach. A local editor praised him: "Phillips knows all there is to know about baseball, having started in the national sport with the Waynesburg College nine. . . . " He had had wide experience, having played on several minor league teams. And he was well known—and liked—locally. He worked hard with a squad of eighteen good candidates. Some thirteen games were played, chiefly against colleges in the tri-state area. The team enjoyed a winning season.[16]

With regard to basketball the most important event was the third Interscholastic Basketball Tournament sponsored by the college on 29 March 1919. Considered "one of the biggest athletic events ever held here," it was a contest among teams from eight high schools including those at Canonsburg, Claysville, Crafton, Waynesburg, and Washington, in Pennsylvania; and Fairview, Farmington, and Wellsburg, in West Virginia. Some eighty students participated. The teams were divided in two divisions; and the winner in each received a beautiful silver cup. A cup was given also to the school with the best cheering section. The tournament aimed to decide championships of Washington and Greene counties. The college's

Athletic Association hoped to make this an annual event, which would be beneficial not only athletically, but socially. "Let's be hospitable" was the oft-heard slogan on the campus.[17]

Intercollegiate football reached a low ebb all over the nation during World War I; as we have seen, it was discontinued at the college. By 1919, however, other institutions were reviving the sport. A local editor maintained, "Waynesburg College should do so, for football is indispensable to a college or a university." Waynesburgers wanted to know about prospects at the college "for a team *soon* (italics in original)." The college desired to field a team, but needed money. Many alumni and businessmen in Waynesburg were willing to give funds for athletics. All concerned—the college administrators, students, alumni, and prominent townsmen—were urged to promote football at the college. A local editor contended that for several years athletics at the college had suffered "not through any fault of the school alone, but partly through the indifference of the townspeople toward the school's athletic efforts."[18] These efforts were not in vain. After McKay's administration intercollegiate football was destined to be revived and to enjoy many years of success.

Other than athletics, certain aspects of student life during McKay's administration are interesting, chiefly because of an almost "about-face" in the college's attitude toward student conduct. The great emphasis was on self-discipline. The college catalogue, after referring to Waynesburg as the "Shiretown," since it was the seat of Greene County, and pointing to the climate as "salubrious beyond compare," praised the high level of social morality:

> For over forty years no licensed bar has projected its befouling presence in our midst nor distilled its brew of hell within our borders. Parents, it is a safe town to which to send your strong boys and clean girls. . . . The best governed body is the least governed body. Our working motto is *semper praesens*, *semper paratus* (always present, always prepared). Self-rule should be right-rule. . . . If one does not acquire self-government in his school days, all else . . . will be worthless, and one's time will have been wasted entirely.

With respect to housing of students, parents were assured: "All homes for the students will be selected and ok-ed [*sic*] by the President. We will adjudge all our girls and boys as ladies and gentlemen, and it will take a mighty effort to prove our opinion fallacious. . . . " Students were warned, however, that "they must not abuse our confidence." If, and when, they ceased to be ladies and gentlemen, they would be liable for expulsion. The attitude toward church attendance was also liberalized. Students were "*expected* to attend the church of their choice each Sunday. . . . " But all worship was on a voluntary basis.[19]

An example of fine student spirit shone through about mid-November 1918, shortly after the armistice was declared. The pressure was off the SATC men; now they could engage in things on the lighter—and different—side of student life. Under the direction of McKay and their commanding officers, these young men held a husking bee on Professor Paul R. Stewart's farm not far from town. On a Saturday forenoon they husked some 300 shocks of corn. Stewart also had a large crop of apples, and one squad was assigned the duty of making cider and supplying the boys with cider and apples. The young men consumed considerable quantities of these delicacies. In addition Stewart gave $25 to the SATC, which was turned over to the officers to spend for the boys as they thought best.[20]

After the war several suggestions were made about a fitting memorial in Greene County "for her illustrious soldier boys, living and dead, who dared their all that liberty should not perish. . . . " A loyal alumnus asked:

> What is a fitting memorial? He then suggested one: In this connection, I, a Greene Countian, a Waynesburg College boy, participant in the Philippine, the Mexican and the "Overseas wars," beg to suggest that we select Waynesburg College as our Memorial; that we at once proceed to make it Greene County's testimonial to her boys and that we ordain it to endure forever and endow it with our gifts so that her glory shall shine resplendent into the very ends of the earth.

McKay fully agreed with these sentiments. He said the college "has repeatedly poured her blood on the altar of freedom. . . . I see no impropriety in this suggested adaptation of the college for the Boys' Memorial, but a very great blessing." The alumnus who made this suggestion signed himself as "A World Warrior," but he obviously was Edward Martin. No other person would fit the description of the "World Warrior."[21]

The SATC program, although short-lived, not only injected new life into the campus, but brought badly needed funds from the federal government. Several payments, ranging from around $3,700 to $4,200, were made to the college during the first half of 1919. This money greatly aided in the payment of current expenses; and even enough money was at hand to authorize McKay to purchase an automobile for his use as the property of Waynesburg College. But both before and after receipt of these funds, the college was hard pressed financially. Tuition, at $25 per term, although higher than ever, plus the Library and Athletic fee of $1.50 per term, plus around $2,000 per year from the Presbyterian Church, U. S. A. did not total enough to keep the budget in balance. The trustees, therefore, were forced to borrow from a local bank in amounts ranging from $1,500 to $3,500 in order to pay faculty salaries and to meet other expenses.[22]

To increase the endowment fund was imperative. By July 1919 the Presbyterian Church, U. S. A. had set up "the Standard" for colleges under its sponsorship. It called for an additional endowment in the amount of $200,000 as soon as possible. The trustees, eager to help raise this money, urged McKay "to seek donations of money, houses, lands, coal lands, bonds and mortgages or other things of value. . . . " By January 1920 the goal for endowment was increased to $500,000. A representative of the Presbyterian College Board then came to Waynesburg, met with trustees of the college, and decided to give every assistance in the campaign. The aim was to raise $500,000 payable in five annual installments. The trustees resolved "that we personally, and as a Board, hereby agree to cooperate with Pres. McKay in securing this sum by the use of the best and most earnest method." They urged the Presbyterian College Board to contribute $100,000 of this sum. The alumni of the college lent their support; local alumni collaborated with those in the Pittsburgh area in order to raise money for the college.[23] But these goals were not reached during McKay's administration.

If funds were lacking, so was an adequate heating system for the buildings. In the early decades coal stoves were used, and they gave way to gas after the turn of the century. As long as natural gas abounded in the area, it was no problem to heat even the four-story main building. By 1919, however, it appears that heating by natural gas had certain drawbacks. The trustees, therefore, considered the installation of a centralized steam-heating system. They chose a committee from their own body and authorized it to raise money necessary for a steam heating plant for the College. The estimated cost was $9,156. The trustees looked for a proper location of the furnace of such a system, and decided on the northwest room in the basement of the main building. The furnace would burn coal, and pipes would carry the steam to heating units in all rooms in the building. But funds were lacking. The trustees moved twice to borrow most of the money; both motions were lost, however. Meanwhile McKay worked hard, and reported on 8 September 1919 that he had secured $3,000 in subscriptions and promises. A local editor gave his moral support to the project: "A young lady from the country says Waynesburg College would be enhanced 100%, if properly steam-heated. It should have been done years ago. Loyal alumni are sending subscriptions from far away. Alumni and friends in Greene County could readily help . . . to install steam heating." The matter dragged on. The college catalogue of 1919-1920 did not mention the money problem; it claimed that "scarcity of labor and materials have delayed the installation of our new heating plant, but it will be done this summer."[24] The project was not to be completed, however, until the late 1920's.

The women's dormitory was constructed as a modern building at the outset. The college catalogue boasted: "The rooms are furnished with couch-bed, bureau, study-table, chairs, and is [*sic*] heated by steam and lighted by electricity. . . . Grounds are very beautiful, there being no lovelier spot in western Pennsylvania devoted to education, and plans for further beautification are constantly being developed."[25] Despite these enticing words, demand for rooms in the dormitory dropped to the nadir. Early in January 1919 the trustees passed a motion to close the dormitory for the winter term. Telephone service in the building was canceled. In what seems an amazing paradox, for some two years the building appears to have been a white elephant.[26]

A windfall for the college came in the spring of 1921, however. The local Hospital Board desired to move the hospital from cramped space in the Blair Building (location of Blair Hotel) on East High Street to more spacious quarters. In March 1921 that body made overtures to the trustees to purchase the dormitory and the ground behind it back to Greene Mount Cemetery; it offered the trustees $75,000 for this property. The trustees promptly appointed a committee to confer with the Hospital Board about the matter. Instead of selling the property, the trustees resolved to rent the dormitory and president's house for hospital purposes for a period of two years from 1 June 1921. The Hospital Board agreed to do all repairing and make necessary alterations at its own expense, and to pay for all fuel, light and water and gas bills, and to keep the building in good repair. Rent on this property was $5,000 per year. The trustees agreed unanimously to this rental; all negotiations were completed by 29 July 1921. But the rental was extended after the expiration of two years.[27]

The college continued to rent most of Hanna Hall to the Waynesburg School Board.[28] With the rentals of the Women's Dormitory and most space in Hanna Hall, the main building was the only one left exclusively for college purposes. While the SATC Unit was on campus, the college leased the Armory from the Waynesburg Armory Board for eight months at $80 per month. This building was needed chiefly as space for feeding this military training unit.[29]

The rentals of Hanna Hall and the Women's Dormitory caused considerable dissatisfaction among alumni. Late in May 1921 a committee of alumni informed the trustees of their desire "to cooperate with the Board to promote the interests of the college. . . . " The alumni suggested some changes: (1) that the college's charter be changed so that trustees could be elected for a term of years; (2) that at least half of the board be alumni and be elected by alumni; and (3) "that this college be operated on a more business [*sic*] method, especially in the executive department." The trustees discussed these matters among themselves, and agreed to supply alumni with data or information concerning college affairs.[30]

One of the most regrettable problems was McKay's poor health. He had suffered for two years as the result of injuries in an automobile accident, which left him blind in one eye and generally frail. Despite his condition, he continued to do his best for the college. Nevertheless, with brutal candor, a note of 31 May 1921 from the Alumni Association suggested:

> That the present administration does not have the support of the citizens and residents of Greene County, and that the Pres. of Waynesburg College is physically unable to perform many duties placed upon him. . . . Therefore, we recommend to your Honorable Body that you declare a vacancy in the Chair of the Presidency of Waynesburg College and that you proceed at your earliest convenience to fill said vacancy.

Accordingly on 10 June 1921, by a majority, the trustees declared the office of the President of the college vacant as of 1 July 1921. Thus McKay was retired. On 22 June 1921 the trustees elected Professor Paul R. Stewart as Acting President of the college.[31]

McKay succumbed on 18 December 1921 in Grove City Hospital, Grove City, Pennsylvania, near the scenes of his boyhood home. He became seriously ill while visiting relatives in that community—and died of a heart attack. His friend, fellow laborer, and successor in the presidency, Paul R. Stewart, said of McKay: "We all loved him in the trying years after the war and remember those days as the most pleasant in our connection with Waynesburg College."[32]

As acting president of the college during the year 1899-1900, McKay served assiduously as a link between Miller and the series of short-term presidents of the institution. On his return in 1918, this time as president, McKay again served as a link between the short-lived administrations and that of Paul R. Stewart. During his three years as president, McKay faced difficulties beyond his own control. His partial blindness and poor physical condition impaired his usefulness; and wartime conditions hurt the institution. Enrollment dropped during the conflict. When peace came, no federal funds were available for the education of returning veterans; and enrollment remained low. Very little was done in the endowment campaign; lack of money was constant. McKay was unable to grapple effectively with these problems.

XIV
STEWART'S STRUGGLES IN THE 1920's

IF ALFRED B. MILLER WAS THE "FATHER" AND "MOSES" OF WAYNESBURG College, Paul R. Stewart was its Regenerator and Redeemer. On taking the helm the two men faced strikingly parallel circumstances. In desperation in 1858, the president of the trustees asked Miller to become president of the college, because there was no alternative.[1] In equally desperate circumstances, late in June 1921, the president of the trustees, Timothy J. Wisecarver, phoned the farmhouse of Professor Paul R. Stewart. Mrs. Stewart answered, learned that her husband was wanted, and went out and called him to the phone. "I was hoeing in the cornfield that morning," said Stewart. "I threw down the hoe and hurried to the house." Wisecarver said: "The trustees had a meeting last night. They couldn't think of any way to save the college. So they voted you as acting president. Come into town and get the keys. I went. By supper time I was in charge of what probably constituted the most impoverished college in the nation." Stewart was to serve as acting president "until a president is elected." Shortly the trustees appointed a committee from their own body to find a president for the college. On 1 January 1923 they unanimously elected Stewart to that position.[2]

Thus began a new and better era for Waynesburg College. For more than two decades, lack of the right kind of leadership had hurt the institution. Nine men had come and gone in rapid succession. Such fast turnover of administrations caused the public—even the alumni—to lack confidence in the college. Some of these men, particularly Houghton, were scholarly and able in some respects. But none of them had all the qualities of Miller or Stewart. What was needed at Waynesburg College was a man who deeply loved, and was totally dedicated to, the institution; who was willing to work for unnumbered hours; and who had a "never-say-die" spirit in the face of adversity. In short, a president, to be successful at the college, had to be a man who yearned to spend unselfishly his energies and his life in service for his students and for humanity. Stewart, like Miller, was such a man. With the advent of Stewart, the short-lived administrations ended.

Stewart started practically from scratch. When he was appointed acting president, college finances were nearly nonexistent. Only one building was in use for college purposes. Student enrollment was sixty-six—one of the lowest in the history of the institution. The college had no faculty, no janitor, no catalog, not even a person to answer the phone. Stewart had no secretary, but he "borrowed" one from a local law office. Lacking an automobile, he borrowed one and started out to recruit students. Shortly the trustees passed a motion to "pay all necessary expenses and furnish [an] automobile to Prof. Stewart in soliciting students."[3]

Stewart struggled not only to solicit students, but also to recruit a faculty. He battled to re-acquire for college use the two buildings then being rented, namely, Hanna Hall and the Women's Dormitory. His most difficult task was in raising the endowment fund. And he faced problems relating to the enforcement of freshman rules and chapel attendance.

Paul R. Stewart was born in a log cabin at Spraggs, eight miles from Waynesburg on 16 March 1887, the son of Ezra De Garmo Stewart, '84, and Lana Waychoff Stewart. The Stewart's first ancestor to come to Greene County was Isaac Stewart, a pioneer settler, who acquired a large area of land by tomahawk right. When Paul was four years old, the family moved to a farm near Waynesburg on which he resided for many years. He attended the local schools and the Academy of Waynesburg College. After completion of work in the Academy, he entered the college and received the A.B. degree in 1909. He married Dessie Rush, one of his classmates. To them were borne two children: Walter Alan Stewart and Ruth Stewart Schenley. Paul briefly taught public school. After completion of his undergraduate work, as we have seen, he served on the faculty of the college from 1910 to 1921. In recognition of his excellent work, his *Alma Mater* conferred upon him the A.M. degree in 1911. Later he did graduate work at Columbia University and won an A.M. degree there in 1916. Subsequently Waynesburg College awarded him the honorary degrees Sc.D. and L.H.D.; Grove City

College honored him with an LL.D.; and West Virginia Wesleyan College, with an Sc.D.[4]

Affectionately called "Prexy," Stewart was successful against great odds, largely because of his unusual philosophy of life. First, he literally thrived on adversity. On one occasion, he referred to "the relation between the product of colleges and so-called hard times. . . . It is a well-known saying that great leaders are not made by prosperity but by adversity." Speaking in 1927, he held that "the temporary financial stringency now existing throughout the nation would bring an increase in the number of youth in colleges generally. He believed "they would be more consecrated due to adversity."[5] Second, he disagreed with the old adage: "Nothing succeeds like success." He contended that anyone who believes that maxim "forgets the nights of planning, the long days of rehearsing before life's great dramas are enacted. Opportunity does not knock at every man's door. Most men must knock at opportunity's door and keep knocking until they find her at home." He then quoted the old saying:

> The heights by great men reached and kept,
> Were not attained by sudden flight.
> But they, while their companions slept,
> Were toiling upward in the night.

Third, he stressed the great need for continuous and unconquerable purpose: "It is this indomitable purpose we are trying to instill into the hearts of Waynesburg College students and alumni. . . . Waynesburg College must no longer be the plaything of circumstances."[6] Fourth, Stewart had a superman's capacity for work. When the trustees selected him as acting president he made "a resolution that he would give an average of 14 or 15 hours each day to the College. . . . "[7] At the outset of his duties for the college in 1910, salaries were low and he eked out a living for himself and his family by the income from his farm, vegetables, and fruit. He "never walked, but ran." He did farm chores in the morning, then ran to the classroom.[8] Fifth, Stewart's great love for, and deep commitment to, the college were exceptional. In this respect he held Miller up as an example which others might emulate: "Dr. Miller saw the vision of a secure Waynesburg College. The power of his love for this institution, stronger than death, calls us to strive toward the realization of the dominant hope of his life. May we be true to that trust."[9]

Joshua Loughran, President 1849-1855

Alfred B. Miller, President 1859-1899

Paul R. Stewart, Acting President, 1921-1923, President 1923-1963, Chancellor, 1963-1973

Bennett M. Rich, President 1963-1974

Hanna Hall. Completed 1851

Plaque on North Morris Street, Wayn

Scene in the park, showing the fountain and "Lake Winetta" to the left

First football team, the "Flying Wedge", 1895

NAIA Football National Champions, 1966

The Lamplighters, Choral Group. Director James D. Randolph on extreme right

Miller Hall from the park. Dedicated 1899

The Library. Completed 1955

Paul R. Stewart Science Building. Dedicated 1964

Buhl Humanities Building. Dedicated 1968

The Gymnasium. Opened 1944

Benedum Hall, Dining Room and Student Center. Erected 1959. Expanded 1971

Thayer Hall, Men's Dormitory. Completed 1958

Martin Hall, Men's Dormitory. Completed 1965

Denny Hall, Women's Dormitory. Completed 1961

Burns Hall, Women's Dormitory. Completed 1967

Stewart had other admirable qualities. A most effective classroom teacher, in addition to his other duties, he taught a variety of subjects including agriculture, astronomy, biology, botany, chemistry, geology, mineralogy, and zoology. He was able to inspire students and to motivate them to do their best. He said: "there is so much joy to be discovered in *whom* you teach as in what you teach (Stewart's italics)." In keeping with long tradition, he was well known for his efforts to help destitute, but worthy, students. During the depression years he gave such students the opportunity to pick apples in his orchard. The apples sold for 40 cents per bushel, if picked from the trees; and 25 cents per bushel, if gathered off the ground. Many bushels annually were brought to the campus for sale to the students. The honor system was used: a student could take what apples he wanted and put the money in a nearby bowl. Shortly everybody would be eating apples. One student reported, however, that he "never saw over four coins in the bowl, but Prexy never complained."[10]

Though Stewart was not a theologian, he was thoroughly familiar with the Bible. He could expound on the meaning of Scriptures clearly and cogently; his commentaries in chapel made students aware of the importance of spiritual things, and aided them in working out a sense of true values. A dynamic orator, Stewart was always in demand as a public speaker; and his performance at commencement and other public events of the college was masterful. Hence he was an excellent public relations man. As a fundraiser he was successful—fortunately, for the very life of the institution depended on a great increase in the endowment fund.

In his struggle to increase enrollment, Stewart faced unusual difficulties. World War I had caused a drop in enrollment at Waynesburg as well as at all colleges in the nation. The local SATC Corps, which numbered 150 men, was disbanded shortly after the armistice. A depression in 1921 hurt many families economically, and made it more difficult to recruit students. Furthermore, classical education was giving way to technical training as a result of the war. The large universities and schools of engineering were attracting most students.[11]

Stewart was determined to add as many students as possible to the 66 enrolled in the college when he became acting president. In 1920 the freshman class numbered only 22, 16 of whom were from Waynesburg, and the rest from Greene County. Stewart aimed to keep doubling each freshman class and to widen his area of operations. From late June to September 1921 he worked sometimes 20 hours a day looking for students and money; in those few weeks he recruited 40 freshmen. In September 1922, in keeping with his resolution, 80 freshmen were enrolled. By that time Stewart had gone beyond Greene County; those freshmen came from all the southwestern counties of Pennsylvania as well as from Illinois, Maryland, Michigan, New York, Ohio, Virginia, and West Virginia. In July 1923 Stewart predicted that 160 freshmen would enroll that fall. By the academic year 1925-1926 enrollment of degree-seeking students had nearly quadrupled the figure for 1920-1921. And overall enrollment in the institution, including students in expression, extension, music, and summer school had increased from 238 in 1920-1921 to 685 in 1925-1926. Waynesburg College was "on the up road."[12]

Students could be admitted to the freshman class in one of three ways: (1) by certificates from approved high schools or academies; (2) by passing an examination administered by the college early in September each year; and (3) by a certificate from the College Entrance Examination Board (CEEB) administered annually in June. Until 1923, students who did not meet these requirements were permitted to enroll in "special courses which do not count toward a degree. If such students succeed, they may later apply these courses toward a degree. They must be mature and work hard." In 1923, however, in keeping with an act of the state legislature, admission requirements became more rigid. Thenceforward only graduates of approved four-year high schools or academies, "or the equivalent" could be admitted. This was a standard of the Association of Colleges and Preparatory Schools of the Middle States "to whose highest credited list Waynesburg [College] hopes to attain shortly."[13]

Community leaders, whose confidence in the college was restored, immediately rallied to Stewart. At the Alumni banquet in the Armory on 22 June 1921, H. D. Freeland, Superintendent of Schools of Greene County, talked on "A Closer Relation Between the High Schools of the County and the College." He said he saw "no reason why Waynesburg College should not secure a large percentage of the high school graduates of 1921, and that he was willing to do all in his power to bring this about." In June 1922 the alumni stated several objectives aimed to support the college: (1) to assist in publishing *The Collegian*; (2) to provide scholarships for worthy students; (3) to raise money for the college by means of an Alumni College Fund Association; (4) to organize, inform, and help Waynesburg College alumni branch associations; (5) to compile records and memorabilia of all living and dead alumni and former students; (6) to publish alumni directories; (7) to suggest trustees for the college; and (8) to plan and execute Alumni Day at commencement time. On 10 April 1924 the Uniontown Alumni Association was organized; its membership included graduates of the college who resided in Fayette County. Within the next two decades other such organizations were established in centers of population where alumni of the college were numerous.[14]

The Waynesburg Board of Trade fully cooperated with Stewart in finding jobs for students on evenings and Saturdays. Some "25 percent of the students were working their way through." Hence the institution came to be called "The Poor Boys' College." A College Employment Bureau was maintained to facilitate contacts between needy students, who wished to work, and the townspeople. Urging townsmen to call this Bureau, a local editor eagerly helped:

> Waynesburg College students can do almost anything—sign painting, table waiting, clerks of all kinds, pipefitting, painting, carpeting, gardening, farming, tree-trimming, lawn-mowing, truck- and car-driving, plumbing, ditch-digging, house-cleaning, addressing envelopes, bookkeeping, type-writing, meat cutting, coal mining, garage work, and stenographic work. . . . Waynesburg College students do not ask, 'How hard is the job'? but 'Where is it'?. . . . Self-help students are good for the college and also, for the community.

In August 1921 the alumni set up several scholarships for meritorious students. In June 1923 other scholarships were given by several women's clubs and by the Federation of Greene County Women.[15] Thus, recruiting, job placement, and financial aid to students were combined to increase enrollment at the college.

At the first opportunity, in June 1921, Stewart gave attention to the most pressing academic matters. He suggested that the college issue a catalogue as soon as possible. And he urged the trustees to "fill all vacancies in faculty."[16] He strived to secure competent teachers. On his recommendation, the trustees shortly employed Professor George F. Dunkleberger, Vice Principal of Southwestern State Normal School, at California, Pennsylvania, as Dean of the College and Professor of Psychology and Education, at a salary of $2,250 per year. Dunkleberger had received the A.B. and A.M. degrees from Susquehanna University; he also held an A.M. degree from the University of Pittsburgh; and he was doing graduate work toward a Ph.D. at New York University. Dunkleberger was widely known as an educator. He served Waynesburg College well by strengthening the courses in psychology and education. Largely as a result of his efforts the college introduced a new degree—the B.S. in Education. But in 1926 he left Waynesburg and accepted a position at Susquehanna University.[17]

Stewart's father, Ezra D. Stewart, also was a member of the faculty. After his graduation from Waynesburg College in 1884, he did graduate work at Harvard University. An efficient man in the classroom, he taught public school for several years at different places, including Garard's Fort, where he met Lana M. Waychoff, whom he married on 2 July 1885; Sunbury, Pennsylvania, where he was assistant principal; Kingwood, West Virginia, where he was principal; and Spraggs, Pennsylvania, where, from 1888 to 1891, he held three good summer normals and taught many teachers of Greene County. In 1891 he joined the faculty of the Normal Department of Waynesburg College. From 1893 to 1896 he served ably as Superintendent of Schools of Greene County. From 1896 until his death in 1928, except for a few years, he taught chiefly mathematics and Greek at Waynesburg College. He succeeded the revered Walter G. Scott as head of the Mathematics Department. Ezra D. Stewart was known as one of the "famous five"—Miller, Scott, Rinehart, Waychoff, and Stewart.[18]

In addition to Dunkleberger and Ezra D. Stewart, other faculty members employed by September 1921 were: Harry S. Todd in history and economics, Helga Colquist in English, Cecil O. Riggs in physics, and Mary Dinsmore as Librarian. On 17 March 1922 Stewart told the trustees that four additional faculty members were needed, but only two—Mary V. Sutton and Mary I. Munnell—were employed. In July 1922 salaries of most of these teachers ranged between $1,600 and $2,250 for the year 1922-1923; Stewart's salary for that year was $2,700.[19] These faculty members were not only skillful classroom teachers, but some had an interest in publication. By December 1922 the following three articles of a scholarly nature were published: George F. Dunkleberger, "Some Aspects of Modern Education"; Cecil O. Riggs, "Some Recent Discoveries in Science"; and Mary Inghram Munnell, "Latin, a Valuable Aid to the Acquisition of Knowledge of Modern Foreign Languages."[20]

Several faculty changes were made in the late 1920's. After Dunkleberger left, the vacancy was filled by James Widdowson from 1926 to 1929. He was replaced in June 1929 by Chauncey Lively. These men served successively as Dean of the College and Professor of courses in education. By 1927 the trustees had hired McLeod

Harvey who taught religion, philosophy, and psychology; and G. Clements Edson had been employed as Field Secretary and professor of Latin. Lively, Harvey, and Edson had earned doctorates—which greatly strengthened the faculty. About the same time Arthur M. Mintier, who held a master's degree in history from the University of Michigan, was appointed to teach history. In the latter half of 1929 Mintier went on an expedition, consisting chiefly of archaeologists from the University of Michigan, to Mesopotamia where they excavated part of the ancient city of Babylon, examined the "Hanging Gardens," and studied archival materials relating to Alexander, the Great. In addition to his duties as a history teacher, Mintier was debate coach. For many years his debaters competed respectably against the best in the Middle West, South and East. They brought glory to, and advertised, Waynesburg College. By the summer of 1929 the School of Music was under the direction of Ellen Reid Carter; the School of Expression under Katherine Arlene Fisher; the Summer Session and Extension under Dr. Harvey; and education courses were taught by Dr. Lively. All were "showing advancing standards."[21]

By the late 1920's two practices had been adopted which helped to maintain faculty morale. One was the monthly dinners, with a faculty committee of two in charge of each. The other was the annual reception for the faculty, given by Stewart and his wife at their home.[22] These affairs were essentially social in nature. The spirit of cooperation and loyalty to the college was fostered.

Stewart's struggle to recruit students and a faculty was equaled only by his efforts to raise funds. When he became acting president of the college, the endowment fund was less that $100,000. He urged alumni and friends of the college to help him financially. Increased endowment was greatly needed; so were two buildings—a science hall and a gymnasium.[23] Early in November 1922 Stewart went to New York and apprised the Presbyterian authorities of the college's needs. Aware of the college's long period of service in Christian education and of Stewart's success in less than two years, in November 1922, the Presbyterian Synod of Pennsylvania recommended the college for a $500,000 increase in endowment. It urged the trustees of the college to plan immediately to raise the first $250,000 of this increased endowment. It resolved to petition the General Board of Education of the Presbyterian Church, U.S.A. to grant $50,000 "of this said $250,000 provided the whole sum shall be raised within a reasonable time." It resolved further to petition the General Educational Board of the Rockefeller Foundation for $50,000 "of this said $250,000. . . . " In March 1923 the General Assembly of the Presbyterian Church, U.S.A. agreed to give $40,000 "on condition that $200,000 is raised."[24]

In May 1923 a bombshell hit the college when the state legislature amended a law of 26 June 1895 relative to college standards. It contained provisions to govern the admission of students and prescribed a certain minimum number of faculty members. But the provision which shook Stewart, the students, alumni, and friends of the college was the one relating to minimum endowment. Signed by Governor Gifford Pinchot on 23 May 1923, it provided that thenceforth no institution would be chartered with power to confer degrees, unless it had a minimum productive endowment of $500,000. Colleges already chartered, if they did not have it, had to reach this figure within four years. Simultaneously a State Council of Education was set up, with some discretionary power over the implementation of this law. It could prescribe additional requirements for some institutions, and make exceptions under some circumstances.[25] Nevertheless, if the college did not abide by this Act, the chances were that it would lose its power to confer degrees. The very life of the institution was in jeopardy.

Fortunately, the college had four years of grace in which to raise endowment to $500,000. The immediate aim was to continue the campaign, already under way, for $250,000; it was hoped this amount could be raised within a year. Then the drive would continue until $500,000 was reached. The campaign was to have been launched in the fall of 1923, some four months after the enactment of the law. But Dr. O. W. Buschgen, financial secretary of the Board of Education of the Presbyterian Church, U.S.A., whose aid was essential, was then too crowded with other such campaigns; he could only make a quick trip to Waynesburg, and survey the situation. The trustees, therefore, decided to postpone "our campaign to come from 1 May to 12 June 1924." Meanwhile, Buschgen would help the college with a publicity campaign. Early in January 1924, Stewart called attention to the act of the legislature: "Remember that the state will soon require $500,000 as the endowment of each college it recognizes." Speaking again just prior to the start of the campaign, he said that during the first seventy-four years of the college's history, only $107,000 had been raised for endowment. Then he mentioned Madison and Monongahela colleges which failed due to lack of endowment. He also called attention to area colleges that succeeded:

Allegheny, Bethany, Geneva, Grove City, Washington and Jefferson, Westminster, and West Virginia Wesleyan. "Church colleges are either secure or dead. Today Waynesburg College is neither secure nor dead." But he warned: "The next generation may see Waynesburg College dead or dying." He showed a ray of hope in the "increased attendance, interest of the alumni, the teacher training program, and so on." Then sorrowfully he stressed "there was NO NOTABLE INCREASE IN OUR PERMANENT RESOURCES (Stewart's capitalization)." He called for $250,000 for endowment by 12 June 1924.[26]

The people got his message. His clarion call reached their hearts —and their pocketbooks. They looked upon the impending plight of the college as they would a great disaster such as a flood, a devastating fire, or other calamity in which human beings suffer— in which those who are fortunate enough to survive and remain strong want to do all in their power to aid the helpless, the homeless, the sick, and the dying. Such circumstances bring out the best in people, and prove that in dire need they will bear one another's burdens. Before the drive could begin, however, the trustees had to borrow $5,000 to get it off the ground. Senator Albert B. Cummins, '67, was invited to be the main speaker at the kickoff dinner on 1 May 1924, but available evidence indicates he was not able to come.[27]

The aim was to raise $250,000 in Greene and Fayette counties, then to continue the drive in wider areas. The Waynesburg Chamber of Commerce endorsed the campaign, and warned that "the college cannot fulfill its mission unless it receives adequate financial support from its constituency and friends. . . . "[28] Business establishments in Waynesburg placed advertisements in local papers: "Join in the crusade to endow Waynesburg College. He who would truly live must give."[29] Waynesburg women became ardent crusaders. They organized a committee and aimed: (1) to conduct prayer meetings on behalf of the drive; (2) to help with getting special subscriptions; and (3) to be ready "for service of all types needed during the work here." These women held prayer meetings in groups gathered in homes and cottages, and asked all women in Waynesburg to have each morning "a short prayer meeting in their homes for the success of the movement."[30]

Alumni rallied to their *Alma Mater*. Members of the graduating class of 1924 all signed a resolution that, in their wills, they would make bequests to the college so "that she may maintain her influence in the cause of Christian education. . . . " Stewart succintly summarized the spirit: "Never in the history of this town has there been such support of any undertaking—never has there been such unanimity of feeling in any cause."[31]

The Presbyterian Church U.S.A. played an important role in the campaign. Late in March 1924, E. R. Pike from its Board of Education came from New York City to confer with local leaders on the start of the drive to raise $250,000 in Greene and Fayette counties. On 16 April 1924 the Endowment Crusade Dinner was held. Dr. William G. Covert, General Secretary of the Board of Education of the church, was speaker of the evening. He bluntly stressed the need of increased endowment: "If you do not secure it, the spirit of moral education of Waynesburg College will go on the rocks." The goal "cannot be reached by the efforts of the few, but by the cooperative efforts of all. I am confident that the two counties are unanimous in the support of the college."[32]

Another dinner, dubbed the "Rainbow Dinner" was held in order to explain the plan of campaign for the town of Waynesburg. Some 200 persons were present, including the officers and their wives from the "city, college, church, and civic organizations."[33] The plan called for teamwork; two teams, one called "The Orange," the other "The Black," were organized; each had a "colonel"; and, in all 110 workers were involved. The goal for the town of Waynesburg was $150,000. A local editor stressed its importance: "Waynesburg was being watched by Pittsburgh and Uniontown. Success here would mean success elsewhere." A "thermometer" was placed on one of the pillars in front of the courthouse, which marked daily the amount raised in Waynesburg. The teams began working on 1 May 1924. By 8 May the "thermometer" showed $100,000. The local editor boasted: "And it will rise today." A week later he exultingly reported: "Victory! Waynesburg goes over the top." Teams of the Orange and Black had reached the $150,000 mark on the thermometer. But the drive was not over. Encouraged by their success, the teams continued to work hard. By the end of the campaign on 12 June, they had raised a grand—and glorious—total of $173,004. Of this sum raised in Waynesburg, $15,325 was given by faculty members and students of the college. Meanwhile, the drive was carried on elsewhere in Greene County; the outside towns and townships were slower in their response than Waynesburgers. Outside Waynesburg the heaviest donors were in Franklin and Cumberland Townships; the Carmichaels area gave substantially. Funds from the Uniontown and Pittsburgh areas were helpful.[34]

By late August 1924 the goal had been reached—and exceeded at $254,000. This together with the $107,000, which was accumulated since 1849, gave the "permanent fund a much more healthy aspect." There was confidence that "we can reach the $500,000 mark by 1927." Many parts of Greene and Fayette counties had not been reached. Furthermore, there were 800 alumni and some 4,000 former students, plus students who had taken work in the Departments of Music and of Expression—all of whom were potential donors.[35]

While the campaign was under way, the trustees looked to G. Clements Edson for information and advice on financial matters. For instance, in January 1925 they desired to dip into the endowment fund for $7,000 to meet current expenses of the college. Edson informed them that such procedure was not wise.[36] On 5 June 1925 he reported that the "grand total of all receipts, including cash and pledges during the year ending on 31 March 1925" was $280,875.[37]

But the deadline year, 1927, came and went—and the endowment fund fell far short of $500,000. By a special dispensation of the state legislature, however, the college was somehow saved. Beyond a doubt that body was aware of the good work done in Waynesburg and in Greene and Fayette counties in 1924; such heroic efforts deserved reward. In any case, in December 1927, Stewart started another drive—this time for $1,000,000 over the next seven years—chiefly for endowment, buildings, and equipment. "The last campaign, which many friends of the college considered too small," he said, "insured the life of the college. The next campaign is for building, for expansion, for efficiency." He then referred to the great development of the Monongahela valley, and contended that the college should "become the equal of any small college in the United States." Many institutions with less age and tradition "have raised a like amount in a short time. . . . We can do the same. . . . " Shortly a dinner meeting was held in the Fort Jackson Hotel—at which the aims of the campaign were stated. The $1,000,000 "would cover everything . . . and would eliminate small debts."[38]

Stewart stressed his unique difficulties in raising large sums. Harking back to a problem that perplexed Miller, namely, that CP members were poor donors to their churches and colleges, he told the trustees: "A constant search should be made for that which this institution has never discovered in its . . . history—a really big giver. . . . The number of people who have made other institutions heirs to their fortunes should put our constituency to shame." Stewart promised the most rigid economy in handling the funds. He predicted that, "in spite of all the difficulties we are facing," the financial picture would improve, the college would prove its ability to be self-sustaining, and the outstanding indebtedness would be paid.[39]

Nevertheless, the drive for $1,000,000 for endowment was not successful. The decade of the 1920's ended, and even half that amount had not been raised. In July 1930 another campaign was started "to increase the endowment of Waynesburg College to $500,000." With D. F. Dunstar of Pittsburgh as general director, it was conducted under the Presbyterian Board of Christian Education. Even this drive was slow in getting under way. In February 1931, the college bulletin warned: "We cannot hope to be accredited unless we build the $300,000 at which we are now rated to the $500,000 mark." Once the latter figure was reached, the campaign would continue in the hope of raising $1,000,000 "in the next few years." Experts in finance in the liberal arts colleges agreed that an endowment of $2,000,000 was necessary for the efficient training of a 500 student unit under modern conditions.[40]

In addition to his struggle to increase endowment, Stewart worked hard to raise funds for the Science Department. On 4 August 1921 he resolved to secure $1,500 for the sciences, chiefly chemistry, as soon as possible; and by 1 November following, he reached his goal. Coming to his aid, on 22 August 1921 the trustees resolved that "we appropriate dollar for dollar up to $1500 toward procuring chemical appliances . . . for said department." Stewart yearned for a science hall. The cost of such a building was estimated, in 1927, to range from $125,000 to $150,000.[41]

The college constantly faced the problem of keeping current expenses within income. Sums received from the Presbyterian Church, U. S. A. varied annually between $2,500 and $5,000.[42] Tuition was comparatively low, but it gradually rose. For the year 1922-1923, for a semester, tuition was $50.00; the athletic fee, $6.00; the library fee, $1.50; and there were also various laboratory fees ranging from $2.00 in geology to $10.00 in an advanced chemistry course. Other expenses at that time were: room, $10.00 per month; board, $7.00 per week; and books, $25.00. Tuition, fees, board, books, and room ran from a total of $400.00 to $450.00 per year.[43] By 1926-1927, tuition per semester was $75.00. Problems presented by perpetual scholarships plagued the college even in the late 1920's. Largely through Stewart's efforts this pernicious system terminated in 1927, when Mary Sayers, '84, a loyal trustee, bought up $3,500 worth of these scholarships and put nearly all of them out of circulation.[44]

As at many colleges in the nation, some students delayed in paying their tuition. To collect it in full was a persistent problem. For example, in June 1924 Stewart showed the trustees "the balance of money due the college from students for tuitions. . . . " The trustees promptly resolved "that hereafter students must pay all tuitions due within two weeks from the beginning of any given term or the matter of an extension of time for payment thereof must be presented to the executive committee" of the trustees, and the decision of this committee was to be conclusive. But this method of collection was not fully effective. Two years later, in June 1926, the faculty came to the aid of the college treasurer by passing a motion that seniors who still owed the college money "shall not be graduated" until such debts were paid. Delinquency of this sort continued, however. In February 1928, in an unusual case, a student attended classes all the preceding semester, and paid nothing. In exasperation, the faculty instructed the registrar to inform the delinquent student's parents "that he is not a member of the college and has not paid last semester's tuition, and that he is residing in town."[45]

Failure to collect tuition on time made it the more difficult to pay current expenses. The college frequently was forced to borrow money from a local bank in order to pay the faculty. It appears too that the funds were not always properly managed. For example, in December 1922 the trustees noted that "teachers' salaries are due but we have no funds in the current expense account to meet the same; in fact, there is an overdraft of approximately $200.00." In order to improve this situation, beginning in December 1924, the trustees called on Edson to help; they declared "'that all checks upon the college treasury be O.K.'d [*sic*] by him before payment." Edson strived to collect funds due the college and to seek a balance between current income and current expenses. Nevertheless, the practice of borrowing money had to be continued in sums running between $2,500 and $5,000.[46]

While Stewart faced manifold problems in the field of finance, he kept abreast of matters relating to the curriculum. In order to strengthen the program to train teachers, by 1921, work toward the B.S. in Education was being offered. After completion of the freshman and sophomore years, one could then obtain a certificate to teach in schools of junior and senior high school grades. Later a student could complete work for the junior and senior years and win the degree B.S. in Education. In order to aid teachers further, the summer normals were continued. Two such sessions were conducted each summer. By attending both, a teacher could add the equivalent of one-half year toward the attaining of a diploma authorizing him to teach. The Department of Public Instruction in Harrisburg desired to concentrate normals at Waynesburg College, and to grant certificates based on the grade of work done by the candidates.[47]

In September 1921, Stewart pointed to the need for Pennsylvania to raise its educational standards: "She is now twenty-one among the states in the union." Knowing that most teachers could not leave their positions to get a college degree, Stewart started Saturday classes in psychology, education, and other courses so that teachers could remain on the job and get an education too. Full college credit was given for all work satisfactorily done. This plan worked well. It helped the teachers; and it helped the college "toward that goal for which all educational institutions stand—the extension of its influence to the greatest number possible."[48]

Several other moves were made to improve the curriculum. By September 1921 the college was cooperating with the undergraduate school of the University of Pittsburgh in the training of engineers. Under this plan, a student could take his first two years' work at Waynesburg College, then transfer to Pitt for his junior and senior years. The aim was to help students "who can't afford to go to Pitt four years." In March 1922 this cooperative plan was amplified to include premedical training; and other institutions were included in the plan. One could take his first two years at Waynesburg, then complete his education in these professions in any one of the following schools: Carnegie Institute of Technology, Massachusetts Institute of Technology, Pennsylvania State University, the University of Pittsburgh, and West Virginia University.[49]

In the belief that "education is a continuing process, beginning at the cradle and ending at the grave," extension courses were offered, starting in 1921. The aim was to help "many intelligent people [who] regret they did not continue their education," and who "want college for cultural purposes." Those taking extension courses were considered special students, and not in line for a degree.[50]

By September 1922 several new courses had been added, including forestry, pre-accounting, business subjects, and journalism. In 1923, after debate was thriving, an English course entitled "Argumentation and Debate" was introduced; offered every semester, most of the students enrolled were members of debating teams.[51] Another curriculum change was the resurrection, in 1924, of graduate work which had been omitted for several years. Courses leading toward the A.M. degree were offered. After a full year of work in residence the candidate was required to submit to "an oral examination before the faculty, stressing the *thesis* (italics in original)."[52]

The semester plan, first effective in the 1922-1923 academic year, was considered an improvement, because it "permits a more adaptable arrangement of courses." Under the preceding system a minimum of 64 *year* hours was required for graduation. Under the semester plan a minimum of 128 semester hours was required for graduation. The normal class schedule for students was 16 hours weekly.[53]

Waynesburg College graduates consistently succeeded wherever they went. They were being admitted to, and were getting on well in, the best professional and graduate schools. They were "hand-forged as opposed to the machine-making of larger schools." Stewart and the faculty could give them individual attention in classrooms and elsewhere on the campus, and could aid them in placement. Stewart exhorted them: "Waynesburg College expects you to make good. You must not be the first to fail."[54]

Students who had specialized in expression and in music also were successful. In the field of music, beyond a doubt the most celebrated young lady to graduate from the college was Helen Denny (later Helen Denny Howard). Late in February 1923, a local newspaper published an article entitled "Waynesburg Girl to Sing in Grand Opera." It referred to a portrait of her adorning "the cover page of the February number of *The Musical Advance*." After graduating from the college, she went to New York City where she appeared in a number of interesting recitals. The article reads: "Her voice is clear, strong, and true, with a remarkable clarity of the intonation. She is particularly commended for the artistry of her interpretations and the depth of feeling she expresses through her voice."[55] Shortly Miss Denny went to Baltimore, Maryland, where she was leading soprano with the De Foe Opera Company. The Baltimore press highly commended her for her splendid singing and realistic interpretations. Subsequently she sang as soloist with a great symphony orchestra in Philadelphia.[56] Miss Denny was most outstanding. But many other musicians of lesser note, trained at Waynesburg College, were successful in their careers.

Reports of students' scholastic standings were regularly sent home to their parents or guardians.[57] Unfortunately there was evidence from time to time of cheating, that perennial evil that plagued so many institutions. In November 1928, at the request of a teacher for concerted action, the faculty "resolved that we . . . exercise very great care in preventing students getting unfair help at written tests and examinations. . . . " This resolution was read to students in chapel; and the faculty called on the Student Council for its cooperation "in upholding the honor of the college through the honor of the individual student."[58]

Turning to a more pleasant aspect of campus life, let us look at the college ring, colors, and seal. Since institutions of higher learning customarily adopt a ring to be worn by their alumni, the faculty and students agreed that the ring of 1923 "shall be standard except the numerals will be changed with each succeeding year—and said ring to be known as the Waynesburg College ring. The ring shall not be worn by any student until his graduation has been approved by the faculty."[59]

In 1929 Stewart threw light on the origin and background of the college seal which is emblazoned on the college ring, and, of course, is stamped into transcripts of students' records and other official documents of the institution. The designer of the college seal was Homer Frye, '10. The lamp signifies the lamp of knowledge. The Latin motto is *Fiat Lux* (Let there be Light). Around the top is *Collegium Waynesburgiense*, the name of the college in Latin. The Roman numerals MDCCCL = 1850, the year in which the college was chartered. The college colors are orange and black. Most of the male students in 1910 were in pre-ministry, and the majority later attended Princeton Theological Seminary. Princeton's colors were orange and black, "so it seemed logical that Waynesburg should adopt these colors also."[60]

In the field of student affairs the most important activity was debating. Revived during the year 1922-1923, interest kept increasing through inter-class and intercollegiate debating. In 1924 a chapter of Alpha Delta Rho Debating Fraternity was organized; membership was limited to participants in intercollegiate debates and oratorical contests. By 1925 Professor A. B. Corey had been employed as debate coach. Shortly he was fortunate to find some excellent candidates for the teams; the cream of the crop came from 1926 to 1930 in Leslie V. Brock, Harland I. Casteel, Oscar G. Enstrom, James R. Johnson, Bennett M. Rich, Kenneth T. Skelton, and Robert S. Steen. On 9 December 1926 a team composed of Brock, Casteel, Skelton, and Steen debated a team from Oxford University on the question: "Resolved that this House favors the Principle of Prohibition." The Waynesburg men admirably upheld the affirmative and defeated Oxford before a large crowd in Alumni Hall. After the debate, one of Oxford's men talked informally on his impressions of America and made a big hit with the audience.[61]

In 1927 Professor Arthur M. Mintier replaced Corey as debate coach. Interest in debating increased; inter-class debating was encouraged; and shortly intercollegiate teams were taking trips into the Middle West and South, and debating some of the best institutions in those regions. Debating was not only an intellectual pursuit; the teams were ambassadors of good will, who favorably advertised Waynesburg College. The trustees regularly set aside funds for debating. On 6 March 1928 a chapter of Tau Kappa Alpha Forensic Fraternity, which rated as one of the largest three fraternities of its type in the United States, was organized on the campus. At the installation of the chapter the charter members were Brock, Casteel, Johnson, Rich, Skelton, and Steen. Professor Mintier was faculty sponsor and member at large.[62] Some of the questions for debate were: "Resolved that the Power of the Press Should Be Diminished"; "Resolved that Further Centralization of Power in the Federal Government is Desirable"; and "Resolved that the United States Should Join the League of Nations." These questions were intellectually stimulating and highly beneficial not only to the debaters, but to the judges and audiences as well. One cannot escape noting the contrast between them and the seemingly naive questions of the nineteenth century like: "Do Whiskers Add to the Appearance of the Masculine Gender"? or "Who Was the Greater—Columbus or Washington"? While the teams consistently competed respectably against their opponents, the most successful year was 1927-1928 when Waynesburg College won 18 and lost only 3 debates. Unfortunately the team lost Brock, Skelton, and Steen by graduation in 1928. The "veterans" in the fall of 1928 were Casteel, Enstrom, Johnson, and Rich; and Samuel Witchell doubled as a debater and as college orator. Fortunately Brock became a member of the faculty and assistant coach of debate in 1928. In the fall of 1929, when Mintier went on his archaeological trip to Mesopotamia, Brock served effectively as debate coach in his absence. By that time Waynesburg's area of debating had been widened to include institutions in the East as well as in the South and Middle West.[63]

In 1928 the debating teams made heroic efforts to restore the literary societies to their former status. These organizations had been moribund for several years. Various attempts to force students to join them were fruitless; and the voluntary scheme was not effective.[64] Stewart and the debaters felt there was still need for them. On 13 April 1928 the affirmative debating teams met to reorganize Philo Society in Philo Hall. The following officers were elected: President, Leslie V. Brock; Vice President, Bennett M. Rich; and Secretary-Treasurer, Van Dyke McDowell. Likewise, on 10 April 1928 the negative debating teams, serving as a nucleus, met in Union Hall and revived Union Society. Officers chosen were: President, Harland I. Casteel; Vice President, James R. Johnson; Corresponding Secretary, Lucille Faddis; Recording Secretary, Isabel Edson; Treasurer, Velma Clovis; and Critic, Kenneth Skelton. With Stewart as chairman, a contest was held between these two societies on 31 May 1928—the first one in nine years. The overall score was six to four in favor of Union. The members of Union then boasted: "We have met the enemy and they are ours, which will be repeated regularly in years to come. Where there is Union there is strength."[65]

Despite such zeal, the days of the literary societies were numbered. But interest in debating kept increasing. During 1928-1929 some twenty students were participating in intercollegiate debates and oratorical contests. Two long trips, and several short ones, were then taken—all by automobile. Waynesburg won over two-thirds of the decisions. More home debates were being held in area high schools in order to get students interested in Waynesburg College. The debaters were making high schools debate conscious, in the hope that teams would be organized at that level.[66] It was physically impossible, however, for the college debaters to participate in the numerous intercollegiate contests, to promote debating in high schools, and to maintain the literary societies. These conditions, plus the strong attraction of varsity athletics and the social sororities and fraternities, terminated the literary societies.

Rules and procedures relating to student conduct were quite different from those of former days. By the middle 1920's, a new day had dawned in which the students themselves aided the administration in the enforcement of such rules. The Men's Tribunal and the Girls' Tribunal had been organized, chiefly for this purpose. They fully cooperated with the faculty in bringing wayward students into line. For example, in December 1926 the Men's Tribunal unanimously recommended to the faculty the suspension of a male student who had failed to wear the freshman cap (the orange and black "dink") and had used the front entrance. The faculty upheld the Tribunal's recommendation and the offender was suspended from the college until he appeared before the Tribunal and complied with its demands.[67]

Two years later the Girls' Tribunal had a real problem on their hands. A freshman girl was "convicted . . . upon the following charges: (1) failing to wear the armband; (2) wearing light hose; (3) refusing to appear before the Girls' Tribunal when summoned; and (4) defying orders of the Tribunal." She was then sentenced "to mop the floor of the main room in the girls' waiting room, the bucket, mop, and all necessary implements being furnished." The recalcitrant completely ignored this sentence. Subsequently the Student Council, the faculty, the Dean of Women, and Stewart in succession, upheld the Girls' Tribunal. But the offender defied them all—and was expelled.[68]

In general, the students complied with the rule on compulsory chapel attendance. Stewart was happy that chapel was well supported. In June 1929, he told the trustees: "Chapel attendance is still excellent and there has never been any tendency such as is lately observed in so many colleges to ask for an elimination of required attendance at these important exercises of the school." Certain groups tended to strengthen chapel. The Y.M.C.A. and Y.W.C.A., inactive in the early and middle 1920's, were reorganized by 1929; they were interested in chapel and in Christian service. Another group was a chapter of the Oxford Fellowship of America, organized on campus by 1927. It was open to all students entering full time Christian service. Made up of pre-ministerial students and others, the local chapter formed gospel teams, which were available to help various churches and pastors in Waynesburg and Greene County.[69]

The Greek letter organizations on campus continued to grow in memberships and importance. They were the chief means of social contacts among students; to belong to one added to one's prestige. In 1925 there were three sororities: Alpha Gamma Theta, Alpha Kappa Phi, and Theta Pi Sigma. At that time the two fraternities, Delta Sigma Phi, and Phi Sigma were thriving. Prior to World War I there was on campus a local fraternity, Theta Psi Omega. It died out during that conflict. By the fall of 1927, several men on campus felt there should be a third social fraternity, and they considered restoring the prewar local. Eventually, however, they decided to go "national," and established a chapter of Phi Lambda Theta.[70] Members of fraternities and sororities were not left on their own at social functions. Dancing was not abhorred as in former years. But the trustees were dubious about the students' ability to discipline themselves under all circumstances. In April 1927 they "directed that all college functions, dances, etc., whether connected with fraternities or otherwise, shall close hereafter not later than 12:30 A.M., and all students and other guests shall depart not later than 1:00 o'clock A.M." Further, chaperons, chosen from the faculty, had to attend these affairs and report any irregularity to the faculty for appropriate action.[71]

The local hospital continued to be housed in the women's dormitory. With Stewart's vigorous efforts as a recruiter of students, enrollment kept rapidly increasing; and housing became more and more of a problem. Local home-owners helped the situation; Stewart and the faculty were grateful for the wholehearted way they opened their homes to roomers and boarders. But Stewart repeatedly reminded the trustees that he wanted to use the dormitory for its intended purpose. In June 1929 he told them:

> The President wishes to keep alive his annual recommendation that just as soon as it is possible to do so facilities should be provided for our student girls. The growth of the student body for the last three years has been mainly among boys, the girls almost standing still in number. Outside the parents residing in and near Waynesburg, few wish to send their daughters to college unless it has dormitory supervision.[72]

Adequate dormitory space or not, the students from time to time had to let off steam. Some of their pranks showed considerable originality and ingeniuty. We get an insight into a few of their antics by their manipulations of "Davy," the human skeleton who reposed in his case many years in the laboratory in the main building and later in the Paul R. Stewart Science Building. The college newspaper for December 1927 contains a splendid cartoon of "Davy" sitting in a chair; the sketch is entitled "My Eternal Wish." "Davy" wishes that someone would procure a mate for him:

> After having spent untold years in these dark halls, in the pond, and hanging on the flagpole, I have resolved to give up my liberty and take unto myself a wife. . . . I am not partial as to race, creed, or previous condition of servitude. Even a Democrat or Prohibitionist would do, if nothing better could be found. If someone gets a mate for me, I can assure him that our relationship would be strictly platonic.[73]

In December 1924 the student newspaper was given a new name. Called *The Collegian* since the turn of the century, it had been an excellent publication with news items of interest to students, faculty, and alumni. Materials relating to athletics, to the literary societies, to Greek letter organizations, to academic matters, and to chapel and other things of the spirit were all included. Editorials were always constructive in nature. With the advent of Stewart to the presidency, however, there was a great boost to the athletic program. Hence the new publication, which at first appeared quarterly, was called *The Yellow Jacket*. And thenceforth all of the college's athletic teams were named "Yellow Jackets," a term appropriately indicative of the sting of this wiry little member of the wasp family.[74] Through the years this paper has been purely a student production. Traditionally the editorial staff has had a faculty advisor. Like its predecessor, *The Yellow Jacket*, though changed in format from *The Collegian*, remains a valuable newspaper.

It became customary for each graduating class to give something of lasting value to the college. Noteworthy was the bronze plaque presented by the class of 1929 on the eightieth anniversary of the founding of the college. It was placed on the Washington Street side of the *Messenger* Building which now houses a men's clothing store. On this site Loughran met his first classes. One of his students was James B. Lazear. Residing in Omaha, Nebraska, in 1929, Lazear, then the oldest living former student, occasionally exchanged letters with Stewart.[75] The graduating class invited him to come and unveil the plaque.[76] Though he was an aged man, he traveled alone from Omaha early in June 1929, arrived in Waynesburg in good spirits, and spoke at the alumni banquet; he also delivered the dedicatory speech at, and unveiled, the plaque.[77] Rectangular in shape, at the middle of the top side is the college seal. At each corner is the traditional oak leaf. The inscription shows that classes met there, beginning in September 1849, pending the erection of the first college building.[78]

While Stewart and the faculty were concerned with affairs of student life in the 1920's, the college gave attention to buildings and grounds in that decade. The steam heating project, started during McKay's presidency, was slow in getting under way. Lack of funds was a drawback. In November 1921, some persons who had made subscriptions to the college during Houghton's administration said they would pay them provided they be applied to the heating plant; and the alumni promised to raise enough money to install it.[79] In October 1922 the trustees directed Stewart to get bids on plans from various firms for the steam heating plant. The following December Stewart reported that he had $5,000 in bona fide subscriptions and cash; he asked the trustees to contract for the heating system and have it put in. By July 1923 construction of the plant supposedly neared completion, but more money was needed. Some four and one-half years later, in January 1928, the college newspaper reported: "Just a little more help and we can put in the steam heating plant we have been working on for so long, and which means so much to the safety of the building as well as the comfort of the student body."[80]

Other improvements were made in the main building. Early in 1923, at Stewart's suggestion, some remodeling was done on the president's office at a cost of $250. Later that year, on the recommendation of a committee of alumni, repairs were made on windows on the north side of Alumni Hall. The chapel on the second floor, adjacent to the Library, was then not large enough. Hence it was moved to Alumni Hall. The library was then enlarged by making the "old chapel" a reading room. In October 1926 a pipe organ was installed in Alumni Hall. Donated by the First Presbyterian Church in Waynesburg, it facilitated training on the pipe organ offered by the Music Department.[81]

The trustees continued to rent Hanna Hall, at $1,200 per year, to the local School Board for five more years after Stewart became president. Four rooms in the building were used as a public school, with some 130 pupils in attendance. Finally, early in May 1926, the trustees resolved to take over Hanna Hall at the end of the year 1925-1926. They told the School Board the building seriously needed repairs and was not in good condition for a public school. Further, the college wanted to use the building, because of increasing enrollment. The college planned, beginning in the year 1926-1927, to use the first and second floors for various offices, classrooms, and auxiliary laboratories. The School Board shortly made other arrangements for the education of the "Hanna Hall" pupils; the voters of Waynesburg Borough overwhelmingly approved a bond issue of $200,000 for their schools, thus assuring better educational facilities for their children. And the college "recaptured" Hanna Hall and resolved to preserve it as one of the "most sacred" buildings on the campus. By June 1929 it had been completely rewired; this measure, plus the placing of fire extinguishers at convenient places, largely removed the menace of fire.[82]

The local hospital was still housed in the Women's Dormitory. Rent at $2,500 per year helped the college cover its current expenses, but it was not always paid promptly. For example, in March 1924 the Hospital Board agreed to "build fire escapes upon the dormitory, pay for same, and be given credit upon the rent overdue." The college badly needed the building to be used for its original purpose, as Stewart repeatedly reminded the trustees. In April 1926 the trustees decided to "take over the dormitory from the Waynesburg Hospital at once. . . . " The following July, however, at the request of the Hospital Board, they agreed to extend the rental one more year, with the understanding that the hospital would vacate the building by 1 July 1927. A committee of three trustees was appointed to negotiate a contract to this effect with the hospital authorities. The trustees threatened that, if the Hospital Board refused to sign it, they would proceed to eject the hospital from the building.[83] Nevertheless, the hospital remained in the building for another decade.

The trustees gave attention to security and maintenance of the college buildings. In May 1928, insurance was fixed at $115,000 on the main building; $19,000 on Hanna Hall; and $39,000 on the Women's Dormitory. The Buildings and Grounds "force" consisted of a janitor, whose wages ranged between $75 and $90 per month, and whatever student assistants were assigned to help him.[84]

In 1925 the possibility of a gymnasium at long last loomed when a lot, located "almost half way between Main Street and the College," was purchased. The gymnasium was to be across the park, with its front facing the main college building; it would supply a long-felt need. The main drawback in building the gymnasium was lack of funds. The college catalogue pleaded: "The advantages are so obvious that surely some philanthropist can be found who will bring to us additional equipment for Christian social service."[85] More than a decade, however, was destined to pass before the gymnasium was constructed.

By April 1929 the trustees faced a problem relating to college grounds. The railroad running through the south side of Waynesburg needed additional land, adjacent to the athletic field, for its right of way. Stewart hoped the anticipated funds from the railroad company might be used as payment toward a stadium. But a stadium was not built. In September 1929 the trustees agreed to accept $5,000 as the minimum settlement "of the trouble with the railroad. . . . "[86]

Stewart and the trustees constantly considered the aesthetic aspects not only of the campus, but also of the contiguous park. In June 1925 the trustees petitioned the town council to pave certain streets around the park.[87] Being a learned botanist, Stewart was interested in trees, particularly in the environs of the college. In 1929, the eightieth anniversary of the founding of the institution, he set an oak near the corner directly in front of Hanna Hall. He "felt that this tree was appropriate to represent the college, because it is a symbol of long life and endurance." Thus the oak became the college tree. Oak leaf impressions in walks on the campus and in bronze dedication tablets here and there in buildings also symbolize strength and longevity. Stewart established the oak tree tradition and expressed his "hopes that it will continue long after he is gone."[88]

Within two years after Stewart became president, the college was recognized academically by larger institutions and by the Department of Public Instruction in Harrisburg. In 1928 the General Alumni Association referred to the advent of Stewart as the time when "the great forward movement" began. From 1922 onward, the officers of that body made great efforts and changed the annual meetings from poorly attended affairs to large, enthusiastic gatherings of two to three hundred members. Thenceforth an alumni bulletin was regularly published; its mailing list steadily increased. The Presbyterian Church, U.S.A. showed its confidence in Stewart in June 1929; at the meeting of the Pennsylvania Synod at Chambersburg, Pennsylvania, he was elected Vice Moderator of that body; and he was appointed also as a member of Synod's Judiciary Committee. He was the first Waynesburger to be chosen to these posts.[89]

Stewart struggled successfully against great odds to save the college in the 1920's. But a dark decade loomed ahead. The depression years continued to challenge him and the entire college family.

XV
THE DEPRESSION YEARS

LIKE ALL INSTITUTIONS OF HIGHER LEARNING, WAYNESBURG SUFFERED from the "Great Depression" which descended over the nation in October 1929. But depression was not new to the campus. As Stewart said humorously: "Waynesburg College has been in a depression since 1849." The economic crash brought hardship to the faculty, students, alumni, and many friends of the college. The endowment fund was still too low. Economic problems were interrelated with those pertaining to the faculty, to student life, to the curriculum, and to the physical plant in the 1930's.

As was customary everywhere, faculty members were assigned duties in addition to teaching. At Waynesburg College, teaching schedules were heavy, ranging usually from fifteen to eighteen hours per week. Frequently a teacher would be working in unrelated fields; for instance, a history teacher might be called upon to teach in the modern languages. Faculty members served on from one to as high as three of the following committees: Library, Athletic Council, Religious Activities, Lectures and Entertainments, Social Activities, Student Publications, Pan-Hallenic, Registration and Scholarship, Attendance, Evening Sessions, and Finance. Teamwork was essential, especially in emergencies. The faculty was expected to set an example by attending chapel; Stewart asked them to sit upon the platform for those exercises. With a view to economy, in the depths of the depression, Stewart requested the faculty to cooperate in "keeping down expenses in details such as lighting, heating, use of supplies, etc." Available evidence shows that a few faculty members did not teach a full "professorial hour" (fifty minutes) at each class period. In keeping with sound scholarship, Stewart asked that all classes be held for the full period. In April 1936 the faculty considered the "serious need for additional chairs for the library reading room" and other "urgent needs such as arm chairs for classrooms and repair of the floors." Adhering to the principle of division of labor, Stewart appointed one teacher to ascertain the cost of replacing the floors; another, the cost of floor coverings; and another, the cost of chairs.[1]

Whenever additional work made great demands on a teacher's time, he received extra pay. There were several examples of this. In September 1937, Stewart was so crowded that he needed an assistant. Hence the trustees appointed Cecil O. Riggs as assistant to the President with power to act at all times in the absence of the President. Riggs had been employed on an eleven months basis, but now he was to receive an additional month's salary. Frank N. Wolf had some six different duties including teaching, athletic coach, athletic manager, supervisor of National Youth Administration (NYA) work, manager of buildings and grounds, and supervisor of the granting of scholarships. In 1939 his salary for teaching and coaching was $270 per month for eleven months; in addition he received $30 per month for serving in the other capacities. Others who received modest sums for additional duty were: Mintier for coaching debate; Mary D. Inghram for serving as Dean of Women; James M. Miller for theatrical work and coach of wrestling; and Michael K. Talpas for assisting Wolf.[2]

In the 1930's faculty salaries ranged from $125 to $250 per month for nine months, but late in that decade the college was hard pressed to pay the faculty. In June 1939 the trustees contemplated a "reduction in salaries for the coming year"; but a motion for such was rejected.[3]

In September 1939 Stewart presented to the trustees a report of his studies during the preceding summer relative to college administration. As a result, he recommended that the deanship be divided between two persons: one, a Dean of the Faculty; the other, a Dean of Students. He defined the duties of a Dean of the Faculty: (1) to preside over the faculty, and in chapel, in the absence of the president; (2) to meet the trustees in the president's absence; (3) to represent the college at all meetings of the Presbyterian Church (presbyteries, synods, general assemblies, etc.) when the president is unable to attend; (4) to aid the president in faculty discipline; and (5) to have charge of all surveys and questionnaires for the college, and be responsible for bringing surveys from the church before the faculty and trustees.[4] Each administrator was a faculty member who handled his administrative duties in addition to teaching a heavy schedule.

Stewart did much to maintain morale by praising faculty members for their devotion to duty. In June 1937 he told the trustees "that very few vacancies ever occur—a healthy sign." The length of service of the faculty, in years, ranged from twenty-seven down to one; the average length of service was nine and one-half years. He then spoke of the quality of the faculty. When he became Acting President, no faculty member had an earned doctorate. In 1937 "all heads of the departments have doctor's degrees or have completed residence requirements for the same."[5]

The faculty suffered a great loss on 2 March 1935, when E. Gertrude Madison passed away. For some ten years she had faithfully served as Dean of Women, Professor of English, and Head of the English Department. Born on 1 March 1871 at Rock Bluff, Nebraska, Miss Madison graduated from Albion College and won her M.A. from Columbia University. She did further graduate work at the University of Wisconsin. Prior to coming to Waynesburg, she had taught briefly at Cornell College in Iowa and at the University of the Philippines.[6] Some ten years after her death, a building on campus was named "Madison Hall" to honor and to commemorate her.

If the faculty suffered from the effects of the depression, so did the students. In June 1930 Stewart told the trustees that: "With great satisfaction we report that we have at last reached the goal set in 1921, a student body of over 300 in the collegiate department alone." As the decade passed, and student recruiting gathered momentum, students were gradually drawn from a wider area. In 1921 only ten percent of students in the collegiate department came from outside Waynesburg; in 1930 seventy percent gave "their addresses from other post offices." Furthermore, students were more carefully selected. In 1935 Stewart reported that "for the first time in many years no senior was deficient at the last faculty meeting before commencement." Stewart also stressed "the paying kind of student"; while the institution remained a "poor boy's college," it was good enough to attract students from the more wealthy families. In order to advertise the college, and as a recruiting technique, by the mid-1930's the college was cooperating with local public school administrations in holding competitive examinations for high school students in Algebra, American History, Biology, and English. Such examinations were administered annually to students from high schools in Greene County. In 1938, in order to step up the recruiting of students, the trustees employed Harry Orndoff to work as Stewart's field assistant. Orndoff was "to serve as a good contact and personnel man with a salary of $150 a month for twelve months and travelling expenses." He went forth to help organize alumni associations and to seek through them new prospective students. On 22 October 1938 Stewart reported an increase of twenty in the freshman class, attributed partly to Orndoff's efforts, partly to a new program in business administration and partly to the reacquisition of the women's dormitory.[7]

The darkest period of the depression was from 1930 into 1933, when no federal funds were available to help youth in any way. In September 1932 a number of girls wrote to the college and indicated they desired to attend, but could not afford to, because of economic conditions. They lacked funds for food and housing, but were willing to work in homes to provide their board and room. Stewart said "this is an unusual chance for many Waynesburg residents to prove that charity really does begin at home." These young ladies were good students; all they asked was a chance to solve the economic problem.[8]

Doubtless most of the girls found opportunities to their liking. But there is evidence that a few property owners took unfair advantage of the students in their plight. In October 1934 the faculty discussed "the long hours required and low wages given to some students working in town while maintaining themselves in the college." The faculty resolved to investigate this situation, and to consider the relation of such work to each student's college schedule. Taken into account were: a student's past academic standing; his present schedule of class and laboratory work; and his work outside of college. A student had to maintain a C average; if his outside work caused his average to drop, he either had to cut down on his schedule of courses or cut down on his outside work.[9]

Destitute, deserving students managed as best they could. Stewart repeatedly referred "to the special courage expressed by a very large proportion of the student body in meeting the almost impossible conditions of the time. By carefully organized self-help and by cooking for themselves in singles and in groups, large numbers are maintaining themselves on the tiny margin of anywhere from $1.25 to $2.00 a week. . . . " Stewart consistently held that graduates of the college "outrivaled in character, scholarship, and service" those of many institutions which were much more affluent.[10]

Fortunately federal funds became available to students early in 1934. Under the Civilian Works Administration (CWA) the college was granted an allotment of $1,995 "for the purpose of helping worthy students."[11] Shortly the college obtained other federal funds through the National Youth Administration (NYA), a broader program than CWA for helping deserving students.

Student activities continued on the upgrade in the 1930's. The Y.M.C.A. and Y.W.C.A. promoted religious and spiritual growth in the student body. The debating teams thrived. By 1930, *The Yellow Jacket*, had become a bi-weekly instead of a monthly publication; its quality remained excellent. An alumni publication, the monthly *Bulletin*, was a means of keeping the alumni in close touch with the college.[12] A yearbook entitled *Mad Anthony*, reminiscent of General "Mad" Anthony Wayne, was published; produced chiefly by the students, its staff was consolidated with that of *The Yellow Jacket* in 1938.[13]

In June 1933 two new student organizations were established. One was Xi Psi Epsilon, an honor society for all students with at least eighty semester hours in the college and an average of 2.0 (on a 3 scale). Its aim was to encourage a high standard of excellence in scholarship and to reward students for such scholarship. The other was "The Sphinx," an honor society for all students after the end of their sophomore year, who had done outstanding work in at least two activities. Its purposes were to stimulate interest in student activities and to foster new activities.[14]

An excellent precedent was set on 1 May 1934 when Stewart crowned Amy Mundell, a senior, as first May queen of Waynesburg College. The coronation took place in a colorful ceremony in front of the fountain in the park. A large audience looked on—with appreciation and approval. A luncheon followed in Call's Dining Room in town. Athletic events, held in the afternoon, consisted of an interclass track meet and a "tennis tilt between Waynesburg and Bethany." A coronation ball was held in the evening. Thus ended a day long to be remembered. On 8 May 1935, Anna Rae Myers was crowned as May queen; Miss Mundell returned to the campus to assist Stewart in the coronation ceremony. Thereafter annually the May queen was selected from the senior class on the basis of poise, personality, beauty, and achievement. This tradition was followed through May 1972 when May Day was abolished and "Spring Weekend" took its place.[15]

A significant movement involving students began in 1936 when the Board of Christian Education and the Board of National Missions of the Presbyterian Church, U.S.A. collaborated with the college in the creation of the Waynesburg College Parish Project. Harry E. Gardner, '34, who studied for the ministry at Princeton Theological Seminary, became a member of the college faculty in 1936. He was appointed to set up and to direct the "Parish Project" (later referred to as "Student Service Project") with the college as headquarters. The broad aim was "to use our Christian groups in the student body to bring to the young people of our area the finest kind of scholastic, social, and religious values." The project was to serve the area comprising Redstone and Washington Presbyteries. Stewart believed that Gardner and the students with whom he worked would be a strong force for patriotism and real Americanization in this area. In 1936 the Nazi juggernaut was rolling ahead relentlessly in Europe; and Communist leaders envisioned world domination. To some extent their influences reached America. Any Christian movement which would tend to counter them was welcomed.[16]

Within a year, Stewart told the trustees: "This project has succeeded beyond our highest dreams." Under Gardner's direction, young men and women went to mining towns and to other underprivileged and underchurched areas to set up Week Day Bible Schools, Vacation Bible Schools, Young Peoples' Associations, and Character Building Schools. The students made reports to Gardner of their activities, and he in turn reported to a local council and to the Board of Christian Education and the Board of National Missions. Stewart expressed his hope that the good example set by the Parish Project might influence other collegiate institutions and other denominations, so that the work might spread all over the nation. He reminded the trustees of the truism "that this college was founded as a definite frontier post in Christian Education." The Parish Project represented the beginning of a new spiritual frontier which should be extended to wider horizons.[17]

By the mid-1930's it was clear that social fraternities and sororities on campus needed more effective control. The highly detailed regulations relating to student conduct in the old days were passe. But young men in the fraternities were inclined to frivolity. For example, in April 1935 a faculty member spoke to his colleagues of "violations of good taste in the outside initiation in one or more of the fraternities," which were symptomatic of a general condition that needed a remedy. Hence, in May 1936 the faculty came forth with its "social regulations" which read:

> All fraternities and sororities, classes, societies, associations, clubs, and other organizations in the college must present to the chairman of

> a Faculty Social and Calendar Committee the date of any proposed social event, the place, and the names of the patrons and patronesses. This information must be in writing. Approval of the chairman of the committee must be secured before the event is definitely arranged. The only places in the Borough of Waynesburg which may be used for dances and parties besides college property and the houses or rooms of fraternities and sororities are: the Armory, the Long Building, the Fort Jackson Hotel, and the social rooms of the various churches when appropriate to the nature of the event.

The Faculty Social and Calendar Committee also recommended that the college provide and pay housemothers for the fraternities and sororities which had houses. Such persons would be representatives of the faculty and responsible to it.[18] The trustees approved this plan, which remained effective for more than three decades.

There was a spirit of rivalry among fraternities and sororities. Competition in the academic sense was desirable; each organization tried to hold an average as near the top as possible. Rivalry during rush week and pledge week was normal and typical. But ill-feeling and resentment often prevailed. One freshman complained:

> The students are divided into a caste system with each fraternity looking down on the others. We say we are Christians, preaching the brotherhood and equality of mankind. Then we speak of our own group and ignore others. . . . When we pledge our love for fellow members, does that release us from our duty to all others?[19]

Late in 1939 two moves were made to improve faculty-student relations. First, a Dean's Council was organized. It consisted of the Dean of the Faculty as Chairman, the Dean of Women as Secretary, the Dean of Students, and the President of the College. Its chief aim was to improve the scheme of selecting sponsors of student activities. Second, the trustees employed a Dean of Students who was in charge of all matters pertaining to student life such as student discipline, relations between students and faculty, and the granting of scholarships. He also was an ex officio member of the Committee on Religious Activities, and a counselor on students' social activities and on student publications.[20]

A problem that became increasingly serious as the years went on was chapel attendance. In March 1933 the editor of the student newspaper lamented that "this year attendance has been poor. The student body shows little interest for reasons unknown. . . . Students should not need to be forced, but should attend voluntarily." Nevertheless in November 1933, the faculty resorted to coercion by the declaration that students having "more than 15 chapel cuts for any semester hereafter shall be subject to suspension." By October 1934 efforts were made to improve chapel exercises. The Sphinx, the Xi Psi Epsilon, and the religious organizations arranged "a system for conducting chapel which should meet with the approval of the student body." A typical program consisted of Scripture reading, a prayer, hymns, and a speaker—if any. The Student Council and the faculty fully supported these efforts. But lack of student interest persisted. Faculty minutes for 16 June 1939 read: "Realizing that the chapel programs have been on a low standard, the Sphinx has decided on a different plan for chapels for the ensuing school year of 1939-40." A Student Chapel Committee, appointed for that year, suggested the following plan: Chapel programs would be held on Monday, Wednesday, and Friday; Stewart would lead on Monday; the Chapel Committee, on Wednesday; and campus organizations in turn, on Friday. A student assembly would meet on Tuesday at which there would be no devotional period. But the students, apparently left to themselves on Tuesdays, either would not attend or, if present, showed a lack of self-discipline.[21]

Student behavior left something to be desired in places other than chapel. In March 1933 a faculty member reported "that a lack of quiet seemed to prevail in the reading room." He also was concerned about the morals of the student body. He said he had heard of drinking among both men and women of the college at dances, and asked the cooperation of the faculty in investigating this condition. Stewart asked to be called into conference in case any further information was obtained. Some students were inclined not only toward these wayward ways, but they absented themselves from class — as they did from chapel. In order to induce them to attend classes, the faculty felt forced to suspend the worst offenders.[22]

While Stewart and the faculty grappled with student affairs, they gave attention to changes in the curriculum. By 1931 a "major" and a "minor" were introduced. A major was not less than 18 nor more than 30 semester hours in one subject, with 1 1/4 honor points times the number of hours, including introductory courses. A minor was not less than 18 semester hours in one subject, including introductory courses, and not less than 18 honor points.[23] In January 1938 the trustees "approved the founding of a school of Business and Finance or Business Administration." In the planning, it was to be copied after such schools as Washington and Jefferson, Grove City, and Westminster. It would be a Business Administration Department with the cultural and academic rather than the commercial viewpoint. In September 1938 the trustees employed Robert Cornish, a graduate of Yale University who was pursuing work at Columbia University toward a doctorate in Business Administration, to serve as head of this new Department. Cornish's salary was $200 per month for the nine-month school period.[24]

In September 1937 the Bible requirement for graduation was set at six semester hours. These were to be "strictly Bible courses"; some of the religious education courses were not acceptable. Students were required to take at least three semester hours of Bible during the first two years.[25]

An innovation came by November 1939, when the Civilian Pilot Training Course was established in cooperation with the Civil Aeronautics Authority (C.A.A.). It was part of a nationwide program designed to be continued for several years. The war situation in Europe was ominous—even for the Americas. The time was at hand for this nation to look at its defenses; and a strong air force would be needed. The unit at the college was directed by Professor Riggs. Some ten students were enrolled at the start. They took a ground school course, which carried four semester hours of college credit; flight training was conducted by R. E. B. Springer at the local airport. Upon completion of the course, the young men were eligible for private pilot licenses.[26]

The academic standing of the college was high in comparison with that of other institutions. The Department of Public Instruction, in Harrisburg, rated it thirteenth from the top of seventy accredited colleges which trained teachers for public school work.[27] In their efforts to maintain sound academic standards, the faculty was careful about "the matter of raising grades"; in June 1933 it proposed two methods of procedure in such cases. The preferred method was repetition of the course. The other permitted a student to pursue work outside of regular class. This method was carefully regulated; not more than two grades could be raised during the entire college course. The professor in charge had to have the faculty's permission in these cases.[28] In order to stay in school, a student had to remain in good academic standing. If he were hopelessly low in any given semester, he was not permitted to register for the next one.[29]

The college always faced an uphill struggle in the field of finance. Early in 1932 the endowment fund approximated $300,000, and the yield from it was low. Due doubtless to the depression, there was a great deal of difficulty in securing the payment of tuitions; and many requests for extension of time were made. The trustees appointed a committee of three from their own body to "pass upon all applications for extension, leniency, etc." Whenver possible they granted such requests. But the college had bills that had to be paid, and collections were urgent.[30]

The drive for funds was constant. In January 1930 the trustees directed Stewart to appoint a committee to confer with the Buhl and Falk Foundations to ascertain if they would assist the college in its need for endowment. In June 1930 Stewart reported that he and Edson had "since last October collected in cash and securities $15,770 of the old endowment pledges." Stewart added: "Every thousand we secure . . . will mean a greater chance of reaching our goal of $500,000." With a view to greater efficiency in the endowment drive, the college's charter was amended in October 1930 to end life membership for trustees. A three-year rotation clause was adopted under which the Board would have twenty-seven members, plus the president of the college. Under the new plan, nine trustees were elected annually, one proposed by the church's Board of Education, three by the General Alumni Association, and five by the existing Board of Trustees.[31] With rotation of this sort, more persons were available to help with endowment and the development of the institution. The Presbyterian Church, U.S.A., and the large foundations were sources of funds. Donations from alumni kept increasing. Stewart exhorted people to make bequests to the college. In February 1938 the trustees called on the College Executive Committee to select a group of women to organize a college Women's Auxiliary to aid the Board of Trustees in furthering the interests of the college. Actuated by moral considerations, in June 1938, the trustees moved "that the various auxiliaries of the Alumni Association be requested not to attempt to raise money by any form of games of chance or gambling devices." Tuition was gradually raised: it was $90.00 per semester in 1935-1936; $95.00 in 1937-1938; and $100.00 in 1939-1940.[32]

Funds were needed not only for current expenses, but for the erection of the gymnasium and for furniture for the women's dormitory. In April 1934 the trustees temporarily took $1,000 from the endowment fund to pay on the gymnasium; they anticipated a legacy of $1,000 which would make possible the return of that sum to endowment. Stewart and the trustees shortly raised $8,000 more for the gymnasium. In May 1936 a campaign was started to raise $25,000 for the gymnasium. Federal Judge John C. Knox, '02, of New York City was main speaker at the kickoff dinner. An eminent jurist and a devoted alumnus, he attributed his success to "a firm father, a sainted mother, and the college which I attended and the town in which it was located. All I am or ever hope to be I owe to what I got here in Waynesburg." Judge Knox had been away for thirty years, "but his heart has always been here." In November 1937, as the trustees looked ahead to the return of the women's dormitory from the hospital to the college, Stewart wondered "where we will get money for furnishing the dormitory? It will take $2,500 or more to get it started." He welcomed suggestions as to how this money could be raised. Early in 1939 he reported that several rooms at the Women's Dormitory were being furnished by clubs and individuals.[33]

After the advent of the "New Deal," the college was fortunate to receive federal funds. In October 1936 the Roosevelt administration approved a Works Progress Administration (WPA) grant of $40,606 for the gymnasium, which "assured completion of the building."[34] Furthermore, for the year 1935-1936 the college received allotments of National Youth Administration (NYA) funds to the extent of $660 a month for nine months. At last deserving students had opportunities to earn money. Some forty-four of them were engaged in constructive work, including work on grounds; repairs on buildings; historical research; labors in laboratories and the library; the collection and labeling of all sorts of botanical, zoological, and geological specimens; and the exhibition of such collections for teaching purposes. Students receiving NYA funds also were instrumental in aiding churches and educational organizations with research problems. For the following year, 1936-1937, the college received NYA funds totaling $6,044.75; some sixty-five students were engaged in the many and varied types of work. Their work was beneficial to the college and to themselves.[35]

Until the late 1930's current expenses were kept within current income. In October 1938, Stewart told the trustees there was a deficit of $5,482.74, "due to the turning over of the dormitory and the loss of rent from the hospital, together with last year's shrinkage of the student body."[36] Many students were attending college on scholarships of one kind or another, which further reduced income. In June 1939 the trustees took action to regulate carefully the scholarship program. And Stewart and his assistant, Orndoff, resolved "to present to the trustees approximately the same sized student body with a phenomenal increase in 'pay students' and a corresponding diminution of scholarships."[37]

Although the current operating budget had been kept in the black until 1938, the college had a number of outstanding debts on which it was paying 6% interest. In the hope of decreasing this rate of interest, in May 1939, one of the trustees, Harland I. Casteel, reported "that a refinancing plan was being considered by the New York Prudential Life Insurance Company whereby the debts of the college would be refinanced at an interest rate of 5%. . . . " After discussing this plan the trustees moved to negotiate a mortgage loan of $100,000 with this company. They would give as security "college real estate located in Waynesburg, plus the pledge of the necessary part of the endowment fund. . . . " Unfortunately the Prudential Life Insurance Company refused to approve this loan. The college was sorely in need of funds to pay its debts. On 14 December 1939 the trustees themselves, therefore, moved that by 1 May 1940 "each trustee be responsible for raising for the college the minimum sum of $100."[38]

In July 1939 the trustees took steps to improve management of the college's funds. Fortunately Richard L. Baily, who was well versed in finance and banking, and who also had the interests of the college at heart, was a trustee. On his motion, the trustees called on Professor Cornish to come into the office and set up books for the coming year. With his training at Yale and Columbia Universities, Cornish was well qualified to handle this assignment.[39] He worked diligently from July until December 1939, during which he made a careful audit of all accounts. On 11 December 1939 he reported to the trustees that "for sometime the college has been operating on an unstable financial basis, and matters are growing consistently worse." On 1 December 1939 the current short-term debt of the college was $18,532.24. As of 11 December the cash balance in the current expense account was $107.99. Current debts had not been paid, and there was no money to pay them. No provision had been made to pay $5,978.76 on unpaid faculty salaries for the preceding year. And, during the fall of 1939, the faculty members received only half of the current salaries due them. Cornish warned: "The seriousness of this situation and its effect in lowering morale of the faculty cannot be overlooked, especially in view of the fact that the cash reserves of many of the faculty have been reduced to the vanishing point, due to the failure of the college to pay last year's salary in full." The financial condition of the college was such that local creditors refused to grant credit beyond $100 maximum with the understanding that these amounts would be paid within thirty days. Many creditors refused to sell to the college except on a cash basis. Cornish expressed his regret that repeated promises had been made to creditors on past due accounts, and most of these promises, made by his predecessors, had been broken. He refused to make further promises to creditors. He pointed out the need for a new financial policy, and contended that immediate steps should be taken to clear up the current indebtedness, "if the college is to regain the confidence of its creditors and faculty." The total fixed indebtedness as of 1 December 1939 was $81,290.19; yearly interest was 6%. According to Cornish, "much of the financial difficulty of the college has been due to the fact that no budgets have been employed in the past, nor has adequate central financial control been exercised." He suggested several ways to improve the situation. First, that "for the operation of next year a complete budget be prepared, and that all departments be required to stay within the allotted budgets." Second, that the amount of scholarships be reduced. Too many scholarships, ranging from $3.00 to $75.00 per student, per semester, were being granted. Such scholarships reduced the income from tuition and fees by nearly 25%; Cornish learned from the Business Office of Washington and Jefferson College "that they consider 10% a fair amount for scholarships." Third, that the payroll be reduced. This could be done, if the number of students receiving scholarships could be reduced. Fourth, as an alternative to three, that tuition be raised. Such a raise would "bring in more receipts and might justify the present payroll." Fifth, that there be more satisfactory accounting for sums paid for travel expense. Cornish revealed that "large sums of money are being advanced to athletic and administrative officers, and when statements are surrendered concerning their expenditure no supporting vouchers are submitted."[40]

If a sound financial operation was essential, equally so was the building program. Without new buildings and adequate maintenance of old ones, the college would be on the downgrade. The most urgent need was a gymnasium. Despite the lack of one, Waynesburg College's athletic teams had competed respectably against their opponents. In the early 1930's basketball was still being played in the Armory, which lacked seating capacity for large crowds; its bleachers were too close to the court which made playing hazardous to players and spectators alike. Furthermore, the Armory was rented only for varsity games. There was no place for intramural sports and for classes in physical education.[41]

In April 1933 the trustees resolved to proceed with plans to build the gymnasium.[42] Fortunately federal funds under the Works Progress Administration (WPA) were available in a collaborative scheme between the college and the Borough of Waynesburg. The plan called for the use of the gymnasium by the college and the community. Construction began in December 1934 when four buildings on the site were razed, and steam shovels started the excavation of the basement area. Some 117 men were employed on the project. Stone for the foundation and walls was obtained from a quarry two miles south of Waynesburg. Architects from The Thayer Company of New Castle, Pennsylvania, prepared plans for the building. Construction proceeded slowly in the winter of 1934-1935; rain and snow retarded progress; and much hard rock was encountered in the excavation. On 12 June 1935, however, Governor George H. Earle spoke at Commencement, after which he laid the cornerstone of the gymnasium at the northeast corner of the structure. A brass box containing several catalogues, a copy of Earle's commencement address, and a commencement program—all were sealed and put beneath the stone. Stewart told the trustees that "all bills are paid to date." But he warned "that the treasury is now dry and to the end of this project we will be forced to live precariously from 'hand to mouth.'" Stewart and the trustees continued to get subscribers and to collect money. Members of the Sphinx, led by Professor Riggs, put up a "gymometer" and aimed to raise $1,000 through donations and efforts of the students. Each student organization helped; and a penny collection was taken, in which the students heartily responded. The "gymometer" steadily rose to the $1,000 mark. In June 1937 Stewart reported that "the sum of $89,000 is now secure in the building, representing over $47,000 from the government, and approximately $42,000 collected from alumni, trustees, and friends." Progress on construction slowly continued. In June 1939, at long last, the building was under roof, at a cost of approximately $210,000. Plans were under way for a quick completion of its chief facilities.[43] Ere long the several teams had a suitable place for basketball and wrestling. And physical education courses could be conducted, and hence added to the curriculum.

In December 1937 the hospital vacated the women's dormitory. Beyond a doubt, the parents of many young women were delighted at the news, for they eschewed institutions which lacked girls' dormitories. Shortly the building was renovated; it was rewired, remodeled, and redecorated. It contained rooms for girls, plus space for an office and an infirmary; it could accommodate 45 students; and the dining room would seat 100 persons. It was expected that 45 young men would eat there in addition to the young women. In taking over the dormitory, the college made possible a much larger proportion of female students. When Stewart took the helm in 1921, in the aftermath of World War I, there were 41 women and 25 men working toward degrees. By late 1937 the men outnumbered the women two to one.[44] The dormitory hopefully would make a better balance between the sexes.

In June 1935 the trustees named the main building "Miller Hall" in memory of President Miller; and the women's dormitory, "Walton Hall" in honor of Senator Walton, who secured the state appropriation for the building. Two additional buildings were acquired. In 1931 the trustees purchased "Varsity Hall," a frame dwelling house on the campus, which was used as a small dormitory and commons for men. In 1937 "Ivyhurst," a spacious brick home located near mid-town, was bequeathed to the college by the late Mrs. Robinson F. Downey, '79. It was used as a student center; and it housed some of the music studios.[45]

With respect to grounds, the College Field contained the gridiron, a one-fifth mile cinder track, and bleachers for a large crowd. In September 1935 the trustees entered into a contract with the Waynesburg School Board whereby the local high school could use College Field for athletic events. The contract was to be in effect for at least five years. In November 1937 W. Walter Montgomery, Principal of Waynesburg High School, proposed to the trustees of the college a plan to obtain a field house at College Field. He pointed out that "there are no toilet facilities or place for . . . players to dress." The Government, planning to dismantle some Civilian Conservation Corps (CCC) camps, "offered lumber and cheap labor to education [*sic*] institutions free." Such lumber and labor would be secured by the high school. And the expense incurred "would apply on the rent. . . . " The trustees approved this proposition, presumably as a temporary measure. In December 1939 they moved to consider the possibilities of erecting a permanent grandstand and field house at the football field. They wanted adequate facilities on the athletic grounds. But they strongly opposed the use of the athletic field for Sunday sports, in line with the policy of the General Assembly of the Presbyterian Church, U.S.A.[46]

In 1937 two important donations of land were made to the college. Mary Sayers gave a lot adjacent to the ground around Miller Hall; it fronted 60 feet on College Street and extended back to a depth of 180 feet. The trustees expressed "the sincere appreciation, not only of the Corporation, but of all friends of the College, for this fine and generous gift." The college also welcomed the gift known as the "Roy J. Waychoff Arboretum." Located some twelve miles east of Waynesburg on a hill above Muddy Creek valley, it consisted of 7 1/2 acres of "virgin forest and excellent, profuse spring flora." Waychoff's widow donated this land in memory of her deceased husband.[47]

Stewart and the faculty continued to work diligently and devotedly during the depression years. The students were denied many material things, but most of them were resourceful and able to manage with whatever was at hand. The coming of the New Deal, with its manifold reforms, aided the college as a whole. Despite drawbacks of one kind or another, the institution continued to progress. As the 1930's closed, however, war clouds in Europe boded ill for the college and for America.

XVI
WORLD WAR II AND ITS AFTERMATH

THE IMPACT OF WORLD WAR II ON INSTITUTIONS OF HIGHER LEARNING was tremendous. For Waynesburg College, as elsewhere, it meant a sharp drop in enrollment; most male students left to enter the nation's armed forces. The resultant economic blow from loss of tuition threatened the life of the college. Once again Stewart sought ways to avert disaster. In the nick of time he secured an Army Air Forces Cadet Training Detachment, the income from which, in the form of federal funds, put the budget in the black. In 1944, after the tide of war turned, the cadet training program terminated, which led to a period of temporary retrenchment. Shortly, however, the veterans began returning in increasing numbers. Under the G. I. Bill they received rather generous financial aid from the federal government for their education. For the convenience of veterans and others residing in Fayette County, the college established the Uniontown Center, designed chiefly for freshmen and sophomores. Soon it was crowded. The overall enrollment kept increasing for several years after the war.

Before the war the faculty compared favorably with those of similar size anywhere. In June 1940, of twenty-one full time members, including the librarian, nine had earned doctorates; eight held the master's degree; and four, the baccalaureate degree. To find money to pay their salaries, however, was a constant problem. In May 1940 it was necessary to transfer $5,000.00 from the endowment fund to the current expense fund in order to pay them. A month later Stewart warned the trustees: "We must practice rigid economy and sacrifice to the utmost. Continued failure to balance the budget will . . . be disastrous to a small institution like Waynesburg College." By belt-tightening during the year 1940-1941, Stewart reported, in June 1941, "that we will, for the first time in the history of the college, finish the year with all salaries paid—and on time to the day."[1] Nevertheless, ere long it was necessary again to dip into the endowment fund in order to pay salaries. When the situation became most critical, Stewart called on the trustees for donations for salaries, and it appears that most of them gave to the cause.[2]

The faculty and administrators assumed heavier burdens as the war spread. In 1942 Cecil O. Riggs and Arthur M. Mintier entered military service. When they left their teaching duties were assumed by other faculty members. In September 1942 Stewart congratulated the faculty on its versatility, and expressed his belief that they could "absorb the work relinquished by the teachers absent this year."[3]

Stewart adopted firm guidelines to control the faculty. If two faculty members were at odds, and could not settle their differences, he wanted to see them both simultaneously "permitting him forthwith an opportunity to study the situation in the light of the general advance of the college. *ON NO ACCOUNT DO MEMBERS OF THE WAYNESBURG COLLEGE STAFF DISCUSS THESE DIFFICULTIES WITH STUDENTS, NOR WITH OTHER STAFF MEMBERS NOT DIRECTLY INVOLVED, AND CERTAINLY NOT IN CLASSES* (Stewart's capitals and italics)." He forewarned that if the student body suspected differences among the faculty, and speak of such, "STAFF MEMBERS IMMEDIATELY DISMISS THE MATTERS AS OF MINOR IMPORTANCE AND ESPECIALLY AS ONES THAT CAN BE HAPPILY ADJUSTED (Stewart's capitals)." He also declared "the faculty will continue by precept and example to demonstrate its personal allegiance to our evangelical churches." He not only encouraged faculty members to attend church, but also chided those who drank alcoholic beverages. He would have faculty members express nothing that would "cause any student to feel that they are not in thorough accord with the wish of the church."[4]

Even before the nation entered the war, certain events brought increasing apprehension to the campus. The fall of France in June 1940 shocked Congress into passing a conscription law, effective on 6 September 1940—the first peacetime draft in our history. Later that month Stewart received a heartening letter from President Roosevelt, who urged students in college to remain there: "We must have well educated and intelligent citizens who have sound judgment in dealing with the difficult problems of today. . . . " Roosevelt advised young people "to continue the normal course of their education, unless and until they are called, so that they will be prepared for their greatest usefulness to their country."[5] By June 1941 several students had already been drafted; others dropped out to take positions, because their older brothers had been called to military duty. Stewart worked hard to recruit freshmen, and enjoyed considerable success even in 1942 and 1943. The great majority who came in 1943, however, were young ladies. During the peak of hostilities, students working toward degrees were chiefly females. With the exodus of so many male students into the armed forces, the NYA program was terminated late in 1942.[6]

Since the airplane was so essential in the war, students became more interested in airplanes than ever before. In December 1940, with aid from Professor Riggs, the Aeronautics Club was organized and affiliated with National Intercollegiate Flying Clubs. Waynesburg was the first college in the tri-state area to join this organization. Its aim was to sponsor flying meetings and to promote flying at the college. Membership was open to all students and alumni of the college. By February 1943 an "Airplane Spotters" group had been organized chiefly by the students. While the possiblity of enemy airplanes reaching the Waynesburg area was rather remote, the students were airplane conscious; many were interested in aircraft identification. In small groups, they regularly kept their eyes skyward, looking for any strange aircraft. But the dean did not take the situation very seriously. He held that students should not miss classes oftener than once in six weeks for this purpose.[7]

While plans were made to stress military training, certain other changes were made in the academic program. In 1940 the undergraduate curriculum was reorganized into upper and lower divisions in line with practice at many other institutions. The plan was to revise the major and minor requirements into fields of concentration, which permitted greater flexibility, but without loss of specialization. In the divisional system, candidates for baccalaureate degrees were required to complete a major course of study in one of the following divisions: language and literature; mathematics and science; history and social studies; philosophy, psychology, education, and religion; and business administration.[8]

Wartime conditions brought great demands for personnel prepared to work successfully both in war-related pursuits and on the home front. Accordingly, in September 1941, the college initiated three two-year programs leading to diplomas, and at the same time placing the student in a position to complete work toward a degree at some later date. First was a two-year pre-nursing curriculum; second, a two-year program designed to prepare one as a doctor's or dentist's receptionist; and third, a two-year secretarial course. In the pre-nursing and pre-medical programs, one could secure a degree with two additional years of training. Such a background would prepare one for further studies in medical school or nursing school.[9]

As war clouds gathered in Europe, the curriculum laid greater stress on military subjects. The course in Aeronautics, when completed, prepared young men to serve the government as flight instructors at the most elementary level and to work as pilots in various ferrying commands.[10] By June 1942 an eight-week glider training program had been established in connection with pilot training. Starting with a class of ten young men, this program, like pilot training, consisted of ground school and flying training. R. E. B. Springer, the flight instructor for pilots, also taught the glider trainees. After completion of the course, some of the young men became glider pilots; some were service pilots; and some, liaison pilots in the Air Corps.[11]

Early in 1942 the Navy Department selected Waynesburg College as one of the institutions to participate in the V-1 program for training naval officers. In this program candidates pursued work leading to the regular baccalaureate degrees. To enter it, a young man had to be from seventeen to twenty years old, be a high school graduate accepted for admission to the college, and be in good standing as of 1 March 1942. Those in this program could enlist in the Navy and come to Waynesburg College as freshmen and, if efficient and studious, remain four years. They also had two other choices: (1) the V-5 program, which represented the Reserve Officers' Division of the air arm of the Navy, in which trainees were permitted to stay only two years at the college; and (2) the V-7 program which included desk and engineering officer training, in which one could remain until graduation. In May 1942, Stewart reported that these programs were progressing.[12] By October 1942 a physical education program had been started, chiefly for members of these reserve units.[13]

After the United States entered hostilities, the college adopted the year around plan, in which students could complete the four years' work in three or, in case of good students, somewhat less. This plan was recommended for students who expected to be called into the armed forces; under it, they could get a degree sooner with obvious benefit both to them and to their country. This acceleration was for the duration. But the four-year program remained for those who wished it.[14]

Shortly after the Pearl Harbor attack, students were drafted in sharply increasing numbers. The drop in enrollment, and hence in income from tuition, created a serious economic problem. Stewart sought ways to solve it. The reserve training programs had been designed chiefly for male students. But they were leaving; with their departure the student body would be greatly reduced; it would consist mainly of females, "4-F" men, and others disqualified for military service. Accordingly, early in 1943 Stewart, accompanied by the Greene County Commissioners and Roy E. Furman, a loyal alumnus of the college and erstwhile member of the state legislature, went to Washington, D. C. to confer with government officials about the possibility of getting an air crew training detachment for the college. There they were greatly assisted by Congressman J. Buell Snyder from the Twenty-fourth District of Greene, Fayette and Somerset counties. Fortunately Snyder was Chairman of the Army and Navy and Civil Functions Appropriations Subcommittee; he also was a true friend of Waynesburg College. If the college could secure a detachment of aviation cadets, the resultant income from the federal government would tide it over its period of financial stress.[15]

Stewart's mission to Washington was successful. On 9 February 1943 he received a telegram from the Chief of the Air Staff stating that the program for the college had been approved; the message requested Stewart to "wire intent" the next day. The trustees promptly accepted the government's proposal and so notified Congressman Snyder.[16]

The program was entitled "Army Air Forces College Training Program (Air Crew)." The local group was called "Ninth College Training Detachment (Air Crew)." Its objective was preparation of Air Crew Students, both mentally and physically, for intensive ground training in the pre-flight schools. In scope it included academic preparation, military training stressing basic military indoctrination and infantry drill, and physical training. Academic instruction, at the college freshman level, included mathematics, physics, history, geography, English, navigation, and Civil Air Regulations. These academic courses were to be taught by the regular college faculty, but eventually four additional faculty members were employed chiefly to handle the heavy schedule in physics and mathematics. Certain essentials of flight instruction and the course in Civil Air Regulations were to be taught at the local airport, where necessary equipment for training was provided. The original plan called for the arrival at the college of 125 cadets on 1 March 1943 and 125 on 1 April 1943. Captain G. L. Weathers of the Army Air Forces, Maxwell Field, Alabama, was commander of the first contingent. Elated over the new program, Stewart said: "Full credit should go to J. Buell Snyder, Congressman from this district, who continually emphasized to government agencies the standards prevailing at the college and the enthusiasm of Greene County toward the program." Stewart also expressed his gratitude to the local officials for their assistance in securing the cadet detachment.[17]

Early in March 1943 an ill omen loomed, which threatened to end plans for the cadet detachment even before it got off the ground. Army engineers, having come to the campus, had approved available housing for the cadets, limiting the number to 200. Later, however, the government's medical examiners arrived and turned down housing facilities. The trustees shortly received a telegram from the Surgeon General's Office stating that at least 500 cubic feet of air space per man must be provided in sleeping quarters. Measurements made by Army officers in Ivyhurst, in the Purman House, and in Walton Hall—where the cadets were to be quartered—showed that this space was not adequate for 200 men; only some 170 men could be accommodated. When it appeared that the college might not get the cadet detachment, Stewart, instead of communicating with the Surgeon General's office, telephoned Congressman Snyder, who promptly came to the rescue. It was he who induced the military authorities to approve the detachment for the college. But the number of cadets on campus was limited to 170—in accord with the government's health regulations. By the end of April 1943, the first contingent of cadets had arrived and the program was under way and working well. They were high grade men from colleges and universities all over the country.[18]

When air crew training got under way the reserve programs were phased out. Nearly all males who were physically and mentally able were inducted; in the fall of 1942, male enrollment was 182; a year later it was 56, including those ineligible for military service due to age, occupation outside of college, or physical disability. The number of female students remained fairly constant; in the fall of 1942, some 121 women were enrolled; a year later the figure was 113.[19] By that time, with the air crew detachment on the upgrade, the college was largely a military training institution.

Air crew training moved at a rapid pace. Although the college had facilities for 170 aviation students, there were never more than 150 in attendance at one time. Each month 30 were transferred from the campus, and 30 arrived to take their places. No cadet remained in attendance at the college for more than five months. Training started on 16 April 1943 and terminated on 28 June 1944, when it was clear that the Axis forces and their dictatorships would disintegrate. Some 575 aviation students received training at the college in this period.[20]

The trustees demonstrated their desire to honor those persons who were in any way connected with the cadet program. On 1 September 1943 they moved that these students "be made alumni of the college in the sense that they would be eligible to attend homecomings, banquets, etc., and enjoy all the privileges accorded to other alumni." Further, each aviation student, upon completion of his required courses, was presented a diploma which made him an alumnus of Waynesburg College. In June 1944 the trustees created the degree Master of Military Administration, which was conferred upon Captain Thomas F. McCullough, Lieutenant Richard H. Eisenstraudt, and Lieutenant John R. Tyler, then the commissioned officers of the detachment. In gratitude to the Honorable J. Buell Snyder, the college conferred upon him the honorary degree Doctor of Laws at commencement on 16 May 1943. A year later, the college honored Lieutenant General Henry H. Arnold, commanding general of United States Army Air Forces, by conferring upon him, *in absentia*, the degree Doctor of Military Science. General Arnold could not attend commencement, because of the press of military duties. Snyder, however, accompanied by two high-ranking officers of the Army Air Forces, was present. Snyder received the scroll which formally conferred the honorary degree on General Arnold, together with the robe and hood, which Snyder was to present personally to Arnold later in a ceremony in Washington, D. C.[21]

The aviation cadets did much to maintain morale. Citizens invited them into their homes and cooperated in other ways "to make their stay with us happy." And happy it was. The cadets frequently livened the whole atmosphere with a favorite song:

I got sixpence; jolly, jolly sixpence;
I got sixpence to last me all my life.
Cause I've got tupence to spend
And tupence to lend,
And tupence to send home to my wife—
Poor wife.

No cares have I to grieve me,
No pretty little girls to deceive me;
Happy as a lark, believe me.
As we go rolling, rolling home.

During their drilling and marching, they sang other songs such as "Show Me the Way to Go Home," "I'm a Yankee Doodle Dandy," and "By the Light of the Silvery Moon."[22]

On 30 October 1943 Homecoming Day exercises took place without a football game. Instead, there was a review of this detachment by its officers, by the Honorable J. Buell Snyder, and by a colonel from the office of Chief of Staff, General George C. Marshall. After the review, Snyder inspected the mess hall and barracks, and chatted informally with the cadets. On the same day the Homecoming Queen, Nell Ross, was crowned; luncheons were held; and a dance was sponsored jointly by the college and the Ninth College Training Detachment. In attendance were aviation cadets, alumni, students, and friends of the college. Congressman Snyder reiterated his feeling of friendliness toward the college. He congratulated the trustees upon the morale of the boys here and also upon the record they were making when they went to other camps for advanced training.[23]

Carefully selected from all over the nation, the cadets helped local people to rid themselves of provincialism. In May 1944, when the program was nearly over, Stewart told the trustees:

> Not one major case of discipline has occurred in the entire period of their stay. . . . Their benefit to this region is inestimable. Waynesburg is an unusual community—cultured—patriotic—thoroughly American—warm in our attitude toward the lads entrusted to us. . . . But, like so many small, cultured communities, we have the great fault of complacency. The Army Air Corps has largely shamed this away. These young men have given us an untrammeled, broad, national viewpoint, showing us by act and inference what we . . . have been missing. We'll be a better community because they have been here.

By June 1945 they had gone. Stewart received many letters from their parents who were happy in the treatment accorded their sons. In order to symbolize forever a bond of loyalty between them and the college, Stewart stated "that each spot trod by a Waynesburg alumnus becomes automatically a part of the Waynesburg College campus. . . . " By the war's end he was receiving many complimentary letters from the erstwhile cadets and other alumni from many parts of the world, "and the symbols 'WC' have been carved on the rocks and trees from the ice of Alaska to the palms of the Pacific."[24]

With the dawn of peace the college continued to seek ways to improve the curriculum. Aware of the college's responsibility to help in the education of leaders in the coal industry, in October 1944, at Stewart's suggestion, a one-year course in mining engineering was added to the curriculum. The aim was to afford miners the opportunity to study toward advancement as managers, foremen, and superintendents. The college did not pretend to compete with large schools and give a degree in mining engineering. Diplomas were granted to all who successfully completed the year's work. For those who could not leave their positions, classes were rotated at night so a candidate could complete the work in two or three years. All courses were college level; credits earned could later be applied toward a degree. This program of study was basic to subsequent studies elsewhere in mining engineering.[25]

Another course added in the post war years was physical education for male students. Offered each semester, it carried one-half semester hour credit and one honor point toward graduation. By June 1949 physical education had expanded in scope, and a Department of Physical Education was established. The purpose was to provide physical education for all members of the student body unless excused because of some physical impairment or participation in a varsity sport. At the outset of this program, however, the course was not required, and only a relatively few students were taking it. The dean lamented that the Physical Education Department was "mainly interested in varsity athletics which is carried on at enormous expense and for the benefit of a few students. . . . "[26] Later, however, physical education was required of all physically able students during the freshman year.[27]

In order to strengthen the curriculum and to aid in the teaching process, Stewart continued to add to the collection in the college museum. Certain geological specimens, for example, were excellent training aids in the "coal" course. Stone implements and other items, both rough and polished, were useful aids in teaching anthropology and archaeology. Indian artifacts helped in these fields, and gave a view of the background of ancient Americans. More modern items such as glass and pottery, secured by Stewart from Greensboro and New Geneva, threw direct light on early industry in the area after the coming of the white men. In April 1949 Stewart acquired from T. B. Stewart, a retired dentist from Lock Haven, Pennsylvania, a great collection of artifacts from Indians in this area, and also from people from Australia, Central America, Continental Europe,

Egypt, England, Ireland, Japan, and South America. This collection, built up over a period of some seventy years, was interesting not only to students in college classes, but to special groups such as pupils from public schools who visited the campus. In 1949 the total college collection contained some 40,000 pieces.[28]

In the field of student activities there was a return to normalcy after the war. In June 1946 the Y.M.C.A., inactive during the conflict, was reorganized with help from the Y.W.C.A. They jointly sponsored the annual Scavenger-Hunt and Wiener Roast for the incoming students during Freshman Week; at Thanksgiving they presented several baskets to needy families in the community; and at Christmas time they "went caroling" here and there in the neighborhood, and brought the season's greetings, thus warming the hearts of many people, particularly of the sick in the local hospital.[29] Debating, discontinued during hostilities, was resumed within the limits permitted by gasoline and tire shortages. With Professors Brock and Mintier as their coaches, the debaters encountered teams from nearby colleges. Under the direction of Professors James Miller and Dawn Logan, The Little Theater group was doing excellent work in drama, despite the fact that most of the members were freshmen and sophomores. By May 1947 the Glee Club was at its all-time largest and best. It put on concerts, furnished music for college functions, and made trips to some of the county high schools.[30]

The Parish Project entered new areas of service. In 1947 Stewart reported that: "At Stringtown, a straggling, incohesive settlement more than two miles long between Carmichaels and the river front, practically all effort toward religious activities had been abandoned." But students in the Parish Project took over a country schoolhouse there, and established a Sunday School which was soon thriving. Largely through the initiative of Gardner and the students, by 1949, two new churches were under construction—one at Crucible, the other at Nemacolin. The Presbyterian Church, U.S.A., in collaboration with the college, aided financially in building these churches. After the Parish Project penetrated these and other underprivileged centers chiefly along the Monongahela River, there was a great decrease in juvenile delinquency in those localities. Furthermore, in 1949 the college had seventy-two ministerial students—an all-time record. It was "considered the chief wellspring of the church in supplying ministers to the seminaries. . . . "[31]

The most colorful student group on campus was organized in 1949. Called the "Kiltie Band," its benefactress was Mary Denny Weaver, '14, a trustee of the college, who generously gave funds for two sets of bagpipes and complete Scotch uniforms, including bonnets, kilts, sashes, gloves, raincoats, and sporrans, for the new band. Having a sense of history, Mrs. Weaver chose the Royal Stewart Plaid for the uniforms; the pattern was that of the Stewart clan of Scottish origin. Stewart expressed his deep gratitude for Mrs. Weaver's gift and thoughtfulness. Her gesture made possible excellent entertainment at athletic events and on other occasions, boosted the financial campaign, and gave the college "a bit of showmanship which up to the present time has been sadly lacking."[32]

The war adversely affected social fraternities on the campus. The membership in each fraternity sharply dropped. The shortage of male students, as a result of the exodus into the armed forces, was partially offset by the coming of the air crew men. By May 1944 the sororities had held several "Sweater Hops," attended by aviation cadets. The Dean of Women reported: "This has helped to create a friendly feeling between the two groups. With very few exceptions our girls deserve praise for their conduct and for their kind helpfulness to the men in training on our campus."[33]

After the war the influx of veterans soon more than compensated for the decrease in enrollment during the conflict. By October 1944, six veterans were already attending the college under the G. I. Bill of Rights. As a recruiting technique, Stewart sent two copies of a special bulletin to all Waynesburg College men and women in the service, including the Ninth College Training Detachment; he asked that the "second copy be passed on to a buddy." This bulletin also went to high school principals and teachers, particularly those who were alumni of Waynesburg College. At that time Stewart read a letter to the trustees, signed by six former aviation students, then in France, expressing their appreciation of Waynesburg College. It was clear that the college had established friendships all over the United States through the 575 men of the Air Corps. The college soon proved to be the best in the region in sympathetic understanding of veterans and their problems. The institution strived to provide housing for veterans, and even to supply garden tracts for married veterans. The G. I. Bill stipulated that any student not above twenty-five years of age, who had been in the armed forces ninety days, exclusive of preliminary training programs, could go to any government-approved college or school of his choice, and the government would pay his tuition and fees and give him base pay at the rate of $50 per month. Those with a disability of ten percent received a base pay of $80 per month.[34]

By 1946 the institution was not large enough to take care of all who sought admission. Many were turned away. In order to be as fair as possible to all, the college established a set of priorities on admissions as follows: (1) our own returning veterans; (2) relatives and friends of our own constituency—student body, faculty, and trustees; (3) students from our own region who would find it a privation if they were refused admission; and (4) strong students from outside. In establishing these priorities, the trustees considered not only our own returning veterans, but also the children of our veterans who had given the last full measure of devotion—and did not return. They passed a motion that the children of Waynesburg College men who died in service in World War II be granted full-tuition scholarships when they came of college age. The alumni backed this plan, which was adopted in many of the best collegiate institutions. There was consensus that such children morally become educational wards of the survivors. The college raised money to support the plan, and welcomed donations from all persons in sympathy with it.[35]

By the year 1945-1946 the student body had reached prewar size, with some 364 students. During the next two years, enrollment skyrocketed to a total of over 1,000 students on the campus and at the Uniontown Center. Of all these, slightly over half (53.5 percent) were taking advantage of the G. I. Bill of Rights. The ratio of men to women was about five to two, approximately as it was before the war.[36]

The trustees gave attention to health services for the students. In June 1945 they employed a registered part-time nurse, who was to dispense information and aid, particularly to female students. A small infirmary was established in a room in Walton Hall. It appears, however, that this service was inadequate—even sporadic. There was no provision for annual physical examinations; and no physician was regularly available. In June 1949 the trustees moved to meet this problem. They employed W. Burdette Clendenning, M. D., as college physician, and Kathryn Rohrbaugh, a registered nurse, as full-time college nurse. All entering freshmen were required to take physical examinations. A study was made of some form of health insurance. And plans were made for a greatly improved physical education program for women. The Dean of Women declared this "is one of our greatest needs. Our girls have even been criticized for their manner of walking."[37]

Through all other developments in the 1940's Stewart and the trustees worked steadily on fund-raising. Knowing that the last decade of the first century of the college's history was an opportune time to raise money, they promoted the "Hundredth Anniversary Campaign," aimed to raise an additional $500,000 for endowment. A centenary celebration was planned to come between September 1949, reminiscent of the days when first classes were held, and September 1950, a century after the charter became effective and the college building was completed. The college was looking ahead hopefully to accreditation. A large increase in endowment was essential to achieve that goal. During the decade, in addition to raising funds, the college hoped to have a new library and science hall and to complete the gymnasium.[38]

The campaign was delayed considerably during the war. But the trustees were very faithful as donors; several gave the suggested $100 and a few went further "and led the President to other gifts." Stewart called on the faculty for help in the drive. Bequests kept coming regularly. Noteworthy was one by Charles Arthur Weaver, husband of Mary Denny Weaver, consisting of one-sixth of a trust fund of over $3,000,000 invested in one of the safest and most conservative trust companies in the United States. The campaign was moving so successfully that the goal was raised from $500,000 to $600,000. The additional $100,000 was to be used to pay off the mortgage, leaving the college free from debt by the Hundredth Anniversary. By October 1948 Stewart had applied for aid to the Richard King Mellon Foundation, and to the older W. L. and May T. Mellon Foundation. He also felt sure that the college was included in the new Benedum Foundation, just being formed. In looking to these Foundations, Stewart was tapping sources of large sums of money. He constantly believed that generous donations would be forthcoming.[39]

Financial support from the Presbyterian Church U.S.A. through its Board of Christian Education continued to increase during the 1940's. The church hoped eventually to give $20,000 annually to the support of the college. In November 1948 Stewart told the trustees that the church was planning to give the college a special gift, which he hoped would be for at least $45,000 in honor of the Hundredth Anniversary.[40] The Board of Christian Education supervised a special drive to raise $100,000 with a three-fold purpose: (1) to finish the gymnasium; (2) to establish endowment for it; and (3) to fireproof Miller Hall. Dr. Lewis Robey was the church's adviser for the campaign; and Edson was the local leader. The value of the gymnasium to the college and to the community was pointed out. With a seating capacity of over 1,000 it would be a great advantage over the Armory.[41]

In October 1943 Governor Edward Martin began serving as honorary chairman of a committee of alumni and friends to raise funds to provide indoor facilities for the gymnasium.[42] It was estimated that $40,000.00 was needed to finish its interior. Of this sum, around $25,000.00 was raised by 25 December 1944. Beginning early in 1945, a plan was devised to raise funds to finish the fifty dormitory rooms on the top floor of the gymnasium; the aim was to have these rooms dedicated to fathers by appreciative sons. By June 1945, twenty-eight rooms had been so dedicated at $250.00 per room. A few fathers expressed their intent to dedicate rooms to sons who lost their lives in the war. The trustees hoped that all fifty rooms would soon be financed in this manner. By December 1945 $40,478.00 had been subscribed. But only $18,713.48 had been collected.[43]

In October 1947 Stewart started still another fund-raising drive —this one for a new library. In Greene County he received two subscriptions of $2,500.00 each for memorial rooms in the library; funds for three memorial carrells had been subscribed; and a donor promised $4,000.00 for the large seminar room. In one day Stewart secured three $1,000.00 subscriptions from alumni in Greensburg.[44]

While the campaign to raise endowment proceeded successfully, the problem of paying faculty salaries and other current expenses was constant. It was critical right after termination of the cadet training program, when funds from the federal government were no longer received. In April 1944 Stewart warned that it would be impossible to retain "all the present faculty for only 150 or 160 students." Meanwhile, he stepped up student-recruiting, which soon met with success, though most new students were girls, and boys who were physically unfit for military service.[45]

When the college could not pay the faculty, it became customary to give due bills for back salaries. This seemed to be a chronic condition. In January 1944 Stewart told the trustees "that due bills for back salaries of the teachers are now five years old and recommended that they be renewed." In April 1945 he reported that he was campaigining for money for teachers' salaries and that he had no doubt that they could be paid that year. In September 1945, when there was an influx of veterans and increased income was expected, Stewart "instructed the office to make payment of back salaries the first charge." By April 1946, income had increased to the point where faculty salaries could be raised; heads of departments were promised $300 per month for nine months; and other faculty members enjoyed raises of twenty percent, to be effective in September 1946. As late as June 1947, however, some faculty salaries were still in arrears; the trustees then moved "that the outstanding balances owed faculty members on back salaries be paid within the next thirty days." In September 1947 Stewart told the trustees that in order to maintain a competent faculty, it would be necessary again to increase the salaries of certain faculty members. Accordingly, the salaries of five were raised approximately ten percent.[46]

It had been customary to pay faculty salaries during the nine-month academic year. Unless they taught summer school, they received no pay checks during the summer. The academic dean repeatedly recommended that the salary for nine months' work be distributed over a twelve-month period as was done in many colleges similar to Waynesburg. Since living expenses were spread throughout the year, salary payments should be similarly spread. Thus the faculty would suffer fewer handicaps. Eventually the trustees acted favorably on this recommendation.[47]

As a requisite for accreditation, in May 1947, steps were taken to provide a retirement plan for the faculty. Stewart recommended to the trustees that the college become affiliated with the Teachers Insurance and Annuity Association (TIAA), the most reputable organization of its kind in the nation. Early in 1948 the college adopted this retirement plan. Unfortunately three faculty members were then too old for inclusion in it. Aware of their long, faithful service, the trustees granted them one-half of their regular salaries during periods of illness and applied this plan to them upon their retirement. All eligible, full-time faculty members were required to enroll in TIAA after the completion of one full year of service.[48]

The problem of raising funds was closely related to development of the physical plant. Since the gymnasium was a joint project of the college and the Council of Waynesburg Borough, there was some question as to how it should be controlled. In order to clarify this situation, in April 1944 the federal government proposed an authority to control the gymnasium project. The town council passed a resolution creating such an authority and turning the lease over to that authority. This was a fifty-year lease; and the authority was empowered to control and do any construction necessary to complete the building. It was believed that this arrangement would show how prior government funds were invested, and put the college in a position to get further federal financial assistance.[49] The building was open to the public on 12 October 1944, and some 1,500 people attended. This event demonstrated public interest in the project. In June 1945 Stewart was chosen President of the Gymnasium Authority, and the Athletic Director, Frank N. Wolf, was a member of the authority. Stewart then told the trustees: "We expect, as the war draws to a close, to put on a very high-grade physical education program, using our athletic staff and senior students as instructors and guides." He also assured the trustees that as long as he was a member of the authority the interests of the college would be protected.[50]

Several buildings were acquired or constructed in the 1940's. Noteworthy was the acquisition, partly by purchase and partly by a gift by former Judge and Mrs. A. H. Sayers, of the Sayers house at the corner of Wayne and Morris Streets. The building, erected in the late 1860's, was Miller's home before and after his wife passed away. It was built of bricks burned from clay obtained just across the street; the excavated area became "Lake Winetta," where gold fish and water lilies still thrive. Originally the house had nine rooms, but additions were built later. For a number of years it was used as a girls' dormitory. The girls dubbed it "Sayers Manor on the Lake."[51] In November 1945 girls were being housed in this home, and in Walton and Varsity Halls. To take care of increasing enrollment of females, a new wing was built on Walton Hall. Ground for this addition was broken in June 1946. In October 1947 the Presbyterian Board of Education granted $22,500 as a challenge gift. Stewart and the trustees met this challenge. By June 1949, the edifice, called "The Corridors," had been completed at a total cost of $88,000. At that time the college owed only $2,545.81 on it.[52]

Stewart grasped the opportunity to acquire surplus military buildings and equipment, either free or at nominal costs under the G. I. education program. Notable was the gift of an officers' club at Camp Reynolds, near Greenville, Pennsylvania, which was moved and reconstructed on the campus by the government, according to floor plans submitted by the college. Having 10,000 square feet of floor space after reconstruction, it was converted into an auditorium, classrooms, a drama workshop, and offices for the English Department. Located across the alley from the present Benedum Hall, it was named "Madison Hall" in memory of E. Gertrude Madison, Professor of English and Dean of Women from 1926 to 1935.[53] The college purchased from the government a three-car dining unit, known as the "Duquesne Diners," located at Duquesne, Pennsylvania. These cars were fully equipped with refrigerators, kitchen equipment, dishes, counters, chairs, and tables. The cost was between $4,500 and $5,000, not including charges for transportation and installation. In May 1947 Stewart, elated over the "Diner deal," spoke of the three units: one was used as a kitchen and the other two were "almost palatial." They relieved the boarding situation, especially for commuting students, faculty members, and others having very little time between classes and laboratories. It was estimated that the Diners, plus the new building donated by the government added the better part of $100,000 to the plant.[54]

In May 1946 the government approved 30 family dwelling units and 100 dormitory units for the college. The aim was to accommodate the influx of students under the G. I. Bill. Housing units were constructed by the government for the use of married veterans on lots leased by the college, in the Bonar Addition in East Waynesburg. By October 1948 the government had given these dwellings to the college. With the aid of Mary Denny Weaver and other trustees, the college purchased the leased land. Mrs. Weaver advanced the money to make the purchase to the end that Veterans' Village would become part of the endowment of the college. In order to house other young men, in October 1947 the college acquired the Waychoff House on Morris Street, adjacent to the campus.[55]

In 1947 the college took steps to improve the science program. The "Old Mill," located on the present site of the Paul R. Stewart Science Building, was purchased and remodeled into a classroom and laboratory building, especially for instruction in chemistry and in physics. Constructed during the Civil War, this building was a flour mill for several decades. Later it housed the first electric company in Waynesburg. Prior to its acquisition by the college, it was used as a warehouse. After it was completely renovated, and modern facilities were installed, it was adequate to take care of the increasing enrollments in chemistry and physics.[56]

In the fall of 1949 a rather unusual building was constructed upon the present site of Benedum Hall. It stemmed from Stewart's long interest in fruit-growing. In June 1949 he reported that his orchard that fall would abound in apples, and he proposed to donate the major portion of the crop to the college. He recommended that the college build a cooler to provide storage for apples. Such a structure, he felt, would always be an advantage to the college; fruit could be bought when the price was low, and could be stored for use the year around. He estimated the cost at $5,000. The trustees promptly moved to borrow this sum; and by early November 1949 the structure was completed. Approximately 1,100 bushels of apples from Stewart's orchard were placed in it. The aims were to supply the college dining halls with apples, and to sell to faculty members, married students, and trustees at less than market prices.[57] It appears, however, that this venture was not long profitable. Eventually the structure was razed before Benedum Hall was built.

In June 1948 Stewart recommended the building of a library. For a half century the library had been housed on the second floor of Miller Hall. It was adequate in the early decades when student enrollment was low. With the sharp increase in enrollment after World War II, however, more space was needed. Accordingly, the trustees purchased a lot on College Heights for $3,000 for the new building; the site overlooked the campus. Governor James H. Duff laid the cornerstone just before Commencement exercises on 12 June 1949. Construction on the foundation proceeded through the summer and fall of 1949. The building was to be modern in all respects with plenty of space for stacks, carrels, reading rooms, offices, and storage. Simultaneously the college acquired the land north of the North Ward School Building, and adjacent to the library; it then owned all the vacant properties in the College Heights section.[58]

In June 1949 the trustees arranged to have permanent lighting facilities installed at College Field. The college also obtained twenty-five acres east of the campus along the Purman Run Road. The aim was to develop another field for outdoor sports. The location was excellent; a steep slope on one side provided a natural setting for bleachers. This area was used as a playground and practice field.[59]

Meanwhile certain improvements were made on campus grounds. By the 1940's the Donley-Schrock Arboretum was flourishing. Started a decade earlier, chiefly by two students, Benjamin F. Donley '35 and Alta Schrock '37, it was an on-campus arboretum composed of native Pennsylvania trees, thus facilitating field trips. After their graduation, other students cared for, and added to, the arboretum. It was a fine asset to the Botany Department.[60]

By June 1948 three good tennis courts to supply one of the crying needs had been constructed. Stewart expressed his happiness about these courts and also about the playground just east of the campus "where students during spare moments can open the throttles of youthful energy."[61] He recalled the old days when the campus consisted of the yard in front of Miller Hall and a hayfield behind it. By 1949, however, the local campus was rapidly expanding. The surroundings were beautiful: "Here the simplicity of the trees, shrubs, and grass plots bring the student closer to the heart of the Creator," said Stewart.[62]

Early in July 1946 the trustees considered the desirability of establishing an extension branch at Uniontown, Pennsylvania, in order to provide more convenient educational facilities for discharged veterans and others in Fayette County and its environs. Shortly Stewart called on Professor Harry E. Gardner to survey the situation there with a view to the establishment of a "Waynesburg College Uniontown Center." Gardner secured classrooms in the Ella Peach School Building. The city library, located nearby, was available to students at the Center. The Third Presbyterian Church, not far distant, promised certain rooms for classes and for chapel. Gardner made progress in his search for faculty members for the Center. Students flocked to it in great numbers. In October 1946 Stewart reported that 256 students were enrolled there; and 623 matriculated on the main campus. He commended Gardner for his splendid work in planning, organizing, and promoting the Uniontown Center. Upon Stewart's recommendation, the trustees gave Gardner the title "Vice President in charge of Uniontown Center," plus extra compensation for his special services on this project.[63]

The Uniontown Center was heartily supported by the Governor of Pennsylvania, the Veterans Administration, and the citizens of Fayette County. It became a feeder for the Waynesburg campus. At first only freshmen were enrolled there, but in 1948 the curriculum was expanded to include courses at the sophomore level.[64]

While the fund-raising campaign was successful and great strides forward were made in the development of the physical plant, the faculty deteriorated in quality. After the war the percentage of earned doctorates sharply dropped, chiefly for two reasons. First, during the conflict the graduate schools could not turn out enough doctorates to meet postwar demand. For the academic year 1946-1947 the faculty consisted of nine with the earned doctorate, thirteen with the master's degree, nineteen with only the bachelor's degree, and two (in voice and violin) with no degree. Second, the salary scale was not attractive; and there was a rapid turnover of teachers—not a good sign. Some teachers had no previous experience in college teaching; others had been retired from other institutions, having reached the age limit. By 1949 the quality of the faculty was so low that the college consultant "advised that we set our goal to obtain a few really topnotch men for the instructional staff."[65]

Though additional teachers were employed, the faculty was heavily overloaded, because of the influx of veterans. In September 1946 Stewart told the faculty it would be necessary "to deputize more jobs than ever before in the history of the college." Simultaneously the teaching schedule was officially set at fifteen hours per week. But Stewart called on the faculty to teach three hours gratis: "If, because of the emergency 18 hours must be scheduled, the extra 3 hours are considered emergency, unofficial, and publicized only as gifts to the veteran cause." Further the schedule was so crowded that some classes ran through the noon hour, and on Saturdays until 1:00 P.M.[66]

The climax of events in the 1940's was the Centennial Celebration on 11 June 1949. After many weeks of planning, it was a day of much pageantry. "The purpose of the pageantry and the parade is to make the people of this community aware of the power of this College," said Stewart. The Centennial Parade was witnessed by an estimated 15,000 people—the largest crowd ever in Waynesburg. Led by the Kiltie Band, it consisted of some 80 different units and was three miles long. It depicted a century of history of the college and of related developments in the community. Noteworthy productions by artists were two large murals—one of Miller, the other of Stewart.[67]

The adversities of World War II tested the viability of the college. From the economic viewpoint, the acquisition of the Army Air Forces training detachment was the most important development; it meant the college would survive. After the war the institution adapted to changing needs, chiefly by the establishment of the Uniontown Center which facilitated the education of veterans and other young people in that area and added economic strength for several years. The 1940's saw a great upsurge in the overall development and growth of the institution. At the end of its first century of life, the college looked ahead hopefully to accreditation by its regional association of institutions of higher learning.

XVII
THE STRUGGLE FOR ACCREDITATION

FROM THE FOUNDING OF COLONIAL COLLEGES THROUGH THE FIRST TWO decades of the twentieth century, there was no standardized procedure by which colleges and universities were evaluated. Hence some institutions fell below others in the quality of their programs. In the interests of greater uniformity, the federal government attempted to rate and standardize all post secondary schools in the United States, but found that such was not possible in a democracy.[1]

By 1920 there was consensus among many educators that the institutions themselves should establish some system of self-evaluation in order to maintain at least minimal standards. Accordingly, universities, colleges, and secondary schools were organized into regional associations. Educators assumed the responsibility to maintain standards in institutions in their respective areas. Waynesburg College has always been located in the Middle States Association of Colleges and Secondary Schools (MSA).

To win accreditation by the MSA was a Sisyphean struggle for the college for nearly three decades. At different times the coveted goal seemed within reach, only to be thwarted by unforeseen circumstances. By September 1923 the college had ended the practice of admitting special students "until they had proven themselves," and had put into effect a new admission requirement, namely, that all entering students must be graduates of approved high schools. This was in keeping with standards set by the MSA. The college then hoped "shortly" to be accredited.[2]

Such hopes were in vain, however. On 12 June 1930, Stewart told the trustees that the college "should at once take steps to place herself on the accredited list of colleges" in the MSA. If it were accredited, it would "be in a much better position" to secure more funds from the church's campaign to raise money in 1932. He urged that $200,000 be raised for endowment, "thus bringing us to the required $500,000 for accrediting purposes." He pointed out the need for a gymnasium and for more building space. In these respects, he said, the college had been surpassed "by practically every other college of the region."[3] Again in June 1939, Stewart said that, with the help of the Board of Christian Education, "we will put on an endowment campaign that will lead us to full accreditment in our regional association."[4]

On 10 June 1941 Stewart reported to the trustees that "we expect to make formal application for recognition by the Middle States Association this summer." He pointed out the high quality of the faculty. Further, a firm of accountants found the financial practices of the college to be sound. This application for accreditation was turned down, however, partly because the college library lacked many books on the Shaw *List*.[5]

Beginning in 1941 efforts were made to acquire more books on this *List*, so-called for C. B. Shaw, Librarian at Swarthmore College. His *List* was the result of a study in which leading educators in all fields were asked to submit titles of one or two books which they considered the "very best in their respective fields." This *List* was used as the standard by which colleges measured their libraries. As of May 1944, after some three years of efforts at improvement, Waynesburg's Library contained only 14 percent of books on the Shaw *List*. It was imperative that this figure be at least doubled.[6]

Several expedients were adopted to secure these books. Each department head submitted titles of books on the *List* needed by his department; these titles, together with prices of the books, were published in a college bulletin. Funds were raised to purchase them. Faculty members were asked to lend to the Library any such books, which were catalogued and made available to students "even if kept at home." Faculty loans of periodicals were also solicited. Efforts were made to secure Shaw *List* books from second-hand bookstores and distribution sales. The alumni were requested to donate books. By May 1944 "book of the month" men were being recruited, including men in military service, who either sent the Library a book each month or gave enough money to purchase one.[7] The campaign to improve the Library continued relentlessly, and eventually this weakness was overcome—thanks to the cooperation of many persons.

Late in October 1944, Stewart, having conferred with members of the Board of Christian Education in Philadelphia, told the trustees that "Waynesburg College must become accredited" by the MSA. Simultaneously he announced his Five-Year Plan for the college, to run from 1944 to 1949, during which the financial goal was $500,000. He believed this increase in funds would go far in the achievement of accreditation. He also had faith that "all obstacles to accreditment" would be surmounted during this period.[8]

On Stewart's recommendation the trustees engaged Harry Morehouse Gage as a consultant on all matters relating to accreditation. Gage was well qualified for this post. A high-ranking man in the church, he had long been an official in the North Central States Association of Colleges and Secondary Schools. He had been president, for varying periods totaling 34 years, of three colleges—Coe, Huron, and Lindenwood. He had also served on the Board of Christian Education, Presbyterian Church, U.S.A. since 1926. Gage visited, and inspected, Waynesburg College several times prior to assumption of his duties as Consultant in November 1947. On 25 February 1947 he told the Waynesburg College faculty that accrediting agencies "are voluntary associations whose purpose it is to evolve standards to be met by their members in carrying out their functions." He stressed self-discipline by the institutions themselves, which was much better than having standards imposed by government. On 8 April 1947 he assured the faculty that accrediting agencies cannot and will not attempt to destroy the independence of church-related colleges. These agencies can best be defined as "cooperative ventures in excellence." He pointed out that, when such an agency evaluates an institution, it first attempts to ascertain its purpose. Then, as the survey progresses, "every activity of the institution is examined in relation to the accomplishing of the institutional purpose." In an understatement, Gage said that "institutions are free to accept these standards or not . . . but . . . it is expedient to conform."[9] Clearly the college faced another crisis. Without accreditation its students would leave, and it would be forced to close its doors.

Gage was most helpful in giving the college the benefit of criticism based on long experience. Early in 1948, however, Dr. Raymond Kistler, President of Beaver College, visited the campus with a view to giving his advice. That institution had recently been accredited by the MSA, and therefore, he too was in a position to give valuable counsel as Waynesburg strived toward the same goal. Gage and Kistler soon saw that, in order to win accreditation, Waynesburg College must immediately take corrective action on four problems. First, faculty salaries must be increased. On 4 March 1948, on Stewart's recommendation, the minimum salary for professors was raised to $3,600 for nine months; and the minimum for instructors, $2,000 for the same period. Fortunately, a retirement plan for the faculty was then being implemented in line with MSA policy. Second, the Library in cramped quarters on the second floor of Miller Hall was still "woefully lacking," despite all efforts to acquire books on the Shaw *List*. The Librarian's salary, $2,250 for nine months, was too low; and her rank as instructor was not adequate. The Library was not being used sufficiently by students and faculty. Third, the college catalogue listed too many courses that were not being regularly offered. It was recommended that courses that could not be presented at least in alternate years be deleted. Fourth, grade distribution sheets showed that grades submitted by some teachers were "skewed too heavily toward the top."[10]

Some faculty members were spread over "too many subjects"; all were overloaded. During the second semester of 1946-1947, when the influx of veterans sharply rose, schedules for most full-time teachers ranged from 15 hours per week upward; one was teaching 24 hours weekly. Classes were large; thirteen teachers had 100 or more students; four had well over 200. By June 1950, however, teaching schedules were "in keeping with standards approved by the accrediting associations." Too many teachers held only the bachelor's degree; early in 1950 the faculty had 15 members with this degree on a total teaching staff of 57. Clearly there was need for more faculty members with higher degrees, especially the earned doctorate.[11]

Certain sins of omission hurt the college. The faculty had no constitution, no bylaws, and no clearly defined policy regarding tenure. As of early 1950 a faculty member was "considered to have tenure after one year's service." But the question of tenure was then "being studied and the term will be defined when the faculty constitution and bylaws are adopted." On 1 March 1949 Stewart had proposed a constitution for the faculty. Based on a model constitution offered by Gage, it was drafted by a faculty committee and put into effect by 1 June 1950.[12] Another significant omission was the lack of an organizational chart which showed the administrative system of the college. The constitution would define the responsibilities of the trustees, the president of the college, the deans, and the standing committees of the faculty; the chart would show them in graphic form. Both were essential to a "well established institution. . . . "[13]

By early 1949 some progress had been made in correcting several of the foregoing weaknesses. At that time the college petitioned the MSA for accreditation and in March, a team from that agency visited and inspected, the college. On that occasion, Stewart "suggested a little 'dressup' and the advancing of suggestions in the matter by faculty members." Evidently the team felt that, while there had been improvement, much was still to be done before accreditation could be granted. "Despite the outcome," the experience was "of value in bringing to the attention of the administration what is expected of a modern, progressive college, and has promoted the idea of self-inspection." Gage was optimistic. He said "if we work," accreditation could be won during the Hundredth Anniversary of the founding of the college.[14]

On 10 June 1949 Stewart listed several obstacles which were still to be surmounted. First, the athletic setup needed complete revision. Athletic scholarships had to be cut down drastically. They, together with other unendowed scholarships, were considered "very weak spots in the college." Second, a library building was desirable, but, according to Stewart, its completion was not necessary to accreditation. Third, the music situation was sharply criticized. According to the examining committee, the college was permitting "certain individuals to use the College name for the advancement of their art." On Stewart's recommendation, this Department was eliminated and, in line with the examining committee's suggestion, attention was given to the music and art needs of the entire student body. Courses in art and drama were added; the conservatory was retained chiefly as a community service. Fourth, the college needed an adequate health service. Fifth, the testing program should be improved. Standard tests had already been added at the sophomore level; and a "high-grade psychologist" would be employed to take charge of various tests desired by the accrediting agencies.[15]

In November 1949 Stewart made a progress report to the MSA. The purpose of the college would be stated in a full page in the catalogue. Eight faculty members with only the bachelor's degree were replaced with those holding the master's degree; others with the bachelor's degree who were not working on higher degrees would not be retained. Teaching schedules had been reduced for several faculty members. Part-time teachers were no longer employed. The Librarian was promoted to assistant professor. Faculty salaries had again been raised. A pre-admission examination assured more careful selection of students. Teaching effectiveness was measured by an adequate testing program. Intercollegiate athletics had been deemphasized and made "subordinate to the physical welfare of the entire student body." The college had a physician and a registered nurse. Proliferation of the college catalogue was corrected when courses not taught were deleted. On an item labeled "efficiency of organization," the examining committee had held that the Registrar, Michael K. Talpas, was too crowded with work. In addition to his duties as Registrar he was laboring efficiently in three other important capacities, namely, Bursar, Book Store Manager, and Purchasing Agent. He was also serving faithfully on the following committees: Allowances, Athletic Council, Centennial, Lectures and Entertainment, Registration and Scholarship, and Self-help and Placement. Stewart assured the examining committee that the present arrangement was "opportunist and experimental. . . . " It met an emergency and proved to be highly successful "because of the unusual ability and character of the Registrar." Stewart promised that Talpas would not be expected to perform such a variety of duties indefinitely, but to relieve him "of financial responsibility immediately would be most unwise."[16]

The year 1949 came and went, and the MSA had not granted accreditation to the college. In March 1950 it sent another inspection committee to the campus and made another survey, guided "by the report of the 1949 committee." Shortly Dr. F. Taylor Jones, Chairman of the MSA, summarized the observations of the examining committee of March 1950. In general, the committee had found that Waynesburg College was sufficiently well organized to do its work, but it "has much more to do." Faculty salaries were still too low, especially at the top. Many faculty members were still overloaded—and so was the administrative staff. Despite these drawbacks, the college's program was well adapted to a good liberal arts education. The fact that it was a small college worked to its advantage. With respect to student clientele, the quality centered about the median. In admissions, the committee held that the college should constantly try to get the "kind of people who can take the program you are prepared to give them." With the exception of the Library, the physical plant was adequate for a good liberal arts program. With respect to finances, the college was making progress, but more money was needed to meet higher salaries and increased costs of buildings and improvements of the physical plant. The committee stressed the need for administrators and faculty members to attend meetings of their respective professional organizations. The college must "help bear the expense of attendance at such meetings." Further, sabbatical leaves were highly desirable in order that faculty members might do research, and thus improve themselves, add to the sum total of knowledge, and be more effective in the classroom.[17]

By June 1950 it was obvious that all the work toward accreditation had "brought about countless improvements." When faculty members were employed, however, Stewart customarily did not tender to them contracts in writing. Instead, as a contemporary teacher put it: "He offered the grasp of a firm hand and the promise of a full partnership with him in all that the college possessed, both fortune and misfortune." Nevertheless, in line with a recommendation of the accrediting agency, on 6 September 1950, Stewart showed the trustees two forms of employment contracts, one to be used for new faculty members, and the other for those who had been granted tenure. On his request, the trustees authorized "the use of these contracts for the present faculty and for any faculty members employed in the future."[18]

The faculty and other college personnel enjoyed certain privileges which helped to maintain morale. Academic freedom prevailed. Waynesburg's motto for more than a century was: "A professor's classroom is his castle." He was free to choose his own methods of teaching, and to teach his courses as he wished, "so long as he was not subversive to the Government of the United States of America." Faculty members also had certain fringe benefits, such as group hospitalization, which was available to all employees of the college. Teachers were to be granted half salary on sabbatical leaves. The retirement plan was highly beneficial. Further, the college began the practice of providing travel expenses for faculty members who attended meetings of their professional associations. In compliance with state law, all employees of the college were covered by Workmen's Compensation Insurance. There was also insurance coverage against burglary, robbery, fire, and injuries to persons in college buildings and at athletic events. Participants in football and basketball were covered by medical expense policies. Collision insurance was carried on all college-owned vehicles.[19]

While all the foregoing improvements were made, or were under way, Stewart and the trustees continued to raise funds. On 3 November 1949, a standard accounting firm, having examined the income and expenditures of the college, reported that the operation was "in conformity with generally accepted accounting principles. . . . " The alumni had come to the aid of their Alma Mater by increased donations. Money was raised by a nationwide telephone campaign.

At the Centennial Celebration on 11-12 June 1949, the financial goal was raised from $500,000 to $750,000. By that time Waynesburg was a synodical college under the Presbyterian Church, U.S.A.—a closer affiliation "which tripled our finances from the church." But the examining comittee felt that the college was spending too much money on intercollegiate athletics. That group was promptly assured that Waynesburg was "trying to abide by the rules of the National Collegiate Athletic Association (NCAA) relative to food expenditures and other expenses for intercollegiate athletics." As the NCAA made rules reducing training table allowances, Waynesburg would act accordingly—and reduce this item in her budget.[20]

With respect to buildings and facilities, the chief drawback was lack of a library building, but this was rapidly being remedied. The new building, visualized as part library and part museum, was under construction early in 1950. It was hoped that it would be completed within two years. In the more spacious quarters there would be plenty of room for the then-existing collection of some 34,000 volumes. Hundreds of additional books and numerous periodicals could be acquired, and space would be available for them. Other improvements which were planned included the remodeling of the chemistry building (the "Old Mill") and the fireproofing of Miller Hall and improving of its halls and stairways.[21]

In the evaluation process the MSA desired to learn not only of the foregoing factors—the purpose, program, organization, and resources of the college—but also of the "outcomes" or results of the overall operation. The paramount question was: How effectively did the college function in the light of its purpose and goals? The answer was to be found chiefly in the degree of success of graduates of the college. At the behest of the MSA, in February 1949 Stewart sent letters to professional and graduate schools in which he asked for a critical estimate of the work of their students who hailed from Waynesburg since 1940.[22] Letters from some of the best graduate schools in the nation indicated that Waynesburg's alumni were successful in their work. Responses to a letter Stewart sent to these alumni showed that they regarded their training at the college as excellent; they expressed thanks "for such good courses at Waynesburg College." In medical schools the record was equally high. During Stewart's administration, beginning in 1921 and running to the date of this survey in 1949, of all Waynesburg students recommended for medical and dental schools, only 3.28 percent failed. The "failure expectancy of all medical schools over a long period of years was 22 to 25 percent." The college attributed its low percentage of failures "to its close and sympathetic attention in the matter of advice and its careful follow-up while the student is in medical college." Students in seminaries, however, did not fare so well. Of six men attending Princeton Seminary in the middle to late 1940's, one left after one term; one was dropped for unsatisfactory work; two were in the "lower groups"; one was a "middler"; and it appears that only one graduated, in 1944. One man attended Union Theological Seminary where he stood in the lower half of his class. Another went to Louisville Presbyterian Seminary where he did average (C+) work; he was burdened by preaching and family responsibilities. Waynesburg men at McCormick, Western, and Hartford Theological Seminaries were doing better-than-average work. The survey on "outcomes" showed that alumni who had entered the teaching profession were "nearly all rated favorably in varying degrees." From 1937 to 1949, 127 returned to their Alma Mater for additional work, chiefly for extension of teacher certification. Some 54 attended graduate school at the University of Pittsburgh; 30, at West Virginia University; others went to the Universities of Colorado, Illinois, Maryland, and a number of others. If we include medical schools, dental schools, and seminaries, alumni of the college, in varying numbers, were attending a total of 54 institutions of higher learning in the 1940's.[23]

Early in November 1950 Stewart told the faculty that the accreditation program was "proceeding well with most obstacles overcome." But he pointed out that the testing program could still be improved. A month later he announced that accreditation, at long last, had been granted by the MSA. Likewise the Department of Public Instruction approved the college's program for training students who were entering the teaching profession. According to Michael K. Talpas, the Registrar, Stewart, on learning that the college was accredited, uttered a prayer of thanks to God, and he humbly asked that Waynesburg College "may continue worthy of this high recognition." After Stewart announced the good news to the faculty, the Reverend Gardner "led the faculty in a prayer of Thanksgiving for accreditation and the many other blessings conferred upon the institution." The faculty then unanimously passed a resolution "extending its respect and honor to President Stewart for his leadership and his dedication over so many years to the advancement of the college. . . . " The faculty further unanimously resolved to commend "Dr. H. M. Gage for all his activities in behalf of the college in its work toward accreditation."[24]

Accreditation had been won. To keep it would require constant efforts at improvement of all facets of the institution.

XVIII
THE ATHLETIC PROGRAM, 1921-1963

THE STRUGGLE FOR ACCREDITATION WAS EQUALED BY THE BATTLE TO RE-new and maintain a strong athletic program. When Stewart took the helm in 1921, the athletic situation had been moribund for several years. He had been an outstanding athlete during his student days at the college, and in Houghton's administration, though inter-collegiate contests were deemphasized, in addition to his teaching duties, Stewart had served successfully as Athletic Director. He naturally hoped to restore athletics to its rightful place, both at the intercollegiate and intramural levels; alumni, students, and friends of the college overwhelmingly concurred; knowing that crowds at games would bring money into Waynesburg, businessmen were willing to support athletics. Through concerted efforts of all interested persons, the college built a strong athletic program. It competed respectably against others in its class and against some of the "big time" institutions as well.

Early in September 1921 the trustees employed Frank N. Wolf as Athletic Director and teacher of Mechanical Engineering and Surveying at a salary of $2,000 per year. A former star at Pennsylvania State College, where he played football, basketball and baseball, Wolf was highly recommended by Hugo Bezedek, head coach at Penn State. Wolf was to coach football, basketball, and baseball and to develop intramural sports. The college did not plan to field a varsity football team in the fall of 1921, but to build a team for 1922. Wolf worked hard, however, from the first with players, most of whom had very little experience. The original plan was changed, and the decision was made "to start football as a preliminary to next year." During that first fall, in 1921, with Harry McHenry as quarterback, Waynesburg defeated California Normal twice, and won against the reserves of Carnegie Institute of Technology; one game was lost to Fairmont Normal.[1] A good start had been made on the gridiron.

The college scheduled ten football games for the 1922 season. Lloyd F. ("Dad") Engle, another Penn State man, served as assistant football coach. Clyde M. Call, a local businessman, became graduate manager of athletics early in 1922. Both Engle and Call were held in highest esteem by officials at the college. They were a good combination in aiding Wolf to reestablish the athletic program. Despite the inexperience of the players, injuries during practice and games, lack of equipment, and an inadequate field, Waynesburg won six out of the ten games in 1922. Wolf was hailed as "one of the best football mentors in the East today." Waynesburg was one of the strongest class B contenders in the tri-state district.[2]

Alumni and friends of the college kept busy raising money for the athletic program. By early 1922 they had boosted their fund to $25,000 to be used to put the college "in the front ranks of major sports." Local businessmen interested in the welfare of the college purchased the old Gibbons Hotel on South Washington Street and gave it to the college to be used as a training house for athletes. The house was remodeled "so men can sleep and eat there." The baseball squad was first to eat at the new training table for all Waynesburg College athletes. The college had a very successful baseball season in the spring of 1922—with 17 wins and 9 losses. "Big time" teams on the schedule included Pitt, Penn State, Carnegie Tech, and Duquesne.[3]

The athletic grounds were owned and maintained by the college. The trustees continued to rent the Waynesburg Armory for use as a basketball room and for other indoor sports. Basketball was conducted for both men and women. At the outset, the men's team was one of the best, and some predicted it would win the tri-state championship in the winter of 1922-1923. But the course of events soon proved othewise. By January 1923 Wolf was facing misfortunes of one form or another, and he was able merely to limp through the schedule—instead of winning the tri-state championship he had hoped for. He became dissatisfied and, after meeting opposition and lack of cooperation along certain lines, he resigned in January 1923. He then went to Williamson, West Virginia, and coached high school there for the next four years. His record there was brilliant; in 1927 his football team won the state championship.[4]

According to Harry McHenry, the best all-around athlete in the college in the early 1920's,[5] the real reason why Wolf left was the fact that the college "wanted to go big time." It appeared to the college's Athletic Council that James B. ("Red") Roberts of Centre College, in Kentucky, was the right man to succeed Wolf. Although Centre was a small institution, it had greatly emphasized football, and its team had defeated Harvard, Princeton, and West Virginia. Roberts was over six feet tall, weighed 250 pounds, and was an All-American; he had played all positions in football. The college employed him as coach of football and basketball. In football he was assisted by "Dad" Engle, also an All-American. With the advent of Roberts, there was great enthusiasm and optimism on campus and among the townspeople. In anticipation of large crowds, the trustees enlarged College Field by adding 75 feet on one end. Plans were made to move the grandstand and to increase the seating capacity by installing new bleachers which would practically form a bowl for football games. Nevertheless, the warm reception accorded Roberts was soon exceeded by disenchantment over his performance. The record of his first—and only—football season shows three wins, four losses, and one tie. He left at the end of the 1923 season.[6]

Meanwhile tennis got under way, chiefly through the initiative and efforts of the students. In June 1922 the editor of *The Collegian* pointed out the advances along other lines of athletics, but lamented that the college had no tennis court. In tennis, he said, "boys and girls play together—the only such sport where this can be done." Shortly a court was prepared on the Milliken property on College Heights, and made available to the students on a temporary basis. Another tennis court, therefore, would soon be needed. By May 1923 this need was met when Mary Sayers generously gave the use of a lot between the main college building (Miller Hall) and her residence, providing the college would do the grading, excavating, and construction of the court. Happy at this offer, the students began work at once. Many gave money, labor, and time, and the work was soon completed. In May 1925 the students sponsored a one-week tennis tourney for the purpose of selecting a varsity team to represent the college in informal matches with other colleges. Lack of a coach hurt the tennis program, but several experienced students coached the others.[7]

After Roberts left, the trustees employed Britain ("Britt") Patterson as athletic coach at a salary of $1,500 for the football season, including spring practice. He had been a tough tackle on the Washington and Jefferson College team in 1912, 1913, and 1914. Subsequently he coached at the University of Detroit, and developed a great team there. He knew the game of football, and was a firm disciplinarian. He too was assisted by "Dad" Engle, and Wendell Scott, one of Waynesburg College's best former players, coached the ends and served as scout. This combination got good results. The football record for 1924 shows seven wins, two losses, and one tie. The college took second place in the Tri-State Conference in football, and rated near the top in basketball.[8]

Despite his success, Patterson left at the end of one season. Records show that control over the college's Athletic Department was inadequate, and the admission of athletes was not systematized. The Athletic Association, which managed athletic affairs, was in debt some $7,500 for goods, equipment, board, and room. An endowment drive, however, had just gained subscriptions in the amount of $18,000, and some subscribers had designated their subscriptions to the athletic fund. Even if coaches came and went, the outlook for athletics was good. The athletic committee of the trustees felt that the revival of athletics was "a very definite and great benefit and it is important that the same be continued."[9]

In March 1925 the trustees employed Roy A. Easterday, D.D.S. of the University of Pittsburgh as Director of Athletics. Aside from his profession as dentist, he had a fine record as a coach. He was to coach football, basketball, and track. Baseball was dropped, and emphasis was laid on track which would furnish diversion for more students and not be so costly. Plans were made immediately to participate in a track meet sponsored by the Tri-State Conference.[10]

Keenly interested in basketball, Easterday immediately promoted a tournament for basketball players from high schools in the tri-state area. The chief aim was to advertise the college to the high schools participating in the games. Lasting a week, the tournament was conducted by Easterday assisted by members of the Athletic Association and by students; each male student in the college helped in some way. It was necessary to see that the visitors were housed and fed, as well as directed in the many games in the tournament. Braddock High School won the Class A division, and received a beautiful full-size silver basketball presented by the Waynesburg Chamber of Commerce. A runner-up in Class A, Charleroi High School received a silver loving cup presented by the Citizens National Bank of Waynesburg. The players respectively won small gold and silver basketballs. The Class B winner was Wadestown High School,

Wadestown, West Virginia. That team was awarded a silver loving cup by Waynesburg College. This tournament proved to be the greatest athletic event ever held in Greene County. Without any question, it did much to promote good relations between the college and the public. Easterday coached both the men's and women's basketball teams, and results were excellent. In two consecutive years the men's team achieved second place in the Tri-State Conference.[11]

Easterday was eager to maintain football at a high level. Assisted by Stewart Simms and "Buck" Jones, he worked the squad long and hard, particularly before games with W. & J., where rivalry was keenest. The college did not expect to beat, but only to play respectable games against, W. & J.—a football power that played in the Rose Bowl in 1921 and remained strong for several years thenceforth. Like all reputable coaches, Easterday hoped that his players would do good work scholastically, and thus maintain their eligibility to remain on the teams. If athletes were down scholastically, efforts were made to motivate them toward higher academic standing; tutoring often helped them. Easterday drew the line on players who were guilty of drunkeness and conduct unbecoming a gentleman; such individuals were dismissed from college.[12] Easterday's football teams had a losing season in 1925, a winning season in 1926, and a most disastrous one in 1927.[13]

In 1927 Easterday left, and the trustees sought his successor. In May 1928 they again employed Wolf as Athletic Director at a salary of $3,000 per year. He was to teach six hours weekly, and to devote his entire time to the interests of the college. He shortly came to town and took an inventory for the coming grid season. Football had sharply declined and, despite Wolf's efforts to rebuild a competitive team, the 1928 season was one of the worst—with no wins, six losses, and two ties.[14]

Such poor results stemmed mainly from existing conditions. The field was inadequate. In 1928 there was a total lack of equipment, and no satisfactory dressing facilities. The Chairman of the Athletic Association told the trustees that "at no school in the tri-state district are visiting teams afforded such miserable accommodations as they must accept here." By June 1929 that Association had improved a room in the basement of the main college building, where equipment could be kept; and shower facilities were installed there for bathing. It was hoped that such improvisations would be only temporary. An adequate field with a track was urgently needed. And, as the

Chairman of the Athletic Association pointed out: "A gymnasium with adequate shower and locker facilities is the most pressing need of the student body. Under the present competitive scheme of obtaining students, who can represent us acceptably on athletic teams, it is almost impossible to attract the type of boy we desire." Money was lacking. The field was not adequately fenced, and people could stand almost anywhere in the environs and witness games without paying admission. Gate receipts were low, and donations from alumni for the athletic program totaled only $12.50 between June 1928 and June 1929. The Chairman of the Athletic Association charitably added: "The fault may lie in lack of contact with alumni who would be willing to help, if requested to do so."[15]

Despite these and other drawbacks, within a year Wolf fielded a strongly competitive football team. In 1929 it won five games, and lost four against rugged opposition; the worst loss was against highly-rated Pitt by a score of 53 to 0. Wolf constantly sought ways to compensate for his lack of material in quantity and quality. He developed a system called "Krazy Kwilt," which stressed speed and deception. It was a combination of the Pitt and other systems consolidated and trimmed to suit the type and amount of material that annually came to Waynesburg. The results obtained by such a system were so satisfactory that subsequently many of Wolf's techniques were adopted by professional teams.[16]

Fortunately improvements were soon made. By 1930 the athletic field had been fenced and equipped for several sports. A one-fifth mile cinder track, several volleyball courts, and practice areas were provided. Seating for some 4,000 spectators was constructed. The college then had six tennis courts; and a varsity tennis team was ready to represent the institution in intercollegiate competition. While these improvements were highly beneficial, a gymnasium was sorely needed. Appeals were made frequently for funds to meet this need. Meanwhile, Professor James M. Miller, a Penn State man, then a member of the English Department, became Faculty Manager of Athletics.[17] All these moves were harbingers of better days for the athletic program.

The 1930's saw an upsurge in football such as the college had never known. The highlights are notable. First, the college defeated Penn State twice—in 1931 by a score of 7 to 0, and in 1932 by 7 to 6. In both games Robert ("Rab" for Rabbit) Currie was the sensational star. In the latter game the score was 6-0 in State's favor with two minutes to play. In a lightning 45-yard sprint, "Rab" took the ball from mid-field to the goal line. Donnelly crashed the line for the touchdown, and then converted the point. This team won the Class B Title, in 1932, after beating Geneva by a score of 6-3. To that time it was the best in the history of the college.[18]

The second highlight in football came in 1935 when Waynesburg, outweighed 20 pounds per man, battled Pitt. Wolf had regularly conducted spring practice, in addition to the rugged training early in the fall, in order to meet such strong competition.[19] Pitt earlier had defeated the college by high scores—53 to 0 in 1929, and 52-0 in 1930. In 1935 Pitt won, 14 to 0, which was considered a moral victory for the college. Arnold Koepka, the Waynesburg quarterback, did excellent punting. This, together with a stubborn Jacket defense, kept the score low. Coach Jock Sutherland of Pitt said: "I can't say too much for the fine defensive game put up by Waynesburg." They "fought hard and showed that they had been well drilled in the fundamentals by their coach, Frank Wolf."[20]

The third high point, which made history, came in 1939, when Waynesburg met Fordham's powerful Rams in the first televised football game at Randall's Island Stadium, New York, on 30 September of that year. Before 8,000 fans, Waynesburg's Robert ("Bob") Brooks, a Greensburg High graduate, raced 63 yards for the first video touchdown, but Fordham went on to a 34-7 victory. The Fordham line was dubbed the "Seven Blocks of Granite." This game, in addition to its historical significance, made money for Waynesburg College; the college's share in gate receipts was $2,750, doubtless one of the highest ever netted. The Jackets of 1939 enjoyed a winning season with six victories, two defeats, and one tie. They won the West Penn Class B title for that year.[21]

Wolf laid great stress on character-building. To do so, he adopted the excellent custom of having all graduating seniors take the "last lap." Symbolic of the end of their college careers, it was run annually on the final day of practice. Just prior to this event, Wolf briefly talked to the men and explained its significance. It was not a ceremony signifying the color and glamour of football, nor was it for cheers by the crowd. It symbolized the mental and physical discipline which helped each man to know, and to have mastery over, himself. The strain of battle had made them better men. Alluding to some defeats, Wolf said: "The spoils of victory might not be theirs, but from their efforts they have gained something far above material rewards. What they have gained is priceless." Then, while teammates silently watched, the seniors, some in tears, slowly trotted around the track, quietly walked off the field, and went to the dressing room—the last time as members of a Waynesburg College football team.[22]

The "Wolfpack" continued to contend valiantly against tough teams, despite lack of facilities. By 1938 a new field house had been projected but, lamented the editor of *The Yellow Jacket*, "the plan doesn't have the backing it deserves. The need is obvious; dressing rooms for the teams and rest rooms for patrons." A press box, so sorely needed, could be had at low cost. Events soon showed that the editor's appeal was not altogether in vain for, in the spring of 1940, practice was held at Flowers Field in Morrisville, just east of Waynesburg, due to extensive repairs at College Field. The squad was then preparing to face formidable foes in the fall of 1940, including Georgetown, Duquesne, Niagara and Youngstown. This team enjoyed a winning season with four victories, three losses (to Duquesne, Georgetown and Niagara), and one tie (with Youngstown).[23]

Records from 1921 to 1941 show that the "Jackets" could win on the gridiron, even though they were constantly handicapped in one way or another. Their opponents frequently outnumbered and outweighed them. Funds, an adequate field house, and the facilities commonly found on other campuses were lacking. Nevertheless, during these two decades, including the years in which Wolf, Roberts, Patterson, and Easterday coached football, their total accumulative results were 84 wins, 82 losses, and 16 ties. This may well be called the "Wolf Era," for he was coach from 1921 to 1922 and from 1928 to 1941, for a total of sixteen years during which his team won 65, lost 63, and tied 10.[24]

From 1921 to World War II the Yellow Jacket basketball teams were even more consistent winners than those on the gridiron. Wolf had starred in basketball as a student at Penn State, and he knew full well how to coach others in this sport. In seventeen seasons his teams won 208 games and lost 141. In this whole period, including the work of two other coaches, the college won 262 games and lost 178. Interestingly enough, some victories were won against "big time" schools such as Pitt and Penn State. And, in its own class, the college handily defeated teams in the tri-state area and others from farther afield.[25]

In 1928 when Wolf returned, and became Athletic Director, the college started intercollegiate wrestling. Professor James M. Miller of the English Department, in addition to his other duties, became coach of wrestling. Lean, wiry, and of average stature, he knew all the techniques of wrestling; and he was a great coach. If we except the 1932-1933 season, he coached wrestling from 1928 to 1942, during which his teams won 48 matches, lost 41, and tied 6. For the most part, the opponents were tri-state teams, hailing from colleges of Waynesburg's class and large universities. Through the 1930's, the teams of Pitt and West Virginia almost invariably fell before Miller's men by lopsided scores.[26] Pitted against such tough opposition, the Yellow Jackets enjoyed phenomenal success.

Prior to World War II, little emphasis was placed on spring sports. In 1925 Professor Cecil O. Riggs coached a tennis team which engaged in a few intercollegiate contests and played certain independent "clubs" in Greene County. From 1926 through 1929, the college had no varsity tennis teams. From 1930 to 1939, if we except 1936, Professor Leslie V. Brock of the Department of History and Government, served as coach of tennis. Tall, lanky, and amiable, Brock was a capable coach. But the teams in these early years only broke about even in wins and losses. Doubtless there was a lack of numbers of players; and available courts left something to be desired. The only other spring sport was golf which was begun in 1936, largely through the initiative of the students. William ("Bill") Goldberg, an undergraduate, served both as player and coach. During the seasons of 1936 and 1937 the golf team won ten and lost six games in varsity competition.[27]

The athletes led a Spartan-like way of life during the depression. Through most of those difficult years, Wolf, his assistant, Michael K. Talpas, and the athletes were "crammed" in Varsity Hall, a frame structure purchased by Stewart in 1931. Located on the present site of the Buhl Humanities Building, it was used as a dormitory and mess hall. The athletes each paid $3.25 weekly for food which was plenteous every fall, but they ate beans by graduation time. In order to assure them some kind of fruit, Stewart brought apples from his farm, placed them in the Hall for sale at 25 cents per bushel for picked apples, 10 cents per bushel for those gathered off the ground, and, generously enough, his sign added: "If you don't have the money, take the apples anyway."[28]

The Pearl Harbor attack, 7 December 1941, terminated intercollegiate athletics for the duration of World War II. Games that had been scheduled in all major sports were canceled. Efforts made as late as October 1943 to maintain basketball and wrestling on limited scales seem to have been fruitless. In May 1944, Stewart advised Wolf that his services were no longer needed. At Wolf's request, the trustees granted him an indefinite leave of absence. Such a grant also was made to Mark ("Mike") Booth, who had assisted Wolf.[29]

As the college looked ahead to post-war athletics, two developments are notable. First, in December 1945 Stewart announced that "no scholarships are to be given for athletes, as such. However, if a man is a good student and eligible for a scholarship as such, the fact that he is an athlete will be no bar."[30] Second, the Purman Run field was a boost to the athletic program. Near the campus, it was convenient to college personnel. The local high school and the college continued to use this field for practice sessions so College Field would be in good condition for games played by both institutions.[31]

In November 1945 John R. Conklin, Chairman of the Athletic Committee of the trustees, reported that during 1946 the college would have all sports—football, basketball, wrestling, and so on. At that time, the local high school desired to use College Field for football, but lights and dressing rooms were lacking. The lights were essential to night games, and the trustees planned to provide them at a cost of $4,500 as soon as possible. By July 1946, however, the lights had not been installed. Arrangements were then made for the college to play for a small rental fee three night games, scheduled for the 1946 season, at Carmichaels High School.[32]

Meanwhile, the college employed Ray Welsh, an alumnus of the college, as Athletic Director and basketball coach. He had been a successful coach at Bridgeton High School in New Jersey. And Asa ("Ace") Wiley, also an alumnus of the college and then Athletic Director at Greensburg High School, was elected coach of football and wrestling. Other sports such as track, baseball, and boxing were to be worked out between the two men. Stewart said "the appointments of these men would take the place of Frank Wolf and Mark Booth respectively, then on indefinite leave." The football season of 1946 was disastrous with no wins, seven losses, and one tie. Wiley had to start from scratch, and his men lacked experience. Furthermore, there was a misunderstanding which apparently stemmed from the college's practice of unwritten contracts between it and its employees. When Wiley was employed in January 1946, he assumed he would receive a long term contract immediately and in writing. By late July 1946, however, he had no such contract. He then tendered his resignation to Stewart. Evidently this problem was soon solved, for Wiley coached football in the fall of 1946—and he left shortly thereafter.[33]

After Wiley's departure, on 12 August 1947 the trustees recalled Wolf from his leave of absence to resume duties as football coach and as Head of the Department of Education. A week later, however, they employed James Stanton ("Stan") Keck, as football coach and Athletic Director. Reasons for this sudden change are not clear. Wolf was to be again on active duty, with his services limited to those of Instructor in Education. He was in failing health, and coaching doubtless would have been too strenuous for him. Unfortunately he died of a cerebral hemorrhage on 3 April 1949 at his home in Mt. Lebanon, just as he was preparing to remove to Waynesburg. His premature death at age fifty-two was mourned by all who knew him. Shortly his former students and players established the Frank N. Wolf Memorial Scholarship Foundation. This fund in the amount of nearly $22,000 has remained on interest which, through the years, has been used to aid worthy students at the college.[34]

With Keck as coach, and Benjamin F. Paul, erstwhile player for the Yellow Jackets, as assistant coach, the football team fared well during the seasons from 1947 through 1950. A Princeton All American and one of Walter Camp's All Time All Americans, Keck was known for his great physical size and even greater heart. He inspired not only the students in college, but also the young townspeople. He extended the use of facilities at College Field and in the gymnasium to all in the neighborhood. During his four seasons as football coach, the team won seventeen games, lost fifteen, and tied three. Three of the losses were to the highly rated "Mountaineers" of West Virginia. By 1950 Keck was suffering from acute high blood pressure, doubtless induced partly by the stress of coaching. Unfortunately he died on 20 January 1951 of a cerebral hemorrhage, at age fifty-three.[35] His passing from the scene, with the same illness that took Wolf, was also premature—and a loss to the college and to football.

After Keck's death the trustees sought new personnel to head the athletic program. By November 1951 they employed James R. Haddick as Athletic Director, Head of the Physical Education Department, coach of basketball and baseball, and assistant football coach. An alumnus of Waynesburg College, Haddick had successfully coached at Plum Township High School and at Wyoming Seminary at Kingston,

Pennsylvania. Two years later he was replaced as Athletic Director by Ray E. Williams, who built up a strong intramural program over the next six years. The new football coach, employed in 1951, was John F. ("Jack") Wiley, also an alumnus of the college, who began a brilliant football career at Richhill Township High School, at Wind Ridge (Jacktown). After entering the college, he became an all-time great tackle under Frank Wolf. Subsequently he entered the armed forces, served with Company K of the 28th Division, and became a commissioned officer. He later joined the Pittsburgh Steelers, and won recognition from the late "Jock" Sutherland under whom he played for two years; he played three more years for the Steelers under coach John Michaelosen. Known as a single wing man, he thoroughly understood all the techniques of football. He was likable in disposition, and sincerely devoted to Waynesburg College. In all respects he was most highly qualified to coach the Yellow Jackets. In four seasons from 1951 to 1954 his team enjoyed a remarkable record of twenty-two wins, nine losses, and one tie. It held the "Mountaineers" of West Virginia to relatively modest scores. And, after the 1954 season, Waynesburg was rated ninth among small colleges in the East. In a super schedule, including three big schools that year, the season result was five wins, two losses, and one tie. This team upset Bowling Green 12 to 7, held Virginia Polytechnic Institute to a 20 to 6 win, lost to Kent State by 26 to 0, and defeated W. & J. by 40 to 12 for the first time in the history of the two schools.[36]

By March 1955 Jack Wiley was beckoned by the Pittsburgh Steelers. In what must have been an attractive offer, he then resigned his position as head coach of the Yellow Jackets and joined the Steelers as line coach. The editor of *The Yellow Jacket* pointed out Wiley's excellent qualities as a coach and as a man: "Waynesburg College owes a lot to Jack for he has done so much to spread the name of Waynesburg over the nation."[37]

When Jack left, he was replaced by John Popovich, who hailed from Monessen, where he had starred in high school. He played college football at St. Vincent from 1939 through 1941, prior to entering the armed forces. After his discharge from military service he played two years for the Steelers, and two for a professional team in Akron, Ohio. In 1952 he enrolled as a student at Waynesburg College, and helped Jack Wiley before becoming head coach. As head football mentor, Popovich continued Wiley's techniques of coaching. In four seasons from 1955 through 1958 his teams won twelve games, lost sixteen, and tied four. The Jackets suffered losing seasons in 1956 and again in 1958. Popovich did not return in 1959.[38]

By September 1959 the trustees had employed Peter Mazzaferro to replace Ray E. Williams as Athletic Director. He was also to coach football, basketball, and track. An alumnus of Centre College, in Kentucky, and holder of a master's degree from Springfield College, in Massachusetts, he had coached football at Ockawamick High School, in New York; and, for two summers, he coached at Camp All America under Clair F. Bee. Mazzaferro worked hard to rebuild football. He was assisted by Charles N. Williams, a graduate of Waynesburg College in 1956, who had played on the football teams coached by Jack Wiley and John Popovich. The first two seasons, 1959 and 1960, were disastrous. But Mazzaferro and his teams enjoyed success in two winning seasons in a row in 1961 and 1962. In April 1963 he resigned, giving as his reason the multifarious duties assigned to him. He said that "in most colleges a man can coach either football or basketball. He cannot do justice to both."[39]

As World War II ended, the college aimed to rebuild basketball. As early as April 1945, Roy E. Furman, loyal alumnus and trustee, reported to the trustees "that in his opinion it would be wise to make plans to have basketball next year. There is quite a lot of interest among other schools of this region and Waynesburg College now has the best facilities of any school in this district." "Such facilities," said Furman, "would help to interest young men who otherwise will go to other schools." Accordingly the trustees voted to resume basketball in 1946, and called on their Athletic Committee to reorganize and administer this sport. By June 1946 Captain Anthony Petri, who returned from military duty to the campus, helped Welsh to lay the foundations for a new athletic program. Still an undergraduate, Petri did much to train a varsity basketball team while at the same time making the honor roll in scholastics.[40]

Although Welsh's basketball team won fourteen games and lost only eight in the 1946-1947 season, he left at the end of one year. The trustees then employed Frank Gustine who had been playing professional baseball for twelve years—nine with the Pittsburgh Pirates—as the new basketball coach. In addition to being skillful both in baseball and basketball, Gustine was a personable man; all Waynesburg College students liked him. His assistant coach was Roger Jorgensen, who received much praise from Gustine: "'Rodge' did an excellent job coaching the Freshmen and in helping with the varsity too." Such teamwork brought good results for, from 1947 to 1950, Gustine's teams won forty-five games and lost twenty-two. Unfortunately for the year 1950-1951, it became necessary to reduce the coaching staff—and Gustine was no longer employed. But Jorgenson carried on the good work for that year and his team won fifteen games and lost only seven. He left, however, at the end of one season. Thenceforth from 1951 to 1963 the college's basketball fortunes remained in a continuous depression; on an average, annual losses more than doubled wins; and the nadir was reached between 1959 and 1963 with only fourteen wins and sixty-six losses.[41] In these later years, the coaches were crowded with so many different duties that it was impossible to do justice to them all.

If the men's basketball team suffered setbacks, the girls' team brought, at least, partial compensation. Called the "Honey Bees" and co-captained by "Cookie" Messick and Elaine Hinkle, in the 1956-1957 season, this team defeated several high school teams in the area, including Waynesburg and Donora. They lost, however, to Geneva College and to the formidable Allis Chalmers team which won the season championship. The Honey Bees carried on vigorously in 1957-1958. They defeated Donora High School, 33 to 19. In what must have been a highly humorous event, they played the male varsity early in March 1958. The boys were at a great disadvantage, however, for they wore boxing gloves. In all the excitement of the game, one boy put the ball in the wrong basket—and the Honey Bees won by 39 to 37. Mary Munnell Rinehart, a member of the college's Modern Language Department, who, we shall recall, played basketball during her student days at the college, was keenly interested in the Honey Bees. The girls began an intramural program with six basketball teams in competition. The trustees commended Lorraine Cassidy for her work in initiating a sports program for girls.[42]

While the male basketball teams lost most of their games from 1951 to 1963, the wrestling teams enjoyed phenomenal success. The Pearl Harbor attack ended wrestling at the college until it was revived by "Ace" Wiley in 1946. That team was highly successful with eight wins, two losses, and one tie. After "Ace" left, the trustees, in October 1947, employed Raymond ("Bucky") Murdock as coach of wrestling. An alumnus of the college, Murdock had wrestled on teams coached by James M. Miller. Murdock completely mastered the science of wrestling; and he was highly proficient in training others in this sport. Fortunately, at the outset Murdock had John R. Conklin, also a master in this sport, as advisory coach. From 1947 to 1963 the Yellow Jacket wrestlers rolled up an incredible record of 122 wins, 21 losses, and 2 ties. Murdock was the coach in this period with the exception of the 1950-1951 and 1951-1952 seasons when he was on military duty, and Conklin carried on most admirably with seventeen victories and no defeats. These were the most successful years in wrestling in the college's history. And, as Stewart said: Conklin did "*all this without money and without price* (Stewart's italics)." In addition to their victories over colleges in their own class, the Yellow Jackets consistently defeated such big time powers as Ohio State, Pitt, Purdue, and West Virginia. They reached the zenith in 1948 when they were co-champions with Michigan State in the Interstate Wrestling Tourney, although Waynesburg College was one of the smallest institutions in the Tourney. Additional honors came a week later when George Lewis, a freshman, won the national intercollegiate championship in the 125 pound class. He was the first athlete at the college to win such honor and distinction. Another Yellow Jacket wrestler to win a national title was "Tony" Gizoni, called "Outstanding Wrestler" by the NCAA in 1951. For three straight seasons the "Jackets" captured the Allegheny Mountain Association Junior Wrestling Tourney in the Downtown Y. M. C. A. in Pittsburgh. Murdock's overall record, amounting to an 84.8 percentage of victories, was so high that he was accepted into the Helms Foundation Hall of Fame.[43]

Despite one of the best records in the history of wrestling, Murdock resigned as wrestling coach in December 1962, effective at the end of the 1962-1963 season. Reasons for his move are not clear. The editor of *The Yellow Jacket* said: "He feels he does not fit into the picture at the college, and felt it better to resign." Immediately Paul F. Bauer, Vice President for Student Personnel Services, told Murdock: "I would like to say again how much the College and the young men who have been wrestlers have benefited from your fine coaching."[44]

In 1947 most spring sports were revived at the varsity level, but they were not strongly emphasized. From then until the end of Stewart's administration, the baseball team broke about even in wins and losses against colleges in the tri-state area. Some baseball players were outstanding. Noteworthy was Joseph J. ("Joe") Zychowski, a pitcher dubbed "WC's Iron Man" from 1952 to his graduation in 1956. In the 1955 season, for example, he struck out 49 batters and walked only 15. Another star, called "baseball's most valuable player" in 1955 was Dominick Christy, Jr., a top first baseman and a skillful batter; in 1955 his batting average was .490. If we except the seasons of 1950, 1951, and 1954 through 1957, varsity golf was played, but the records were not impressive. From 1947 to 1949 the varsity tennis team, coached by Edward J. ("Joaquin") Patterson, then a student, enjoyed two winning seasons. From 1950 through 1957, varsity tennis was abandoned. From 1958 through 1963 Professor Robert J. Bowden served as tennis coach in addition to his other duties. Lack of adequate courts hurt tennis; a macadam-top court was not constructed until 1956. Stewart had hoped for such a court for thirty years, and, at last, it became a reality. Shortly, additional courts were hard-surfaced. Cross country races were not introduced until 1958, and this sport was not strong until after 1963.[45]

Track was not stressed in the postwar years. In the spring of 1949 some students became interested in it, and a track meet took place on 4 May 1949 at West Virginia University with the "Mountaineers," the Yellow Jackets, and a team from Bethany College as participants. It appears that track was neglected from then until the spring of 1955, when "several boys were working hard to revive varsity track" at the college.[46] But it was not established on a lasting basis.

In accord with the old maxim "a sound mind in a strong body," an intramural program was maintained for all students. It afforded those who did not participate in varsity athletics the means by which they could keep in shape. By 1950 this program included badminton, table tennis, volleyball, tumbling, and bowling. Female students also engaged in these sports. In Physical Education classes they also stressed softball and basketball. By 1958 horseshoe-pitching courts were provided. Touch football was then popular, chiefly among male students.[47]

The athletic program in the postwar years was benefited by the interest and support of the faculty. In December 1953 the faculty chose from its own body a Committee on Athletics. It consisted of four faculty members, the Dean of Men, and the Director of Athletics. As a standing committee, its functions were: (1) to cooperate with the Athletic Department in the promotion of intercollegiate and intramural athletic programs; (2) to supervise the enforcement of the eligibility code adopted by the faculty as of 1 May 1952 "and any further rulings on eligibility which the faculty may . . . see fit to adopt . . . "; (3) to supervise the scheduling of athletic events; and (4) to assume responsibility for disciplinary action which may be necessary, and "which does not otherwise fall within the authority of other administrative officers." This committee, in cooperation with the Athletic Department, did much to maintain a good athletic program. It ascertained that the college was complying with rules laid down by the NCAA and NAIA.[48]

In the late 1950's certain steps were taken to strengthen varsity athletics. For many years eighteen scholarships "had been permitted to boys who were playing football." But, on 10 October 1959, the trustees increased this number to twenty-two, or two full teams. Likewise scholarships were provided for ten basketball players, or two full teams. At that time only eight scholarships, enough for one team, were permitted for wrestling. On 20 January 1960, however, the trustees increased the number of wrestling scholarships from eight to twelve. Another move aimed "to promote a rational athletic program in western Pennsylvania" was the establishment, by 1958, of the Western Pennsylvania Intercollegiate Athletic Conference. Paul Sullivan of the Pittsburgh *Sun-Telegraph* proposed such a conference in October 1957, when a constitution was drafted and approved by presidents and athletic directors of the following institutions: Carnegie Institute of Technology, Duquesne, Geneva, Grove City, St. Francis, St. Vincent, Waynesburg and Westminster. Sports included in the competition were football, basketball, baseball, tennis, golf, swimming, track, cross country, and rifle. The Conference met annually, and each year a president of one of the member institutions was elected as its president. In May 1962 Stewart was so elected and, on 14 November 1962, the Conference met at Waynesburg. At such meetings a main item on the agenda was aid to student athletes; efforts were made to maintain equity in this respect so that no one institution would take unfair advantage of the others.[49]

A survey made early in 1958 threw much light on the college's athletic program. It revealed that scholasticism was valued more highly than athletic skill; athletes were held to the same academic standards as other students; and research showed that their range of IQ's was somewhat higher than for nonathletes. Efforts were made to recruit good athletes, but the coaches regularly issued a general call to the student body, urging them to come out for the teams; the door was always kept open for competition in the hope of finding the best material possible. Athletes were aided financially on the basis of their ability as athletes, but only 5 percent of the total college budget was used for athletics—in line with financial policies at similar institutions. While victories were highly desirable, no coach was dependent for his position on producing a winning team. In general there was every evidence of good sportsmanship on the part of coaches, athletes, and members of the student body.[50]

In sum, the name of Wolf dominates the football and basketball pictures from 1921 to World War II. Bright highlights can clearly be seen in the postwar period, particularly in football with Jack Wiley as coach, and, in wrestling, with Bucky Murdock as mentor. In all major sports the Yellow Jackets performed valiantly. Setbacks were suffered, chiefly in minor sports, which were not stressed. When we consider the depression of the 1930's, the lack of a gymnasium, the few facilities, and the inadequate athletic field, the overall results were remarkable. Much credit is due Stewart, certain trustees like John R. Conklin, and the outstanding coaches; the entire college family and the townspeople deserve praise for their support. And we must not forget Waynesburg College men who entered the coaching profession, for many of them guided other athletes to Waynesburg. For instance, in September 1953, Stewart spoke of Waynesburg men who were coaching in Fayette County: "Waynesburg College has ten alumni coaching high school teams in that county," which was more than those coming from Pitt, W. & J., Penn State, and Slippery Rock combined.[51]

XIX
END OF AN ERA

THIS CHAPTER DEALS WITH DEVELOPMENTS DURING THE LAST THIRTEEN years of Stewart's administration, ending on 1 July 1963. Rapid strides were made in the building program and in the acquisition of land and other property. Likewise, fund-raising moved ahead at a steady pace. Faculty members enjoyed gradual raises in salaries; and certain fringe benefits were adopted, which made their lot happier than ever before. In line with a nationwide trend, students were showing signs of discontent with traditional rules relative to their conduct, but they were not yet ready for revolts which were to plague many other campuses. In many ways the college was making progress. The main drawback, however, was deterioration in the academic program. Waynesburg College, as we know, was accredited in 1950. Had all gone well in accord with the established practice of re-evaluations every decade, her accreditation would have been reaffirmed in 1960. But that year—and five more—passed before the desired goal was reached. The college went through a serious crisis in which its very life was in jeopardy. Through 1960 little was done to come to grips with the realities of the situation. And from 1961 to 1963 dissensions and personality clashes among faculty members and administrators precluded the possibility of full cooperation in finding solutions, particularly to academic problems.

Let us turn first to affairs of student life. By 1950 student government, vested in the Student Council, had little power. That body was interested chiefly in such things as May Day, and the selection of the May Queen and the Homecoming Queen. To some extent it cooperated with the faculty in the control of student conduct, such as checking attendance at chapel. But by 1963 the members of Student Council had become reluctant to record chapel attendance lest they be "in danger of losing a friend."[1]

Stewart often expressed his happiness that student conduct in general was much better in the 1950's than it was in his student days when

> there was no student government, and the student mind was constantly concocting methods of self assertion. The president gazes upon his Board of Trustees and sees among them schoolmates and students of his early instructional years. They know full well . . . how often chairs hung like festoons from telephone wires; how old Davy, the skeleton, appeared in Lake Winetta, in the president's chair in chapel, and in many other untoward places. There is still a place in Hanna Hall where the old cow chewed the window sill. [But now] the safety valves of student government, intramural athletics, varsity athletics, student participation in chapel, miscellaneous student organizations, and even fraternity and sorority initiations, have made the college pranks which we knew in our day practically a thing of the past.[2]

The college catalogue apprised all students that "conduct befitting a lady or a gentleman is expected at all times of Waynesburg College students." Despite this warning, the behavior of some students left much to be desired. The editor of *The Yellow Jacket* tried to shame such offenders:

> Students talk during lectures in class. Dorm radios blare, doors bang, and merry voices sing at 7:00 A.M., or earlier. . . . Garbage and trash are dumped out windows and strewn everywhere—despite the presence of trash cans. Telephones are tampered with until the company threatens to remove them all. School furniture and property are defaced with such love notes as "John Loves Mary." In cafeteria line . . . rude boys rush in, go to the head of the line and push everyone back—like hogs going for a trough.[3]

Student opposition to compulsory chapel continued. In 1955 the editor of *The Yellow Jacket* held that "you don't show a man how to worship God by twisting his arm. . . . A man learns to worship only when the atmosphere around him is conducive to meditation with his God." Students showed passive resistance in chapel by inattention and by refusing to join in singing. Confronted with such opposition, various expedients were adopted in the hope of improving the situation. By 1962 a student could meet chapel requirements, at least in part, by attending a variety of cultural activities such as the Artist Series and the Faculty Lecture Series. A year later a system of chapel points was established as part of the requirement for graduation. A student received one point each time he attended chapel or a convocation; eighty points were required for graduation. Failure to maintain these requirements subjected the offender to the same penalties as academic probation. Despite all efforts to induce students to attend chapel, their opposition kept mounting.[4]

Attendance at classes was a constant problem. A few teachers did not take absences seriously. The government required an attendance record on all veterans; and it was necessary to keep track of dropouts. The dean exhorted faculty members to be diligent in the recording of absentees each day. Beginning in 1958, any student who was absent from class for the equivalent of four weeks received an automatic failing grade in the course. On days before, and right after, vacations such as Christmas and Easter, each absence meant a double cut.[5] But all such measures were of little avail.

Older students (over twenty-one) and veterans could discipline themselves, while most freshmen could not. Consequently, beginning in 1959, these more mature male students were not required to reside in dormitories. By 1958 revised student handbooks were available for both male and female students. These publications contained the latest regulations and gave students valuable counsel concerning life on the campus.[6]

In the interests of sound scholasticism, students were not allowed to participate in extracurricular activities if their academic records were low. In his first semester of attendance, a freshman was eligible for such if he ranked in the upper three-fifths of his high school graduating class. Upperclassmen on academic probation were not permitted to hold offices in fraternities, sororities, and other organizations, or to participate in intercollegiate athletics. The Parish Project came to be considered the largest single factor in the financial and spiritual development of the college. Because of its success, it became the model for similar organizations elsewhere in the nation.[7]

Other student groups engaged in activities aimed at campus and community betterment. The Y. W. C. A. in collaboration with other student organizations, provided religious instruction and worship services at the nearby Youth Development Center—an institution for young women who needed help. The Theta Chi Fraternity and the Beta Sigma Omicron Sorority aided the Waynesburg Committee in behalf of Muscular Dystrophy. Students and faculty members regularly gave blood when the Red Cross Bloodmobile visited the campus. By 1954 interested students established the college's first short-wave radio station (W3YGE), which gave amateurs a chance to gain experience and served as a link in the Pennsylvania Civil Defense communication system. The Kiltie Band performed admirably and colorfully at football games and other college events. The Lamplighters, the college chorus under the direction of the capable James D. Randolph presented renditions of the highest type at such affairs as commencement, and they annually traveled and presented concerts at colleges, universities, and churches chiefly in the northeastern part of the nation. Likewise the debating team went on tours mainly in the Middle West and South and debated questions of current interest.[8]

Certain changes took place among social fraternities and sororities in the 1950's. In May 1951, the Delta Sigma Phi Fraternity moved from its house on East Franklin Street to its more spacious home on West Wayne Street. The Phi Sigma Fraternity, a "local," became affiliated with Phi Sigma Kappa, a national group. Kappa Phi Nu, another "local," joined with the Theta Chi national fraternity. And in 1958 a chapter of Tau Kappa Epsilon Fraternity was organized on the campus. Certain changes also took place among sororities: Alpha Gamma Theta, "a local," changed to Pi Kappa Psi, a national organization; and Theta Pi Sigma, another "local," joined Alpha Delta Pi, a national sorority. In 1960 a chapter of Beta Sigma Omicron Sorority was installed on the campus. By that time an Interfraternity Council had been organized at the college. Having jurisdiction over member fraternities, it aimed to cause closer friendship and coordination among them. But rules relative to fraternities and sororities were hard to enforce.[9]

One of the main drawbacks to morale among students was the lack of an adequate student union. Fortunately, by 1956 the south room in the basement of the new Library was set aside for this purpose. Here students could relax, play games, listen to records, and obtain candy and soft drinks. The room was nearly soundproof and students studying in the library above were not disturbed by any noise from the recreation room. While this student union was inadequate, it helped to boost student morale until a much more spacious place was later provided in the basement of Benedum Hall.[10]

If student life was carefully regulated, so were affairs of the faculty. The first faculty constitution was promulgated in 1951. From 1925 until that year the faculty had from time to time adopted bylaws to guide and govern them. The new constitution contained the essence of these bylaws, plus other regulations. In September

1953 the constitution and other basic documents were published in a pamphlet entitled *Documents Pertaining to the Government of the College*. The first constitution was rather confusing, because it contained overlapping materials relating to the faculty and the trustees. A revision, made in 1960, did not fully clarify the document. It was not until 1965, in another revision, that the powers and duties of the faculty and the trustees were clearly defined. The faculty constitution originally provided that all full-time members of the faculty had the right of suffrage after one year of service.[11]

The faculty constitution called for a three-dean system. Accordingly, in January 1952, Lester T. Moston was chosen Dean of the Faculty; Charles L. Bryner became Dean of Men; and Mary D. Inghram became Dean of Women. In addition to their new administrative duties, all three continued to teach.[12]

Although the constitution and bylaws defined the rights, duties, and responsibilities of the faculty, administrators, and trustees, Stewart continued firmly to control the faculty. But he regularly came forth with slogans which gave the faculty new aspirations and higher goals. Examples are "Vitalized Teaching Year," "Library Year," "Mark Hopkins Year," and "The Year of New Horizons." He urged faculty members to follow the example set by "The Great Teacher by Galilee or on the Mount. . . . " For He was the epitome of "love, sacrifice, and devotion to those taught. . . . " Stewart frequently praised and encouraged all who labored assiduously and unselfishly for the college.[13]

It appears that, until the late 1950's, the faculty was not organized on a departmental basis. As we have seen, a divisional system was earlier instituted. But in January 1954 Dean Moston called attention to "considerable confusion concerning departmental jurisdiction and some misunderstanding as to the identity of the Heads of Departments." He held that action should be taken to set up an orderly basis of authority within the departments and to reduce the amount of independent administrative action taken by various subordinate members of the faculty. In March 1955 the faculty was still hazy on such questions as: "What is a department and who are our department heads? . . . " By September 1958, as an outgrowth of the self-evaluation, the faculty was organized into eight departments, and heads had been chosen for six, as follows: Business Administration and Secretarial, Professor James P. Rice; English and Fine Arts, Professor Robert J. Bowden; History and Social Studies, Professor Arthur M. Mintier; Mathematics, Professor Lester T. Moston;

Science, Professor Charles L. Bryner; Religion and Philosophy, Professor Harry E. Gardner; Psychology and Education; and Language. For the last two departments, heads had not yet been appointed, but Professor Gardner was to oversee their organization. In November 1958 Gardner reported "we are getting the department system organized so it could operate."[14]

The faculty was also organized into committees. In December 1950 the Faculty Conference Committee was formed chiefly to hear complaints by faculty members and to provide a direct channel by which they could bring their ideas before the trustees. In April 1953 a Student-Faculty Committee was created to serve as a liaison between the student body and the faculty and administration. Other faculty committees included the Committee on Committees which annually would recommend to the President members of all standing committees; the Committee on Financial Aid to Students; the Library Committee; the Curriculum Development Committee; and the Committee on Registration and Scholarship.[15]

From the mid-1950's on there was a tendency to employ too many teachers with only the bachelor's degree. As of September 1960, there were eight with earned doctorates, forty-nine with the master's degree, nineteen with the bachelor's degree, and two with no degree. Teaching schedules were heavy, running generally from fifteen to eighteen hours per week. In general, classes were large, and the student-teacher ratio was dangerously high. There was a relatively rapid turnover of teachers from year to year. The low salary scale, plus the fact that topflight faculty members were in short supply, were the main difficulties in maintaining a strong faculty.[16]

Increases in faculty salaries came slowly. Prior to accreditation, salaries had been raised, but as of June 1955 the scale for nine months' work ranged from $1,800 to $5,500. Gardner pointed out that, in filling faculty vacancies, it was necessary in some cases to offer salaries that were higher than the scale set for professors already employed. He asked for salary increases in order to prevent inequalities that might make for bad morale in the faculty. Hence, by October 1956 the minimum salary scale ranged from $3,000 for one with the bachelor's degree to $5,000 for one with an earned doctorate. In June 1957 Stewart reported: "Forced to pay increasingly higher salaries, we have increased tuition." Another raise by June 1960 set the salary scale at a "low" of $3,800 for an instructor to a "high" of $8,200 for a professor, and a further increase was planned. In June 1961, Charles B. Stoy, Jr., Vice President for

Business and Finance, reported that salaries then compared favorably with those of other similar colleges. In administrative costs, Waynesburg ranked among the lowest in the Presbyterian group.[17]

Likewise certain new fringe benefits added to the security of faculty members. In 1960 they came under the College Retirement Equities Fund (CREF) which, in addition to TIAA income, provided an income upon retirement which "floated" with the current value of the dollar as determined by the stock market. By 1963 a plan of major medical insurance was adopted to cover the high costs of prolonged hospitalization.[18]

The financial campaign forged ahead from 1950 to 1963. The main sources of income merit our attention. First, tuition and fees for room and board were gradually raised. In 1951 tuition was $160 per semester, and the room and board rate was $216 per semester. In 1963 tuition per semester was $350, and board and room totaled $366. These costs were low in comparison with those of other institutions—in keeping with tradition. The departure of male students for service in the Korean War in 1951 and 1952 caused a sharp drop in enrollment. The resulting decrease in tuition caused temporary hardship in balancing the current budget. In April 1954 Stewart askcd the trustees to help battle for student enrollment for the next two or three years. After that a sharp increase in enrollment was anticipated. By October 1956 the following groups were given a special tuition rate of $50 per semester less than the regular rate: ministers in service, children of ministers, children of faculty members, and preministerial students.[19]

The second main source of income was from gifts and bequests from foundations, friends of the college, and alumni. The most consistent donor was Mary Denny Weaver who stood ready constantly to help the college when funds were low. In addition to her gifts for the Kiltie Band and other musical activities of the college, she purchased a new car for Stewart, paid his fee for membership in the Duquesne Club in Pittsburgh, and headed a drive for funds for a science hall to be named in his honor. Another donor was Michael L. Benedum, dubbed the "Great Wildcatter" for his interest in oil production, who partially endowed a chair in geology and gave funds to help pay for the dining hall named in his honor. Noteworthy were annual gifts from Vira I. Heinz to be used to send every summer some meritorious student on a study tour of Europe. Notable also was a $100,000 gift from the Richard K. Mellon Foundation for the dormitory campaign. Among several bequests was one from Thomas D. Whittles, first football coach at the college and later a renowned Presbyterian minister; the income from it was to go annually to a deserving ministerial student. By 1960 the college was receiving gifts from seven foundations, including the Ford Foundation which gave $67,000 in December 1955. Meanwhile the alumni were giving regularly to the college. By 1958 they were organized on a nationwide basis with John W. Knox '30 as chairman. The nation was subdivided into regions where alumni were relatively concentrated such as Waynesburg—Greene County, Uniontown—Fayette County, the Pittsburgh area, the Seaboard area, the Cleveland area, the Pacific Coast area, and so on.[20]

The third source of funds was the United Presbyterian Church in the U.S.A. Its Board of Christian Education, by 1954, was giving the college an annual appropriation of $5,250; in that year an additional $2,139.75 was given "realizing that post-veteran years are difficult ones." Support also was received from this denomination's Synod of Pennsylvania, beginning in 1961; this added income boosted the total amount from the church for the year 1960-1961 to $26,731.23.[21]

The fourth source was from the federal government. A law of 1951 entitled "Housing for Educational Institutions" provided that any institution of higher learning could obtain federal loans to build dormitories, to be repaid over a period of forty years at 2 3/4 percent interest. In 1957 the college negotiated such a loan to build a men's dormitory, and by June 1960 a similar loan was approved for a girl's dormitory.[22]

In February 1952 Stewart began a campaign to increase the endowment fund from $415,000 to $1,000,000. The campaign slogan was: "A million-dollar-endowed and debtless Waynesburg College by 1959." Stewart held that, although endowment had increased in the last ten years, it was still not enough for the perpetuation of a college such as Waynesburg. The movement gained momentum in 1954 when Michael L. Benedum became its leader. Shortly Cy Hungerford, the highly respected cartoonist for the *Pittsburgh Post-Gazette*, lent a helping hand by drawing an appropriate cartoon which appeared in the campaign bulletin and in the local newspapers. With the concerted effort of Stewart, the trustees, faculty, students, alumni, and friends, the amount collected rose steadily. It was $867,000 by March 1958, at which time the original goal was raised to $1,200,000. Subsequently this figure was reached, and the sights were again set much higher. In February 1960 Joseph W. Ray, Jr., President of the Board of Trustees, said: "We should soon begin to announce a goal of $4 million in endowment." Stewart said he would not object to a goal of $10 million dollars by 1975.[23]

It is abundantly clear that the Uniontown Center made money for Waynesburg College. The Korean War caused a temporary drop in enrollment and income. But before and after that conflict, the Center was a profitable operation. In April 1957, a financial report for the preceding ten years showed a profit of $115,546.25 at the Center. A year later the college's current budget at the campus showed a deficit of $20,000, but the net gain from the Center largely offset it. It appears that until 1960 there were two separate and distinct budgets—one for the campus and one for the Center. In April of that year, however, the trustees merged these funds in one common account which was to be used either at the campus or the Center.[24]

The Center was considered such an important part of the overall institution that in October 1962 a campaign was begun to raise $300,000 to construct a building in Uniontown, which would be adequate for the educational needs of college-bound young folks in that area. By February 1963 some $200,000 in gifts and pledges had been raised, and it was confidently expected that the goal of $300,000 could be reached.[25] Subsequently, however, this plan was abandoned, and the Center was turned over to the Pennsylvania State University.

By 1959 plans were under way for a new science hall, and money had to be found for this purpose. Mary Denny Weaver lent the college $50,000 at four percent interest per annum in order to purchase certain properties adjacent to the "Old Mill" as the site of the science building. She also became National Chairman of the Science Hall Campaign. Shortly students, trustees, faculty, alumni, and friends of the college donated to this fund.[26]

There were still times when the college was hard pressed to pay current expenses. Money was borrowed to meet the June payroll and other bills in 1954, probably because of decreased income from tuition as a result of lower enrollment during the Korean War. Borrowing became necessary to meet September payrolls in 1957, 1958, and 1960. Each year the athletic program either broke even financially or operated at a loss. The College Book Store, while run by the college, operated in the red. Beginning in 1958, however, W. Ralph Headlee, an alumnus of the college, took it over under a lease agreement with the trustees. He operated the store efficiently, and the college received regularly a part of the profits therefrom.

Interspersed between critical periods in the current budget, the college operated in the black. At certain times, particularly at registration, large sums then accumulated and were not needed immediately for current operations. At such times, Charles B. Stoy, Jr., the college's business manager, ever conservative and careful about funds, favored the investment of some of this money in short-term United States Government securities. By 1963 it was evident that the lean years in the current budget could be offset by better years when the operation was in the black.[27]

Keeping the budget in balance over the long pull, however, was not an easy task. It required the know-how of men well versed in banking and finance. The college was fortunate to have such a man in Richard L. Baily, a trustee. By June 1951 Baily, as head of the trustees' Special Committee on the Budget, brought the budget into balance. Stewart then rejoiced that "we may be able to proclaim a tiny current surplus." Looking at the budget realistically, Baily later reported that the accounting system and records were not satisfactory. Officials on the church's Board of Christian Education concurred with him. It was imperative to set up a satisfactory accounting system, and to employ a competent accountant. Accordingly, in August 1958 the trustees retained Robert Harper, a Certified Public Accountant from Uniontown, Pennsylvania, who was to study the college's accounting system, to recommend whatever changes were necessary, and to train and supervise the College staff in the new system. In line with Harper's suggestion, the college promptly purchased a Front Office machine by which cash receipts and student accounts could be handled in one operation. Such a machine was a great time-saver; with it, records could more easily be kept current. In October 1959 Joseph W. Ray, Jr., President of the Board of Trustees, commended Harper for doing a "fine job in revising the accounting system of the college. . . . For the first time . . . we feel that we have an accounting system which is in line with approved methods of accounting for colleges and universities." Harper promised to continue to supervise the system, but he felt that in the future the job would be relatively simple.[28]

If the trustees were wise in adopting an approved accounting system, they were equally so in the investment of the endowment fund. This money was consistently invested conservatively in the safest stocks and bonds. The largest investments were in public utilities. As of October 1960 their total market value was $751,760, approximately half of which was put into public utilities; the largest single investment was in American Telephone and Telegraph. The trustees were regularly commended for the high quality predominating throughout these investments.[29]

Expansion of the physical plant kept pace with fund-raising. From 1950 to 1963 the college acquired additional land and other property, chiefly in the environs of the campus. A building program, hitherto without parallel, was under way.[30]

In October 1951 the trustees faced a perplexing problem referred to as the "cemetery matter." The town council was then expecting to rescind an ordinance of 1920 which restricted burials of human bodies in Greene Mount Cemetery beyond a certain established line, and to draw up a new ordinance permitting such burials on a triangular plot at the end of North Washington Street and adjoining college property. Stewart explained that such expansion of the cemetery would have a harmful effect on the recruiting of students. Parents would be reluctant to send their daughters to the college "when they see that the dormitory is so very near a cemetery plot." Property owners on College Heights concurred with Stewart; the proposed expansion of the cemetery would lower the value of their property. The matter was settled in May 1954 when the college and the town council reached a compromise. The trustees then purchased from the Greene Mount Cemetery Company eight lots which were to serve as a buffer zone between the cemetery and land already belonging to the college. Thenceforth graves would not be too near the campus.[31]

In the expansion program the college literally leaped westward to Florissant, Colorado, in the Rocky Mountains—a paradise for geologists. By April 1954 Stewart had made a new friend there in Alexander Comstock Kirk, a rancher and former Ambassador to Russia and Italy. Kirk, with evident interest in geology, offered to sell the college some land on which there was a dwelling house for the nominal price of $1,000. The trustees promptly approved this purchase. Kirk's beneficence made possible the establishment of the Rocky Mountain Geology Station at Florissant. Shortly the college added a geology major to the curriculum; and a geology department became reality. By 1957 advanced courses in geology were being conducted at this station under the direction of Professor James B. Schroyer. In successive summers Stewart went to Florissant, where he and Schroyer taught and inspired geology students, some of whom became outstanding scholars.[32]

The college acquired a number of private homes in Waynesburg, which were used, mostly temporarily, as student dormitories, for classroom purposes, or for faculty offices. Adjacent to the campus the college added Rhodes Hall, Leonard Hall, and the "Khiva." The Mary Sayers House, with its adjoining land, rounded out the front of the campus. By September 1956 three other houses were purchased: the Rinehart House on East Wayne Street became the President's Home; to the rear, two houses facing Franklin Street were to be used as faculty residences; Mary Denny Weaver gave generously toward the purchase of these homes. Located on the east campus overlooking the town was Knox House, acquired and used briefly as a dormitory for upperclass women. A building out of town, located at Crucible, Pennsylvania, was donated by the Crucible Steel Company, and used for activities sponsored by the Parish Project.[33]

In April 1953 the college faced a critical situation in which a state investigator complained about unsanitary conditions at College Field. He apprised Stewart of the rules and regulations laid down by the Pennsylvania Department of Health, and urged that they be complied with as soon as possible. In essence the rules required "that ample, free toilet facilities, for both sexes, be provided where large crowds of persons are assembled for periods of time witnessing such events." Seating capacity at the field was over 2,000 persons; adequate sewage disposal could be provided by the Borough of Waynesburg. Such facilities obviously would be appreciated by the alumni of Waynesburg College and Waynesburg High School, as well as the ardent sports fans of the community. But it appears that adequate facilities were not provided until September 1959, when a field house was constructed. A simple building with two dressing rooms, two rooms for coaches, and a room for officials, it was made of material already at hand, including steel received a number of years earlier from war surplus. The total cost of the building was less than $5,000. The college renewed rental of the field to the local high school for $1,000 per year for a five-year period. The trustees borrowed money to finance the building, and the anticipated income from rent was used as collateral. In October 1960 Stewart told the trustees, "The football field is in better condition than ever. All bleachers have been painted and the field generally made to appear more attractive. . . . Lavatory facilities have been installed."[34]

The new library building, needed for many years, was under construction by February 1952. It was designed in a small way on the plan of the Carnegie Library-Museum at Pittsburgh. It would contain two interesting rooms. One was the Trans-Appalachian Room placed by Thomas H. Hudson, '94, William M. Hudson, '92, and certain heirs of Stephen L. Mestrezat, '69 whose pioneer ancestor in these parts was a personal friend of Albert Gallatin. This room became the repository for the Charles M. Ewing Collection, one of the best in southwestern Pennsylvania, for use by research historians interested in this area. The other was the French Room, made possible by a generous bequest of Bessina Hoge in honor of her daughter Margaret Hoge Reavis. In her will Mrs. Hoge named Mary Denny Weaver as the person to supervise the building and arrangement of the French Room. Mrs. Hoge left the college furniture, rugs, draperies, and other materials reminiscent of the reigns of Louis XIV and Louis XV, plus a fund the interest from which was to be used to maintain the room. A study area in the Library, dedicated in honor of Don C. Longanecker, Jr., a former student of the college who gave his life for his country in France during World War II, was finished and furnished by his parents. Another benefactor of the Library was Charles G. Reigner, poet, publisher, and President of the H. M. Rowe Company, in Baltimore, Maryland, which had long published textbooks. Through his generosity, the Charles G. Reigner Library Collection was established with the intent to donate $500 annually for the purchase of books helpful to students entering the ministry or the teaching profession. The Library building was completed by 23 May 1955 when the students carried all the books from the "old Library" on the second floor of Miller Hall to the "new Library." Under the supervision of May P. Clovis, the Librarian, and her staff, the students performed yeoman service and moved the books in an orderly manner. When the building was completed, the front, with the Ionic style was not then constructed; these columns were added during the summer of 1960.[35]

The need for a new dining hall was critical. Accordingly, in April 1958 ground was broken for it just west of Walton Hall on the site where Leonard Hall, Rhodes Hall, and "the Khiva" were located. This building was so constructed that two dormitory wings could later be added. On 27 May 1958 the cornerstone was laid with appropriate ceremonies. The facility, spacious and modern in all respects, was named Benedum Hall in honor of Michael L. Benedum, who gave funds for it. The downstairs area was set aside as a student union. A snack bar adjoining it was a great improvement over the old college diner of World War II vintage which had long been a hangout for students.[36]

By June 1958 Stewart and the trustees were planning to construct a new science building and a fund-raising campaign for that purpose was under way. The "Old Mill" in which chemistry classes had met was inadequate, but it burned in December 1958. Immediately a chemistry laboratory was set up in temporary quarters in the basement of the gymnasium located just across Washington Street; this would suffice until a new science hall was constructed. A five-story structure, on the site of the "Old Mill" plus the adjacent ground, was planned: the first floor for a geology museum and specimens; the second for geology classes and chemistry laboratories; the third for classrooms; the fourth for physics; and the fifth for biology laboratories and classrooms. A greenhouse was to be located on the roof. Faculty offices would be on each floor. The building would be a lasting monument to Stewart—and it was named the "Paul R. Stewart Science Building." Hopes for federal funds to finance it were dashed in October 1962 when Congress failed to pass a bill providing aid for the construction of academic facilities. But the college's fund-raising campaign was highly successful; by February 1963, some $600,000 had been raised in gifts and reliable pledges, which made possible the start of construction a month later. The base bid for the building was $988,900. The college borrowed funds, on a long term loan, to pay the balance. Fittingly enough, a sculptor created a bust of Stewart which reposes near the main entrance to the building.[37]

By 1960 housing for girls was critically deficient. Accordingly a women's dormitory was constructed, chiefly with federal funds, adjacent to Benedum Hall; the two were connected by a covered passageway. The new structure was named Denny Hall in honor of Mary Denny Weaver and her sisters, Josephine Denny and Helen Denny Howard.[38]

By 1951 housing for men was most inadequate. Some 280 men were living in private homes in Waynesburg, many of them under unhappy conditions. The college had some housing units for veterans on Bonar Avenue, but there was always a waiting list for them. A few married students were living in private homes and paying exorbitant rent. In order to alleviate these conditions, the college obtained federal funds for the construction of a men's dormitory in the area back of the Library. By October 1958 the building was erected. Called "Thayer Hall," it could comfortably house 128 men. But it was still not adequate to meet needs. By February 1963 plans for another men's dormitory were under way. It was patterned on a "new type of construction such as is now in use at the Bethany campus." Named Joseph W. Ray Hall in honor of the President of the Board of Trustees and of his father who also was a trustee and President of the Board, and located on the north side of the campus, it would house 60 students.[39] These halls did much to improve housing on the campus.

While new buildings were being constructed, the old were not neglected. The floors and stairways in Miller and Hanna Halls had deteriorated through the years; splintered wood and weak spots here and there were constant hazards; fire could the more easily engulf a whole building. In February 1952, Stewart called attention to the need to fireproof Miller Hall. At the outset, the plan called for a terrazo covering on the first floor and the replacing of the stairways with steel and concrete. Funds were lacking, but Mary Denny Weaver made loans at a low interest rate so the work could move forward. Gradually, room by room, the building was fireproofed and, by June 1963, this project was nearly complete. Likewise Hanna Hall was fireproofed on the inside; and sandblasted, painted, and waterproofed on the outside. By 1958 a centralized heating system was planned for Hanna Hall, and it was later installed.[40] These were sacred buildings, and it was imperative that they be preserved.

Improvements in Miller and Hanna Halls made classrooms more attractive—and safe from fire. But more classroom space was sorely needed. Classes were being conducted wherever space could be found—in paneled rooms in the dungeon-like basement of Miller Hall, in the Library, and so on. Moreover, the infirmary was most inadequate. It was much too small and badly in need of paint, repairs, and modern furniture.[41]

As the financial structure was strengthened and the physical plant was improved, attention was given to the curriculum. Through the 1950's the Curriculum Development Committee initiated all changes in the curriculum. By 1960 this committee was abolished by vote of the faculty and the duties were assigned to the heads of departments. In 1952 the trustees passed a resolution that provided for the granting of degrees to law school graduates who took their pre-legal training at Waynesburg, but did not complete residence requirements for a degree. By 1960 the Fine Arts offerings had been improved; they included courses in art, music, and drama. Noteworthy was Drama 305, entitled Radio and Television Technique, in which the college cooperated with Educational Television Station WQED in Pittsburgh.[42]

While rapid strides forward had been made in fund-raising, in the acquisition of land and other property, and in the building program, the college was deteriorating in its academic standing. In September 1953 Stewart spoke to the faculty about the "Cycle of Empire." He warned that:

> Nations—dynasties—institutions seem to pass through the stages of pioneering characterized by a rough and ready simplicity, followed by a period of expansion . . . and this followed by decadence. . . . The President feels that in one way and one way alone can this College look forward to empire without decadence. That way is by suppressing self-desire and substituting an unselfish, friendly spirit of service to our fellow men. . . .[43]

One irate senior, shortly before his graduation, deplored "the faculty cliques and personal smallness and even petty jealousies, which give little inspiration. . . . These faults can be attributed to inbreeding and the lack of a fresh breeze of academic stimulation. . . . " The accrediting committees were pointing out certain weaknesses, including the tendency to try to do too much without adequate facilities, administrative action taken without waiting for faculty consideration, lack of coordination in the counseling program, the need to avoid provincialism by affiliation with national academic and professional societies, and the need for more efficient organization of the teaching departments.[44]

The college looked ahead in the hope its accreditation would be reaffirmed n 1960. To that end, in 1956 Stewart appointed Professor Harry E. Gardner as chairman of a Self-Evaluating Committee. Subcommittees were organized, and every member of the faculty had a part in the self-evaluation. The aim was to increase the academic efficiency of the college and to solve the many problems of increased enrollment.[45]

The report of the Self-Evaluating Committee was completed and published on 7 April 1958. Among its most salient recommendations were: (1) that the college move immediately to restate and clarify its objectives; (2) that the constitution and bylaws for faculty and administration and the bylaws of the trustees be revised and altered to rectify omissions and inconsistencies; (3) that a committee be appointed to revise the catalogue; (4) that conditions concerning tenure be clarified; (5) that a full-time professional member be added to the library staff; (6) that the problem of scholarships and financial aid to students be studied and clarified; (7) that consideration be given to increased resources through alumni; (8) that more classroom space be made available; (9) that entrance tests be given to high school students graduating in the bottom three-fifths of their classes; (10) that a faculty committee undertake a study of faculty grading standards; and (11) that the work load of faculty members not be too burdensome. The only recommendation on improvement of the quality of the faculty was that an item be included in each departmental budget to cover costs of attendance at professional meetings. But nothing was said about the need for more faculty members with earned doctorates or about financial aid and leaves for those who might wish to further their education.[46]

In June 1958 the faculty resolved to continue this self-study and "to put into effect the recommendations . . . wherever practicable." On the advice of F. Taylor Jones, Executive Secretary of the MSA, Stewart requested the trustees to secure two able consultants to survey the findings of the faculty, visit the campus, and make additional recommendations. The consultants were Dr. Raymond Haupert, President of Moravian College, and Dr. Edward F. Clark, S. J., Academic Vice President of Fordham University. These scholars visited the Waynesburg campus late in May 1958 and studied the self-evaluation report. They returned the following October and made further study of the operations of the college. After their second visit they made several recommendations for improvement of the institution. First, "there must be equality of teaching" on the campus and the Uniontown Center, which "might be attained by general syllabi of courses taught" in both places. Second, some faculty members were giving too many A and B grades. Third, the student-faculty ratio was too high for efficient pedagogy. Fourth, the administrative organization of the college would have to be revamped to bring it in line with accepted practices in other similar institutions. The counselors suggested four administrative offices with well defined areas of responsibility: Vice President-Academic; Vice President-Personnel Services; Vice President-Finances; and Vice President-Public Relations, Plans, and Development. The trustees promptly concurred in this change. They also agreed, in line with another suggestion, to a closer integration of administration for the campus and the Uniontown Center. Fifth, the counselors contended that administrative officers spent too much time teaching; they held that division of labor would make for greater efficiency both in teaching and in administration. Sixth, on the advice of the consultants, the trustees directed Stewart to find "a strong academic dean" who has "stability and who has had experience as an Assistant Dean in one of our large universities."[47]

On the basis of these recommendations, the faculty began to re-evaluate its self-evaluation. Moreover, in June 1959, the MSA, having considered the college's self-study, sent new questionnaires for use by faculty committees as they worked on a report to be submitted to that agency, which was to evaluate the college in the fall of 1960. This questionnaire dealt chiefly with the objectives of the college and with the academic program. Certain questions revealed the prevailing academic weakness. An example is: "How do you give recognition and prestige to good student scholarship and help the students to understand the importance and desirability of intellectual attainment, other than through election to honorary societies?" The answer was: "Almost every faculty member feels that this is our weakest area." Mention was then made of an honors day, instituted in 1959, when students with high academic standing were recognized and presented certain awards for their achievements. The self-evaluation committee continued to work on its several tasks. In order to give it more time, the visitation from MSA was postponed from the fall of 1960 until the week of 12 February 1961. The inspection team was headed by Dr. Morley Mays, Academic Dean of Juniata College, who paid a pre-evaluation visit to the college on 28 October 1960.[48]

This team was on the campus from 12 to 15 February 1961, studying all facets of the institution. Its report, dated 13 March 1961, was very critical of the college. Accreditation continued temporarily, "with the understanding that far-reaching changes would be made in the College's administrative organization, its curriculum, its faculty, and its facilities." In particular, the curriculum needed revision. Accordingly, an *ad hoc* committee met with the Curriculum Development Committee, consisting of department heads. They, together with the faculty, hoped to strengthen and modernize the curriculum. Much work had to be done by 1 October 1961, when another report would be due the accrediting agency. Early in June 1961 Dr. William A. Morrison, General Secretary of the Board of Christian Education of the United Presbyterian Church, U. S. A. visited the campus and stressed that: "The Church is very much concerned that all its colleges maintain accreditation in the regional accrediting associations."[49]

Meanwhile Stewart looked for a strong academic dean who would be able to do the job that had to be done at Waynesburg. The trustees believed they had the right man early in August 1961, when Dr. Paul D. Walter of the University of Pittsburgh was employed as Vice President for Academic Affairs and Professor of Psychology. Walter was highly recommended by Dr. Stanton Crawford, venerable Dean of the Faculties of the University of Pittsburgh. Walter held two baccalaureate degrees from Marion College in Indiana, a master's degree from Indiana University in Indiana, and a Ph. D. from the University of Pittsburgh. He had been an able administrator at the University of Pittsburgh, having served in the different capacities of Assistant Dean of the School of Business Administration, Acting Director of the Bureau of Business Research, and Associate Dean of the School of General Studies. Joseph W. Ray, Jr., President of the Board of Trustees, Richard L. Baily, a member of that board, and Dr. Morrison interviewed Walter; and Morrison approved his appointment to the position. Ray "explained that Dr. Walter is to have full responsibility for all academic affairs of the College, thus freeing President Stewart for work in public relations, fund raising, etc."[50]

When Walter was employed, the duties of administrative officers were defined in line with suggestions made by Dr. F. Taylor Jones and by Dr. Morrison. In addition to Stewart as President and to Walter as Vice President for Academic Affairs, other top administrative posts were filled as follows: The Reverend Paul Bauer, Vice President in Student Personnel Services; the Reverend J. E. Victor Carlson, Vice President in Planning and Development; and Charles B. Stoy, Jr., Vice President in Business Affairs and Finance. Shortly the trustees set salaries for these men, with Stewart receiving a salary slightly higher than that of Walter.[51]

Walter immediately went about his new assignment with great determination to bring the college up to standards set by the accrediting agencies and approved by the church. First, he upgraded the faculty. He deplored the fact that some teachers "exhibit bizarre idiosyncracies, and, as the Middle States report phrases it so pungently, 'eschew all manner of sophistication.'"[52] One of his chief aims was to increase the number of faculty members with earned doctorates. As of October 1961 there were fifty full-time and thirteen part-time teachers. Of these, seven had the earned doctorate; forty-two, the master's degree; and fourteen held only the bachelor's degree. Walter held that fifty percent of the faculty should have the "terminal degree." He was remarkably successful in recruiting faculty members for, within a year, those with earned doctorates more than doubled in number. He encouraged faculty members to further their education and to remain at the college. At his behest, in February 1962, the trustees provided that faculty members studying for the doctorate might borrow from the college for tuition, with no interest being charged; and 25 percent of the loan itself would be forgiven for each year the recipient remained on the faculty. In order to make faculty positions more attractive, Walter recommended an increase in salaries, particularly for the three upper ranks; a major medical and insurance plan for all faculty members; full remission of tuition for faculty children and spouses; and a new retirement plan in which one could voluntarily retire at age sixty-two, lose tenure and be employed on a year-to-year basis at age sixty-five, with compulsory retirement at age seventy. In April 1963 the trustees went on record as supporting these recommendations. The accrediting agencies, both MSA and the Department of Public Instruction (DPI), also favored them. Walter exhorted faculty members to come to him with their problems rather than to take them directly to the trustees. He also wanted full democratic action in the faculty by eliminating the provision that none could enjoy the right of suffrage until after one year of service. He wanted immediate suffrage for all full time members, but could not get it.[53]

Second, Walter wanted to recruit better students. Admission standards had been low. As of September 1961, fifty-one percent of the incoming class ranked in the lower three-fifths of their high school classes. Within a year, however, the standard was raised. In November 1962, the Director of Admissions reported: "We have moved from readily accepting any 'warm body' who appears at the door—either with or without money in hand. We have heeded . . . the suggestions of the Middle States Association . . . that we *ought* to be drawing more and more students from the upper three-fifths of their graduating classes in high school (italics in original)." By January 1963 this goal was reached.[54]

Third, Walter raised standards relative to the students' academic standing. Prior to his coming, on an honor point system based on 4, 3, 2, 1, and 0 for letter grades A, B, C, D, and F respectively, a student was put on academic probation his first semester if his cumulative average was lower than 1.5; a 2 (or C) was not required until his sixth semester. For the academic year 1960-1961, of 930 students enrolled, 435 were below a C average; this did not include those who were suspended or dropped. Calling this "disgraceful," in October 1961 Walter announced that thenceforth a C average would be a minimum among upperclassmen. In a chapel period, he talked to the students on "How to Study," stressing the importance of proper study habits, note-taking, preparations for examinations, and the differences between high school and college. On telling the students that "the faculty must be improved," they applauded him loudly. The editor of *The Yellow Jacket* praised Walter's program, saying: "If the academic norm is not raised, the deadwood will remain."[55]

Fourth, under Walter's direction the Uniontown Center was integrated with the campus. The Registrar supervised registration at both places; faculty members began teaching at both; and the Director of the Center was responsible to the Vice President for Academic Affairs. The quality of instruction was greatly raised at the Center, and it was no longer considered undesirable or inferior.[56]

Fifth, at Walter's suggestion certain changes were made in the curriculum. Overlapping courses were eliminated in the fields of religion, philosophy, psychology, and education. Minor changes were made in courses in the natural sciences, foreign languages, history, and business administration departments. Some twenty changes were made in the English and fine arts offerings. A new development was the initiation of advanced placement for credit, effective in September 1962. Upon passing thorough examinations in certain areas of learning, students could receive credit. This was a progressive measure—one where the capabilities of the better student were recognized.[57]

Sixth, an innovation by Walter was the introduction of advanced registration, including prepayment of tuition and fees. Such procedure would avoid the mass confusion which occurred the day before classes began, and the frantic working until two or three in the morning so that classes could begin on time. The irritations at having classes canceled, new sections created, and times of meeting altered—these and other problems would be nonexistent under the new system.[58]

Seventh, Walter contended that the Library should have more books and scholarly magazines. In October 1961 it had 51,764 books, whereas the average number for colleges of Waynesburg's size in this area was 73,100 volumes. Waynesburg had 280 magazines in all; the average for area colleges of like size was 374. The Library at the Center had only 764 books and 80 periodicals.[59]

The MSA had criticisms other than those along academic lines. By June 1962 it had recommended the employment of a Buildings and Grounds Superintendent, and the trustees chose William L. Millikin, Jr., to that position. It also called for a new statement of the philosophy and objectives of the college. Accordingly, a committee of five faculty members re-drafted this statement which was more concise and more cogent than any earlier attempts. It was included in the 1962-1963 catalogue of the college.[60]

While Walter and his fellow administrators were trying to improve the college on all fronts, the MSA kept in touch with the situation. In April 1962 Dr. F. Taylor Jones visited the campus, interviewed Stewart and the four vice presidents, and "was encouraged by the progress we have made." He returned a month later and again expressed his agreeable surprise at the progress. But he said another visitation would be made in the fall of 1962. This visitation by an MSA committee, headed by Dr. Eric Faigle, Vice President of Syracuse University, occurred in November 1962, for the purpose of meeting administrators, trustees, and faculty members. Faculty members were permitted to say anything they pleased provided they believed what they said was true. Despite Walter's reforms, Faigle's Committee was even more critical of the college than the one headed by Dr. Mays early in 1961. The Faigle report concluded:

> The problems of Waynesburg College are so deep seated that the visiting group felt it would take considerable time to solve many of them. Although the present administration has made an effort to meet the recommendations of the Middle States team in 1961, it has not made adequate headway. The salary scale . . . especially at the upper levels, is still woefully inadequate to meet the competition for first rate faculty. Moreover, office space, library facilities, student quality, teaching load, and general working conditions, while improving, . . . had fallen so far behind that heroic efforts are needed, not merely steady improvement.

Faigle's team held that efforts to add Ph. D.'s should continue, but there should be a recognition that not all Ph. D.'s are capable faculty members. For faculty, Waynesburg College had drawn too heavily from West Virginia University and the University of Pittsburgh; more members should come from farther afield. The team sensed that faculty morale was low. "The faculty," they felt, "appears to have no viable part in College affairs. . . . " They feared that once the specific suggestions of the MSA report were met, the college would stagnate and retrogress. They lamented that the Library was not being used entirely for the purpose for which it had been built; part of it was used as classrooms, part for storage space, and part for plant maintenance uses. Progress had been made. But the MSA gave the college more time to solve some of its major problems. Its recommendations made to the college were also sent to the annual meeting of the MSA at Atlantic City on 6-7 December 1962. Stewart and Walter attended this meeting. The MSA once more postponed any action on reaffirming the regional accreditation of the college.[61]

In academic standing and in other ways, the college was also responsible to the DPI in Harrisburg which had authority to grant or withdraw "program approval" for the several fields in which students were trained to teach in public schools. A team of ten professional individuals from collegiate institutions elsewhere in Pennsylvania visited the campus on 18-19 March 1963 and evaluated the educational curriculum. As a result, fortunately, in no area did certification cease. Approval was delayed in physics; and the History and Social Science Department was criticized adversely, because its faculty schedules were too heavy. All other areas were approved. The DPI had a number of recommendations including more office space for faculty members, a new education program providing for a full semester of professional work, reduction of teaching schedules to twelve hours per week, reduction in size of classes, replacement of all teachers without an earned doctorate or who were not working toward one, no further employment of alumni of the college in order to prevent inbreeding, encouragement of faculty members to attend professional meetings, improvement in the quality of the student body, and an increase in tuition. Most of these recommendations were also made by the MSA.[62]

All went well for Walter for slightly more than a year—the "honeymoon" period during which he praised Stewart and the faculty for their cooperation. By December 1962, however, dissensions in the faculty began to impede his program. He lamented that two factions had formed—"one for progress and change and one against all changes." He reminded all of "the importance of progress to maintain accreditation. If the reactionaries should take the reins, Waynesburg would lose accreditation, the better students and faculty would leave, the building program would be stymied, but if the faculty and administration would cooperate, Waynesburg College would progress."[63]

The accrediting association—and the inexorable march of time—called for a change of presidents of the college. Accordingly, Stewart announced his retirement as President on 2 February 1963, to become effective as of 1 July 1963. Aware of his long devotion to the college and of his great abilities as a fund-raiser and public relations man, the accrediting association recommended that he be retained with the title of "Chancellor" so he could continue his efforts in these areas. Stewart told the trustees that he still wanted to work along these lines. Concurring with his wishes, they accepted his resignation as President of the College and gave him the title "Chancellor," with the understanding that his chief duty would be fund-raising. It is abundantly clear that the trustees deeply appreciated Stewart, because of his long, unselfish service to the college. Plans were immediately made to honor him at the forthcoming Alumni Day activities. And the Waynesburg Junior Chamber of Commerce named him as their "Man of the Year."[64]

Shortly a committee of six trustees, with Richard L. Baily as Chairman, began the search for a new president of the college. In the event that none was elected by 1 July 1963, this committee contemplated the possibility that an acting president might be appointed, and that a trustee might serve in that capacity on a temporary basis, pending the election of a president.[65]

Meanwhile, Walter became impatient, because his academic program was hampered. When he was employed, he was considered "leader in all academic matters." But dissensions in the faculty became increasingly disenchanting to him. Beginning in January 1963, the trustees imposed certain restrictions on his activities which curtailed his effectiveness. In the belief that his position was no longer tenable nor desirable, he resigned on 2 May 1963. The trustees quickly accepted his resignation.[66] Without any question, Walter had done much to strengthen the academic standing of the college.

In sum, from 1950 to 1963 Stewart made many strides forward. The campus was greatly expanded, and the building program was unparalleled in the history of the college. In public relations he was unexcelled. In fund-raising he was highly successful; thus he was able largely to offset a certain stigma handed down by Cumberland Presbyterians who were never known to be generous donors to their churches and colleges. But the gravest handicap was academic decadence. When Stewart retired as President, the college's accreditation still was not reaffirmed. And much remained to be done before that target was reached.[67]

XX
THE TRANSFORMATION OF THE COLLEGE

WHEN STEWART RESIGNED THE PRESIDENCY OF THE COLLEGE, A SEARCH committee of trustees considered several candidates and concluded that Dr. Bennett Milton Rich was best qualified for the position. The trustees offered him the position and he accepted it late in May 1963.[1] His duties began on 1 July 1963. Born in Rices Landing, Pennsylvania, on 8 June 1909, he graduated from Cumberland Township High School at nearby Carmichaels, and from Waynesburg College, with the A. B. degree, in 1930. During his senior year at Waynesburg he was president of the student body. He taught from 1930 to 1938 at his high school *Alma Mater*. Having chosen political science as his specialty, he won the M. A. degree in 1932, and the Ph. D. in 1941, both from the University of Michigan. In May 1974 he was awarded two honorary degrees: an LL. D. by Geneva College, and an L. H. D. by Waynesburg College. For the academic year 1940-1941 he was a Brookings Fellow, which aided him in his research. During 1941-1942 he was a member of the Political Science Department of the University of Pennsylvania. He entered the United States Army in 1942 and, four years later, he was separated from active duty in the rank of lieutenant colonel, having served chiefly in the office of the Provost Marshal General. Right after the war he spent a summer as consultant for the office of United States Military Government in Germany. In 1946 he began teaching political science at Rutgers University. He was the first Director of Rutgers' Bureau of Government Research when it was founded in 1950. He served for ten years at that post and, according to Dr. Mason W. Gross, President of Rutgers University, Rich did much to develop that Bureau into "an instrument of ever-increasing value to every level of government in the state of New Jersey."

Rich produced two scholarly books: *The Presidents and Civil Disorder*, in 1941; and *The Government and Administration of New Jersey*, in 1957. In 1953-1954 he was Visiting Associate Professor and Acting Director of the Institute of Public Administration at the University of Michigan. Subsequently he served one summer as consultant to the Institute of Public Administration at the University of the Philippines. He is a member of several honorary fraternities and professional associations. From 1967 to 1973 he was a member of the Board of Trustees of the Middle States Association of Colleges and Secondary Schools. He is a good family man with a gracious wife and three fine children—two sons and a daughter.[2]

The chief difficulty facing Rich was the reaffirmation of the college's accreditation. There were many interrelated problems such as fund raising, the faculty, the physical plant, admissions of students, the academic program, and so on. As the accrediting team reported late in 1962, the college had fallen so far behind that heroic efforts were needed to set things aright. It had not kept pace with profound changes in American higher education in the twentieth century, which stemmed chiefly from the lasting effects of German scholarship with its higher criticism and from the theory of evolution. These changes were: (1) the gradual termination of the classical curriculum, which gave way to greater emphasis on science; and (2) a new kind of professor. The classically trained teacher who attempted to teach a wide variety of unrelated subjects was being replaced by the expert who mastered one area of knowledge. While more and more institutions were recruiting experts for their faculties, as late as the 1950's, Waynesburg had faculty members who were teaching too heavy schedules, spread over too wide areas of subject material. As examples, in 1951, the college catalogue listed one faculty member as "Instructor in French, Chemistry, and Education"; another as "Instructor in Psychology and Spanish"; and the Dean of Women taught French and Piano. In addition to changes in curricula and the advent of the expert, other new values were substituted for the old in American higher education. Noteworthy was the end of compulsory chapel on campus after campus, but it persisted at Waynesburg, despite increasing student opposition, until the late 1960's.[3]

Rich was inaugurated as President of Waynesburg College on 12 October 1962 in an impressive ceremony attended by representatives from some 200 colleges, universities, and learned societies. On the same occasion Stewart was installed as Chancellor of the College.

In his inaugural address Rich spoke of the main strengths of the college—the record of service to society of the alumni for over a century, and the new Chancellor's "service for the last 53 years, 42 of them as President of the College." He called attention to the importance of the faculty in the success or failure of the college. He declared: "The college does not exist for the glory of the administration. The administration exists for the glory of the college—to perform the thousand and one services needed for a smoothly operating institution." In order to help him always to keep this correct concept of administration he suggested to the faculty "that a chapter of that ancient and honorable body, The American Association of University Professors, be established on the campus." He then described how the accreditation process works, and why accreditation was essential to the life of any institution of higher learning. "Reaffirmation of this accreditation becomes a prime responsibility," he said. Efforts to strengthen the faculty would continue. The college would tighten admission standards, and it would seek the most able students regardless of race, creed, or color. As always, it would try to extend more financial aid to talented but needy students in Greene and Fayette counties. Rich called on all to "Come, labor on" in the achievement of these worthy goals.[4]

Being an alumnus of Waynesburg College, Rich felt a deep sense of devotion to it, akin to that of Miller and Stewart. He quietly, methodically, and patiently went about the manifold tasks before him. He got along amicably with Stewart, who declared at the inaugural ceremonies: "My prayers and support will be with Dr. Rich."[5]

Shortly Rich established his administrative organization. At his suggestion, the trustees called Dr. G. Wayne Smith, Chairman of the Department of History and Political Science at Fairmont State College, to the all-important position of Academic Dean. Smith had won his M. A. and Ph. D. degrees at West Virginia University. Having specialized in American History, with emphasis on West Virginia History, he had taught at Marshall University, Huntington, West Virginia, and, on a part-time basis, at West Virginia University, prior to his post at Fairmont State. He was a member of several honorary societies, including Phi Beta Kappa, and a number of professional associations. He had published several scholarly articles and a biography of Nathan Goff, Jr., West Virginia's most popular Republican leader in the post-Civil War period. The position of Dean of Student Life was filled by Alexander G. Sidar, Jr., who had been Assistant Director of Admissions at Rutgers University from 1955 until 1962, when he was promoted to Associate Director in the same post. Sidar received his B. S. degree in 1946 and the Ed. M. degree in 1947—both at Rutgers University. He had served in the United States Army Air Forces during 1945 and 1946 as a pilot instructor.[6] Rich retained Charles B. Stoy, Jr., as Vice President for Business and Finance; and J. E. Victor Carlson, as Vice President for Public Relations, Plans, and Development. Meanwhile, at Rich's suggestion, the Board of Trustees was reorganized, and cut, from eight committees to four; under the new arrangement there was a trustee committee for each of the four administrative areas—Academic Matters; Student Life; Development, Alumni, and Public Relations; and Finance and Property. The duties of each of these committees were clearly specified.[7]

Cognizant of these administrative changes, the MSA gave the college an additional period of time to correct some of its deficiencies and to solve some of its major problems. It was deemed best to start from scratch and to conduct another self-evaluation of the entire institution. Rich told the faculty that one major goal would be to prove Waynesburg's academic respectability to the various agencies, but that he was confident the college could go far beyond the minimum requirements. He held that "principal emphasis has to be on developing the teaching program. There are areas of subject matter where we have been weak—places where we have never had the faculty to make it possible for every student to have the best possible liberal arts offerings." Rich told the trustees that faculty salaries all over the nation were sharply rising and, in order to meet the competition for topflight faculty members, the college's salary scale must be raised accordingly.[8]

Undaunted by still staggering problems, in the fall of 1963 Rich and Smith organized the faculty into eleven institutional self-evaluation committees. Each proceeded promptly with its assigned task, and the work of all was carefully collated. Rich "urged the faculty to state Waynesburg's case fully, carefully, and truthfully."[9]

The college was scheduled for a full-scale re-evaluation in the spring of 1965. On 14 April 1964 Dr. F. Taylor Jones of the MSA, visited the campus and conferred with the administrative staff and the Curriculum Development Committee. At that time the evaluation by MSA was deferred from the spring to the fall of 1965 in order not to rush too greatly the several committees in producing the reports required by MSA. Ever in close touch with the situation,

Jones again visited the campus on 16 September 1964. He said that Dr. Frederick Miller, President of Lebanon Valley College, who had considerable experience in conducting such evaluations, would head the team which would visit Waynesburg in the fall of 1965. Jones fortunately added: "Very rarely does an evaluating team come in and either 'kill off' an institution or say, 'All is well for another ten years.' The usual plan is to suggest that the institution do certain things and make a series of progress reports." Miller first visited the campus on 21-22 April 1965. He reminded the faculty members once again of the purposes of MSA and assured them that the visitation committee was a fact-finding and not a fault-finding body: "They come as constructive critics, not as carping censors." Plans were then made for Miller's team to return on 10-12 October 1965 when the full-scale re-evaluation would be conducted.[10]

Meanwhile the several committees were busy preparing materials for the "Self-Evaluation Report for the Middle States Association of Colleges and Secondary Schools, Commission on Institutions of Higher Education," dated 1 September 1965. A product of the collective, integrated action of many persons, it presented a clear, concise, correct, complete, cogent picture of Waynesburg College. We shall here examine only the most salient features of this report.[11]

Improvement of the faculty was the first consideration. The aim was to recruit an increasing number of members with the earned doctorate, who had proven to be competent in the classroom. Rich and Smith desired that 50 percent of the faculty would hold earned doctorates, but, as of May 1964, Smith "was quite certain that the accrediting association would approve the progress we have made."[12] Walter had made progress in improving the faculty. His efforts, plus those that immediately followed, raised the percentage of full-time faculty with earned doctorates from 14 for the academic year 1961-1962 to 39.2 for 1964-1965. In the same period the percentage with only a bachelor's degree decreased from 12 to 7.9. By 1968, 42 percent of the full-time faculty had earned doctorates. The great majority of the newly employed doctors had published scholarly works, including books and articles in the best magazines in their respective specialties.[13]

In order to recruit and to hold first-rate faculty members, several measures had to be taken. First, salaries had to be raised. Although the college raised salaries for full-time faculty members almost every year after 1960, its scale lagged behind those of comparable institutions. For example, the average salary for the year 1964-1965 was $7,461, while the average in colleges and universities in Pennsylvania was $9,025; and Waynesburg ranked 53 among 80 institutions in the state. Under those conditions, the college obviously had a problem of raiding by other institutions. It was not until 1967 that Waynesburg's faculty salary scale approached those of other similar colleges. And by the early 1970's it was competitive with those of the overwhelming majority of collegiate institutions in the nation.[14]

Second, the program of fringe benefits for the faculty was highly attractive. In addition to a good retirement plan, adequate health insurance, and remission of tuition for faculty children and spouses, the college would aid faculty members in securing homes, and in moving to Waynesburg. In all, these fringe benefits, as of 1971, were estimated to range in value annually from $1,139 for an instructor to $1,861 for a professor.[15]

Several other developments helped to create an atmosphere in which faculty members would be happy. Sabbatical leaves and leaves of absence without pay were permissible, but they had to be for a genuinely educational activity, such as study, research, writing, or travel. Though the college had no publish or perish policy, research was encouraged. The teaching schedule was twelve hours weekly for regular faculty members, and nine hours for departmental chairmen; the usual number of daily preparations did not exceed three. Keeping the principle of division of labor in mind, teachers taught, and administrators performed duties in the management of the college. Teaching assignments were based chiefly upon one's academic preparation. Efforts were made to keep classes relatively small; the desirable range was from 15 to 25 students with a maximum of 30. Academic freedom prevailed, but along with it went responsibility. The tenure policy provided that any teacher above the rank of instructor, who had served the college for five years would be granted tenure "unless by September 1 of the fifth year notice has been given of non-reappointment for the sixth year." And, beginning in 1963, there was no restriction as to race, color, or creed in the extending of tenure. The foregoing policies went a long way, as Rich told the trustees in October 1963, "to create a scholarly climate of opinion where each faculty member feels that he has dignity; that he counts, and that he is being adequately rewarded for his effort."[16]

That the faculty was given an important role in college affairs is shown by the creation, in the fall of 1963, of the Curriculum Development and Planning Committee (later changed to Faculty

Planning and Development Committee). This was a "working committee" of faculty members. Its immediate task was to review the philosophy and objectives of the college and to study the faculty constitution with a view to its revision. A clearer statement was needed on such matters as academic freedom, rank, promotions, tenure, leaves of absence, sabbatical leaves, and so on. There was some question about the definition of members of the faculty. According to custom, the director of athletics was a member of the faculty, but assistant librarians were not. On 25 March 1965 May P. Clovis, the Librarian, who held faculty rank as an associate professor, requested faculty rank for the assistant librarians. But this move was slow in coming; in 1968, for the first time, the assistant librarian was listed in the college catalogue as an assistant professor; and in May 1970, at the request of the faculty, the trustees granted that professional librarians holding professorial rank be given status as members of the teaching faculty.[17] By the spring of 1965 the statement of policy for the faculty, the faculty constitution and bylaws, and the bylaws of the Board of Trustees had all been revised and rewritten. They were included, together with other basic documents, in a pamphlet entitled *Documents Pertaining to the Government of the College*, dated September 1965.[18] It was carefully compiled, well written, and concise.

In line with Rich's suggestion in his inaugural address, the faculty shortly organized a chapter of the American Association of University Professors (AAUP) which was concerned not only with the welfare of the faculty, but also the good of the college as a whole. The chapter shortly engaged in several projects including the judging of teaching effectiveness, working conditions, and fringe benefits. Officers of the local chapter kept abreast of guidelines of the national organization which were included regularly in the *AAUP Bulletin*. The college attempted to adhere to these guidelines. The local chapter dealt chiefly with local problems. Without any doubt, it raised faculty morale and worked to the advantage of the entire institution. Of its officers and members, Rich said: "I applaud their action."[19]

In order to encourage faculty members along the creative line, a Faculty Research Committee was established to administer a faculty research fund. Faculty members could submit to this committee descriptions of their research projects and apply for grants. The committee carefully considered them, and allotted funds in proportion to the scope and importance of each project. While the total amount of this fund was not great, it aided faculty members to cover expenses of travel, lodging, use of research equipment, paper, typing of manuscripts, and so on.[20]

If a strong faculty was essential to a sound academic program, equally so were carefully selected students. In 1963 enrollments at Waynesburg, as at all collegiate institutions in the nation, were increasing, and it was generally assumed that this trend would continue. Applications for admission exceeded by far the number of acceptances. Though numbers of applicants were high, the college carried on "a vigorous recruiting campaign in order to get our share of bright students," and rather consistently 85 percent of entering freshmen were from the top three-fifths of their high school classes. The student body became increasingly cosmopolitan, with more students coming from New Jersey, New York, Maryland and some ten other states, and from three or four foreign countries. In 1963 approximately 85 percent still came from Pennsylvania, however. Efforts were made to recruit more black students. The aim was to reduce, beginning in 1964, over the next five-year period, the proportion of men to women students from 2.2 men to 1 woman to 1.5 to 1.[21] Despite increases in tuition and competition from other institutions, enrollments continued to rise in the 1960's.

From July 1963 to December 1965, in addition to strengthening the faculty and student body, rapid strides ahead were made in other areas. All seemed well for the visitation by the MSA evaluation team headed by Miller on 10-12 October 1965. On 15 October Rich told the trustees: "the members were, for the most part, real pros. They went about their work quietly and efficiently and . . . obtained a tremendous amount of information about the operation of the institution." Before they left they "had many suggestions for improvement, but there were also several areas in which the college was commended for its actions. We will now await the written report and the final decision of the Middle States Commission." It was expected that the decision would be made early in December when the Commission held its annual convention in Atlantic City, New Jersey.[22]

On 10 November 1965, Rich told the faculty about his meeting with the evaluation team, and he warned that we "have much to do in the next few years." Curriculum revision was needed. And the faculty was organized into both divisions and departments; the organization should be changed either to one or the other for the sake of consistency. On 7 December 1965 Rich received the report that the accreditation of the college had been reaffirmed. Immediately he announced the good news to the faculty. Accreditation meant, however, that in the view of independent observers, the college met only minimum requirements. It did "not mean that it has arrived academically." The evaluation confirmed that some areas were sufficiently strong, while others should be stronger. The accrediting agency asked for a progress report by 1 October 1967 with respect to the four following recommendations: (1) that a closer relationship between aims and objectives and curricular offerings should be effected; (2) that the trustees redouble their efforts to seek new friends and sources of funds to lighten the heavy burden of debt; (3) that more precise job descriptions and lines of authority be developed in administrative offices, particularly in student personnel services and in public relations; and (4) that greater efforts be made to promote the general intellectual life of the campus. By December 1967 the MSA had received and accepted this progress report. Meanwhile, the DPI in Harrisburg had given program approval in all academic fields, and teaching certificates would "be granted to Waynesburg College graduates in these fields merely on certification that they had completed the work."[23]

The recruiting of better faculty members and students went a long way toward the reaffirmation of the college's accreditation. But progress along other lines—the curriculum, fund-raising, and the physical plant—was also essential to the achievement of that goal. Beginning in 1964 certain changes were made in the core curriculum, a group of courses deemed necessary for an "educated person," which were required of all students working toward baccalaureate degrees. Included in the core were certain courses in the broad areas of the humanities, the natural and physical sciences, and the social sciences. There were no basic changes in the core curriculum until 1973, when it became much more flexible; in the "new core" the only requirement was two semesters of English composition; students were given a wider variety of choice of courses than ever before. But they were still held in a general way to the main areas of a liberal arts program. Another innovation was a two-year program leading to the degree Associate of Science in Business Administration designed to train young people for careers in business and industry.[24]

Noteworthy were certain changes in the several sciences. The geology program was revamped in line with recommendations of national leaders in the field and the geology staff. According to Hollis Dole, Assistant Secretary of the Interior, who visited the college in October 1972, the Paul R. Stewart mineral collection was "one of the best I have seen in a long time. . . . " Dole said there was increasing need for geologists. The physics major was eliminated, chiefly because there were not enough teachers in that specialty. But the introductory physics courses were retained. By May 1968 a new major in earth and space science was added to the curriculum. It would prepare teachers who planned to work in this specialty in secondary schools, and it would provide an excellent foundation for those who went to graduate school for further study. With the great emphasis on the space program in the nation, there was increasing need for persons with such expertise. With respect to chemistry, on 11 November 1970 Rich announced that the college was placed on the approved list of the American Chemical Society, thanks to the leadership of Dr. Robert B. LaCount, chairman of the Chemistry Department. The inspection committee of that Society was "very favorably impressed with the facilities at Waynesburg and especially with the enthusiasm, interest, and capability of the staff." Of 103 accredited four-year colleges and universities in Pennsylvania, Waynesburg was one of 37 to win such recognition.[25]

Certain other curricular developments are notable. In keeping with a nationwide trend, a course in the history of black people was added. An internship program for accounting majors was introduced, in which a student in his senior year left the campus for a time and worked with an accounting firm; the practical experience thus gained was most beneficial to him. An interdisciplinary colloquium was added. At the outset it was intended mainly for faculty members and students interested in ecology. An attempt in 1967 to establish a Reserve Officers Training Corps (ROTC) on campus ended in failure, chiefly due to lack of student interest; another attempt, in 1971, failed because of opposition from some students and faculty members. In the belief that it would attract students, a Fine Arts major was established early in 1972, which included courses in Art, Drama, and Music.[26]

An innovation came in October 1970, when the college joined the Regional Council for International Education (RCIE). With a membership of some thirty collegiate institutions in the tri-state area, the aim of RCIE was "to bring about a global perspective on the campuses of its member institutions in order to overcome the culture-bound approach which still characterizes American education." The main feature of RCIE was its overseas program of study for undergraduates at Verona, Italy, and at Basel, Switzerland. Under arrangements between member institutions and RCIE, a student could take his junior year's work at either of these centers and receive full credit for it toward graduation from his "home institution." Students bound for either center lived with local families in each and studied the language spoken in each. In addition to a heavy schedule of courses, they took field trips to cultural centers in each nation. The RCIE also sponsored an institute for faculty members, which met near Cleveland, Ohio, for two-day sessions four times annually. Each year the program dealt with a different area of the world. Scholarly papers were presented at each session, followed by discussions relevant to the topic under consideration. The college regularly sent two faculty members to this institute. The RCIE further sponsored seminars for faculty members and students at member institutions and in foreign nations.[27]

By 1968 certain departmental changes were made. The duties of departmental chairmen had already been specified. Now their term of service was set at three years, at the end of which they were eligible for reappointment. Although they might have tenure as faculty members, they did not have such as chairmen. For their duties as chairmen they did not receive additional pay, but their teaching schedules were reduced from twelve to nine hours per week. By 1970 the Science Department, was divided into three Departments—one for Biology, one for Chemistry and Physics, and one for Geology. And the Department of Education and Psychology was separated into two Departments—one for Education and one for Psychology. Similarly, by 1972 the Department of English and Fine Arts was divided into two—one for English and one for Fine Arts.[28] The other departments, which remained intact, were: History and Social Sciences; Modern Foreign Languages; Mathematics; Business Administration; and Religion and Philosophy.

The Academic Standards Committee and the faculty attempted to maintain respectable standards in the administration of the curriculum. Entering freshmen were required to make certain scores on tests produced by the College Entrance Examination Board (CEEB). In order to avoid academic probation, students were required to maintain a 2.000 (C) academic quotient. Aware that this standard was too rigorous for freshmen while they were making the adjustment to college-level work, by 1966 the faculty lowered the academic quotient for them to 1.750. By 1965 the college would give credit to students for college-level courses completed in secondary schools; those who made satisfactory scores (3 or higher) on advanced placement tests of the "College Board" also were considered for advanced standing or placement. In April 1964 the faculty took concerted action to encourage students to spell correctly, to build their vocabularies, and to express themselves clearly in English. In admirable cooperation with the Department of English, all faculty members resolved "to apply the strictest feasible standards of mechanical accuracy to written work done in the classes they teach. . . . " And all departments agreed to require the form for research papers that was taught in the Freshman English course, which was based on the best available handbook in English. The faculty grappled with the perennial problems of plagiarism and cheating; procedures were adopted for handling such cases consistently, with due regard for precedent—and fairness to the accused.[29]

The faculty constantly exhorted students to do their utmost toward ever greater academic achievement. Honor students were regularly given the opportunity to become candidates for Danforth fellowships under the Danforth Foundation. Departmental honors were awarded annually at commencement to seniors who did outstanding work in each department. Beginning in 1964, class honors were awarded to honor students in each of the four classes. By 1970 an annual honors banquet was held for honor students in all four classes; here students received various awards such as dictionaries, scholarly books, and subscriptions to scholarly magazines in their respective areas of study. Qualified students had the opportunity to join any of several honor societies on the campus.[30]

While the faculty and administration were concerned with the curriculum and affairs of academe, the college faced financial problems, which were intertwined with all the others. As events were to prove, Rich had a logical approach to finances. He wanted to increase the endowment fund, but he felt impelled to do two other things at the same time; one was to upgrade the student body, the other to upgrade the faculty. Tuition could not be raised until these two things had been done, which would take a year or two. It was imperative immediately to raise faculty salaries and to employ more faculty members. As of December 1963 the faculty had no political scientist and no sociologist; there was only one economist on the faculty, and he lacked the earned doctorate. To strengthen the faculty, therefore, took priority over the erection of new buildings. At that time the total debt of the college was $737,580; deficits for the academic years 1963-1964 and 1964-1965 averaged approximately $65,000 for each year. While the trustees deplored the size of the debt and were unhappy about deficits, they supported the administration in its move to upgrade the faculty and the student body.[31]

Fund-raising continued without letup. The first drive, known as the "New Achievements Campaign," was started late in 1963 with a view to raising $1,875,000 by 1968. The chief sources of gifts were alumni, friends of the college, the church (including the U. P. Church of the U. S. A., its Synod of Pennsylvania, and individual churches), corporations, foundations, and civic organizations. The four major goals of the campaign were: (1) to attract additional faculty members of high competence; (2) to increase financial support for talented, but needy students; (3) to increase the endowment fund; and (4) to pay the balance, or $554,000, due on the Paul R. Stewart Science Building and to equip it for more efficient uses. A donor could designate his gift for any one of these purposes; and undesignated gifts were to be distributed equally among the four general areas.[32]

The New Achievements Campaign was combined with another drive, beginning in April 1965, when the Buhl Foundation, aware of the college's great need of a humanities building, gave the college $250,000 on the condition that the college raise an additional $500,000 by 1 December 1966. On learning that this, the "largest single gift ever offered to Waynesburg College," was in the offing, Rich was ready to "jump up and down with joy." Shortly the trustees gratefully accepted this challenge, and the fund-raising drive was under way. Another most generous gift was $250,000 from Lieutenant General and Mrs. Richard K. Mellon of Pittsburgh; it was an unrestricted grant for general development of the institution, hence any portion of it could be used for the new building. The United Presbyterian Church, U. S. A., from its "50 Million Fund" for all its colleges, gave the college $180,000. The number of alumni donors increased steadily from seven percent in 1959, when annual alumni fund drives began, to 30 percent by 1973; by that time more than 35 percent of all gifts came from alumni. By January 1966, the drive had gone over the top—and beyond; gifts and pledges totaled $685,131. On learning of this result, the Buhl Foundation notified Rich that the condition of its $250,000 grant for the Humanities Building was satisfied. The goal was reached nearly a year before the deadline. Construction of the building could start, while additional funds were being raised to offset inflation and other costs; when completed, it would be debt free. Fortunately, in May 1966 the college received a federal grant of $322,000 under Title I of the Higher Education Facilities Act of 1965; and an "Appalachian" grant of $98,000 was welcomed. With these grants, plus all the other funds raised, erection of the building was assured.[33]

In February 1967 plans were made for another fund drive, known as the "125th Anniversary Campaign." More extensive than previous campaigns, it was expected to reach all alumni and friends all over the United States, who would be asked to make pledges over a four-year period. The aim was to secure $2,650,000 to meet the following urgent needs: $1,850,000 to build a new campus center, to renovate and modernize old buildings, and to pay the balance due on the Paul R. Stewart Science Building; and $800,000 for the endowment fund. On 26 September 1969 the campaign was kicked off at a dinner in Benedum Hall with Dr. Henry Steele Commager, the renowned American historian, as main speaker. The campaign proceeded admirably with full cooperation of the administration, alumni, trustees, students, and friends of the college. By October 1971, 56 percent of the projected total had been raised. Thenceforth anticipated large gifts were not forthcoming and, in late 1973, it appeared that the goal of $2,650,000 would not be reached by 1974. Meanwhile, early in 1973, the Benedum Foundation gave $50,000 on the condition that the college raise an additional $95,400 by 30 June 1973. This challenge grant was to be applied to the debt on Benedum Hall. In this effort, students conducted a telethon to alumni, parents, and friends of the college for a total of sixteen days in late January and early February 1973. This challenge grant was met—and exceeded by the deadline date. As Rich looked ahead to retirement, another fund drive entitled "Transition in Strength" was started. The aim was to raise $2,500,000 between 1 July 1973 and December 1976. This money was to be allotted in varying sums for academic distinction, current operations, scholarships and loans, library additions, renovations of the physical plant, endowment and reduction of debts.[34]

Alumni, foundations, trustees, and friends of the college continued to be its main sources of revenue. In the late 1960's, gift income averaged annually around $500,000; nearly 20 percent of this went for current operating expenses, and, by 1971, changing economic conditions caused this percentage to increase. Annual support from the United Presbyterian church, U. S. A. declined sharply from $22,000 in 1967 to zero by 1973; funds from its Synod of Pennsylvania also decreased from $38,000 in 1967 to $27,000 in 1973. The state legislature could not appropriate money for independent colleges, but the state could grant scholarships and loans to college and university students. For the year 1971-1972, for example, the college received $238,000 in state scholarships. Under this program, many students bound for Waynesburg were aided by the state. By 1970 some federal money under the Economic Opportunity Grants program was also available to Waynesburg's students. The college continued to help talented, needy students; parents of such students were asked to submit confidential statements, indicating what part, if any, of their children's expenses they could pay. Selected students were then aided on the basis of this information. The independent colleges of Pennsylvania needed, and tried to get, more financial aid from the legislature. Rich lamented "that educators were notably poor lobbyists," and added: "The independent colleges particularly have shied away from the legislature. . . . " The Commission of Independent Colleges and Universities (CICU) had long stressed the important role of such institutions and of their need of financial support from the state.[35]

Funds from the federal government were available for certain purposes. The college could, and did, borrow federal money at low interest rates to build dormitories, because such loans were self-liquidating. Colleges receiving these funds had to abide by the Civil Rights Act of 1964, which forbade discrimination against persons on the ground of race, color, or national origin.[36]

The endowment fund rose rapidly. Its book value on 30 June 1963 was $1,223,507. Ten years later it had grown to $2,678,759, an increase of 119 percent. The market value of the endowment fund on 30 June 1973 was $2,905,599. Plant investment increased from $3,765,966 in 1963 to $9,237,649 in 1973. And in that decade, assets of the college more than doubled from $6,106,091 to $13,325,843.[37]

As the fund-raising campaigns proceeded, so did expansion and improvement of the physical plant. In May 1965 the trustees could foresee that the new interstate highway (I-79) would shortly bring Waynesburg within "50 minutes of Pittsburgh," put the college within that metropolitan area, and cause a rise in the price of property in Greene County. Their Development Committee held that all the real estate on the east side of Morris Street and north of Franklin Street should be college property. The open ground could be used in the intramural program and for nonvaristy as well as for varsity sports.[38]

Shortly an aerial survey was made of the campus and 100 acres in four directions around it. And an architect was employed to develop a Master Plan for it. A ten-year plan was projected. In addition to the science building and the humanities building, it called for the construction of a maintenance building, a men's dormitory, a women's dormitory, a campus center, a social science building, and a chapel. The plan also called for replacement of the old wing of Walton Hall; improvements and alterations in the gymnasium, Miller Hall, Hanna Hall, the Library, and College Field; the conversion of the student center in Benedum Hall to dining facilities; and the addition of tennis courts. The estimated total cost of these developments was $8,830,000.[39]

In May 1964 the college acquired the Fred Gordon farm. Its location some seven miles south of town was near the right of way of the new interstate highway. Its value would rise in the years ahead, but the college was fortunate to have such a generous bequest even for the immediate future. Its 174 acres were well situated, partly in a verdant valley and partly on gently rolling hills. With its two ponds, its superb timber tracts, its luxuriant vegetation, and its fertile soil it was an excellent auxiliary recreational and educational facility for the college.[40]

As additional property was acquired, new buildings were built, and old ones were renovated, the trustees provided for greater security of the college. In September 1966 they named John Rock, erstwhile member of the Pennsylvania State Police force, as Director of Campus Security. Their chief aim was to provide additional security and protection for students and the physical plant from outside influences. For several years Rock had been stationed in Waynesburg, and he well knew the community and the college. As Stoy put it: "We are fortunate to have a man of Mr. Rock's capabilities to direct this operation."[41]

The problem of lack of classroom space, which seriously plagued the college, was largely solved when two new buildings were ready for use. The Paul R. Stewart Science Building was dedicated on 20 September 1964. It had excellent classrooms, laboratories, and offices. A large auditorium in the Science Building was named the "Snyder Auditorium" in honor of William Penn Snyder, Jr., and in recognition of the support and assistance of the Snyder family.[42] After considerable debate among the trustees over the choice of a site, the Buhl Humanities Building was constructed on the area between the North Ward School and the Knox House and dedicated on 13 October 1968. It had sixteen classrooms, four seminar rooms, a lecture hall, a language laboratory, a band and choral practice room, art studios, a faculty lounge, and faculty offices. The lecture hall was named "McCance Auditorium" in honor of Pressly H. McCance, Director of the Buhl Foundation. Shortly it housed four Departments: English, Fine Arts, Modern Languages, and History and Social Sciences. The Stewart and Buhl buildings were attractive in design and modern in all respects.[43]

Student housing was greatly improved by the construction of new dormitories. "Ray Hall" was dedicated on 22 September 1963. It was used the first year as a men's dormitory, but in September 1964 it was changed to a women's dormitory; this made possible an increase of females entering the freshman class, but the college was temporarily hard-pressed to find enough room for male students.[44] Fortunately another men's dormitory was shortly constructed and named "Martin Hall" in honor of General Edward Martin. With this additional space for men, it was no longer necessary to use the Gymnasium Dormitory, considered substandard and a handicap to the recruiting program. That space thenceforth was used for student activities including Student Council, *Mad Anthony*, *The Yellow Jacket*, and the college radio station.[45] By late 1967 another women's dormitory had been constructed north of Denny Hall; it was named "Ross Burns Hall" in memory of Ross Burns, an alumnus, and long a devoted trustee of the college.[46] In 1971 Walton Hall ceased to be used as a dormitory. Shortly the college was renting it to the Intermediate Unit of the public school system for classroom purposes; certain "special education" groups were meeting there. The other end of that structure, long known as "The Corridors," and of more modern design, by 1973, was being used by the sororities, and for art studios.[47]

The college provided additional housing for married students. After World War II twelve housing units for married students were constructed, and the rent was $35 per month. In August 1970 the trustees planned to erect eight two-bedroom units, at a cost of $119,400, on college-owned land on the corner of Liberty Avenue and Walnut Street, just east of Purman Run Field. But, in January 1971, the local Planning Commission denied the College permission to erect these housing units on the Liberty Street site. The trustees then considered the Bonar Avenue site where the first Veterans Housing Project was located. There was plenty of room near that Project for the new units, and they were built there. These eight units were well equipped; older ones were also available for married students. Rents were most reasonable.[48]

Of the old buildings, Miller Hall received most attention. In August 1963, Ray, the President of the Board of Trustees, said "that it is essential for the prestige of the College at this point to have executive offices that are adequately furnished and attractively decorated." Accordingly, Stewart, as Chancellor, was provided with a renovated office. The office of the President and the adjacent one for his secretary were remodeled. Faculty mailboxes and the telephone switchboard were moved from the secretary's office to more appropriate places on the first floor of Miller Hall. New furniture, chandeliers, carpet, and drapes at the windows greatly improved the aesthetic qualities of those offices.[49]

Fireproofing of Miller Hall continued, and by 1964 it was completed on the first two floors. At that time old members of the literary societies were contributing funds to fireproof the third floor. By 1970 Alumni Hall, where chapel had been held for many years, had been completely remodeled. The stage, permanent seats, and pipe organ were removed. The stained glass windows were repaired. A cement floor replaced the wooden, splintery floor; the room was painted and fully carpeted. On 8 October 1971 a large crowd assembled there to hear a program entitled "An Evening of Music." On this pleasant occasion, Mrs. James T. Sutton presented to the college a piano of the finest quality, in memory of her late husband. The trustees desired to preserve Miller's portrait which had hung in that room for many years; it was cleaned and oiled as part of the Alumni Hall project.[50]

Early in 1971 a spacious, attractive conference room was finished and furnished on the second floor of Miller Hall. It was named "the Martin Room" in honor of General Edward Martin. Logs on each side of the fireplace came from the cabin in which he was born. The Martin family furnished funds for this fine facility.[51]

Numerous other changes were made in Miller Hall. By the late 1960's the first and second floors were entirely remodeled; administrative offices took up space which had formerly been used as classrooms. On the third floor a few classrooms and offices were located on either side of Alumni Hall. But on the fourth, the attic, one could still see signs of the Chicken Coop, the improvised basketball court of long ago.

Significant improvements were made in the Library. Noteworthy was a generous gift from Robert D. Thompson, '48, of Washington,

Pennsylvania, for the "Ellen Troutman Thompson Memorial Room" in memory of his wife, a deceased member of the Class of 1951, and a former student assistant in the Library. Located on the second floor of the Library, this is a spacious attractive room; it is used for periodicals, microfilms, government documents, and musical collections. The Librarian, May P. Clovis, rejoiced over this room, because of its great value to students and faculty.[52] An appreciable gift from Mrs. Warren S. Ege of Washington, D. C. was used to establish a room in memory of her father, the Honorable John Clark Knox, '02. Named the "John Clark Knox Memorial Room," it was located on the ground floor of the Library. With modern furniture and "a few pieces of Victorian influence," and indirect lighting and the best heating and ventilating systems, it is a quiet, comfortable place to study. With its predominant colors of red, beige, and green, its aesthetic qualities are striking.[53] Plans were made to establish on the top floor of the Library, adjacent to the "Thompson Room," a room in memory of Professor Arthur M. Mintier, the long-time history teacher and debate coach. Funds for it were solicited from the alumni, and by April 1971 some $4,000 had been pledged.[54] This room became a repository for collections useful to historians.

The gymnasium cried most loudly for improvements. It was described as "a large and solid structure . . . erected on a financial shoestring bit by bit" and "never finished." The ceiling was never completed. The lighting was poor. The outside of the building needed to be cleaned and pointed. Renovation of locker rooms was long overdue. It was the girls who suffered most because of the lack of facilities. Such deficiencies were the chief cause of student complaints. The administration and trustees resolved to remedy these conditions as soon as practicable. But the overall operation was of such proportions that it could not be accomplished in a short time. Improvements were planned in three steps: (1) to remove the Maintenance Department from the basement area intended originally for a swimming pool and to add a second floor in the large space thus vacated; (2) to construct a new building for the Maintenance Department and for storage of supplies; and (3), as a long term objective, to secure land on the west side of the gymnasium where an addition could be built for an expanded intramural program and a swimming pool. The first project, a most imperative one, was a new basketball floor. It had been in poor condition for several years. Beginning in June 1971, the "gods" came to the aid of the basketball squad by sending torrential rains, which clogged drains in the roof and caused leaks which warped the floor, making it useless. But by October 1971, in time for the forthcoming season, a new hardwood floor had been constructed, and better lights and new backboards were installed. Pending completion of these improvements, the basketball squad practiced on the Waynesburg Central High School's basketball court. Fortunately other renovations were made in the basement, the gymnastics room, and the locker area.[55]

Conditions at College Field were still unsatisfactory. Track teams and baseball squads from the college and the local high school practiced and played there. The crowded situation was somewhat alleviated in April 1966 when the Waynesburg Recreation Board gave a field near the town's sewage disposal plant for use by both institutions. The seating capacity at College Field was inadequate. In anticipation of a large crowd at the football game with Fairmont State College in 1968, that event was moved to Uniontown—to the consternation of some people in Waynesburg. By the fall of 1969, toilet facilities at the Field were enlarged by concrete block construction. The building in which teams met was improved by the installation of a ceiling and by additional lighting. The field was newly fenced; and bleachers which were "not permanent" were installed. These improvements were helpful, but it appears that they were intended to be temporary, pending the "possibility that other fields may be built—possibly by the county commissioners or by the school district—which the College would be able to use."[56]

Cognizant of Waynesburg's constantly changing character from a chiefly commuting college to a largely resident institution, in September 1967, the trustees resolved that the next project in the way of facilities on the campus should be a student center. Tentative plans called for a building on the site of Madison Hall, located southward across the street from Benedum Hall, plus additional, adjacent ground which would be most spacious, and would have all the recreational facilities one could desire for a student center.[57] Experience elsewhere had shown the desirability of combining student centers with dining facilities; in this arrangement such centers were most frequently used. Hence it was contemplated that Benedum Hall dining room would be joined to the new center. But these plans were too grandiose; funds were not sufficient for this purpose. And unfortunately overall fund-raising had, by 1970, slowed to the point where it was necessary to "reorder our priorities." The plan for the new center as such was abandoned. Instead the whole of Benedum Hall was extended south to the street, thus enlarging not only the dining area but the existing student center as well. Cost of this project was $500,000, part of which was available from the 125th Anniversary Fund. Such expansion provided, to some extent, the facilities originally planned, and thus achieved some measure of the original goal. The enlarged facility was "a small scale version of the larger student center we hope to have some day."[58]

While work proceeded on the expansion of Benedum Hall, the trustees were negotiating with directors of the Central Greene School District for the acquisition of North Ward School. For more than a century this building was a geographic misfit; it was located in the heart of the campus, which had expanded around it. For some three decades Stewart had hoped the college could own this property, and he had raised funds for this purpose. As early as April 1941 he talked with the trustees about purchase of the school, but no immediate action was taken. Early in 1966 a committee of trustees, on conferring with the school directors about possible purchase, learned that the building would still be needed as a public school for a few more years. It had been built in two stages. The original structure of four rooms was erected in 1863; it was named the "Union School"; the four front rooms were added in 1882. It was an elementary school, but the first high school in Greene County was established there in 1899, utilizing two rooms on the top floor. By October 1969 the building had deteriorated to the point where it was unsafe for use. It was then closed, and the 205 pupils were transferred to South Ward School.[59]

The building was vacant about three years. Almost immediately after it was abandoned, vandals began breaking the windows; the lawn was unkempt; and maintenance on the property was nearly nil. In January 1971 Rich told the trustees "this does not make a good impression on parents or other visitors to the campus, who assume that it is a college building." The trustees then were determined to acquire that site before someone decided to purchase it for a commercial enterprise of some kind.[60]

After lengthy negotiations with the school board, early in February 1972, the trustees purchased North Ward School for $42,500. They then faced the problem of either renovating or razing the building; consideration was given to both the architectural and historical standpoints. The architect who examined the structure said that "architecturally the original building was a gem. . . . " But the overall edifice had so deteriorated that it could not be salvaged. Hence in September 1972 the trustees took action to demolish the building and to prepare the area for intramural activities or parking.[61] Within a few days the building was razed. And students shortly were using the area (a lot 180 feet square) for recreation and exercise.

In October 1971 the trustees arranged to purchase another structure located in the heart of the campus, just behind Miller Hall. Called the "Challen W. Waychoff property," long ago it was a cottage where needy male students resided and cooked for themselves.[62] In more recent years, large additions had been built around the original edifice. Overall, it was a spacious, modern dwelling house in which the widow of the late Judge Waychoff resided. After her death, the trustees purchased it, and made it available, at reasonable rent, to administrators or to faculty members.

Purchase of North Ward School and of the Waychoff property rounded out the campus and made it contiguous in all its parts. The trustees constantly looked for ways to improve and beautify the campus and its environs, including the adjacent park. For example, in January 1966 they appointed a committee to confer with the Park Commission about the possibility of constructing crosswalks in Monument Park, in the east portion of the overall area of the old commons; the trustees offered to share in the cost of such an installation. The Park Commission's funds, however, were limited; and it was planning to use available money to rebuild the fountain and repair walks in College Park in front of Miller Hall. Nevertheless, the crosswalks in Monument Park were constructed with funds provided by the college, largely because the walks were necessary for students who crossed that area in going to classes, dormitories, and the dining hall.[63]

The administration and trustees considered the acquisition of two pieces of property in the business area of Waynesburg. One was the Fort Jackson Hotel, for many years the best in town. Overtures were made to the college in August 1963, September 1968, and April 1970. For one reason or another these offers were turned down. The Hotel was visualized as a possible dormitory, but it was located too far from the campus. Early in 1971 a committee of the trustees considered a proposal to remodel the Hotel into apartments to be leased to the college for use by married students. This proposal too was rejected.[64] The other building was known as the "Long Building," long the largest department store in Waynesburg. It was contemplated that this structure might be converted into a dormitory, but it too was off-campus too far; this distance would present tremendous control problems.[65] The trustees did not purchase it.

In September 1966 the Gulf Oil Company indicated its desire to acquire "Ivyhurst" from the college. At length such negotiations were completed. Located in mid-town, this was an ideal site for a filling station, which shortly was constructed there.[66]

The administrative staff, faculty, and trustees heeded Rich's call to "Come, labor on." In a spirit of excellent cooperation, they raised standards so that, after an impartial, objective evaluation by reputable scholars from the regional accrediting agency, accreditation could be reaffirmed. And, at Rich's exhortation, they strived toward higher goals and aimed to "go far beyond minimum requirements." In so doing, to a large extent, they transformed the college. The faculty was strengthened enormously; it was led in paths of true erudition and effective pedagogy. Fund-raising attained far higher figures than ever. Expansion of, and improvements on, the physical plant reached unprecedented proportions. In the total effort, the college won self-respect and, because it did so, it won the respect of its peers elsewhere. At long last, it "reached the mainstream" of higher education in America.

XXI
STUDENT LIFE, 1963-1974

In this period students were becoming increasingly restless under the regulations of college life. As elsewhere in the nation, they were demanding a role in the government and administration of the college; they wanted some voice in their own destiny as students. They showed discontent, particularly because of rules relating to social life on the campus. As always, they were interested in extracurricular activities. By the mid-1960's, partly by careful recruiting and partly by good fortune, the college had many students who proved not only their academic excellence, but also their superb ability as athletes.

Shortly after a freshman arrived for his first semester, he attended a series of orientation meetings. Most important from the scholastic viewpoint was academic orientation at which his departmental chairman discussed the scope and nature of the student's work and made suggestions about study habits, note-taking, use of the library, and so on. In other sessions the Dean of Student Life talked to the men about social activities and social behavior; and the Dean of Women did likewise to the women students.[1] Each freshman received a copy of the *Student Handbook* which contained general information about the college and the town. Unlike its antecedent a century before, it lacked detailed regulations relating to morality. It did, however, contain student life policies on drugs, firearms, gambling, hazing, drinking alcoholic beverages, use of motor vehicles, manner of dress, quiet hours, visiting privileges, and so forth.

Proctors, later called "resident advisers," aided in maintaining discipline in dormitories.[2] By 1968 all male freshmen and sophomores, all male scholarship-holders, all males with on-campus jobs, and "others that the College may designate," were required to live in the residence halls.[3] By 1970 senior women in good academic standing were permitted to reside off campus. While male students residing in dormitories could come and go as they wished, female students were still restricted in their hours. By 1971, however, only freshman girls were rigidly held accountable for specific hours. Late in 1973, the Human Relations Commission, a state agency, asked that regulations be equal for men and women. That body was somewhat critical of the traditional double standard of rules relative to housing on the campus. In October 1973, in line with a nationwide trend, some sixty students, including males and females, expressed their desires for co-ed dorm life. Though they were a small percentage of the student body, they contended that such was "a necessary part of college life at Waynesburg." In April 1974 the faculty voted down a recommendation that co-ed housing be optional. But it seemed only a matter of time until this practice would reach the campus—since it was becoming more prevalent over the nation. Another nationwide trend in the spring of 1974 was "streaking," in which a student in the nude rushed rapidly from one point to another in the presence of other persons. It reached the Waynesburg College campus early in March when two young men, clad only in tennis shoes and socks took a run around the park. Others took shorter runs on the campus and in certain buildings. Student reaction varied. In general, female students were highly embarrassed. But, of some "27 males contacted, only one seriously thought streakers were insane."[4]

Most members of the social fraternities resided in their respective houses. Women were permitted in first floor lounges of fraternity houses during certain hours. Nonfraternity men were not allowed in fraternity houses after 7:00 p. m. on Friday and Saturday, except for certain social events. By 1970 faculty members no longer chaperoned fraternity dances and parties. Thenceforth, officers of fraternities were to keep their own houses in order.[5]

The college had a policy of approved housing for students who were permitted to reside in private homes in the area. Customarily the deans visited local homes and saw what facilities were available; on the basis of such visitations, they compiled lists of approved homes to be given to students. The recent Civil Rights laws, however, required the college to list as approved only those houses whose owners signed a statement that they would not discriminate against students because of race, creed, or color. As of 1970 only ten were willing to sign this statement, which obviously limited the college's housing policy.[6]

To reside in private off-campus housing was generally deemed a privilege, and the college warned that a "corollary responsibility goes with this privilege." Each student was urged to conduct himself in such a way as not to bring discredit to the institution or community. Despite this exhortation, a growing minority of these students were trouble-makers. Their unbecoming behavior brought increasing hostility between them and the townsmen. In January 1971 the Executive Board of the Alumni Association expressed its concern over these conditions, asked for an investigation of the conduct of these students, and suggested the possibility of some kind of control. But the problem was serious. College officials could not enter private homes; each owner was responsible for residents in his house. The college did take action, however, to curb such misbehavior. When complaints reached the Student Life Office, the deans promptly investigated them. If students had violated college regulations or the laws of the land, and had damaged the institution's public reputation, they were subject to disciplinary action, which might include the loss of their off-campus housing privilege, suspension, dismissal, or expulsion.[7]

The perennial problem of absences from class persisted—and perplexed the faculty. As of November 1965, six absences in all (excused and unexcused) from class were permitted. A year later this figure was dropped in favor of a more general statement that a student was expected "to attend all scheduled class and laboratory periods for which he is enrolled." This policy still was unworkable. Consequently, by 1971 each faculty member was permitted to determine his own attendance policy. Individual policies were widely variable, ranging between extreme severity to the utmost leniency on class cuts.[8]

By 1967 compulsory chapel attendance was abolished and, instead of chapel, a system of convocations, which counted one point each, was established. Six convocations were held each semester; they might or might not be religious in character. Each student was required to attend four of the six convocations each semester—for a total of 32 points—in order to graduate. The students even opposed this system. Therefore, by 1969 the college terminated these convocations.[9]

But the end of compulsory chapel did not mean that "God was dead" on the campus. Soon many students showed an inherent interest in religion in their own ways. In the search for truth and in efforts to work out a philosophy of life, they began meeting freely and informally for exchanges of ideas. In the fall of 1967, the Reverend Robert W. Cahn, a graduate of Princeton Theological Seminary, was appointed Director of Religious Life on the campus; subsequently he was elevated to Dean of Student Life. Young, personable, and learned, he continued to be keenly interested in religious life on the campus and he encouraged students in work they were already doing in their quest for identity and a true sense of values. In February 1972 he reported:

> There is more religious ferment on campus now than there has been for many years. . . . Someone recently commented that in the calendar of events there are more Bible study and prayer meetings listed than anything else. Every week a Bible study and prayer group is meeting in the coffeehouse and every Wednesday evening another . . . group is meeting in the Science Hall. Student initiative has brought to the campus a number of groups with a clear-cut religious message. One of these groups came to the campus in connection with the Billy Graham crusade last fall. A special table has been set up in the Student Union which offers Christian literature for sale.[10]

While many students considered the search for eternal verities dearer than life itself, others—the immature—were vexed by rules, and they were inclined to frivolity or outright offenses. Hazing was strictly prohibited, but it became a problem at times. For example, in September 1969, after some complaints the faculty voted to limit hazing to the carrying of posters and the wearing of freshman dinks.[11] Smoking in classrooms and halls had always been prohibited. But this rule was frequently violated in the halls and, to a lesser extent, in classrooms. In January 1971 the faculty voted down a motion to permit smoking in classrooms, and thus held to tradition.[12]

In April 1965 the faculty expressed its displeasure with "Hell Week" and moved to direct the Fraternity Advisory Council to curtail it so that it no longer interfered with scholastic work. Shortly use of the expression "Hell Week" was abandoned in favor of "Help Week," which was infinitely more desirable. Under the new system, pledges to fraternities were not subjected to inane activities which might be detrimental to their health; instead they were urged to spend the week in careful study, in attendance at all classes and laboratories for which they were scheduled, and in work of a constructive nature.[13]

By the late 1960's irresponsible students were reporting bomb alerts to the administration. One wonders about their motives. In any case, there were several such alerts—and all proved to be phony. The perpetrators of such shenanigans were either unaware of, or did not care about, the resultant inconveniences to great numbers of students. In order to cope with the situation, Michael Talpas, the Registrar, prepared a "Rooms Available" summary which enabled faculty members to choose alternate meeting places in case of bomb threats.[14]

A serious offense was uncovered, in May 1972, in the use of campus telephones: it was ascertained that students had "found some method of by-passing the controls and making long distance calls without paying the toll." Within two and one-half months the total bill reached an incredible $10,000. Fortunately the telephone company was able to trace the calls, "and caught about 98 per cent of the offenders." Collections shortly began, and it was expected that most of this bill would be paid by the culprits.[15]

The illegal use of drugs by students was not evident until April 1966. In the first case of this kind on campus, three students and one ex-student participated in a party at a man's apartment downtown at which marijuana was smoked. The three students were promptly suspended. Thenceforth, the Student Life Office was alert to the possibility of a drug problem, but it was difficult to ferret out the facts. In May 1968 rumors were rife that students were illegally using drugs, but they were investigated and no evidence was found to support them.[16] In the spring of 1970, however, an objective survey, made by a sociology instructor on the faculty, showed that 43 percent of the male students and 25 percent of the female students had smoked marijuana. The survey revealed that, in most instances, these students were classified as "tasters," or those who had not smoked "the weed" more than three times. A smaller percentage of students used stimulants, known as "uppers," such as "speed" and methedrine. A still smaller percentage used depressants ("downers") such as tranquilizers and barbituates; about the same percentage confessed using hallucinogens such as LSD and mescaline. Practically no students were using the harder drugs such as morphine, heroin, and cocaine.[17] The college warned all students that misuse of marijuana and other drugs was against the laws of the land; and the institution would not protect them from prosecution under the laws. Moreover, the illegal use of drugs would lead to suspension, dismissal, or expulsion. But college policy was not entirely punitive. It recognized "that students who have taken or are taking marijuana and other drugs may need and wish to seek counseling." The college counselor, physicians, and deans were ready to help students with such problems.[18]

If there were sordid sides of student life, there were compensations in constructive extracurricular activities in which students engaged wholeheartedly. By 1970 the college had a new marching band, thanks to efforts by its able Director, Professor Allen C. Emerick. Supplied with new uniforms, new instruments, and new music, its members were most dedicated; they would represent the college well. The "Lamplighters," led by Professor James D. Randolph, were second to none in performance at such ceremonies as commencement and baccalaureate; and on tours to various institutions in the eastern part of the nation, they were excellent advertisers of Waynesburg College.[19]

Another fine extracurricular activity was the college's new radio station WKUL, successor to W3YGE of 1954 vintage, which began broadcasting on 18 October 1970. Students resurrected this project. Those first in charge were: Jerry Rutkowski, station manager; Wayne Gnatuk, public relations; Mike Todd, program director; and Gary Stewart, music director. Backed by the student government and the administration, these boys got some help in the form of literature from the local station, WANB; and technicians from Slippery Rock State College aided them in setting up the equipment. During the academic year, it broadcasted regularly from noon to midnight; its programs were of interest to students and faculty. It was a good means of communication between both. For example, in February 1973, Mark Kennedy, then student manager of WKUL, offered the station to all faculty members who had something to present to the student body. He announced to the faculty that one of the students had completed 150 consecutive hours as a disc jockey in a project to raise money for Greene County Memorial Hospital and to publicize the Benedum Challenge for the College. He asked the faculty for donations to the local hospital.[20]

There were other ways by which students served constructively. Those interested in journalism joined *The Yellow Jacket* staff; others worked on the school yearbook, *The Mad Anthony*; and still others produced the literary magazine, *The Courtier*. Some maintained the coffee house, called "Cross Roads," a place for campus dialogue, musical entertainment, film presentations, and group meetings. Here members of the administrative staff and the faculty met with students and discussed problems of mutual concern, such as tuition increases.[21]

By 1971 each residence hall was allotted a small budget for "certain activities to help fill the void in terms of social life." Christmas parties were held in the dormitories; and religious seasons, such as Advent, were observed. Part of Madison Hall was set aside for recreation early in 1969; pool tables, ping pong tables, and a television set were placed there for use by students. Early in 1971 more equipment for recreation and exercise was made available in the gymnasium. The philosophy of the Student Life Office was "to use all these facilities to the fullest extent for the benefit of our students."[22]

Of all extracurricular activities, the students were most outstanding in intercollegiate athletics. The football team merits first consideration, for it won the national championship in 1966. The story has been told in an excellent pamphlet entitled *The Road to the Championship*, edited by Richard D. Kunkle, '57, and published in 1966. The building of this team began in the fall of 1963 when Michael J. ("Mo") Scarry assumed his duties as Athletic Director and coach of football and basketball at the college. He had been a great athlete at Duquesne High School and at Waynesburg College, where he played football and basketball from 1939 to 1942 under the legendary Frank Wolf. After a hazardous tour of military duty in World War II, he entered professional football in which he was highly successful. Later he successfully coached football at Western Reserve University, Santa Clara University, Washington State University, and Loras College (in Iowa).[23] Having played football for Waynesburg, he felt a strong sense of devotion to the college.

As football coach, Scarry enjoyed winning seasons in 1963, 1964, and 1965. Shortly after the 1963 season, he was named "Coach of the Year" by the Pittsburgh Curbstone Coaches. After the 1964 season he was inducted into the NAIA Hall of Fame. In March 1965 the Waynesburg Junior Chamber of Commerce presented him a plaque for outstanding service to Waynesburg College and to the community of Waynesburg. After the 1965 season, the Yellow Jackets captured the West Penn Conference grid title.[24]

When Scarry was employed, he was promised some help in the way of a basketball coach. A tight budget, however, caused delay in providing funds to pay such a coach until plans were made for the budget for 1966-1967. Meanwhile, as we shall see, Scarry's basketball team was suffering setbacks. And he received an attractive offer from the Washington Redskins of the National Football League. There he would be an assistant coach, working with Otto Graham, his old friend, who was head coach of that organization. Scarry then faced a dilemma. He liked Waynesburg; his relationship with the college and the townspeople was excellent. As he put it: "It was the hardest decision I've had to make since beginning coaching." But he resigned, effective 31 March 1966.[25]

When Scarry left, certain changes were made in the Athletic Department. Coach Clayton P. Ketterling was appointed Athletic

Director; he continued as wrestling coach and assistant football coach. In keeping with plans for a head basketball coach, Harold O. King was chosen to that position. And, from some 43 applicants, Carl De Pasqua was selected as head football coach. Born in Williamsport, Pennsylvania, he had been a top player in high school there. In 1950 he won the A.B. degree at the University of Pittsburgh where he played at quarterback and "lettered in all four backfield positions." When he came to Waynesburg, he was a veteran of fifteen years of coaching. At Waynesburg he was assisted by Ketterling, King, and William Hardisty.[26]

During spring practice in 1966, the football squad, including 24 lettermen, showed great enthusiasm. De Pasqua said the team would be successful if this order were followed: "defense, the punting game, and the offense. . . . " He hoped that "performance on the field of play will distinguish each boy in his own right."[27]

His hopes were not in vain. The team won all nine of its regularly scheduled games—some by lopsided scores. Next they won a play-off game by a score of 30-27 against the "Cowboys" of New Mexico Highlands University, at Albuquerque, on 26 November 1966. Such games were sponsored by the National Association of Intercollegiate Athletics (NAIA), the nation's largest organization for colleges of moderate enrollment with sound athletic philosophies and programs. After the game, in accord with NAIA policy, both head coaches exchanged presents at a banquet in Albuquerque. De Pasqua gave New Mexico Highlands University Coach Jack Schofield a coal miner's hat, lamp, and belt symbolic of the bituminous coal area in southwestern Pennsylvania; Schofield then presented De Pasqua a hand-carved replica of New Mexico's state bird, the Road Runner. In the game both teams played admirably and showed fine sportsmanship. On returning to Waynesburg the team was given a rousing reception. They were banqueted in the local Elks Club, where De Pasqua received an award from that organization. On the same occasion, the Greene County Court presented the "Distinguished Performance Award" to coaches and members of the Yellow Jacket Team. Judge Glenn R. Toothman made the presentation—the first one of its kind—to De Pasqua. Waynesburg College was Pennsylvania's first finalist in an NAIA championship game.[28]

After the victory over New Mexico Highlands University, the Yellow Jackets turned their attention to Tulsa, Oklahoma, location of the game for the national championship, on 10 December 1966. Their opponent in that game was Whitewater State University,

Whitewater, Wisconsin, one of some ten campuses which comprised Wisconsin State University. In its playoff game, Whitewater trounced Central College, located at Pella, Iowa, by a score of 41 to 18.[29]

The Yellow Jackets received many messages wishing them good luck in Tulsa. William W. Scranton, Governor of Pennsylvania, wired Waynesburg his wishes: "Whitewash Whitewater." In what De Pasqua called a "Cinderella experience," Waynesburg clobbered Whitewater 42 to 21. Following the game a banquet was held at which a large red-and-blue Champions' Banner and the magnificent five and one-half foot silver traveling trophy were presented to the Yellow Jackets; and each teammate received a wrist watch. In accord with NAIA policy, gifts symbolic of the area represented by each team were exchanged between the two coaches: De Pasqua gave Coach Forrest Perkins, of Whitewater, a coal miner's cap, belt, and lamp; and Perkins reciprocated with a traditional Wisconsin cheese.[30]

On learning that the Yellow Jackets were the national champions, the jubilation at the college and in Waynesburg was without parallel in the annals of both. Reminiscent of some victories in the old days, students "rushed pell-mell to the courthouse steps" where an impromptu victory rally was held. Students quickly put up banners and signs, "Waynesburg—No. 1 in the Nation." Wilma Milliken, Mayor of Waynesburg, issued a special proclamation setting aside 12 December 1966 as a day of general rejoicing and urging "the entire citizenry to display flags and college banners and thereby share in the joy of our college community."[31]

Many praises were heaped upon the champions. According to Joseph A. Axelson, Assistant Executive Secretary of the NAIA, "the Waynesburg players best exemplified the Association's basic concepts of the ideal American college athlete both as individuals as well as athletes."[32] On 12 December 1966, Rich congratulated the team, saying they "were a credit to the college." The faculty passed a motion to congratulate the team on the outstanding season and on "their daily preparation and weekly performance in athletics." Trustee Jack Wiley, who saw the game at Tulsa, said "the college and the community could be proud of them."[33]

On 5 February 1967, the college administration honored the champions at a banquet in Benedum Hall, to which their parents were invited. With Jack Wiley as master of ceremonies and some 400 in attendance, the occasion was most pleasant. De Pasqua said the attitude of the team was "the finest I have ever seen in any team." At the end of the banquet, Rich presented each player a personalized memorial plate with each 1966 game and score imprinted on it.[34]

In addition to honors from the Waynesburg area, De Pasqua and the champions were lauded on a wider scale. He was named "Outstanding Coach" in the tri-state area. And on 10 January 1967, at a banquet in Washington, D. C. the Washington Touchdown Club presented him an award acclaiming "the 1966 Waynesburg College football team as the 'top small-college' team in the nation." In March 1967 De Pasqua received the Knute Rockne Touchdown Club's Coach-of-the-Year award, at Kansas City, Missouri.[35]

The team enjoyed another winning season in 1967. It lost only one game—against Fairmont State College, 7-0. After that season, De Pasqua received an attractive offer from the Pittsburgh Steelers. He resigned in order to join the coaching staff of that professional football organization.[36]

Shortly Dr. Darrell J. Lewis replaced De Pasqua as head football coach. A dentist by profession, Lewis had been a star quarterback for three years for the University of Pittsburgh. Subsequently he had served on "Pitt's" coaching staff. Lewis was fortunate to inherit several stars, who had played under De Pasqua and Scarry. The Yellow Jackets had three more consecutive winning seasons in 1968, 1969, and 1970. After the 1968 season, Lewis was named West Penn Conference "Coach of the Year."[37]

In 1971 the football fortunes of the Yellow Jackets fell, and the Yellow Jackets suffered their first losing season in eleven years—with two wins, seven losses, and no ties. The 1972 season was even more disastrous—with one win and eight losses. On 10 January 1973 Lewis resigned.[38]

Immediately the administration and trustees sought a new football coach. From some 45 applicants, they chose Hayden Buckley to the position. At that time, in light of the economic situation, they made a change in the administrative organization of the Athletic Department. Buckley became Athletic Director as well as head football coach. Ketterling was shifted from the post of Athletic Director to Assistant Director of Financial Aid; he retained his duties as head wrestling coach and golf coach.[39]

Buckley was well qualified for the tasks ahead. He won the A. B. degree at Ohio Wesleyan University, and the M. Ed. at Kent State University. He began his coaching career in high school and, in 1959, was named "Ohio Valley Coach of the Year." Subsequently he had successful coaching experience at Washington University, at the University of Virginia, and at West Virginia University. He came to Waynesburg on 1 March 1973, and immediately attacked the main problem—recruiting. On 14 August 1973 Buckley, assisted by full-time coaches William Hardisty and John Westenhaver and by part-time coaches Ernest Benedict, Larry Piper, Frank Mosier and William Tornabene, began working with a 70-man squad, 41 of whom were freshmen. Buckley believed there was plenty of potential in these freshmen, and added: "With hard work, I'm confident they will be able to help us in the future." With able assistants, a goodly number of players, and a strong sense of dedication, improvement seemed certain. As Buckley said: "The only way for us to go is up." The road upward was started in the 1973 season with three wins and five losses; 1974 saw six wins and three losses. The players showed they could compete respectably against their rivals.[40]

If the football team reached the top among small colleges in the nation, and later floundered, the wrestling team under Ketterling continued to be a consistent winner. From 1963 to 1974 the wrestling teams achieved an admirable overall record of 121 wins, 41 losses, and 3 ties. In 1965, in their respective weight classes, "Tony" Gusic and "Mike" Zrimm became Waynesburg's first NAIA national champions. In 1969 "Dick" Pollock took third place, in his class, at the NAIA Tournament; and "Bob" Flint and "Bill" Buchanan took fifth place in their classes. In 1970 Pollock repeated with a third place; and in 1971 he came out fourth.[41]

With such records made by his grapplers, Ketterling came into the limelight not only on the national scene, but also on the world scene. In October 1972 he was named chairman of the national selection committee for the NAIA Hall of Fame. And, two months later, the NAIA Executive Committee appointed him to the United States Olympic Wrestling Games Committee for a term ending after the 1976 Olympic Games.[42]

Of the major sports, basketball continued to suffer most from 1963 to 1972. Beginning in 1963, as we have seen, Scarry was head basketball coach in addition to his onerous duties as Athletic Director and head football coach. At the outset of his first season as basketball coach, he lamented the lack of hustle and spirit in his team. At the end of that season, with 6 wins and 14 losses, Scarry said: "This has been the toughest year of my life, even though I've had losing seasons before." In three seasons, 1963 to 1966, his teams won 19 games and lost 47.[43] When Scarry left, the trustees employed Harold O. King, who held a B. S. from

Michigan State University, as head basketball coach. But the team continued to lose: from 1966 to 1969 it won 12 games and lost 59. After that last season, King left.[44]

Shortly the trustees named Rudolph ("Rudy") Marisa as head basketball coach and tennis coach. A native of Fredericktown, Pennsylvania, Marisa won his bachelor's degree from Pennsylvania State University, and his master's degree in Physical Education from West Virginia University. He was chosen because of his superior knowledge of the game and his past experiences in the area. He was a star player as an undergraduate. And his coaching career was excellent: at Dunbar High School, in his first year as coach there, he gave the school its first winning season in eleven years; and from 1960 to 1966, he coached at Albert Gallatin High School, and produced two WPIAL sectional championships—in 1961 and 1964. He was well qualified to bring a new era in basketball to the college.[45]

During 1970-1971, Marisa produced a team which gave the college its first winning season (13 wins, 10 losses) in twenty years. The team suffered reverses in the 1971-1972 season, but it bounded back in 1972-1973 and won 14 and lost 10 games; this was considered the best team the college had had in some twenty-two years. In the 1973-1974 Marisa guided his team to 15 wins and only 6 losses. After that season he received two honors: NAIA District 18 "Coach of the Year," and "All-District Coach of the Year."[46]

From 1963 through 1971 the varsity baseball team continued to endure losing seasons. But, under Hardisty, the Yellow Jackets surged upward in 1972 and completed the best season since 1955, with 10 wins and 8 losses. The next season brought even better results with a 10-5 record, and entry into the NAIA District 18 playoffs in Pittsburgh. Unfortunately the Yellow Jackets were eliminated in these games. But their season record was one of the best in the annals of athletics at the college.[47]

During the decade from 1964 through 1973 the cross country team, under Coach Tom Ciminel, enjoyed a majority of winning seasons. In all "meets" they were competing against strong teams in the tri-state area.[48]

In the mid-1960's the varsity golf team, coached by Joseph ("Joe") Conklin showed much improvement over their predecessors for more than two decades. Beginning in 1968, with Ketterling as coach, the golfers won consistently each year through 1973. In May 1973 the Yellow Jackets placed ninth from a field of thirteen golf teams in the NAIA District 18 Golf Championship meeting at the New Castle Country Club.[49]

Varsity tennis, with the exception of the years 1950 to 1957 when there was no team, had been in the doldrums since 1949. The Yellow Jackets had enjoyed their last winning seasons in 1947 and 1948 with Edward J. ("Joaquin") Patterson, '49, as coach. "Joaquin," as he was affectionately called, was a star tennis player in Waynesburg High School and in Waynesburg College, where he was both coach and captain of the team. Well liked by his players, he was "probably the best tennis player ever to come out of Greene County. . . . " Fortunately for the college, he returned in 1964 to serve, along with Eugene Strosser, as tennis coach. Patterson was then Assistant Superintendent of Schools, for Special Education, in Greene County. The results of his skill, leadership, and dedication to his Alma Mater were soon apparent: in 1965 the team won 6 matches and lost 3; and in 1966, with a record of 10 wins and 1 loss, the Yellow Jackets were West Penn Champions. By that time, Patterson had joined the faculty of the college and had been appointed Chairman of the Psychology Department. With this full schedule, it was impossible for him to continue his labors for the tennis team. Consequently a series of losing seasons again set in. It was 1971, with Marisa as coach, before the tennis team got on the winning trail with 5 wins and 4 losses. The team was again on the upgrade; the record for 1973 was 6 wins and 2 losses.[50]

While the varisty athletes, who comprised a minority of the student body, competed respectably against their opponents, the college provided an intramural program for the great majority of students who otherwise would have lacked facilities for recreation and physical exercise. In 1972 chess, swimming, weight-lifting, and wrestling were added to the usual sports for males. Intramural sports for females included archery, badminton, basketball, golf, softball, tennis, and volleyball. Available evidence shows that a high percentage of students engaged in these sports. For example, in 1972-1973, when Jay H. Payne, Jr., was in charge of this program, in a total enrollment of some 1,000 students, males were participating as follows: 250 in basketball, 235 in football, 251 in softball, 238 in volleyball, and lesser numbers in the other sports. The aim was to offer every male student the opportunity to participate regardless of his level of ability. Beginning in the fall of 1973, John Westenhaver succeeded Payne as director of the intramural program, and as an assistant football coach. Under the tutelage of these likable, young coaches, some students became sufficiently adept in intramural sports to join varsity teams.[51]

The administration and trustees constantly tried to promote the general welfare of the students and to maintain a strong athletic program. The overall results were commendable.

XXII
PROBLEMS AND PROSPECTS

DURING RICH'S ADMINISTRATION CERTAIN PROBLEMS AROSE WHICH had never before confronted the college. Some stemmed from the views and actions of young, liberal-minded members of the faculty who wanted to break away from tradition. In accord with a national trend, students made new demands on the administration, faculty, and trustees; they increasingly resented rules and regulations; and they were intolerant of supervision of their social and sexual activities. Problems were posed by the acts of a director of religious activities, by a dispute over an avowed Communist who was invited to speak on the campus, by obscene language and beer advertisements in *The Yellow Jacket*, by the race question, by a series of programs called "sexuality week," and by the unionization of nonacademic personnel. It took a great deal of thought, tact, and patience to find solutions to these problems. To crack down on small, determined minorities either in the faculty, among nonacademic personnel, or in the student body might further aggravate problems and lead to violence, strikes, or even open rebellion. Another problem, different in character, was the Uniontown Center, which was transferred to Pennsylvania State University. Still another was the decline in enrollment and the consequent decrease in income from tuition in the early 1970's. But these obstacles were largely surmounted, and the college looked optimistically to the future.

The rapidly changing attitude of students should be considered first, because it was related to other problems. In April 1965 Alexander G. Sidar, Jr., Dean of Student Life, told the trustees:

> There is a movement on the part of college students to press for rights in the college community which are beginning to infringe on the right

> of the faculty to teach, the right of the administrators to administer, and even the right of trustees to discharge their obligations in the government of the institution. In the next few years all colleges can expect to be faced with student demonstrations of one kind or another. . . . It is possible that in a few years they will reach the Waynesburg campus and the trustees should be aware of this trend. . . . Waynesburg students at the moment are restless, but not mutinous.[1]

The new student movement had such strong implications that, by 1968, the American Association of University Professors (AAUP) and four other leading professional organizations endorsed a document entitled "Joint Statement of the Rights and Freedoms of Students." This document was so significant that Rich desired all the trustees to become familiar with it. He explained that it did "not apply only to Waynesburg College, but to 2,300 colleges across the country." Students everywhere were making demands relating to such matters as "conduct of the faculty, the keeping of students' records, [and] the judiciary system whereby students may be dismissed. . . . " Rich pointed to the need for establishing legal procedures in almost every phase of college life. The AAUP, while considerate of students' rights and freedoms, opposed any action by students which might disrupt the regular and essential operation of institutions. Many of the policies set forth in the "Joint Statement" were already in force at Waynesburg College.[2]

By October 1970 this movement reached the Waynesburg campus. The student governing body, known as the Student Senate,[3] then came forth with a variety of "campus grievances." With regard to the curriculum, it proposed an interdepartmental day to discuss course offerings; it would drop physical education, religion, and foreign language requirements. It expressed the students' desire for guidance services and information for graduates. The students also wanted all faculty and trustee meetings open to them, and student membership on the Board of Trustees. They demanded that "double jeopardy be ended"; customarily, if a student committed a crime in town, he was punished by the local civil authorities and also by the college. They wanted "a review board, consisting of students only, to investigate student charges of inefficiency against administrators and faculty, and to make evaluations and recommendations to the President of the College." A long list of other demands included improvement in the infirmary's facilities and hours; a student-run bookstore; housing for sororities; permission to smoke in the cafeteria; "no dressup day on Sunday"; laundry facilities, refrigerators and milk in dormitories; student use of kitchens in dormitories;

more cigarette and vending machines; more parking facilities; more improvements in rooms; open dormitories on weekends; better food; and chocolate milk in the cafeteria.[4]

The Student Senate, doubtless aware that some of these demands were either impracticable or utopian, did not insist that they all be met. At its weekly meetings it was concerned chiefly with things that had always interested students such as plans for Homecoming, the election of the May Day Queen and her court, the choice of "Campus Cover Girl," participation in fund-raising for the college and the local hospital, and the promotion of extracurricular activities. Instead of having students on the Board of Trustees, the Student Senate was content to have two students on the Student Life Committee of that body; the aim was "to have student input on matters concerning the student body." The Student Senate welcomed trustees and members of the administrative staff to its meetings for the purpose of better communication. For example, it was grateful to Stoy for his comments on the financial operation of the institution; and to Trustee W. Robert Thompson for his light on a possible R. O. T. C. program for the college. By and large, the trustees did not object to having students as members of their Student Life Committee, but they opposed student membership on the Board of Trustees.[5] By 1970 students, selected by the Student Senate, were regularly attending faculty meetings; and some were serving on faculty committees. By the fall of 1972 the students were organized into committees somewhat parallel to the faculty committee system. The student "academic committee" was interested in an objective evaluation of the faculty; and in a pass-fail system in which weak students could take twelve semester-hours, out of the total needed for graduation, on a pass-fail basis.[6] Relations between the faculty, students, and trustees in general remained cordial. Lines of communication were kept open. In times of tension, cooler heads prevailed. Fortunately the college did not suffer from violence, destruction, and death which visited numerous other institutions in the nation.

In May 1967 the administration faced a serious problem commonly called the "Benson affair." For some years the college had needed a strong religious leader—one capable of stirring interest in chapel and in conducting other religious activities on the campus. In August 1966 the trustees employed the Reverend Dennis C. Benson, Jr., a preacher at Faith United Presbyterian Church, Tinley Park, Illinois, as Director of Religious Activities. Benson held an A. B. from the University of Michigan, and a B. D. from McCormick

Theological Seminary. He was the sort of man who appealed to youth; he was young, and had lots of energy and a dynamic personality. He was highly recommended for the position. Rich felt that "he will fit in well and meet the needs of our student body." Benson's duties were to develop and coordinate religious activities on campus, to counsel students, to establish liaison with local churches, and to advise student religious groups.[7] Since he would be working chiefly with students, he was assigned to the Student Life Office headed by Dean Sidar.

Benson vigorously plunged into his work, but he soon met adverse criticism and outright opposition. Believing in equality of the races, he condemned the local attitude toward blacks as a "middle class suburban world view." He wondered if local barbershops served all regardless of race, if any student could get off-campus housing in college-approved homes regardless of color of skin, and if blacks dated whites. Black students told him they were not accepted on campus. Hence Benson established SNARE, a student group dedicated to promoting racial equality. He contended that students should have a voice in everything, to become mature; in the belief that they should be free to express their grievances, he began a movement dubbed "Operation Upswing." Wanting "to make people think," he created a coffeehouse called the "Salt Cellar"—a dark, simply furnished room where students could have coffee and cogitate.[8]

In February 1967 Benson was adversely criticized, because of his unconventional methods. A trustee lamented "that the Salt Cellar is dark, not too clean, and the use of wine, whiskey, brandy bottles, etc., for table decorations is in poor taste. . . . " He also deplored a news sheet produced by promoters of that rendezvous. Rich asked for patience in making judgments of Benson. He called Benson "a dedicated individual who has good support from the churches in this area."[9] But Benson's "impact on the total student body was limited and he was not able to work completely or effectively within the structure of the student life office." The problem was essentially an internal one "involving failure to work within the organizational structure." Further, "his methods were suspect and led to a lack of confidence in his value to the college."[10] For these reasons Benson's contract was not renewed.

On learning of Benson's dismissal, a highly vocal, determined minority of the faculty came to his defense. They pointed out his merits in a faculty meeting, and moved that he be re-employed. The motion was lost. The dissenters still complained, and showed their unhappiness at a demonstration for Benson at commencement.

There a small group of students, joined by a few others in the community, "marched for Benson." Fortunately they did nothing to disrupt proceedings on that occasion.[11]

During the Benson controversy, another one arose over a Communist who was to speak on the campus. In November 1966, apparently without informing Rich of their plans, some faculty members invited Dr. Herbert Aptheker, Director of the American Institute of Marxist Studies, to speak in chapel on "A Marxist Interpretation of the Civil War," late in January 1967. Immediately there was apprehension over Aptheker's advent, which was delayed until 25 April 1967. Previously he had spoken at Latrobe, Pennsylvania, and "there was a disturbance. Some in Waynesburg feared there would be one here." There was some feeling among the trustees that the program should be canceled. Rich said on 2 February 1967, "that if the invitation is withdrawn now, some members of the faculty would be very much upset, and he expressed confidence that the situation could be handled without any harm to the College." In order to mollify the controversy, Rich said he would insist that there be at least one other speaker on the program to counter Aptheker's arguments. Accordingly, Dr. David MacDonald, a specialist on the reconstruction period after the Civil War, from the University of Pittsburgh, was scheduled to speak with Aptheker at the chapel program, on the morning of 25 April 1967; and in the afternoon, at the Student Center, Dr. John Williams, Chairman of the Political Science Department of West Virginia University, plus some members of Waynesburg's own faculty, were to be on a panel discussion with Aptheker. But the idea of a balanced program evoked much opposition from some faculty members and students. Early in March, some trustees, fearing possible violence and destruction to property, felt that the program should be canceled. To cancel it at that late date, however, "would be a sign of weakness and would promote discomfort among faculty and students." Rich lucidly pointed to the basic problem by saying "that the crux of the situation is not Dr. Aptheker particularly, but whether or not the College as an educational institution is open enough to let persons of varied opinions come in and talk to the students."[12] The controversy ended when, shortly before the program was to take place, Rich received word from Aptheker that Mrs. Aptheker was in serious condition resulting from surgery. Aptheker expressed regrets that he could not keep his appointment.[13]

Two notable developments resulted chiefly from this controversy. First, available evidence suggests that a few individuals declared they would no longer support the college financially.[14] Second, in the hope of avoiding other similar conflicts, the college adopted a speaker's policy. Liberal in nature, it permitted students to hear speakers "who represent another thought pattern, another value system, or another culture. Such encounters are the laboratories of learning." It made clear, however, that "the viewpoints expressed by speakers who came to the campus do not necessarily reflect the views of those who study, teach, or administer at Waynesburg College."[15]

If the Benson and Aptheker problems were perplexing, equally so was obscene language in *The Yellow Jacket*. The college was not alone in facing such a problem; many collegiate newspapers over the nation were in the hands of minorities of students who seemed bent on testing one of the basic tenets upon which the republic was founded, namely, freedom of the press. Late in 1969 and early in 1970, *The Yellow Jacket* had several accounts by students which included obscene words. Shortly alumni, trustees, and parents of some students complained about such language and contended that it reflected badly on the college. Rich explained that "freedom of the press has never been absolute." He also was instrumental in establishing a "College Publication Review Board," consisting of faculty members, administrators, and students, to set up guidelines for college publications. Simultaneously, the editor of *The Yellow Jacket* wrote a letter to the trustees in which he protested a recent increase in tuition. Several trustees felt the boy should have been ousted from school "or at least should have been removed as editor of *The Yellow Jacket*." Meanwhile more obscenities appeared in this newspaper. By April 1970, Rich had issued a statement ordering the cessation of the use of words deemed to be indecent. The editor held that, if the paper was to be censored, it would be difficult to get a staff to produce it, "because nobody wants to work under conditions which involve censorship. . . . " Furthermore, some students might start "an underground paper with all its attendant viciousness." Shortly a beer advertisement appeared in several issues of *The Yellow Jacket*—to the consternation of several trustees. And Rich's moratorium on certain words was broken twice. Removal of the editor was then contemplated, but he promised that "no incident would occur for the remainder of the year."[16]

Trouble over the newspaper started again shortly after the opening of the semester in the fall of 1970. The College Publication Review Board had been working on a temporary basis without participation of all members of the newspaper staff. Hence on 18 September

1970, *The Yellow Jacket* staff temporarily suspended publication of the paper, "because it did not agree with the plan put into effect by the administration on an interim basis." By 1 October 1970 a document resulting from the labors of faculty members, students, administrators, and the Publications Review Board was acceptable to the Student Senate, the faculty, the administration, and the trustees. Publication of the paper resumed on 9 October 1970.[17] It appears that the paper still contained filthy language, because on 10 November 1970, publishers of *The Democrat Messenger*, which printed *The Yellow Jacket*, announced they would no longer do so "until editors delete the 'smut' from its pages." An official of *The Democrat Messenger* said: "It's not only degrading to us, but the staff at the college as well."[18] The controversy continued for several weeks; demands to close down the paper were countered by pleas for freedom of the press. Finally students realized the unfavorable publicity given the college, and they used restraint the rest of the year.[19]

By the middle and late 1960's the question of racial discrimination came to the fore. A century after the Civil War, black people all over the nation were demanding equality; recent civil rights acts aimed to guarantee it, but to achieve it in fact was difficult. In March 1965 an incident arose on the Waynesburg campus, which, although not directly related to any local problem, was indicative of the nationwide feeling about equality. The Reverend James Reeb of Boston, Massachusetts, had just been beaten to death in Selma, Alabama, for speaking out in favor of political equality. Shortly thereafter Dr. W. Landis Jones, Assistant Professor of Political Science at the college, led a march in sympathy for civil rights from the campus to the courthouse steps, "protesting the treatment of Negroes and whites who participated in the Negro voter movement in Selma, Alabama." In a brief talk, Jones called for equality of civil rights in fact "so blacks could join clubs, fraternities, sororities, and unions." He called Reeb "a man who laid down his life for his fellowmen."[20]

The college made every effort to comply with civil rights legislation. It attempted to assure that off-campus housing was nondiscriminatory by sending a letter to local home owners, asking them to accept students as roomers without discrimination. But only a small percentage complied with this request. The college tried to recruit more black students and to employ blacks as faculty members and administrators. At Rich's behest, consideration was given to inclusion on the Board of Trustees "individuals representing other phases of our clientele," such as Roman Catholics, Jews, and blacks. By April 1970 the college established a Race Relations Committee consisting of 14 members including faculty, administrators, and students, which came forth with a "Recommended Policy Statement" which declared: "Every person associated formally with Waynesburg College in its internal institutional life, whether a member of the faculty, staff, or student body, is to be free from discrimination based on race, creed, color, or national origin." It further declared that the college would conduct its relations with local organizations "beyond the campus in such a way that the integrity of its non-discriminatory policy shall not be jeopardized."[21]

The college aimed to improve the lot of nonacademic personnel. In February 1965, Stoy called attention to the good program of fringe benefits for the faculty, and added: "There is a need for fringe benefits for non-academic personnel, clerical staff, maintenance people, cooks, etc." He called on the appropriate committee of trustees "to study this problem and work out a program" to help such personnel. But action on this matter came slowly. In February 1969 the trustees considered granting to any employee of the college remission of tuition charges for children or spouse. It had been customary to extend this privilege only to faculty members and their families. Instead of remission of full tuition, however, the trustees provided "for remission of one-half tuition to the spouse of a full-time non-professional employee. . . . "[22] Early in 1970 a policy of granting sick leave to full-time nonacademic personnel was established. A retirement policy provided for their retirement at age 65, but they could work beyond that age, up to 70, by mutual agreement "between the employer and employee. . . . " Nonacademic personnel had insurance coverage, including major medical insurance, which was increased by June 1970.[23]

In the fall of 1970 the college encountered a labor problem, after the United State Department of Labor examined the college payroll and found that women employees were not paid the same hourly rate as men employees. Women were engaged chiefly in dusting, sweeping, and cleaning in toilet and shower rooms; they did not operate scrubbing machines or do other heavy work. But the federal labor investigator claimed "that 70 per cent of the time the man is doing the same work women are doing." He insisted on the principle of "equal pay for equal work," as provided by the Fair Labor Standards Act of 1938. The investigator also found that the college had a practical nurse on duty, who lived in the infirmary, and was available at night if a student became ill. He contended that, if she were awakened in the night to care for a student, the college owed her for an additional eight-hour day. By April 1971, after a hearing in Philadelphia, a settlement was worked out. The college had to pay all cleaning and maintenance personnel at the same rate; and the practical nurse was to be paid back wages due her. Job descriptions for each type of work were to be drawn up.[24]

Late in 1971, certain nonacademic personnel, including maintenance workers, secretaries, and food service employees, indicated their desire to become unionized. Shortly the trustees petitioned the National Labor Relations Board (NLRB) "to hold an election to determine whether or not the people really want a union." The election was held on 1 February 1972, and the vote was 44 to 24 in favor of affiliation with the Service Employees International Union, AFL-CIO. The chairman of the drive to unionize was Glenn De Poe. The aims of unionization were "job security, fringe benefits, and salary increases." This labor organization had earlier unionized employees of Greene County and of the local hospital. It had done likewise with employees at the University of Pittsburgh and at Washington and Jefferson College. Waynesburg College was the last to be affected. The Finance and Property Committee of the trustees felt "that the integrity and judgment of Mr. Stoy should be relied upon to negotiate a fair and equitable contract." That Committee wanted to avoid a strike, but it was aware there was "a limit to the financial ability of the college to meet exorbitant demands." Stoy was able to negotiate satisfactorily with the new labor organization on campus. On 6 December 1972, on behalf of the college, he signed "the first Union contract ever signed by Waynesburg College." Fortunately the college was financially able to meet the demands of the union. But Rich warned: "We may see harder times than we are now having. . . . The labor problem will get worse as the years go on."[25]

In the spring of 1972, a series of meetings lasting a week, and referred to as the "sexuality seminar" led to heated argument. Planned by a committee composed of faculty and students, the aim was to show the relationship between Christian principles and teaching about sexuality. One of the programs, dealing with homosexuality, was most controversial. Sponsors of the seminar contended that the students had gained "an enormous educational experience" by seeing how homosexuality was a sick way of life. But some of the trustees, chiefly those who attended parts of the seminar, had other views. One said "he regretted the reaction of the outside community and felt that the week was costly." Another lamented that "he had read more about sex in *The Yellow Jacket* than he had seen in any other paper. This paper is read by other people," and harm "is done to the College." He contended that this seminar "split the community [and] the Board of Trustees, and we cannot afford to have a repetition."[26] No such seminar was presented in 1973 and 1974.

If student affairs posed problems for the faculty, administration, and trustees, so did the Uniontown Center. When Rich took the helm the Center was still thriving, although enrollment had started to decline in 1960. Despite this, in the fall of 1963, plans were made to construct a "new Uniontown Extension Building," which hopefully would solve the recruiting problem there. The college took steps to acquire property on which the building was to be constructed, and a fund-raising campaign was begun for that purpose. The estimated cost of construction was $297,000. By May 1964, of this sum, the college had approximately $100,000 in cash, and pledges amounting to about $125,000. It was assumed that not all pledges would be paid, and that there would be a shortage of about $100,000. To equip the building would require at least an additional $50,000. It was obvious that more money must be raised, and the college looked chiefly to the people of Uniontown and Fayette County for help. Working together, it was visualized that, within three years, the college would: (1) construct the building; (2) step up the recruiting policy, backed by financial aid from the Fayette community; (3) adhere to high admission standards like those at the Waynesburg campus; and (4) develop a "vigorous and well-qualified administrative staff at the Center." Steps of this nature would "keep faith with the people of Fayette County." On 21 May 1964, Rich recommended that a committee of trustees be appointed to work with the administrative staff on these plans.[27]

Between May and September 1964, however, the picture changed completely. In the interim civic and college leaders made a special study of the higher educational needs of Fayette County. The aim was to discover what kind of program would be best for "the broad and varied vocational needs of post-high school young people." By the fall of 1964 Pennsylvania State University wished to establish centers at Beaver, Sharon, and Uniontown. Waynesburg was delayed in building the new Center by faulty titles to the property which the college needed. Decline in enrollment at the Center continued. Waynesburg could offer only a four-year liberal arts program, which many students in Fayette County could not afford. But Pennsylvania State University could offer two-year technical courses to qualify young people for jobs in industry as engineers, draftsmen, and so on; it could provide better recreational facilities; and it also could offer courses leading toward a degree in liberal arts. For these reasons it seemed feasible and desirable to transfer the Center to Penn State. The change was to be gradual. Waynesburg College students at the Center "were assured of their continued good standing . . . and their transfer to the [Waynesburg] campus." Rich gave assurance that all contributions to a Waynesburg College building in Uniontown would be handled honorably. Donors were given four choices as to how their cash gifts or pledges could be used: (1) in the proposed Penn State operation; (2) by Waynesburg College in its current fund drive; (3) by return to the donor; or (4) "divided among the above choices as you may desire." The transfer was mutually advantageous to Waynesburg College, to Pennsylvania State University, and to the young people of Fayette County.[28] Ere long the University constructed a spacious, well equipped, new building on Route 119 north from Uniontown, and Hugh M. Barclay, former Director of the Center for Waynesburg College, was chosen to a similar post for Pennsylvania State University.

By 1971 certain problems arose relative to the faculty, stemming partly from the economic situation and partly from a lack of communication between the faculty and administration. In February 1971 Rich pointed out the ill effects of inflation, which made it impossible to stabilize costs. "Even now," he added, "our salary level, for nearly all categories of employees, is below the median for institutions of our size; Waynesburg ranked 67th out of 89 institutions currently surveyed." To permit the institution to go backward in the care and support of its staff would be self-defeating.[29] By September 1971 the wage-price freeze, imposed by the federal government on the nation, put the college in a difficult situation. Faculty contracts called for an automatic annual increment of five percent, but the freeze temporarily made this impossible. Rich wanted to grant the faculty its regular increment, but the law had to be obeyed.[30] It appears, however, that the law made special provision for faculty members, for their increments were paid after the freeze ended, thus making it possible for the college to fulfill its contracts. The economic situation appeared so tenuous, however, that, by September

1972, five faculty members were notified that they would not be offered contracts for 1973-1974. But subsequently, the financial situation was better than expected; and a large sector of the student body complained about the dismissal of these teachers. Consequently, in February 1973 the trustees rescinded the notices of nonreappointment to the five faculty members. They also restored the regular five percent annual salary increment for the faculty, which had been temporarily reduced to three percent. To meet added costs, tuition and board charges were increased $200 for the year 1973-1974.[31]

Some faculty members felt the faculty should have been informed about conditions which led to the notices of nonreappointment to their five colleagues. They expressed their sentiments at a staff seminar late in August 1972. As a result, Rich established a special "Advisory Committee on College Matters, consisting of 15 members including administrators, faculty, and students." This group was to meet "at least once a month" in the hope of effecting better communication within the institution as a whole. One means to this end was a faculty newsletter, started late in 1972, which contained dialogue between faculty members and administrators, plus news items of interest to all. It served a useful purpose.[32]

Rich wanted to do everything possible "to make the faculty member happy. One is an increase in the pay check." To continue such increases was imperative, because "a part of the problem is the trend of the times." Three different organizations were in keen competition to unionize faculties. These were the National Education Association, the American Federation of Teachers, and the American Association of University Professors. As we have seen, Waynesburg had a chapter of the AAUP, but it was not very active. The AAUP had long opposed unionization of faculty, "feeling that it was unprofessional." By 1973, however, it entered the movement, because it did not want to "lose out to the two other organizations. . . . " Rich expressed the "hope that the faculty will not organize," but sooner or later the college might face this problem.[33]

An ill omen for the future was the decline in enrollments, beginning in the early 1970's. As late as 1965, there was too much optimism about future enrollments in institutions all over the nation; it was then impossible to foresee changing conditions which later caused such a decline. At the college, plans were made to enroll a maximum of 1,500 students by 1975. By late 1966, however, a figure of 1,200 or 1,300 appeared "to be a more realistic aim," chiefly because of the tuition gap between private colleges and state colleges.[34] Most families could not afford to send their children to private institutions, when they could annually save from $1,000 to $1,500 by sending them to state institutions.

By 1971 other factors affected the situation. Community colleges were springing up in many places, and their tuition was low. The draft law had been changed so that many students did not feel "they must go to college as a refuge." By 1964 there had been a "40 percent increase in the number of 18-year olds going to college, and institutions geared themselves to take care of that increase." By 1972, however, this increase had "plateaued out" and there was a slight dip in the college-age population. Most colleges in the tri-state area were then "down 20 percent in applications, as is Waynesburg." Enrollment at Waynesburg dropped from 1,008 in January 1970 to 868 in January 1974.[35]

In February 1972 Rich expressed alarm at the decline in enrollment and the consequent drop in income from tuition. He alluded to progress since July 1963. By careful management, in 1971 there was a surplus of $316,588 in the fund for current expenses. But Rich wanted the college to continue its operations in the black. On 15 January 1974 he asked departmental chairmen "to get every dollar out of the budget they possibly can," since a sharp drop in enrollment was expected for 1974-1975.[36]

The college stepped up its recruiting program and made efforts to decrease the attrition rate. The admissions staff relied more than ever on the alumni for help. Alumni communicated with prospective students in localities where they resided, gave names of such students to the Admissions Office, and aided admission officials locally in the recruiting process. Admissions personnel increased their visits to high schools from 360 in 1971 to 480 in 1972. Beginning in February 1974, the students conducted telethons in which they phoned to prospective students in their home communities. The Presbyterian Church, U. S. A. helped in the recruiting process. Its ministers told young people in their respective congregations about the advantages of attending Waynesburg College. By early 1974 the Pennsylvania-West Virginia Synod's office was sending to the college names of juniors and seniors, who were Presbyterians, in high schools in its area. Exceedingly helpful in terms of local public relations was the annual science institute. Beginning in 1968, on every Saturday in each February, juniors and seniors from high schools in Fayette, Greene, and Washington counties were invited to the campus to participate in the Institute; these students gained a clear insight into the work of scientists at the college level. In January 1972, Rich called attention to this Institute, and asked the faculty "to do a lot of searching to see if there are things the faculty can do" to make the college "more attractive in reference to curriculum, scheduling, etc." Shortly other departments contemplated institutes somewhat like that of the sciences. By 1974 the Admissions Office was collaborating with the Veterans Office in Pittsburgh in the hope of recruiting more veterans. Efforts were made to recruit more students from junior colleges and community colleges. One drawback to recruiting from community colleges stemmed from graduation requirements; after completing the two years' work offered by community colleges, a student could not complete the requirements for graduation from Waynesburg in two additional years. Further, it was difficult to recruit transfer students, because of lack of financial aid for them; most such aid went to freshmen, and at mid-year little money was left to help transfer students.[37]

Declining enrollment in the early 1970's resulted in a decrease in tuition income, the main source of revenue. But other sources of revenue were either reduced or terminated. As we have seen, by 1972, funds from the United Presbyterian Church, U. S. A. dropped to zero; and by January 1974 the annual sum received from its West Virginia-Pennsylvania Synod was $28,000.[38] In the state scholarship program, $1,200 per year was awarded to select students.[39]

The private colleges needed more state aid. To this end, in 1970, a "Master Plan" for higher education in Pennsylvania was drawn up. It included reports from community colleges, state colleges, and state-related institutions, "but nothing from the area of the private colleges." It was hoped that Pennsylvania would follow New York's plan by which independent colleges in that state annually received $400 for each graduate.[40] Such hopes seemed in vain, however. In October 1971 Pennsylvania's Governor, Milton Shapp, told a gathering of college presidents "that more money will not be forthcoming for education." He warned them not to expect institutional grants. He added that "education . . . now will have to take second place to such things as recreation, welfare, prison reform, etc., which now rank above education in the minds of the people." By January 1974 the Pennsylvania Association of Colleges and Universities proposed that state grants be raised from $1,200 to $2,000 per year and that the income level for eligible families be raised from $15,000 to $20,000. The second feature of this proposal would give the college a grant of $600 for each student who received a state grant. Later that year the legislature acted as follows: the state grant remained at $1200; the income level for eligible families was set at $18,000; and the college annually would receive up to $400 for each student holding a state grant.[41]

Gift income to the college decreased after 1970. But in this same period, the alumni, aware of the economic situation, increased their gifts. Most big gifts in the 1960's were from sources that were either no longer available or questionable by 1971. Lack of funds from the church hurt the college; the "50 Million Fund" ended; Richard King Mellon had passed away; the Buhl Foundation had changed its policy, which "precludes gifts we need most"; and bequests were unpredictable in number and dollar amount.[42]

As elsewhere in the nation, while income decreased, expenses increased at the college. Raises in faculty salaries and in costs of labor, supplies, and equipment resulted in a deficit of $100,284 for the academic year 1969-1970. Fortunately, however, an operating surplus of some $290,000 absorbed this deficit.[43]

The plight of private colleges in general, and of Waynesburg in particular, apparently caused some apprehension among the trustees. In April 1970 a trustee asked Rich "if the private colleges will not disappear." Rich answered that of the 46 Presbyterian-related colleges "four or five . . . are right now 'on the rocks.' Waynesburg College is much stronger than some; much worse off than others." Early in February 1971 Rich said: "A recent study of 41 independent colleges and universities showed 11 in serious trouble, 18 headed for trouble, and only 12 in good financial condition. Happily, Waynesburg is not now in serious difficulty, but neither does it have the resources that permit any degree of complacency on the part of the trustees and staff."[44]

Rich resorted to various means to keep the college economically sound. Better contacts with foundations and corporations were sought. It was recognized that more of the college family might help in attracting financial aid to the college. The new "Honor Club," recognizing donors who gave at least $500 annually to the college, was renamed the "Paul R. Stewart Club" in order to lend prestige to that group—and to increase its numbers.[45]

Efforts were made to save money. The plan to build a large student center was abandoned, and a more modest one was created in the expansion of Benedum Hall. Steps were then taken to reduce some departmental funds. Retiring faculty members or those leaving the college for other reasons were not to be replaced. Secretarial positions were combined, where possible. And Rich asked the staff to "bear down as hard as possible on non-personnel items, such as supplies, furniture, and equipment." The budget could be balanced by personnel cuts, but such would be a last resort. In January 1972 the trustees found a good way to save money needed "to finance the Benedum Hall expansion by borrowing from our current funds surplus" rather than by seeking loans from commercial sources as they did for the science building. These economy moves, plus a $150 raise in tuition and a $50 increase in board for 1973-1974 helped the financial situation. The 1973-1974 budget was based on an estimated enrollment of 950.[46] Fortunately the figure as of September 1973 was slightly higher. The Admissions Office had done an excellent job in recruiting.

The college continued its close relationship with the United Presbyterian Church, U. S. A. In May 1966 the trustees' Committee on Development

> recommended to the Board of Trustees that in the event there should ever be a question of Waynesburg's continuing its historic position as a college related to the United Presbyterian Church in the U. S. A., or its becoming a publicly controlled institution, it be affirmed by this board that Waynesburg College maintain this church relationship, and this is to become a basic tenet of all long-range planning.

On 13 January 1974 Rich attended a meeting of the Presbyterian College Union in St. Louis. This is an organization of the presidents of all Presbyterian-related colleges and universities. By that time the church had been reorganized, and Waynesburg College came under the Pennsylvania-West Virginia Synod, a new regional arrangement in which West Virginia was incorporated with Pennsylvania. The main topic of discussion in St. Louis was a document entitled *The Church and Related Colleges and Universities, A Statement of Mutual Responsibilities*. This statement was approved by the faculty and trustees of Waynesburg College. The church would "regard the colleges and universities as independent corporate institutions. . . . " In order that they would be eligible for federal grants, it was understood that they were not under the control of the church. The church would also encourage the collegiate institutions in their work, and its synods would aid them financially. The responsibilities of the colleges and universities were essentially to provide opportunities for teaching and learning, to offer courses in religion stressing the Judeo-Christian tradition, and to maintain full accreditation by the regional accrediting agencies. Mutually the church and its educational institutions would "commit themselves to support the struggle for full recognition of all persons as children of God."[47]

In April 1969 officials from the Synod of Pennsylvania visited the campus "to determine the feasibility of having the Synod meeting here in 1970." Customarily the Synod met at various Presbyterian colleges in the state, but it had not recently come to Waynesburg because of lack of dormitory space. Synod officials toured the campus, and they concluded they "had never before seen such consistently good dormitories." Hence plans were made for the Synod to come to Waynesburg, for the first time since 1913.[48] The college hosted the Synod on 16-19 June 1970. Some 208 delegates from 14 presbyteries across Pennsylvania represented one-half million members. The stress was on missionary work throughout the world; the delegates were also interested in social problems.[49]

A sign of close relations with the church as a whole came on 29 March 1973 when the college welcomed Dr. C. Willard Heckel, Moderator of the United Presbyterian General Assembly, to the campus. Heckel, a professor of law and Dean of the School of Law at Rutgers University, was the main speaker on the 123rd Charter Day of Waynesburg College. The next year the Moderator of the General Assembly was Dr. Clinton M. Marsh. The college was fortunate to secure him as speaker at the Charter Day celebration on 26 March 1974, which marked the beginning of a year-long celebration of the 125th Anniversary of the founding of the college.[50]

Early in 1972 the administration planned for a self-study of the college "in preparation for a Middle States visitation" during 1973-1974.[51] The accreditation of the college was reaffirmed in 1965. In keeping with the established practice of such reaffirmations every ten years, another was not due until 1975. But, in February 1973, Rich announced his plan to retire on 30 June 1974. Therefore, it seemed desirable to get on quickly with the self-study so that accreditation could be reaffirmed before the new president took office. To that end ten faculty committees worked, each on its assigned task, in expectation of a visit by an accreditation team in September or October 1973. The labors of these committees were much lighter than they had been a decade before. In 1973 the college was academically strong; some 48 percent of the faculty had earned doctorates; and efforts were constantly made to increase this percentage, and to recruit only faculty members who were also topnotch classroom teachers. A survey of graduates of the college from 1967 to 1971 showed that 95.3 percent of them rated their academic preparation at Waynesburg from satisfactory to excellent. The physical plant was the best in the history of the college: classrooms were spacious and designed in every way to facilitate the educational process; laboratories were well equipped; the Library was adequate in all respects; and dormitories were spacious, comfortable, and conducive to study. The college was financially sound. For all these reasons, as Rich said, there was "no cause to be alarmed at the arrival of a Middle States team." On 31 January 1974 the Commission on Higher Education of the MSA reaffirmed the college's accreditation. Its report to the faculty, administration, and trustees read in part:

> Waynesburg is not "on the rocks" by any means. It has excellent facilities, a good faculty, an effective administration, and a student body of reasonable size and ability. Annual enrollment fluctuations are troublesome, but they will continue to occur. The capital debt situation is not at all bad. . . . Future capital needs for facilities are not unreasonably high and if the past record of the College in meeting its facilities' needs can be continued, there seems little reason for official pessimism.[52]

Shortly before the college's accreditation was reaffirmed for the next decade, the entire college family and many other people were saddened by Stewart's death, on 27 January 1974, of a massive stroke suffered in mid-December 1973 from which he had not recovered. He had been in declining health for more than a year; and he was confined to his home for several months prior to his passing away in the local hospital. As long as he was able, as Chancellor of the college, he had gone daily to his office and had continued to work devotedly, chiefly by raising funds. On 30 January the college officially closed so the faculty, administrative staff, students, and others could attend the funeral in the First United Presbyterian Church in Waynesburg. To mourners crowded in the church, the Reverend William M. Meyer spoke of Stewart's long, unselfish service to the college, saying that "Prexy" took seriously Christ's words: "He who is the greatest must become servant." Meyer concluded that the living could honor the memory of Stewart most, if they rededicated themselves to keeping "Waynesburg College alive and vital as a Christian institution and as an integral part of this community's life. . . . " The "Lamplighters" sang hymns, closing the service with "Down Through the Ages," composed long ago by Stewart, which epitomized his constant prayer for Waynesburg College. He was buried in Greene County Memorial Park.[53]

As a means of raising funds, Stewart often had requested people to remember Waynesburg College in making their wills. In keeping with that practice, he left the institution a generous bequest in money, real estate, and his collections of Indian artifacts, fossils, minerals and rocks. In his will he requested "that the Indian archaeological collection, known as the Gay Shriver (Frank Bryan) collection remain intact and be exhibited, as it is 'probably the best Archaic collection in the United States.' " As professor, president, and chancellor, Stewart loyally served Waynesburg College for nearly sixty-four years. And, as a writer for the *Pittsburgh Post-Gazette* put it: He "still serves. . . . He died recently, but the college will continue to benefit from his life," because of "his nationally acclaimed collection of Indian artifacts. . . . "[54]

Rich took a rational approach to the solution of problems. When faced with dilemmas and conflicting claims of individuals or groups, he sought a middle course which hopefully would reconcile both sides. Always resorting to democratic thought and action, he used the committee system to "talk out" problems in the hope of arriving at solutions. He made every effort to keep lines of communication open. His tact, patience, and efforts to see problems in proper perspective doubtless went a long way in keeping peace on the Waynesburg campus.

On its 125th Anniversary Waynesburg College is stronger than at any time in its history. The prospect of declining enrollment and the resultant decrease in income will be the main problems for Waynesburg—as for all institutions of higher learning—in the foreseeable future. Hopefully solutions will be found, for small, liberal arts colleges are an essential element in American education. They are important because their size permits small classes and a closer relationship between teachers and students. In this sense they have a distinct advantage over large universities. Commager lucidly explains the chief differences between large and small institutions:

> Much of student discontent has been aggravated by, and directed against, the great, impersonal multiversity that appears to treat students as interchangeable parts in a giant educational machine. . . . The [liberal arts] college can, in this situation, make sure that it does indeed offer the traditional advantages—a genuine community, an easygoing relationship between trustees and administration on the one side, students and faculty on the other, amid tranquility and freedom from secular pressures.[55]

Members of the Waynesburg College family, including all alumni, owe much to the labors of men and women, both living and dead, who have served the institution. The college has surmounted seemingly insuperable obstacles. It is still capable of surmounting others.

On 11 April 1974 the trustees took action which augured well for the future when they selected Dr. Joseph F. Marsh as the next president of the college, to succeed Rich on 1 July 1974. A twelve-member search committee of trustees, faculty members, and students had worked diligently for several months screening more than 150 candidates for the position. Dr. Marsh is a native of Charleston, West Virginia. After a tour of duty in the United States Navy during World War II in which he was commissioned as an ensign, he completed work for the A. B. degree *magna cum laude* at Dartmouth College in 1947. He won the M. P. A. degree at Harvard from the Graduate School of Public Administration; and he did advanced research in British public administration at Oxford University. In 1968 Davis and Elkins College awarded him the honorary degree LL. D. After teaching at Dartmouth from 1952 to 1959, Dr. Marsh became president of Concord College, Athens, West Virginia, serving there from 1959 to 1973. On assuming that post, he was one of the youngest college presidents in the nation.

Ewing B. Pollock, President of the Board of Trustees, on announcing Dr. Marsh as the new president, used a three-word summary: "outstanding professional competence." Rich complimented the trustee-faculty-student search committee for doing a good job, and added: "Dr. Marsh is a splendid choice. The college is most fortunate to obtain an individual whose training and experience are so admirably suited to the present needs of the institution." In accepting the appointment, Dr. Marsh said: "Personally and professionally, I am extremely pleased and honored to accept the invitation of the Board of Trustees to become president of Waynesburg College. . . . " Looking to the challenges ahead, he declared: "With the dedicated help of trustees, faculty, students, administrators, alumni, and friends, I am convinced that Waynesburg will realize continued progress."[56]

On 22 October 1974, at a special convocation held in the First Presbyterian Church of Waynesburg, Marsh was installed as the twelfth president of the college, and it was then visualized that his formal inauguration would be held in the spring of 1975. Marsh termed the location "a symbolic reaffirmation of the College's historic beginnings. . . . " The most salient points in his excellent installation address merit our attention. In speaking of the strengths of the college, he praised the faculty and staff and their commitment to the welfare of the students, and expressed his happiness that students were participating in every facet of college life. He called on all who serve the college to provide "assistance—academic, personal, and financial—that will enable our students to grow spiritually and intellectually." He solicited trustee involvement in the affairs of the college, particularly "in the development of a long-range plan, new policies, new programs, fund raising, capital improvements and so on." And he was assured of such service by the trustees.

With respect to the curriculum, changes would be made as conditions in society changed. A move to meet a present demand is the mining education program, approved by both labor and management. It will be beneficial to miners of bituminous coal as that industry spreads westward in Greene County and taps one of the richest, untouched reserves in the earth. Looking farther ahead to another demand, Marsh said "the Regional Industrial Development Corporation of Southwestern Pennsylvania and the National Planning Association project a 54 percent increase in government-related jobs in this part of the state by 1980." To meet this demand Marsh suggested that "we should consider the possibility of offering an undergraduate program in public administration."

Knowing that history is a never-ending stream, Marsh admirably linked the past, present, and future of the college. Aware of society's great need to stress religion and morality, those paramount values of long ago, he said: "We already have done initial investigation leading to the proposal of a religious education program." As Margaret Bell Miller, more than a century ago, exhorted her students to love Waynesburg College, so Marsh gave "*an admonition*: 'No one should tamper with a college who does not know and love it greatly' " (Marsh's italics). Marsh then urged all to accept *a charge* given by Sir Eric Ashley, who held that a strong institution must fulfill two conditions: "It must be sufficiently stable to sustain the ideal which gave it birth, and sufficiently responsive to concerns relevant to the society which supports it" (Marsh's italics). Quoting the English poet, Swinburne, "All our past acclaims our future. . . . " Marsh's conclusion was succinct and lucid: "The first light of this College was as a flickering candle, but the light did not go out. Today, we have a light which flames brightly. In the future, the light of Waynesburg College will shine ever more widely and strongly."

Explanation of the Notes

In the early years titles of original documents pertaining to the college were long, and they varied from year to year or from one period to another. This was true of minutes of meetings of the trustees, faculty, the Board of Trust, the literary societies, alumni meetings, and so on; likewise catalogues of the college had long, wordy titles. For the sake of brevity and consistency these have all been shortened in the notes.

In referring to books, the first citation in each chapter includes the name of the author, title, place and date of publication, and page number. Thereafter, within the chapter, only the surname of the author and the page number are included. If two authors of books have the same surname and they are both cited in a chapter, the usual bibliographical information is given for each on the first reference. In following references within the chapter, for one work the surname of the author and page number are included; for the other, the surname of the author, a shortened form of the title, and page number are given.

In referring to articles from scholarly magazines, the name of the author, title of the article, name of the magazine, date, and page number are included in the first reference in each chapter. Thereafter within the chapter, the author's surname, an abbreviated form of the title, the name of the magazine, date, and page numbers are given.

Some notes contain incidental comments which throw additional light on material in the text. Others are explanatory in nature, and aimed to clarify relevant parts of the text. Some individual notes contain several references to the same subject matter in the text. In such instances great masses of detail have been condensed into general statements, so that the book would not reach encyclopedic proportions.

CHAPTER I

1. Nelson M. Blake, *A History of American Life and Thought* (New York, 1963), p. 14; Thomas A. Bailey, *The American Pageant: a History of the Republic*, 2nd ed. (Boston, 1961), pp. 67, 74; Ben M. Barrus, Milton L. Baughn, and Thomas H. Campbell, *A People Called Cumberland Presbyterians* (Memphis, Tenn., 1972), p. 8; J. E. Wright and Doris S. Corbett, *Pioneer Life in Western Pennsylvania* (Pittsburgh, 1968), pp. 141, 144-145.

2. Henry Jones Ford, *The Scotch-Irish in America* (Princeton, N. J., 1915), pp. 360, 379-381.

3. William Warren Sweet, ed., *Religion on the American Frontier, 1783-1840*, vol. II, *The Presbyterians* (New York, 1964), pp. 4-5; Barrus, Baughn, and Campbell, pp. 9-10.

4. An academy was founded also in Washington, Pennsylvania, which shortly became Washington College. Committee on Publication, *History of the Presbytery of Washington* (Philadelphia, 1889), pp. 166-392; Samuel P. Bates, *History of Greene County, Pa.* (Chicago, 1888), pp. 361-362, 491. A good biography of McMillan is Dwight R. Guthrie, *John McMillan, The Apostle of Presbyterianism in the West, 1752-1833* (Pittsburgh, Pa., 1952).

5. Blake, p. 200; Barrus, Baughn, and Campbell, pp. 32-34; Wright and Corbett, pp. 146-147.

6. Blake, p. 43; *The Cumberland Presbyterian*, 13 March 1884, p. 2.

7. Ford, pp. 413, 415.

8. Blake, pp. 72-73, 75-76.

9. Blake, pp. 192-194; B. W. McDonnold, *History of the Cumberland Presbyterian Church*, 2nd ed. (Nashville, Tenn., 1888), p. 9; William W. McKinney, ed., *The Presbyterian Valley* (Pittsburgh, Pa., 1958), p. 237.

10. The term "Cumberland" was given to the borderland between Kentucky and Tennessee by Scotch-Irish settlers there in honor of the Duke of Cumberland, their hero who led Scotsmen and beat the "English Jacobites" in a battle in Scotland in April, 1746, which secured administrative and legal reforms beneficial to Scotland. News of this victory reached these migrants as they were moving westward. Happily they named many things in the area "Cumberland"—the Gap, Trail, Valley, Mountains, River, Country, and so forth. See McKinney, pp. 237-238; McDonnold, pp. 7, 10-11, 39-40; William H. Black, "The CP Church: Its Origin, Distinctive Features, and the Grounds for Preserving Its Denominational Integrity," *Journal of the Presbyterian Historical Society*, I, (Dec. 1901), pp. 189-204. See also William Ferguson, *Scotland from 1689 to the Present* (New York, 1968), pp. 152-154.

11. Blake, p. 71. See also T. C. Blake, *The Old Log House, a History and Defense of the Cumberland Presbyterian Church* (Nashville, Tenn., 1878), pp. 65, 268; J. V. Stephens, *The Causes Leading to the Organization of the Cumberland Presbyterian Church* (Nashville, Tenn., 1898), p. 94; *The Cumberland Presbyterian*, 15 March 1877, p. 1; 13 March 1884, p. 2; Boyd Crumrine, ed., *History of Washington County, Pennsylvania, with Biographical Sketches of Many of Its Pioneers and Prominent Men* (Philadelphia, 1882), pp. 410-411.

12. Stephens, pp. 25, 45; McDonnold, pp. 5, 48-50; McKinney, p. 239; *The Cumberland Presbyterian*, 29 Nov. 1883, p. 1. Noteworthy was the truly militant CP missionary, Sumner Bacon, dubbed the "Apostle of Texas." He was the first Protestant preacher to enter Texas, in 1829, when it was still under Mexican rule. He was rough, wore buckskin, and carried a Colt's revolver in one hand and the Bible in the other. See Barrus, Baughn, and Campbell, pp. 135-137.

13. Sweet, pp. 282-283, 339-340, 380; Blake, *The Old Log House*, pp. 56-58; Mc-

Kinney, pp. 240-241; *The Cumberland Presbyterian*, 7 June 1877, p. 4. There were several other fragmentations of Presbyterianism. The most important one was variously called Christian, Disciples of Christ, and Campbellites. This church was strong in states along the Ohio River. Bethany College in the West Virginia Panhandle was its child. Another schism was known as the "Shakers," who were highly emotional and pacifist. Prior to the Civil War the Presbyterians, like Methodists and Baptists, split into Northern and Southern churches over the question of slavery. The CP Church, however, remained united. There are nine Presbyterian bodies in the United States today, and numerous other branches in other nations. See Charles A. Johnson, *The Frontier Camp Meeting, Religious Harvest Time* (Dallas, Texas, 1955), pp. 71, 76-77; Blake, pp. 197-198; *The Cumberland Presbyterian*, 31 July 1884, p. 3.

14. *The Cumberland Presbyterian*, 16 Sept. 1845, p. 70; 11 Jan. 1877, p. 1; 19 Jan. 1882, p. 3; McDonnold, p. 1; Sweet, pp. 696-697; Barrus, Baughn, and Campbell, pp. 205-206.

15. After graduation from Waynesburg College, Gordon spent a year in a medical college after which he was an apprentice under Dr. J. B. Laidley, a physician, in Carmichaels. His co-workers in Japan were the Reverends A. D. Hail, J. B. Hail, Alice Orr and Julia Leavitt. They founded CP churches in Osaka, Kioto, Sanda, and other places. By 1880 a CP presbytery was established in Japan. See McDonnold, p. 440; *The Cumberland Presbyterian*, 19 May 1871, p. 1; 28 Feb. 1873, p. 1; 20 Jan. 1876, p. 4; 28 Sept. 1876, p. 4; 8 March 1877, p. 1; 5 Dec. 1878, p. 1; 30 Jan. 1879, p. 1; 10 July 1879, p. 1; 23 Feb. 1882, p. 1; 1 June 1882, p. 5.

16. *The Cumberland Presbyterian*, 22 Dec. 1881, p. 1. The Committee of Five consisted of Henry Cary, Luther Day, Ephraim Post, Odell Squier and William Stockdale.

17. *The Cumberland Presbyterian*, 22 Dec. 1881, p. 1; 12 Jan. 1882, p. 1; 19 Jan. 1882, p. 1; McDonnold, p. 275.

18. McKinney, pp. 243-244.

19. *The Cumberland Presbyterian*, 12 Jan. 1882, p. 1; 26 Jan. 1882, p. 1; McDonnold, p. 278; Fred Cochran, *A History of the West Union Presbyterian Church and Community* (Plain Grove, Pa., 1947), pp. 4-5. The ruling elders who served both at Old Concord and West Union were Luther Day and Odell Squier; they and William Stockdale were members of the Committee of Five.

20. *The Cumberland Presbyterian*, 2 Feb. 1882, p. 1; 26 Feb. 1885, p. 1.

21. McKinney, pp. 105, 243; McDonnold, pp. 273-274, 285-287; *The Cumberland Presbyterian*, 22 Dec. 1881, p. 1; 12 Jan. 1882, p. 1. The circular plate on the front of the Bethel United Presbyterian Church reads: "Bethel CP Church: Fiftieth Anniversary Celebrated, May 20th, 1883."

22. Fred High, *Waynesburg, Prosperous and Beautiful* (Waynesburg, Pa., 1973), p. 14. Here is a good picture, which shows the location of the first CP Church in relation to the North Ward public school which stood nearby until it was razed in 1972. See also *The Cumberland Presbyterian*, 12 Aug. 1880, p. 1; *The Democrat Messenger* (Waynesburg) 4 Aug. 1931, p. 1; 6 Oct. 1941, pp. 1, 5; McDonnold, p. 283; Bates, pp. 359-360.

23. *The Cumberland Presbyterian*, 31 March 1846, p. 291; 22 Sept. 1871, p. 2.

24. Bates, pp. 360, 362. CP churches in Greene County were located at Carmichaels, Clarksville, Claylick, Hewitt's (at Rices Landing), Jefferson, Muddy Creek, Nineveh, Waynesburg, West Union, and Wind Ridge. The Claylick Church shows the close harmony between CP members and Methodist Protestants. Beginning in 1874, congregations of these churches built, and shared, a small frame church which still stands in a secluded, rustic valley not far from Rutan. See Irene McQuay and Robert Foltz, eds.,

"A Brief History of the Claylick Methodist Church, Greene County, Pennsylvania," 1 Sept. 1964. I am indebted to A. O. Hougland of Rutan for a copy of this history.

25. *The Cumberland Presbyterian*, 5 Oct. 1882, p. 1; McDonnold, pp. 527-528; *The Waynesburg Republican*, 3 July 1890, p. 1.

26. *The Cumberland Presbyterian*, 7 June 1877, p. 1.

27. McDonnold, pp. 201, 214-216, 218-220; *The Cumberland Presbyterian*, 23 Sept. 1845, p. 78; 4 Aug. 1846, p. 433; 3 March 1881, p. 7. From 1906, after the merger of the CP and Presbyterian churches, until 1946 Cumberland University was sponsored by the latter denomination. From 1946 until 1951 it was under Baptist control. Since 1951 it has been a two-year nondenominational junior college. See *Cumberland College of Tennessee Bulletin, Catalogue Issue* (Lebanon, Tenn., 1970), p. 17.

28. *St. Louis Observer*, 25 Nov. 1886, p. 8; see also *Lincoln College, 1969/70 Catalog* (Lincoln, Ill.), pp. 10-12. Shortly after 1906 the name was changed from Lincoln University to Lincoln College. After operating for several years as a four-year institution, it was changed to a junior college with a two-year program in the liberal arts. Until 1953 it was sponsored by the Presbyterians, but then the connection was severed; since then the college has been an inter-faith institution.

29. McDonnold, p. 527; *The Cumberland Presbyterian*, 15 June 1876, p. 1; *Bulletin of Trinity University* (San Antonio, Texas, 1971), pp. 11, 15.

30. The other CP collegiate institutions were Bethel College, McKenzie, Tennessee; Beverly College, Beverly, Ohio; Cane Hill College in Arkansas; Cumberland Female College, McMinnville, Tennessee; Greenwood Seminary for Women, Lebanon, Tennessee; Madison College, Uniontown, Pennsylvania; McGee College, College Mound, Missouri; Missouri Valley College, Marshall, Missouri; Spring Hill Institute, Kemper County, Mississippi; and Ward's Seminary, Nashville, Tennessee. See McDonnold, pp. 527, 559, 561, 563-568, 570-571; *The Cumberland Presbyterian*, 25 Feb. 1875, pp. 1-2; 15 June 1876, p. 1; 10 April 1884, p. 4; Barrus, Baughn, and Campbell, p. 227.

31. James Hadden, *A History of Uniontown, The County Seat of Fayette County, Pennsylvania* (n. p., 1913), pp. 483-486. See also *Souvenir Book of the Golden Jubilee of St. John The Baptist Greek Catholic Church* (Uniontown, Pa., 1951), p. 15. I am indebted to the Very Reverend Sebastian Sabol, O. S. B. M., First Superior and Pastor of the Carpathian Branch of the Basilian Fathers, for a copy of this excellent publication, and for a copy of the *Dedication Book of Saint John The Baptist Parochial School* (Uniontown, Pa., 28 April 1927).

32. Hadden, pp. 485-486; Crumrine, pp. 192, 200.

33. Hadden, pp. 486-487, 490.

34. Hadden, p. 491.

35. McDonnold, pp. 527-529.

36. Hadden, p. 493; McDonnold, pp. 528-529.

37. McDonnold, pp. 530-531; Hadden, pp. 494-495; George P. Schmidt, *The Liberal Arts College: A Chapter in American Cultural History* (New Brunswick, N. J., 1957), p. 133.

38. Hadden, pp. 494-495.

39. McDonnold, pp. 530-531; Hadden, p. 496.

40. McDonnold, pp. 530-531.

41. Hadden, pp. 496-497.

42. McDonnold, pp. 530-531; Hadden, pp. 496-497; William Hanna, *History of Greene County, Pa.* (n. p., 1882), pp. 178-179.

43. McDonnold, pp. 530-531; *The Cumberland Presbyterian*, 15 July 1845, p. 5.

44. *The Cumberland Presbyterian*, 25 Nov. 1845, p. 145.

45. *The Cumberland Presbyterian*, 7 Oct. 1845, p. 95; 11 Aug. 1846, pp. 447-448; McDonnold, pp. 530-531. After the

CP church abandoned Madison, the college was almost moribund for the next four years. Shortly it came under Methodist Protestant control, and it continued to suffer misfortunes. Beginning in 1854, the college was split into two irreconcilable factions over the question of slavery. By mid-1857 its doors closed. Its buildings, with two acres, were sold at a sheriff's sale on 7 March 1859 for $850. They were used thereafter for a variety of schools, of variable duration, including a female institute, seminary, school for soldiers' orphans, and an academy, until March 1912, when the property was sold to the congregation of St. John the Baptist Greek Catholic Church for $10,000. See Hadden, pp. 500-518.

46. *The Cumberland Presbyterian*, 25 Nov. 1845, p. 145; L. K. Evans, *Pioneer History of Greene County, Pennsylvania* (Waynesburg, Pa., 1941), pp. 159-160; McDonnold, pp. 531-532.

47. McDonnold, pp. 531-532; *The Cumberland Presbyterian*, 24 Nov. 1846, p. 40; 13 Aug. 1869, p. 1. For several years the institution at Beverly operated as an academy. Attempts in the late 1860's to make it a college ended in failure.

48. Hanna, pp. 178-179; Hadden, p. 533; Evans, p. 156.

49. J. A. Caldwell, *Illustrated Historical Centennial Atlas of Greene County, Pennsylvania* (Condit, Ohio, 1876), p. 17; Solon J. Buck and Elizabeth H. Buck, *The Planting of Civilization in Western Pennsylvania* (Pittsburgh, Pa., 1939), p. 397.

50. Schmidt, p. 31; Howard L. Leckey, *The Ten Mile Country and Its Pioneer Families*, 7 vols. (Waynesburg, Pa., 1950), IV, 12-13; Evans, pp. 72, 75, 149; Blake, pp. 191, 194; Hanna, p. 179; Greene County, Register and Recorder, Deed Book, No. 1, p. 659.

51. Evans, p. 74. See also Pennsylvania, *Laws of the Commonwealth of Pennsylvania*, 1809-1812, V. 154. I am indebted to C. Robert McCall, an attorney in Waynesburg, for procuring for me a photostatic copy of the unpublished Act, dated 20 March 1810, reposing in archives in Harrisburg, Pennsylvania, which established Greene Academy, named the trustees, and gave details relative to the beginning and operation of the institution.

52. T. S. Crago, "Greene Academy," *Western Pennsylvania Historical Magazine*, VII (1924), 121-133; *The Democrat Messenger* (Waynesburg), 16 Jan. 1920, p. 1; Bates, pp. 324, 327; Evans, pp. 156-157; Greene County, Register and Recorder, Deed Book No. 2, p. 536.

53. Blake, p. 194; *Fieldview*, Feb. 1903, p. 3; *The Democrat Messenger* (Waynesburg), 21 July 1922, p. 5; McDonnold, pp. 528-530.

54. *Catalogue of the Officers and Students of Greene Academy, Carmichaeltown, Pa.*, 1851 (Washington, Pa. 1851), pp. 2-4.

55. *Catalogue . . . of Greene Academy . . . 1851*, p. 11.

56. *Catalogue . . . of Greene Academy . . . 1851*, pp. 9-10; *Reunion of Teachers and Students of Greene Academy* (n. p., 1900), pp. 19-20.

57. Mrs. Almira B. Kerr, Iowa City, Ia., to Miss S. A. Diem, 8 Aug. 1900, in *Reunion of Teachers and Students of Greene Academy*, 1900, pp. 21-22. Mrs. Kerr, then over eighty years old, asked to be excused from the reunion, but she wrote this letter instead.

58. *Catalogue . . . of Greene Academy . . . 1851*, pp. 7, 11; Robert E. Boyle, ed., *Carmichaels: A Story of Two Centuries of Progress, 1767-1967* (Carmichaels, Pa., 1967), p. 24.

59. *The Cumberland Presbyterian*, 3 Nov. 1846, p. 16; T. S. Crago, "Greene Academy," *Western Pennsylvania Historical Magazine*, VII (1929), 129; *Reunion of Teachers and Students of Greene Academy*, 1900, pp. 19-20; Andrew J. Waychoff, *Local History* (Waynesburg, Pa., 1926), No. 183; *Catalogue . . . of*

Greene Academy . . . 1851, p. 11; Boyle, p. 24.

60. *Reunion of Teachers and Students of Greene Academy*, 1900, pp. 8-9. See "*A Program, Annual Literary Contest of the Clio and Erodelphian Literary Societies of Greene Academy* (Carmichaels, 22 Sept. 1853), Stewart files. See also *Catalogue . . . of Greene Academy . . . 1851*, pp. 10-11.

61. In accord with state law, on 16 March 1865, the trustees of Greene Academy conveyed the institution to the Carmichaels Borough School District. It was used as a public school until 1893, when the more spacious Borough school opened nearby. From 1893 to 1920, it was the local post of the Grand Army of the Republic (GAR). From 1920 into the 1950's, it was used as an apartment building. Subsequently, the town council took it over. An attempt to restore it in 1967, on the occasion of the town's bicentennial, ended in failure. But on 18 February 1972 plans were made to convert it into the Greene Academy of Arts. Led by Glenn R. Toothman, President Judge of the Greene County Courts, a group of interested citizens met in the courthouse in Waynesburg, created a nonprofit corporation, and discussed steps to be taken to restore the building. As of 1974, reconstruction is well under way. Under the capable leadership of Alvin D. Laidley, the first president of the organization, Greene Academy of Arts bids fair to continue its progress. See *Catalogue . . . of Greene Academy . . . 1851*, pp. 5-8, 12; Waychoff, No. 183; *The Waynesburg Independent*, 27 Aug. 1896, p. 15; Bates, pp. 327, 491; *The Waynesburg Republican*, 17 Jan. 1872, p. 4; 7 April 1885, p. 3; 16 March 1886, p. 4; *The Democrat Messenger* (Waynesburg), 16 Jan. 1920, p. 1; 12 Feb. 1972, p. 1; *Observer-Reporter* (Washington, Pa.), 14 Feb. 1972, p. B-7; 21 Feb. 1972, p. B-6.

62. Evans, p. 157. For pictures taken at the reunion at Greene Academy in 1900 see High, p. 132.

CHAPTER II

1. *The Fieldview*, I (June 1903), p. 2; B. W. McDonnold, *History of the Cumberland Presbyterian Church*, 2nd ed. (Nashville, Tenn., 1888), pp. 328-329.

2. The Hathaway home, built of brick in 1853 after Carmichaels lost its bid for the college, is located near the left bank of Muddy Creek as one goes downstream about a quarter mile below Greene Academy. It is still in good condition, and the family of the late Thomas Hathaway resides in it. See Andrew J. Waychoff, *Local History* (Waynesburg, 1926), No. 183. See also George P. Schmidt, *The Liberal Arts College: A Chapter in American Cultural History* (New Brunswick, N. J., 1957), pp. 6, 11-12.

3. Bates, pp. 329-330; *The Washington Observer*, 11 June 1949, p. 27; *WC Catalogue*, 1920-1921, pp. 12-13; McDonnold, p. 533; T. S. Crago, "Greene Academy," *Western Pennsylvania Historical Magazine*, VII (1929), 127-128; *The Collegian*, XII (May 1911), 2. See also *The Waynesburg Republican*, 15 Feb. 1917, p. 1, for the full list of first subscribers for the college building.

4. *The Waynesburg Independent*, 27 Aug. 1896, p. 12; Fred High, *Waynesburg, Prosperous and Beautiful* (Waynesburg, 1973), p. 37; L. K. Evans, *Pioneer History of Greene County, Pennsylvania* (Waynesburg, 1941), p. 37; *The Yellow Jacket*, 14 Nov. 1969, p. 2.

5. In later years Waynesburg's healthful location was often stressed in catalogues: "The water is plentiful and pure; the mountain air, refreshing and invigorating. . . . " Further, as one came on the railroad to town he saw "scenery not less

grand than are the scenic views among the foothills of the Alps in Switzerland." Another inducement for parents to send their sons and daughters to Waynesburg was "the fact that for more than two decades the city of Waynesburg has been free from licensed saloons." See *WC Bulletin*, July, 1914, pp. 9-10.

6. Evans, p. 157.

7. *The Washington Observer*, 11 June 1949, p. 18; *The Waynesburg Republican*, 21 Jan. 1897, p. 1; Bates, pp. 333-334; Blanche Loughran Brown to President [Paul R.] Stewart, 8 March 1949, Stewart files.

8. McDonnold, p. 533; Bates, pp. 329-330.

9. Evans, p. 157. At present there is a men's clothing store on the first floor of this building.

10. Evans, p. 157; *The Yellow Jacket*, 12 Nov. 1955, p. 4; High, p. 14.

11. *A Program*: *Dedication of the First Baptist Church of Waynesburg, Pa.*, 9 Dec. 1962; *The Yellow Jacket*, 23 Nov. 1957, p. 3; High, p. 97; *The Woman's Centennial Paper, Commemorating the Settlement of Greene County* (Waynesburg, Pa., 26-27 Aug. 1896), unpaged, Registrar's files; Schmidt, pp. 129, 133, 139; *The Collegian*, March 1916, p. 8.

12. McDonnold, p. 533; *WC Catalogue*, 1853, p. 2; 1920-1921, pp. 12-13; *The Yellow Jacket*, 12 Nov. 1955, p. 4; Evans, p. 160.

13. The charter also provided for a body of stockholders who were to have a voice in the election of trustees. See McDonnold, p. 534; Evans, pp. 157-158; Bates, pp. 330-333.

14. Shortly the number of trustees was increased to twenty-one, and the legislature was requested to supplement the charter so that the Pennsylvania Presbytery could elect twelve trustees and the stockholders nine of that body. But in practice, for many years, the Synod appointed all trustees. See Trustees' Minutes, 19 April 1853; Commonwealth of Pennsylvania, *Laws of Pennsylvania*, 1850, No. 231, pp. 283-285. See also *The Collegian*, March 1916, p. 8.

15. James B. Lazear to President [Paul R.] Stewart, 13 Dec. 1930, Registrar's files.

16. *The Waynesburg Republican*, 14 Nov. 1901, p. 4; James B. Lazear to President [Paul R.] Stewart, 13 Dec. 1930, Registrar's files.

17. *The Cumberland Presbyterian*, 8 April 1875, p. 1; *The Woman's Centennial Paper, Commemorating the Settlement of Greene County* (Waynesburg, Pa., 26-27 Aug. 1896), unpaged, Registrar's files.

18. Trustees' Minutes, 14 Oct. 1853; *The Washington Observer*, 11 June 1949, p. 30; *The Yellow Jacket*, 23 Nov. 1957, p. 3; *Fieldview* I (June, 1903), pp. 3-4; McDonnold, p. 533; *The Woman's Centennial Paper, Commemorating the Settlement of Greene County*, (Waynesburg, Pa., 26-27 Aug. 1896), unpaged, Registrar's files. Even at Oberlin College, where coeducation began in 1837, there was discrimination against female students. They could graduate, but were not allowed to speak at commencement. A girl graduate was compelled to write an essay for the program, but a male classmate read it while she sat in silence on the platform. See Schmidt, pp. 132-133. See also Bates, pp. 332-333.

19. Trustees' Minutes, 8 April 1852, 12 April 1852, 27 April 1852, Aug. 1853, 24 Feb. 1854. See also *The Yellow Jacket*, 12 Nov. 1955, p. 4.

20. Evans, p. 159. See the Plan of Hanna Hall, undated, Stewart files. See also Waychoff, No. 192; Nelson M. Blake, *A History of American Life and Thought* (New York, 1963), pp. 79-80; *The Washington Observer*, 1 July 1960, p. 10. I am indebted to Russell Raymont, an alumnus of the college, for a description of the construction of Hanna Hall. Some years ago Raymont and fellow workers reno-

vated the building. In so doing they discovered the large iron rods which support the upper portion of the edifice.

21. Henry S. Commager, "Has the Small College a Future," *Saturday Review*, 21 Feb. 1970, p. 62; Schmidt, pp. 43-44.

22. *WC Catalogue*, 1853, pp. 7, 14; Blake, p. 388; Schmidt, pp. 158-159; *The Yellow Jacket*, 8 Dec. 1961, p. 2.

23. *WC Catalogue*, 1853, pp. 7-8.

24. *WC Catalogue*, 1853, p. 12. It is difficult to ascertain just what subject material was covered in some of these courses. For example, the course in "Moral Science," was variously called "Moral Philosophy," "Metaphysics," and "Ethics." It covered a wide variety of material including ethics, political science, sociology, economics, and psychology. In aggregate, it would approximate today's social sciences. See Schmidt, pp. 46-47.

25. *WC Catalogue*, 1853, p. 14; *WC Catalogue*, 1855, unpaged; Trustees' Minutes, 14 Oct. 1853; High, p. 14.

26. Bates, pp. 311, 323; *WC Catalogue*, 1853, pp. 10-11, 13. In 1853 there were 83 males and 58 females enrolled; of these, respectively, 35 and 21 were in the Preparatory Department. Three females from Ohio were the only ones from "out of state."

27. *WC Catalogue*, 1853, p. 13; Trustees' Minutes, 18 April 1853.

28. Henry S. Commager, "Has the Small College a Future," *Saturday Review*, 21 Feb. 1970, p. 62; *WC Catalogue*, 1853, pp. 13-14; Trustees' Minutes, 27 March 1854.

29. Minutes of Philo Society, 11 Feb. 1851; 7 Aug. 1851; 18 Sept. 1851; 22 Sept. 1851; James B. Lazear to President [Paul R.] Stewart, 13 Dec. 1930, Registrar's files.

30. High, p. 32.

31. In June 1911 Mrs. Martha Bayard Howard spoke briefly at a meeting of the Philo Society. She was a member of the first class of females which graduated in 1852. See Minutes of Philo Society, June 1911.

32. *The Waynesburg Times*, 12 Sept. 1911, unpaged; Minutes of Philo Society, June 1911; High, pp. 30, 32.

33. Minutes of Philo Society, 20 June 1851; 18 Sept. 1851; Minutes of Emma Willard Society, 5 Aug. 1853.

34. *Constitution and By-Laws and Rules of Order of the Philomathean Literary Society, Waynesburg College, adopted 1852, revised 1897 and 1903*, (Waynesburg 1903), Registrar's files; Minutes of Philo Society, 23 May 1851; 9 Jan. 1852; June 1911.

35. For examples of fines see Minutes of Philo Society, 23 May 1851; 23 Jan. 1852; 30 June 1852; 27 Aug. 1852; 25 Feb. 1853; Minutes of Emma Willard Society, 20 Nov. 1851; 30 Aug. 1854.

36. Minutes of Philo Society, 24 July 1851. Philo's financial report for November 1851 shows that 35 cents was spent for candles, 62 1/2 cents for candlesticks, $5.00 for ribbon and badges, and $10.00 for the services of a band. See Minutes of Philo Society, 6 Nov. 1851. In February 1856 four members were suspended from Philo for debts ranging from 25 to 87 1/2 cents. One owed Philo's library $1.00. See Minutes of Philo Society, 8 Feb. 1856. See also High, pp. 30, 32.

37. Minutes of Emma Williard [*sic*] Society, 23 Nov. 1851; 12 Dec. 1851; 23 June 1853; 30 Aug. 1854; Minutes of Philo Society, 31 July 1851; 9 Jan. 1852; 23 Jan. 1852; 21 Jan. 1853; Schmidt, p. 98.

38. Minutes of Philo Society, 20 June 1851; 25 June 1851; 20 Nov. 1851. See also *The Waynesburg Times*, 12 Sept. 1911, unpaged.

39. Minutes of Philo Society, 10 Nov. 1851; 13 Nov. 1851.

40. Minutes of Philo Society, 20 Nov. 1851; 9 Sept. 1853; 15 June 1855; High, p. 32.

41. *The Literary Visitor*, ed. by a Joint Committee from the Literary Societies of

Waynesburg College, Waynesburg College, May 1854; *The Literary Pearl*, ed. by a Joint Committee from the Literary Societies of Waynesburg College, July 1858, Registrar's files.

42. Evans, p. 159; Records of Board of Trust, undated.

43. Jesse Lazear was of French lineage. His parents were pioneer settlers along Crabapple Run not far from Wind Ridge in Greene County. He had a son and a grandson who became famous. The son was James Burbridge Lazear, one of Loughran's students at Greene Academy and in Waynesburg College's first classes in September 1849. He shortly transferred to West Point, and subsequently he went with his parents to Baltimore, Maryland, where they engaged in the wholesale grocery business. As a national bank examiner late in the nineteenth century, he became one of the best known financial men of the trans-Mississippi West. The grandson was Dr. Jesse W. Lazear who became "a noted physician, and in 1900 he gave his life in the discovery of the cause of *yellow fever* in Havanah [*sic*]." See James B. Lazear, Omaha, Nebr., to Ida Lazear Thomas, Kirksville, Ohio, 10 June 1929, author's files. See also *The Cumberland Presbyterian*, 9 July 1869, p. 8; 25 Oct. 1877, p. 4; William Hanna, *History of Greene County, Pennsylvania* (n. p., 1882), p. 276; Bates, p. 838; Trustees' Minutes, 8 April 1852; 17 Jan. 1853. I am indebted to Mary F. Thomas of Newark, Ohio, for information on the genealogy of the Lazear clan and for the letter from James B. Lazear to Ida L. Thomas.

44. McDonnold, pp. 539-540; Trustees' Minutes, 7 Feb. 1854; 3 Aug. 1855. Several documents entitled "Perpetual Scholarships" are in the Stewart files. See also Evans, pp. 161-162.

45. Trustees' Minutes, 27 April 1852; 19 April 1853; 14 Oct. 1853; *The Woman's Centennial Paper . . . 1896*, unpaged.

46. Trustees' Minutes, 18 April 1853; 24 Feb. 1854; 3 Aug. 1855; McDonnold, pp. 534-535; Bates, p. 333; Evans, p. 161.

47. Valedictory Address on Behalf of the Senior Class of 1855 at Waynesburg College, Registrar's files. After Loughran left Waynesburg he went west and continued his labors as educator and pastor in several places. His first wife was Lucinda Crawford, a granddaughter of William Crawford, a pioneer who settled near Carmichaels on what is known as the "Mel Stephenson farm." Loughran married her in 1836; to them three children were born. She died during their stay in Hazel Green, Wisconsin, from 1856 to 1858. Here he conducted a "collegiate institution." In 1858 he became pastor of the Presbyterian Church of Waukon, Iowa, and "took charge of the college there." In 1860 he was remarried, this time to Jennie Dodd of Polo, Illinois, and they became parents of three daughters and a son. From 1863 to 1872, he was in the Methodist Conference, and preached to Methodists in Missouri. In 1872 he returned to Waukon, Iowa, established a seminary there, and continued his teaching and preaching. In 1884 he moved to White Lake, South Dakota, where he was principal of the school for two years; he then became pastor of the Presbyterian Church there. He suffered a heart attack, and died on 7 January 1897, full of years, and mourned by his wife, children, and members of the church he had faithfully served. See James B. Lazear to President [Paul R.] Stewart, 13 Dec. 1930, Registrar's files; Blanche Loughran Brown to President [Paul R.] Stewart, 8 March 1949, Stewart files. Mrs. Brown was one of Loughran's two surviving daughters. She enclosed an obituary entitled "He is Gone," taken from the local newspaper published at White Lake, South Dakota, at the time of his death. See also *The Waynesburg Republican*, 21 Jan. 1897, p. 1; Evans, pp. 35-36.

CHAPTER III

1. *The Washington Observer*, 11 June 1949, p. 30; Mrs. Bernarda Bryson Shahn to President [Paul R.] Stewart, 16 Dec. 1965, Stewart files; B. W. McDonnold, *History of the Cumberland Presbyterian Church*, 2nd ed. (Nashville, Tenn., 1888), p. 535.

2. Mrs. Bernarda Bryson Shahn to President [Paul R.] Stewart, 16 Dec. 1965, Stewart files. Weethee was a great uncle of Mrs. Shahn. The second coming of Christ is recorded in Acts I, 9-11; it is referred to over 300 times in the New Testament alone. See Merrill C. Tenney, general ed., *Pictorial Bible Dictionary* (Nashville, Tenn. 1968), p. 765. See also *The History of the Hocking Valley* (Chicago, Ill., 1883), "Personal and Biographical Sketch of Jonathan Perkins Weethee," (a typewritten copy), Stewart files; *The Waynesburg Republican*, 14 Nov. 1901, p. 4.

3. McDonnold, p. 535.

4. *The Democrat Messenger* (Waynesburg), 10 June 1949, p. 1; *The Washington Observer*, 11 June 1949, p. 30; *The Collegian*, March 1916, p. 8; Katherine Scott, "Strict Rules for Coeds Are Not New; Night Dates Were Banned 89 Years Ago," *The Philadelphia Record*, 31 Jan. 1932, p. 8; [Chancellor Paul R.] Stewart to Mrs. Bernarda Bryson Shahn, 23 Dec. 1965, Stewart files; L. K. Evans, *Pioneer History of Greene County, Pennsylvania* (Waynesburg, Pa., 1941), p. 161. After it was concluded that the institution was "one College with male and female departments," bylaws were adopted which prescribed the duties of the president of the college and the principal of the female department. See Samuel P. Bates, *History of Greene County, Pennsylvania* (Chicago, 1888), pp. 333-334. Margaret L. Needham was the first woman at Waynesburg College and the first in Pennsylvania to receive a diploma conferring on her the Bachelor of Science degree. See also *The Waynesburg Republican*, 30 May 1929, p. 4.

5. Bates, pp. 333-334.

6. *WC Catalogue*, 1857, pp. 4, 6-9, 11-14, 17. See also *Laws and Regulations of Waynesburg College, at Waynesburg, Greene County, Pa.*, 1857, revised 1869, (Waynesburg, Pa. 1869), p. 1.

7. Bates, p. 312; *Program of 42d Annual Session of Greene County Teachers' Institute*, 1908, unpaged. A state law in 1867 made teachers' institutes obligatory in all counties of Pennsylvania.

8. *Laws and Regulations of Waynesburg College, 1857*, pp. 1-2.

9. *Laws and Regulations of Waynesburg College, 1857*, p. 2.

10. *Laws and Regulations of Waynesburg College, 1857*, pp. 2-4; George P. Schmidt, *The Liberal Arts College, A Chapter in American Cultural History* (New Brunswick, N. J., 1957), p. 71.

11. *Laws and Regulations of Waynesburg College, 1857*, pp. 4-5.

12. *Laws and Regulations of Waynesburg College, 1857*, pp. 6-7.

13. Katherine Scott, "Strict Rules for Coeds Are Not New; Night Dates Were Banned 89 Years Ago," *The Philadelphia Record*, 31 Jan. 1932, p. 8; *Laws and Regulations of Waynesburg College, 1857*, p. 7.

14. *Laws and Regulations of Waynesburg College, 1857*, pp. 5-6.

15. Minutes of Philo Society, 7 Dec. 1855; 18 Sept. 1856; 12 Dec. 1856; *Laws and Regulations of Waynesburg College*, 1857, p. 7.

16. Katherine Scott, "Strict Rules for Coeds Are Not New; Night Dates Were Banned 89 Years Ago," *The Philadelphia Record*, 31 Jan. 1932, p. 8.

17. James B. Lazear to President [Paul R.] Stewart, 13 Dec. 1930, Registrar's files; *The Waynesburg Republican*, 14 Nov. 1901, p. 4; Bates, p. 334; McDonnold, p. 535; Evans, p. 161.

18. Evans, p. 161. When Weethee left, his salary was in arrears and no attempt was made to pay it until he submitted a

claim twenty years later. In December 1878 the trustees applied $300 on the debt due Weethee, but they owed him $424.40. It appears that the balance was never paid. See Trustees' Minutes, 30 Aug. 1878; 3 Dec. 1878; 31 Dec. 1878; 25 Jan. 1879.

19. Bates, p. 334; McDonnold, p. 535; Evans, p. 161; *The Waynesburg Republican*, 14 Nov. 1901, p. 4. Weethee had a rather checkered career after leaving Waynesburg which included teaching, preaching, writing, geological research, and promoting a railroad company. Through it all he kept watching for the second coming of Christ. After his resignation in 1858 he returned to Ohio and began teaching in his own home. He spent nearly all his savings on furniture, apparatus, and expansion of his plant. His institution was chartered as "Weethee College," but it closed for lack of money and students in 1869. He then became a member of the Board of Directors of the Ohio Central Railroad and remained in that post until 1875. Briefly he became interested in geological research to ascertain the mineral resources in various parts of Athens County, Ohio. From 1876 until his death on 8 August 1899 he spent his time in retirement at his home some ten miles north of Athens. While in retirement he wrote religious articles for various newspapers and magazines which circulated widely in the United States and in several foreign countries. To the very last he kept "looking for that blessed hope, the appearing of the Great God, even our Savior, Jesus, the Christ." He was buried in Dover Township in Athens County. See *The History of the Hocking Valley* (Chicago, 1883), "Personal and Biographical Sketch of Jonathan Perkins Weethee," (a typewritten copy), Stewart files. See also *The Washington Observer*, 11 June 1949, p. 30.

CHAPTER IV

1. L. K. Evans, *Pioneer History of Greene County, Pennsylvania* (Waynesburg, 1941), p. 161; Samuel P. Bates, *History of Greene County, Pennsylvania* (Chicago, 1888), pp. 334-340. The mortality rate was very high among newly founded colleges in the nation between 1790 and 1860. Of 43 established in Ohio in that period, 26 were defunct by the latter date; like figures for Georgia were 46 and 39; and for Missouri 85 and 77. See George P. Schmidt, *The Liberal Arts College, A Chapter in American Cultural History* (New Brunswick, N. J., 1957), p. 11.

2. Bates, pp. 331-332, 337-338; *The Waynesburg Daily Times*, 30 Jan. 1902, p. 1; Evans, p. 160; *Program of Forty-Second Annual Session of the Greene County Teachers' Institute* (Waynesburg, Pa., 1908), unpaged. See also *WC Bulletin*, June-July 1927, pp. 1-2.

3. *The Cumberland Presbyterian*, 30 July 1869, p. 1; 6 Aug. 1869, p. 1; 29 May 1874, p. 1; 27 April 1882, p. 1.

4. *The Cumberland Presbyterian*, 1 July 1870, p. 1.

5. *The Cumberland Presbyterian*, 21 July 1871, p. 1; 22 Feb. 1877, p. 1; 24 May 1877, p. 2. See also Nelson M. Blake, *A History of American Life and Thought* (New York, 1963), pp. 208-209; William W. Sweet, *Religion on the Frontier*, 1783-1840, vol. II, *The Presbyterians* (New York, 1964), pp. 65-66.

6. *The Cumberland Presbyterian*, 21 July 1871, p. 1; *St. Louis Observer*, 21 Oct. 1886, p. 2.

7. *The Cumberland Presbyterian*, 29 Oct. 1869, p. 2; 21 Dec. 1876, p. 1; 15 Dec. 1881, p. 3; *The Collegian*, March 1916, p. 7.

8. *The Cumberland Presbyterian*, 29

Oct. 1869, p. 2; 24 Dec. 1869, p. 1; *The Collegian*, II (Nov. 1900), p. 7.

9. *The Cumberland Presbyterian*, 24 Jan. 1873, p. 1; 16 Jan. 1874, p. 1. The church newspaper aided Miller in his crusade against the use of tobacco by giving instructions aimed literally to wash away the sin: "A thorough course of bathing to eliminate tobacco from the system will make the struggle much less severe, and prove the greatest aid that can be given. . . . No drink but water, and that may be drank [*sic*] as freely as desired. To allay the craving for tobacco, hold cold water or pieces of ice in the mouth." See *The Cumberland Presbyterian*, 26 Aug. 1870, p. 3.

10. *The Cumberland Presbyterian*, 31 July 1879, p. 2; 21 Aug. 1879, p. 2.

11. *The Cumberland Presbyterian*, 10 Sept. 1869, p. 1.

12. Blake, p. 215.

13. *The Cumberland Presbyterian*, 17 Sept. 1869, p. 2. This newspaper published an article which contained radical views on women's dress and activities. It read in part: "Why must a being, because she is a girl, screw up her ribs, wear thin stockings and shoes in winter, [and] learn no art or trade by which she can support herself? . . . " Girls "shouldn't waste money on corsets and high-heeled shoes." They should "play ball, skate, run races, and play like boys! . . . Don't be a dead weight on your parents." See *The Cumberland Presbyterian*, 26 July 1883, p. 3.

14. Blake, pp. 207-208; *The Waynesburg Republican*, 17 Jan. 1882, p. 3.

15. *The Waynesburg Republican*, 22 April 1884, p. 3; 3 Oct. 1889, p. 1. The "Old County Home" was temporarily abandoned in 1964, when the new Curry Home opened on the opposite side of "Old Route 21." Since June 1970 the Greene County Historical Society has occupied the old building.

16. Evans, pp. 161-162.

17. *The Cumberland Presbyterian*, 16 July 1869, p. 1; 6 Dec. 1872, p. 1.

18. *The Cumberland Presbyterian*, 24 Dec. 1869, pp. 2-3; Trustees' Minutes, 11 Sept. 1869; 4 Jan. 1870; 23 Aug. 1878; 17 Sept. 1878. By contrast, in 1870 when Miller was pleading for funds and Waynesburg's endowment was $40,000 and bearing little interest, Wooster College was just founded by the more affluent Presbyterians. Wooster's building, then under construction, cost $150,000; her endowment was $250,000 and she had two men "in the field" raising more money. In addition to the collegiate department, she soon set up a medical department and a law school. See *The Cumberland Presbyterian*, 30 Sept. 1870, p. 5.

19. *The Cumberland Presbyterian*, 24 June 1870, p. 5; 19 June 1871, p. 1; 1 Dec. 1871, p. 1; 16 Feb. 1872, p. 5; 1 Nov. 1872, p. 1.

20. *The Cumberland Presbyterian*, 24 Jan. 1873, p. 1.

21. *The Cumberland Presbyterian*, 11 Nov. 1880, p. 1.

22. *The Cumberland Presbyterian*, 3 Aug. 1882, p. 4.

23. *The Cumberland Presbyterian*, 27 Nov. 1884, p. 1.

24. *WC Catalogue*, 1891-1892, p. 38; 1898, pp. 44-45; Evans, p. 159.

25. *The Cumberland Presbyterian*, 18 March 1870, p. 2.

26. *The Cumberland Presbyterian*, 13 Jan. 1871, p. 1; 3 Feb. 1871, p. 1; 3 March 1871, p. 1.

27. *The Cumberland Presbyterian*, 18 March 1870, p. 2; 19 Dec. 1873, p. 1; 10 March 1881, p. 4; 27 July 1882, p. 2; 23 Aug. 1883, p. 5; *The Waynesburg Republican*, 20 March 1872, p. 4. The college was perplexed by the perennial problem of those students who did not promptly pay their tuition and fees. For example, in July 1879 the trustees directed their treasurer "to collect immediately the

amounts due from irregular students for the past two terms. . . . " See Trustees' Minutes, 29 July 1879.

28. *WC Catalogue*, June 1897, pp. 57-59.

29. *The Cumberland Presbyterian*, 21 Aug. 1879, p. 1; 3 Nov. 1881, p. 1.

30. *The Waynesburg Republican*, 14 Nov. 1901, p. 4. See also A. J. Waychoff Scrapbook, Stewart files.

31. *The Cumberland Presbyterian*, 4 Nov. 1870, p. 1; 22 June 1876, p. 1; 29 June 1876, p. 1.

32. *The Cumberland Presbyterian*, 22 June 1876, p. 1.

33. *The Cumberland Presbyterian*, 29 Aug. 1873, p. 1; 25 Jan. 1877, p. 4; Blake, p. 200.

34. *The Cumberland Presbyterian*, 11 Jan. 1877, p. 1.

35. *The Cumberland Presbyterian*, 18 Jan. 1877, p. 1.

36. *The Cumberland Presbyterian*, 18 Jan. 1877, p. 1; 25 Jan. 1877, p. 4; 1 Feb. 1877, p. 2.

37. *The Cumberland Presbyterian*, 25 March 1875, p. 1.

38. *The Cumberland Presbyterian*, 19 Feb. 1885, p. 2.

39. *St. Louis Observer*, 13 Jan. 1887, p. 12. Miller's reference here to the "double tale of brick, while withholding the straw" is taken from Exodus 5:16. The best grade of brick then had straw as binding material. Hence "withholding the straw" implies limited resources and struggle. Pharaoh abused the Israelites, many of whom were engaged in brick-making. He decreed that they were no longer to be supplied with straw, but were to find their own straw and to continue production as usual. They then went all over Egypt "to gather stubble for straw." Consequently Moses repeatedly implored Pharaoh to "let my people go." See Merrill C. Tenney, general ed., *Pictorial Bible Dictionary* (Nashville, Tenn. 1968), pp. 132-133.

40. Blake, p. 202; *The Cumberland Presbyterian*, 22 Aug. 1873, p. 4; 16 Jan. 1874, p. 1.

41. *The Cumberland Presbyterian*, 9 May 1873, p. 5; 4 Aug. 1881, p. 1; 1 Dec. 1881, p. 5; 1 Nov. 1883, p. 5; 26 March 1885, p. 5; *The Waynesburg Republican*, 28 March 1877, p. 3; 8 Aug. 1895, p. 1.

42. *The Cumberland Presbyterian*, 27 Feb. 1874, p. 5; 15 Feb. 1877, p. 5.

43. *The Cumberland Presbyterian*, 4 Dec. 1884, p. 1.

44. *The Cumberland Presbyterian*, 24 Nov. 1871, p. 1; 29 Aug. 1873, p. 1; 24 Jan. 1873, p. 1; 13 Sept. 1883, p. 4; Blake p. 389.

45. A. B. Miller, *Doctrines and Genius of the Cumberland Presbyterian Church* (Nashville, Tenn., 1892), pp. 5, 11.

46. *The Cumberland Presbyterian*, 16 July 1869, p. 1; 3 Sept. 1869, p. 1; 1 Oct. 1869, p. 1.

47. *The Cumberland Presbyterian*, 23 May 1873, p. 1; *The Collegian*, Feb. 1902, pp. 5-6; March 1916, p. 7.

48. *The Cumberland Presbyterian*, 18 Jan. 1877, p. 1; Blake, p. 425.

49. Program of *Forty-Second Annual Session of the Greene County Teachers' Institute* (Waynesburg, Pa., 1908), unpaged; Bates, p. 314. Miller occasionally resorted to the horse and buggy, rented from a local livery stable, particularly when bound for places outside of Greene County. Such transportation was sometimes hazardous. For example, late in April 1889, accompanied by his son, Howard, he drove to Old Concord, preached there in the morning, and started for the Fairview church, some three miles distant, in the afternoon. On the way the horse ran off, throwing them out of the buggy and injuring them. See *The Waynesburg Republican*, 26 April 1889, p. 1.

50. *The Waynesburg Republican*, 20 Sept. 1871, p. 1; 22 May 1883, p. 3; *The Cumberland Presbyterian*, 19 June 1874, p. 5.

51. *The Cumberland Presbyterian*, 19 Nov. 1869, p. 1.

52. *The Cumberland Presbyterian*, 14 April 1881, p. 1; 21 April 1881, p. 1.

53. *The Cumberland Presbyterian*, 5 May 1881, p. 2; 2 June 1881, p. 4.

54. *The Cumberland Presbyterian*, 24 Dec. 1869, p. 2.

55. *The Cumberland Presbyterian*, 11 April 1878, p. 1.

56. *The Cumberland Presbyterian*, 1 Sept. 1871, p. 5.

57. *The Cumberland Presbyterian*, 12 Aug. 1875, p. 4.

58. *The Cumberland Presbyterian*, 28 Oct. 1875, p. 1; 4 Nov. 1875, p. 2.

59. *The Cumberland Presbyterian*, 4 Nov. 1875, p. 2.

60. *The Cumberland Presbyterian*, 18 Nov. 1875, p. 1.

61. *The Cumberland Presbyterian*, 6 Jan. 1876, p. 5.

62. *The Cumberland Presbyterian*, 24 May 1877, p. 4.

63. *The Collegian*, Feb. 1902, pp. 3-4.

CHAPTER V

1. *WC Catalogue*, 1871-1872, pp. 26-27.

2. *WC Catalogue*, 1871-1872, pp. 24, 26-27.

3. *WC Catalogue*, June 1898, pp. 59-60, 63-64.

4. Faculty Minutes, 20 June 1888.

5. Faculty Minutes, 16 Dec. 1892; 19 Dec. 1892; 10 Feb. 1893; 19 Feb. 1898; 7 March 1898; L. K. Evans, *Pioneer History of Greene County, Pennsylvania* (Waynesburg, Pa., 1941), p. 164.

6. Faculty Minutes, 24 May 1895; 25 May 1896; 8 Dec. 1897; 10 Dec. 1897; 13 Dec. 1897; 14 Dec. 1897.

7. Trustees' Minutes, 30 April 1878; *WC Catalogue*, 1885-1886, p. 27; Faculty Minutes, 26 Jan. 1885; H. Laura Inghram, Kirby, Pa., to Louise M. Hook, Waynesburg, Pa., 11 May 1949, Stewart files.

8. Faculty Minutes, 9 Dec. 1878; 16 Dec. 1878; 27 Jan. 1879; 11 March 1879; 31 March 1879; 27 Sept. 1880; 9 May 1881; 4 Nov. 1887; 2 Oct. 1891; *WC Catalogue*, 1888-1889, p. 28.

9. Faculty Minutes, 20 June 1879; 10 Oct. 1881; 17 Oct. 1881; 31 Oct. 1881.

10. *The Waynesburg Republican*, 18 Dec. 1890, p. 1.

11. Faculty Minutes, 4 May 1894; 18 May 1894; 7 June 1898.

12. Faculty Minutes, 14 Feb. 1898; 27 June 1898.

13. Faculty Minutes, 13 June 1894; 25 May 1895; 10 Nov. 1899.

14. Faculty Minutes, 22 Nov. 1880; 14 April 1884; 19 May 1884; 22 Nov. 1897.

15. Trustees' Minutes, 13 Feb. 1869.

16. Faculty Minutes, 18 April 1881; 2 May 1881; 16 May 1881; 17 April 1882; 31 March 1884.

17. Faculty Minutes, 6 Feb. 1882; 18 Oct. 1894.

18. Minutes of Emma Willard Society, 23 June 1859; 21 July 1859; 11 Aug. 1859; 1 Feb. 1861; 28 May 1863; 8 Sept. 1864.

19. Minutes of Philo Society, 31 July 1863.

20. Program of Philomathean Literary Society, 4 Sept. 1868, Registrar's files; Faculty Minutes, 21 Nov. 1881; 4 June 1890.

21. Minutes of Philo Society, 13 Jan. 1865; 28 April 1865.

22. Minutes of Emma Willard Society, 19 Dec. 1859; *The Washington Observer*, 11 June 1949, p. 26.

23. Minutes of Philo Society, 22 May 1874; 29 May 1874; 5 June 1874; 19 June 1874.

24. Minutes of Philo Society, 10 July 1874; 17 July 1874.

25. Minutes of Philo Society, 21 Jan. 1876; 20 July 1877.

26. *The Cumberland Presbyterian*, 21 Aug. 1879, p. 5.

27. *The Washington Observer*, 11 June 1949, p. 26; Minutes of Philo Society, 6 Nov. 1863; 20 Nov. 1863; Thomas A. Bailey, *The American Pageant: A History of the Republic*, 2nd ed. (Boston, 1961), pp. 531-532.

28. One of these janitors was John M. Howard, who later became a leader in the CP Church and a regular contributor of articles to *The Cumberland Presbyterian.* See Minutes of Philo Society, 10 March 1865.

29. Minutes of Philo Society, 15 July 1863.

30. Minutes of Philo Society, 27 Nov. 1863; Trustees' Minutes, 4 Jan. 1870.

31. *Waynesburg College Crayon*, Jan. 1891, p. 2; *WC Catalogue*, 1888-1889, p. 31; 1891-1892, pp. 22-23; *Dedication Exercises of Philo Hall*, 30 June 1890, Registrar's files; George P. Schmidt, *The Liberal Arts College: A Chapter in American Cultural History* (New Brunswick, N. J., 1957), p. 99.

32. *The Washington Observer*, 11 June 1949, p. 26; *St. Louis Observer*, 15 April 1886, p. 13.

33. Minutes of Philo Society, 22 Aug. 1862.

34. Minutes of Philo Society, 11 Feb. 1865; 17 Feb. 1865; 24 Feb. 1865.

35. Minutes of Philo Society, 31 Jan. 1878; Trustees' Minutes, 17 March 1880; *The Cumberland Presbyterian*, 18 Sept. 1874, p. 1; *St. Louis Observer*, 15 April 1886, p. 13; Faculty Minutes, 8 Jan. 1897.

36. *The Cumberland Presbyterian*, 23 March 1876, p. 1; R. F. Downey, Waynesburg, Pa., to W. B. Mathews, Charleston, W. Va., 2 Sept. 1903. Stewart files.

37. *The Waynesburg Republican*, 23 April 1896, p. 1; Faculty Minutes, 30 April 1897; 29 April 1898.

38. "Report of Librarian of Emma Willard and Philo Societies," Summer 1875; and Philo Literary Society, Library Record, 8 March 1877. See also Minutes of Philo Society, 1 Jan. 1883.

39. Trustees' Minutes, 27 Feb. 1874; 1 Oct. 1878; Faculty Minutes, 14 Oct. 1878; 23 Jan. 1882.

40. *WC Catalogue*, 1871-1872, p. 24.

41. *The Cumberland Presbyterian*, 25 May 1882, p. 1; *WC Catalogue*, 1885-1886, p. 28; June 1896, p. 23; June 1898, p. 41.

42. See the Registrar's files for copies of these programs.

43. Nelson M. Blake, *A History of American Life and Thought* (New York, 1963), p. 273.

44. *The Yellow Jacket*, 15 Sept. 1955, p. 2; 11 June 1949, p. 24.

45. *The Waynesburg Republican*, 20 Sept. 1871, p. 2; *The Washington Observer*, 11 June 1949, pp. 24-25.

46. Schmidt, pp. 198-201.

47. *The Yellow Jacket*, Dec. 1924, pp. 2-3. Whittles became a noted clergyman. A graduate in the Class of 1896, he returned to Waynesburg in 1924, when he was preaching in Duluth, Minnesota. He saw his *Alma Mater* beat Bethany College. He was especially interested in the contrast between the teams of 1895 and 1924. See also "The Yellow Jacket's, Waynesburg College Football Records," revised 1968, pp. 1-2.

48. *The Yellow Jacket*, 22 Oct. 1932, p. 2; 29 Feb. 1936, p. 3; *The Washington Observer*, 11 June 1949, p. 4.

49. *The Waynesburg Republican*, 2 Sept. 1897, p. 1; 16 Sept. 1897, p. 1; 14 Oct. 1897, p. 1; 21 Sept. 1899, p. 1; 26 Sept. 1899, p. 1; *The Yellow Jacket*, Dec. 1924, p. 9; *The Washington Observer*, 11 June 1949, p. 27. See also "The Yellow Jacket's, Waynesburg College Football Records," revised 1968, pp. 1-2.

50. *The Waynesburg Republican*, 31 Jan. 1895, p. 1; 8 April 1897, p. 1.

51. *WC Catalogue*, 1885-1886, p. 30;

The Cumberland Presbyterian, 29 Sept. 1871, p. 2; 21 Sept. 1876, p. 4; *The Waynesburg Republican*, 12 March 1891, p. 1.

52. *WC Catalogue*, 1891-1892, pp. 21-22; June 1898, p. 41; M. Anstice Harris to President [Paul R.] Stewart, 2 Nov. 1951, Stewart files.

53. *WC Catalogue*, June 1896, p. 29.

54. *WC Catalogue*, Sept. 1865, p. 8; *The Washington Observer*, 11 June 1949, pp. 21, 30. That some students sympathized with the South, and cast their lot with the Confederacy, was realistically portrayed in the college's Centennial Parade in Waynesburg on 11 June 1949. Two "opposing" detachments participated: one was "The Northern Cavalry"; the other, "The Southern Cavalry." Clad respectively in blue and gray uniforms, and sporting full beards characteristic of the time, these units added greatly to the pageantry of that day's activities. See Souvenir Program, *Waynesburg College Centennial Parade* (Waynesburg, Pa., 11 June 1949), p. 2, Registrar's files.

55. *The Cumberland Presbyterian*, 30 Sept. 1870, p. 1; 25 July 1873, p. 4.

56. *The Waynesburg Republican*, 18 Oct. 1871, p. 3; *The Cumberland Presbyterian*, 5 March 1885, p. 5.

57. *The Cumberland Presbyterian*, 21 July 1871, p. 1; 19 Jan. 1872, p. 1.

58. *The Waynesburg Republican*, 14 Feb. 1895, p. 1.

59. Faculty Minutes, 18 July 1879.

CHAPTER VI

1. George P. Schmidt, *The Liberal Arts College: A Chapter in American Cultural History* (New Brunswick, N. J., 1957), p. 35; *WC Catalogue*, June 1898, p. 59; *The Collegian*, March 1916, p. 7; Trustees' Minutes, 5 May 1880; Andrew J. Waychoff, *Local History* (Waynesburg, 1926), No. 52.

2. *The Cumberland Presbyterian*, 14 Oct. 1870, p. 1. See also Nelson M. Blake, *A History of American Life and Thought* (New York, 1963), p. 200.

3. *The Cumberland Presbyterian*, 3 July 1874, p. 5.

4. Trustees' Minutes, 30 April 1878; 5 Oct. 1880.

5. Samuel P. Bates, *History of Greene County, Pennsylvania* (Chicago, 1888), pp. 338-339.

6. Bates, pp. 339-340.

7. *The Cumberland Presbyterian*, 29 April 1870, p. 2; B. W. McDonnold, *History of the Cumberland Presbyterian Church*, 2nd ed. (Nashville, Tenn., 1888), p. 536; *The Waynesburg Republican*, 14 Nov. 1901, p. 4; A. B. Miller, *Funeral Discourse of Professor Milton E. Garrison. . . .* (Pittsburgh, Pa., 1870), pp. 5-7.

8. *The Cumberland Presbyterian*, 26 Oct. 1876, p. 5.

9. Trustees' Minutes, 2 July 1878; 31 July 1878; 1 Aug. 1878; 6 Aug. 1878.

10. Trustees' Minutes, 6 Aug. 1878.

11. Trustees' Minutes, 6 Aug. 1878.

12. Trustees' Minutes, 11 Oct. 1878.

13. Trustees' Minutes, 12 Dec. 1878; 21 March 1879; 6 May 1879.

14. Trustees' Minutes, 4 Nov. 1879.

15. Trustees' Minutes, 24 Dec. 1879.

16. *The Waynesburg Republican*, 12 Oct. 1883, p. 1.

17. *The Waynesburg Republican*, 19 July 1871, p. 4; 14 Nov. 1901, p. 4.

18. William Hanna, *History of Greene County, Pa.* (n. p., 1882), pp. 184-185.

19. *The Waynesburg Republican*, 27 Sept. 1871, p. 2; 19 June 1913, p. 1.

20. McDonnold, p. 537; *The Cumberland Presbyterian*, 19 June 1874, p. 2; *The Waynesburg Republican*, 4 March 1874, p. 3; 11 June 1891, p. 1; 5 March 1896, p. 1. A baby born to the Millers died in infancy. A son, Albert Barnes Miller,

attended Waynesburg College, and he graduated from Pennsylvania Dental College, in Philadelphia, in 1893. He returned to Waynesburg and became an itinerant dentist, practicing in several places in Greene County. Unfortunately he died of Bright's disease in 1895. For several years prior to his death, he and his wife, Jennie Wilson Miller, resided in his father's home, and aided in the home management. A daughter, Mrs. Jessie Miller Maxwell, died in 1900. Survivors after that time were Mrs. Lida Simpson, Mrs. Lucy Beach, Mrs. Haddie Minor, Howard B. Miller, and Alfred T. Miller, '99. See *The Waynesburg Daily Times*, 30 Jan. 1902, p. 1. See also Bates, pp. 683-685; *The Waynesburg Republican*, 11 June 1891, p. 1; 25 June 1891, p. 1.

21. Trustees' Minutes, 28 April 1874.

22. *The Cumberland Presbyterian*, 19 June 1874, p. 2.

23. *The Cumberland Presbyterian*, 18 Sept. 1874, p. 1; 25 March 1875, p. 1; 20 Sept. 1877, p. 1; 4 Nov. 1880, p. 1; *The Waynesburg Republican*, 30 June 1875, p. 3.

24. *The Democrat Messenger* (Waynesburg), 27 April 1928, p. 1. See also *The Margaret Bell Miller School Dedication Program*, Waynesburg, Pa., 1 June 1928. By 1969 the new Waynesburg Central High School was constructed just east of town, and high school students attend there. The Margaret Bell Miller School, in excellent condition, is now (1974) being used as a "middle school."

25. *The Washington Observer*, 11 June 1949, p. 30; *WC Bulletin*, Oct. and Nov. 1927, pp. 1, 3; *The Cumberland Presbyterian*, 17 June 1870, p. 4; 8 Nov. 1883, p. 5; *The Waynesburg Republican*, 14 Nov. 1901, p. 4; Faculty Minutes, 21 Sept. 1896; Trustees' Minutes, 12 June 1917; Trustees' Minutes, Adrian College, 17 June 1890.

26. *WC Bulletin*, Dec. 1927, pp. 1, 3; *The Waynesburg Republican*, 1 Dec. 1910, p. 1; *The Washington Observer*, 11 June 1949, p. 30.

27. *WC Bulletin*, Dec. 1927, p. 3; *The Waynesburg Republican*, 25 July 1895, p. 1; 1 Dec. 1910, p. 1; *The Washington Observer*, 11 June 1949, p. 30.

28. Trustees' Minutes, 21 March 1879; 31 July 1879; 31 Aug. 1880. Albert McGinnis was the son of John McGinnis of Ten Mile, Pennsylvania, who, early in the present century, was one of the ruling elders of the Pleasant Hill Presbyterian Church located near that village. The CP missionaries founded this church in 1833. See Arthur W. McGinnis, Westbury, New York, to Lois Westfall, Secretary to Chancellor [Stewart], Waynesburg College, 27 Aug. 1966, Stewart files. See also Fred Cochran, "Pleasant Hill Presbyterian Church, 1833-1973" (Ten Mile, Pa., 1973), p. 12.

29. *The Cumberland Presbyterian*, 18 Oct. 1883, p. 5; 8 Nov. 1883, p. 5; 19 June 1884, p. 4; *The Waynesburg Republican*, 4 Aug. 1887, p. 1.

30. Program of *Forty-Second Annual Session of the Greene County Teachers' Institute* (Waynesburg, Pa., 1908), unpaged.

31. *WC Bulletin*, Jan.-Feb. 1929, pp. 1-2; *The Democrat Messenger* (Waynesburg), 27 Nov. 1945, pp. 1, 5; Faculty Minutes, 25 Sept. 1894. See also "List of Principals of the Female Seminary, Principals of the Female Department, and Deans of Women," Stewart files.

32. *The Waynesburg Republican*, 20 June 1895, p. 1. Goodnight was a leader in the CP Church before the union with the United Presbyterian Church, U. S. A. in 1905. In the CP Church that survived after that union, his services were outstanding. He was stated clerk at meetings of its General Assembly from 1907 through 1914. See Ben M. Barrus, Milton L. Baughn, and Thomas H. Campbell, *A People Called Cumberland Presbyterians* (Memphis, Tenn., 1972), p. 518.

33. *The Cumberland Presbyterian*, 17 June 1870, p. 4; 19 May 1871, p. 1; *The Waynesburg Republican*, 24 Feb. 1887, p. 1.

34. Trustees' Minutes, 8 Dec. 1879.

35. Faculty Minutes, 1 Oct. 1878; 7 Jan. 1880; 2 Oct. 1882; 21 Sept. 1896.

36. *The Waynesburg Republican*, 12 March 1891, p. 1; Edward Martin, *Always Be On Time, An Autobiography* (Harrisburg, Pa., 1959), pp. 9-10.

37. *The Waynesburg Republican*, 18 June 1879, p. 4; Faculty Minutes, 5 July 1880.

38. Trustees' Minutes, 31 July 1878; 30 Aug. 1878; 11 Oct. 1878; 18 March 1879; 21 March 1879.

39. Trustees' Minutes, 19 Feb. 1879; 1 July 1879; 13 May 1880; 31 Aug. 1880.

40. *The Waynesburg Republican*, 29 Nov. 1871, p. 2; *The Cumberland Presbyterian*, 23 March 1882, p. 4; Trustees' Minutes, 4 March 1879; 8 Dec. 1879.

41. Trustees' Minutes, 31 July 1879.

42. Trustees' Minutes, 17 Sept. 1878; 3 Sept. 1879.

43. Trustees' Minutes, 3 Sept. 1879; 8 Dec. 1879.

44. Trustees' Minutes, 27 Dec. 1880.

45. Schmidt, p. 95.

46. Trustees' Minutes, 19 Feb. 1879; 31 Aug. 1880.

47. Trustees' Minutes, 3 Dec. 1878; 24 June 1879; 15 Dec. 1879; Faculty Minutes, 19 March 1897.

48. *The Waynesburg Republican*, 10 Jan. 1872, p. 3.

49. *WC Catalogue*, 1888-1889, p. 16; Schmidt, p. 92.

50. Bates, p. 337.

51. *The Collegian*, March 1916, p. 7.

CHAPTER VII

1. George P. Schmidt, *The Liberal Arts College, A Chapter in American Cultural History* (New Brunswick, N. J., 1957), pp. 43-45.

2. *WC Catalogue*, 1871-1872, pp. 1-3; 1886-1887, p. 32; Trustees' Minutes, 20 Feb. 1879; 12 July 1881.

3. *WC Catalogue*, 1871-1872, p. 15; 1885-1886, p. 32; 1888-1889, pp. 6-7; June 1898, p. 7; Schmidt, p. 69.

4. *WC Catalogue*, 1871-1872, pp. 15-18; June 1898, p. 7.

5. *WC Catalogue*, 1871-1872, p. 18; 1882-1883, p. 21; June 1898, p. 7.

6. *The Waynesburg Republican*, 8 Sept. 1875, p. 3.

7. *The Cumberland Presbyterian*, 7 Oct. 1870, p. 1; 6 Oct. 1871, p. 1. The Dio Lewis system of physical culture was named for Dr. Dio Lewis, a health advocate whose father was a drunkard. Dr. Lewis collaborated with temperance-minded women in founding the Women's Christian Temperance Union (WCTU) in 1874. See *Democrat Messenger* (Waynesburg), 12 Feb. 1974, p. 4.

8. *WC Catalogue*, 1892-1893, p. 25; June 1896, p. 20; June 1897, p. 28.

9. *WC Catalogue*, 1871-1872, pp. 19-20; *The Cumberland Presbyterian*, 4 Feb. 1875, p. 8; 31 March 1881, p. 8.

10. Faculty Minutes, 10 March 1884; 2 June 1884; *The Cumberland Presbyterian*, 18 Oct. 1883, p. 5; 19 June 1884, p. 4; *The Waynesburg Republican*, 4 Aug. 1887, p. 1.

11. Andrew J. Waychoff, *Local History* (Waynesburg, 1926), No. 52, No. 184.

12. *WC Catalogue*, 1871-1872, p. 18; 1885-1886, p. 19; Faculty Minutes, 2 June 1879; *St. Louis Observer*, 22 July 1886, pp. 12-13.

13. *WC Catalogue*, 1890-1891, pp. 15-16; 1891-1892, p. 13.

14. B. W. McDonnold, *History of the Cumberland Presbyterian Church*, 2nd

ed. (Nashville, Tenn., 1888), pp. 538-539; *The Cumberland Presbyterian*, 26 Oct. 1876, p. 1; 20 Sept. 1877, p. 1.

15. *The Cumberland Presbyterian*, 28 March 1878, p. 2; 31 March 1881, p. 8.

16. *The Waynesburg Republican*, 23 Aug. 1871, p. 3.

17. *WC Catalogue*, 1885-1886, p. 10.

18. *WC Catalogue*, 1891-1892, pp. 15-16.

19. Faculty Minutes, 4 Nov. 1880.

20. *WC Catalogue*, 1885-1886, p. 9.

21. *WC Catalogue*, 1885-1886, p. 11; June 1897, p. 29.

22. Schmidt, pp. 71, 160, 180, 289; Nelson M. Blake, *A History of American Life and Thought* (New York, 1963), p. 388.

23. *WC Catalogue*, 1891-1892, pp. 17-18.

24. Faculty Minutes, 26 June 1894.

25. Faculty Minutes, 27 March 1895.

26. Farabee is a legend. After teaching at Harvard, he became Curator of the Museum of the University of Pennsylvania. The latter institution sponsored his explorations in South America, Mexico, and Iceland. He and Theodore Roosevelt were warm friends, for they had much in common in their expeditions in the jungles of South America. President Warren G. Harding appointed him to head a commission from the United States at Peru's Centennial Celebration of independence in 1921. President Woodrow Wilson chose Farabee as a cartographer and ethnographer on the commission of experts, who accompanied him to the Peace Conference at Versailles, France, in 1919. After some thirty-five blood transfusions, at age sixty, Farabee died of a blood disease contracted while exploring in the Amazon valley. See *The Waynesburg Republican*, 6 July 1916, p. 1; 12 Dec. 1918, p. 1; 9 Jan. 1919, p. 1; 22 May 1919, p. 1; 14 July 1921, p. 1.

27. *WC Catalogue*, June 1896, pp. 12-13.

28. Faculty Minutes, 9 Nov. 1896.

29. *WC Catalogue*, 1890-1891, p. 19; 1891-1892, p. 27; 1892-1893, p. 28; June 1894, p. 29; June 1896, pp. 30-31; June 1897, p. 46; June 1898, p. 47; 1899-1900, p. 43; 1900-1901, p. 33.

30. See Registrar's files for this and similar certificates of deportment and scholastic standing of students.

31. Faculty Minutes, 10 Feb. 1879; 12 April 1880; 26 Sept. 1887; 20 March 1894.

32. Faculty Minutes, 5 Feb. 1892.

33. Faculty Minutes, 24 June 1891; 16 Jan. 1894; 20 Jan. 1896.

34. Faculty Minutes, 26 Sept. 1879.

35. Faculty Minutes, 9 Jan. 1882.

36. Faculty Minutes, 2 Feb. 1880; 13 June 1880; 27 June 1881; 13 Feb. 1882.

37. Faculty Minutes, 19 Sept. 1879; 20 Sept. 1879.

38. Faculty Minutes, 12 July 1880.

39. Faculty Minutes, 23 Aug. 1894.

40. Faculty Minutes, 23 June 1884.

41. Faculty Minutes, 5 June 1891; 2 Oct. 1891; 25 March 1896.

42. Faculty Minutes, 25 May 1888, 22 Feb. 1890.

43. Faculty Minutes, 24 June 1891.

44. Faculty Minutes, 1 March 1895.

45. Faculty Minutes, 29 Oct. 1899; 26 Jan. 1900.

46. Faculty Minutes, 1 April 1884.

47. *WC Catalogue*, 1871-1872, p. 28; *The Cumberland Presbyterian*, 2 Sept. 1870, p. 1; 12 Aug. 1875, p. 4.

48. See Commencement Programs, 22 Sept. 1859, 20 Sept. 1864, 10 Sept. 1867. See also *The Cumberland Presbyterian*, 6 Oct. 1871, p. 1.

49. Faculty Minutes, 24 June 1880; 2 June 1882; 28 Jan. 1884; 28 June 1887.

50. Faculty Minutes, 28 June 1890; 15 May 1896; 12 May 1897.

51. Freeman said Waynesburg had "not grown into a city as it would have done long ago, had it been in the Prairie state, [but] it has greatly improved in appearance and shows on every hand the evidences of prosperity." See *The Cumberland Presbyterian*, 14 Oct. 1879, p. 1.

52. *The Cumberland Presbyterian*, 7 Sept. 1876, pp. 1, 4.

53. *The Cumberland Presbyterian*, 6 Oct. 1871, p. 1.

54. *The Cumberland Presbyterian*, 7 Sept. 1876, p. 1; 18 Sept. 1874, p. 1.

55. Nora M. High to President [Paul R.] Stewart, 18 Jan. 1949, Stewart files; *Waynesburg College Crayon*, Jan. 1891, p. 2. I am indebted to Mrs. Katherine Biddle Nolf, '41, for the rare copy of this newspaper.

56. *The Cumberland Presbyterian*, 1 April 1870, p. 5; 12 Aug. 1875, p. 4; 27 Sept. 1872, p. 1; *The Waynesburg Republican*, 20 March 1872, p. 3; 8 Sept. 1875, p. 3.

57. *The Cumberland Presbyterian*, 18 Sept. 1874, p. 1; 1 April 1875, p. 5.

58. Schmidt, pp. 69-70.

CHAPTER VIII

1. *The Cumberland Presbyterian*, 10 Nov. 1881, p. 1.

2. L. K. Evans, *Pioneer History of Greene County, Pennsylvania* (Waynesburg, Pa., 1941), p. 162; Samuel P. Bates, *History of Greene County, Pennsylvania* (Chicago, 1888), pp. 319, 341-342; J. A. Caldwell, *Illustrated Historical Centennial Atlas of Greene County, Pennsylvania* (Condit, Ohio, 1876), p. 18; *Annual Catalogue*, Monongahela College, 1890-1891, pp. 2, 27-28; *The Cumberland Presbyterian*, 17 Dec. 1874, p. 1; 2 May 1878, p. 5.

3. Evans, p. 162.

4. *The Cumberland Presbyterian*, 17 Dec. 1874, p. 1; Program of the *Forty-Second Annual Session of the Greene County Teachers' Institute* (Waynesburg, Pa., 1908), unpaged.

5. *The Waynesburg Republican*, 16 Aug. 1871, p. 4.

6. *The Cumberland Presbyterian*, 20 Sept. 1877, p. 1; 3 Feb. 1881, p. 1.

7. Trustees' Minutes, 13 May 1880; 22 July 1880; 6 Aug. 1880; *The Yellow Jacket*, 19 Nov. 1955, p. 1; Evans, p. 162.

8. B. W. McDonnold, *History of the Cumberland Presbyterian Church* 2nd ed. (Nashville, Tenn., 1888), p. 539.

9. *The Cumberland Presbyterian*, 29 Nov. 1872, p. 1; 23 May 1873, p. 1; 19 Sept. 1873, p. 1.

10. Trustees' Minutes, 6 Aug. 1878; 5 Aug. 1879; 3 Sept. 1879; 4 Nov. 1879.

11. *The Cumberland Presbyterian*, 8 April 1880, p. 7.

12. Trustees' Minutes, 19 June 1880.

13. Trustees' Minutes, 31 July 1878.

14. Evans, pp. 163-164.

15. Trustees' Minutes, 30 April 1878; 15 Dec. 1879; 15 Jan. 1880; 5 Oct. 1880; *The Cumberland Presbyterian*, 9 Oct. 1874, p. 1; 5 Oct. 1876, p. 5; 26 Oct. 1876, p. 5; 15 Nov. 1877, p. 1; 13 Nov. 1879, p. 5; 23 Sept. 1880, p. 5.

16. Trustees' Minutes, 9 Nov. 1877; 31 July 1878; 4 March 1879; 18 April 1879; 30 July 1879; 3 Sept. 1879; 8 Dec. 1879.

17. Trustees' Minutes, 31 July 1879; 5 May 1880; 5 Oct. 1880; *The Waynesburg Republican*, 23 July 1875, p. 3; 11 Aug. 1875, p. 3.

18. Trustees' Minutes, 11 Aug. 1880; 14 Jan. 1881; 16 March 1881; 17 March 1881; 5 April 1881; 18 July 1881.

19. *The Waynesburg Republican*, 20 April 1881, p. 3.

20. *The Waynesburg Republican*, 2 Oct. 1883, p. 3; *St. Louis Observer*, 15 July 1886, p. 16.

21. *St. Louis Observer*, 15 July 1886, p. 16.

22. *The Cumberland Presbyterian*, 26 Nov. 1884, p. 2; 23 Nov. 1882, p. 1; Evans, p. 162.

23. Trustees' Minutes, 30 April 1878; *The Cumberland Presbyterian*, 7 June 1877, p. 4.

24. *The Cumberland Presbyterian*, 6 June 1878, p. 4; 2 June 1881, p. 4.

25. *The Cumberland Presbyterian*, 23 March 1876, p. 1; 8 March 1877, p. 1.

26. *The Cumberland Presbyterian*, 23 March 1876, p. 1; 11 July 1878, p. 4.

27. *The Cumberland Presbyterian*, 17 Dec. 1874, p. 1; 9 Aug. 1877, p. 5; 1 Nov. 1877, p. 1; 14 June 1883, p. 1; Evans, p. 163.

28. Evans, p. 163; *The Cumberland Presbyterian*, 1 Nov. 1877, p. 1; 16 Oct. 1879, p. 1.

29. *The Cumberland Presbyterian*, 23 March 1876, p. 1; Trustees' Minutes, 22 Aug. 1877.

30. *The Cumberland Presbyterian*, 22 July 1880, pp. 1, 4; 7 Oct. 1880, p. 5.

31. *The Cumberland Presbyterian*, 10 March 1881, p. 4.

32. *The Cumberland Presbyterian*, 4 Aug. 1881, p. 5; 11 Aug. 1881, p. 5; 8 Sept. 1881, p. 1; 13 Oct. 1881, p. 1; 10 Nov. 1881, p. 1.

33. Trustees' Minutes, 29 March 1881; 31 May 1881; 24 June 1881; 13 July 1881; Evans, p. 163.

34. *The Cumberland Presbyterian*, 5 Oct. 1882, p. 1; 13 Sept. 1883, p. 5.

35. *St. Louis Observer*, 9 Dec. 1886, p. 1.

36. *The Waynesburg Republican*, 8 May 1890, p. 1.

37. *St. Louis Observer*, 6 Jan. 1887, p. 16.

38. *The Yellow Jacket*, 19 Nov. 1955, p. 1; Evans, p. 163. See also relevant documents in Stewart files.

39. *The Cumberland Presbyterian*, 4 March 1875, p. 1; 4 Jan. 1877, p. 1; 15 Nov. 1877, p. 1. Miller's estimate of 803,000 bricks to complete the building was far short of the number eventually needed. As construction progressed more bricks were made, and the total number in the building is 1,400,012. See Evans, p. 162.

40. *The Cumberland Presbyterian*, 21 Aug. 1879, p. 1; *The Waynesburg Republican*, 25 June 1879, p. 3.

41. *The Cumberland Presbyterian*, 21 Aug. 1879, p. 1; Trustees' Minutes, 1 July 1879; 18 July 1879.

42. Hymn sung at the laying of the cornerstone of Waynesburg College, 10 Sept. 1879, from Mrs. Samilda Rose Keigley's Scrap Book, by her daughter Mrs. T. J. Rose, Stewart files. See also A. B. Miller to the Friends of Education (Waynesburg, Pa., 27 Aug. 1879), unpaged, Registrar's files.

43. *The Waynesburg Republican*, 28 June 1881, p. 3; *The Cumberland Presbyterian*, 1 July 1880, p. 4; 4 Nov. 1880, p. 1; 4 Aug. 1881, p. 1; Trustees' Minutes, 5 April 1881, 1 July 1881.

44. *The Waynesburg Republican*, 7 April 1885, p. 3; *The Cumberland Presbyterian*, 20 July 1882, p. 1; 11 Sept. 1884, p. 1.

45. *WC Catalogue*, 1885-1886, p. 26; *The Waynesburg Republican*, 24 Feb. 1887, p. 1; *St. Louis Observer*, 26 Aug. 1886, p. 13.

46. *WC Catalogue*, 1885-1886, pp. 25, 31; 1888-1889, p. 29; *The Yellow Jacket*, 8 Dec. 1961, p. 2.

47. McDonnold, p. 539; *Waynesburg Independent*, 11 Sept. 1890, p. 4.

48. Alumni Association Minutes, 1 July 1885; 26 June 1889; 26 June 1895; 25 June 1896; *WC Catalogue* 1888-1889, pp. 29-30; *The Cumberland Presbyterian*, 17 Dec. 1874, p. 1; Constitution of the Alumni Association, 1871, Stewart files; *Waynesburg Independent*, 3 July 1890, p. 1.

49. *WC Catalogue*, June 1897, p. 45.

50. *WC Catalogue*, 1882-1883, p. 39; *The Cumberland Presbyterian*, 12 Jan. 1882, p. 1; 8 June 1882, p. 1.

51. *The Cumberland Presbyterian*, 17 Dec. 1874, p. 2; 7 June 1877, p. 4; 14 Oct. 1880, p. 1.

52. *The Cumberland Presbyterian*, 25 Dec. 1879, p. 5.

53. *The Cumberland Presbyterian*, 22

July 1880, p. 4; 23 Sept. 1880, p. 5; 7 Oct. 1880, p. 5; 14 Oct. 1880, p. 1.

54. *The Cumberland Presbyterian*, 3 Feb. 1881, p. 1; 25 Aug. 1881, p. 4; 1 Sept. 1881, p. 1.

55. *The Cumberland Presbyterian*, 24 Feb. 1881, p. 1. It was not unusual for needy colleges to receive property "in kind." For example Harvard, the first colonial college, in the early years, gladly received livestock as income, but the animals had to be fat and in good condition; otherwise they were "sent back" to donors. A student could pay his tuition with a fat cow. Harvard also welcomed all kinds of grain as income. See Margery Somers Foster, *"Out of Small Beginnings . . ." An Economic History of Harvard College in the Puritan Period, 1636 to 1712* (Cambridge, Mass., 1962), pp. 21, 27, 49.

56. *The Cumberland Presbyterian*, 13 Oct. 1881, p. 1.

57. *The Cumberland Presbyterian*, 12 Jan. 1882, p. 1.

58. *The Cumberland Presbyterian*, 8 June 1882, p. 1; 15 June 1882, p. 4; 13 July 1882, p. 1.

59. *The Cumberland Presbyterian*, 4 Aug. 1881, p. 1; 10 Aug. 1882, p. 1.

60. *The Cumberland Presbyterian*, 10 Aug. 1882, p. 1; 15 Feb. 1883, p. 4; 22 Feb. 1883, p. 1.

61. *The Cumberland Presbyterian*, 8 Nov. 1883, p. 5; 13 Dec. 1883, p. 5.

62. *The Waynesburg Republican*, 25 March 1884, p. 3.

63. *The Cumberland Presbyterian*, 24 July 1884, p. 2; *St. Louis Observer*, 13 Jan. 1887, p. 9.

64. Faculty Minutes, 25 Sept. 1894; *WC Catalogue*, 1892-1893, p. 36.

65. Evans, p. 164; *The Waynesburg Republican*, 19 Aug. 1897, p. 1; 21 Oct. 1897, p. 1; 27 Oct. 1898, p. 1; 28 Sept. 1899, p. 1.

66. *The Cumberland Presbyterian*, 20 Sept. 1877, p. 1; 15 Nov. 1877, p. 1; Bates, p. 547. A good description of the "W. & W." railroad is Bates, pp. 354-357.

67. *The Waynesburg Republican*, 20 April 1881, p. 3. Within a decade after its completion, the "W. & W." Railroad was taken over by the Pennsylvania Railroad Company. Competition from automobiles, buses, and trucks forced termination of service on the "W. & W." in 1927. The Pennsylvania Railroad Company, however, has kept the right of way, in case new coal mines open in the area. In 1966 a small car was still run over the track once weekly, in order to maintain legal claim to the route. In 1958 the "Pennsy" generously presented the last narrow gauge locomotive to the Greene County Historical Society. See George Swetnam, "Once-A-Week-Railroad," *The Pittsburgh Press*, 21 Aug. 1966, (Family Magazine, pp. 4-5). See also Bates, p. 547.

68. *The Waynesburg Republican*, 21 Feb. 1872, p. 3; 19 Sept. 1877, p. 2.

69. *The Waynesburg Republican*, 28 June 1881, p. 3; 16 Jan. 1883, p. 3; 6 March 1883, p. 3; 27 Feb. 1883, p. 3; 5 Aug. 1884, p. 3.

70. *The Waynesburg Republican*, 14 June 1894, p. 1; 6 July 1899, p. 1.

71. *The Cumberland Presbyterian*, 23 Aug. 1883, p. 4.

72. *The Cumberland Presbyterian*, 19 June 1884, p. 4.

73. *St. Louis Observer*, 29 July 1886, p. 8.

74. McDonnold, p. 541; Bates, p. 328; *The Waynesburg Independent*, 27 Aug. 1896, p. 12.

75. William Hanna, *History of Greene County, Pennsylvania* (n. p., 1882), p. 104.

76. *St. Louis Observer*, 29 April 1886, p. 13; *The Waynesburg Republican*, 14 Nov. 1889, p. 1; 30 July 1890, p. 1; 10 Oct. 1895, p. 1.

77. *The Waynesburg Republican*, 27 April 1899, p. 1; 29 June 1899, p. 1; 6 July 1899, p. 1.

78. *The Cumberland Presbyterian*, 21 Aug. 1879, p. 1.

79. Evans, p. 164. Other figures have

been given on the college's endowment as of 1899. One source claims "there was a productive endowment of $40,000 and a non-productive endowment of $20,000." See Ben M. Barrus, Milton L. Baughn, and Thomas H. Campbell, *A People Called Cumberland Presbyterians* (Memphis, Tenn., 1972), p. 229.

80. *WC Catalogue*, 1899-1900, p. 51; Evans, p. 164.

81. *The Fieldview*, June 1903, p. 4; Bates, p. 340.

CHAPTER IX

1. *The Waynesburg Republican*, 5 March 1896, p. 1; 19 Oct. 1899, p. 1; *WC Catalogue*, 1899-1900, pp. 4-5. The Millers resided for many years in what is now called "Sayers Manor" at the corner of Wayne and Morris Streets. After Mrs. Miller died, Miller continued to live there until 1896 after his son, Albert Barnes Miller, a dental surgeon, died. Thenceforward, Miller made his home in a room in Hanna Hall until his death. Shortly before his retirement as President, his residence was sold to A. I. Cooke for $5,200. Cooke made some improvements on it, and resided there. Many years later the college acquired it; and in recent years it has been used as a dormitory. See *The Washington Observer*, 11 June 1949, p. 30.

2. *The Waynesburg Republican*, 6 July 1899, p. 1; 12 Oct. 1899, p. 1.

3. Trustees' Minutes, 10 Sept. 1900.

4. *St. Louis Observer*, 9 Dec. 1886, p. 3; *The Waynesburg Republican*, 14 Nov. 1901, p. 4; *The Fieldview*, June 1903, p. 5; *The Collegian*, April 1900, p. 9; June 1900, p. 13; July 1900, pp. 6, 12; Faculty Minutes, faculty members for 1899-1900. McKay was also a promoter for the Wabash Railroad Company in its plan to build a line from Uniontown, to cross the Monongahela River at McCann's Ferry, come through Carmichaels to Waynesburg, and run thence north to Washington, Pennsylvania. Nothing came of this plan, however. At that time there was keen competition among three companies to construct another railroad in Greene County. The Pennsylvania Railroad Company had "taken over" the "W. & W." And the Baltimore and Ohio Railroad Company projected a rail line through the county. See *The Waynesburg Republican*, 30 Oct. 1902, p. 1.

5. *The Fieldview*, June 1903, pp. 6-7; *The Waynesburg Republican*, 13 Sept. 1900, p. 1; Trustees' Minutes, 20 Sept. 1900; *The Collegian*, July 1905, p. 4.

6. *WC Catalogue*, 1901-1902, pp. 49-50.

7. *The Democrat Messenger* (Waynesburg, Pa.), 10 June 1949, p. 1; Trustees' Minutes, 10 Sept. 1900; 20 Sept. 1900; 21 Nov. 1900; 17 Jan. 1901; 20 June 1901; 19 June 1902; 13 Sept. 1902; 24 June 1903; 7 Sept. 1903; 14 Oct. 1903; 20 June 1904; 18 July 1904; *WC Catalogue*, 1902-1903, p. 2. Miss Acklin resigned on 18 January 1903, which was a loss to the college. The trustees tried to induce her to stay—to no avail. See Trustees' Minutes, 24 April 1903. See also *The Waynesburg Republican*, 18 Feb. 1904, p. 1.

8. Trustees' Minutes, 10 Sept. 1900; 23 Nov. 1900.

9. *WC Catalogue*, 1901-1902, pp. 52-53; 1902-1903, p. 54; 1903-1904, p. 72.

10. Trustees' Minutes, 1 Aug. 1901; 18 Sept. 1901.

11. *WC Catalogue*, 1901-1902, p. 12; *The Collegian*, Oct. 1901, p. 14; Nov. 1901, pp. 8, 11, 15; *The Waynesburg Republican*, 14 Nov. 1901, p. 4. See also the *Official Program of the Half-Century Celebration of Waynesburg College*, 1901, Stewart files.

12. Trustees' Minutes, 6 Dec. 1901; 18 Dec. 1901; 5 Dec. 1902; 24 June 1903;

The Collegian, March 1902, p. 12; Oct. 1902, p. 6. In the midst of the fund-raising campaign, Turner took time to attend the installation of Woodrow Wilson as President of Princeton University in October 1902. See *The Waynesburg Republican*, 17 May 1917, p. 1.

13. Trustees' Minutes, 24 April 1903.

14. Faculty Minutes, 30 Nov. 1900; 22 April 1901; 26 April 1901; 27 Jan. 1902; 19 June 1903.

15. Faculty Minutes, 11 May 1900; 1 March 1901; 12 Dec. 1902; 6 March 1903.

16. Faculty Minutes, 10 Oct. 1902; *The Collegian*, Dec. 1902, p. 1.

17. Faculty Minutes, 13 Sept. 1901; *The Collegian*, Oct. 1902, p. 2; Trustees' Minutes, 24 June 1903.

18. Trustees' Minutes, 5 Dec. 1902; 24 April 1903.

19. *The Collegian*, March 1900, p. 10; Minutes of Philo Society, 20 June 1901; 4 Dec. 1903. For the year 1899-1900 Edward Martin was president of Philo Society; and Charity Scott was its secretary. On 1 December 1908 they were happily married. He later referred to his marriage as "the most important event of my life." See Edward Martin *Always Be On Time, An Autobiography* (Harrisburg, Pa., 1959), p. 20. See also Minutes of Philo Society, 20 Oct. 1899.

20. *Waynesburg College Crayon*, Jan. 1891, p. 2; *The Collegian*, March 1900, p. 3.

21. Faculty Minutes, 15 Nov. 1901; 25 April 1902; 2 May 1902; 11 May 1902.

22. Minutes of Philo Society, 11 Jan. 1901; Faculty Minutes, 28 Feb. 1901; 1 March 1901.

23. Faculty Minutes, 17 Oct. 1901; 14 Feb. 1902; 21 Feb. 1902; 11 April 1902; 30 May 1903; 16 June 1903; *The Collegian*, April 1900, p. 7.

24. *The Collegian*, March 1900, p. 10.

25. *The Collegian*, March 1900, pp. 12-13; Oct. 1900, p. 6; *WC Catalogue*, 1901-1902, pp. 45-46.

26. *WC Catalogue*, 1901-1902, p. 46; *The Collegian*, March 1900, pp. 12-13; Oct. 1900, p. 6.

27. *The Collegian*, March 1900, p. 14; Oct. 1902, p. 8.

28. *The Collegian*, Feb. 1903, p. 2; *The Fieldview*, June 1903, p. 8.

29. *The Fieldview*, June 1903, p. 8; *The Collegian*, Feb. 1903, p. 2; March 1903, pp. 11-12; May 1903, pp. 3-4; Trustees' Minutes, 24 April 1903.

30. *The Collegian*, Oct. 1902, p. 1.

31. Trustees' Minutes, 7 Sept. 1903.

32. *The Collegian*, May 1900, p. 3; April 1901, p. 7; May 1901, p. 7.

33. *The Collegian*, Dec. 1902, p. 13; April 1903, p. 12; *The Waynesburg Republican*, 26 May 1904, p. 1.

34. *The Waynesburg Republican*, 7 Dec. 1899, p. 1. See also "Waynesburg College Football Records," revised 1968, p. 1.

35. *The Waynesburg Republican*, 27 Sept. 1900, p. 1; *The Collegian*, March 1900, p. 14; "Waynesburg College Football Records," revised 1968, p. 1.

36. *The Collegian*, Oct. 1900, pp. 9, 14.

37. *The Collegian*, Sept. 1901, p. 9.

38. *The Collegian*, Oct. 1902, p. 8; Nov. 1902, p. 9; Dec. 1902, pp. 12-13; "Waynesburg College Football Records," revised 1968, pp. 1-2.

39. *The Collegian*, Jan. 1903, p. 2.

40. *The Collegian*, Oct. 1903, p. 7; Trustees' Minutes, 7 Sept. 1903; "Waynesburg College Football Records," revised 1968, p. 2.

41. *The Collegian*, March 1900, p. 14; Oct. 1902, p. 8; Dec. 1902, p. 13; *The Yellow Jacket*, 15 Sept. 1955, p. 2.

42. *The Collegian*, Oct. 1902, p. 8; Dec. 1902, p. 13; April 1903, p. 11.

43. *WC Catalogue*, 1900-1901, pp. 4, 10-11, 17-18; 1901-1902, pp. 15, 24; 1903-1904, p. 36.

44. Faculty Minutes, 22 March 1901; 17 Oct. 1902; *WC Catalogue*, 1900-1901, pp. 17, 50-51, 52-54; 1901-1902, p. 70; 1902-1903, p. 21; 1903-1904, p. 24.

45. *The Collegian*, Jan. 1901, p. 12. The total enrollment in all departments in 1901-1902 was 418. The faculty had 18 members in all. See *WC Catalogue*, 1901-1902, p. 70.

46. *WC Catalogue*, 1900-1901, p. 27.

47. Faculty Minutes, 16 March 1900; 14 June 1901; 5 June 1903.

48. Faculty Minutes, 27 Dec. 1900; 27 Sept. 1901; 21 March 1902.

49. Faculty Minutes, 29 Nov. 1901; 6 Dec. 1901; 13 Dec. 1901; 8 June 1903.

50. Faculty Minutes, 20 June 1901.

51. Faculty Minutes, 5 April 1901; 12 April 1901; 17 May 1901.

52. Faculty Minutes, 24 May 1901; 7 June 1901.

53. Faculty Minutes, 7 June 1900; 25 Oct. 1902.

54. *The Collegian*, July 1904, p. 3; Trustees' Minutes, 20 June 1904; Alumni Association Minutes, 15 June 1904; Faculty Minutes, 4 May 1903.

55. Trustees' Minutes, 18 Jan. 1901; 6 Dec. 1901; 19 June 1902; 24 June 1903; 25 March 1904; 5 July 1904; *The Collegian*, Jan. 1901. p. 7.

56. *WC Catalogue*, 1903-1904, pp. 63-64; *The Collegian*, Jan. 1904, p. 5; *The Yellow Jacket*, 8 Dec. 1961, p. 2.

57. *WC Catalogue*, 1900-1901, p. 63; Alumni Association Minutes, 27 June 1900; 19 June 1901.

58. *WC Catalogue*, 1900-1901, p. 63; *The Collegian*, May 1901, p. 7; *The Waynesburg Republican*, 26 March 1903, p. 1.

59. Alumni Association Minutes, 19 June 1901; 18 June 1902.

60. *The Collegian*, Oct. 1902, p. 2; *WC Catalogue*, 1903-1904, p. 3; Trustees' Minutes, 24 April 1903; 25 March 1904. By 1904 the number of trustees was increased to twenty-seven. See *WC Catalogue*, 1904-1905, p. 3.

61. *The Waynesb[illegible]rg Republican*, 10 Jan. 1901, p. 1; 14 [illegible]n. 1904, p. 1; *The Fieldview*, June 1[illegible] p. 8.

62. *The Colle[illegible]* April 1901, p. 14; July 1901, p. [illegible] [illegible]an. 1902, pp. 12-14; Faculty Minute[illegible] Jan. 1902.

63. Faculty [illegible]utes, 30 Jan. 1902; *The Washingto[illegible] [illegible]bserver*, 11 June 1949, p. 30; *The Wa[illegible]esburg Republican*, 16 Jan. 1902, p. 1; *[illegible]e Collegian*, Feb. 1902, pp. 3-4.

64. *The Waynesburg Daily Times*, 30 Jan. 1902, p. 2; 1 Feb. 1902, p. 1; *The Washington Observer*, 11 June 1949, p. 30.

65. *The Waynesburg Republican*, 6 Feb. 1902, p. 1; *The Collegian*, Feb. 1902, pp. 3-4, 6-8; Faculty Minutes, 31 Jan. 1902.

66. Faculty Minutes, 21 Feb. 1902.

67. Alumni Association Minutes, 18 June 1902.

68. Faculty Minutes, 31 Jan. 1902.

69. *WC Catalogue*, 1901-1902, p. 9.

70. *The Waynesburg Republican*, 5 Feb. 1903, p. 1.

71. *The Waynesburg Republican*, 18 Feb. 1904, p. 1; 26 May 1904, p. 1.

72. Trustees' Minutes, 6 June 1904; 13 June 1904; *The Waynesburg Republican*, 16 June 1904, p. 1; *The Collegian*, July 1904, p. 4.

73. Trustees' Minutes, 13 June 1904; 15 June 1904; *The Waynesburg Republican*, 16 June 1904, p. 1; *The Collegian*, July 1904, p. 4.

74. Trustees' Minutes, 13 June 1904; 20 June 1904; 5 July 1904; *The Collegian*, July 1905, p. 4.

CHAPTER X

1. *The Waynesburg Republican*, 4 Aug. 1904, p. 1; Trustees' Minutes, 1 Aug. 1904; *The Collegian*, Oct. 1904, p. 4.

2. Trustees' Minutes, 3 May 1905; 21 June 1905; 20 July 1905; *The Waynesburg Republican*, 27 July 1905, p. 1; 3 Aug.

1905, p. 1; 3 March 1906, p. 1; *The Collegian*, May 1906, p. 7.

3. Trustees' Minutes, 4 Sept. 1905.

4. *The Waynesburg Republican*, 1 Aug. 1912, p. 1. See also the account of Bucher in Stewart [illegible]

5. *The Waynes*[illegible] *Republican*, 7 Sept. 1905, p. 1; 14 [illegible]t. 1905, p. 1; 16 Jan. 1908, p. 1; Truste[illegible]inutes, 21 June 1906; 9 Sept. 1907; *W*[illegible]*atalogue*, 1905-1906, p. 3.

6. Trustees' Minutes [illegible]4 Jan. 1908; *The Waynesburg Republica*[illegible] 16 Jan. 1908, p. 1; 21 Sept. 1911, p. 1; 1 Aug. 1912, p. 1; *The Collegian*, May 1908, p. 1; Nov. 1909, p. 2.

7. *The Collegian*, May 1908, p. 1; *WC Bulletin*, March 1931, pp. 1-2.

8. Trustees' Minutes, 14 Jan. 1908; 5 May 1908; *The Waynesburg Republican*, 6 Feb. 1908, p. 1; *The Collegian*, July 1908, p. 12.

9. Trustees' Minutes, 17 June 1910; 16 June 1911; *The Waynesburg Republican*, 9 March 1911, p. 1; 6 April 1911, p. 1; 22 June 1911, p. 1. Hudson rendered excellent service for Blackburn College, where he was president from 1912 to 1931. He raised it from an obscure college to one of the best in the Middle West. There he began the "self-help plan," which was later used in many other colleges. See *WC Bulletin*, March 1931, pp. 1-2.

10. Trustees' Minutes, 20 Sept. 1904.

11. *The Waynesburg Republican*, 25 Feb. 1904, p. 1; 2 June 1904, pp. 2-3; 6 Oct. 1904, p. 1; 20 April 1905, p. 1; 25 May 1905, p. 1; 7 June 1906, p. 1; 6 Dec. 1906, p. 1; *The Cumberland Presbyterian*, 18 Nov. 1880, p. 1. Not all CP churches rejoined the parent church. CP congregations in Kentucky, Tennessee, and indeed in all the South Central states perpetuated the CP Church, despite a long, bitter struggle with the Presbyterian Church, U. S. A. At the end of 1970 membership in the CP Church totaled 87,823; there was a smaller group, the CP Church (Colored). Those CP churches which merged with the Presbyterian Church, U. S. A. were chiefly in the North, where the change to one church came gradually and peacefully over a period of some twenty years. See Ben M. Barrus, Milton L. Baughn, and Thomas H. Campbell, *A People called Cumberland Presbyterians* (Memphis, Tenn., 1972), pp. 323-352, 484, 509.

12. *The Waynesburg Republican*, 12 Jan. 1905, p. 1.

13. Trustees' Minutes, 22 March 1905; 16 May 1905; *The Collegian*, Feb. 1905, p. 7. The members of the newly constituted Board of Trustees were: N. H. Biddle, L. D. Brown, N. W. Carter, R. L. Crawford, N. S. Danley, R. F. Downey, A. B. Elliott, N. B. Evans, W. T. Hays, F. P. Iams, James Inghram, I. H. Knox, W. J. Kyle, A. F. Lewis (ex-officio), S. L. Mestrezat, R. W. Parkinson, J. G. Patton, J. A. F. Randolph, J. W. Ray, J. B. F. Rinehart, John Rose, Timothy Ross, H. G. Teagarden, J. T. Ullom, D. S. Walton, T. J. Wisecarver, and J. C. Work. See *The Waynesburg Republican*, 12 Jan. 1905, p. 1.

14. William W. McKinney, ed., *The Presbyterian Valley* (Pittsburgh, 1958), pp. 339-340.

15. Trustees' Minutes, 20 July 1905; 21 June 1907; 9 Sept. 1907; 18 June 1908; 19 June 1909; *WC Catalogue*, 1909-1910, pp. 2-3.

16. *The Collegian*, Feb. 1910, pp. 1-4.

17. *WC Catalogue*, 1908-1909, p. 27.

18. *WC Catalogue*, 1905-1906, pp. 44-45; *WC Bulletin*, Jan. 1909.

19. *WC Catalogue*, 1908-1909, pp. 39-40.

20. *WC Catalogue*, 1909-1910, pp. 35-37, 39.

21. *WC Catalogue*, 1905-1906, pp. 44-45.

22. *WC Catalogue*, June 1907, p. 35; 1908-1909, p. 36; 1909-1910, p. 37.

23. *WC Catalogue*, 1909-1910, pp. 14-34; *The Collegian*, March 1911, p. 5; May 1911, pp. 7-8.

24. *The Waynesburg Republican*, 9 March 1911, p. 1.

25. *WC Catalogue*, 1904-1905, pp. 74-75; 1909-1910, pp. 38-39.

26. *WC Catalogue*, 1909-1910, pp. 39-40.

27. *WC Catalogue*, 1905-1906, pp. 73-74.

28. *The Collegian*, June 1905, p. 13; Nov. 1905, p. 4; Dec. 1907, pp. 3-4.

29. *The Collegian*, Oct. 1904, p. 5; July 1905, p. 7. At that time the athletic field had a covered grandstand and some bleachers; it was surrounded by a board fence. See also "Waynesburg College Football Records," revised 1968, p. 2.

30. *The Collegian*, Nov. 1904, p. 4.

31. *The Collegian*, Jan. 1906, p. 8.

32. *The Waynesburg Republican*, 28 Nov. 1907, p. 1; Trustees' Minutes, 31 May 1907; 18 June 1908.

33. *The Waynesburg Republican*, 5 March 1908, p. 1.

34. *WC Bulletin*, Oct. 1908, p. 10; *The Collegian*, Dec. 1908, pp. 8-9, 14; July 1909, p. 28; "Waynesburg College Football Records," revised 1968, p. 2.

35. Edward Martin, *Always Be On Time, An Autobiography* (Harrisburg, Pa., 1959), p. 22.

36. Trustees' Minutes, 23 June 1910; *The Collegian*, Oct. 1909, p. 10; Nov. 1910, pp. 13-14; May 1911, p. 12; "Waynesburg College Football Records," revised 1968, p. 2.

37. *The Washington Observer*, 11 June 1949, pp. 23, 25; *WC Catalogue*, 1905-1906, pp. 73-74.

38. *The Waynesburg Republican*, 4 Feb. 1909, p. 1; 18 Feb. 1909, p. 1; *The Collegian*, July 1909, p. 28.

39. *The Collegian*, Jan. 1910, p. 4.

40. *The Collegian*, March 1911, p. 7; May 1911, pp. 8-9.

41. *WC Catalogue*, 1905-1906, pp. 73-74; *The Waynesburg Republican*, 28 May 1908, p. 1; 19 Nov. 1908, p. 1; *The Collegian*, July 1909, p. 28.

42. *The Waynesburg Republican*, 21 April 1910, p. 1.

43. *The Waynesburg Republican*, 15 June 1905, p. 1.

44. *The Collegian*, Nov. 1904, p. 8; *The Waynesburg Republican*, 30 March 1905, p. 1.

45. R. F. Downey, '67, to William B. Matthews, Esq., 12 July 1906, Stewart files; Minutes of Philo Society, 7 March 1908; 18 Feb. 1910.

46. *WC Catalogue*, 1905-1906, pp. 48-49.

47. *The Waynesburg Republican*, 25 June 1908, p. 1.

48. *The Waynesburg Republican*, 5 Jan. 1911, p. 1; 30 March 1911, p. 1.

49. *The Collegian*, May 1911, pp. 4-5.

50. *WC Catalogue*, 1904-1905, p. 76.

51. Trustees' Minutes, 19 June 1909.

52. *WC Catalogue*, 1904-1905, p. 77.

53. *WC Catalogue*, 1905-1906, p. 83; 1906-1907, p. 75.

54. Trustees' Minutes, 22 Feb. 1906.

55. Trustees' Minutes, 26 April 1907; 3 June 1909; 19 June 1909; 17 June 1910; 13 Oct. 1910; 26 April 1911; 20 May 1911; *The Waynesburg Republican*, 3 Nov. 1910, p. 1; 24 Nov. 1910, p. 1.

56. Trustees' Minutes, 20 June 1906; 9 July 1906; *The Waynesburg Republican*, 12 July 1906, p. 1.

57. Trustees' Minutes, 3 Aug. 1909; 25 Nov. 1910.

58. Trustees' Minutes, 20 June 1907; 14 Sept. 1907; 18 June 1908; *The Waynesburg Republican*, 23 May 1907, p. 1; 20 June 1907, p. 1; Alumni Association Minutes, 19 June 1907.

59. Trustees' Minutes, 20 Sept. 1904; 26 April 1907; 31 May 1907; *WC Catalogue*, 1909-1910, p. 99.

60. See examples in Trustees' Minutes, 1 Aug. 1904; 21 June 1906; 31 May 1907; 21 June 1907; 6 July 1907; 1 July 1908; 9 Dec. 1910.

61. Trustees' Minutes, 19 June 1907; 6 July 1907; 14 Jan. 1908; *The Waynesburg Republican*, 11 July 1907, p. 1; 3 Sept.

1908, p. 1; *WC Bulletin*, Oct. 1908, p. 9; *The Yellow Jacket*, 10 Sept. 1971, pp. 1, 5.

62. *WC Catalogue*, 1905-1906, p. 71.

63. Trustees' Minutes, 20 Sept. 1904.

64. Trustees' Minutes, 6 July 1907; 3 June 1909; 12 March 1910; 17 June 1910.

65. Trustees' Minutes, 12 March 1910.

CHAPTER XI

1. Trustees' Minutes, 22 June 1911.

2. *The Waynesburg Collegian*, Dec. 1922, p. 11; *The Waynesburg Republican*, 20 June 1911, p. 1; *WC Bulletin*, Jan. 1932, pp. 1-2.

3. *The Waynesburg Republican*, 5 Oct. 1911, p. 1; 19 Oct. 1911, p. 1; *The Athenian*, Waynesburg College, Waynesburg, Pa., 1912.

4. Trustees' Minutes, 22 April 1912.

5. *The Waynesburg Republican*, 9 May 1912, p. 1.

6. Trustees' Minutes, 28 Aug. 1911; 9 May 1912; 14 June 1912; *The Waynesburg Republican*, 16 May 1912, p. 1; 13 June 1912, p. 1; *WC Bulletin*, Aug. 1912, p. 4; Dec. 1913, p. 10; *The Collegian*, Nov. 1912, p. 2.

7. *The Waynesburg Republican*, 3 Dec. 1914, p. 1; 28 Jan. 1915, p. 1.

8. Trustees' Minutes, 17 Aug. 1912; *The Waynesburg Republican*, 22 Aug. 1912, p. 1; *WC Bulletin*, Dec. 1913, p. 5; *WC Catalogue*, Aug. 1913, pp. 4-5; July 1914, pp. 4-5.

9. Trustees' Minutes, 13 June 1913.

10. Trustees' Minutes, 15 July 1914.

11. Trustees' Minutes, 13 June 1913.

12. Trustees' Minutes, 14 June 1912; 17 Aug. 1912; *WC Bulletin*, Aug. 1912, pp. 48-49, 52; Aug. 1913, p. 55; *The Waynesburg Republican*, 9 Jan. 1913, p. 1.

13. Trustees' Minutes, 13 June 1913.

14. *The Waynesburg Republican*, 14 Nov. 1912, p. 1.

15. *The Waynesburg Republican*, 13 Aug. 1914, p. 3; Trustees' Minutes, 15 July 1914; Faculty Minutes, 26 Feb. 1915.

16. Faculty Minutes, 26 Sept. 1914; 13 Oct. 1914.

17. Faculty Minutes, 8 Dec. 1914.

18. Faculty Minutes, 22 Jan. 1915; *Waynesburg College Alumni Directory* (Waynesburg, Pa., 1966), p. 92; Trustees' Minutes, 11 June 1915.

19. William H. Carpenter, Provost of Columbia University, to President Ezra F. Baker, 1 May 1915, Trustees' Minutes, 3 May 1915.

20. Trustees' Minutes, 13 June 1913; *WC Bulletin*, Dec. 1913, p. 1; *The Collegian*, Nov. 1912, p. 12.

21. *The Waynesburg Republican*, 23 Oct. 1913, p. 1; 30 Oct. 1913, p. 1; *The Collegian*, Oct. 1913, pp. 8, 10.

22. Trustees' Minutes, 15 July 1914.

23. *The Waynesburg Republican*, 13 June 1912, p. 1; 14 April 1913, p. 1; Trustees' Minutes, 13 June 1913.

24. Trustees' Minutes, 13 June 1913; 26 Dec. 1913; *The Waynesburg Republican*, 4 Dec. 1913; p. 1; *WC Bulletin*, Dec. 1913, pp. 1, 3-5.

25. Trustees' Minutes, 15 July 1914.

26. Trustees' Minutes, 16 March 1914; 15 July 1914; 22 Jan. 1915.

27. Trustees' Minutes, 15 July 1914; 12 Sept. 1914.

28. *The Waynesburg Republican*, 25 June 1914, p. 1.

29. Trustees' Minutes, 22 Jan. 1915.

30. Trustees' Minutes, 13 Sept. 1912; 13 June 1913; 12 Sept. 1914; *The Collegian*, Nov. 1912, p. 10; Jan. 1913, p. 12; *WC Bulletin*, Aug. 1912, pp. 73-74; *The Waynesburg Republican*, 16 Jan. 1913, p. 1.

31. Faculty Minutes, 3 Nov. 1914; 4 Nov. 1914; "Waynesburg College Football Records," revised 1968, pp. 1, 3.

32. *The Collegian*, Dec. 1912, p. 12; Jan. 1913, p. 2; *The Waynesburg Republican*, 16 Jan. 1913, p. 1.

33. Trustees' Minutes, 13 June 1913.

34. Trustees' Minutes, 13 June 1913.

35. *WC Bulletin*, Aug. 1913, p. 69.

36. Trustees' Minutes, 15 July 1914.

37. Minutes of Philo Society, 25 Oct. 1912; 12 Dec. 1913; *The Collegian*, Jan. 1913, p. 3.

38. Minutes of Philo Society, 4 March 1914; 3 April 1914; Trustees' Minutes, 15 July 1914; Faculty Minutes, 26 Sept. 1914.

39. Faculty Minutes, 26 Sept. 1914.

40. Faculty Minutes, 22 Feb. 1915.

41. Faculty Minutes, 17 March 1915.

42. Trustees' Minutes, 13 June 1913; *The Waynesburg Republican*, 23 Oct. 1913, p. 1.

43. Trustees' Minutes, 13 June 1913.

44. Trustees' Minutes, 26 Dec. 1913.

45. Trustees' Minutes, 4 Jan. 1913; 13 June 1913.

46. Trustees' Minutes, 14 June 1912; 17 Aug. 1912.

47. Faculty Minutes, 20 Oct. 1914, Trustees' Minutes, 22 Jan. 1915.

48. *Suggestions by Friends of Waynesburg College*, n. p., 26 Dec. 1913, Registrar's files.

49. *The Waynesburg Independent*, 27 May 1914, p. 4.

50. Trustees' Minutes, 11 June 1915.

CHAPTER XII

1. *The Waynesburg Republican*, 6 May 1915, p. 1; 10 June 1915, p. 1; 17 June 1915, p. 1; Trustees' Minutes, 11 June 1915.

2. *The Waynesburg Collegian*, Feb. 1918, p. 1; *WC Catalogue*, July 1915, pp. 4-5; *WC Bulletin*, Jan. 1916, p. 7.

3. *The Waynesburg Collegian*, Feb. 1918, pp. 1, 3.

4. *The Waynesburg Republican*, 13 April 1916, p. 1; 8 June 1916, p. 1.

5. *WC Catalogue*, 1918, p. 2.

6. *The Waynesburg Republican*, 7 Sept. 1916, p. 1.

7. *The Waynesburg Collegian*, March 1918, pp. 2-3.

8. *The Collegian*, Oct. 1916, p. 1.

9. R. F. Downey, '67 to William B. Matthews, Esq., Charleston, W. Va., 21 June 1917, Stewart files.

10. *The Democrat Messenger* (Waynesburg), 25 Aug. 1916, p. 1.

11. Trustees' Minutes, 3 April 1916; 12 June 1917; *The Democrat Messenger* (Waynesburg), 12 May 1916, p. 1; *The Waynesburg Republican*, 11 May 1916, p. 1; *WC Bulletin*, Jan. 1916, p. 7.

12. Trustees' Minutes, 3 Dec. 1915; 28 June 1917; *The Waynesburg Republican*, 16 Sept. 1915, p. 1; 13 Jan. 1916, p. 1.

13. Faculty Minutes, 5 April 1917.

14. Faculty Minutes, 11 April 1917.

15. *The Waynesburg Republican*, 7 Oct. 1915, p. 1.

16. Faculty Minutes, 5 April 1917; 20 Nov. 1917.

17. Faculty Minutes, 4 April 1916; 23 Sept. 1916; *WC Catalogue*, 1916-1917, pp. 18-30.

18. *The Waynesburg Republican*, 11 Jan. 1917, p. 1; *WC Catalogue*, 1916-1917, p. 30.

19. *WC Catalogue*, 1915-1916, p. 33; 1916-1917, p. 11.

20. *The Waynesburg Republican*, 2 Sept. 1915, p. 1; 13 Jan. 1916, p. 1; *WC Bulletin*, Jan. 1916, pp. 2-4.

21. *The Waynesburg Republican*, 19 Oct. 1916, p. 1.

22. *The Waynesburg Republican*, 16 Sept. 1915, p. 1.

23. *The Waynesburg Republican*, 2 Sept. 1915, p. 1; 16 Sept. 1916, p. 1;

WC Catalogue, 1915-1916, p. 14; 1916-1917, p. 55; 1918, p. 44; Trustees' Minutes, 9 June 1916.

24. Faculty Minutes, 3 May 1917; *The Collegian*, March 1917, p. 5.

25. *WC Catalogue*, 1918, p. 41.

26. Faculty Minutes, 7 June 1915.

27. "Inaugural Address of Herbert Pierrepont Houghton," 14 June 1916, Stewart files.

28. *The Collegian*, April 1917, p. 14.

29. *The Waynesburg Republican*, 16 Sept. 1915, p. 1; "Waynesburg College Football Records," revised 1968, pp. 1, 3; Faculty Minutes, 11 Jan. 1917.

30. Faculty Minutes, 1 March 1917.

31. Trustees' Minutes, 12 June 1917; 28 June 1917.

32. *WC Catalogue*, 1915-1916, p. 26.

33. *The Waynesburg Republican*, 6 Jan. 1916, p. 1; 22 June 1916, p. 1.

34. *The Collegian*, Dec. 1915, p. 5; *The Waynesburg Republican*, 6 Jan. 1916, p. 1.

35. *The Waynesburg Republican*, 20 Jan. 1916, p. 4; 27 Jan. 1916, pp. 1, 4; 17 Feb. 1916, p. 4; 24 Feb. 1916, p. 4; 18 Jan. 1917, p. 4; 25 Jan. 1917, p. 4; 10 Jan. 1918, p. 1.

36. *The Collegian*, Feb. 1917, pp. 9, 11; March 1918, p. 1; *The Waynesburg Republican*, 18 Oct. 1917, p. 4. I am indebted to Mary Munnell Rinehart for certain information about the team on which she played. She says they "tried several times to beat Pitt, but were overwhelmed by numbers and size."

37. *The Waynesburg Collegian*, April 1918, p. 1; May 1918, p. 2.

38. *The Waynesburg Republican*, 2 Dec. 1915, p. 1; 1 Feb. 1917, p. 1; 1 March 1917, p. 1; Trustees' Minutes, 12 June 1917.

39. Minutes of Philo Society, 13 June 1917; *The Waynesburg Republican*, 15 June 1916, p. 1.

40. Faculty Minutes, 14 June 1915; 1 March 1917; 12 Feb. 1918; 21 May 1918.

41. Faculty Minutes, 15 Sept. 1917.

42. *The Waynesburg Republican*, 17 Feb. 1916, p. 1.

43. *The Waynesburg Republican*, 30 March 1916, p. 1; 13 April 1916, p. 1; 20 April 1916, p. 1.

44. *The Waynesburg Republican*, 12 April 1917, p. 1; *The Collegian*, April 1917, p. 1.

45. *The Waynesburg Collegian*, March 1918, p. 1.

46. *The Waynesburg Republican*, 17 Jan. 1918, p. 1; *The Democrat Messenger* (Waynesburg), 8 Feb. 1918, p. 1.

47. *The Collegian*, Feb. 1917, pp. 14-15; April 1917, p. 9.

48. *The Collegian*, Jan. 1913, p. 12; June 1916, pp. 23, 25.

49. Trustees' Minutes, 12 June 1917; *The Waynesburg Republican*, 13 Jan. 1916, p. 1.

50. *The Waynesburg Republican*, 17 May 1917, p. 1.

51. *The Waynesburg Republican*, 17 May 1917, p. 1; 24 May 1917, p. 1; Trustees' Minutes, 3 Dec. 1915; 2 Feb. 1917; 8 March 1917; 9 April 1917; 16 April 1917; 8 May 1917; *The Collegian*, Feb. 1917, p. 13.

52. *The Waynesburg Republican*, 31 May 1917, p. 1; *The Democrat Messenger* (Waynesburg), 8 June 1917, p. 1.

53. Trustees' Minutes, 5 June 1917; *The Waynesburg Republican*, 7 June 1917, p. 1; *The Democrat Messenger* (Waynesburg), 8 June 1917, p. 1.

54. Trustees' Minutes, 7 Aug. 1916; *The Collegian*, Feb. 1917, p. 13.

55. *The Waynesburg Republican*, 10 Feb. 1916, p. 1; *WC Catalogue*, 1917, p. 44; *The Collegian*, Feb. 1917, p. 7.

56. *The Waynesburg Republican*, 19 Aug. 1915, p. 1.

57. Trustees' Minutes, 3 Dec. 1915.

58. Trustees' Minutes, 9 June 1916; 12 June 1917; 28 June 1917.

59. Trustees' Minutes, 7 Aug. 1916; 30 Nov. 1917; *The Waynesburg Republican*, 6 Sept. 1917, p. 1.

60. *The Waynesburg Republican*, 31

Jan. 1918, p. 1; *The Democrat Messenger* (Waynesburg), 1 Feb. 1918, p. 1; *The Waynesburg Collegian*, Feb. 1918, p. 1; Trustees' Minutes, 26 April 1918; 10 May 1918.

61. Herbert P. Houghton to W. T. Hays, Treasurer of Waynesburg College, 2 April 1916, Registrar's files.

62. Trustees' Minutes, 31 March 1917; 26 April 1918.

63. Houghton's career was somewhat varied after he left Waynesburg. After brief tenure as president of Carroll College, he studied theology and became a priest of the Protestant Episcopal Church. He was curate in St. Paul's Church, in Milwaukee, Wisconsin, from 1920 to 1923. He then joined the faculty of Carleton College, in Northfield, Minnesota, and taught from 1923 to 1929; simultaneously he also served as rector of All Saints Church in Northfield; from 1940 to 1950, he was Chairman of Carleton College's Classical Department. He died at Wellesley Hills, Massachusetts, on 12 May 1964, at age eighty-four. See *New York Times*, 13 May 1964, p. 47.

CHAPTER XIII

1. Trustees' Minutes, 20 May 1918; *The Waynesburg Republican*, 23 May 1918, p. 1; 11 July 1918, p. 1.

2. *WC Bulletin*, April 1932, pp. 1-2.

3. Trustees' Minutes, 20 May 1918; 6 July 1920; 31 May 1921; *WC Catalogue*, 1919-1920, p. 7; *The Waynesburg Republican*, 15 May 1919, p. 1.

4. *The Waynesburg Republican*, 15 July 1920, p. 1; *The Democrat Messenger* (Waynesburg), 18 July 1919, p. 5; 9 July 1920, p. 1.

5. Trustees' Minutes, 6 July 1920; 31 May 1921; 10 June 1921; 16 June 1921.

6. *WC Catalogue*, 1919-1920, p. 11.

7. *WC Catalogue*, 1920-1921, p. 3; 1921-1922, p. 3.

8. *WC Catalogue*, 1919-1920, p. 39; Trustees' Minutes, 10 June 1921.

9. Trustees' Minutes, 6 Nov. 1918; *The Waynesburg Collegian*, Oct. 1918, p. 7; *The Waynesburg Republican*, 19 Sept. 1918, p. 1; *The Washington Observer*, 11 June 1949, pp. 30-31.

10. *The Waynesburg Collegian*, Nov. 1918, p. 2.

11. *The Waynesburg Collegian*, Dec. 1918, p. 1; *The Waynesburg Republican*, 26 Dec. 1918, p. 1; *WC Catalogue*, 1919-1920, p. 40.

12. *WC Catalogue*, 1919-1920, pp. 34-35.

13. Trustees' Minutes, 17 Sept. 1919; *WC Catalogue*, 1921-1922, p. 61.

14. Trustees' Minutes, 2 July 1919; 31 May 1921; Faculty Minutes, 10 March 1919.

15. *WC Catalogue*, 1919-1920, pp. 44-45.

16. *The Pittsburgh Gazette Times*, 3 May 1919, p. 13; *The Democrat Messenger* (Waynesburg), 25 March 1921, p. 1; 22 April 1921, p. 1; 20 May 1921, p. 1; *The Waynesburg Republican*, 31 March 1921, p. 1.

17. *The Waynesburg Collegian*, March 1919, p. 5; *The Waynesburg Republican*, 27 March 1919, p. 1.

18. *The Democrat Messenger* (Waynesburg), 12 Dec. 1919, p. 1.

19. *WC Catalogue*, 1919-1920, pp. 9, 43, 48, 55.

20. *The Waynesburg Republican*, 21 Nov. 1918, p. 1.

21. The "World Warrior's" reference here to the "Mexican" War is obviously to the military campaign in the spring and summer of 1916 in search of "Pancho" Villa. See "A World Warrior" to Dr. J. W. McKay, 21 May 1919; J. W. McKay

to "A World Warrior," 22 May 1919, *WC Catalogue*, 1919-1920, pp. 53-55.

22. *WC Catalogue*, 1919-1920, p. 64; Trustees' Minutes, 6 Dec. 1918; 2 Jan. 1919; 17 June 1919; 30 June 1919; 20 Dec. 1919; 25 March 1920; 6 July 1920; 29 March 1921.

23. Trustees' Minutes, 2 July 1919; 17 June 1920; Alumni Association Minutes, 16 June 1920; *The Waynesburg Republican*, 1 Jan. 1920, p. 1.

24. Trustees' Minutes, 2 Jan. 1919; 14 July 1919; 9 Aug. 1919; 8 Sept. 1919; 17 Sept. 1919; *The Waynesburg Republican*, 4 Sept. 1919, p. 1; *WC Catalogue*, 1919-1920, pp. 39, 42, 51.

25. *WC Catalogue*, 1919-1920, p. 39.

26. Trustees' Minutes, 2 Jan. 1919; 30 Nov. 1920; *WC Catalogue*, 1919-1920, pp. 41-42.

27. Trustees' Minutes, 29 March 1921; 5 April 1921; *The Yellow Jacket*, 10 Sept. 1971, pp. 1, 5; *The Democrat Messenger* (Waynesburg) 29 July 1921, p. 1.

28. Trustees' Minutes, 17 Sept. 1919; 6 July 1920; 30 Nov. 1920.

29. Trustees' Minutes, 17 Oct. 1918.

30. Trustees' Minutes, 26 May 1921.

31. Trustees' Minutes, 31 May 1921; 10 June 1921; *WC Bulletin*, April 1932, p. 2; *The Democrat Messenger* (Waynesburg), 17 June 1921, p. 1; 24 June 1921, p. 1.

32. *The Waynesburg Republican*, 22 Dec. 1921, p. 1; *WC Bulletin* April 1932, p. 2; *The Collegian*, 20 Jan. 1922, p. 1.

CHAPTER XIV

1. L. K. Evans, *Pioneer History of Greene County, Pennsylvania* (Waynesburg, Pa. 1941), p. 161.

2. Trustees' Minutes, 22 June 1921; 27 June 1921; 1 Jan. 1923; Bernard Ikeler, "Stewart of Waynesburg," *Presbyterian Life*, 1 May 1963, pp. 9-10; *The Democrat Messenger* (Waynesburg), 5 Jan. 1923, p. 1; *The Waynesburg Collegian*, Jan. 1923, pp. 1, 3.

3. Trustees' Minutes, 22 June 1921; Ikeler, "Stewart of Waynesburg," *Presbyterian Life*, 1 May 1963, pp. 9-10, 37.

4. Trustees' Minutes, 12 June 1924; *The Waynesburg Collegian*, Jan. 1923, p. 1; *WC Bulletin*, Dec. 1913, pp. 18-19; June 1928, pp. 1-2; *WC Catalogue*, 1971, p. 127; *The Waynesburg Republican*, 30 June 1921, p. 1; *The Yellow Jacket*, 12 March 1953, p. 1.

5. *The Waynesburg Republican*, 25 Aug. 1927, p. 1.

6. *The Collegian*, 15 Dec. 1921, p. 1.

7. Trustees' Minutes, 2 Feb. 1963.

8. See biographical sketch of Stewart, Stewart files.

9. *The Waynesburg Collegian*, May 1924, p. 1.

10. Ikeler, "Stewart of Waynesburg," *Presbyterian Life*, 1 May 1963, pp. 9-10, 37; *WC Bulletin*, Dec. 1913, pp. 18-19; *The Waynesburg Collegian*, Jan. 1923, p. 1.

11. *The Washington Observer*, 11 June 1949, pp. 30-31.

12. Ikeler, "Stewart of Waynesburg," *Presbyterian Life*, 1 May 1963, pp. 9-10, 37; *The Washington Observer*, 11 June 1949, pp. 30-31; *The Democrat Messenger* (Waynesburg), 22 Sept. 1922, p. 1; *The Waynesburg Republican*, 27 Sept. 1922, p. 1; 19 July 1923, p. 1; 13 May 1926, p. 1; Trustees' Minutes, 11 June 1925.

13. Commonwealth of Pennsylvania, *Laws of the General Assembly . . .* (Harrisburg, Pa., 1923), p. 319, No. 206, Section 6; *The Waynesburg Republican*, 20 Sept. 1923, p. 1; *The Democrat Messenger* (Waynesburg), 16 Sept. 1921, p. 1; *WC Catalogue*, 1920-1921, pp. 15-16.

14. *The Waynesburg Republican*, 23 June 1921, p. 1; Alumni Association

Minutes, 14 June 1922; *WC Catalogue*, 1923-1924, p. 74.

15. *The Waynesburg Republican*, 4 Aug. 1921, p. 1; 17 Aug. 1922, p. 1; 26 April 1923, p. 1; Alumni Association Minutes, 15 June 1923.

16. Trustees' Minutes, 27 June 1921.

17. *The Waynesburg Republican*, 28 July 1921, p. 1; 2 Sept. 1926, p. 1; *The Collegian*, 20 Jan. 1922, p. 1; *WC Catalogue*, 1920-1921, pp. 7-8.

18. *WC Bulletin*, June 1928, pp. 1-2; *The Democrat Messenger* (Waynesburg), 22 June 1928, p. 1; *The Waynesburg Republican*, 21 June 1928, p. 1; 1 Nov. 1928, p. 4. Waychoff died on 16 January 1927, having been stricken with paralysis. He had spent most of his life in the service of the college. See *The Waynesburg Republican*, 20 Jan. 1927, p. 1; *The Democrat Messenger* (Waynesburg), 21 Jan. 1927, p. 1; *WC Catalogue*, 1926-1927, p. 2.

19. Trustees' Minutes, 4 Aug. 1921; 7 Sept. 1921; 1 Nov. 1921; 17 March 1922; 21 July 1922.

20. *The Waynesburg Collegian*, Dec. 1922, pp. 5-10.

21. *The Waynesburg Republican*, 15 Aug. 1929, p. 1; 30 Jan. 1931, p. 1; *WC Catalogue*, 1927-1928, pp. 5-6; Trustees' Minutes, 5 June 1929; 13 June 1929.

22. Faculty Minutes, 21 Nov. 1928.

23. *The Collegian*, 24 June 1922, p. 1.

24. Trustees' Minutes, 24 Nov. 1922; 27 April 1923; *The Waynesburg Republican*, 16 Nov. 1922, p. 1; 8 March 1923, p. 1.

25. Commonwealth of Pennsylvania, *Laws of the General Assembly . . .* passed at the session of 1923 (Harrisburg, Pa., 1923), p. 319, No. 206, Section 6; Session of 1895, pp. 327-331, No. 244; Session of 1909, pp. 206-207, No. 141. The law of 1923 resurrected the one of 1895, and set $500,000 as the amount of endowment needed, *in addition* to buildings, grounds, and equipment. The law of 1895 called for at least six full-time professors in a college; another, in 1909, changed this to "three regular professors and two or more instructors or fellows"; and the law of 1923 required at least eight professors.

26. *The Waynesburg Collegian*, May 1924, pp. 5-6; *The Waynesburg Republican*, 8 Nov. 1923, p. 1; 3 Jan. 1924, p. 1; *The Democrat Messenger* (Waynesburg), 29 Aug. 1924, p. 1.

27. Trustees' Minutes, 13 March 1924; 29 April 1924. Senator Cummins died of a heart attack on 30 July 1926, at age seventy-six. He had been one of Iowa's United States senators since 1908. Born near Carmichaels, Pennsylvania, on 15 February 1850, he attended public school and Waynesburg College. Shortly before graduation, he went to Iowa without his diploma, but later received it as of the class of 1867. See *The Yellow Jacket*, 10 Aug. 1926, pp. 1-3, 8.

28. *The Waynesburg Republican*, 20 March 1924, p. 1.

29. *The Democrat Messenger* (Waynesburg), 21 March 1924, p. 1.

30. *The Waynesburg Republican*, 10 April 1924, p. 1.

31. *The Waynesburg Collegian*, May 1924, pp. 5-6.

32. *The Waynesburg Republican*, 27 March 1924, p. 1; 17 April 1924, p. 1; *The Democrat Messenger* (Waynesburg), 21 March 1924, p. 1; Alumni Minutes, 11 June 1924.

33. *The Waynesburg Republican*, 10 April 1924, p. 1.

34. *The Waynesburg Republican*, 17 April 1924, p. 1; 8 May 1924, p. 1; 15 May 1924, p. 1; 12 June 1924, p. 1; *The Democrat Messenger* (Waynesburg), 2 May 1924, p. 1; 11 July 1924, p. 5.

35. *The Waynesburg Republican*, 3 Jan. 1924, p. 1; *The Democrat Messenger* (Waynesburg), 29 Aug. 1924, p. 1.

36. Trustees' Minutes, 12 Aug. 1924; 23 Sept. 1924; 17 Jan. 1925; *The Yellow Jacket*, Dec. 1924, p. 13.

37. *The Waynesburg Republican*, 7 May 1925, p. 1; Trustees' Minutes, 29 May 1925; 5 June 1925.

38. *The Democrat Messenger* (Waynesburg), 9 Dec. 1927, p. 1; *The Waynesburg Republican*, 8 Dec. 1927, p. 1; Trustees' Minutes, 2 Dec. 1927.

39. Trustees' Minutes, 13 June 1929.

40. *The Democrat Messenger* (Waynesburg), 18 July 1930, p. 1; *WC Bulletin*, Feb. 1931, p. 2.

41. Trustees' Minutes, 22 Aug. 1921; 1 Nov. 1921; 21 July 1922; *WC Catalogue*, 1927-1928, p. 66.

42. Trustees' Minutes, 21 July 1922; 18 Jan. 1929; 13 June 1929.

43. *WC Catalogue*, 1922-1923, pp. 67-68.

44. *WC Catalogue*, 1925-1926, p. 91; 1926-1927, p. 95; Trustees' Minutes, 30 April 1926; 7 April 1927. See also "Perpetual Scholarships," Stewart files.

45. Trustees' Minutes, 12 June 1924; 10 June 1926; 16 Feb. 1928.

46. Trustees' Minutes, 2 Dec. 1921; 17 March 1922; 15 Dec. 1922; 12 Dec. 1924; 17 Jan. 1925; 10 June 1927.

47. *WC Catalogue*, 1920-1921, pp. 23-25, 75.

48. *The Waynesburg Republican*, 29 Sept. 1921, p. 1; 27 April 1922, p. 1; *The Democrat Messenger* (Waynesburg), 30 Sept. 1921, p. 1.

49. *The Waynesburg Republican*, 1 Sept. 1921, p. 1; *The Democrat Messenger* (Waynesburg), 3 March 1922, p. 1; 7 Aug. 1925, pp. 1-2.

50. *WC Catalogue*, 1921-1922, p. 34.

51. *The Waynesburg Republican*, 21 Sept. 1922, p. 1; *WC Catalogue*, 1923-1924, p. 48.

52. *WC Catalogue*, 1924-1925, p. 21; 1926-1927, p. 26.

53. Trustees' Minutes, 21 July 1922; *The Democrat Messenger*, (Waynesburg), 3 March 1922, p. 1; *WC Catalogue*, 1920-1921, pp. 19-20.

54. *The Democrat Messenger* (Waynesburg), 7 Aug. 1925, pp. 1-2; *The Waynesburg Republican*, 13 Aug. 1925, p. 1.

55. *The Democrat Messenger* (Waynesburg), 23 Feb. 1923, p. 1.

56. *The Waynesburg Republican*, 12 July 1923, p. 1.

57. *WC Catalogue*, 1926-1927, pp. 23-24; Faculty Minutes, 21 Jan. 1926; 3 Feb. 1926; Trustees' Minutes, 12 Aug. 1924.

58. Faculty Minutes, 3 Feb. 1926; 13 Nov. 1928; 8 Jan. 1929; 5 Feb. 1929; 26 Feb. 1929.

59. *WC Catalogue*, 1922-1923, p. 74.

60. I am indebted to Michael K. Talpas, '38, and now Registrar of the college, for this information, which was recorded in 1929.

61. *The Waynesburg Republican*, 10 Jan. 1924, p. 1; 4 Nov. 1926, p. 1; 18 Nov. 1926, p. 1; 16 Dec. 1926, p. 1; Faculty Minutes, 6 Oct. 1925; *WC Catalogue*, 1924-1925, p. 85.

62. *WC Catalogue*, 1928-1929, p. 70; Faculty Minutes, 26 Oct. 1926; 12 Dec. 1927; 23 Jan. 1928; Trustees' Minutes, 14 June 1928.

63. *The Yellow Jacket*, Oct. 1928, p. 9; Nov. 1928, p. 7; 1 Nov. 1929, p. 1.

64. *WC Catalogue*, 1921-1922, p. 67; 1923-1924, pp. 72-73.

65. *WC Catalogue*, 1925-1926, p. 96; 1927-1928, pp. 63-64; *The Yellow Jacket*, Senior number, 1928, pp. 30-31; Oct. 1928, pp. 8-9. See also Program of Union-Philo Literary Contest, Alumni Hall, 31 May 1928, Registrar's files.

66. Trustees' Minutes, 13 June 1929.

67. Faculty Minutes, 6 Dec. 1926.

68. Faculty Minutes, 6 Dec. 1928.

69. Faculty Minutes, 14 Nov. 1927; 13 Nov. 1928; 8 Jan. 1929; Trustees' Minutes, 11 June 1925; 13 June 1929; *The Yellow Jacket*, Oct. 1925, p. 12; *WC Catalogue*, 1925-1926, p. 96; 1926-1927, p. 100.

70. *The Yellow Jacket*, March 1925, pp. 8-9; Senior No. 1928, p. 25.

71. Trustees' Minutes, 7 April 1927.

72. Trustees' Minutes, 11 June 1925; 13 June 1929; *The Waynesburg Republican*, 16 Sept. 1926, p. 1.

73. *The Yellow Jacket*, Dec. 1927, p. 6.

74. *The Democrat Messenger* (Waynesburg), 19 Dec. 1924, p. 1; Faculty Minutes, 23 Oct. 1925; *WC Catalogue*, 1925-1926, p. 97.

75. *WC Bulletin*, April 1928, unpaged, Stewart files; Evans, p. 157.

76. *WC Bulletin*, Jan.-Feb. 1929, p. 4, Stewart files.

77. *The Waynesburg Republican*, 6 June 1929, p. 1; *WC Bulletin*, Sept. 1929, pp. 1-2, Stewart files.

78. After serving a number of years as cashier of a local bank, Jesse Lazear went into business in Baltimore, Maryland. In his dedicatory address at the plaque, his son, James B. Lazear, said the first flat car on the Waynesburg and Washington Railroad carried the body of his father, who died in Baltimore on 2 September 1877, from Washington to Hackney Station in southern Washington County, about two miles from the boundary between Washington and Greene counties. By that time, the railroad had been constructed only to Hackney. Many Waynesburgers drove there to meet the train. They formed a funeral cortege and followed the hearse to Waynesburg, where Jesse was buried. James B. Lazear died in a hospital in Omaha, Nebraska, on 7 March 1931, and was buried in Denver, Colorado, for many years the headquarters of his work as national bank examiner of the West. See *WC Bulletin*, Sept. 1929, pp. 1-2; March 1931, pp. 1-2; *The Democrat Messenger* (Waynesburg), 5 July 1929, p. 1.

79. Trustees' Minutes, 1 Nov. 1921.

80. Trustees' Minutes, 10 Oct. 1922; 15 Dec. 1922; *The Waynesburg Republican*, 19 July 1923, p. 1; *The Democrat Messenger* (Waynesburg), 7 Dec. 1923, p. 1; *The Yellow Jacket*, Jan. 1928, p. 3.

81. Trustees' Minutes, 23 Feb. 1923; 29 July 1926; *The Democrat Messenger* (Waynesburg), 8 Oct. 1926, p. 1; Alumni Association Minutes, 15 June 1923; *The Yellow Jacket*, 8 Dec. 1961, p. 2.

82. *The Democrat Messenger* (Waynesburg), 7 May 1926, p. 1; 21 May 1926, p. 1; *The Waynesburg Republican*, 6 May 1926, p. 1; *WC Catalogue*, 1926-1927, pp. 13-14; Trustees' Minutes, 27 June 1921; 22 Aug. 1921; 15 June 1922; 14 June 1923; 12 June 1924; 30 April 1926; 13 June 1929.

83. Trustees' Minutes, 13 March 1924; 29 April 1924; 30 April 1926; 29 July 1926.

84. Trustees' Minutes, 22 Aug. 1921; 15 Dec. 1922; 9 May 1928; 9 Aug. 1929.

85. *WC Catalogue*, 1924-1925, pp. 86-87; *The Yellow Jacket*, March 1925, p. 3.

86. Trustees' Minutes, 12 April 1929; 13 June 1929; 5 Sept. 1929.

87. Trustees' Minutes, 5 June 1925.

88. I am indebted to Michael K. Talpas for the information concerning the oak tree tradition. See Registrar's files.

89. *WC Catalogue*, 1924-1925, pp. 14-15; 1927-1928, p. 65; 1928-1929, p. 72; *The Democrat Messenger* (Waynesburg), 28 June 1929, p. 1.

CHAPTER XV

1. Faculty Minutes, 26 Sept. 1933; 11 Oct. 1934; 8 Jan. 1935; 7 April 1936.

2. Trustees' Minutes, 21 Sept. 1937; 5 June 1939; 8 July 1939.

3. Trustees' Minutes, 12 April 1935; 7 Aug. 1935; 17 Jan. 1936; 7 Sept. 1938; 13 June 1939; 8 July 1939.

4. Trustees' Minutes, 11 Sept. 1939.

5. Trustees' Minutes, 16 June 1937.

6. *WC Bulletin*, Aug. 1935, pp. 1-2; Faculty Minutes, 25 Feb. 1935; 2 March 1935.

7. Trustees' Minutes, 12 June 1930; 12 June 1935; 10 June 1936; 20 Jan. 1937; 29 April 1937; 14 June 1938; 22 Oct. 1938; 8 July 1939; Faculty Minutes, 9 March 1936.

8. *The Democrat Messenger* (Waynesburg), 20 Sept. 1932, p. 1.

9. Faculty Minutes, 16 Oct. 1934; 4 Dec. 1934; 8 Jan. 1935.

10. Trustees' Minutes, 13 June 1934; 12 June 1935; 14 June 1938.

11. Trustees' Minutes, 13 June 1934.

12. Trustees' Minutes, 12 June 1930; 10 June 1936; 29 April 1937; *The Yellow Jacket*, 1 April 1932, p. 1.

13. Faculty Minutes, 4 Oct. 1938.

14. *The Yellow Jacket*, June 1933, unpaged.

15. *The Democrat Messenger* (Waynesburg), 1 May 1934, p. 1; *The Yellow Jacket*, 8 May 1935, p. 1; Dean Robert W. Cahn to the author, 15 April 1974.

16. Trustees' Minutes, 10 June 1936.

17. Trustees' Minutes, 16 June 1937.

18. Faculty Minutes, 2 April 1935; 5 May 1936; *The Yellow Jacket*, 1 Oct. 1937, p. 4.

19. *The Yellow Jacket*, 2 May 1936, p. 2; 5 Nov. 1938, p. 1.

20. Trustees' Minutes, 11 Sept. 1939; Faculty Minutes, 6 Nov. 1939; 7 Nov. 1939.

21. Faculty Minutes, 27 Sept. 1931; 14 March 1933; 8 Nov. 1933; 5 Dec. 1933; 12 April 1938; 16 June 1939; 5 Dec. 1939; *The Yellow Jacket*, 3 March 1933, p. 2; 2 Oct. 1934, p. 2.

22. Faculty Minutes, 14 March 1933; 8 Nov. 1933; 9 March 1937.

23. *WC Catalogue*, 1930-1931, p. 20; 1931-1932, p. 23.

24. Faculty Minutes, 4 Jan. 1938; Trustees' Minutes, 14 June 1938; 7 Sept. 1938.

25. Faculty Minutes, 20 Sept. 1937.

26. Faculty Minutes, 6 Nov. 1939.

27. *The Democrat Messenger* (Waynesburg), 12 Feb. 1932, p. 1.

28. Faculty Minutes, 7 June 1933.

29. Faculty Minutes, 8 Feb. 1933; 8 Feb. 1937.

30. Trustees' Minutes, 11 April 1930; 2 April 1931; 20 Jan. 1933; *The Democrat Messenger* (Waynesburg), 26 Jan. 1932, p. 1.

31. *The Democrat Messenger* (Waynesburg), 17 Oct. 1930, p. 1; Trustees' Minutes, 10 Jan. 1930; 12 June 1930; 10 Oct. 1930; Waynesburg College, *Documents Pertaining to the Government of the College* (Waynesburg, Pa., Sept. 1965), pp. 28-30.

32. Trustees' Minutes, 10 June 1936; 20 Jan. 1937; 29 April 1937; 16 June 1937; 4 Feb. 1938; 14 June 1938; 10 Feb. 1939; Faculty Minutes, 1 April 1937; *WC Catalogue*, 1935-1936, pp. 21-22; 1937-1938, pp. 22-23; 1939-1940, p. 22.

33. Trustees' Minutes, 28 April 1934; 13 June 1934; 13 Nov. 1937; 10 Feb. 1939; *The Democrat Messenger* (Waynesburg), 26 May 1936, p. 1.

34. *The Democrat Messenger* (Waynesburg), 29 Oct. 1936, p. 1.

35. Trustees' Minutes, 10 June 1936; 16 June 1937.

36. Trustees' Minutes, 22 Oct. 1938.

37. Trustees' Minutes, 13 June 1939; 14 June 1939; 24 June 1939.

38. Trustees' Minutes, 5 May 1939; 23 June 1939; 8 July 1939; 15 Dec. 1939.

39. Trustees' Minutes, 28 July 1939.

40. Trustees' Minutes, Auditor's Report, 11 Dec. 1939.

41. *The Yellow Jacket*, 1 April 1933, p. 1.

42. Trustees' Minutes, 15 April 1933; 11 Dec. 1934; *The Democrat Messenger* (Waynesburg), 18 April 1933, p. 1; 2 June 1933, p. 1.

43. Trustees' Minutes, 2 Jan. 1935; 12 June 1935; 16 June 1937; 14 June 1939; *The Yellow Jacket*, 24 Jan. 1935, p. 1; 13 Feb. 1935, p. 1; *The Democrat Mes-*

senger (Waynesburg), 14 Dec. 1934, p. 1; 4 Jan. 1935, p. 1; 13 June 1935, pp. 1, 5.

44. Trustees' Minutes, 14 June 1938; 22 Oct. 1938; *The Yellow Jacket*, 11 Dec. 1937, p. 1.

45. Trustees' Minutes, 12 June 1935; *WC Catalogue*, 1937-1938, p. 14. Mrs. Downey's husband was the Honorable Robinson F. Downey, one of the best men in the service of the college and the community of Waynesburg. From 1885 to 1905 he was a member of the Board of Trust of Waynesburg College. In 1905, when the CP and Presbyterian churches reunited, he became a trustee of the college, and remained so until his death on 19 December 1923. See *WC Bulletin*, Feb. 1930, pp. 1-2; Jan. 1937, pp. 1-2.

46. Trustees' Minutes, 24 Sept. 1935; 20 Jan. 1937; 13 Nov. 1937; 15 Dec. 1939; *WC Catalogue*, 1937-1938, p. 14.

47. Trustees' Minutes, 29 April 1937; 7 June 1937; *WC Catalogue*, 1937-1938, p. 14.

CHAPTER XVI

1. Trustees' Minutes, 28 May 1940; 11 June 1940; 10 June 1941; 26 Sept. 1941.

2. Trustees' Minutes, 15 April 1943; 29 April 1943; 27 April 1945; 31 July 1946; 19 Oct. 1946.

3. Trustees' Minutes, 23 Jan. 1942; 14 Sept. 1942; 29 Sept. 1942.

4. Faculty Minutes, 1 Dec. 1942; 21 Sept. 1946; 15 Sept. 1948.

5. President Franklin D. Roosevelt to President Paul R. Stewart, *The Yellow Jacket*, 25 Sept. 1940, pp. 1, 4.

6. Trustees' Minutes 10 June 1941; 29 May 1942; 16 May 1943.

7. *The Yellow Jacket*, 10 Dec. 1940, p. 1; Faculty Minutes, 2 Feb. 1943.

8. Trustees' Minutes, 11 June 1940; 10 Dec. 1940.

9. Trustees' Minutes, 26 Sept. 1941; 29 April 1943; *WC Catalogue*, 1944-1945, pp. 39-42.

10. *WC Catalogue*, 1939-1940, p. 42; 1941-1942, p. 35; *WC Bulletin*, Jan. 1942, pp. 1-2.

11. Trustees' Minutes, 27 June 1942; *The Yellow Jacket*, 17 Oct. 1942, p. 2.

12. Trustees' Minutes, 29 May 1942; *WC Catalogue*, 1941-1942, pp. 36-37.

13. *The Yellow Jacket*, 17 Oct. 1942, p. 2.

14. *WC Catalogue*, 1942-1943, p. 2; Trustees' Minutes, 23 Jan. 1942.

15. *The Democrat Messenger* (Waynesburg), 18 Feb. 1943, p. 1.

16. Trustees' Minutes, 10 Feb. 1943; Faculty Minutes, 11 Feb. 1943.

17. Trustees' Minutes, 10 Feb. 1943; 21 March 1944; Faculty Minutes, 11 Feb. 1943; *The Democrat Messenger* (Waynesburg), 15 Feb. 1943, p. 1; 18 Feb. 1943, p. 1; *The Yellow Jacket*, 5 Feb. 1943, p. 1; *WC Catalogue*, 1943-1944, pp. 5-6.

18. Faculty Minutes, 4 March 1943; Trustees' Minutes, 22 March 1943; 29 April 1943. I am indebted to Lois Westfall, Stewart's secretary, and to Michael K. Talpas, Registrar, for certain details relative to securing the air crew detachment for the college. The military authorities were not favorably impressed with the Waynesburg airport; one of the inspectors told Stewart that conditions there "were abominable." See Trustees' Minutes, 1 Sept. 1943.

19. Trustees' Minutes, 16 May 1943; 20 May 1944.

20. Trustees' Minutes, 28 Jan. 1944; 20 May 1944; 2 June 1945.

21. *WC Catalogue*, 1943-1944, p. 31; 1944-1945, p. 88; Trustees' Minutes, 1 Sept. 1943; 29 April 1943; 27 June 1944; *The Democrat Messenger* (Waynesburg), 16 May 1944, p. 1; 19 May 1944, p. 1. Unfortunately Snyder died nearly two years later. The trustees were grieved at

the loss of one "who so long and faithfully aided us in our governmental connections in Washington, D. C." See Trustees' Minutes, 1 June 1946.

22. See the Air Corps songs, Stewart files. See also Trustees' Minutes, 16 May 1943; 30 Oct. 1943.

23. Trustees' Minutes, 30 Oct. 1943; *WC Bulletin*, March 1944, pp. 1-2; *The Yellow Jacket*, 30 Oct. 1943, p. 1.

24. Trustees' Minutes, 29 April 1943; 20 May 1944; 27 June 1944; 2 June 1945; *WC Catalogue*, 1943-1944, p. 31. A service center for the cadets was provided in the *Messenger* Building. The owners of that structure, Harry Rothenberg and Associates, kindly rented it for a nominal sum to the college. It was used not only by the cadets, but by other service men on vacation. See also *WC Bulletin*, July 1944, p. 9.

25. Trustees' Minutes, 28 Oct. 1944; *WC Catalogue*, 1944-1945, pp. 42-43.

26. Faculty Minutes, 10 Oct. 1946; 6 May 1947; Trustees' Minutes, 10 June 1949.

27. Faculty Minutes, 6 May 1947.

28. *The Democrat Messenger* (Waynesburg), 14 April 1949, pp. 1-2; 26 Oct. 1949, p. 8; 9 Dec. 1949, pp. 1, 3.

29. Trustees' Minutes, 2 June 1946; 5 June 1948; 10 June 1949.

30. Trustees' Minutes, 2 June 1945; 31 May 1947.

31. Trustees' Minutes, 31 May 1947; 17 Oct. 1947; 10 June 1949; 5 Nov. 1949; *The Washington Observer*, 11 June 1949, p. 22.

32. Trustees' Minutes, 10 Feb. 1949; 5 Nov. 1949; *WC Catalogue*, 1949-1950, p. 28; *The Evening Standard* (Uniontown), 7 Jan. 1949, p. 7.

33. Faculty Minutes, 21 May 1944; Trustees' Minutes, 20 May 1944; 2 June 1945.

34. Trustees' Minutes, 8 Sept. 1944; 28 Oct. 1944; 20 March 1946; *WC Catalogue*, 1944-1945, pp. 2-3.

35. Trustees' Minutes, 2 June 1945; 10 Nov. 1945; 1 June 1946; 31 May 1947; 5 June 1948. See also *The Democrat Messenger* (Waynesburg), 22 Dec. 1944, p. 1.

36. Trustees' Minutes, 1 June 1946; 31 May 1947; 5 June 1948.

37. Trustees' Minutes, 2 June 1945; 10 June 1949; 30 Aug. 1949; 5 Nov. 1949.

38. Trustees' Minutes, 11 June 1940; 29 May 1942; 20 May 1944; *The Yellow Jacket*, 21 Feb. 1940, p. 1.

39. Trustees' Minutes, 11 June 1940; 29 May 1942; 1 June 1946; 31 May 1947; 8 Nov. 1947; 16 Oct. 1948; 10 June 1949; Faculty Minutes, 5 Dec. 1944.

40. Trustees' Minutes, 23 Jan. 1948; 5 June 1948; 1 Nov. 1948.

41. *The Yellow Jacket*, 4 Oct. 1940, p. 1.

42. Edward Martin, '01, took the oath of office as Governor of Pennsylvania in a simple ceremony in Harrisburg on 19 January 1943. For the oath, he used the Bible which he carried through all his military and political campaigns. Charity Scott, his college sweetheart and later his wife, gave it to him when he left Waynesburg College to enter the Spanish American War. The book was badly worn by the ravages of time and constant reading. See *The Democrat Messenger* (Waynesburg), 19 Jan. 1943, pp. 1, 3; 20 Jan. 1943, p. 1; 23 Oct. 1943, pp. 1, 5.

43. Faculty Minutes, 5 Dec. 1944; 2 June 1945; 12 Dec. 1945.

44. Trustees' Minutes, 17 Oct. 1947.

45. Trustees' Minutes, 21 April 1944.

46. Trustees' Minutes, 28 Jan. 1944; 17 April 1945; 15 Sept. 1945; 3 April 1946; 14 June 1947; 9 Sept. 1947.

47. Trustees' Minutes, 5 June 1948; 10 June 1949; 30 Aug. 1949.

48. Faculty Minutes, 27 May 1947; Trustees' Minutes, 12 Jan. 1948; 1 Oct. 1948.

49. Trustees' Minutes, 21 April 1944.

50. Trustees' Minutes, 27 June 1944; 28 Oct. 1944; 2 June 1945. Shown there was the "G. I. Collection" sent to Stewart by erstwhile students from many parts of the world. It consisted of more than 1,000 specimens. See Trustees' Minutes, 5 June

1948; *WC Catalogue*, 1948-1949, pp. 19-21; *The Washington Observer*, 11 June 1949, p. 3.

51. Trustees' Minutes, 15 May 1943; 30 Oct. 1943; 28 Oct. 1944; *The Democrat Messenger* (Waynesburg), 21 Oct. 1943, pp. 1, 5; *The Yellow Jacket*, 30 Oct. 1943; p. 1; *WC Catalogue*, 1943-1944, p. 9; *WC Bulletin*, July 1944, p. 9.

52. Trustees' Minutes, 10 Nov. 1945; 12 Dec. 1945; 1 June 1946; 17 Oct. 1947; 5 June 1948; 10 June 1949.

53. Faculty Minutes, 12 Nov. 1946; Trustees' Minutes, 31 May 1947; 5 June 1948; *The Democrat Messenger* (Waynesburg), 13 Nov. 1946, p. 1; *WC Catalogue*, 1946-1947, p. 14.

54. Trustees' Minutes, 31 July 1946; 31 May 1947. The federal government generously gave the college two trucks; and a deep freeze unit which was installed in Walton Hall. Other gifts included a new C-46 airplane, several airplane engines of various makes, a cut-away engine for demonstration purposes, a link trainer, "and various parts and instruments." The college also purchased seventy-five double-deck beds at $2.00 per bed. Stewart urged the trustees to "please watch for advertisements . . . where we may obtain scientific equipment such as microscopes, chemical and physical apparatus and supplies, dormitory furniture, gymnasium and other athletic equipment, etc. SUCH AN OPPORTUNITY TO EQUIP OUR COLLEGE MAY NEVER COME AGAIN (Stewart's capitalization)." See Trustees' Minutes, 1 June 1946; 19 Oct. 1946; 5 June 1948.

55. Trustees' Minutes, 31 May 1947; 17 Oct. 1947; 16 Oct. 1948; *WC Catalogue*, 1948-1949, pp. 17-18; *The Democrat Messenger* (Waynesburg), 1 May 1946, p. 1.

56. Trustees' Minutes, 31 May 1947; 17 Oct. 1947; 8 Nov. 1947; 16 Oct. 1948; *WC Catalogue*, 1946-1947, p. 14; *The Washington Observer*, 11 June 1949, p. 21.

57. Trustees' Minutes, 25 June 1949; 30 Aug. 1949; 5 Nov. 1949; Faculty Minutes, 8 Nov. 1949. In July 1946 the trustees employed a night watchman to guard the college against fires and other dangers. A year later they created the office of Superintendent of Buildings and Grounds and defined his duties. See Trustees' Minutes, 12 July 1946; 12 Aug. 1947.

58. Trustees' Minutes, 5 June 1948; 14 June 1948; 28 April 1949; 30 Aug. 1949; 5 Nov. 1949; *WC Bulletin*, 1 Oct. 1949, p. 1; *The Democrat Messenger* (Waynesburg), 11 May 1949, p. 1.

59. Trustees' Minutes, 10 June 1949; 25 June 1949; 15 Aug. 1949; *The Washington Observer*, 11 June 1949, p. 21.

60. *WC Catalogue*, 1948-1949, pp. 17-18.

61. Trustees' Minutes, 5 June 1948.

62. Trustees' Minutes, 10 June 1949.

63. Trustees' Minutes, 3 July 1946; 31 July 1946; 10 Oct. 1946; *WC Catalogue*, 1946-1947, p. 3.

64. Faculty Minutes, 21 Sept. 1946; Trustees' Minutes, 31 May 1947; 5 June 1948; 4 Sept. 1948; 10 June 1949.

65. *WC Catalogue*, 1946-1947, pp. 5-6; Trustees' Minutes, 5 June 1948; 10 June 1949.

66. Trustees' Minutes, 2 June 1945; 3 April 1946; 21 Sept. 1946.

67. Trustees' Minutes, 28 April 1949; 10 June 1949; *WC Bulletin*, 1 Oct. 1949, p. 2.

CHAPTER XVII

1. Trustees' Minutes, 8 April 1947.

2. *The Waynesburg Republican*, 20 Sept. 1923, p. 1.

3. Trustees' Minutes, 12 June 1930; *WC Bulletin*, X (Feb. 1931), p. 2.

4. Trustees' Minutes, 14 June 1939.

5. Trustees' Minutes, 10 June 1941; 28 July 1941; n. d. Nov. 1941.

6. Trustees' Minutes, 20 May 1944.

7. Faculty Minutes, 13 Jan. 1941; 3 Nov. 1942; 31 May 1944; 5 Dec. 1944; Trustees' Minutes, 28 Jan. 1944; 21 April 1944; 20 May 1944; 28 Oct. 1944; 12 Dec. 1945.

8. Trustees' Minutes, 28 Oct. 1944.

9. Trustees' Minutes, 19 Oct. 1946; 8 April 1947; 31 May 1947; 28 April 1949; Faculty Minutes, 7 Jan. 1947; 25 Feb. 1947; 4 March 1947. See also "Data for Middle States," Waynesburg College, 15 Feb. 1950, Registrar's files.

10. Faculty Minutes, 7 April 1942; 6 Jan. 1949; 13 Dec. 1948; Trustees' Minutes, 28 Jan. 1944; 8 April 1947; 31 May 1947; 23 Jan. 1948; 4 March 1948; 5 June 1948; 28 April 1949. See also "Data for Middle States," Waynesburg College, 15 Feb. 1950, Registrar's files.

11. "Data for Middle States," Waynesburg College, 15 Feb. 1950, Registrar's files; Faculty Minutes, 13 Dec. 1948; Trustees' Minutes, 28 Jan. 1944.

12. "Data for Middle States," Waynesburg College, 15 Feb. 1950, Registrar's files; Faculty Minutes, 1 March 1949; Trustees' Minutes, 10 June 1950.

13. Faculty Minutes, 13 Dec. 1948; 1 June 1950.

14. Faculty Minutes, 1 March 1949; Trustees' Minutes, 10 June 1949.

15. Trustees' Minutes, 10 June 1949; 25 June 1959.

16. Paul R. Stewart to Ewald B. Nyquist, Columbia University, New York, 10 Nov. 1949, Registrar's files; "Data for Middle States," Waynesburg College, 15 Feb. 1950, Registrar's files.

17. Trustees' Minutes, 25 March 1950; 10 June 1950.

18. Trustees' Minutes, 10 June 1950; 6 Sept. 1950; Faculty Minutes, 12 Feb. 1974.

19. "Data for Middle States," Waynesburg College, 15 Feb. 1950, Registrar's files.

20. Tenney and Co. Accountants and Auditors to the Board of Trustees of Waynesburg College, 3 Nov. 1949, Registrar's files; "Data for Middle States," Waynesburg College, 15 Feb. 1950, Registrar's files.

21. "Data for Middle States," Waynesburg College, 15 Feb. 1950, Registrar's files; *WC Catalogue*, 1950-1951, pp. 19-23.

22. Paul R. Stewart to Dr. Gaius Slosser, Western Theological Seminary, 11 Feb. 1949, Registrar's files. This letter is a sample of the kind sent to several institutions where Waynesburg's graduates were pursuing work leading toward higher degrees.

23. "Data for Middle States," Waynesburg College, 15 Feb. 1950, Registrar's files.

24. Faculty Minutes, 7 Nov. 1950; 5 Dec. 1950; *The Yellow Jacket*, Dec. 1950, p. 2.

CHAPTER XVIII

1. Trustees' Minutes, 7 Sept. 1921; *The Democrat Messenger* (Waynesburg), 9 Sept. 1921, p. 1; *The Collegian*, 15 Dec. 1921, p. 1.

2. *The Collegian*, 31 March 1922, p. 1; *The Waynesburg Collegian*, new ser. (Nov. 1922), pp. 25-26; *The Yellow Jacket*, Dec. 1924, p. 26; "Waynesburg College Football Records," rev. 1968, p. 13; *WC Catalogue*, 1922-1923, p. 72.

3. *The Democrat Messenger* (Waynesburg), 21 April 1922, p. 3; 23 June 1922, p. 3; *The Collegian*, 15 May 1922, p. 1; *WC Catalogue*, 1921-1922, p. 69.

4. Trustees' Minutes, 2 Dec. 1921; *The Democrat Messenger* (Waynesburg) 2 Feb. 1923, p. 1; 4 April 1949, pp. 1-2; *The Waynesburg Collegian*, Jan. 1923, p. 20; *WC Catalogue*, 1921-1922, p. 69; *The Yellow Jacket*, 13 April 1949, p. 1.

5. McHenry, a graduate of California High School, California, Pennsylvania, was a student at Penn State for over a year, after which he transferred to Waynesburg College and graduated in 1923. At Penn State he played with Wolf as a teammate. At Waynesburg, with Wolf as his coach, he was captain in three sports—football, basketball, and baseball. McHenry was relatively small of stature, but "did a big man's job well." He played on every team that represented Waynesburg College. See *The Waynesburg Collegian*, May 1923, p. 9.

6. *The Waynesburg Collegian*, April 1923, p. 7; May 1923, pp. 3-4; *The Democrat Messenger* (Waynesburg), 16 March 1923, p. 1; *WC Catalogue*, 1922-1923, p. 7; 1923-1924, p. 8; "Waynesburg College Football Records," rev. 1968, p. 13.

7. *The Collegian*, 24 June 1922, p. 2; *The Waynesburg Republican*, 17 May 1923, p. 1; *The Yellow Jacket*, May 1925, p. 3.

8. Trustees' Minutes, 13 Dec. 1923; *WC Catalogue*, 1923-1924, p. 8; 1924-1925, p. 86; *The Waynesburg Republican*, 20 Dec. 1923, p. 1; "Waynesburg College Football Records," rev. 1968, p. 13.

9. Trustees' Minutes, 12 Aug. 1924.

10. Trustees' Minutes, 11 March 1925; *The Yellow Jacket*, March 1925, p. 3; *The Waynesburg Republican*, 5 March 1925, p. 1; *WC Catalogue*, 1924-1925, p. 8; 1925-1926, p. 8; 1926-1927, p. 8.

11. *The Yellow Jacket*, May 1925, pp. 2, 5; Trustees' Minutes, 15 Dec. 1927; *WC Catalogue*, 1927-1928, p. 64.

12. Faculty Minutes, 2 Nov. 1926; 10 Nov. 1926; 10 Oct. 1927; *The Waynesburg Republican*, 23 Sept. 1926, p. 1.

13. "Waynesburg College Football Records," rev. 1968, p. 13.

14. Trustees' Minutes, 9 May 1928; *The Yellow Jacket*, senior number, 1928, p. 34; "Waynesburg College Football Records," rev. 1968, p. 13.

15. Trustees' Minutes, 10 June 1929.

16. *The Yellow Jacket*, 4 Oct. 1940, p. 3.

17. *WC Catalogue*, 1930-1931, pp. 80-81; *The Yellow Jacket*, 28 April 1930, p. 3.

18. Other stars on this team, in addition to "Rab" and Adam Donnelly, were Mark ("Mike") Booth, William ("Bull") Brnjas, James ("Killer") Conroy, Benjamin ("Ben") Donley, Thomas ("Tom") Holland, Wettie Mancuso, Benjamin ("Ben") Parker, William ("Billy") Paul, Fred Rollason, John Ross, Louis ("Lou") Rozzi, Andrew ("Andy") Sepsi, Alexander ("Alex") Ufema, and Asa ("Ace") Wiley. See *The Yellow Jacket*, 14 Oct. 1932, pp. 2-3; 23 Nov. 1932, p. 1; 8 Feb. 1944, p. 3. Until 1931 when the college acquired Varsity Hall, many of these men roomed and dined in Hanna Hall, and sometimes the fare was not sumptuous. See *The Yellow Jacket*, 28 Oct. 1932, p. 3. See also "Waynesburg College Football Records," rev. 1968, p. 14.

19. In addition to his coaching duties, Wolf continued his education, working toward a master's degree. In June 1933 the college conferred an earned master's degree upon him. See Faculty Minutes, 7 June 1933.

20. *The Yellow Jacket*, 18 March 1933, p. 3; 2 Oct. 1935, p. 3; *The Democrat Messenger* (Waynesburg), 30 Sept. 1935, p. 6; "Waynesburg College Football Records," rev. 1968, pp. 13-14.

21. *The Pittsburgh Press* (Family Magazine), Sunday, 1 Oct. 1972, p. 10; *The Yellow Jacket*, 4 Oct. 1940, p. 3; Trustees' Minutes, 30 Nov. 1939; "Waynesburg College Football Records," rev. 1968, p. 14; *The Washington Observer*, 11 June 1949, p. 22.

22. *The Yellow Jacket*, 22 Nov. 1940, p. 3.

23. In 1940 the football team was still strong. Wolf was fortunate to "have at his command an experienced and tried bunch of boys." See *The Yellow Jacket*,

29 Oct. 1938, p. 2; 6 April 1940, p. 3; "Waynesburg College Football Records," rev. 1968, p. 14.

24. The Athletic Department has carefully compiled, and keeps current, data on coaches and players. Figures are available for 1921 and subsequent years for all kinds of statistics and records. See "Waynesburg College Football Records," rev. 1968, pp. 41-62. Early in June 1973 the college received six national honors from the National Association of Intercollegiate Athletics (NAIA) for its brochures on athletics, edited by R. Terry Murdock. See *The Democrat Messenger* (Waynesburg), 5 June 1973, p. 6.

25. "Waynesburg College Basketball Guide," 1972-1973, pp. 25, 28, 31, 33. Most brilliant in basketball was Clair F. Bee. In 1922, having heard of the college's "athletic renaissance," he and two friends came from Troy, New York, to Waynesburg. En route they "ran out of money, and ate raw corn, fruit, and vegetables." After graduation in 1925, Bee coached basketball at Mansfield, Ohio, High School, and his team won a sectional championship. He next coached successfully at Rider College. He went thence to Long Island University where his teams rolled on to thirty-three consecutive conquests. They were always a drawing card at Madison Square Garden's weekly doubleheaders. According to NCAA figures, Bee was the "winningest major college basketball coach of all time," with a "21-year record of 410 victories against 86 losses for an .827 winning percentage." See *Times-West Virginian* (Fairmont), 10 Feb. 1974, p. 14-A. See also *The Yellow Jacket*, 23 March 1936, p. 3.

26. "Waynesburg College Wrestling Guide," 1972-1973, pp. 33, 47-48.

27. "Waynesburg College Spring Sports," 1973, pp. 18, 22.

28. *The Yellow Jacket*, 13 March 1936, p. 3; 17 Feb. 1967, p. 6.

29. *The Democrat Messenger* (Waynesburg), 14 Jan. 1943, p. 1; Trustees' Minutes, 1 Sept. 1943; 30 Oct. 1943; 18 May 1944; 9 Nov. 1945; 4 Feb. 1946.

30. Faculty Minutes, 4 Dec. 1945; Trustees' Minutes, 14 June 1947.

31. Trustees' Minutes, 19 Oct. 1946; 31 May 1947; 10 Nov. 1959; *WC Catalogue*, 1953-1954, p. 31; *The Yellow Jacket*, 1 April 1949, p. 5.

32. Trustees' Minutes, 10 Nov. 1945; 25 July 1946.

33. Trustees' Minutes, 4 Feb. 1946; 29 July 1946; 10 June 1949.

34. From 1944 until his death, Wolf was on the staff of the Veterans Administration as Chief of Rehabilitation Training. He had a beautiful, gracious daughter named "Frankie," who was Homecoming Queen at Waynesburg College in 1951. See *The Yellow Jacket*, 13 April 1949, p. 1; 25 May 1949, p. 3; 3 Nov. 1951, p. 5; *WC Catalogue*, 1947-1948, p. 7; Trustees' Minutes, 12 Aug. 1947; 19 Aug. 1947; 5 June 1948; *The Democrat Messenger* (Waynesburg), 4 April 1949, pp. 1-2. For the Frank N. Wolf Memorial Scholarship Foundation see *WC Catalogue*, 1950-1951, p. 29, and subsequent catalogues.

35. Trustees' Minutes, 5 June 1948; *The Yellow Jacket*, 26 Jan. 1951, p. 5; "Waynesburg College Football Guide," 1972, pp. 45, 59-60.

36. Trustees' Minutes, 23 May 1951; 5 Nov. 1951; 7 June 1952, 5 June 1954; 8 June 1957; *The Yellow Jacket*, 3 Nov. 1951, p. 5; 21 Jan. 1955, p. 4; 4 March 1955, p. 4; "Waynesburg College Football Guide," 1972, pp. 45, 60.

37. As the "Jacket" coach, "Jack" Wiley had some outstanding players. Noteworthy was John Barish who starred in football and wrestling. He was six feet two inches tall, weighed 245, and was well proportioned. In the 1954 season he was placed on the All District Squad, the All Pennsylvania Team, and the NAIA All American Team. He joined the

Washington Redskins after leaving Waynesburg College. See *The Yellow Jacket*, 4 March 1955, p. 4; 24 May 1955, p. 1.

38. *The Yellow Jacket*, 1 Oct. 1955, p. 3; "Waynesburg College Football Guide," 1972, pp. 45, 60-61.

39. Trustees' Minutes, 24 Sept. 1959; *The Yellow Jacket*, 13 Feb. 1959, p. 5; 25 Sept. 1959, p. 2; 9 April 1963, p. 1; "Waynesburg College Football Guide," 1972, p. 45.

40. Trustees' Minutes, 27 April 1945; 2 June 1945; 1 June 1946.

41. Trustees' Minutes, 5 June 1948; 25 June 1949; *The Yellow Jacket*, 15 March 1949, p. 3; "Waynesburg College Basketball Guide," 1972-73, pp. 25, 34-38.

42. *The Yellow Jacket*, 8 Dec. 1956, p. 3; 18 Jan. 1958, p. 1; 15 March 1958, p. 1.

43. *The Yellow Jacket*, 1 April 1949, p. 5; 26 Jan. 1952, p. 5; 15 Jan. 1953, p. 3; 21 Jan. 1955, p. 1; Trustees' Minutes, 22 Oct. 1947; 9 June 1951; *The Washington Observer*, 11 June 1949, p. 24. In addition to such wrestling champions as Gizoni and Lewis, the "Jacket" squad had men who were interesting in other ways. Notable was the Reverend Ray Carlson, dubbed "Our Wrasslin' Reverend," who was pastor of the Jefferson Methodist Church in addition to his duties as a student and wrestler. In nearly four years he lost only one bout; his record was one of the best in the nation. The fans were impressed, because he momentarily bowed in prayer just before each bout. He said he was "not grandstanding," and prayed "so there would be little notice of it." Showing his implicit faith, he added: "Everything we have we owe to the Lord—wrestling included. I do the practicing and training and the Lord does the rest." See *The Yellow Jacket*, 18 Feb. 1955, p. 4. See also "Waynesburg College Wrestling Guide," 1972-73, pp. 33, 36, 39, 42, 44-45, 48-50.

44. Trustees' Minutes, 2 Feb. 1963; *The Yellow Jacket*, 7 Dec. 1962, p. 1.

45. "Waynesburg College Spring Sports Guide," 1973, pp. 12-13, 17-18, 22-23; *The Yellow Jacket*, 20 May 1955, p. 4; 24 May 1955, p. 2; 27 Oct. 1956, p. 1; 3 Feb. 1959, p. 5; 10 April 1959, p. 3; Trustees' Minutes, 7 June 1958. See also "Waynesburg College Cross Country Guide," 1972, pp. 12-13.

46. *The Yellow Jacket*, 1 April 1949, p. 5; 4 March 1955, p. 4.

47. Trustees' Minutes, 10 June 1950; 7 June 1958.

48. Faculty Minutes, 3 Dec. 1953; 10 Jan. 1958; Trustees' Minutes, 13 Oct. 1962.

49. Trustees' Minutes, 18 Oct. 1957; 7 June 1958; 10 Oct. 1959; 20 Jan. 1960; 2 June 1962; 13 Oct. 1962; Faculty Minutes, 10 Jan. 1958.

50. Faculty Minutes, 10 Jan. 1958.

51. Faculty Minutes, 9 Sept. 1953.

CHAPTER XIX

1. WC, Registrar's files, 15 Feb. 1950; Trustees' Minutes, 7 June 1958; 28 Oct. 1961; 2 Feb. 1963.

2. Trustees' Minutes, 9 June 1951; 7 June 1952; 5 June 1954.

3. *WC Catalogue*, 1956-1957, p. 41; *The Yellow Jacket*, 12 Dec. 1958, p. 2.

4. Trustees' Minutes, 10 June 1950; 9 June 1951; 7 June 1952; 5 June 1954; 2 June 1962; Faculty Minutes, 1 June 1950; 7 Feb. 1951; 1 May 1951; 14 Feb. 1952; 8 Feb. 1955; *The Yellow Jacket*, 16 March 1951, p. 1; 12 Nov. 1955, p. 2; 22 March 1958, p. 2; 14 Dec. 1962, p. 1; *WC Catalogue*, 1963-64, pp. 24-25.

5. Faculty Minutes, 14 Sept. 1954; 7-8-9 Sept. 1958; 6 Oct. 1960; 14 Nov. 1962.

6. Trustees' Minutes, 1 Aug. 1958; 6 June 1959; *WC Catalogue*, 1952-1953, p. 57; *The Yellow Jacket*, 3 Nov. 1951, p. 4.

7. Faculty Minutes, 13 Dec. 1948; 6 March 1951; 7 May 1952; Trustees' Minutes, 9 June 1951; 7 June 1952; 5 June 1954; 11 June 1955; 28 Oct. 1961; James W. Hoffman, "The Community is Their Job." *Presbyterian Life*, IV (31 March 1951), pp. 11-14.

8. Trustees' Minutes, 10 June 1950; 7 June 1952; 5 June 1954; 28 Oct. 1961; 2 Feb. 1963; *WC Catalogue*, 1954-1955, p. 42; *The Yellow Jacket*, April 1951, p. 1; 21 Jan. 1955, p. 1; *The Democrat Messenger* (Waynesburg), 25 March 1961, p. 1.

9. Trustees' Minutes, 5 June 1954; 9 June 1956; 8 June 1957; 7 June 1958; 6 June 1959; 3 Dec. 1959; 3 June 1961; 2 June 1962; *The Yellow Jacket*, 3 March 1961, p. 1; 19 May 1961, p. 1; *Mad Anthony*, 1951, p. 98.

10. Trustees' Minutes, 9 June 1956; 1 June 1963.

11. Faculty Minutes, 1 May 1951; 1 Dec. 1960; 5 Jan. 1961; 15 Nov. 1961; Waynesburg College, *Documents Pertaining to the Government of the College* (Waynesburg, Pa., Sept. 1953), pp. 28-29. See also the revision of this publication, dated September 1965, pp. 41-44 for bylaws of the trustees and pp. 47-52 for the constitution and bylaws of the faculty.

12. *The Yellow Jacket*, 26 Jan. 1952, pp. 1, 4; Trustees' Minutes, 9 June 1951.

13. Faculty Minutes, 3 March 1950; 10 Sept. 1952; 7 Oct. 1952; 9 Sept. 1953; 8 Feb. 1955; 7-8-9 Sept. 1958; 6 Sept. 1960; 3 Nov. 1960; 11 Sept. 1961; Trustees' Minutes, 7 April 1958.

14. Faculty Minutes, 5 Jan. 1954; 1 March 1955; 7-8-9 Sept. 1958; 6 Nov. 1958.

15. Trustees' Minutes, 14 Dec. 1950; Faculty Minutes, 1 April 1953; 6 Sept. 1960.

16. Trustees' Minutes, 10 June 1950; 7 June 1952; 5 June 1954; 11 June 1955; 9 June 1956; 7 June 1958; 3 June 1960; 3 June 1961.

17. Trustees' Minutes, 11 June 1955; 27 Aug. 1955; 13 Oct. 1956; 8 June 1957; 3 June 1960; 3 June 1961.

18. Trustees' Minutes, 7 June 1952; 8 Oct. 1955; 1 June 1963; Faculty Minutes, 5 March 1959; 3 March 1960; 8 April 1960.

19. Trustees' Minutes, 24 Feb. 1951; 5 April 1954; 30 Jan. 1956; 13 Oct. 1956; 18 Feb. 1957; 10 Feb. 1958; *WC Catalogue*, 1951-1952, p. 45; 1962-1963, p. 39.

20. Trustees' Minutes, 24 Feb. 1951; 5 Nov. 1951; 18 Feb. 1952; 7 June 1958; 20 Jan. 1960; 3 June 1960; 2 June 1962; 13 Oct. 1962; Faculty Minutes, 10 Sept. 1962; *The Lamp*, March 1958; *WC Catalogue*, 1952-1953, p. 38; 1953-1954, p. 42; *WC Bulletin*, 18 Feb. 1951, p. 1; *The Yellow Jacket*, 17 March 1956, p. 2.

21. Trustees' Minutes, 5 June 1954; 3 June 1961; 28 Oct. 1961.

22. Trustees' Minutes, 9 June 1951; 18 Feb. 1957; 22 July 1957; 9 Sept. 1957; 24 Sept. 1959; 10 Oct. 1959; 3 June 1960.

23. Trustees' Minutes, 18 Feb. 1952; 2 March 1953; 6 June 1953; 30 June 1953; 5 April 1954; 9 Oct. 1954; 23 Oct. 1954; 11 June 1955; 7 April 1958; 17 Feb. 1960; *The Lamp*, March 1958; Faculty Minutes, 10 Sept. 1952; *The Yellow Jacket*, 19 Nov. 1954, p. 1.

24. Trustees' Minutes, 24 Feb. 1951; 8 Oct. 1955; 9 June 1956; 12 April 1957; 18 Oct. 1958; 6 April 1959; 10 Oct. 1959; 4 April 1960. I am indebted to Hugh M. Barclay, who was Director of Waynesburg College's Uniontown Center, for data showing how profitable financially the Center was for the institution as a whole.

25. Trustees' Minutes, 13 Oct. 1962; 14 Nov. 1962; 13 Dec. 1962; 2 Feb. 1963; 1 April 1963.

26. Trustees' Minutes, 16 Feb. 1959; 10 Oct. 1959; 20 Jan. 1960; 4 April 1960; 3 June 1960; 2 Feb. 1963.

27. The trend in the current budget can be followed in Trustees' Minutes, 24 Feb. 1951; 5 June 1954; 14 March 1955; 8 Oct.

1955; 9 June 1956; 3 Sept. 1957; 1 Aug. 1958; 18 Oct. 1958; 16 Jan. 1959; 10 Oct. 1959; 20 Jan. 1960; 4 Aug. 1960; 15 Oct. 1960; 28 Oct. 1961; 13 Oct. 1962; 1 April 1963; 1 June 1963.

28. Trustees' Minutes, 9 June 1951; 13 Oct. 1956; 1 Aug. 1958; 18 Oct. 1958; 10 Oct. 1959.

29. Trustees' Minutes, 15 Sept. 1958; 21 Sept. 1959; 5 Oct. 1960.

30. Trustees' Minutes, 9 June 1956.

31. Trustees' Minutes, 12 Oct. 1951; 5 Nov. 1951; 24 May 1954.

32. Trustees' Minutes, 5 April 1954; 8 June 1957. On 6 October 1955 Stewart, his family, and friends of the college felt a deep sense of bereavement when Stewart's son, Dr. Walter Alan Stewart, lost his life in an airplane crash. Having been inspired by his father and having won a Ph. D. at the Colorado School of Mines, Walter Alan Stewart was already highly esteemed in the field of geology. He had his own prospecting firm; he and his fellow geologists "located a good deposit of uranium." See *The Yellow Jacket*, 14 Oct. 1955, p. 1. See also Trustees' Minutes, 8 Oct. 1955.

33. Trustees' Minutes, 10 June 1950; 31 Oct. 1953; 5 April 1954; 8 Oct. 1955; 8 June 1957; 9 Sept. 1960; 1 June 1963; *WC Catalogue*, 1954-1955, pp. 26-27; 1957-1958, p. 17; *The Yellow Jacket*, 14 Jan. 1956, p. 3; 3 March 1956, p. 1; 17 March 1956, p. 2; 29 Sept. 1956, p. 1.

34. Trustees' Minutes, 9 May 1953; 24 Sept. 1959; 15 Oct. 1960.

35. Trustees' Minutes, 18 Feb. 1952; 7 July 1952; 2 March 1953; 11 June 1955; 2 April 1956; 18 Oct. 1957; 10 Feb. 1958; *WC Catalogue*, 1952-1953, p. 28; 1957-1958, p. 15; 1959-1960, pp. 19-20; *The Democrat Messenger* (Waynesburg), 28 April 1956, pp. 1, 8; *The Yellow Jacket*, 4 June 1955, p. 3; 17 March 1956, p. 2; 25 Jan. 1958, p. 1; 21 Oct. 1960, p. 2; 8 Dec. 1961, p. 2; *The Lamp*, Sept. 1968, p. 4.

36. Trustees' Minutes, 4 April 1955; 30 Jan. 1956; 10 Feb. 1958; 14 June 1958; 13 Oct. 1962; *The Yellow Jacket*, 26 April 1958, p. 1; 2 June 1958, p. 1; 11 Dec. 1959, p. 5; *WC Catalogue*, 1959-1960, p. 18.

37. Trustees' Minutes, 7 June 1958; 30 Dec. 1958; 16 Feb. 1959; 3 March 1959; 5 Oct. 1960; 3 April 1961; 12 July 1962; 13 Oct. 1962; 2 Feb. 1963; Faculty Minutes, 8 Jan. 1959; 9 Oct. 1959; *The Yellow Jacket*, 24 April 1959, p. 1; 27 Feb. 1963, pp. 1-2.

38. Trustees' Minutes, 9 Oct. 1954; 4 April 1955; 8 June 1957; 7 June 1958; 15 Oct. 1960; 3 June 1961; 13 Oct. 1962; *WC Catalogue*, 1952-1953, p. 25; 1958-1959, p. 18; 1961-1962, p. 11; *The Yellow Jacket*, 11 Nov. 1960, p. 1; 6 Oct. 1961, p. 2; 13 Oct. 1961, p. 1.

39. Trustees' Minutes, 9 June 1951; 31 Oct. 1953; 15 Dec. 1955; 9 Sept. 1957; 1 Aug. 1958; 18 Oct. 1958; 6 June 1959; 2 Feb. 1963; 1 June 1963; *WC Catalogue*, 1958-1959, p. 18; *The Yellow Jacket*, 9 April 1963, p. 1.

40. Trustees' Minutes, 18 Feb. 1952; 18 Oct. 1952; 2 March 1953; 25 Nov. 1958; 2 June 1962; 12 July 1962. In 1850, when the foundation for Hanna Hall was being excavated, a locust seed sprouted in the loose dirt nearby, took root, and grew into one of the largest locust trees in the entire region. It was a "time barometer" for alumni who measured its circumference upon graduation—and years later upon returning to the campus for reunions. When age caused it to deteriorate, every effort was made to save it. But it became "too hazardous for life and limb of students and others who pass under it." It was, therefore, cut down in December 1971 at age 121. See *The Yellow Jacket*, 12 Nov. 1955, p. 4; 8 Nov. 1971, p. 6.

41. Trustees' Minutes, 13 Oct. 1956; 6 June 1959; 17 Feb. 1960.

42. Trustees' Minutes, 24 Feb. 1951; 18 Feb. 1952; 24 May 1954; 9 June 1956; 3 June 1960; Faculty Minutes, 7 Feb. 1951; 4 April 1952; 5 Nov. 1959; 8 April 1960;

WC Catalogue, 1951-1952, p. 63; 1953-1954, p. 3; *The Yellow Jacket*, Feb. 1951, p. 1. The college promoted certain activities in the fields of archaeology and geology. In the summer of 1955 a team of archaeologists from Carnegie Museum spent nine weeks working on a site near Waynesburg pointed out by Stewart. Under the supervision of Dr. William Mayer-Oakes, the group found many relics and artifacts relating to the early Monongahela Indians who flourished between 1100 and 1400 A.D. For their convenience, these archaeologists were quartered at the college during their stay here. Another instance of collaboration began in 1956 when the college installed a seismology station provided by Columbia University under a Federal Research Grant of $10,000. This station recorded earthquake shocks from all over the world, and it helped scientists of many nations during the International Geophysical Year of 1957-1958. Professor James B. Schroyer, Director of the Earthquake Research Laboratory, trained advanced geology students to use the seismograph. See *The Yellow Jacket*, 1 Oct. 1955, p. 1; 20 Oct. 1956, p. 5; *The Lamp*, Feb. 1961, p. 4.

43. Faculty Minutes, 9 Sept. 1953.

44. *The Yellow Jacket*, 26 Jan. 1952, p. 2; Faculty Minutes, 6 Oct. 1953.

45. Trustees' Minutes, 9 June 1956; 8 June 1957; *The Yellow Jacket*, 11 Oct. 1958, p. 1.

46. See "Report of Self-Evaluation by Waynesburg College," Waynesburg, Pennsylvania, 7 April 1958, pp. 1-5, entitled "Recommendations."

47. Trustees' Minutes, 7 June 1958; 6 Nov. 1958; 4 Dec. 1958; 17 Dec. 1958; 3 March 1959; 6 April 1959; *The Yellow Jacket*, 5 Dec. 1958, p. 1. Available records show that standards relative to grades were low. The faculty did not effectively cope with this problem. See Faculty Minutes, 10 Dec. 1951; 2 June 1952; 3 Feb. 1953; 6 Oct. 1953; 2 March 1954; 1 March 1955; 7-8-9 Sept. 1958; 5 March 1959; 9 Oct. 1959.

48. Trustees' Minutes, 6 June 1959; 4 April 1960; 3 June 1960; Faculty Minutes, 8 Jan. 1960; 3 March 1960; 2 April 1960; 6 Oct. 1960; 28 Oct. 1960.

49. Faculty Minutes, 5 Jan. 1961; 2 March 1961; 11 Sept. 1963; Trustees' Minutes, 3 April 1961, 3 June 1961.

50. Trustees' Minutes, 18 Aug. 1961; *The Center Sentinel* (Uniontown), 17 Oct. 1961, p. 4; *WC Catalogue*, 1962-1963, p. 123.

51. Trustees' Minutes, 18 Aug. 1961; 2 April 1962.

52. Faculty Minutes, 5 Feb. 1959; 14 March 1962; Trustees' Minutes, 2 June 1962.

53. Trustees' Minutes, 28 Oct. 1961; 2 June 1962; 2 Feb. 1963; 1 April 1963; 1 June 1963; Faculty Minutes, 13 Feb. 1962; 4 Jan. 1963.

54. Trustees' Minutes, 9 June 1951; 18 Aug. 1961; 28 Oct. 1961; 9 June 1959; 3 June 1961; 1 June 1963; Faculty Minutes, 9 Oct. 1959; 11 Sept. 1961; 1 March 1962; 19 Nov. 1962; 29 Nov. 1962; 17 Jan. 1963.

55. *The Yellow Jacket*, 20 Oct. 1961, p. 1; 27 Oct. 1961, p. 1; 3 Nov. 1961, p. 2; 8 Dec. 1961, p. 2; Trustees' Minutes, 28 Oct. 1961; Faculty Minutes, 15 Dec. 1961; *WC Catalogue*, 1960-1961, pp. 50-51.

56. Trustees' Minutes, 28 Oct. 1961; 2 June 1962; 13 Oct. 1962.

57. Trustees' Minutes, 2 June 1962.

58. Trustees' Minutes, 2 June 1962.

59. Trustees' Minutes, 28 Oct. 1961.

60. Trustees' Minutes, 2 June 1962; Faculty Minutes, 13 Dec. 1962; 28 Feb. 1963; *WC Catalogue*, 1962-1963, pp. 2-3.

61. Trustees' Minutes, 2 June 1962; 2 Feb. 1963; Faculty Minutes, 14 Nov. 1962; 11 Sept. 1963; *The Yellow Jacket*, 7 Dec. 1962, pp. 1-2.

62. Trustees' Minutes, 2 Feb. 1963; 1 April 1963; Faculty Minutes, 29 March 1963.

63. Faculty Minutes, 13 Dec. 1962.

64. Trustees' Minutes, 2 Feb. 1963; Faculty Minutes, 18 Feb. 1963; *The Yellow Jacket*, 4 Feb. 1963, p. 1; *The Waynesburg Republican*, 4 July 1963, p. 1. See also "An Evaluation of Waynesburg College, Waynesburg, Pennsylvania: A Report Prepared by a Committee Representing The Commission on Institutions of Higher Education of the Middle States Association of Colleges and Secondary Schools," 13 March 1961, p. 8. At the sixtieth reunion of Stewart's class in 1969, Herschel Williams, President of the Class of 1919, conferred on Stewart the title "Mr. Waynesburg College" by which he had been known for years by many former students and friends. See *The Lamp*, Sept. 1969, p. 11.

65. Trustees' Minutes, 2 Feb. 1963.

66. Trustees' Minutes, 1 June 1963. After Walter left Waynesburg, he returned to the administrative staff of the University of Pittsburgh. He was assigned to the Johnstown Center, where an expansion program was under way on a 136-acre campus. See *The Yellow Jacket*, 4 May 1963, p. 1; 8 May 1963, p. 1.

67. Trustees' Minutes, 2 June 1962; 1 June 1963.

CHAPTER XX

1. Trustees' Minutes, 24 May 1963.

2. *The Waynesburg Republican*, 10 Oct. 1963, p. 2; *The Yellow Jacket*, 4 Sept. 1963, p. 1; *The Democrat Messenger* (Waynesburg), 24 May 1929, p. 1; 15 May 1974, p. 2; 20 May 1974, pp. 1-2; *The Observer-Reporter* (Washington, Pa.), 15 May 1974, p. A-15.

3. George P. Schmidt, *The Liberal Arts College: A Chapter in American Cultural History* (New Brunswick, N. J., 1957), pp. 146-147, 166-167, 181-182, 191-192; *WC Catalogue*, 1951-1952, pp. 6-8, 54; Faculty Minutes, 11 Sept. 1963.

4. Trustees' Minutes, 12 Oct. 1963; *The Yellow Jacket*, 11 Oct. 1963, p. 2.

5. *The Yellow Jacket*, 11 Oct. 1963, p. 3.

6. *The Yellow Jacket*, 4 Sept. 1963, p. 1.

7. *WC Catalogue*, 1964-1965, p. 127; 1965-1966, p. 121; Trustees' Minutes, 3 Feb. 1964; 6 April 1964; *The Lamp*, May 1965, p. 2. During the decade 1963 to 1973 the Board of Trustees suffered loss by the deaths of some of its most dedicated members including Ross Burns, John Conklin, Ralph Garrison, John D. Garvin, Edward Martin, D. Ray Murdock, Chauncy W. Parkinson, Lloyd E. Pollock, Joseph W. Ray, Jr., W. Robert Thompson, and Mary Denny Weaver. Illness forced the resignation of Joseph W. Ray, Jr., as President of the Board on 1 October 1968. The trustees immediately elected Richard L. Baily as Ray's successor. Baily served as President of that body until 11 September 1970, when his resignation became effective. He had been a trustee since 1 January 1923. His successor as President of the Board was Ewing B. Pollock, a trustee for several years who had been very faithful and helpful to the college. See Trustees' Minutes, 2 Feb. 1965; 3 April 1967; 7 Oct. 1968; 11 Sept. 1970; 1 Feb. 1971; 5 Feb. 1973; *The Waynesburg Republican*, 27 Feb. 1964, p. 10; 24 March 1967, p. 1; 28 Aug. 1970, p. 8; 1 Dec. 1972, p. 2; 19 Jan. 1973, p. 6.

8. Faculty Minutes, 11 Sept. 1963; Trustees' Minutes, 11 Oct. 1963; *The Waynesburg Republican*, 10 Oct. 1963, p. 1.

9. Faculty Minutes, 7 Oct. 1964; 18 Nov. 1964.

10. Faculty Minutes, 11 Dec. 1963; 3 Sept. 1964; 17 Sept. 1964; 8 Dec. 1964; 24 Feb. 1965; 12 April 1965; 22 April 1965; 4 Oct. 1965; Trustees' Minutes, 3

Feb. 1964; 6 April 1964; 24 May 1964; 19 Sept. 1964; 2 Feb. 1965; 22 May 1965; 15 Sept. 1965.

11. Trustees' Minutes, 15 Sept. 1965.

12. Trustees' Minutes, 23 May 1964; *The Lamp*, Jan. 1965, pp. 2-3.

13. Trustees' Minutes, 11 Oct. 1963; 2 Feb. 1965; 9 Sept. 1966; 8 Sept. 1967; 13 Sept. 1968; "Self-Evaluation Report for the Middle States Association of Colleges and Secondary Schools," 1 Sept. 1965, pp. 3, 102-104.

14. Trustees' Minutes, 10 Sept. 1964; 19 Sept. 1964; 2 Feb. 1965; 8 Feb. 1966; 4 April 1966; 21 May 1966; 3 April 1967; 4 May 1967; 3 Feb. 1969; "Self-Evaluation Report for the Middle States Association," 1 Sept. 1965, pp. 36, 41; Faculty Handbook, Waynesburg College, 1971-72, p. 17.

15. "Self-Evaluation Report for the Middle States Association," 1 Sept. 1965, pp. 14-16; Faculty Handbook, Waynesburg College, 1971-72, pp. 18-22.

16. "Self-Evaluation Report for the Middle States Association," 1 Sept. 1965, pp. 13-15, 43-44, 48. In 1943 the trustees accepted the standards of the Presbyterian Church, U. S. A. which stated that regular faculty members should be those who professed faith in Jesus Christ as Lord. In 1963, however, they adopted new guide lines of the church in which nothing was said of church membership. See Faculty Minutes, 23 Oct. 1963; Trustees' Minutes, 11 Oct. 1963; 15 May 1971; *The Lamp*, Jan. 1965, pp. 2-3.

17. Faculty Minutes, 23 Oct. 1963; 18 Nov. 1964; 15 March 1965; 25 March 1965; Trustees' Minutes, 2 Feb. 1965; 16 May 1970; *WC Catalogue*, 1966-1967, p. 133.

18. Faculty Minutes, 12 April 1965; 15 April 1965; 22 April 1965; 9 Sept. 1965; Trustees' Minutes, 24 March 1965; 22 May 1965.

19. Faculty Minutes, 23 Oct. 1963; 11 Dec. 1963; 4 May 1964; 9 Sept. 1965; 9 Dec. 1969; *The Lamp*, Jan. 1965, pp. 2-3.

20. Faculty Minutes, 17 Sept. 1964; 4 Oct. 1965; *The Lamp*, Jan. 1965, pp. 2-3. From 1965 to 1972 the college mourned the deaths of several faculty members including Professor Arthur M. Mintier on 24 August 1965; Associate Professor Jeanne Shelby Mosier on 6 November 1966; Associate Professor Harry K. Martin on 8 August 1972; Professor Harry E. Gardner on 24 Nov. 1972. A deep sense of bereavement was also felt after the death of Dessie Rush Stewart, wife of Chancellor Paul R. Stewart, on 5 March 1969. See *The Lamp*, May 1969, p. 6. See also *The Waynesburg Republican*, 2 Sept. 1965, p. 8; 7 March 1969, p. 1; Trustees' Minutes, 5 Feb. 1973; *WC Catalogue*, 1973-1974, p. 130.

21. Trustees' Minutes, 11 Oct. 1963; 3 Feb. 1964; 19 Sept. 1964; 2 Feb. 1965; 5 April 1965; 15 Sept. 1965; 11 Sept. 1970; 10 Sept. 1971; *The Lamp*, Jan. 1965, pp. 2-3.

22. Rich to the Board of Trustees, 15 Oct. 1965, Trustees' Minutes.

23. Trustees' Minutes, 24 Nov. 1965; 29 Nov. 1965; 17 Jan. 1966; Faculty Minutes, 10 Nov. 1965; 9 Dec. 1965; 18 Dec. 1967; *The Lamp*, Dec. 1965, p. 3; Jan. 1966, p. 2.

24. Trustees' Minutes, 6 April 1964; 5 April 1965; 19 Feb. 1974; *WC Catalogue*, 1973-1974, p. 55; Faculty Minutes, 5 Dec. 1972; 12 Feb. 1974; *The Democrat Messenger* (Waynesburg), 12 Feb. 1974, p. 1.

25. Trustees' Minutes, 5 April 1965; 20 July 1967; 18 May 1968; Faculty Minutes, 8 May 1968; 11 Nov. 1970; *The Lamp*, Oct. 1971, pp. 2-3; *The Waynesburg Republican*, 20 Oct. 1972, p. 7. By June 1964, Dr. Oscar R. Clovis, '13 had added to the college's Indian Archaeological Collection many specimens from the Adena culture of the Ohio valley. These artifacts came from the greatest flint area in the United States, namely, Flint Ridge some three miles northeast of Columbus, Ohio. The Adena culture built the mounds at Moundsville, West Virginia, and else-

where in the area. Their era was from a few centuries B. C. to 400 A. D. See *The Waynesburg Republican*, 18 June 1964, p. 3. See also *The Observer-Reporter* (Washington, Pa.), 18 Oct. 1972, p. A-11.

26. Faculty Minutes, 27 Nov. 1967; 20 April 1971; 16 Dec. 1971; Trustees' Minutes, 2 Feb. 1970; *The Waynesburg Republican*, 6 June 1969, p. 6; *The Yellow Jacket*, 21 Jan. 1972, p. 1; *WC Catalogue*, 1973-1974, pp. 85-88.

27. Faculty Minutes, 19 Jan. 1971; 23 Feb. 1971; *The Lamp*, Dec. 1970, p. 10; *WC Catalogue*, 1973-1974, p. 53.

28. Trustees' Minutes, 2 Feb. 1968; 7 April 1969; 11 Sept. 1970; 20 May 1972.

29. *WC Catalogue*, 1962-1963, p. 44; 1965-1966, pp. 32, 35; Faculty Handbook, 1971-72, pp. 28, 38-39; Faculty Minutes, 19 March 1964; 23 April 1964; 6 May 1964; 31 Oct. 1967; 28 March 1968; 4 Nov. 1969; 11 Nov. 1970.

30. *WC Catalogue*, 1965-1966, p. 37; Faculty Minutes, 24 March 1970; *The Yellow Jacket*, 17 April 1972, p. 2; *The Waynesburg Republican*, 27 May 1965, p. 1.

31. Trustees' Minutes, 11 Oct. 1963; 3 Dec. 1963; 23 May 1964; 2 Feb. 1965; 15 Sept. 1965; 29 Nov. 1965; 9 Sept. 1966; 8 Sept. 1967; 13 Sept. 1968; 5 Nov. 1969; 7 April 1971; 19 Feb. 1974; Faculty Minutes, 11 Dec. 1963; 8 Dec. 1965; 11 Nov. 1970. Figures on the gradual increase in tuition, fees, and costs of room and board are given in the trustees' minutes. As of August 1973 the estimated total for campus resident students was $1,515.00 per semester. See *WC Catalogue*, 1973-1974, p. 21. I am indebted to President Rich for figures on annual surpluses or deficits from 1963 to 1973. Six years showed surpluses; in the other four there were planned deficits, and the overall operation for the decade was well in the black.

32. Trustees' Minutes, 3 Dec. 1963; 3 Feb. 1964; 2 March 1964; 6 April 1964; 23 May 1964; 15 Sept. 1965; 8 Feb. 1966; *The Waynesburg Republican*, 19 March 1964, p. 1.

33. Trustees' Minutes, 19 April 1965; 28 April 1965; 22 May 1965; 15 Sept. 1965; 18 Jan. 1966; 26 Jan. 1966; 8 Feb. 1966; 4 April 1966; Faculty Minutes, 6 May 1965; 28 April 1966; 11 May 1966; *The Waynesburg Republican*, 6 May 1965, p. 1; 22 Jan. 1966, p. 1; *The Lamp*, Sept. 1965, pp. 1-2. I am indebted to J. E. Victor Carlson for data on alumni donors to the college.

34. Trustees' Minutes, 2 Feb. 1967; 2 Feb. 1968; 3 Feb. 1969; 16 June 1969; 12 Sept. 1969; 2 Feb. 1970; 16 May 1970; 11 Sept. 1970; 8 Sept. 1972; 5 Feb. 1973; 19 May 1973; 19 Feb. 1974; Faculty Minutes, 4 Sept. 1969; *The Lamp*, July 1970, p. 6; Oct. 1971, p. 9; July 1973, p. 1; *The Waynesburg Republican*, 14 April 1972, p. 1; *The Yellow Jacket*, 29 Jan. 1973, p. 1. See also the excellent pamphlet entitled *The Waynesburg Story* (Waynesburg, Pa., n. d.), pp. 9-13.

35. Trustees' Minutes, 19 Sept. 1964; 2 Feb. 1965; 29 Nov. 1965; 2 Feb. 1967; 2 Feb. 1968; 24 May 1969; 1 Feb. 1971; 15 May 1971; 2 Feb. 1972; 20 May 1972; Faculty Minutes, 23 Oct. 1963; 31 Jan. 1968; *WC Catalogue*, 1968-1969, pp. 27-28.

36. Trustees' Minutes, 22 May 1965; 4 April 1966; 9 Sept. 1966; *The Waynesburg Republican*, 10 March 1966, p. 1.

37. *The Lamp*, Oct. 1973, p. 5.

38. Trustees' Minutes, 22 May 1965.

39. Trustees' Minutes, 8 Feb. 1966; 8 Sept. 1967.

40. Trustees' Minutes, 2 March 1964; 6 April 1964; 23 May 1964; *WC Catalogue*, 1964-1965, p. 15.

41. *The Yellow Jacket*, 30 Sept. 1966, p. 1.

42. Trustees' Minutes, 23 May 1964; 2 Feb. 1970; *The Yellow Jacket*, 16 Sept. 1964, p. 1; *The Waynesburg Republican*, 24 Sept. 1964, p. 1; *WC Catalogue*, 1964-1965, p. 12.

43. Trustees' Minutes, 18 Feb. 1966;

16 June 1966; 2 Feb. 1967; 13 Sept. 1968; Faculty Minutes, 22 Feb. 1966; 30 March 1967; *The Yellow Jacket*, 30 Sept. 1966, p. 1; *The Waynesburg Republican*, 20 Sept. 1968, p. 1; *WC Catalogue*, 1968-1969, p. 10.

44. Trustees' Minutes, 19 Sept. 1964; *The Yellow Jacket*, 25 Sept. 1963, p. 1; *WC Catalogue*, 1963-1964, p. 14.

45. Trustees' Minutes, 6 April 1964; 2 Feb. 1965; 10 Sept. 1971; *The Yellow Jacket*, 18 Feb. 1966, p. 1; *WC Catalogue*, 1964-1965, p. 14; *The Waynesburg Republican*, 24 Feb. 1966, p. 1.

46. Faculty Minutes, 29 March 1966; 1 Sept. 1966; 31 Oct. 1967; Trustees' Minutes, 26 March 1968; *WC Catalogue*, 1968-1969, p. 12.

47. Trustees' Minutes, 10 Nov. 1967; 1 Feb. 1971; 15 May 1971; *The Yellow Jacket*, 10 Sept. 1971, pp. 1, 5; *WC Catalogue*, 1973-1974, p. 13.

48. Trustees' Minutes, 17 Aug. 1970; 11 Sept. 1970; 5 Jan. 1971; 1 Feb. 1971; 7 April 1971; 2 Feb. 1972; *The Waynesburg Republican*, 28 Aug. 1970, p. 1; 20 Nov. 1970, p. 1; *WC Catalogue*, 1973-1974, p. 12.

49. Trustees' Minutes, 12 Aug. 1963.

50. Trustees' Minutes, 23 May 1964; 8 Sept. 1967; 7 April 1969; 12 Sept. 1969; 11 Sept. 1970; 1 Feb. 1971; 15 May 1971; 10 Sept. 1971; *The Lamp*, Dec. 1970, p. 5; Dec. 1971, p. 1.

51. Trustees' Minutes, 1 Feb. 1971; 7 April 1971; 20 May 1972.

52. Trustees' Minutes, 8 July 1965; *The Yellow Jacket*, 22 April 1966, p. 1; *The Waynesburg Republican*, 9 Sept. 1966, p. 5.

53. Trustees' Minutes, 13 Sept. 1968; 7 Oct. 1968; 5 Jan. 1971; *The Yellow Jacket*, 16 Oct. 1970, p. 7; *The Waynesburg Republican*, 15 Jan. 1971, p. 6. Relations between the Library and the local area were excellent. For example, early in October 1964 the Pennsylvania Library Association, at its annual meeting in Pittsburgh, commended the Library "as the college or university library which planned and administered the outstanding observance of National Library Week" that year. Librarian May P. Clovis received the Certificate of Award. The Assistant Librarian, Sarah J. Olmstead, had made posters featuring community use of the Library. The theme was: "The Library Welcomes the Community and The Community Aids the College Library." See *The Yellow Jacket*, 7 Oct. 1964, p. 1.

54. Trustees' Minutes, 7 April 1971.

55. Trustees' Minutes, 1 Feb. 1971; 7 April 1971; Faculty Minutes, 7 Sept. 1971; *The Yellow Jacket*, 8 Oct. 1971, p. 3.

56. Trustees' Minutes, 8 Feb. 1966; 26 March 1968; 13 Sept. 1968; 24 May 1969; 16 June 1969; 5 Jan. 1971; 7 April 1971; *The Waynesburg Republican*, 7 April 1966, p. 7.

57. Trustees' Minutes, 8 Sept. 1967; 2 Feb. 1968; 18 May 1968.

58. Trustees' Minutes, 18 May 1968; 5 Nov. 1969; 2 Feb. 1970; 1 Feb. 1971; *The Lamp*, Sept. 1970, p. 2.

59. *The Waynesburg Republican*, 31 Oct. 1969, p. 1; Trustees' Minutes, 25 April 1941; 8 Feb. 1966.

60. Trustees' Minutes, 5 Jan. 1971.

61. Trustees' Minutes, 22 Oct. 1971; 2 Feb. 1972; 29 Feb. 1972; 8 Sept. 1972; *The Observer-Reporter* (Washington, Pa.), 10 Feb. 1972, p. B-8; *The Democrat Messenger* (Waynesburg), 23 Sept. 1972, p. 1.

62. Trustees' Minutes, 22 Oct. 1971.

63. Trustees' Minutes, 17 Jan. 1966; 18 Feb. 1966.

64. Trustees' Minutes, 12 Aug. 1963; 22 Nov. 1963; 26 March 1968; 13 Sept. 1968; 6 April 1970; 17 Aug. 1970; 5 Jan. 1971.

65. Trustees' Minutes, 20 May 1967.

66. Trustees' Minutes, 9 Sept. 1966.

CHAPTER XXI

1. Trustees' Minutes, 11 Oct. 1963.
2. Trustees' Minutes, 13 Dec. 1963; 23 May 1964; Faculty Minutes, 19 March 1964.
3. *WC Catalogue*, 1968-1969, p. 41.
4. Dean Robert W. Cahn to the author, 23 April 1974; Faculty Planning and Development Committee to the Faculty, 5 March 1974; *Student Handbook*, Waynesburg College, 1971-72, pp. 20-21; Student Senate Minutes, 13 Nov. 1973; *The Democrat Messenger* (Waynesburg), 2 Oct. 1973, p. 1; *WC Catalogue*, 1968-1969, p. 41; Trustees' Minutes, 11 Oct. 1963; 19 May 1973; 3 Dec. 1973. Students in some colleges had accepted the gender revolution matter-of-factly. Males and females shared rooms and even bathrooms. See "The New Campus Rebels: Women," *Newsweek*, 10 Dec. 1973, p. 120. See also *The Yellow Jacket*, 15 March 1974, pp. 1, 7.
5. Trustees' Minutes, 19 Sept. 1964; Faculty Minutes, 10 Nov. 1965; *Student Handbook*, Waynesburg College, 1971-72, p. 17.
6. Trustees' Minutes, 16 May 1970.
7. *Student Handbook*, Waynesburg College, 1971-72, p. 16; Trustees' Minutes, 16 May 1970; 1 Feb. 1971.
8. Faculty Minutes, 10 Nov. 1965; 1 Nov. 1966; 6 May 1971; *WC Catalogue*, 1967-1968, p. 38.
9. Faculty Minutes, 26 Sept. 1963; 31 Aug. 1967; *The Yellow Jacket*, 5 Nov. 1965, p. 2; *WC Catalogue*, 1966-1967, p. 34; 1967-1968, pp. 38-39; 1968-1969, p. 40.
10. Trustees' Minutes, 2 Feb. 1972; Faculty Minutes, 1 Oct. 1970; *The Yellow Jacket*, 17 Nov. 1967, p. 1; *The Waynesburg Republican*, 9 Oct. 1970, p. 1.
11. *Student Handbook*, Waynesburg College, 1971-72, p. 14; Faculty Minutes, 4 Sept. 1969.
12. Faculty Minutes, 19 Jan. 1971.
13. Faculty Minutes, 22 April 1965; 4 Oct. 1965.
14. Faculty Minutes, 27 March 1972.
15. Trustees' Minutes, 20 May 1972.
16. Trustees' Minutes, 4 April 1966; 2 Feb. 1968; 18 May 1968.
17. J. Robert Lilly, "Partial Analysis of a Survey: Drug Use/Abuse," Waynesburg College, Waynesburg, Pa., Spring 1970.
18. *Student Handbook*, Waynesburg College, 1970-71, p. 27; 1971-72, p. 13.
19. Trustees' Minutes, 19 Sept. 1964; 2 April 1973; *The Yellow Jacket*, 9 Oct. 1970, p. 7.
20. *The Yellow Jacket*, 23 Oct. 1970, p. 1; Trustees' Minutes, 15 May 1971; Faculty Minutes, 6 Feb. 1973.
21. Trustees' Minutes, 19 Sept. 1964; *Student Handbook*, Waynesburg College, 1971-72, p. 31.
22. Trustees' Minutes, 3 Feb. 1969; 1 Feb. 1971.
23. *The Yellow Jacket*, 4 Sept. 1963, p. 6; Trustees' Minutes, 24 May 1963.
24. *The Waynesburg Republican*, 17 Oct. 1963, p. 9; 2 Jan. 1964, p. 7; 4 March 1965, p. 1; 11 Nov. 1965, p. 7; *The Yellow Jacket*, 18 Nov. 1964, p. 4; "Waynesburg College Football Guide," 1972, p. 61.
25. Trustees' Minutes, 29 Nov. 1965; 8 Feb. 1966; *The Waynesburg Republican*, 10 Feb. 1966, p. 7; *The Yellow Jacket*, 18 Feb. 1966, p. 1.
26. *The Yellow Jacket*, 1 April 1966, p. 1; 26 April 1966, p. 3; *The Waynesburg Republican*, 31 March 1966, p. 7; 16 Sept. 1966, p. 7; Trustees' Minutes, 4 April 1966.
27. *The Yellow Jacket*, 13 Sept. 1966, p. 3; *The Waynesburg Republican*, 15 April 1966, p. 9.
28. *The Washington Observer*, 28 Nov. 1966, pp. 9, 22; 29 Nov. 1966, p. 14; 1 Dec. 1966, p. 14; 6 Dec. 1966, p. 19; *The Democrat Messenger* (Waynesburg), 1 Dec. 1966, pp. 1, 6; *The Waynesburg Republican*, 2 Dec. 1966, p. 1.
29. *The Democrat Messenger* (Waynesburg), 30 Nov. 1966, p. 8; 10 Dec. 1966, p. 6.
30. *The Washington Observer*, 12 Dec.

1966, p. 19; *The Democrat Messenger* (Waynesburg), 12 Dec. 1966, p. 6.

31. *The Washington Observer,* 12 Dec. 1966, pp. 1, 4, 8, 10; *The Waynesburg Republican,* 16 Dec. 1966, p. 1; *The Pittsburgh Post-Gazette,* 12 Dec. 1966, p. 27; *The Democrat Messenger* (Waynesburg), 12 Dec. 1966, p. 1.

32. *The Brownsville Telegraph,* 13 Dec. 1966, p. 2. Some men on the championship team were outstanding. "Rich" Dahar, ace halfback, and "Tim" McNeil, stellar linebacker, were selected to the NAIA All-American team; and "Joe" Righetti, middle guard, "Fran" Bedont, defensive tackle and "Joe" Hornak, defensive end, received honorable mention. Other top performers were quarterbacks Don Paull and John Huntey; end Don Herrmann; field goal and conversion man, "Ben" Falcone; and flanker Dan Dvorchak. Those elected to the West Penn Conference All-Star Team were: "Bob" Babish, "Fran" Bedont, Henry Brehm, "Rich" Dahar, Frank DeStefano, "Tony" Fusarelli, "Joe" Hornak, Eric Johnson, "Bob" Miltenberger, "Tim" McNeil, "Joe" Righetti, and "Rich" Ripepi. For other honors and for records, both individual and team, see *The Road to the Championship.* See also *The Washington Observer,* 31 Dec. 1966, p. 24; *The Democrat Messenger* (Waynesburg), 7 Dec. 1966, p. 8; 14 Dec. 1966, p. 8; 15 Dec. 1966, p. 6; 31 Dec. 1966, p. 6; 13 Nov. 1967, p. 6.

33. Faculty Minutes, 13 Dec. 1966; Trustees' Minutes, 2 Feb. 1967.

34. *The Washington Observer,* 6 Feb. 1967, p. 20; *The Democrat Messenger* (Waynesburg), 6 Feb. 1967, p. 8; *The Waynesburg Republican,* 10 Feb. 1967, p. 7.

35. *The Democrat Messenger* (Waynesburg), 16 Jan. 1967, p. 1; 6 Feb. 1967, p. 8; *The Washington Observer,* 12 Jan. 1967, p. 18; *The Brownsville Telegraph,* 12 Jan. 1967, p. 13.

36. *The Yellow Jacket,* 9 Feb. 1968, p. 3; "Waynesburg College Football Guide," 1972, p. 62.

37. *The Yellow Jacket,* 28 March 1968, p. 1; 28 Nov. 1968, p. 4; 6 Dec. 1968, p. 4; *The Waynesburg Republican,* 29 March 1968, p. 7; 29 Nov. 1968, p. 7; 3 Jan. 1969, p. 7; 21 Nov. 1969, p. 5. On 25 October 1969 several men were selected to the Waynesburg College Sports Hall of Fame: Paul R. ("Prexy") Stewart, "for his meritorious service to the school's overall sports program"; Michael J. ("Mo") Scarry, athlete and coach; Raymond ("Bucky") Murdock, wrestling coach; and Victor A. ("Tony") Gizoni, Marcus Davies, Robert ("Bob") Brooks, and Wettie Mancuso—all athletes. See *The Lamp,* Dec. 1969, p. 5. On 9 April 1970, the entire college family was shocked and saddened by the sudden death of star quarterback Don Paull in the Youghiogheny River, near Ohiopyle. Paull was one of five athletes who went to "shoot the rapids" in that river. In whirlpool water, their rafts capsized, and all but Paull swam to shore and were saved. Paull's undergraduate work was nearly completed at the time of his death. At Commencement in May 1970 his name appeared on the program "In Memoriam," and the diploma he would have received was sent to his parents. See *The Waynesburg Republican,* 17 April 1970, p. 1. See also Faculty Minutes, 6 May 1970.

38. "Waynesburg College Football Guide," 1972, pp. 9, 62; *The Waynesburg Republican,* 17 Nov. 1972, p. 7; *WC Catalogue,* 1973-1974, p. 126.

39. *The Waynesburg Republican,* 12 Jan. 1973, p. 3.

40. *The Democrat Messenger* (Waynesburg), 13 Aug. 1973, p. 6; 11 Nov. 1974, p. 7; *The Waynesburg Republican,* 23 Feb. 1973, p. 3; *The Yellow Jacket,* 26 Feb. 1973, p. 1; Faculty Minutes, 20 March 1973; *The Observer-Reporter* (Washington, Pa.), 19 Nov. 1973, p. B-3.

41. *The Waynesburg Republican,* 18 March 1965, p. 9; 25 March 1965, p. 7; 14 March 1969, p. 7; 20 March 1970, p. 7; 19 March 1971, p. 7; 30 March 1973, p. 5; "Waynesburg College Wrestling Guide," 1972-73, pp. 33, 40; *The Demo-*

crat Messenger (Waynesburg), 8 Feb. 1974, p. 6.

42. *The Waynesburg Republican*, 20 Oct. 1972, p. 6; *The Yellow Jacket*, 1 Dec. 1972, p. 1. Other Yellow Jacket wrestlers were honored from 1968 to 1973. Early in 1968 former Coach Raymond ("Bucky") Murdock and Victor ("Tony") Gizoni were inducted into the NCAA Wrestling Hall of Fame. Early in 1970 Murdock was elected to the NAIA Hall of Fame. In April 1973 he was inducted into the Western Pennsylvania Chapter of the Pennsylvania Sports Hall of Fame. He was already a member of the Helms Hall of Fame and the Waynesburg College Sports Hall of Fame. See *The Waynesburg Republican*, 6 March 1970, p. 5; 20 April 1973, p. 7. See also *The Lamp*, July 1973, p. 8.

43. *The Waynesburg Republican*, 28 Nov. 1963, p. 9; 12 March 1964, p. 7; "Waynesburg College Basketball Guide," 1972-73, p. 25.

44. "Waynesburg College Basketball Guide," 1972-73, p. 25; *The Yellow Jacket*, 31 Jan. 1969, p. 4; Trustees' Minutes, 3 Feb. 1969.

45. *The Yellow Jacket*, 18 April 1969, p. 1; *The Lamp*, May 1969, p. 7; Dec. 1969, p. 9; *The Waynesburg Republican*, 18 April 1969, p. 7.

46. *The Waynesburg Republican*, 23 March 1973, p. 2; 30 March 1973, p. 5; *The Lamp*, Dec. 1970, p. 13; Jan. 1973, p. 8; "Waynesburg College Basketball Guide," 1972-73, p. 25; *The Democrat Messenger* (Waynesburg), 25 Feb. 1974, p. 7; 6 March 1974, p. 6; 11 March 1974, p. 6; 12 March 1974, p. 8.

47. *The Waynesburg Republican*, 5 May 1972, p. 3; 18 May 1973, p. 5; 25 May 1973, p. 5; "Waynesburg College Spring Sports Guide," 1973, pp. 12-13.

48. "Waynesburg College Cross Country Guide," 1972, p. 12; *The Yellow Jacket*, 16 Sept. 1963, p. 4; *The Waynesburg Republican*, 11 Nov. 1965, p. 7.

49. "Waynesburg College Spring Sports Guide," 1973, pp. 16-18; *The Waynesburg Republican*, 9 April 1964, p. 7; 11 May 1973, p. 5.

50. *The Waynesburg Republican*, 26 March 1964, p. 7; "Waynesburg College Spring Sports Guide," 1973, p. 22. I am indebted to R. Terry Murdock, Sports Information Director for the college, for data on season results on spring sports for 1973, which were too late to be included in the excellent series of brochures he compiled for the Athletic Department. Of all spring sports, track received least attention. See *The Waynesburg Republican*, 9 April 1964, p. 7; 28 April 1972, p. 5; 5 May 1972, p. 3.

51. *Student Handbook*, Waynesburg College, 1971-72, p. 39. I am grateful to Jay H. Payne, Jr., Intramural Director in 1972-1973, for a copy entitled "Men's Intramural Association Summary," 1972-1973, which contains full information on this program. See also *The Lamp*, July 1973, p. 8.

CHAPTER XXII

1. Trustees' Minutes, 5 April 1965.

2. Trustees' Minutes, 13 Sept. 1968; Faculty Minutes, 28 Jan. 1969.

3. The Student Senate consisted of a president and four vice presidents, who were elected at large, and senators elected on a geographical basis in order to get better representation of the entire student body. The Student Senate selected students who attended faculty meetings. The president of that body selected students who served on certain faculty-student committees. See Trustees' Minutes, 10 Sept. 1971.

4. *The Yellow Jacket*, 9 Oct. 1970, pp. 1, 4, 7.

5. Trustees' Minutes, 15 May 1971; 22 Oct. 1971; 2 Feb. 1972; Student Senate

Minutes, 13 Oct. 1970; 4 Nov. 1970; 19 Oct. 1971; 1 Dec. 1971; 4 April 1972.

6. *WC Catalogue*, 1970-1971, pp. 142-143; Student Senate Minutes, 12 Oct. 1971; 26 Sept. 1972; Faculty Minutes, 29 Feb. 1972; 11 April 1972; *The Yellow Jacket*, 22 Nov. 1971, p. 1; *The Lamp*, Oct. 1971, p. 3.

7. Trustees' Minutes, 11 Aug. 1966; *The Yellow Jacket*, 13 Sept. 1966, p. 1.

8. *The Yellow Jacket*, 3 March 1967, p. 2; 14 April 1967, p. 4; *The Waynesburg Republican*, 26 May 1967, p. 1.

9. Trustees' Minutes, 2 Feb. 1967.

10. *The Yellow Jacket*, 27 Aug. 1967, p. 1; *The Waynesburg Republican*, 26 May 1967, p. 4; Faculty Minutes, 16 May 1967.

11. Faculty Minutes, 12 May 1967; 16 May 1967; 20 May 1967; *The Waynesburg Republican*, 26 May 1967, p. 1.

12. Trustees' Minutes, 2 Feb. 1967; 7 March 1967; *The Yellow Jacket*, 3 March 1967, p. 2; 14 April 1967, p. 1.

13. *The Yellow Jacket*, 28 April 1967, p. 4.

14. Trustees' Minutes, 13 Sept. 1968.

15. *The Yellow Jacket*, 17 March 1967, p. 1; Trustees' Minutes, 7 March 1967; 7 April 1969; 7 Oct. 1971.

16. Trustees' Minutes, 2 Feb. 1970; 6 April 1970; 16 May 1970; *The Yellow Jacket*, 16 Jan. 1970, p. 1.

17. *The Yellow Jacket*, 18 Sept. 1970, p. 1; Faculty Minutes, 1 Oct. 1970; *The Waynesburg Republican*, 25 Sept. 1970, p. 1.

18. *The Democrat Messenger* (Waynesburg), 10 Nov. 1970, p. 1; Trustees' Minutes, 2 Feb. 1972.

19. *The Lamp*, Oct. 1971, pp. 4-5.

20. *The Yellow Jacket*, 25 March 1965, p. 1.

21. Trustees' Minutes, 2 Feb. 1968; 3 Dec. 1968; 7 April 1969; 24 May 1969; 9 Feb. 1970; 22 April 1970; 1 Feb. 1971; 15 May 1971; 2 April 1973.

22. Trustees' Minutes, 2 Feb. 1965; 3 Feb. 1969; 7 April 1969.

23. Trustees' Minutes, 2 Feb. 1970; 6 April 1970; 8 June 1970.

24. Trustees' Minutes, 11 Sept. 1970; 1 Feb. 1971; 7 April 1971; 15 May 1971.

25. Right after Stoy signed the college's first union contract, he gave me the pen he used in signing it. I am grateful to him for it. See C. B. Stoy, Jr., to the author, 6 Dec. 1972. See also Trustees' Minutes, 2 Feb. 1972; 8 Sept. 1972; *The Yellow Jacket*, 7 Feb. 1972, p. 1; *Observer-Reporter* (Washington, Pa.), 2 Feb. 1972, p. B-10.

26. Trustees' Minutes, 3 April 1972.

27. Trustees' Minutes, 11 Oct. 1963; 3 Dec. 1963; 21 May 1964.

28. Trustees' Minutes, 1 Sept. 1964; 19 Sept. 1964; 18 Dec. 1964; 5 April 1965; Faculty Minutes, 3 Nov. 1964; 18 Nov. 1964; *The Waynesburg Republican*, 1 Sept. 1964, p. 1; *The Lamp*, Jan. 1966, p. 5.

29. Trustees' Minutes, 1 Feb. 1971.

30. Trustees' Minutes, 10 Sept. 1971.

31. Trustees' Minutes, 8 Sept. 1972; 5 Feb. 1973; Faculty Minutes, 6 Feb. 1973.

32. Faculty Minutes, 5 Sept. 1972; 7 Nov. 1972.

33. Trustees' Minutes, 20 May 1972; 19 May 1973.

34. Faculty Minutes, 1 Nov. 1966.

35. Faculty Minutes, 31 Jan. 1972; Trustees' Minutes, 10 Sept. 1971; 2 Feb. 1972; 19 May 1973; Office of the Registrar, "Report to the Faculty," 18 Jan. 1974; *The Democrat Messenger* (Waynesburg), 8 Sept. 1973, p. 1.

36. Trustees' Minutes, 2 Feb. 1972; Faculty Minutes, 15 Jan. 1974.

37. Trustees' Minutes, 10 Sept. 1971; 19 Feb. 1974; Faculty Minutes, 31 Jan. 1972; 12 Feb. 1974; *The Yellow Jacket*, 12 Feb. 1973, p. 1; *The Lamp*, Jan. 1974, p. 2.

38. Trustees' Minutes, 2 Feb. 1967; 1 Feb. 1971; 20 May 1972; 5 Feb. 1973; Faculty Minutes, 31 Jan. 1972; 15 Jan. 1974.

39. Trustees' Minutes, 13 Sept. 1968.

40. Trustees' Minutes, 2 Feb. 1967; 11 Sept. 1970; Faculty Minutes, 30 March 1971.

41. Faculty Minutes, 20 Oct. 1971; 14 Jan. 1974; *The Democrat Messenger* (Waynesburg), 12 June 1974, p. 1; Dean Robert W. Cahn to the author, 23 Jan. 1975.

42. Trustees' Minutes, 1 Feb. 1971; 8 Sept. 1972; 3 Dec. 1973.

43. Trustees' Minutes, 7 April 1969.

44. Trustees' Minutes, 6 April 1970; Faculty Minutes, 8 Sept. 1970; 1 Feb. 1971.

45. Trustees' Minutes, 3 Dec. 1973.

46. Trustees' Minutes, 1 Feb. 1971; 2 Feb. 1972; 5 Feb. 1973; Faculty Minutes, 31 Jan. 1972; 1 May 1973.

47. Trustees' Minutes, 21 May 1966; 3 Dec. 1973; Faculty Minutes, 14 Jan. 1974; *The Church and Related Colleges and Universities, A Statement of Mutual Responsibilities*, the United Presbyterian Church, U. S. A., New York, 1973.

48. Trustees' Minutes, 7 April 1969.

49. *The Lamp*, July 1970, pp. 2-3.

50. Faculty Minutes, 20 March 1973; *The Yellow Jacket*, 6 April 1973, p. 3; Trustees' Minutes, 19 Feb. 1974.

51. Trustees' Minutes, 3 April 1972.

52. Trustees' Minutes, 20 May 1972; 5 Feb. 1973; 3 Dec. 1973; Elizabeth J. McCormack, Chairman, Commission on Higher Education, to Bennett M. Rich, 31 Jan. 1974; "Report to the Faculty, Administration, Trustees of Waynesburg College by An Evaluation Team representing the *Commission on Higher Education of the Middle States Association*," 21-24 October 1973, p. 3; Waynesburg College, "Institutional Self-Study Report for the Middle States Association of Colleges and Secondary Schools," Waynesburg, Pennsylvania, 1 Sept. 1973. See also *Observer-Reporter* (Washington, Pa.), 26 Oct. 1973, p. A-8; 8 Feb. 1974, p. A-8; *The Democrat Messenger* (Waynesburg), 26 Oct. 1973, p. 2; 9 Feb. 1974, p. 1.

53. Rich to Faculty, Staff, and Students, 28 Jan. 1974; *The Democrat Messenger* (Waynesburg), 28 Jan. 1974, p. 1; 31 Jan. 1974, p. 1; *Observer-Reporter* (Washington, Pa.), 28 Jan. 1974, pp. A-1, A-12; *The Telegraph* (Brownsville), 28 Jan. 1974, p. 2; *Times-West Virginian* (Fairmont), 3 Feb. 1974, p. 8-B; *The Lamp*, Jan. 1974, pp. 1, 4.

54. *Observer-Reporter* (Washington, Pa.), 2 Feb. 1974, p. A-10; *Pittsburgh Post-Gazette*, 7 Feb. 1974, p. 23.

55. Henry Steele Commager, "Has the Small College a Future," *Saturday Review*, 21 Feb. 1970, p. 64.

56. *The Democrat Messenger* (Waynesburg), 18 April 1974, p. 2; *Observer-Reporter* (Washington, Pa.), 18 April 1974, p. B-8.

INDEX

BELMONT COLLEGE LIBRARY